Distributed
Algorithms

The Morgan Kaufmann Series in Data Management Systems
Series Editor, Jim Gray

Distributed Algorithms

Nancy A. Lynch

Morgan Kaufmann Publishers, Inc.
San Francisco, California

Sponsoring Editors Bruce M. Spatz/Diane D. Cerra
Production Manager Yonie Overton
Production Editor Julie Pabst
Cover Design Ross Carron Design
Cover Photograph Scott Camazine
Copyeditor Sharilyn Hovind
Proofreaders Ken DellaPenta, Jennifer McClain, and Gary Morris
Composition Ed Sznyter, Babel Press
Printer Courier Corporation

Morgan Kaufmann Publishers, Inc.
Editorial and Sales Office
340 Pine Street, Sixth Floor
San Francisco, CA 94104-3205
USA
Telephone 415/392-2665
Facsimile 415/982-2665
Internet mkp@mkp.com
Order toll free 800/745-7323

Library of Congress Cataloging-in-Publication Data is available for this book.
ISBN 1-55860-348-4

To Dennis, Patrick, and Mary

Contents

Preface

Distributed algorithms are algorithms designed to run on hardware consisting of many interconnected processors. Pieces of a distributed algorithm run concurrently and independently, each with only a limited amount of information. The algorithms are supposed to work correctly, even if the individual processors and communication channels operate at different speeds and even if some of the components fail.

Distributed algorithms arise in a wide range of applications, including telecommunications, distributed information processing, scientific computing, and real-time process control. For example, today's telephone systems, airline reservation systems, banking systems, global information systems, weather prediction systems, and aircraft and nuclear power plant control systems all depend critically on distributed algorithms. Obviously, it is important that the algorithms run correctly and efficiently. However, because the settings in which they run are so complicated, the design of such algorithms can be an extremely difficult task.

This book contains a comprehensive introduction to the field of distributed algorithms—a collection of the most significant algorithms and impossibility results, all presented in a simple automata-theoretic setting. Mathematical proofs are given (or at least sketched) for virtually all of the results. Algorithms are analyzed according to precisely defined complexity measures. Altogether, this material provides an excellent foundation for a deep understanding of distributed algorithms.

This book has been written with several audiences in mind. First, it is organized as a textbook for a first-year graduate computer science course, especially for students interested in computer systems, theory, or both. It can also be used as a text for a short course for designers of distributed systems. Finally, it is intended as a reference manual for designers, students, researchers, and anyone else interested in the field.

The book contains algorithms for many typical problems, including problems of consensus, communication, resource allocation, and synchronization, in several different system settings. The algorithms and results are organized according to basic assumptions about the distributed setting. The first level of organization is according to the *timing model*—synchronous, asynchronous, or partially synchronous—and the second level is according to the *interprocess communication mechanism*—shared memory or message passing. Several chapters are devoted to each type of system model; the first chapter in each group presents a formal model for that type of system, while the rest of the chapters contain the algorithms and impossibility results. Throughout, the presentation is rigorous, yet it is firmly grounded in intuition.

Because this field is so large and active, this book does not attempt to cover everything. The results that are included have been selected because they are the most fundamental. These are not always the optimal results, in terms of the complexity measures; they are generally those that are simple and that illustrate important general methods of design or reasoning.

This book will make you familiar with many of the most important problems, algorithms, and impossibility results in the area of distributed computing. You will be able to recognize the problems when they arise in practical settings, apply algorithms like the ones contained here to solve them, and invoke the impossibility results to argue that the problems are not solvable. The book will also give you a good feeling for the various system models and their capabilities, so that you can design new algorithms yourself (or even prove new impossibility results). Finally, this book should convince you that it is feasible to reason carefully about distributed algorithms and systems: to model them formally, give precise specifications for their required behavior, prove rigorously that they satisfy their specifications, identify appropriate complexity measures, and analyze them according to these measures.

Using this Book

Prerequisites.   The only prerequisites for reading the book are knowledge of basic college-level discrete mathematics (including mathematical induction and asymptotic analysis), some programming skill, and reasonable familiarity with computer systems. The sections about randomized algorithms also require knowledge of basic probability. An undergraduate-level course about sequential algorithms and their analysis is helpful, but not necessary.

Chapter dependencies.   This book has been designed so that the material using the different models can be read fairly independently. An outline of significant chapter dependencies is presented in Figure A. For example, if you prefer to move quickly to the material on asynchronous networks, you can skip Chapters

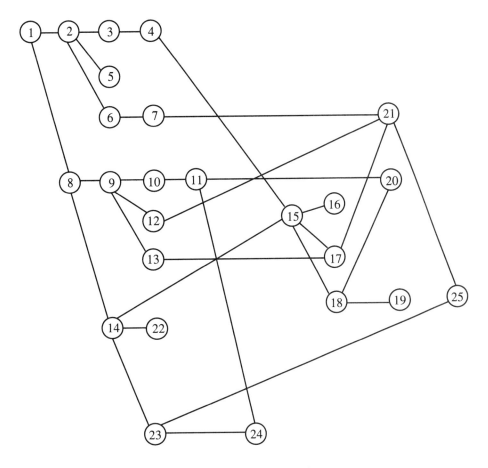

Figure A: Chapter dependencies.

5–7. You can also read a good part of the algorithm chapters without reading the modelling chapters on which they are formally dependent.

Starred sections. This book contains several sections whose titles are starred in the table of contents. These sections contain material that is less fundamental or more advanced than the other sections. You can omit these sections on a first reading without much harm.

Courses. Preliminary versions of this book have been used for many years in an introductory graduate-level course at MIT, and for three years in a summer course for system designers in computer software and applications companies. This book contains enough material for a one-year course, so you will have to select material for shorter courses (but watch the chapter dependencies).

For example, in a one-semester course emphasizing asynchronous network computing, you could cover Chapters 3, 4, 6, 7.2, 12, and 14–21, referring to material from the modelling chapters (Chapters 2, 8, and 9) and filling in a few definitions from Chapters 10, 11, and 13 as needed. In a one-semester course emphasizing a thorough study of distributed consensus, you could cover Chapters 2–9, 12, 13.1, 15, 17, 21, 23, and 25. There are many other possibilities. If you yourself are a researcher in this area, then you might want to supplement this book as a course text with more advanced or specialized results from the research literature in your favorite area.

In a one-week or two-week short course for system designers, you could cover the highlights of all the chapters, discussing key results and key proof ideas at a high level instead of presenting a lot of detail.

Errors.   I would appreciate hearing about any errors that you find in the book, as well as receiving any other constructive suggestions you may have. Suggestions for additional problems would be especially welcome. Please email your comments to distalgs@theory.lcs.mit.edu.

Acknowledgments

It is impossible to acknowledge all the people who contributed to the production of this book, since it is the product of many years of teaching and research, involving interactions with many, many students and research colleagues. I will try, though.

The book is the final version of the lecture notes for MIT's graduate course 6.852. The students in the many passes through this course suffered through my early attempts to organize the material. The students were especially helpful in 1990 and 1992, when they helped to prepare on-line versions of the lecture notes. Course teaching assistants Ken Goldman, Isaac Saias, and Boaz Patt-Shamir helped immensely in developing the notes. Jennifer Welch and Rainer Gawlick also helped out as teaching assistants during other passes through the course.

Many students and colleagues contributed to my own understanding of the material by working with me on some of the results that appear here or by discussing other people's work. These include Yehuda Afek, Eshrat Arjomandi, Hagit Attiya, Baruch Awerbuch, Bard Bloom, Alan Borodin, James Burns, Soma Chaudhuri, Brian Coan, Harish Devarajan, Danny Dolev, Cynthia Dwork, Alan Fekete, Michael Fischer, Greg Frederickson, Eli Gafni, Rainer Gawlick, Ken Goldman, Art Harvey, Maurice Herlihy, Paul Jackson, Jon Kleinberg, Leslie Lamport, Butler Lampson, Victor Luchangco, Yishay Mansour, Michael Merritt,

Michael Paterson, Boaz Patt-Shamir, Gary Peterson, Shlomit Pinter, Stephen Ponzio, Isaac Saias, Russel Schaffer, Roberto Segala, Nir Shavit, Liuba Shrira, Jørgen Søgaard-Andersen, Eugene Stark, Larry Stockmeyer, Mark Tuttle, Frits Vaandrager, George Varghese, Bill Weihl, Jennifer Welch, and Lenore Zuck. Two of these people deserve special credit: my mentor Michael Fischer, for starting work with me in 1978 on what was then a small but promising-looking research area, and my student Mark Tuttle, whose M.S. thesis work defined and developed the I/O automaton model.

I would also like to thank Ajoy Datta, Roberto De Prisco, Alan Fekete, Faith Fich, Rainer Gawlick, Shai Halevi, Jon Kleinberg, Richard Ladner, John Leo, Victor Luchangco, Michael Melliar-Smith, Michael Merritt, Daniele Micciancio, Boaz Patt-Shamir, Anya Pogosyants, Stephen Ponzio, Sergio Rajsbaum, Roberto Segala, Nir Shavit, Mark Smith, Larry Stockmeyer, Mark Tuttle, George Varghese, Jennifer Welch, and Lenore Zuck for reading portions of drafts of the book and contributing many useful comments. Ajoy, Faith, and George, especially, suffered through the effort of teaching their classes from early versions of the book and provided many suggestions. And I want to thank Joanne Talbot for her tireless work on formatting, drawing diagrams, preparing the bibliography, making endless copies, and more. David Jones helped with some of the formatting. I also thank John Guttag, Paul Penfield, and others in the MIT EECS Department for arranging for me to have the free time that I needed to write. Bruce Spatz at Morgan Kaufmann was, once again, encouraging and helpful to me in this daunting endeavor. He always seemed to provide exactly the right suggestions. And Julie Pabst and Diane Cerra at Morgan Kaufmann helped immensely in the final stages of production. Thanks also to Ed Sznyter of Babel Press for his LATEX expertise.

Last and most of all, I want to thank my unboundedly patient family, Dennis, Patrick, and Mary Lynch, for tolerating all my work on this book and taking care of absolutely everything else in the meantime. Thanks especially to Dennis for cooking all those excellent seafood dinners (not to mention renovating both the bathroom and the laundry room) while I spent all my time at my computer!

Nancy A. Lynch
Cambridge, Massachusetts

Chapter 1

Introduction

1.1 The Subject Matter

The term *distributed algorithms* covers a large variety of concurrent algorithms used for a wide range of applications. Originally, this term was used to refer to algorithms that were designed to run on many processors "distributed" over a large geographical area. But over the years, the usage of this term has been broadened, so that it now includes algorithms that run on local area networks and even algorithms for shared memory multiprocessors. This has happened because it has become recognized that the algorithms used in these various settings have a great deal in common.

Distributed algorithms arise in many applications, including telecommunications, distributed information processing, scientific computing, and real-time process control. An important part of the job of building a system for any of these applications is the design, implementation, and analysis of distributed algorithms. The algorithms that arise, and the problems that they are designed to solve, form the subject matter of the field of study covered in this book.

There are many different kinds of distributed algorithms. Some of the attributes by which they differ include

- *The interprocess communication (IPC) method:* Distributed algorithms run on a collection of processors, which need to communicate somehow. Some common methods of communication include accessing shared memory, sending point-to-point or broadcast messages (either over a long distance or local area network), and executing remote procedure calls.

- *The timing model:* Several different assumptions can be made about the timing of events in the system, reflecting the different types of timing information that might be used by algorithms. At one extreme, processors can be completely synchronous, performing communication and computation in perfect lock-step synchrony. At the other extreme, they can be completely asynchronous, taking steps at arbitrary speeds and in arbitrary orders. In between, there are a wide range of possible assumptions that can be grouped together under the designation *partially synchronous*; in all of these cases, processors have partial information about the timing of events. For example, processors might have bounds on their relative speeds or might have access to approximately synchronized clocks.

- *The failure model:* The hardware upon which an algorithm runs might be assumed to be completely reliable. Or, the algorithm might need to tolerate some limited amount of faulty behavior. Such faulty behavior can include processor failures: processors might just stop, with or without warning; might fail transiently; or might exhibit more severe *Byzantine failures*, where a failed processor can behave arbitrarily. Faulty behavior can also include failures of the communication mechanisms, including message loss or duplication.

- *The problems addressed:* Of course, the algorithms also differ in the problems that they are supposed to solve. The typical problems that are considered are those that arise in the application areas mentioned above. They include problems of resource allocation, communication, consensus among distributed processors, database concurrency control, deadlock detection, global snapshots, synchronization, and implementation of various types of objects.

Some kinds of concurrent algorithms, such as Parallel Random Access Machine (PRAM) algorithms and algorithms for fixed-connection networks (for example, arrays, trees, and hypercubes), are not covered in this book. The algorithms presented here are distinguished within the larger class of concurrent algorithms by having a higher degree of *uncertainty* and more *independence of activities*. Some of the types of uncertainty and independence that the algorithms in this book must contend with include

- unknown number of processors

- unknown network topology

- independent inputs at different locations

- several programs executing at once, starting at different times, and operating at different speeds

- processor nondeterminism

- uncertain message delivery times

- unknown message ordering

- processor and communication failures

Fortunately, not every algorithm has to contend with all of these types of uncertainty!

Because of all this uncertainty, the behavior of distributed algorithms is often quite difficult to understand. Even though the code for an algorithm may be short, the fact that many processors execute the code in parallel, with steps interleaved in some undetermined way, implies that there are many different ways in which the algorithm can behave, even for the same inputs. Thus, it is generally impossible to understand the algorithm by predicting exactly how it will execute. This can be contrasted with other kinds of parallel algorithms such as PRAM algorithms, for which we can often predict exactly what the algorithm will do at every point in time. For a distributed algorithm, instead of understanding everything about its behavior, the best that we usually can do is to understand certain selected *properties* of its behavior.

The study of distributed algorithms has developed over the past 15 years into a fairly coherent field. The general style of work in this field is more or less as follows. First, problems of significance in practical distributed computing are identified, and abstract versions of these problems, suitable for mathematical study, are defined. Then, algorithms that solve the problems are developed. These are described precisely and proved to solve the stated problems, and their complexity, according to various measures, is analyzed. In designing such algorithms, we typically try to minimize their complexity. Also, impossibility results and lower bounds are proved, demonstrating limitations on what problems can be solved and with what costs. Underlying all of this work are mathematical models for distributed systems.

These results comprise a very interesting mathematical theory. But they are more than a mathematical theory: the problem statements can be used to formulate specifications for portions of real systems, the algorithms can (in many cases) be engineered for practical use, and the impossibility results can help to tell designers when to stop trying to build something. All of these results, as well as the underlying mathematical models, can provide designers with assistance in understanding the systems they build.

1.2 Our Viewpoint

This book contains a study of the field of distributed algorithms. Because this field is so large and active, we cannot give an exhaustive study. Since we have had to select, we have tried to choose the most fundamental results in the area, both theoretically and practically speaking. These are not always the optimal results in terms of the complexity measures; instead, we have favored those that are simple and that illustrate important general methods of design or reasoning. The results we present involve a small number of problems that are typical of this area, including leader election, network searching, spanning tree construction, distributed consensus, mutual exclusion, resource allocation, construction of objects, synchronization, global snapshots, and reliable communication. These problems recur in many different applications. We consider the same problems in several different system models.

One feature of this book is that we present all the algorithms, impossibility results, and lower bounds in terms of a more or less unified formal framework. This framework consists of a small number of formal, automata-theoretic models for various types of distributed systems, together with some standard ways of reasoning about systems using the models. Our framework is automata-theoretic, rather than being based on any particular formal language or formal proof logic; this allows us to present results in terms of basic set-theoretic mathematics without worrying too much about language details. It also allows flexibility, in that a variety of languages and logics could be used to describe and reason about algorithms in the same framework. Using a formal framework permits a rigorous treatment of all the results.

Some more remarks about rigor are in order. A rigorous treatment is especially important in the area of distributed algorithms because of the many subtle complications that arise. Without such care, it is difficult to avoid mistakes. However, it is not clear how we could make a completely rigorous presentation both reasonably short and intuitively understandable. In this book, we compromise and use a mixture of intuitive and rigorous reasoning. Namely, we give precise descriptions of appropriate formal models. We sometimes give precise descriptions of algorithms in terms of the formal models, sometimes English descriptions, and sometimes both. The degree of rigor in correctness arguments for algorithms varies greatly: sometimes we give rather formal proofs and sometimes only intuitive sketches. We hope, however, that we have provided enough tools for you to expand our intuitive sketches into formal proofs when you want to. We generally present impossibility arguments rather rigorously, in terms of the formal models.

Because there are so many different settings and problems to consider, it is not obvious how best to organize the presentation of the material. We have chosen to organize it primarily according to the formal models—in particular, according to those aspects of the models that seem to make the most difference in the results, and secondarily by abstract problem statements. The deepest distinctions among the models seem to be based on timing assumptions, but IPC mechanisms and failure assumptions are also important factors.

The timing models we consider are the following.

- *The synchronous model:* This is the simplest model to describe, to program, and to reason about. We assume that components take steps simultaneously, that is, that execution proceeds in synchronous rounds. Of course, this is not what actually happens in most distributed systems, but the synchronous model can be useful anyway. Understanding how to solve a problem in the synchronous model is often a useful intermediate step toward understanding how to solve it in more realistic models. For example, it is sometimes possible for a real distributed system to "simulate" a synchronous system. Also, impossibility results for the synchronous model carry over directly to less well-behaved models. On the other hand, it is impossible or inefficient to implement the synchronous model in many types of distributed systems.

- *The asynchronous model:* Here we assume that the separate components take steps in an arbitrary order, at arbitrary relative speeds. This model is also reasonably simple to describe, although there are a few subtleties, mainly involving *liveness* considerations. It is harder to program than the synchronous model because of the extra uncertainty in the order of events. However, the asynchronous model does allow the programmer to ignore specific timing considerations. Since the asynchronous model assumes less about time than is guaranteed by typical distributed systems, algorithms designed for the asynchronous model are general and portable: they are guaranteed to run correctly in networks with arbitrary timing guarantees. On the other hand, the asynchronous model sometimes does not provide enough power to solve problems efficiently, or even to solve them at all.

- *The partially synchronous (timing-based) model:* Here we assume some restrictions on the relative timing of events, but execution is not completely lock-step as it is in the synchronous model. These models are the most realistic, but they are also the most difficult to program. Algorithms designed using knowledge of the timing of events can be efficient, but they can also be fragile in that they will not run correctly if the timing assumptions are violated.

The next basis we use for classification is the IPC mechanism. In this book, we consider both shared memory and message passing. We present the shared memory model first, because it is more powerful and simpler to understand, and because many of the techniques and results for the shared memory setting can be adapted for use in the network setting. Next, we organize the material according to the problem studied. And finally, we study many of the problems under different failure assumptions. You should see, as we present the same problems in a variety of different models, that apparently minor differences in assumptions can make a big difference in the results. We have tried to identify and highlight such differences.

We have tried to make our presentation as *modular* as possible by composing algorithms to obtain other algorithms, by developing algorithms using levels of abstraction, and by transforming algorithms for one model into algorithms for other models. This helps greatly to reduce the complexity of the ideas and allows us to accomplish more with less work. The same kinds of modularity can serve the same purposes in practical distributed system design.

1.3   Overview of Chapters 2–25

The specific topics that this book covers are as follows.

Models and proof methods.   The material on formal models and proof methods is presented in separate chapters—Chapters 2, 8, 9, 14, and 23—heading the major subdivisions of the book (synchronous network algorithms, asynchronous shared memory algorithms, asynchronous network algorithms, and partially synchronous algorithms). This material is isolated into separate chapters for easy reference. You may prefer to skip some of the modelling material on the first reading, returning to it as needed for understanding the material in the succeeding "algorithm chapters." We have tried to construct the book so that the algorithm chapters can be read, and mostly understood, without too much formal modelling work.

The models we use are all based on state machines, often having an infinite number of states and usually having explicit names associated with their transitions. A state machine can be used to model either a component of a distributed system or an entire distributed system. Each state of the machine represents an instantaneous snapshot of the component or system, including such information as the state of the memory of each processor, the program counter for each running program, and the messages that are in transit in the communication system. The transitions describe changes that occur in the system, such as the sending or receipt of a message, or the changes caused by some local computation. We present separate state machine models for synchronous networks, asynchronous systems, and timing-based systems.

One important use of a formal model for distributed systems is as a basis for specification of the problems to be solved and verification of algorithm correctness. Such specification and verification can be done using many stylized and ad hoc methods. However, certain methods are used so frequently that we describe them explicitly in the modelling chapters. These include the method of *invariant assertions* and the method of *simulations*. An invariant assertion is a property that is true of all reachable states of a system. Assertions are generally proved by induction on the number of steps in a system execution. A simulation is a formal relationship between a pair of systems, one representing the problem to be solved and another representing the solution, or one representing a high-level, abstract solution and another a detailed solution. Simulation relationships are also generally proved using induction.

Chapter 2 contains the first model, for synchronous networks. It is a very simple model that just describes synchronized rounds of message exchange and computation. Chapter 8 contains a general model for asynchronous systems, the *input/output automaton* (*I/O automaton*) model. The name of the model refers to its explicit distinction between input and output transitions, that is, those communicated to the system by its environment and those communicated to the environment by the system. In an I/O automaton, several transitions may be possible from any given state; for example, transitions involving different processors may be performed in any order. Since the model allows so much flexibility in the order of transitions, a notion of liveness is included, allowing us to express the notion that certain transitions must eventually happen. A useful feature of this model is that it has a parallel composition operation, which allows a combination of system components modelled as I/O automata also to be modelled as an I/O automaton. Often, the correctness of a composed automaton can be proved in a modular fashion, based on proofs of the correctness of its components.

The model in Chapter 8 is general enough to describe both asynchronous shared memory systems and asynchronous networks (as well as many other types of asynchronous systems); Chapters 9 and 14 contain the additional structure needed to tailor the model for shared memory systems and message-passing systems, respectively.

Finally, in Chapter 23, we present models for timing-based systems. These models are, once again, state machines, but this time the states include information about timing, such as the current time and scheduled times for various events. These models allow us to describe typical constructs for timing-based systems, such as local clocks and timeouts.

Synchronous network algorithms. The simplest model that we consider (that is, the one with the least uncertainty) is the synchronous network model, in which all the processors communicate and compute in synchronous rounds. We do not consider synchronous shared memory algorithms, since these constitute a large subject of study in their own right (see the Bibliographic Notes at the end of this chapter). In the network setting we assume that the processors are located at the nodes of a graph or digraph, G, and communicate with their neighbors using messages sent along the edges of G.

In Chapters 3–7, we consider several typical distributed problems in synchronous networks. In Chapter 3, we begin with a simple example involving computation in ring networks. The problem is to *elect a unique leader* in a ring network, assuming that the processors at the nodes are identical except for *unique identifiers* (*UIDs*). The main uncertainty here is that the set of UIDs actually possessed by the processors is unknown (although it is known that no two processors have the same UID); in addition, the size of the network is usually unknown. The main application for this problem is a local area ring network that operates as a token ring, in which there is always supposed to be a single token circulating, giving its current owner the sole right to initiate communication. Sometimes, however, the token gets lost, and it becomes necessary for the processors to execute an algorithm to regenerate the missing token. This regeneration procedure amounts to electing a leader. We present some basic complexity-theoretic results about the leader-election problem. In particular, we prove bounds for the time and the amount of communication (i.e., the number of messages) that are required.

Next, in Chapter 4, we give a brief survey of basic algorithms used in more general networks. Specifically, we describe some algorithms used to solve such fundamental problems as *electing a leader*, conducting a *breadth-first search*, finding *shortest paths*, finding a *minimum spanning tree*, and finding a *maximal independent set* of nodes. Typical forms of uncertainty here are unknown UIDs and an unknown network graph.

Then, in Chapters 5 and 6, we consider problems of *reaching consensus* in a distributed network. These are problems in which a collection of distributed processors are required to reach a common decision, even if there are initial differences of opinion about what that decision ought to be. Many different consensus problems arise in practice: for example, the processors could be monitoring separate altimeters on board an aircraft and could be attempting to reach agreement about the altitude. Or the processors could be carrying out separate fault diagnosis procedures for some other system component and could be attempting to combine their individual diagnoses into a common decision about whether or not to replace the component.

The uncertainty that we consider here stems not only from differences in initial opinions, but also from *failures*, either of links or of processors. In Chapter 5, we consider the case where links can fail by losing messages. In Chapter 6, we consider two different types of processor failures: stopping failures, where faulty processors can, at some point, just stop executing their local protocols, and Byzantine failures, where faulty processors can exhibit completely arbitrary behavior (subject to the limitation that they cannot corrupt portions of the system to which they have no access). We present bounds on the number of tolerable faults, on the time, and on the amount of communication.

Finally, in Chapter 7, we consider some extensions and variations on the basic consensus problems, including *agreement on a small set of values* rather than just a single value, *approximate agreement* on a real value, and *distributed database commit*.

Asynchronous shared memory algorithms. After warming up with synchronous algorithms (in which there is only a little uncertainty), we begin the more difficult study of asynchronous algorithms. Now we no longer assume that processors operate in lock-step synchrony, but rather that they can interleave their steps in an arbitrary order, with no bounds on individual processor speeds. Typically, the interactions with the external world (via input and output events) are ongoing, rather than just involving an initial input and final output. The results in this setting have a very different flavor from those for synchronous networks.

Chapters 10–13 contain asynchronous shared memory algorithms. The first problem we consider, in Chapter 10, is that of *mutual exclusion*. This is one of the most fundamental problems in the area of distributed algorithms, and historically the first problem to receive serious theoretical study. Essentially, the problem involves managing access to a single, indivisible resource that can only support one user at a time. Alternatively, it can be viewed as the problem of ensuring that certain portions of program code are executed within *critical regions*, where no two programs are permitted to be in critical regions at the same time. This problem arises in both centralized and distributed operating systems. Besides the basic uncertainty about the order of steps, there is also uncertainty about which users are going to request access to the resource, and when.

We present a series of shared memory mutual exclusion algorithms, starting with a classical algorithm invented by Dijkstra in 1965, and proceeding through a series of algorithms with successively better correctness guarantees. Most of these results are based on shared memory that can only be accessed using read and write operations; for this read/write shared memory model, we also present a lower bound on the number of shared variables that must be used. We also consider the problem using a stronger type of shared memory—read-modify-write memory; for this case, we give upper and lower bounds on the size of the needed shared memory. In addition to presenting the algorithms and lower bounds, we also use the mutual exclusion problem as a case study to illustrate many concepts of general importance for asynchronous distributed algorithms. These concepts include the general modelling methods; notions of atomicity, fairness, progress, and fault-tolerance; invariant assertion and simulation proofs; and time analysis techniques.

In Chapter 11, we discuss generalizations of the mutual exclusion problem to more complicated *resource allocation* problems; these involve more resources and have more elaborate requirements about their usage patterns. For example, we consider the *Dining Philosophers* problem, a prototypical resource allocation problem involving allocation of pairwise shared resources in a ring of processors.

In Chapter 12, we reconsider *consensus* problems in the asynchronous shared memory model. The main result of this chapter is the fundamental fact that a very basic consensus problem cannot be solved in this setting in the presence of faults, if the shared memory supports only read and write operations. In contrast, stronger types of shared memory, such as read-modify-write memory, admit simple solutions to this problem.

Next, in Chapter 13, we present *atomic objects*. Up to this point in the book, we assume that all accesses by processors to shared memory are instantaneous. Atomic objects admit separate invocation and response actions, but otherwise behave very similarly to instantaneous-access shared variables. We define atomic objects and prove basic results showing how they can be used to construct systems; in particular, they can be used in place of shared variables. We also consider several algorithms that implement powerful atomic objects using weaker primitives—either shared variables or atomic objects of weaker types. An interesting property that these algorithms have is *wait-freedom*, which means that any operation on the implemented object must complete regardless of the failure of other concurrent operations.

We show how to implement a *snapshot atomic object* using read/write shared memory; a snapshot atomic object admits a *snapshot* operation that returns values for all the memory locations at once. We also show how to implement a *multi-writer/multi-reader atomic object* using single-writer read/write shared memory.

Asynchronous network algorithms. In Chapters 15–22, we proceed to the study of algorithms that operate in asynchronous networks. As for synchronous networks, the system is modelled as a graph or digraph with processors at the nodes and communication links on the edges, but now the system does not operate in rounds. Now, messages can arrive at arbitrary times and the processors can take steps at arbitrary speeds. The system components can be said to be more "loosely coupled" than they are in either the synchronous network setting or the asynchronous shared memory setting. Thus, the amount of uncertainty in the model is again increased.

We begin in Chapter 15 by reconsidering the problems and algorithms of Chapter 4 in the asynchronous network setting. For example, we reconsider the problems of leader election, breadth-first search and shortest paths, broadcast and convergecast, and minimum spanning tree. Although some of the algorithms carry over to the new setting with little change, most of them require significant modification. In particular, it is rather difficult to extend the simple synchronous minimum spanning tree algorithm of Chapter 4 to the asynchronous setting.

Chapter 15 should convince you that the task of programming asynchronous networks is difficult. This difficulty motivates the following four chapters, Chapters 16–19, where we introduce four techniques for simplifying the task. These techniques are formulated as *algorithm transformations* that allow an asynchronous network to simulate simpler or more powerful models. These transformations permit algorithms designed for the simpler or more powerful models to run in the more complex asynchronous network model.

The first technique, described in Chapter 16, is the introduction of a *synchronizer*. A synchronizer is a system component that enables asynchronous networks (without failures) to simulate the synchronous networks of Chapters 2–4 (those without failures). We give efficient implementations and contrast these implementations with a lower bound result that seems to say that any such simulation must be inefficient. The apparent contradiction turns out to depend on the type of problem being solved.

The second technique, described in Chapter 17, is the simulation of the asynchronous shared memory model by the asynchronous network model. This permits asynchronous shared memory algorithms such as those developed in Chapters 10–13 to be used in asynchronous networks.

The third technique, described in Chapter 18, is the assignment of consistent *logical times* to events in an asynchronous distributed network. This technique can be used to allow an asynchronous network to simulate one in which the nodes have access to perfectly synchronized real-time clocks. An important use of this capability is to allow an asynchronous network to simulate a centralized (nondistributed) state machine.

Chapter 19 contains our fourth technique, the monitoring of asynchronous network algorithms while they run. This might be done, for example, for the purpose of debugging, for producing backup versions, or for detecting *stable properties* of the algorithm. A stable property is one that, once it occurs, will persist forever; examples are system *termination* or *deadlock*. It turns out that a fundamental primitive that helps in the detection of stable properties is the ability to produce a *consistent global snapshot* of the state of the distributed algorithm. We show some ways in which such a snapshot can be produced and describe how a snapshot can be used to detect stable properties.

Having developed some powerful tools, we return to considering specific problems in the asynchronous network setting. In Chapter 20, we revisit the problem of resource allocation. For example, we show some ways of solving the mutual exclusion and Dining Philosophers problems in asynchronous networks.

In Chapter 21, we consider the problem of computing in an asynchronous network in the presence of stopping faults. First, using a transformation developed in Chapter 17, we show that the impossibility result for consensus carries over from the shared memory setting to the network setting. We then consider some ways around this inherent limitation; for instance, we give a *randomized algorithm* to solve consensus, show how to solve consensus using modules known as *failure detectors*, and show how to reach *approximate agreement* rather than exact agreement.

In Chapter 22, we consider the *data link* problem. Data link protocols are designed to implement a reliable communication link in terms of unreliable underlying channels. We begin by presenting the Alternating Bit protocol, a simple protocol that, in addition to being interesting in its own right, is also well known as a standard case study in the field of concurrent algorithm verification. We also present a variety of other algorithms and impossibility results for this problem, for settings in which different types of failure behavior are considered for the underlying channels.

Partially synchronous algorithms. Partially synchronous models lie properly between synchronous and asynchronous models. In partially synchronous models, we assume that processors have some knowledge of time, for example, access to real time or approximate real time, or some type of timeout facility. Or, we might assume that processor step times and/or message delivery times are between known upper and lower bounds. Since partially synchronous systems have less uncertainty than asynchronous systems, you might think that they ought to be easier to program. However, there are extra complications that arise from the timing—for example, algorithms are often designed so that their correctness depends crucially on timing assumptions. Thus, algorithms and proofs for the partially synchronous setting are often more complicated than those for the asynchronous setting.

In Chapter 24, we present upper and lower bounds for the time requirements of solving the mutual exclusion problem in the timed setting, while in Chapter 25, we obtain upper and lower bounds for consensus. Since partially synchronous distributed algorithms are a subject of current research, the results we present for this model are necessarily preliminary.

1.4   Bibliographic Notes

The major source for the material in this book is the research literature, especially the many papers presented in the Association for Computing Machinery's annual symposium on Principles of Distributed Computing (PODC). Other symposia that contain a substantial number of papers in this area include the annual symposia on Foundations of Computer Science (FOCS), Theory of Computing (STOC), and Parallel Algorithms and Architectures (SPAA), and the annual Workshop on Distributed Algorithms (WDAG). Much of this work has also appeared by now in computer science journals such as the *Journal of the ACM, Distributed Computing, Information and Computation*, the *SIAM Journal on Computing, Acta Informatica*, and *Information Processing Letters*. The results in these papers are presented in terms of a great many different models and at varying levels of rigor.

There have been a few previous attempts to collect and summarize some of the material in this area. The chapter by Lamport and Lynch on distributed computing in the *Handbook of Theoretical Computer Science* [185] is a sketchy overview of some of the modelling and algorithmic ideas. Two books by Raynal [249, 250] present descriptions of the areas of mutual exclusion algorithms and asynchronous network algorithms, respectively. Another book, by Raynal and Helary [251], presents results on network synchronizers. Chandy and Misra [69] present a substantial collection of distributed algorithms, in terms of the UNITY programming model. Tel [276] presents another view of the field.

Results about the PRAM model for synchronous shared memory systems are collected in a paper by Karp and Ramachandran [166]. Results about synchronous parallel algorithms for fixed-connection networks are collected in a book by Leighton [193]. Lynch, Merritt, Weihl, and Fekete [207] and Bernstein, Hadzilacos, and Goodman [50] present many algorithms for concurrency control and recovery in distributed data processing systems. Hadzilacos and Toueg [143] present results about the implementation of distributed systems based on communication systems with an atomic broadcast primitive.

This book uses many concepts from graph theory. A standard reference for these is the classical book by Harary [147].

1.5 Notation

We collect here some mathematical notation that we use throughout the book.

$\mathbb{N}$ denotes the natural numbers, $\{0, 1, 2, \ldots\}$.

$\mathbb{N}^+$ denotes the positive natural numbers, $\{1, 2, \ldots\}$.

$R^{\geq 0}$ denotes the nonnegative real numbers.

R^+ denotes the positive real numbers.

λ denotes the empty string.

If β is any sequence and S is any set, then $\beta | S$ denotes the subsequence of β consisting of all the elements of S in β.

Part I

Synchronous Network Algorithms

The first part of this book consists of Chapters 2–7. These chapters contain algorithms and lower bound results for the *synchronous network model*, in which processors in a network take steps and exchange messages in synchronous rounds.

The first chapter in this part, Chapter 2, just presents our formal model for synchronous networks. You can skip this chapter for now and return to it as you need to while reading the algorithm chapters, Chapters 3–7. Chapter 3 deals with the simple problem of *electing a unique leader in a ring network*. Chapter 4 contains a survey of basic algorithms used in synchronous networks based on arbitrary graphs. Chapters 5 and 6 deal with basic problems of *reaching consensus* in synchronous networks, in the presence of link and processor failures, respectively. Finally, Chapter 7 contains extensions and variations of the basic consensus problems.

Chapter 2

Modelling I: Synchronous Network Model

This is the shortest chapter in the book. That is because all it has to accomplish is to present a simple computational model for synchronous network algorithms. We present the model separately so that you can use this chapter as a convenient reference while reading Chapters 3–7.

2.1 Synchronous Network Systems

A *synchronous network system* consists of a collection of computing elements located at the nodes of a directed network graph. In Chapter 1, we referred to these computing elements as "processors," which suggests that they are pieces of hardware. It is often useful to think of them instead as logical software "processes," running on (but not identical to) the actual hardware processors. The results that we present here make sense in either case. We will use the convention of calling the computing elements "processes" from now on in the book.

In order to define a synchronous network system formally, we start with a directed graph $G = (V, E)$. We use the letter n to denote $|V|$, the number of nodes in the network digraph. For each node i of G, we use the notation *out-nbrs$_i$* to denote the "outgoing neighbors" of i, that is, those nodes to which there are edges from i in the digraph G, and *in-nbrs$_i$* to denote the "incoming neighbors" of i, that is, those nodes from which there are edges to i in G. We let *distance(i, j)* denote the length of the shortest directed path from i to j in G, if any exists; otherwise *distance$(i, j) = \infty$*. We define *diam*, the *diameter*, to be the maximum *distance(i, j)*, taken over all pairs (i, j). We also suppose that we have some fixed message alphabet M, and we let *null* be a placeholder indicating the absence of a message.

Associated with each node $i \in V$, we have a *process*, which consists formally of the following components:

- *states$_i$*, a (not necessarily finite) set of *states*

- *start$_i$*, a nonempty subset of *states$_i$* known as the *start states* or *initial states*

- *msgs$_i$*, a *message-generation function* mapping *states$_i$* × *out-nbrs$_i$* to elements of $M \cup \{null\}$

- *trans$_i$*, a *state-transition function* mapping *states$_i$* and vectors (indexed by *in-nbrs$_i$*) of elements of $M \cup \{null\}$ to *states$_i$*

That is, each process has a set of states, among which is distinguished a subset of start states. The set of states need not be finite. This generality is important, since it permits us to model systems that include unbounded data structures such as counters. The message-generation function specifies, for each state and outgoing neighbor, the message (if any) that process i sends to the indicated neighbor, starting from the given state. The state-transition function specifies, for each state and collection of messages from all the incoming neighbors, the new state to which process i moves.

Associated with each edge (i, j) in G, there is a *channel*, also known as a *link*, which is just a location that can, at any time, hold at most a single message in M.

Execution of the entire system begins with all the processes in arbitrary start states, and all channels empty. Then the processes, in lock-step, repeatedly perform the following two steps:

1. Apply the message-generation function to the current state to generate the messages to be sent to all outgoing neighbors. Put these messages in the appropriate channels.

2. Apply the state-transition function to the current state and the incoming messages to obtain the new state. Remove all messages from the channels.

The combination of the two steps is called a *round*. Note that we do not, in general, place restrictions on the amount of computation a process does in order to compute the values of its message-generation and state-transition functions. Also note that the model presented here is deterministic, in the sense that the message-generation function and the state-transition function are (single-valued) functions. Thus, given a particular collection of start states, the computation unfolds in a unique way.

Halting. So far, we have not made any provision for *process halting*. It is easy, however, to distinguish some of the process states as *halting states*, and specify that no further activity can occur from these states. That is, no messages are generated and the only state transition is a self-loop. Note that these halting states do not play the same role in these systems as they do in traditional finite-state automata. There, they generally serve as *accepting states*, which are used to determine which strings are in the language computed by the machine. Here, they just serve to halt the process; what the process computes must be determined according to some other convention. The notion of accepting state is normally not used for distributed algorithms.

Variable start times. Occasionally, we will want to consider synchronous systems in which the processes might begin executing at different rounds. We model this situation by augmenting the network graph to include a special *environment node*, having edges to all the ordinary nodes. The job of the associated *environment process* is to send special *wakeup* messages to all the other processes. Each start state of each of the other processes is required to be *quiescent*, by which we mean that it does not cause any messages to be generated, and it can only change to a different state as the result of the receipt of a *wakeup* message from the environment or a non-*null* message from some other process. Thus, a process can be awakened either directly, by a *wakeup* message from the environment, or indirectly, by a non-*null* message from another, previously awakened, process.

Undirected graphs. Sometimes we will want to consider the case where the underlying network graph is undirected. We model this situation within the model we have already defined for directed graphs simply by considering a directed graph network with bidirectional edges between all pairs of neighbors. In this case, we will use the notation $nbrs_i$ to denote the neighbors of i in the graph.

2.2 Failures

We will consider various types of failures for synchronous systems, including both *process failures* and *link (channel) failures*.

A process can exhibit *stopping failure* simply by stopping somewhere in the middle of its execution. In terms of the model, the process might fail before or after performing some instance of Step 1 or Step 2 above; in addition, we allow it to fail somewhere in the middle of performing Step 1. This means that the process might succeed in putting only a subset of the messages it is supposed to produce into the message channels. We will assume that this can be *any* subset—

we do not think of the process as producing its messages sequentially and failing somewhere in the middle of the sequence.

A process can also exhibit *Byzantine failure*, by which we mean that it can generate its next messages and next state in some arbitrary way, without necessarily following the rules specified by its message-generation and state-transition functions.

A link can fail by losing messages. In terms of a model, a process might attempt to place a message in a channel during Step 1, but the faulty link might not record the message.

2.3   Inputs and Outputs

We still have not provided any facility for modelling inputs and outputs. We use the simple convention of encoding the inputs and outputs in the states. In particular, inputs are placed in designated input variables in the start states; the fact that a process can have multiple start states is important here, so that we can accommodate different possible inputs. In fact, we normally assume that the *only* source of multiplicity of start states is the possibility of different input values in the input variables. Outputs appear in designated output variables; each of these records the result of only the first write operation that is performed (i.e., it is a *write-once* variable). Output variables can be read any number of times, however.

2.4   Executions

In order to reason about the behavior of a synchronous network system, we need a formal notion of a system "execution."

A *state assignment* of a system is defined to be an assignment of a state to each process in the system. Also, a *message assignment* is an assignment of a (possibly *null*) message to each channel. An *execution* of the system is defined to be an infinite sequence

$$C_0, M_1, N_1, C_1, M_2, N_2, C_2, \dots ,$$

where each C_r is a state assignment and each M_r and N_r is a message assignment. C_r represents the system state after r rounds, while M_r and N_r represent the messages that are sent and received at round r, respectively. (These may be different because channels may lose messages.) We often refer to C_r as the state assignment that occurs at *time r*; that is, time r refers to the point just after r rounds have occurred.

If α and α' are two executions of a system, we say that α is *indistinguishable* from α' with respect to a process i, denoted $\alpha \overset{i}{\sim} \alpha'$, if i has the same sequence of states, the same sequence of outgoing messages, and the same sequence of incoming messages in α and α'. We also say that α and α' are *indistinguishable to process i through r rounds* if i has the same sequence of states, the same sequence of outgoing messages, and the same sequence of incoming messages up to the end of round r, in α and α'. We also extend these definitions to the situation where the executions being compared are executions of two different synchronous systems.

2.5 Proof Methods

The most important proof method for reasoning about synchronous systems involves proving *invariant assertions*. An invariant assertion is a property of the system state (in particular, of the states of all the processes) that is true in every execution, after every round. We allow the number of completed rounds to be mentioned in assertions, so that we can make claims about the state after each particular number r of rounds. Invariant assertions for synchronous systems are generally proved by induction on r, the number of completed rounds, starting with $r = 0$.

Another important method is that of *simulations*. Roughly speaking, the goal is to show that one synchronous algorithm A "implements" another synchronous algorithm B, in the sense of producing the same input/output behavior. The correspondence between A and B is expressed by an assertion relating the states of A and B, when the two algorithms are started on the same inputs and run with the same failure pattern for the same number of rounds. Such an assertion is known as a *simulation relation*. As for invariant assertions, simulation relationships are generally proved by induction on the number of completed rounds.

2.6 Complexity Measures

Two measures of complexity are usually considered for synchronous distributed algorithms: time complexity and communication complexity.

The *time complexity* of a synchronous system is measured in terms of the number of rounds until all the required outputs are produced, or until the processes all halt. If the system allows variable start times, the time complexity is measured from the first round in which a *wakeup* occurs, at any process.

The *communication complexity* is typically measured in terms of the total number of non-*null* messages that are sent. Occasionally, we will also take into account the number of bits in the messages.

The time measure is the more important measure in practice, not only for synchronous distributed algorithms but for all distributed algorithms. The communication complexity is mainly significant if it causes enough congestion to slow down processing. This suggests that we might want to ignore it and just consider time complexity. However, the impact of the communication load on the time complexity is not just a function of an individual distributed algorithm. In a typical network, many distributed algorithms run simultaneously, sharing the same network bandwidth. The message load added to a link by any single algorithm gets added to the total message load on that link, and thus contributes to the congestion seen by all the algorithms. Since it is difficult to quantify the impact that any one algorithm's messages have on the time performance of other algorithms, we settle for simply analyzing (and attempting to minimize) the number of messages generated by individual algorithms.

2.7   Randomization

Instead of requiring the processes to be deterministic, it is sometimes useful to allow them to make random choices, based on some given probability distributions. Since the basic synchronous system model does not permit this, we augment the model by introducing a new *random function* in addition to the message-generation and transition functions, to represent the random choice steps. Formally, we add a $rand_i$ component to the automaton description for each node i; for each state s, $rand_i(s)$ is a probability distribution over some subset of $states_i$. Now in each round of execution, the random function $rand_i$ is first used to pick new states, and the $msgs_i$ and $trans_i$ functions are then applied as usual.

The formal notion of execution used in a randomized algorithm now includes not only state assignments and message assignments, but also information about random functions. Specifically, an *execution* of the system is defined to be an infinite sequence

$$C_0, D_1, M_1, N_1, C_1, D_2, M_2, N_2, C_2, \ldots,$$

where each C_r and D_r is a *state assignment* and each M_r and N_r is a message assignment. D_r represents the new process states after the round r random choices.

Claims about what is computed by a randomized system are usually probabilistic, asserting that certain results are achieved with at least a certain probability. When such a claim is made, the intention is generally that it is supposed to hold for all inputs and, in case of systems with failures, for all failure patterns. To model the inputs and failure patterns, a fictitious entity called an *adversary* is usually assumed to control the choices of inputs and occurrences of failures, and the probabilistic claim asserts that the system behaves well in competition with any allowable adversary. General treatment of these issues is beyond the scope of this book; we will just provide special case definitions as they are needed.

2.8 Bibliographic Notes

The general notion of a state machine model has its roots in the traditional finite-state automaton model. Basic material on finite-state machines appears in many undergraduate textbooks such as those of Lewis and Papadimitriou [195] and Martin [221]. The particular kind of state machine model defined here is extracted from numerous papers in distributed computing theory, for example, the Byzantine agreement paper by Fischer and Lynch [119].

The idea of invariant assertions seems to have been first proposed by Floyd [124] for sequential programs and generalized by Ashcroft [15] and by Lamport [175] for concurrent programs. Similar ideas have appeared in many other places. The idea of simulations also has numerous sources. One of the most important is the early work on data abstraction in sequential programs embodied, for example, in Liskov's programming language CLU [198] and in work of Milner [228] and Hoare [158]. Later work that extended the notion to concurrent programs includes papers by Park [236], Lamport [177], Lynch [203], Lynch and Tuttle [218], and Jonsson [165].

Chapter 3

Leader Election in a Synchronous Ring

In this chapter, we present the first problem to be solved using the synchronous model of Chapter 2: the problem of *electing a unique leader* process from among the processes in a network. For starters, we consider the simple case where the network digraph is a ring.

This problem originally arose in the study of local area *token ring* networks. In such a network, a single "token" circulates around the network, giving its current owner the sole right to initiate communication. (If two nodes in the network were to attempt simultaneously to communicate, the communications could interfere with one another.) Sometimes, however, the token may be lost, and it becomes necessary for the processes to execute an algorithm to regenerate the lost token. This regeneration procedure amounts to electing a leader.

3.1   The Problem

We assume that the network digraph G is a ring consisting of n nodes, numbered 1 to n in the clockwise direction (see Figure 3.1). We often count mod n, allowing 0 to be another name for process n, $n + 1$ another name for process 1, and so on. The processes associated with the nodes of G do not know their indices, nor those of their neighbors; we assume that the message-generation and transition functions are defined in terms of local, relative names for the neighbors. However, we do assume that each process is able to distinguish its clockwise neighbor from its counterclockwise neighbor. The requirement is that, eventually, exactly one process should output the decision that it is the leader, say by changing a special *status* component of its state to the value *leader*. There are several versions of

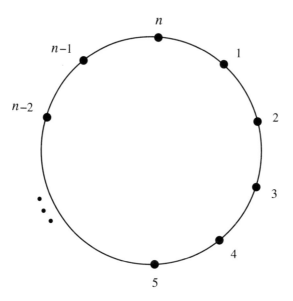

Figure 3.1: A ring of processes.

the problem:

1. It might also be required that all non-leader processes eventually output the fact that they are not the leader, say by changing their *status* components to the value *non-leader*.

2. The ring can be either *unidirectional* or *bidirectional*. If it is unidirectional, then each edge is directed from a process to its clockwise neighbor, that is, messages can only be sent in a clockwise direction.

3. The number n of nodes in the ring can be either known or unknown to the processes. If it is known, it means that the processes only need to work correctly in rings of size n, and thus they can use the value n in their programs. If it is unknown, it means that the processes are supposed to work in rings of different sizes. Therefore, they cannot use information about the ring size.

4. Processes can be identical or can be distinguished by each starting with a *unique identifier (UID)* chosen from some large totally ordered space of identifiers such as the positive integers, $\mathbb{N}^+$. We assume that each process's UID is different from each other's in the ring, but that there is no constraint on which UIDs actually appear in the ring. (For instance, they do not have to be consecutive integers.) These identifiers can be restricted to be

manipulated only by certain operations, such as comparisons, or they can admit unrestricted operations.

3.2 Impossibility Result for Identical Processes

A first easy observation is that if all the processes are identical, then this problem cannot be solved at all in the given model. This is so even if the ring is bidirectional and the ring size is known to the processes.

Theorem 3.1 *Let A be a system of n processes, n > 1, arranged in a bidirectional ring. If all the processes in A are identical, then A does not solve the leader-election problem.*

Proof. Suppose that there is such a system A that solves the leader-election problem. We obtain a contradiction. We can assume without any loss of generality that each process of A has exactly one start state. This is so because if each process has more than one start state, we could simply choose any one of the start states and obtain a new solution in which each process has only one start state. With this assumption, A has exactly one execution.

So consider the (unique) execution of A. It is straightforward to verify, by induction on the number r of rounds that have been executed, that all the processes are in identical states immediately after r rounds. Therefore, if any process ever reaches a state where its *status* is *leader*, then all the processes in A also reach such a state at the same time. But this violates the uniqueness requirement.   □

Theorem 3.1 implies that the only way to solve the leader-election problem is to break the symmetry somehow. A reasonable assumption derived from what is usually done in practice is that the processes are identical except for a UID. This is the assumption we make in the rest of this chapter.

3.3 A Basic Algorithm

The first solution we present is a fairly obvious one, which we call the *LCR algorithm* in honor of Le Lann, Chang, and Roberts, from whose papers this algorithm is extracted. The algorithm uses only unidirectional communication and does not rely on knowledge of the size of the ring. Only the leader performs an output. The algorithm uses only comparison operations on the UIDs. Below is an informal description of the *LCR* algorithm.

LCR algorithm (informal):

Each process sends its identifier around the ring. When a process receives an incoming identifier, it compares that identifier to its own. If the incoming identifier is greater than its own, it keeps passing the identifier; if it is less than its own, it discards the incoming identifier; if it is equal to its own, the process declares itself the leader.

In this algorithm, the process with the largest UID is the only one that outputs *leader*. In order to make this intuition precise, we give a more careful description of the algorithm in terms of the model of Chapter 2.

LCR algorithm (formal):

The message alphabet M is exactly the set of UIDs.

For each i, the states in $states_i$ consist of the following components:

> u, a UID, initially i's UID
> *send*, a UID or *null*, initially i's UID
> *status*, with values in $\{unknown, leader\}$, initially *unknown*

The set of start states $start_i$ consists of the single state defined by the given initializations.

For each i, the message-generation function $msgs_i$ is defined as follows:

> send the current value of *send* to process $i + 1$

Actually, process i would use a relative name for process $i+1$, for example, "clockwise neighbor"; we write $i + 1$ because it is simpler. Recall from Chapter 2 that we use the *null* value as a placeholder indicating the absence of a message. So if the value of the *send* component is *null*, this msg_i function does not actually send any message.

For each i, the transition function $trans_i$ is defined by the following pseudocode:

> *send* := *null*
> if the incoming message is v, a UID, then
>   case
> $v > u$: *send* := v
> $v = u$: *status* := *leader*
> $v < u$: do nothing
>   endcase

The first line of the transition function definition just cleans up the state from the effects of the preceding message delivery (if any). The rest of the code contains the interesting work—the decision about whether to pass on or discard the incoming UID, or to accept it as permission to become the leader.

This description is written in what should be a reasonably readable programming language, but note that it has a direct translation into a process state machine in the model in Chapter 2. In this translation, each process state consists of a value for each of the variables, and the transitions are describable in terms of changes to the variables. Note that the entire block of code written for the $trans_i$ function is supposed to be executed indivisibly, as part of the processing for a single round.

How do we go about proving formally that the algorithm is correct? Correctness means that exactly one process eventually performs a *leader* output. Let $i_{\max}$ denote the index of the process with the maximum UID, and let $u_{\max}$ denote its UID. It is enough to show that (1) process $i_{\max}$ outputs *leader* by the end of round n, and (2) no other process ever performs such an output. We prove these two properties, respectively, in Lemmas 3.2 and 3.3.

Here and in many other places in the book, we attach the subscript i to a state component name to indicate the instance of that state component belonging to process i. For example, we use the notation u_i to denote the value of state component u of process i. We generally omit the subscripts when writing the process code, however.

Lemma 3.2 *Process i_{max} outputs leader by the end of round n.*

Proof. Note that $u_{\max}$ is the initial value of variable $u_{i_{\max}}$, the variable u at process $i_{\max}$, by the initialization. Also note that the values of the u variables never change (by the code), that they are all distinct (by assumption), and that $i_{\max}$ has the largest u value (by definition of $i_{\max}$). By the code, it suffices to show the following invariant assertion:

> **Assertion 3.3.1** *After n rounds, $status_{i_{max}} = leader$.*

The normal way to try to prove an invariant such as this one is by induction on the number of rounds. But in order to do this, we need a preliminary invariant that says something about the situation after smaller numbers of rounds. We add the following assertion:

> **Assertion 3.3.2** *For $0 \leq r \leq n-1$, after r rounds, $send_{i_{max}+r} = u_{max}$.*

(Recall that addition is modulo n.) This assertion says that the maximum value appears in the *send* component at the position in the ring at distance r from $i_{\max}$.

It is straightforward to prove Assertion 3.3.2 by induction on r. For $r = 0$, the initialization says that $send_{i_{max}} = u_{max}$ after 0 rounds, which is just what is needed. The inductive step is based on the fact that every node other than i_{max} accepts the maximum value and places it into its *send* component, since u_{max} is greater than all the other values.

Having proved Assertion 3.3.2, we use its special case for $r = n - 1$ and one more argument about what happens in a single round to show Assertion 3.3.1. The key fact here is that process i_{max} accepts u_{max} as a signal to set its *status* to *leader*.   □

Lemma 3.3 *No process other than i_{max} ever outputs the value leader.*

Proof.   It is enough to show that all other processes always have *status* = *unknown*. Again, it helps to state a stronger invariant. If i and j are any two processes in the ring, $i \neq j$, define $[i, j)$ to be the set of indices $\{i, i+1, \ldots, j-1\}$, where addition is modulo n. That is, $[i, j)$ is the set of processes starting with i and moving clockwise around the ring up to and including j's counterclockwise neighbor. The following invariant asserts that no UID v can reach any *send* variable in any position between i_{max} and v's original home i:

> **Assertion 3.3.3** *For any r and any i, j, the following holds. After r rounds, if $i \neq i_{max}$ and $j \in [i_{max}, i)$ then $send_j \neq u_i$.*

Again, it is straightforward to prove the assertion by induction; now the key fact used in the proof is that a non-maximum value does not get past i_{max}. This is because i_{max} compares the incoming value with u_{max}, and u_{max} is greater than all the other UIDs.

Finally, Assertion 3.3.3 can be used to show that only process i_{max} can receive its own UID in a message, and hence only process i_{max} can output *leader*.   □

Lemmas 3.2 and 3.3 together imply the following:

Theorem 3.4 *LCR solves the leader-election problem.*

Halting and *non-leader* outputs.   As written, the *LCR* algorithm never finishes its work, in the sense of all the processes reaching a halting state. We can augment each process to include halting states, as described in Section 2.1. Then we can modify the algorithm by allowing the elected leader to initiate a special *report* message to be sent around the ring. Any process that receives the *report* message can halt, after passing it on. This strategy not only allows processes to halt, but could also be used to allow the non-leader processes to output *non-leader*. Furthermore, by attaching the leader's index to the *report* message, this strategy could also allow all the participating processes to output the identity of the leader. Note that it is also possible for each non-leader node to output *non-leader* immediately after it sees a UID greater than its own; however, this does not tell the non-leader nodes when to halt.

    In general, halting is an important property for a distributed algorithm to satisfy; however, it cannot always be achieved as easily as in this case.

Complexity analysis. The time complexity of the basic *LCR* algorithm is n rounds until a leader is announced, and the communication complexity is $O(n^2)$ messages in the worst case. In the halting version of the algorithm, the time complexity is $2n$ and the communication complexity is still $O(n^2)$. The extra time needed for halting and for the *non-leader* announcements is only n rounds, and the extra communication is only n messages.

Transformation. The preceding two remarks describe and analyze a general transformation, from any leader-election algorithm in which only the leader provides output and no process ever halts, to one in which the leader and the non-leaders all provide output and all processes halt. The extra cost of obtaining the extra outputs and the halting is only n rounds and n messages. This transformation works for any combination of our other assumptions.

Variable start times. Note that the *LCR* algorithm works without modification in the version of the synchronous model with variable start times. See Section 2.1 for a description of this version of the model.

Breaking symmetry. In the problem of electing a leader in a ring, the key difficulty is breaking symmetry. Symmetry-breaking is also an important part of many other problems that need to be solved in distributed systems, including *resource-allocation* problems (see Chapters 10–11 and 20) and *consensus* problems (see Chapters 5–7, 12, 21, and 25).

3.4   An Algorithm with $O(n \log n)$ Communication Complexity

Although the time complexity of the *LCR* algorithm is low, the number of messages used by the algorithm seems somewhat high, a total of $O(n^2)$. This might not seem significant, because there is never more than one message on any link at any time. However, in Chapter 2, we discussed why the number of messages is an interesting measure to try to minimize; this is because of the possible network

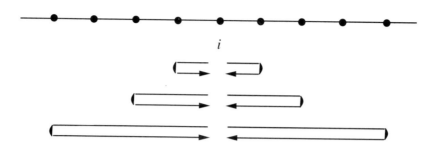

Figure 3.2: Trajectories of successive tokens originating at process i in the *HS* algorithm.

congestion that can result from the total communication load of many concurrently running distributed algorithms. In this section, we present an algorithm that lowers the communication complexity to $O(n \log n)$.

The first published algorithm to reduce the worst-case complexity to $O(n \log n)$ was that of Hirschberg and Sinclair, so we call this algorithm the *HS algorithm*. Again, we assume that only the leader needs to perform an output, though the transformation at the end of Section 3.3 implies that this restriction is not important. Again, we assume that the ring size is unknown, but now we allow bidirectional communication.

As does the *LCR* algorithm, the *HS* algorithm elects the process with the maximum UID. Now every process, instead of sending its UID all the way around the ring as in the *LCR* algorithm, sends it so that it travels some distance away, then turns around and comes back to the originating process. It does this repeatedly, to successively greater distances. The *HS* algorithm proceeds as follows.

HS algorithm (informal):

Each process i operates in phases $0, 1, 2, \ldots$. In each phase l, process i sends out "tokens" containing its UID u_i in both directions. These are intended to travel distance 2^l, then return to their origin i (see Figure 3.2). If both tokens make it back safely, process i continues with the following phase. However, the tokens might not make it back safely. While a u_i token is proceeding in the outbound direction, each other process j on u_i's path compares u_i with its own UID u_j. If $u_i < u_j$, then j simply discards the token, whereas if $u_i > u_j$, then j relays u_i. If $u_i = u_j$, then it means that process j has received its own UID before the token has turned around, so process j elects itself as the leader.

All processes always relay all tokens in the inbound direction.

Now we describe the algorithm more formally. This time, the formalization requires some bookkeeping to ensure that tokens follow the proper trajectories.

For instance, flags are carried by the tokens indicating whether they are travelling outbound or inbound. Also, hop counts are carried with the tokens to keep track of the distances they must travel in the outbound direction; this allows the processes to figure out when the directions of the tokens should be reversed. Once the algorithm is formalized in this way, a correctness argument of the sort given for LCR can be provided.

HS algorithm (formal):

The message alphabet M is the set of triples consisting of a UID, a *flag* value in $\{out, in\}$, and a positive integer *hop-count*.

For each i, the states in *states*$_i$ consist of the following components:

> u, of type UID, initially i's UID
> *send+*, containing either an element of M or *null*,
>   initially the triple consisting of i's UID, *out*, and 1
> *send−*, containing either an element of M or *null*,
>   initially the triple consisting of i's UID, *out*, and 1
> *status*, with values in $\{unknown, leader\}$, initially *unknown*
> *phase*, a nonnegative integer, initially 0

The set of start states *start*$_i$ consists of the single state defined by the given initializations.

For each i, the message-generation function *msgs*$_i$ is defined as follows:

> send the current value of *send+* to process $i + 1$
> send the current value of *send−* to process $i − 1$

For each i, the transition function *trans*$_i$ is defined by the following pseudocode:

> *send+* := *null*
> *send−* := *null*
> if the message from $i − 1$ is (v, out, h) then
>   case
> $v > u$ and $h > 1$: *send+* := $(v, out, h − 1)$
> $v > u$ and $h = 1$: *send−* := $(v, in, 1)$
> $v = u$: *status* := *leader*
>   endcase
> if the message from $i + 1$ is (v, out, h) then
>   case
> $v > u$ and $h > 1$: *send−* := $(v, out, h − 1)$
> $v > u$ and $h = 1$: *send+* := $(v, in, 1)$
> $v = u$: *status* := *leader*
>   endcase
> if the message from $i − 1$ is $(v, in, 1)$ and $v > u$ then

$send+ := (v, in, 1)$
if the message from $i + 1$ is $(v, in, 1)$ and $v > u$ then
   $send- := (v, in, 1)$
if the messages from $i - 1$ and $i + 1$ are both $(u, in, 1)$ then
   $phase := phase + 1$
   $send+ := (u, out, 2^{phase})$
   $send- := (u, out, 2^{phase})$

As before, the first two lines just clean up the state. The next two pieces of code describe the handling of outbound tokens: tokens with UIDs that are greater than u_i are either relayed or turned around, depending on the *hop-count*, and the receipt of u_i causes i to elect itself the leader. The next two pieces of code describe the handling of inbound tokens: they are simply relayed. (A trivial *hop-count* of 1 is used for inbound tokens.) If process i receives both of its own tokens back, then it goes on to the next phase.

Complexity analysis. We first analyze the communication complexity. Every process sends out a token in phase 0; this is a total of $4n$ messages for the token to go out and return, in both directions. For $l > 0$, a process sends a token in phase l exactly if it receives both its phase $l - 1$ tokens back. This is exactly if it has not been "defeated" by another process within distance 2^{l-1} in either direction along the ring. This implies that within any group of $2^{l-1} + 1$ consecutive processes, at most one goes on to initiate tokens at phase l. This can be used to show that at most

$$\left\lfloor \frac{n}{2^{l-1} + 1} \right\rfloor$$

processes altogether initiate tokens at phase l. Then the total number of messages sent out at phase l is bounded by

$$4 \left(2^l \cdot \left\lfloor \frac{n}{2^{l-1} + 1} \right\rfloor \right) \leq 8n.$$

This is because phase l tokens travel distance 2^l. Again, the factor of 4 is derived from the fact that the token is sent out in both directions—clockwise and counterclockwise—and that each outbound token must turn around and return.

The total number of phases that are executed before a leader is elected and all communication stops is at most $1 + \lceil \log n \rceil$ (including phase 0), so the total number of messages is at most $8n(1 + \lceil \log n \rceil)$, which is $O(n \log n)$, with a constant factor of approximately 8.

The time complexity for this algorithm is just $O(n)$. This can be seen by noting that the time for each phase l is $2 \cdot 2^l = 2^{l+1}$ (for the tokens to go out and return). The final phase takes time n—it is an incomplete phase, with tokens only travelling outbound. The next-to-last phase is phase $l = \lceil \log n \rceil - 1$, and its time complexity is at least as great as the total time complexity of all the preceding phases. Thus, the total time complexity of all but the final phase is at most

$$2 \cdot 2^{\lceil \log n \rceil}.$$

It follows that the total time complexity is at most $3n$ if n is a power of 2, and $5n$ otherwise. The rest of the details are left as an exercise.

Variable start times. The *HS* algorithm works without modification in the version of the synchronous model with variable start times.

3.5 Non-Comparison-Based Algorithms

We next consider the question of whether it is possible to elect a leader with fewer than $O(n \log n)$ messages. The answer to this problem, as we shall demonstrate shortly with an impossibility result—a lower bound of $\Omega(n \log n)$—is negative. That result, however, is valid only in the case of algorithms that manipulate the UIDs using comparisons only. (*Comparison-based algorithms* are defined in Section 3.6 below.)

In this section, we allow the UIDs to be positive integers and permit them to be manipulated by general arithmetic operations. For this case, we give two algorithms, the *TimeSlice algorithm* and the *VariableSpeeds algorithm*, each of which uses only $O(n)$ messages. The existence of these algorithms implies that the lower bound of $\Omega(n \log n)$ cannot be proved for the general case.

3.5.1 The *TimeSlice* Algorithm

The first of these algorithms uses the strong assumption that the ring size n is known to all the processes, but only assumes unidirectional communication. In this setting, the following simple algorithm, which we call the *TimeSlice algorithm*, works. It elects the process with the minimum UID.

Note that this algorithm uses synchrony in a deeper way than do the *LCR* and *HS* algorithms. Namely, it uses the non-arrival of messages (i.e., the arrival of *null* messages) at certain rounds to convey information.

> **TimeSlice algorithm:**
>
> Computation proceeds in phases 1, 2, ... , where each phase consists of n consecutive rounds. Each phase is devoted to the possible circulation, all the way around the ring, of a token carrying a particular UID. More

specifically, in phase v, which consists of rounds $(v-1)n+1,\ldots,vn$, only a token carrying UID v is permitted to circulate.

If a process i with UID v exists, and round $(v-1)n+1$ is reached without i having previously received any non-*null* messages, then process i elects itself the leader and sends a token carrying its UID around the ring. As this token travels, all the other processes note that they have received it, which prevents them from electing themselves as leader or initiating the sending of a token at any later phase.

With this algorithm, the minimum UID $u_{\min}$ eventually gets all the way around, which causes its originating process to become elected. No messages are sent before round $(u_{\min}-1)n+1$, and no messages are sent after round $u_{\min} \cdot n$. The total number of messages sent is just n. If we prefer to elect the process with the maximum UID rather than the process with the minimum, we can simply let the minimum send a special message around after it is discovered in order to determine the maximum. The communication complexity is still $O(n)$.

The good property of the *TimeSlice* algorithm is that the total number of messages is n. Unfortunately, the time complexity is about $n \cdot u_{\min}$, which is an unbounded number, even in a fixed-size ring. This time complexity limits the practicality of the algorithm; it is only useful in practice for small ring networks in which UIDs are assigned from among the small positive integers.

3.5.2   The *VariableSpeeds* Algorithm

The *TimeSlice* algorithm shows that $O(n)$ messages are sufficient in the case of rings in which processes know n, the size of the ring. But what if n is unknown? It turns out that in this case, also, there is an $O(n)$ message algorithm, which we call the *VariableSpeeds algorithm* for reasons that will become apparent in a moment. The *VariableSpeeds* algorithm uses only unidirectional communication.

Unfortunately, the time complexity of the *VariableSpeeds* algorithm is even worse than that of the *TimeSlice* algorithm: $O(n \cdot 2^{u_{\min}})$. Clearly, no one would even think of using this algorithm in practice! The *VariableSpeeds* algorithm is what we call a *counterexample algorithm*. A *counterexample algorithm* is one whose main purpose is to show that a conjectured impossibility result is false. Such an algorithm is generally not interesting by itself—it is neither practical nor particularly elegant from a mathematical viewpoint. However, it does serve to show that an impossibility result cannot be proved.

Here is the algorithm.

VariableSpeeds algorithm:

Each process i initiates a token, which travels around the ring, carrying the UID u_i of the originating process i. Different tokens travel at different rates. In particular, a token carrying UID v travels at the rate of 1 message transmission every 2^v rounds, that is, each process along its path waits 2^v rounds after receiving the token before sending it out.

Meanwhile, each process keeps track of the smallest UID it has seen and simply discards any token carrying an identifier that is larger than this smallest one.

If a token returns to its originator, the originator is elected.

As for the *TimeSlice* algorithm, the *VariableSpeeds* algorithm guarantees that the process with the minimum UID is elected.

Complexity analysis. The *VariableSpeeds* algorithm guarantees that by the time the token carrying the smallest identifier $u_{\min}$ gets all the way around the ring, the second smallest identifier could only get at most halfway around, the third smallest could only get at most a quarter of the way around, and in general, the kth smallest could only get at most $\frac{1}{2^{k-1}}$ of the way around. Therefore, up to the time of election, the token carrying $u_{\min}$ uses more messages than all the others combined. Since $u_{\min}$ uses exactly n messages, the total number of messages sent, up to the time of election, is less than $2n$.

But also, note that by the time $u_{\min}$ gets all the way around the ring, all nodes know about this value, and so will refuse to send out any other tokens. It follows that $2n$ is an upper bound on the total number of messages that are *ever* sent by the algorithm (including the time after the *leader* output).

The time complexity, as mentioned above, is $n \cdot 2^{u_{\min}}$, since each node delays the token carrying UID $u_{\min}$ for $2^{u_{\min}}$ time units.

Variable start times. Unlike the *LCR* and *HS* algorithms, the *VariableSpeeds* algorithms cannot be used "as is" in the version of the synchronous model with variable start times. However, a modification of the algorithm works:

Modified *VariableSpeeds* algorithm:

Define a process to be a *starter* if it receives a *wakeup* message strictly before (i.e., at an earlier round than) receiving any ordinary (non-*null*) messages.

Each starter i initiates a token to travel around the ring, carrying its UID u_i; non-starters never initiate tokens. Initially, this token travels "fast," at the rate of one transmission per round, getting passed along by all the non-starters that are awakened by the arrival of the token, just until it first arrives at a starter. (This could be a different starter, or i itself.) After the token arrives at a starter, the token continues its journey, but from now on at the "slow" rate of one transmission every 2^{u_i} rounds.

Meanwhile, each process keeps track of the smallest starter's UID that it has seen and discards any token carrying an identifier that is larger than this smallest one. If a token returns to its originator, the originator is elected.

The modified *VariableSpeeds* algorithm ensures that the starter process with the minimum UID is elected. Let $i_{\text{min-start}}$ denote this process.

Complexity analysis. We count the messages in three classes.

1. The messages involved in the initial fast transmission of tokens. There are just n of these.

2. The messages involved in the slow transmission of tokens, up to the time when $i_{\text{min-start}}$'s token first reaches a starter. This takes at most n rounds from when the first process awakens. During this time, a token carrying UID v could use at most $\frac{n}{2^v}$ messages, for a total of at most $\sum_{v=1}^{n} \frac{n}{2^v} < n$ messages.

3. The messages involved in the slow transmission of tokens, after the time when $i_{\text{min-start}}$'s token first reaches a starter. This analysis is similar to that for the basic *VariableSpeeds* algorithm. By the time the winning token gets all the way around the ring, the kth smallest starter's identifier could only get at most $\frac{1}{2^{k-1}}$ of the way around. Therefore, the total number of messages sent, up to the time of election, is less than $2n$. But by the time the winning token gets all the way around the ring, all nodes know about its value, and so will refuse to send out any other tokens; thus, $2n$ is an upper bound on the number of messages in this class.

Thus, the total communication complexity is at most $4n$.

The time complexity is $n + n \cdot 2^{u_{\text{min-start}}}$.

3.6   Lower Bound for Comparison-Based Algorithms

So far, we have presented several algorithms for leader election on a synchronous ring. The *LCR* and *HS* algorithms are comparison based, and the latter achieves a communication complexity bound of $O(n \log n)$ messages and a time bound of $O(n)$. The *TimeSlice* and *VariableSpeeds* algorithms, on the other hand, are not comparison based, and use $O(n)$ messages, but have a huge running time. In this section, we show a lower bound of $\Omega(n \log n)$ messages for comparison-based algorithms. This lower bound holds even if we assume that communication is bidirectional and the ring size n is known to the processes. In the next section, we show a similar lower bound of $\Omega(n \log n)$ messages for non-comparison-based algorithms with bounded time complexity.

The result of this section is based on the difficulty of *breaking symmetry*. Recall the impossibility result in Theorem 3.1, which says that, because of symmetry, it is impossible to elect a leader in the absence of distinguishing information such as UIDs. The main idea in the following argument is that a certain amount of symmetry can arise even in the presence of UIDs. In this case, the UIDs allow symmetry to be broken, but it might require a large amount of communication to do so.

Recall that we are assuming throughout this chapter that the processes in the ring are all identical except for their UIDs. Thus, the start states of the processes are identical except for designated components that contain the process UID. In general, we have not imposed any constraints on how the message-generation and transition functions can use the UID information.

We assume for the rest of this chapter (this section and the next) that there is only one start state containing each UID. (As in the proof of Theorem 3.1, this assumption does not cause any loss of generality.) The advantage of this assumption is that it implies that the system (with a fixed assignment of UIDs) has exactly one execution.

A comparison-based algorithm obeys certain additional constraints, expressed by the following slightly informal definition. A UID-based ring algorithm is *comparison based* if the only ways that the processes manipulate the UIDs are by copying them, by sending and receiving them in messages, and by comparing them for $\{<, >, =\}$.

This definition allows a process, for example, to store any of the various UIDs that it has encountered and to send them out in messages, possibly combined with other information. A process can also compare the stored UIDs and use the results of these comparisons to make choices in the message-generation and state-transition functions. These choices could involve, for example, whether or not to send a message to each of its neighbors, whether or not to elect itself the leader, whether or not to keep the stored UIDs, and so on. The important fact is that all of the activity of a process depends only on the relative ranks of the UIDs it has encountered, rather than on their particular values.

The following formal notion is used to describe the kind of symmetry that can exist, even with UIDs. Let $U = (u_1, u_2, \dots, u_k)$ and $V = (v_1, v_2, \dots, v_k)$ be two sequences of UIDs, both of the same length k. We say that U is *order equivalent* to V if, for all $i, j, 1 \leq i, j \leq k$, we have $u_i \leq u_j$ if and only if $v_i \leq v_j$.

Example 3.6.1   Order equivalence

The sequences $(5, 3, 7, 0)$, $(4, 2, 6, 1)$, and $(5, 3, 6, 1)$ are all order equivalent if the UID set is the natural numbers with the usual ordering.

Notice that two sequences of UIDs are order equivalent if and only if the corresponding sequences of relative ranks of their UIDs are identical. Two technical definitions follow. A round of an execution is said to be *active* if at least one (non-null) message is sent in it. The *k-neighborhood* of process i in ring R of size n, where $0 \le k < \lfloor n/2 \rfloor$, is defined to consist of the $2k + 1$ processes $i - k, \ldots, i + k$, that is, those that are within distance at most k from process i (including i itself).

Finally, we need a definition of what it means for process states to be the same, except for the particular choices of UIDs they contain. We say that two process states s and t *correspond* with respect to sequences $U = (u_1, u_2, \ldots, u_k)$ and $V = (v_1, v_2, \ldots, v_k)$ of UIDs provided that the following hold: all the UIDs in s are chosen from U, all the UIDs in t are chosen from V, and t is identical to s except that each occurrence of u_i in s is replaced by an occurrence of v_i in t, for all i, $1 \le i \le k$. *Corresponding messages* are defined analogously.

We can now prove the key lemma for our lower bound, Lemma 3.5. It says that processes that have order-equivalent k-neighborhoods behave in essentially the same way, until information has had a chance to propagate to the processes from outside the k-neighborhoods.

Lemma 3.5 *Let A be a comparison-based algorithm executing in a ring R of size n and let k be an integer, $0 \le k < \lfloor n/2 \rfloor$. Let i and j be two processes in A that have order-equivalent sequences of UIDs in their k-neighborhoods. Then, at any point after at most k active rounds, processes i and j are in corresponding states, with respect to the UID sequences in their k-neighborhoods.*

Example 3.6.2   Corresponding states

Suppose that the sequence of UIDs in process i's 3-neighborhood is $(1, 6, 3, 8, 4, 10, 7)$ (where process i's UID is 8), and the sequence in process j's 3-neighborhood is $(4, 10, 7, 12, 9, 13, 11)$ (where process j's UID is 12). Since these two sequences are order equivalent, Lemma 3.5 implies that processes i and j remain in corresponding states with respect to their 3-neighborhoods, as long as no more than three active rounds have occurred. Roughly speaking, the reason this is so is that if there are only three active rounds, there has not been any opportunity for information from outside the order-equivalent 3-neighborhoods to reach i and j.

Proof (of Lemma 3.5). Without loss of generality, we may assume that $i \neq j$. We proceed by induction on the number r of rounds that have been performed in the execution. For each r, we prove the lemma for all k.

Basis: $r = 0$. By the definition of a comparison-based algorithm, the initial states of i and j are identical except for their own UIDs, and hence they are in corresponding initial states, with respect to their k-neighborhoods (for any k).

Inductive step: Assume that the lemma holds for all $r' < r$. Fix k such that i and j have order-equivalent k-neighborhoods, and suppose that the first r rounds include at most k active rounds.

If neither i nor j receives a message at round r, then by induction (for $r - 1$ and k), i and j are in corresponding states just after $r - 1$ rounds, with respect to their k-neighborhoods. Since i and j have no new input, they make corresponding transitions and end up in corresponding states after round r.

So assume that either i or j receives a message at round r. Then, round r is active, so the first $r - 1$ rounds include at most $k - 1$ active rounds. Note that i and j have order-equivalent $(k - 1)$-neighborhoods, and likewise for $i - 1$ and $j - 1$ and for $i + 1$ and $j + 1$. Therefore, by induction (for $r - 1$ and $k - 1$), we have that i and j are in corresponding states after $r - 1$ rounds, with respect to their $(k - 1)$-neighborhoods, and similarly for $i - 1$ and $j - 1$, and for $i + 1$ and $j + 1$.

We proceed by case analysis.

1. At round r, neither $i - 1$ nor $i + 1$ sends a message to i.

   Then, since $i - 1$ and $j - 1$ are in corresponding states after $r - 1$ rounds, and likewise for $i + 1$ and $j + 1$, we have that neither $j - 1$ nor $j + 1$ sends a message to j at round r. But this contradicts the assumption that either i or j receives a message at round r.

2. At round r, $i - 1$ sends a message to i but $i + 1$ does not.

   Then, since $i - 1$ and $j - 1$ are in corresponding states after $r - 1$ rounds, $j - 1$ also sends a message to j at round r, and that message corresponds to the message sent by $i - 1$ to i, with respect to the $(k - 1)$-neighborhoods of $i - 1$ and $j - 1$, and hence with respect to the k-neighborhoods of i and j. For similar reasons, $j + 1$ sends no message to j at round r. Since i and j are in corresponding states after round $r - 1$, and receive corresponding messages, they remain in corresponding states, this time with respect to their k-neighborhoods.

3. At round r, $i + 1$ sends a message to i but $i - 1$ does not.

   Analogous to the previous case.

4. At round r, both $i - 1$ and $i + 1$ send messages to i.

A similar argument.   □

Lemma 3.5 tells us that many active rounds are necessary to break symmetry if there are large order-equivalent neighborhoods. We now define particular rings with the special property that they have many order-equivalent neighborhoods of various sizes.   Let $c, 0 \leq c \leq 1$, be a constant, and let R be a ring of size n. Then R is said to be *c-symmetric* if for every l, $\sqrt{n} \leq l \leq n$, and for every segment S of R of length l, there are at least $\lfloor \frac{cn}{l} \rfloor$ segments in R that are order equivalent to S (counting S itself).[1]

If n is a power of 2, then it is easy to construct a ring that is $\frac{1}{2}$-symmetric. Specifically, we define the *bit-reversal ring* of size n as follows. Suppose that $n = 2^k$. Then we assign to each process i the integer in the range $[0, n - 1]$ whose k-bit binary representation is the reverse of the k-bit binary representation of i (we use 0^k as the k-bit binary representation of n, identifying n with 0).

Example 3.6.3   Bit-reversal ring

For $n = 8$, we have $k = 3$, and the assignment is as in Figure 3.3.

Lemma 3.6 *Any bit-reversal ring is $\frac{1}{2}$-symmetric.*

Proof.   Left as an exercise.[2]   □

For values of n that are not powers of 2, there also always exist *c*-symmetric rings, though the general case requires a smaller constant c.

Theorem 3.7 *There exists a constant c such that, for all $n \in \mathbb{N}^+$, there is a c-symmetric ring of size n.*

The proof of Theorem 3.7 involves a fairly complicated recursive construction.[3] It is not possible to produce the needed ring simply, say by starting with the bit-reversal ring for the next smaller power of 2 and just adding some extra processes; these extra processes would destroy the symmetry.

So we can assume, for any n, that we have a *c*-symmetric ring R of size n. The following lemma states that if such a ring elects a leader, then it must have many active rounds.

---

[1] Try to ignore the square root lower bound condition—it is just a technicality.

[2] Note that for the bit-reversal ring, there is no need for the square root lower bound condition.

[3] This is where the square root lower bound condition arises.

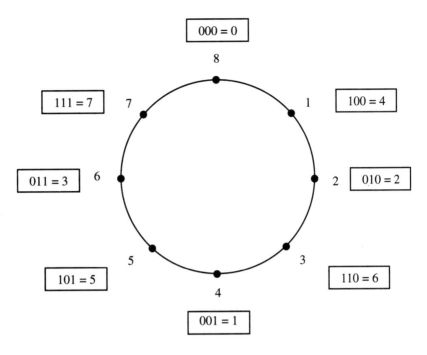

Figure 3.3: Bit-reversal ring of size 8.

Lemma 3.8 *Let A be a comparison-based algorithm executing in a c-symmetric ring of size n, and suppose that A elects a leader. Suppose that k is an integer such that $\sqrt{n} \leq 2k+1$ and $\left\lfloor \frac{cn}{2k+1} \right\rfloor \geq 2$. Then A has more than k active rounds.*

Proof. We proceed by contradiction. Suppose that A elects a leader, say process i, in at most k active rounds. Let S be the k-neighborhood of i; S is a segment of length $2k + 1$. Since the ring is c-symmetric, there must be at least $\left\lfloor \frac{cn}{2k+1} \right\rfloor \geq 2$ segments in the ring that are order equivalent to S, counting S itself. Thus, there is at least one other segment that is order equivalent to S; let j be the midpoint of that segment. Now, by Lemma 3.5, i and j remain in equivalent states throughout the execution, up to the election point. We conclude that j also gets elected, a contradiction. $\qquad\square$

Now we can prove the lower bound.

Theorem 3.9 *Let A be a comparison-based algorithm that elects a leader in rings of size n. Then there is an execution of A in which $\Omega(n \log n)$ messages are sent by the time the leader is elected.[4]*

---

[4]The $\Omega(n \log n)$ expression hides a fixed constant, independent of n.

Proof.   Fix c to be the constant whose existence is asserted by Theorem 3.7, and use that theorem to obtain a c-symmetric ring R of size n. We consider executions of the algorithm in ring R.

Define $k = \left\lfloor \frac{cn-2}{4} \right\rfloor$. Then $\sqrt{n} \leq 2k+1$ (provided n is sufficiently large), and $\left\lfloor \frac{cn}{2k+1} \right\rfloor \geq 2$. It follows by Lemma 3.8 that there are more than k active rounds, that is, that there are at least $k+1$ active rounds.

Consider the rth active round, where $\sqrt{n} + 1 \leq r \leq k+1$. Since the round is active, there is some process i that sends a message in round r. Let S be the $(r-1)$-neighborhood of i. Since R is c-symmetric, there are at least $\left\lfloor \frac{cn}{2r-1} \right\rfloor$ segments in R that are equivalent to S. By Lemma 3.5, at the point just before the rth active round, the midpoints of all these segments are in corresponding states, so they all send messages.

Now let $r_1 = \lceil \sqrt{n} \rceil + 1$ and $r_2 = k+1 = \left\lfloor \frac{cn-2}{4} \right\rfloor + 1$. The argument above implies that the total number of messages is at least

$$\sum_{r=r_1}^{r_2} \left\lfloor \frac{cn}{2r-1} \right\rfloor \geq \sum_{r=r_1}^{r_2} \frac{cn}{2r-1} - r_2.$$

The second term is $O(n)$, so it suffices to show that the first term is $\Omega(n \log n)$. We have

$$\sum_{r=r_1}^{r_2} \frac{cn}{2r-1} = \Omega\left(n \sum_{r=r_1}^{r_2} \frac{1}{r} \right)$$
$$= \Omega\left(n \left(\ln r_2 - \ln r_1 \right) \right)$$

by an integral approximation of the sum,

$$= \Omega\left(n \left(\ln\left(\left\lfloor \frac{cn-2}{4} \right\rfloor + 1 \right) - \ln(\lceil \sqrt{n} \rceil + 1) \right) \right)$$
$$= \Omega(n \log n).$$

This is as needed.   □

3.7   Lower Bound for Non-Comparison-Based Algorithms*

Can we describe any lower bounds on the number of messages for the case of non-comparison-based algorithms? Although the $\Omega(n \log n)$ barrier can be broken in this case, it is possible to show that this can only happen at the cost of large time complexity. For example, suppose that the time until leader election is bounded by t. Then, if the total number of UIDs in the space of identifiers is sufficiently large—say, greater than some particular fast-growing function $f(n, t)$—then there is a subset U of the identifiers on which it is possible to show that the algorithm behaves "like a comparison-based algorithm," at least through t rounds. This implies that the lower bound for comparison carries over to the time-bounded algorithm using identifiers in U.

We give somewhat more detail, but our presentation is still just a sketch. We will define the fast-growing function $f(n, t)$ using *Ramsey's Theorem*, which is a kind of generalized Pigeonhole Principle. In the statement of the theorem, an n-subset is just a subset with n elements, and a coloring just assigns a color to each set.

Theorem 3.10 (Ramsey's Theorem) *For all integers n, m, and c, there exists an integer $g(n, m, c)$ with the following property. For every set S of size at least $g(n, m, c)$, and any coloring of the n-subsets of S with at most c colors, there is some subset C of S of size m that has all of its n-subsets colored the same color.*

We begin by putting each algorithm into a *normal form,* in which each state simply records, in LISP S-expression format, the initial UID plus all the messages ever received, and each non-*null* message contains the complete state of its sender. Certain of these S-expressions are then designated as *election* states, in which the process is identified as having been elected as the leader. If the original algorithm is a correct leader-election algorithm, then the new one (with the modified output convention) is also, and the communication complexity is the same.

Our lower bound theorem is as follows.

Theorem 3.11 *For all integers n and t, there exists an integer $f(n, t)$ with the following property. Let A be any (not necessarily comparison-based) algorithm that elects a leader in rings of size n within time t and uses a UID space of size at least $f(n, t)$. Then there is an execution of A in which $\Omega(n \log n)$ messages are sent by the time the leader is elected.*

Proof Sketch. Fix n and t. Without loss of generality, we only consider algorithms in normal form. Since the algorithms involve only n processes and proceed for only t rounds, all the S-expressions that arise have at most n distinct arguments and at most t parenthesis depth.

Now for each algorithm A, we define an equivalence relation $\equiv_A$ on n-sets (i.e., sets of size n) of UIDs; roughly speaking, two n-sets will be said to be equivalent if they give rise to the same behavior for algorithm A. More precisely, if V and V' are two n-sets of UIDs, then we say that $V \equiv_A V'$ if, for every

S-expression of depth at most t over V, the corresponding S-expression over V' (generated by replacing each element of V with the same rank element within V') gives rise to the same decisions, in algorithm A, about whether to send a message in each direction and about whether or not the process is elected as leader.

Because the S-expressions in the definition of the equivalence relation have at most n arguments and at most t depth, there are only finitely many $\equiv_A$ equivalence classes; in fact, there is an upper bound on the number of classes that does not depend on the algorithm A, but only on n and t. Let $c(n,t)$ be such an upper bound.

Now fix algorithm A. We describe a way of coloring n-sets of UIDs, so we can apply Ramsey's Theorem. Namely, we just associate a color with each $\equiv_A$ equivalence class of n-sets, and color all the n-sets in that class by that color.

Now define $f(n,t) = g(n, 2n, c(n,t))$, where g is the function in Theorem 3.10, and consider any UID space containing at least $f(n,t)$ identifiers. Then, Theorem 3.10 implies the existence of a subset C of the UID space, containing at least $2n$ elements, such that all n-subsets of C are colored the same color. Take U to be the set consisting of the n smallest elements of C.

Then we claim that the algorithm behaves exactly like a comparison algorithm through t rounds, when UIDs are chosen from U. That is, every decision made by any process, about whether to send a message in either direction or about whether the process is a leader, depends only on the relative order of the arguments contained in the current state. To see why this is so, fix any two subsets W and W' of U, of the same size—say m. Suppose that S is an S-expression of depth at most t with UIDs chosen from W, and S' is the corresponding S-expression over W' (generated by replacing each element of W with the same rank element within W'). Then W and W' can be extended to sets V and V', each of size exactly n, by including the $n - m$ largest elements of C. Since V and V' are colored the same color, the two S-expressions gives rise to the same decisions about whether to send a message in each direction and about whether or not the process is elected as leader.

Since the algorithm behaves exactly like a comparison algorithm through t rounds, when UIDs are chosen from U, Theorem 3.9 yields the lower bound. $\square$

3.8   Bibliographic Notes

The impossibility result of Section 3.2 seems to be a part of the ancient folklore of this area; one version of this result, for a different model, appears in a paper by Angluin [13]. The *LCR* algorithm is derived from one developed by Le Lann

[191], with optimizations due to Chang and Roberts [71]. The *HS* algorithm is due to Hirschberg and Sinclair [156].

There have been a series of improvements in the constant in the $O(n \log n)$ upper bound, culminating in a bound of approximately $1.271n \log n + O(n)$, by Higham and Przytycka [155]; this bound works for the unidirectional case. Peterson [239] and Dolev, Klawe, and Rodeh [97] have given $O(n \log n)$ algorithms for the unidirectional case.

The *TimeSlice* algorithm also seems to be folklore, but is similar to the election strategy used in the MIT token ring network. The *VariableSpeeds* algorithm was developed by Frederickson and Lynch [127], and simultaneously by Vitanyi [282].

The lower bound results, both for comparison-based and for non-comparison-based algorithms, are due to Frederickson and Lynch [127]. Another construction of c-symmetric rings is carried out by Attiya, Snir, and Warmuth [27]. Ramsey's Theorem is a standard result of combinatorial theory, and is presented, for example, in the graph theory book of Berge [47].

The paper by Attiya, Snir, and Warmuth [27] contains other results about limitations of computing power in synchronous rings, using proof techniques similar to those used in Section 3.6.

3.9 Exercises

3.1. Fill in more of the details for the inductive proof of correctness of the *LCR* algorithm.

3.2. For the *LCR* algorithm,

   (a) Give a UID assignment for which $\Omega(n^2)$ messages are sent.

   (b) Give a UID assignment for which only $O(n)$ messages are sent.

   (c) Show that the average number of messages sent is $O(n \log n)$, where this average is taken over all the possible orderings of the processes on the ring, each assumed to be equally likely.

3.3. Modify the *LCR* algorithm so that it also allows all the non-leader processes to output *non-leader*, and so that all the processes eventually halt. Present the modified algorithm using the same style of "code" that we used for the *LCR* algorithm.

3.4. Show that the *LCR* algorithm still works correctly in the version of the synchronous model allowing variable start times.

3.5. Carry out a careful proof of correctness for the *HS* leader-election algorithm, using the invariant assertion style used for *LCR*.

3.6. Show that the *HS* algorithm still works correctly in the version of the synchronous model allowing variable start times.

3.7. Suppose that the *HS* leader-election algorithm is modified so that successive powers of k are used for path lengths, $k > 2$, instead of successive powers of 2. Analyze the time and communication complexity of the modified algorithm, similarly to the way the original *HS* algorithm is analyzed in the book. Compare the results to those for the original algorithm.

3.8. Consider modifying the *HS* algorithm so that the processes only send tokens in one direction rather than both.

   (a) Show that the most straightforward modification to the algorithm in the text does not yield $O(n \log n)$ communication complexity. What is an upper bound for the communication complexity?

   (b) Add a little more cleverness to the algorithm in order to restore the $O(n \log n)$ complexity bound.

3.9. Design a unidirectional leader-election algorithm that works with unknown ring size, and only uses $O(n \log n)$ messages in the worst case. Your algorithm should manipulate the UIDs using comparisons only.

3.10. Give code for a state machine to express the *TimeSlice* leader-election algorithm.

3.11. Describe a variant of the *TimeSlice* algorithm that saves time at the expense of additional messages, by allowing some number k of UIDs instead of just one to circulate in each phase. Prove the correctness of your algorithm and analyze its complexity.

3.12. Give code for a state machine to express the *VariableSpeeds* leader-election algorithm.

3.13. Show that the unmodified *VariableSpeeds* algorithm does not necessarily have the desired $O(n)$ communication complexity if processes can wake up at different times.

3.14. Prove the best *lower* bound you can for the number of rounds required, in the worst case, to elect a leader in a ring of size n. Be sure to state your assumptions carefully.

3.15. Give an explicit description of the bit-reversal ring for $n = 16$.

3.16. Prove that the bit-reversal ring of size $n = 2^k$ is $\frac{1}{2}$-symmetric, for any $k \in \mathbb{N}^+$.

3.17. Design a c-symmetric ring for non-powers of 2, for some value of $c > 0$.

3.18. Consider the problem of electing a leader in a synchronous ring of size n, where n is known to all the processes and the processes have no UIDs. Devise a *randomized* leader-election algorithm, that is, one in which the processes can make random choices in addition to just following their code deterministically. State carefully the properties that your algorithm satisfies. For example, is it absolutely guaranteed to elect a unique leader, or is there a small probability that it will fail to do this? What are the expected time and message complexities of your algorithm?

3.19. Consider a synchronous bidirectional ring of unknown size n, in which processes have UIDs. Give upper and lower bounds on the number of messages required for all the processes to compute $n \bmod 2$.

Chapter 4

Algorithms in General Synchronous Networks

In Chapter 3, we presented algorithms and lower bounds for the problem of leader election in very simple synchronous networks—unidirectional and bidirectional rings. In this chapter, we consider a larger collection of problems in a larger class of synchronous networks. In particular, we present algorithms for *leader election*, *breadth-first search (BFS)*, finding *shortest paths*, finding a *minimum spanning tree (MST)*, and finding a *maximal independent set (MIS)*, in networks based on arbitrary graphs and digraphs.

The problem of leader election arises when a process must be selected to "take charge" of a network computation. The problems of breadth-first search, finding shortest paths, and finding a minimum spanning tree are motivated by the need to build structures suitable for supporting efficient communication. The problem of finding a maximal independent set arises from the problem of network resource allocation. (We will revisit many of these problems and algorithms later, in Chapter 15, in the context of asynchronous networks.)

In this chapter, we consider an arbitrary, strongly connected network digraph $G = (V, E)$ having n nodes. (Sometimes we will restrict attention to the case where all edges are bidirectional, i.e., where the graph is undirected.) We assume, as usual for synchronous systems, that the processes communicate only over the directed edges of the digraph. In order to name the nodes, we assign them the indices $1, \ldots, n$, but, unlike the ring's indices, these have no special connection to the nodes' positions in the graph. The processes do not know their indices, nor those of their neighbors, but refer to their neighbors by local names. We do assume that if a process i has the same process j for both an incoming and outgoing neighbor, then i knows that the two processes are the same.

4.1   Leader Election in a General Network

We start by reconsidering the problem of leader election, this time in a network based on an arbitrary strongly connected digraph.

4.1.1   The Problem

We assume that the processes have unique identifiers (UIDs), chosen from some totally ordered space of identifiers; each process's UID is different from each other's in the network, but there is no constraint on which UIDs actually appear. As in Chapter 3, the requirement is that, eventually, exactly one process should elect itself the leader, by changing a special *status* component of its state to the value *leader*. As in Chapter 3, there are several versions of the problem:

1. It might also be required that all non-leader processes eventually output the fact that they are not the leader, by changing their *status* components to *non-leader*.

2. The number n of nodes and the diameter, *diam*, can be either known or unknown to the processes. Or, an upper bound on these quantities might be known.

4.1.2   A Simple Flooding Algorithm

We give a simple algorithm that causes both leaders and non-leaders to identify themselves. The algorithm requires that the processes know *diam*. The algorithm just floods the maximum UID throughout the network, so we call it the *FloodMax algorithm*.

> ### *FloodMax* algorithm (informal):
>
> Every process maintains a record of the maximum UID it has seen so far (initially its own). At each round, each process propagates this maximum on all of its outgoing edges. After *diam* rounds, if the maximum value seen is the process's own UID, the process elects itself the leader; otherwise, it is a non-leader.

The code for process i follows.

> ### *FloodMax* algorithm (formal):
>
> The message alphabet is the set of UIDs.
>
> ***states*$_i$ consists of components:**
> u, a UID, initially i's UID
> *max-uid*, a UID, initially i's UID

$status \in \{unknown, leader, non\text{-}leader\}$, initially $unknown$
$rounds$, an integer, initially 0

$msgs_i$:
if $rounds < diam$ then
     send $max\text{-}uid$ to all $j \in out\text{-}nbrs$

$trans_i$:
$rounds := rounds + 1$
let U be the set of UIDs that arrive from processes in $in\text{-}nbrs$
$max\text{-}uid := \max(\{max\text{-}uid\} \cup U)$
if $rounds = diam$ then
     if $max\text{-}uid = u$ then $status := leader$
     else $status := non\text{-}leader$

It is easy to see that *FloodMax* elects the process with the maximum UID. More specifically, define $i_{\max}$ to be the index of the process with the maximum UID, and $u_{\max}$ to be that UID. We show the following:

Theorem 4.1 *In the FloodMax algorithm, process $i_{\max}$ outputs leader and each other process outputs non-leader, within diam rounds.*

Proof. It is enough to prove the following assertion:

> **Assertion 4.1.1** *After diam rounds, $status_{i_{max}} = leader$ and $status_j = non\text{-}leader$ for every $j \neq i_{max}$.*

The key to the proof of Assertion 4.1.1 is the fact that after r rounds, the maximum UID has reached every process that is within distance r of $i_{\max}$, as measured along directed paths in G. This condition is captured by the invariant:

> **Assertion 4.1.2** *For $0 \leq r \leq diam$ and for every j, after r rounds, if the distance from i_{max} to j is at most r, then $max\text{-}uid_j = u_{max}$.*

In particular, in view of the definition of the diameter of the graph, Assertion 4.1.2 implies that every process has the maximum UID by the end of *diam* rounds. To prove Assertion 4.1.2, it is useful to have the following additional auxiliary invariants:

> **Assertion 4.1.3** *For every r and j, after r rounds, $rounds_j = r$.*

> **Assertion 4.1.4** *For every r and j, after r rounds, $max\text{-}uid_j \leq u_{max}$.*

Assertions 4.1.2, 4.1.3, and 4.1.4, specialized to $r = diam - 1$, plus an argument about what happens at round *diam*, imply Assertion 4.1.1 and therefore the result.

□

The *FloodMax* algorithm can be regarded as a kind of generalization of the *LCR* algorithm of Section 3.3, because the *LCR* algorithm also floods the maximum value throughout the (ring) network. However, note that the *LCR* algorithm does not require any special knowledge about the network, such as its diameter. In *LCR*, a process is elected simply when it receives its own UID in a message, rather than after a specified number of rounds as in *FloodMax*. This strategy is particular to ring networks and does not work in general digraphs.

Complexity analysis.   It is easy to see that the time until the leader is elected (and all other processes know that they are not the leader) is *diam* rounds. The number of messages is $diam \cdot |E|$, where $|E|$ is the number of directed edges in the digraph, because a message is sent on every directed edge for each of the first *diam* rounds.

Upper bound on the diameter.   Note that the algorithm also works correctly if the processes all know an upper bound d on the diameter rather than the diameter itself. The complexity measures then increase so that they depend on d rather than *diam*.

4.1.3   Reducing the Communication Complexity

There is a simple optimization[1] that can be used to decrease the communication complexity in many cases, although it does not decrease the order of magnitude in the worst case. Namely, processes can send their *max-uid* values only when they first learn about them, not at every round. We call this algorithm *OptFloodMax*. The modification to the code for *FloodMax* is as follows.

OptFloodMax algorithm:

$states_i$ **has an additional component:**
new-info, a Boolean, initially *true*

$msgs_i$**:**
if *rounds* < *diam* and *new-info* = *true* then
    send *max-uid* to all $j \in$ *out-nbrs*

---

[1] "Optimization" is not really the appropriate word to use here. "Improvement" would be better, but "optimization" is standard usage.

$trans_i$:

$rounds := rounds + 1$
let U be the set of UIDs that arrive from processes in *in-nbrs*
if $\max(U) > max\text{-}uid$ then *new-info* := *true* else *new-info* := *false*
$max\text{-}uid := \max(\{max\text{-}uid\} \cup U)$
if $rounds = diam$ then
    if $max\text{-}uid = u$ then $status := leader$ else $status := non\text{-}leader$

It is easy to believe that this modification yields a correct algorithm. How can we prove this formally? One way is to carry out another invariant assertion proof similar to the one for *FloodMax*. However, this would involve repeating a lot of the work we have already done for the earlier proof. Instead of starting from scratch, we give a proof based on relating the *OptFloodMax* algorithm formally to the *FloodMax* algorithm. This is a simple example of the use of the *simulation* method for verifying the correctness of distributed algorithms.

Theorem 4.2 *In the OptFloodMax algorithm, process i_{max} outputs leader and each other process outputs non-leader, within diam rounds.*

Proof. It is enough to prove the following assertion, analogous to Assertion 4.1.1 in the proof for *FloodMax*.

Assertion 4.1.5 *After diam rounds, $status_{i_{max}} = leader$ and $status_j = non\text{-}leader$ for every $j \neq i_{max}$.*

We start by proving a preliminary invariant that says that a process's *new-info* flag is always set to *true* whenever there is new information that the process is supposed to send at the next round. More specifically, it says that if any outgoing neighbor of i does not know a UID at least as great as the maximum UID known by i, then i's *new-info* flag must be *true*.

Assertion 4.1.6 *For any r, $0 \leq r \leq diam$, and any i, j, where $j \in out\text{-}nbrs_i$, the following holds: after r rounds, if $max\text{-}uid_j < max\text{-}uid_i$ then $new\text{-}info_i = true$.*

Assertion 4.1.6 is proved by induction on r. The basis case, $r = 0$, is true because all the *new-info* flags are initialized to *true*. For the inductive step, consider any particular processes i and j, where $j \in out\text{-}nbrs_i$. If $max\text{-}uid_i$ increases in round r, then $new\text{-}info_i$ gets set to *true*, which suffices. On the other hand, if $max\text{-}uid_i$ does not increase, then the inductive hypothesis implies that either $max\text{-}uid_j$ was already sufficiently large, or else $new\text{-}info_i = true$ just before round r. In the former case, $max\text{-}uid_j$ remains sufficiently large because the value never decreases. In the latter case, the new information is sent from i to j at round r, which causes $max\text{-}uid_j$ to become sufficiently large.

Now, to prove that *OptFloodMax* is correct, we imagine running it side by side with *FloodMax*, starting with the same UID assignment. The heart of the proof is a *simulation relation*, which is just an invariant assertion that involves the states of both algorithms after the same number of rounds.

> **Assertion 4.1.7** *For any* r, $0 \leq r \leq diam$, *after* r *rounds, the values of the u, max-uid, status, and rounds components are the same in the states of both algorithms.*

The proof of the simulation assertion, Assertion 4.1.7, is carried out by induction on r, just as for the usual sorts of assertions involving only a single algorithm. The interesting part of the inductive step is showing that the *max-uid* values remain identical.

So consider any i, j, where $j \in out\text{-}nbrs_i$. If $new\text{-}info_i = true$ before round r, then i sends the same information to j in round r in *OptFloodMax* as it does in *FloodMax*. On the other hand, if $new\text{-}info_i = false$ before round r, then i sends nothing to j in round r in *OptFloodMax*, but sends $max\text{-}uid_i$ to j in round r in *FloodMax*. However, Assertion 4.1.6 implies that, in this case, $max\text{-}uid_j \geq max\text{-}uid_i$ before round r, so the message has no effect in *FloodMax*. It follows that i has the same effect on $max\text{-}uid_j$ in both algorithms. Since this is true for all i and j, it follows that the *max-uid* values remain identical in both algorithms.

Assertions 4.1.7 and 4.1.1 together imply Assertion 4.1.5, as needed.   □

The method we just used to prove the correctness of *OptFloodMax* is often useful for proving the correctness of "optimized" versions of distributed algorithms. First, an inefficient but simple version of the algorithm is proved correct. Then a more efficient but more complicated version of the algorithm is verified by proving a formal relationship between it and the simple algorithm. For synchronous network algorithms, this relationship generally takes the form used above—an invariant involving the states of both algorithms after the same number of rounds.

Another improvement. It is possible to reduce the number of messages in the *FloodMax* algorithm slightly further. Namely, if a process i receives a new maximum from a process j that is both an incoming neighbor and an outgoing neighbor, that is, with which it has bidirectional communication, then i need not send a message in the direction of j at the next round.

It is possible to elect a leader in a general digraph network with UIDs, but in which no information about n or *diam* is available to the processes. We suggest that you stop here and try to construct an algorithm to do this. One possibility is to introduce an auxiliary protocol that allows each process to calculate the diameter of the network. Ideas presented later in this chapter might also be useful.

4.2 Breadth-First Search

The next problem we consider is that of performing a breadth-first search (BFS) in a network based on an arbitrary strongly connected directed graph having a distinguished source node. More precisely, we consider how to establish a *breadth-first spanning tree* for the digraph. The motivation for constructing such a tree comes from the desire to have a convenient structure to use as a basis for broadcast communication. The BFS tree minimizes the maximum communication time from the process at the distinguished node to all other processes in the network (under the simplifying assumption that it takes the same amount of time for a message to traverse each communication channel).

The BFS problem and its solutions are somewhat simpler in the case where all pairs of neighbors have bidirectional communication, that is, where the network graph is undirected. We will indicate the simplifications for this case.

4.2.1 The Problem

We define a *directed spanning tree* of a directed graph $G = (V, E)$ to be a rooted tree that consists entirely of directed edges in E, all edges directed from parents to children in the tree, and that contains every vertex of G. A directed spanning tree of G with root node i is *breadth-first* provided that each node at distance d from i in G appears at depth d in the tree (that is, at distance d from i in the tree). Every strongly connected digraph has a breadth-first directed spanning tree.

For the BFS problem, we suppose that the network is strongly connected and that there is a distinguished *source node* i_0. The algorithm is supposed to output the structure of a breadth-first directed spanning tree of the network graph, rooted at i_0. The output should appear in a distributed fashion: each process other than i_0 should have a *parent* component that gets set to indicate the node that is its parent in the tree.

As usual, processes only communicate over directed edges. Processes are assumed to have UIDs but to have no knowledge of the size or diameter of the network.

4.2.2 A Basic Breadth-First Search Algorithm

The basic idea for this algorithm is the same as for the standard sequential breadth-first search algorithm. We call this algorithm *SynchBFS*.

SynchBFS algorithm:

At any point during execution, there is some set of processes that is "marked," initially just i_0. Process i_0 sends out a *search* message at round 1, to all of its outgoing neighbors. At any round, if an unmarked process receives a *search* message, it marks itself and chooses one of the processes from which the *search* has arrived as its parent. At the first round after a process gets marked, it sends a *search* message to all of its outgoing neighbors.

It is not hard to see that the *SynchBFS* algorithm produces a BFS tree. To show this formally, we can prove the invariant that after r rounds, every process at distance d from i_0 in the graph, $1 \leq d \leq r$, has its *parent* pointer defined; moreover, each such pointer points to a node at distance $d - 1$ from i_0. This invariant can, as usual, be proved by induction on the number of rounds.

Complexity analysis. The time complexity is at most *diam* rounds. (Actually, this analysis can be refined a little, to the maximum distance from the particular node i_0 to any other node.) The number of messages is just $|E|$—a *search* message is transmitted exactly once on each directed edge.

Reducing the communication complexity. As for the *FloodMax* algorithm, it is possible to reduce the number of messages slightly: a newly marked process need not send a *search* message in the direction of any process from which it has already received such a message.

Message broadcast. The *SynchBFS* algorithm can easily be augmented to implement message broadcast. If a process has a message m that it wants to communicate to all of the processes in the network, it can simply initiate an execution of *SynchBFS* with itself as the root, *piggybacking* message m on the *search* message it sends in round 1. Other processes continue to piggyback m on all their *search* messages as well. Since the tree eventually spans all the nodes, message m is eventually delivered to all the processes.

Child pointers. In an important variant of the BFS problem, it is required that each process learn not only who its parent in the tree is, but also who all of its children are. In this case, it is necessary for each process receiving a *search* message to respond to that message with a *parent* or *non-parent* message, telling the sender whether or not it has been chosen by the recipient as the parent.

If bidirectional communication is allowed between all pairs of neighbors, that is, if the network graph is undirected, then there is no difficulty—and little extra cost—in adding this extra communication. However, since we are allowing pairs of neighbors with only unidirectional communication, some of the *parent* and *non-parent* messages may need to be sent via indirect routes. For example, a *parent* or *non-parent* message could be sent via a new execution of *SynchBFS*, using piggybacking as above. In order for such a message to be recognized by its intended recipient, the message should also carry the UID of the intended recipient (plus a local name by which the recipient knows the sender), which should therefore itself be piggybacked on the original *search* message. Note that many executions of these *SynchBFS* "subroutines" can go on in parallel. In order to fit our formal model, in which at most one message can be sent on each link at each round, it may be necessary to combine many messages into one.

For a directed graph with unidirectional communication on some edges, in addition to outputting parent and child pointers, it may also be useful to have processes output information about the shortest routes from children to their parents. Such information could be produced, for example, using additional executions of *SynchBFS*.

Complexity analysis. If the graph is undirected, then the total time to compute a BFS tree, including child pointers, is $O(diam)$, and the communication complexity is $O(|E|)$.

Even if some of the pairs of neighbors have unidirectional communication, the time to compute the tree plus child pointers is still only $O(diam)$, because the extra BFS executions can all go on in parallel. In this case, the total number of messages is $O(diam|E|)$, because at most $|E|$ messages can be sent at each of the $O(diam)$ rounds. However, because a message might contain information from up to $|E|$ concurrent BFS executions, there might be as many as $|E|b$ bits in a message, where b is the maximum number of bits needed to represent a single UID. This yields a total of $O(diam|E|^2b)$ bits of communication. A smaller bound on the total number of bits can be obtained by noting that each of the (at most $|E|$) concurrent BFS executions uses at most $|E|$ messages, each having at most b bits. So the total number of communication bits is at most $O(|E|^2b)$.

Termination. How can the source process i_0 tell when the construction of the tree has been completed? If each *search* message is answered with either a *parent* or *non-parent* message, then after any process has received responses for all of its *search* messages, it knows who all its children in the BFS tree are and knows that they have all been marked. So, starting from the leaves of the BFS tree, notification of completion can be "fanned in" to the source: each process can send notification of completion to its parent in the tree as soon as (a) it has received responses for all its *search* messages (so that it knows who its children are and knows that they have been marked), and (b) it has received notification of completion from all its children. This type of procedure is called a *convergecast*.

If the graph is undirected, then the total time to compute a BFS tree, including child pointers, and to propagate notification of completion back to the source is $O\left(diam\right)$ and the communication complexity is only $O\left(|E|\right)$. If unidirectional communication is allowed, then the total time, including notification of completion, is $O\left(diam^2\right)$. The reason the behavior is quadratic is that the notification has to proceed sequentially, one level at a time in the tree. The total number of messages is $O\left(diam^2|E|\right)$ and the total number of communication bits is at most $O\left(|E|^2b\right)$.

4.2.3   Applications

Breadth-first search is one of the most basic building blocks for distributed algorithms. We give some examples here of how the *SynchBFS* algorithm can be used or augmented to help in performing other tasks.

Broadcast.   As we mentioned earlier, a message broadcast can be implemented along with the establishment of a BFS tree. Another idea is first to produce a BFS tree with child pointers, as described above, and then to use the tree to conduct the broadcast. The message need only be propagated along edges from parents to their children. This allows the work of constructing the BFS tree to be reused, because many messages can be sent on the same tree. Once the BFS tree has been constructed, the additional time to broadcast a single message is only $O\left(diam\right)$, and the number of messages is only $O\left(n\right)$.

Global computation.   Another application of BFS trees is the collection of information from throughout the network or, more generally, the computation of a function based on distributed inputs. For example, consider the problem in which each process has a nonnegative integer input value and we want to find the sum of all the inputs in the network. Using a BFS tree, this can be done easily (and efficiently) as follows. Starting from the leaves, "fan in" the results in a convergecast procedure, as follows. Each leaf sends its value to its parent; each parent waits until it gets the values from all its children, adds them to its own input value, and then sends the sum to its own parent. The sum calculated by the root of the BFS tree is the final answer.

Assuming that the BFS tree has already been constructed, and assuming bidirectional communication on all tree edges, this scheme requires $O\left(diam\right)$ time and $O\left(n\right)$ messages. The same scheme can be used to compute many other functions, for example, the maximum or minimum of the integer inputs. (What is required is that the function be associative and commutative.)

Electing a leader. Using *SynchBFS*, an algorithm can be designed to elect a leader in a network with UIDs, even when the processes have no knowledge of n or *diam*. Namely, all the processes can initiate breadth-first searches in parallel. Each process i uses the tree thereby constructed and the global computation procedure just described to determine the maximum UID of any process in the network. The process with the maximum UID then declares itself to be the leader, and all others announce that they are not the leader. If the graph is undirected, the time is $O\left(diam\right)$ and the number of messages is $O\left(n \cdot |E|\right)$.

Computing the diameter. The diameter of the network can be computed by having all processes initiate breadth-first searches in parallel. Each process i uses the tree thereby constructed to determine *max-dist$_i$*, defined to be the maximum distance from i to any other process in the network. Each process i then reuses its breadth-first tree for a global computation to discover the maximum of the *max-dist* values. If the graph is undirected, the time is $O\left(diam\right)$ and the number of messages is $O\left(n \cdot |E|\right)$. The diameter thus computed could be used, for example, in the leader-election algorithm *FloodMax*.

4.3 Shortest Paths

Now we examine a generalization of the BFS problem. Again, we consider a strongly connected directed graph, with the possibility of unidirectional communication between some pairs of neighbors. This time, however, we assume that each directed edge $e = (i, j)$ has an associated nonnegative real-valued *weight*, which we denote by *weight(e)* or *weight$_{i,j}$*. The weight of a path is defined to be the sum of the weights on its edges. The problem is to find a shortest path from a distinguished source node i_0 in the digraph to each other node in the digraph, where a *shortest path* is defined to be a path with minimum weight.[2] A collection of shortest paths from i_0 to all the other nodes in the digraph constitutes a subtree of the digraph, all of whose edges are oriented from parent to child.

As for breadth-first search, the motivation for constructing such a tree comes from the desire to have a convenient structure to use for broadcast communi-

---

[2]The mixture of measures of weight and distance is unfortunate, but traditional.

cation. The weights represent costs that may be associated with the traversal of edges, for instance, communication delay or a monetary charge. A shortest paths tree minimizes the maximum worst-case cost of communicating with any process in the network.

We assume that every process initially knows the weight of all its incident edges, or, more precisely, that the weight of an edge appears in special *weight* variables at both its endpoint processes. We also assume that each process knows the number n of nodes in the digraph. We require that each process should determine its parent in a particular shortest paths tree, and also its distance (i.e., the total weight of its shortest path) from i_0.

If all edges are of equal weight, then a BFS tree is also a shortest paths tree. Thus, in this case, a trivial modification of the simple *SynchBFS* tree construction can be made to produce the distance information as well as the *parent* pointers.

The case where weights can be unequal is more interesting. One way to solve the problem is by the following algorithm—a version of the Bellman-Ford sequential shortest paths algorithm.

BellmanFord algorithm:

Each process i keeps track of *dist*, the shortest distance from i_0 it knows so far, together with *parent*, the incoming neighbor that precedes i in a path whose weight is *dist*. Initially, $dist_{i_0} = 0$, $dist_i = \infty$ for $i \neq i_0$, and the *parent* components are undefined. At each round, each process sends its *dist* to all its outgoing neighbors. Then each process i updates its *dist* by a "relaxation step," in which it takes the minimum of its previous *dist* value and all the values $dist_j + weight_{j,i}$, where j is an incoming neighbor. If *dist* is changed, the *parent* component is also updated accordingly. After $n - 1$ rounds, *dist* contains the shortest distance, and *parent* the parent in the shortest paths tree.

It is not hard to see that, after $n - 1$ rounds, the *dist* values converge to the correct distances. One way to argue the correctness of *BellmanFord* is to show (by induction on r) that the following is true after r rounds: Every process i has its *dist* and *parent* components corresponding to a shortest path among those paths from i_0 to i consisting of at most r edges. (If there are no such paths, then $dist = \infty$ and *parent* is undefined.) We leave the details for an exercise.

Complexity analysis. The time complexity of the *BellmanFord* algorithm is $n - 1$, and the number of messages is $(n - 1)|E|$.

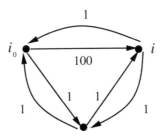

Figure 4.1: Shortest paths stabilize only after 2 rounds, though $diam = 1$.

Example 4.3.1   Time complexity of *BellmanFord*

You might suspect that by analogy with *SynchBFS*, the time complexity of *BellmanFord* is actually *diam*. An example that indicates why this is not the case is shown in Figure 4.1. In this example, it takes 2 rounds for the correct distance, 2, from i_0 to i to stabilize, since the path along which that distance is realized has two edges. However, the diameter is only 1.

The *BellmanFord* algorithm also works using an upper bound on n in place of n itself. If no such bound is known, it is possible to use techniques such as those described in Section 4.2 to discover one.

4.4   Minimum Spanning Tree

The next problem we consider is that of finding a minimum, or minimum-weight, spanning tree (MST) in an undirected graph network with weighted edges. Again, the main use for such a tree is as a basis for broadcast communication. A minimum-weight spanning tree minimizes the total cost for any source process to communicate with all the other processes in the network.

4.4.1   The Problem

A *spanning forest* of an undirected graph $G = (V, E)$ is a forest (i.e., a graph that is acyclic but not necessarily connected) that consists entirely of undirected edges in E and that contains every vertex of G. A *spanning tree* of an undirected graph G is a spanning forest of G that is connected. If there are weights associated with the undirected edges in E, then the *weight* of any subgraph of G (such as a spanning tree or spanning forest of G) is defined to be the sum of the weights of its edges.

Recall that we formalize the underlying undirected graph within our directed graph model as a directed graph having bidirectional edges between all pairs of neighbors. As in Section 4.3, we assume that each directed edge $e = (i, j)$ has an associated nonnegative real-valued *weight*, $weight(e) = weight_{i,j}$, only this time, we assume that for all i and j, $weight_{i,j} = weight_{j,i}$. We assume that every process initially knows the weight of all its incident edges, or, more precisely, that the weight of an edge appears in *weight* variables at both its endpoint processes. We assume that the processes have UIDs and know n. The problem is to find a minimum-weight (undirected) spanning tree for the entire network; specifically, each process is required to decide which of its incident edges are and which are not part of the minimum spanning tree.

4.4.2   Basic Theory

All known MST algorithms, sequential as well as concurrent, are based on the same simple theory, which we describe in this subsection. The basic strategy for constructing a minimum spanning tree involves starting with the trivial spanning forest consisting of n single nodes and repeatedly merging components along connecting edges until a spanning tree is produced. In order to end up with a minimum spanning tree, it is important that the merging occur only along certain selected edges—namely, those that are minimum-weight outgoing edges of some component. Justification for this method of selection is provided by the following lemma.

Lemma 4.3 *Let $G = (V, E)$ be a weighted undirected graph, and let $\{(V_i, E_i) : 1 \le i \le k\}$ be any spanning forest for G, where $k > 1$. Fix any i, $1 \le i \le k$. Let e be an edge of smallest weight in the set*

$$\{e' : e' \text{ has exactly one endpoint in } V_i\}.$$

Then there is a spanning tree for G that includes $\bigcup_j E_j$ and e, and this tree is of minimum weight among all the spanning trees for G that include $\bigcup_j E_j$.

Proof.   By contradiction. Suppose the claim is false—that is, that there exists a spanning tree T that contains $\bigcup_j E_j$, does not contain e, and is of strictly smaller weight than any other spanning tree that contains $\bigcup_j E_j$ and e. Now consider the graph T' obtained by adding e to T. Clearly, T' contains a cycle, which has another edge $e' \ne e$ that is outgoing from V_i.

By the choice of e, we know that $weight(e') \ge weight(e)$. Now, consider the graph T'' constructed by deleting e' from T'. Then T'' is a spanning tree for G, it contains $\bigcup_j E_j$ and e, and its weight is no greater than that of T. But this contradicts the claimed property of T. $\square$

Lemma 4.3 provides the justification for the following general strategy for constructing an MST.

General strategy for MST:
Start with the trivial spanning forest that consists of n individual nodes and no edges. Then repeatedly do the following: Select an arbitrary component C in the forest and an arbitrary outgoing edge e of C having minimum weight among the outgoing edges of C. Combine C with the component at the other end of e, including edge e in the new combined component. Stop when the forest has a single component.

Lemma 4.3 can be used in an inductive proof to show that, at any stage in the construction, the forest is a subgraph of an MST. Several well-known sequential MST algorithms are special cases of this general strategy. For example, the *Prim-Dijkstra algorithm* begins by distinguishing one of the initial single-node components and repeatedly adds the minimum-weight outgoing edge from the current component, each time attaching a single new node until a complete spanning tree is obtained. For another example, the *Kruskal algorithm* repeatedly adds the minimum-weight edge among all the edges that join two separate components in the current spanning forest, thus combining components until there is only one component, which is the final spanning tree.

In order to use this general strategy in a distributed setting, it would be nice to be able to extend the forest with several edges determined concurrently. That is, each of several components could determine its minimum-weight outgoing edge independently, and then all of the determined edges could be added to the forest, thereby causing several combinations of components to occur all at once. But Lemma 4.3 does not guarantee the correctness of this parallel strategy. In fact, the strategy is not correct, in general.

Example 4.4.1 Cycle creation in parallel MST algorithm

Consider the graph in Figure 4.2. The dots represent components in the spanning forest. The three edges with weight 1 are the only outgoing edges. If the components choose their minimum-weight outgoing edges as depicted by the arrows, a cycle would be created.

The cycle problem is avoidable, however, in the special case where all the edges have distinct weights. This is because of the following lemma.

Lemma 4.4 *If all edges of a graph G have distinct weights, then there is exactly one MST for G.*

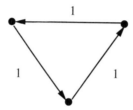

Figure 4.2: A cycle created by concurrent choices of minimum-weight outgoing edges.

Proof.   The proof is similar to the proof of Lemma 4.3. Suppose that there are two distinct minimum-weight spanning trees, T and T', and let e be the minimum-weight edge that appears in only one of the two trees. Suppose (without loss of generality) that $e \in T$. Then the graph T'' obtained by adding e to T' contains a cycle, and at least one other edge in that cycle, e', is not in T. Since the edge weights are all distinct and since e' is in only one of the two trees, we must have $weight(e') > weight(e)$, by our choice of e. Then removing e' from T'' yields a spanning tree with a smaller weight than T', which is a contradiction.
$\square$

Now reconsider the general strategy for the case where the graph has distinct edge weights, and so, by Lemma 4.4, there is a unique MST. In this case, at any stage of the construction, any component in the forest has exactly one minimum-weight outgoing edge (which we abbreviate, unpronounceably, as MWOE). Lemma 4.3 implies that if we begin the stage with a forest, all of whose edges are in the unique MST, then all of the MWOEs, for all components, are also in the unique MST. So we can add them all at once, without any danger of creating a cycle.

4.4.3   The Algorithm

We present a distributed algorithm for constructing an MST in an arbitrary weighted undirected graph, following the general strategy described in the previous subsection. Since components will be allowed to combine concurrently, we assume that edge weights are all distinct; near the end of this subsection, we will say how this assumption can be removed. We call the algorithm *SynchGHS* because it is based on an asynchronous algorithm developed by Gallager, Humblet, and Spira. (We will present the asynchronous algorithm, called simply *GHS*, in Section 15.5.)

SynchGHS algorithm:

The algorithm builds the components in "levels." For each k, the level k components constitute a spanning forest, where each level k component consists of a tree that is a subgraph of the MST. Each level k component has at least 2^k nodes. Every component, at every level, has a distinguished leader node. The processes allow a fixed number of rounds, which is $O(n)$, to complete each level.

The algorithm starts with level 0 components consisting of individual nodes and no edges. Suppose inductively that the level k components have been determined (along with their leaders). More specifically, suppose that each process knows the UID of the leader of its component; this UID is used as an identifier for the entire component. Each process also knows which of its incident edges are in the component's tree.

To get the level $k + 1$ components, each level k component conducts a search along its spanning tree edges for the MWOE of the component. The leader broadcasts search requests along tree edges, using the message broadcast strategy described in Section 4.2. Each process finds, among its incident edges, the one of minimum weight that is outgoing from the component (if there is any such edge); it does this by sending *test* messages along all non-tree edges, asking whether or not the other end is in the same component. (This determination is made by comparing the component identifiers.) Then the processes convergecast this local minimum-weight edge information toward the leader, taking minima along the way. The minimum obtained by the leader is the MWOE of the entire component.

When all level k components have found their MWOEs, the components are combined along all these MWOEs to form the level $k + 1$ components. This involves the leader of each level k component communicating with the component process adjacent to the MWOE, to tell it to mark the edge as being in the new tree; the process at the other end of the edge is also told to do the same thing.

Then a new leader is chosen for each level $k + 1$ component, as follows. It can be shown that for each group of level k components that get combined into a single level $k + 1$ component, there is a unique edge e that is the common MWOE of *two* of the level k components in the group. (We argue this below.) We let the new leader be the endpoint of e having the larger UID. Note that this new leader can identify itself using only information available locally.

Finally, the UID of the new leader is propagated throughout the new component, using a broadcast.

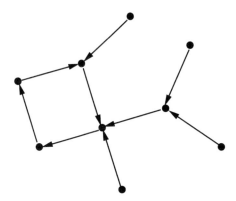

Figure 4.3: A graph in which each node has exactly one outgoing edge. Note the unique cycle.

Eventually, after some number of levels, the spanning forest consists of only a single component containing all the nodes in the network. Then a new attempt to find a MWOE will fail, because no process will find an outgoing edge. When the leader learns this, it broadcasts a message saying that the algorithm is completed.

A key to the algorithm is the fact that, among each group of level k components that get combined, there is a unique (undirected) edge that is the common MWOE of both endpoint components. In order to see why this is so, consider the *component digraph* G', whose nodes are the level k components that combine to form one level $k + 1$ component and whose edges are the MWOEs. G' is a weakly connected digraph in which every node has exactly one outgoing edge. (A digraph is *weakly connected* if its undirected version, obtained by ignoring the directions of all the edges, is connected.) So we can use the following property:

Lemma 4.5 *Let G be a weakly connected digraph in which each node has exactly one outgoing edge. Then G contains exactly one cycle.*

Proof.   The proof is left as an exercise.   □

Example 4.4.2   Graph with one outgoing edge per node

Figure 4.3 shows an example of a graph in which each node has exactly one outgoing edge.

We apply Lemma 4.5 to the component digraph G' to obtain the unique cycle of components. Because of the way G' was constructed, successive edges in the cycle must have nonincreasing weights; therefore, the length of this cycle cannot be greater than 2. So the length of the unique cycle is exactly 2. But this corresponds to an edge that is the common MWOE of both adjacent components.

In the *SynchGHS* algorithm, it is crucial that the levels be kept synchronized. This is needed to ensure that when a process i tries to determine whether or not the other endpoint j of a candidate edge is in the same component, both i and j have up-to-date component UIDs. If the UID at j is observed to be different from that at i, we would like to be certain that i and j really are in different components, not just that they haven't yet received their component UIDs from their leaders. In order to execute the levels synchronously, processes allow a predetermined number of rounds for each level. To be certain that all the computation for the round has completed, this number will be $O(n)$; note that $O(diam)$ rounds are not always sufficient. The need to count this number of rounds is the only reason that the nodes need to know n. (In Section 15.5, when we revisit this algorithm in the asynchronous network setting, we will use a different strategy for synchronizing the components.)

Complexity analysis. Note first that the number of nodes in each level k component is at least 2^k. This can be shown by induction, using the fact that at each level, each component is combined with at least one other component at the same level. Therefore, the number of levels is at most $\log n$. Since each level takes time $O(n)$, it follows that the time complexity of *SynchGHS* is $O(n \log n)$. The communication complexity is $O((n + |E|) \cdot \log n)$, since at each level, $O(n)$ messages are sent in total along all the tree edges, and $O(|E|)$ additional messages are required for finding the local minimum-weight edges.

Reducing the communication. It is possible to reduce the number of messages to $O(n \log n + |E|)$ by using a more careful strategy to find local minimum-weight edges. This improvement causes an increase in the time complexity, although it does not increase its order of magnitude. The idea is as follows.

Each process marks its incident edges as "rejected" when they are found to lead to a node in the same component; thereafter, there is no need to test them again. Also, at each level, the remaining candidate edges are tested one at a time, in order of increasing weight, just until the first one is found that leads outside the component (or until the candidate edges are exhausted).

With this improvement, the number of messages sent over tree edges is, as before, $O(n \log n)$. We carry out an amortized analysis of the number of messages used for finding local minimum-weight edges. Each edge gets tested and rejected at most once, for a total of $O(|E|)$. An edge that is tested and is found to be the local minimum-weight edge, but not the MWOE for the entire component, may be tested again. However, there is at most one such exploration originating at each node at each level, adding up to a total of $O(n \log n)$. The total communication complexity is thus $O(n \log n + |E|)$.

The strategy just described has another advantage. Since each node marks both its incident edges that are in the MST and those that are not in the tree, there is no need for the final phase in which the leader notifies everyone that the algorithm is completed. Each node can simply output the information about its adjacent edges as it is discovered.

Non-unique edge weights. Now consider the MST problem for a graph whose edge weights are not necessarily distinct. In this case, the *SynchGHS* algorithm can be used, with a small modification. Note first that the *SynchGHS* algorithm only manipulates the weights using $\{<, >, =\}$ comparisons.

Given arbitrary edge weights, we can derive a set of distinct *edge identifiers* using the UIDs. The identifer of an edge (i, j) is the triple $(weight_{i,j}, v, v')$, where v and v' are the UIDs of i and j, with $v < v'$. (Thus, (i, j) and (j, i) have the same edge identifier.) A total ordering is defined among the edge identifiers, based on lexicographic order among the triples.

Since *SynchGHS* manipulates the weights using comparisons only, we can run it using the edge identifiers in place of the (real-valued) weights; the resulting execution will be the same as if *SynchGHS* were running with a set of unique weights satisfying the same ordering relationships. A tree is thus produced. We leave as an exercise the task of showing that this tree is in fact an MST for the original graph.

Leader election. Once an MST (or any spanning tree) is known for a network based on an undirected graph, it is easy to elect a unique leader, provided UIDs are available. Namely, the leaves of the spanning tree begin a convergecast along the paths of the tree; each internal node waits to hear from all but one of its neighbors before sending a message to its remaining neighbor. If a node hears from all its neighbors without having itself sent out a message, it declares itself the leader. Also, if two neighboring nodes get messages from each other at the same round, then one of them, say, the one with the larger UID, declares itself the leader. The total additional complexity of this leader-election procedure (after the MST is constructed) is just $O(n)$ time and $O(n)$ messages.

Combining this with the MST complexity analysis, we see that, starting with a weighted undirected graph in which the nodes know n (but not *diam*), a leader can be elected in time $O(n \log n)$, with $O(n \log n + |E|)$ communication.

4.5 Maximal Independent Set

The final problem we consider in this chapter is that of finding a *maximal independent set* (*MIS*) of the nodes of an undirected graph. A set of nodes is called an *independent set* if it contains no pair of neighboring nodes, and an independent set is said to be *maximal* if it cannot be increased to form a larger independent set by the addition of any other nodes. Note that an undirected graph can have many different maximal independent sets. We do not require the largest possible maximal independent set—any will do.

The MIS problem can be motivated by problems of allocating shared resources to processes in a network. The neighbors in the graph G might represent processes than cannot simultaneously perform some activity involving shared resources (for example, database access or radio broadcast). We might wish to select a set of processes that could be allowed to act simultaneously; in order to avoid conflict, these processes should comprise an independent set in G. Furthermore, for performance reasons, it is undesirable to block a process if none of its neighbors is active; thus, the chosen set of processes should be maximal.

4.5.1 The Problem

Let $G = (V, E)$ be an undirected graph. A set $I \subseteq V$ of nodes is said to be *independent* if for all nodes $i, j \in I$, $(i, j) \notin E$. An independent set I is *maximal* if any set I' that strictly contains I is not independent. The goal is to compute a maximal independent set of G. More specifically, each process whose index is in I should eventually output *winner*, that is, should set a special *status* component of its state to the value *winner*, and each process whose index is not in I should output *loser*.

We assume that n, the number of nodes, is known to all the processes. (We could, alternatively, use an upper bound on n.) We do not assume the existence of UIDs.

4.5.2 A Randomized Algorithm

It is not hard to show that in some graphs, the MIS problem cannot be solved if the processes are required to be deterministic. The argument is similar to the one in the proof of Theorem 3.1. In this section, we present a simple solution that uses *randomization* to overcome this inherent limitation of deterministic systems. To be precise, we note that the randomized algorithm actually solves a weaker problem than the one that is stated above, in that it will have a (probability zero) possibility of never terminating. We call this algorithm *LubyMIS*, after Luby, its discoverer.

LubyMIS is based on the following iterative scheme, in which an arbitrary nonempty independent set is selected from the given graph G, the nodes in this set and all of their neighbors are removed from the graph, and the process is repeated. If W is a subset of the nodes of a graph, then we use $nbrs(W)$ to denote the set of neighbors of nodes in W.

> Let *graph* be a record with fields *nodes*, *edges*, and *nbrs*, initialized to
>> the indicated components of the original graph G.
> Let I be a set of nodes, initially empty.

```
while graph.nodes ≠ φ do
    choose a nonempty set I' ⊆ graph.nodes that is independent in graph
    I := I ∪ I'
    graph := the induced subgraph³ of graph on graph.nodes − I' − graph.nbrs(I')
end while
```

It is not hard to see that this scheme always produces a maximal independent set. To see why it is independent, note that at each stage, the selected set I' is independent, and we explicitly discard from the remaining graph all neighbors of vertices that are put into I. To see why it is maximal, note that the only nodes that are removed from consideration are neighbors of nodes that are put into I.

The key question in implementing this general scheme in a distributed network is how to choose the set I' at each iteration. Here is where randomization is used. In each stage, each process i chooses an integer val_i in the range $\{1, \dots, n^4\}$ at random, using the uniform distribution. The reason for the use of n^4 as a bound is that it is sufficiently large so that, with high probability, all processes in the graph will choose distinct values. (We do not carry out this calculation in this book, but instead refer you to Luby's research paper.) Once the processes have chosen these values, we define I' to consist of all the nodes i that are local *winners*, that is, those nodes i such that $val_i > val_j$ for all neighbors j of i. This obviously yields an independent set, since two neighbors cannot simultaneously defeat each other.

In this implementation it is possible, if the random choices are unlucky, that the set I' might be empty at some stages; those stages will be "useless," accomplishing nothing. Provided the algorithm does not reach a point after which it keeps performing useless stages forever, we can simply ignore the useless stages and assert that *LubyMIS* correctly follows the general scheme. We will, how-

---

[3] The *induced subgraph* of a graph G on a subset W of its nodes is defined to be the subgraph (W, E'), where E' is the set of edges of G that connect nodes in W.

ever, have to take the useless stages into account in the analysis. The algorithm follows.

LubyMIS algorithm (informal):

The algorithm works in *stages*, each consisting of three rounds.

Round 1: In the first round of a stage, the processes choose their respective *val*s and send them to their neighbors. By the end of round 1, when all the *val* messages have been received, the winners—that is, the processes in I'—know who they are.

Round 2: In the second round, the winners notify their neighbors. By the end of round 2, the losers—that is, the processes having neighbors in I'—know who they are.

Round 3: In the third round, each loser notifies its neighbors. Then all the involved processes—the winners, the losers, and the losers' neighbors— remove the appropriate nodes and edges from the graph. More precisely, this means the winners and losers discontinue participation after this stage, and the losers' neighbors remove all the edges that are incident on the newly removed nodes.

We now describe the algorithm more formally in our model. As described in Section 2.7, each process uses a special random function $rand_i$, which it applies at each round prior to applying the $msgs_i$ and $trans_i$ functions. Here, we use *random* to indicate a random choice from $\{0, \dots, n^4\}$, using the uniform distribution.

LubyMIS algorithm (formal):

states_i:
$round \in \{1, 2, 3\}$, initially 1
$val \in \{1, \dots, n^4\}$, initially arbitrary
awake, a Boolean, initially *true*
rem-nbrs, a set of vertices, initially the neighbors in the original graph G
$status \in \{unknown, winner, loser\}$, initially *unknown*

rand_i:
if *awake* and $round = 1$ then $val := random$

msgs_i:
if *awake* then
    case
        $round = 1$:
            send *val* to all nodes in *rem-nbrs*
        $round = 2$:
            if $status = winner$ then

        send *winner* to all nodes in *rem-nbrs*
    round = 3:
      if *status* = *loser* then
        send *loser* to all nodes in *rem-nbrs*
  endcase

In the following code, we identify 3 with 0, modulo 3.

trans$_i$:
if *awake* then
  case
    round = 1:
      if *val* > *v* for all incoming values *v* then *status* := *winner*
    round = 2:
      if a *winner* message arrives then *status* := *loser*
    round = 3:
      if *status* ∈ {*winner*, *loser*} then *awake* := *false*
      rem-nbrs := *rem-nbrs* − {*j* : a *loser* message arrives from *j*}
  endcase
  round := (*round* + 1 mod 3)

Note that *LubyMIS* still works correctly if, at some stages, some neighboring processes choose the same random values.

4.5.3   Analysis*

We have already argued that, provided that *LubyMIS* does not stall, executing useless stages forever, it will produce an MIS. Now we claim that with probability one, the algorithm in fact does not stall. More specifically, we claim that at any stage of the algorithm, the expected number of edges removed from the remaining graph is at least a constant fraction of the total number of remaining edges; this implies that there is a constant probability that at least a constant fraction of the edges is removed. In turn, this implies that the expected number of rounds until termination is $O(\log n)$. It also implies that, with probability one, the algorithm does in fact terminate.

The complete analysis of *LubyMIS* can be found in Luby's original paper; it involves substantial counting arguments about graphs. We just state the main technical lemma without proof, and indicate how it is used to obtain the needed results. For the next three lemmas, fix $G = (V, E)$ and, for an arbitrary node $i \in V$, define

$$sum(i) = \sum_{j \in nbrs_i} \frac{1}{d(j)} \, ,$$

where $d(j)$ is the degree of j in G. Here is the technical lemma:

Lemma 4.6 *Let I' be defined as in one stage of the LubyMIS algorithm. Then, for every i in the graph just before the stage,*

$$\Pr[i \in nbrs(I')] \geq \frac{1}{4} \min \left(\frac{sum(i)}{2}, 1 \right).$$

Using Lemma 4.6, we obtain the bound on the expected number of edges removed from the graph:

Lemma 4.7 *The expected number of edges removed from G in a single stage of LubyMIS is at least $\frac{|E|}{8}$.*

Proof. The algorithm ensures that every edge with at least one endpoint in $nbrs(I')$ is removed. It follows that the expected number of edges removed is at least

$$\frac{1}{2} \sum_{i \in V} d(i) \cdot \Pr[i \in nbrs(I')].$$

This is because each vertex i has the indicated probability of having a neighbor in I'; if this is the case, then i is removed, which causes the deletion of all of its $d(i)$ incident edges. The factor of $\frac{1}{2}$ is included to compensate for possible overcounting of removed edges, since each edge has two endpoints that could cause its deletion.

We next plug in the bound from Lemma 4.6, concluding that the expected number of removed edges is at least

$$\frac{1}{8} \sum_{i \in V} d(i) \cdot \min \left(\frac{sum(i)}{2}, 1 \right).$$

Breaking this up according to which term of the *min* is less, this is equal to

$$\frac{1}{8} \left(\frac{1}{2} \sum_{i:sum(i)<2} d(i) \cdot sum(i) + \sum_{i:sum(i)\geq 2} d(i) \right).$$

Now we expand the definition of $sum(i)$ and also write $d(i)$ as a trivial sum, obtaining

$$\frac{1}{8} \left(\frac{1}{2} \sum_{i:sum(i)<2} \sum_{j \in nbrs_i} \frac{d(i)}{d(j)} + \sum_{i:sum(i)\geq 2} \sum_{j \in nbrs_i} 1 \right).$$

Note that each undirected edge (i,j) contributes two summation terms to the expression in parentheses, one for each direction; in each case, the sum of these two terms is greater than 1. So the total is at least $\frac{|E|}{8}$. □

Lemma 4.7 can be used to conclude

Lemma 4.8 *With probability at least $\frac{1}{16}$, the number of edges removed from G in a single stage of LubyMIS is at least $\frac{|E|}{16}$.*

Using both Lemmas 4.7 and 4.8, we conclude:

Theorem 4.9 *With probability one, LubyMIS eventually terminates. Moreover, the expected number of rounds until termination is $O(\log n)$.*

Randomized algorithms.   The technique of randomization is used frequently in distributed algorithms. Its main use is to break symmetry. For example, the leader-election and MIS problems cannot be solved in general graphs by deterministic processes without UIDs because of the impossibility of breaking symmetry. In contrast, these problems can be solved using randomization. Even when there are UIDs, randomization may allow symmetry to be broken faster.

One problem with randomized algorithms, however, is that their guarantees of correctness and/or performance might only hold with high probability, not with certainty. In designing such algorithms, it is important to make sure that the crucial properties of the algorithm are guaranteed with certainty, not probabilistically. For example, any execution of *LubyMIS* is guaranteed to produce an independent set, regardless of the outcomes of the random choices. The performance, however, depends on the luckiness of the random choices. There is even a (probability zero) possibility that all processes will repeatedly choose the same value, thereby stalling progress forever. Whether or not these are serious drawbacks to the algorithm depends on the application for which it is used.

4.6   Bibliographic Notes

The *FloodMax* and *OptFloodMax* algorithms appear to be folklore. Afek and Gafni [6] have developed complexity bounds for leader election in complete synchronous networks. The *SynchBFS* algorithm is based on the standard sequential breadth-first search algorithm appearing, for example, in [83]. The *BellmanFord* algorithm is a distributed version of a sequential algorithm developed (separately) by Bellman and Ford [43, 125].

The *SynchGHS* algorithm is a synchronized (and therefore considerably simplified) version of the well-known asynchronous MST algorithm developed by Gallager, Humblet, and Spira. The *LubyMIS* algorithm and its analysis appear in a paper by Luby [200].

An example of a (probability zero) execution of a randomized algorithm in which the processes keep making the same choice appears in [271].

4.7 Exercises

4.1. Fill in more details in the correctness proof for the *FloodMax* algorithm.

4.2. In terms of n, the number $diam|E|$ of messages used in the *FloodMax* algorithm is easily seen to be $O\left(n^3\right)$. Either produce a class of digraphs in which the product $diam|E|$ really is $\Omega(n^3)$ or show that no such class of digraphs exists.

4.3. For the *OptFloodMax* algorithm, either prove a smaller upper bound than $O\left(n^3\right)$ on the number of messages or exhibit a class of digraphs and corresponding UID assignments in which the number of messages is $\Omega(n^3)$.

4.4. Consider the "further optimized" version of *OptFloodMax* described at the end of Section 4.1.3, which prevents processes from resending *max-uid* information to processes from which they have previously received the same information.

(a) Give code for this algorithm, in the same style as the other code in this chapter.

(b) Prove the correctness of your algorithm by relating it to *OptFlood-Max*, using the same sort of simulation strategy used in the proof of correctness for *OptFloodMax* itself (i.e., in the proof of Theorem 4.2).

4.5. (a) Write the code for the *SynchBFS* algorithm.

(b) Prove the correctness of your algorithm using invariant assertions.

(c) Do the same—parts (a) and (b)—for the *SynchBFS* algorithm with child pointers.

(d) Do the same—parts (a) and (b)—for the *SynchBFS* algorithm with child pointers and notification of completion.

4.6. Consider the optimized version of *SynchBFS* described in Section 4.2.2, which prevents processes from sending *search* messages to processes from which they have previously received such messages.

(a) Give code for this algorithm.

    (b) Prove the correctness of your algorithm by relating it to *SynchBFS*, using the same sort of simulation strategy used in the proof of correctness for *OptFloodMax* (i.e., in the proof of Theorem 4.2).

4.7. Describe in detail an algorithm that extends *SynchBFS* to produce not only child pointers, but also information about shortest routes from children in the BFS tree to their parents. This information should be distributed along those paths so that each process on a path knows the next process along the path. Analyze the time and communication complexity.

4.8. Describe in detail an algorithm that extends *SynchBFS* to allow the source process i_0 to broadcast a message to all other processes and obtain an acknowledgment that all processes have received it. Your algorithm should use $O\left(|E|\right)$ messages and $O\left(diam\right)$ time. You may assume that the network graph is undirected.

4.9. Analyze the time and communication complexity of the global computation scheme, the leader-election scheme and the diameter computation scheme at the end of Section 4.2, assuming that communication is allowed to be unidirectional between some pairs of neighbors.

4.10. Devise the most efficient leader-election algorithm you can, for a strongly connected directed network in which the processes have UIDs but do not have any knowledge of the number of nodes in or diameter of the network.

    (a) Do this assuming that communication is bidirectional between every pair of neighbors, that is, that the network graph is undirected.

    (b) Do this without making this assumption.

Analyze.

4.11. Develop the most efficient algorithm you can for finding the total number of nodes in a strongly connected directed network in which the processes have UIDs.

    (a) Do this assuming that communication is bidirectional between every pair of neighbors, that is, that the network graph is undirected.

    (b) Do this without making this assumption.

Analyze.

4.12. Develop the most efficient algorithm you can for finding the total number of edges in a strongly connected directed network in which the processes have UIDs.

(a) Do this assuming that communication is bidirectional between every pair of neighbors, that is, that the network graph is undirected.

(b) Do this without making this assumption.

Analyze.

4.13. Develop the most efficient algorithm you can, for an arbitrary undirected graph network, to determine a minimum-height rooted spanning tree. You may assume the processes have UIDs, but there is no distinguished leader node.

4.14. (a) Give code for the *BellmanFord* shortest paths algorithm.

(b) Prove its correctness using invariant assertions.

4.15. Give code for the *SynchGHS* algorithm.

4.16. Prove Lemma 4.5.

4.17. In the *SynchGHS* algorithm, show that it is not the case that $O(diam)$ rounds are always sufficient to complete each level of the computation.

4.18. Show that the version of *SynchGHS* that uses edge identifiers in place of edge weights (described near the end of Section 4.4) in fact produces an MST.

4.19. *Research Question:* Come up with a better synchronous minimum spanning tree algorithm than *SynchGHS*—better in terms of the time complexity, the communication complexity, or both.

4.20. Give code for the convergecast algorithm outlined at the end of Section 4.4, which elects a leader given an arbitrary spanning tree of an undirected graph network.

4.21. Give the best upper and lower bounds you can for the problem of establishing an arbitrary spanning tree in an undirected graph network. You may assume UIDs, but no weights. State carefully what assumptions you use about the processes' knowledge of the graph.

4.22. Consider a *line network*, that is, a linear collection of n processes $1, \ldots, n$, where each process is bidirectionally connected to its neighbors. Assume that each process i can distinguish its left from its right and knows whether or not it is an endpoint.

Assume that each process i initially has a very large integer value v_i and that it can hold in memory only a constant number of such values at any time. Design an algorithm to sort the values among the processes, that is, to cause each process i to return one output value o_i, where the multiset of outputs is equal to the multiset of inputs and $o_1 \leq \ldots \leq o_n$. Try to design the most efficient algorithm you can both in terms of the number of messages and the number of rounds. Prove your claims.

4.23. Prove that, under the assumptions given in Section 4.5, but assuming that the processes are deterministic rather than probabilistic, there are some graphs in which it is impossible to solve the MIS problem. Find the largest class of graphs you can for which your impossibility result holds.

4.24. Suppose that *LubyMIS* is executed in a ring of size n. Estimate the probability that any particular edge is removed from the graph in one iteration of the algorithm.

Chapter 5

Distributed Consensus with Link Failures

In this and the next two chapters, we study problems of *reaching consensus* in a distributed network. In such problems, each of the processes in the network begins with an initial value of a particular type and is supposed to eventually output a value of that same type. The outputs are required to be the same— the processes must *agree*—even though the inputs can be arbitrary. There is generally a *validity condition* describing the output values that are permitted for each pattern of inputs.

When there are no failures of system components, consensus problems are usually easy to solve, using a simple exchange of messages. To make matters more interesting, the problems are usually considered in settings that include failures. In this chapter, we consider basic consensus problems in the presence of communication failures, while in Chapter 6, we consider process failures. Chapter 7 contains some variations on the basic problems, also in the presence of process failures.

Consensus problems arise in many distributed computing applications. For example, processes may attempt to reach agreement on whether to commit or abort the results of a distributed database transaction. Or processes may try to agree on an estimate of an airplane's altitude based on the readings of multiple altimeters. Or they may attempt to agree on whether to classify a system component as faulty, given the results of separate diagnostic tests performed by separate processes.

The particular consensus problem that we present in this chapter is called the *coordinated attack problem*; it is a fundamental problem of reaching consensus in a setting where messages may be lost. We begin by presenting a basic impossibility result for deterministic systems, and then explore the possibilities for randomized solution. We show that the problem can be solved by a randomized algorithm, with a certain (substantial) probability of error. Moreover, that probability of error turns out to be unavoidable.

5.1　The Coordinated Attack Problem—Deterministic Version

We begin with an informal (in fact, ambiguous) problem statement, in terms of a battlefield scenario.

> Several generals are planning a coordinated attack from different directions, against a common objective. They know that the only way the attack can succeed is if all the generals attack; if only some of the generals attack, their armies will be destroyed. Each general has an initial opinion about whether his army is ready to attack.

> The generals are located in different places. Nearby generals can communicate, but only via messengers that travel on foot. However, messengers can be lost or captured, and their messages may thus be lost. Using only this unreliable means of communication, the generals must manage to agree on whether or not to attack. Moreover, they should attack if possible.

> (We suppose that the "communication graph" of generals is undirected and connected, and that all of the generals know the graph. We also assume that there is a known upper bound on the time it takes for a successful messenger to deliver a message.)

If all the messengers are reliable, then all the generals can send messengers to all the other generals (possibly in several hops), saying whether or not they are willing to attack. After a number of "rounds" equal to the diameter of the "communication graph," all the generals will have all of this information. Then they can all apply a commonly agreed-upon rule to make the same decision about attacking: for example, they can decide to attack exactly if all the generals want to do so.

In a model in which messengers may be lost, this easy algorithm does not work. It turns out that this is not just a problem with this algorithm: we show that there is no algorithm that always solves this problem correctly.

The real computer science problem behind this description is the commit problem for distributed databases. This problem involves a collection of processes that have participated in the processing of a database transaction. After this processing, each process arrives at an initial "opinion" about whether the transaction ought to be *committed* (i.e., its results made permanent and released for the use of other transactions) or *aborted* (i.e., its results discarded). A process will generally favor committing the transaction if all its local computation on behalf of that transaction has been successfully completed, and will favor aborting the transaction otherwise. The processes are supposed to communicate and eventually to agree on one of the outcomes, *commit* or *abort*. If possible, the outcome should be *commit*.

Before proving the impossibility result, we state the problem more formally and remove the ambiguities. We consider n processes indexed by $1, \ldots, n$, arranged in an arbitrary undirected graph network, where each process knows the entire graph, including the process indices. Each process starts with an input in $\{0, 1\}$ in a designated state component. We use 1 to denote "attack," or *commit*, and 0 to denote "don't attack," or *abort*. We use the same synchronous model that we have been working with so far, except that now we allow any number of messages to be lost during the course of an execution. (See Section 2.2 for the definition.) The goal is for all the processes to eventually output decisions in $\{0, 1\}$, by setting special *decision* state components to 0 or 1. There are three conditions imposed on the decisions made by the processes:

Agreement: No two processes decide on different values.

Validity:

1. If all processes start with 0, then 0 is the only possible decision value.

2. If all processes start with 1 and all messages are delivered, then 1 is the only possible decision value.

Termination: All processes eventually decide.

The agreement and termination requirements are the natural ones. The validity requirement is just one possibility—there are several useful alternatives. Validity conditions, in general, express the notion that the value decided upon should be "reasonable"; for instance, in this case, the trivial protocol that always decides 0 is ruled out by part 2 of the validity requirement. The particular validity condition we have stated above is quite weak: for example, if even one process starts with 1, the algorithm is allowed to decide 1, and if all processes start with 1 and even one message is lost, the algorithm is allowed to decide 0. The weak formulation is appropriate because our main focus in this chapter is on impossibility results. It turns out that even this weak version of the problem is impossible to solve in any graph with two or more nodes.

We prove the impossibility result for the special case of two nodes connected by one edge. We leave it as an exercise for you to show that impossibility for this case implies impossibility for any graph with two or more nodes. In this proof, we use the formal definitions of executions and indistinguishability ($\sim$) given in Chapter 2.

Theorem 5.1 *Let G be the graph consisting of nodes 1 and 2 connected by a single edge. Then there is no algorithm that solves the coordinated attack problem on G.*

Proof.   By contradiction. Suppose a solution exists, say algorithm A. Without loss of generality, we may assume that, for each process, there is only one start state containing each input value; this implies that the system has exactly one execution for a fixed assignment of inputs and fixed pattern of successful messages. Also without loss of generality, we may assume that both processes send messages at every round in A, since we can always force them to send dummy messages.

Let α be the execution that results when both processes start with value 1 and all messages are delivered. By the termination requirement, both eventually decide, and by the validity condition, part 2, both decide on the value 1. Suppose that both decide within r rounds. Now let α_1 be the same as α, except that all messages after the first r rounds are lost. In α_1, both processes also decide on 1 within r rounds. The communication pattern in α_1 is represented in Figure 5.1. The edges represent messages that are delivered; messages sent but not delivered are simply not drawn.

Starting from α_1, we now construct a series of executions, each of them indistinguishable from its predecessor in the series with respect to one of the processes; it will follow that all of these executions must have the same decision value.

Let α_2 be the execution that is the same as α_1, except that the last (round r) message from process 1 to process 2 is not delivered (see Figure 5.2). Then, although process 2 may go to different states after round r in executions α_1 and α_2, this difference never gets communicated to process 1; therefore $\alpha_1 \overset{1}{\sim} \alpha_2$. Since process 1 decides 1 in α_1, it also decides 1 in α_2. By the termination and agreement properties, process 2 also (eventually) decides 1 in α_2.

Next, let α_3 be the same as α_2, except that the last message from process 2 to process 1 is lost. Since $\alpha_2 \overset{2}{\sim} \alpha_3$, process 2 decides 1 in α_3, and by termination and agreement, so does process 1.

Continuing in this way, by alternately removing the last message from process 1 and from process 2, we eventually reach an execution α' in which both processes

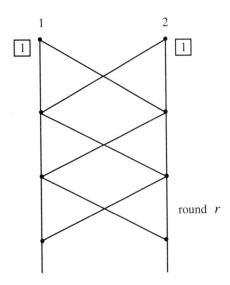

Figure 5.1: Pattern of message exchanges in execution α_1.

start with 1 and no messages are delivered. By the same reasoning as above, both processes are forced to decide 1 in this case.

But now consider the execution α'' in which process 1 starts with 1 but process 2 starts with 0, and no messages are delivered. Then $\alpha'' \overset{1}{\sim} \alpha'$, and hence process 1 still decides 1 in α'', and so does process 2, by termination and agreement. But $\alpha'' \overset{2}{\sim} \alpha'''$, where α''' is the execution in which both processes start with 0 and no messages are delivered. So process 2 decides 1 in α'''. But this yields a contradiction, because the validity condition, part 1, requires that both processes decide 0 in α'''. $\qquad\square$

Theorem 5.1 describes a fundamental limitation on the capabilities of distributed networks. It suggests that there is little that can be done to solve basic consensus problems such as the distributed database commit problem in the face of unreliable communication. However, some versions of this problem must be solved in real systems. In order to cope with the limitation of Theorem 5.1, it is necessary to strengthen the model or relax the problem requirements.

One approach is to make some probabilistic assumptions about the loss of messages, while keeping the processes deterministic. Then we must allow for some possibility of violating the agreement and/or validity condition. We leave the development of an algorithm for this setting for an exercise. A second approach is to allow the processes to use randomization, again allowing some

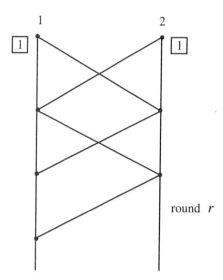

Figure 5.2: Pattern of message exchanges in execution α_2.

possibility of violating the agreement and/or validity condition; we discuss this approach in Section 5.2.

5.2 The Coordinated Attack Problem—Randomized Version

In this section, we consider the coordinated attack problem in the setting where processes can be randomized. As in the previous section, we consider n processes arranged in an arbitrary, known, undirected graph network. Each process starts with an input in $\{0, 1\}$ in a designated state component; we assume that for each process, there is exactly one start state containing each input value. For this section, we assume that the protocol terminates within a fixed number $r \geq 1$ of rounds; specifically, that by the end of round r, each process is required to output a decision in $\{0, 1\}$ by setting its *decision* variable to 0 or 1. We assume that a message is sent along each edge at each round k, $1 \leq k \leq r$, and that any number of these messages may be lost.

The goal is essentially the same as before, except that now we weaken the problem statement to allow for some probability of error. Namely, we use the same validity condition as before, but weaken the agreement condition to allow a small probability ϵ of disagreement. We obtain upper and lower bound results for the achievable values of ϵ, in terms of the number r of rounds. As you will see, the achievable values of ϵ are not small.

5.2.1 Formal Modelling

In formalizing this problem, we must be clear about the meaning of the probabilistic statements—the situation is more complicated than it was for the MIS problem in Section 4.5. The complication is that the execution that is produced depends not only on the results of the random choices, but also on which messages are lost. We do not want to assume that message losses are determined randomly. Rather, we imagine that they are determined by some "adversary" that tries to make things as difficult as possible for the algorithm; we evaluate the algorithm by considering its worst-case behavior over the class of all possible adversaries.

Formally, we define a *communication pattern* to be any subset of the set

$$\{(i, j, k) : (i, j) \text{ is an edge in the graph, and } 1 \le k\}.$$

A communication pattern γ is defined to be *good* if $k \le r$ for every $(i, j, k) \in \gamma$ (for this chapter only—we will use another notion of "goodness" in Chapter 6). A good communication pattern represents the set of messages that are delivered in some execution: if (i, j, k) is in the communication pattern, then it means that a message sent by i to j at round k succeeds in getting delivered.

The notion of *adversary* that we use here is an arbitrary choice of

1. An assignment of input values to all the processes

2. A good communication pattern

For any particular adversary, any particular set of random choices made by the processes determines a unique execution. Thus, for any particular adversary, the random choices made by the processes induce a probability distribution on the set of executions. Using this probability distribution, we can express the probability of events such as the processes all agreeing. To emphasize the role of the adversary, we use the notation Pr^B for the probability function induced by a given adversary B.

We now restate the coordinated attack problem in this probabilistic setting. The statement uses the parameter ϵ, $0 \le \epsilon \le 1$.

Agreement: For every adversary B,

$$Pr^B[\text{some process decides 0 and some process decides 1}] \le \epsilon.$$

Validity: Same as before.

We do not require a termination condition, because we have already assumed that all processes decide within r rounds. Our goals are to find an algorithm with the smallest possible value of ϵ and to prove that no smaller value of ϵ can be achieved.

5.2.2 An Algorithm

For simplicity, we restrict attention in this and the following subsection to the special case of an n-node complete graph. We leave the extensions to arbitrary graphs as exercises. For this special case, we present a simple algorithm that achieves $\epsilon = \frac{1}{r}$.

The algorithm is based on what processes know about each other's initial values and on what they know about each other's knowledge of the initial values, and so on. We need some definitions to capture such notions of knowledge.

First, for any communication pattern γ, we define a reflexive partial ordering $\leq_\gamma$ on pairs of the form (i, k), where i is a process index and k is a time, $0 \leq k$. (Recall from Chapter 2 that "time k" refers to the point in the execution just after k rounds have occurred.) This ordering represents information flow between the various processes at various times. We define the relation by

1. $(i, k) \leq_\gamma (i, k')$ for all i, $1 \leq i \leq n$, and all k, k', $0 \leq k \leq k'$.

2. If $(i, j, k) \in \gamma$, then $(i, k - 1) \leq_\gamma (j, k)$.

3. If $(i, k) \leq_\gamma (i', k')$ and $(i', k') \leq_\gamma (i'', k'')$, then $(i, k) \leq_\gamma (i'', k'')$.

The first case describes information flow at the same process. The second case describes information flow from the sender to the receiver of a message. The third case just takes the transitive closure. Similar information-flow ideas will appear later in the book, for example, in Chapters 14, 16, 18, and 19.

Now for any good communication pattern γ, we define the *information level,* $level_\gamma(i, k)$ of any process i at any time k, $0 \leq k \leq r$, recursively. There are three cases:

1. $k = 0$:
   Then define $level_\gamma(i, k)$ to be 0.

2. $k > 0$ and there is some $j \neq i$ such that $(j, 0) \not\leq_\gamma (i, k)$:
   Then define $level_\gamma(i, k)$ to be 0.

3. $k > 0$ and $(j, 0) \leq_\gamma (i, k)$ for every $j \neq i$:
   Then for each $j \neq i$, let l_j denote $\max\{level_\gamma(j, k') : (j, k') \leq_\gamma (i, k)\}$.

(This is the largest level that i knows j has reached.) Note that $0 \leq l_j \leq k - 1$ for all j. Then define $level_\gamma(i, k)$ to be $1 + \min\{l_j : j \neq i\}$.

In other words, each process starts out at level 0; when it hears from all the other processes, it advances to level 1. When it hears that all the other processes have reached level 1, it advances to level 2, and so on. If B is an adversary with communication pattern γ, we sometimes write $level_B(i, k)$ to mean $level_\gamma(i, k)$.

Example 5.2.1 Information level

Suppose that $n = 2$ and $r = 6$. Let γ be the good communication pattern consisting of exactly the following triples:

$$(1, 2, 1), (1, 2, 2), (2, 1, 2), (1, 2, 3), (2, 1, 4), (1, 2, 5), (2, 1, 5), (1, 2, 6)$$

Communication pattern γ is depicted in Figure 5.3. The information levels for processes 1 and 2, at times k, $0 \leq k \leq 6$, are as indicated by the labels.

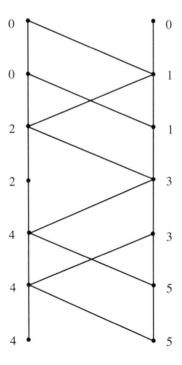

Figure 5.3: Good communication pattern γ.

The following lemma says that the information levels of different processes always remain within 1 of each other.

Lemma 5.2 *For any good communication pattern* γ, *any* k, $0 \leq k \leq r$, *and any* i *and* j, $|level_\gamma(i,k) - level_\gamma(j,k)| \leq 1$.

Proof.   The proof is left as an exercise.   □

The following lemma says that, in the case where all messages are delivered, the information level is equal to the number of rounds.

Lemma 5.3 *If* γ *is the "complete" communication pattern containing all triples* (i,j,k), $1 \leq k \leq r$, *then* $level_\gamma(i,k) = k$ *for all* i *and* k.

Proof.   The proof is left as an exercise.   □

The idea of the algorithm, which we call *RandomAttack*, is as follows:

RandomAttack algorithm (informal):

Each process i keeps explicit track of its level, with respect to the communication pattern that occurs in the execution, in a variable *level*. Also, process 1 chooses a random *key* value, an integer in the range $[1, r]$; this value is piggybacked on all messages. In addition, the initial values of all processes are piggybacked on all messages.

After r rounds, each process decides 1 exactly, if its calculated *level* is at least as large as *key* and it knows that all processes' initial values are 1.

RandomAttack algorithm (formal):

The message alphabet consists of triples of the form (L, V, k), where L is a vector assigning an integer in $[0, r]$ to each process index, V is a vector assigning a value in $\{0, 1, undefined\}$ to each process index, and k is either an integer in $[1, r]$ or *undefined*.

states$_i$:
rounds $\in \mathbb{N}$, initially 0
decision $\in \{unknown, 0, 1\}$, initially *unknown*
key $\in [1, r] \cup undefined$, initially *undefined*
for every j, $1 \leq j \leq n$:
    val(j) $\in \{0, 1, undefined\}$; initially *val(i)* is i's initial value and
        val(j) $= undefined$ for all $j \neq i$
    level(j) $\in [-1, r]$; initially *level(i)* $= 0$ and *level(j)* $= -1$ for all $j \neq i$

The variable *level(j)* is used to keep track of the largest level for process j that is known (through a chain of messages) to process i. For $j \neq i$, before i has heard anything from j, *level(j)* has the default value -1. In the random function *rand$_i$*, we use *random* to indicate a random choice of an integer in $[1, r]$, using the uniform distribution.

rand$_i$:
if $i = 1$ and $rounds = 0$ then $key := random$

msgs$_i$:
send (L, V, key) to all j, where L is the $level$ vector and V is the val vector

trans$_i$:
$rounds := rounds + 1$
let (L_j, V_j, k_j) be the message from j, for each j from which a message arrives
if some $k_j \neq undefined$ then $key := k_j$
for all $j \neq i$ do
    if some $V_{i'}(j) \neq undefined$ then $val(j) := V_{i'}(j)$
    if some $L_{i'}(j) > level(j)$ then $level(j) := \max \{L_{i'}(j)\}$
$level(i) := 1 + \min \{level(j) : j \neq i\}$
if $rounds = r$ then
    if $key \neq undefined$ and $level(i) \geq key$ and $val(j) = 1$ for all j then
        $decision := 1$
    else $decision := 0$

In this code, the third line sets the *key* component; it does not matter if it is set more than once, since all values of *key* that get passed around are the same. The fifth line sets the *val* components for processes $j \neq i$, again with no danger of conflicting assignments. The sixth line updates the *level* components for processes $j \neq i$; these are intended to contain the largest levels that i knows about, for all the other processes. Next, i updates its own *level* component, setting it to be one more than the smallest level it knows about for any of the other processes. Finally, if this is the last round r, then i decides according to the rule described earlier.

Theorem 5.4 *RandomAttack solves the randomized version of the coordinated attack problem, for* $\epsilon = \frac{1}{r}$.

Proof.   The key to the proof is just the claim that the algorithm correctly calculates the levels. That is, in any execution of *RandomAttack*, with any good communication pattern γ, for any k, $0 \leq k \leq r$, and for any i, after k rounds, the value of $level(i)_i$ is equal to $level_\gamma(i, k)$. Also, after k rounds, if $level(i)_i \geq 1$, then key_i is defined and $val(j)_i$ is defined for all j; moreover, these values are equal to the actual *key* chosen by process 1 and the actual initial values, respectively.

Termination of the *RandomAttack* algorithm is obvious. For validity, if all processes have initial value 0, then obviously 0 is the only possible decision value. Now suppose that all processes start with 1 and all messages are delivered. Then Lemma 5.3 and the fact that the algorithm correctly calculates the levels imply that for each i, $level(i)_i = r$ at the point in round r where the decision is made.

Since $level(i)_i = r \geq 1$ at this point, it follows that key_i is defined and $val(j)_i$ is defined for all j. Since all possible key values are less than or equal to r, 1 is the only possible decision value.

Finally, we consider agreement. Let B be any adversary; we show that

$$Pr^B[\text{some process decides 0 and some process decides 1}] \leq \epsilon.$$

For each i, let l_i denote the value of $level(i)_i$ at the time process i makes its decision (in round r). Then Lemma 5.2 implies that all the values l_i are within one of each other. If the chosen value of key is strictly greater than $\max\{l_i\}$, or if there is some process with an initial value of 0, then all processes decide 0. On the other hand, if $key \leq \min\{l_i\}$ and all processes have initial value 1, then all processes decide 1. So the only case where disagreement is possible is where $key = \max\{l_i\}$. The probability of this event is $\frac{1}{r} = \epsilon$, since $\max\{l_i\}$ is determined by the adversary B and key is uniformly distributed in $[0, r]$. □

Example 5.2.2   Behavior of *RandomAttack*

Consider the case where $n = 2$ and $r = 6$. Consider the adversary B that supplies input 1 for both processes, together with the good communication pattern γ of Example 5.2.1. Let $\epsilon = \frac{1}{6}$. Theorem 5.4 says that the probability of disagreement for adversary B is at most ϵ. In fact, this probability is exactly ϵ: if the value of key chosen by process 1 is 5, then process 1 decides 0 and process 2 decides 1; if $key \leq 4$, then both decide 1; and if $key = 6$, then both decide 0.

On the other hand, if the adversary supplies any other combination of inputs together with communication pattern γ, then the probability of disagreement is 0, since both processes decide 0.

Using the ideas in the proof of Theorem 5.4, we can see that *RandomAttack* satisfies stronger validity conditions than we have so far claimed. Namely, we can show:

Validity:

1. If any process starts with 0, then 0 is the only possible decision value.

2. For any adversary B for which all the initial values are 1,

$$Pr^B[\text{all processes decide 1}] \geq l\epsilon,$$

where l is the minimum level of any process at time r in B.

The second of these properties might be useful in some applications, such as warfare or distributed database commit, where it is considered desirable to favor the positive outcome. If, for example, only a single message is lost, then the probability of coordinated attack is guaranteed to be high, at least $\frac{r-1}{r}$. The proof that *RandomAttack* satisfies the stronger validity conditions is left as a simple exercise.

5.2.3 A Lower Bound on Disagreement

Now we show that it is not possible to do much better than the bound described in Theorem 5.4. (Recall from the previous subsection that we are only considering n-node complete graphs.)

Theorem 5.5 *Any r-round algorithm for the randomized coordinated attack problem has probability of disagreement at least $\frac{1}{r+1}$.*

For the remainder of this section, we assume a particular r-round algorithm A that solves the coordinated attack problem with disagreement probability ϵ in an n-node complete graph; we show that $\epsilon \geq \frac{1}{r+1}$.

In order to prove the theorem, we need one more definition. If B is any adversary, γ its communication pattern, and i any process, then we define another adversary, $prune(B, i)$. Adversary $prune(B, i)$ simply "prunes out" information that i does not hear about in B. $B' = prune(B, i)$ is defined as follows:

1. If $(j, 0) \leq_\gamma (i, r)$, then j's input in B' is the same as it is in B, and otherwise it is 0.

2. A triple (j, j', k) is in the communication pattern of B' exactly if it is in the communication pattern of B and $(j', k) \leq_\gamma (i, r)$.

That is, adversary B' includes all the messages that i knows about in B, but no others, and B' specifies that all the inputs that i does not know about in B are 0. The following lemma says that the pruned version of an adversary is sufficient to determine the probability distribution of outputs.

Lemma 5.6 *If B and B' are two adversaries, i is a process, and $prune(B, i) = prune(B', i)$, then $Pr^B[i \text{ decides } 1] = Pr^{B'}[i \text{ decides } 1]$.*

Proof. The proof is left as an exercise. $\qquad\square$

The proof of Theorem 5.5 is based on the following lemma.

Lemma 5.7 *Let B be any adversary for which all initial values are 1 and let i be any process. Then*

$$Pr^B[i \ decides \ 1] \le \epsilon(level_B(i,r) + 1).$$

Proof.   By induction on $level_B(i,r)$.

Basis: Suppose $level_B(i,r) = 0$. Define $B' = prune(B,i)$. Then $prune(B',i) = B' = prune(B,i)$, so by Lemma 5.6,

$$Pr^B[i \ decides \ 1] = Pr^{B'}[i \ decides \ 1]. \tag{5.1}$$

Since $level_B(i,r) = 0$, there must be some process $j \ne i$ such that $(j,0) \not\leq_\gamma (i,r)$, where γ is the communication pattern of B. Then adversary B' specifies an initial value of 0 for j and includes no messages with destination j in its communication pattern. It follows that $prune(B',j)$ is the trivial adversary for which all the initial values are 0 and there are no messages in the communication pattern. Let B'' denote this trivial adversary. Then $prune(B'',j) = B'' = prune(B',j)$, so by Lemma 5.6,

$$Pr^{B'}[j \ decides \ 1] = Pr^{B''}[j \ decides \ 1].$$

The validity condition implies that

$$Pr^{B''}[j \ decides \ 1] = 0,$$

so therefore

$$Pr^{B'}[j \ decides \ 1] = 0.$$

But since there is at most probability ϵ of disagreement, we have that

$$|Pr^{B'}[i \ decides \ 1] - Pr^{B'}[j \ decides \ 1]| \le \epsilon.$$

Therefore,

$$Pr^{B'}[i \ decides \ 1] \le \epsilon,$$

which by Equation 5.1 implies that

$$Pr^B[i \ decides \ 1] \le \epsilon,$$

as needed.

Inductive step: Suppose $level_B(i,r) = l > 0$, and suppose that the lemma holds for all levels less than l. Define $B' = prune(B,i)$. Then Lemma 5.6 implies that

$$Pr^B[i \ decides \ 1] = Pr^{B'}[i \ decides \ 1]. \tag{5.2}$$

Since $level_B(i, r) = l$, the definition of *level* implies that there must be some process j such that $level_{B'}(j, r) \leq l - 1$. By the inductive hypothesis,

$$Pr^{B'}[j \text{ decides } 1] \leq \epsilon \left(level_{B'}(j, r) + 1\right)$$
$$\leq \epsilon l.$$

But since there is at most probability ϵ of disagreement, we have that

$$|Pr^{B'}[i \text{ decides } 1] - Pr^{B'}[j \text{ decides } 1]| \leq \epsilon.$$

Therefore,

$$Pr^{B'}[i \text{ decides } 1] \leq \epsilon(l + 1),$$

which by Equation 5.2 implies that

$$Pr^{B}[i \text{ decides } 1] \leq \epsilon(l + 1),$$

as needed. ☐

We can now prove the theorem.

Proof (of Theorem 5.5). Let B be the adversary for which all inputs are 1 and no messages are lost. The probability that all processes decide 1 is at most the probability that any of them decides 1, which is, by Lemma 5.7, at most $\epsilon(level_B(i, r) + 1) \leq \epsilon(r + 1)$. But the validity condition says that all processes must decide 1 in all executions generated by this adversary B; hence the probability that all decide 1 must be exactly 1. This implies that $\epsilon(r+1) \geq 1$, that is, that $\epsilon \geq \frac{1}{r+1}$, as needed. ☐

5.3   Bibliographic Notes

The coordinated attack problem was originated by Gray [142] in order to model the problem of distributed database commit. The impossibility result for the deterministic version of the problem is also due to Gray [142]. The results on randomized coordinated attack are derived from work of Varghese and Lynch [281].

5.4   Exercises

5.1. Show that a solution to the (deterministic) coordinated attack problem for any nontrivial connected graph implies a solution for the simple graph consisting of two processes connected by one edge. (Therefore, this problem is unsolvable in any nontrivial graph.)

5.2. Consider the following variant of the (deterministic) coordinated attack problem. Assume that the network is a complete graph of $n > 2$ participants. The termination and validity requirements are the same as those in Section 5.1. However, the agreement requirement is weakened to say: "If any process decides 1, then there are at least two that decide 1." (That is, we want to rule out the case where one general attacks alone, but allow two or more generals to attack together.) Is this problem solvable or unsolvable? Prove.

5.3. Consider the coordinated attack problem with link failures for the simple case of two processes connected by an edge. Suppose that the processes are deterministic, but the message system is probabilistic, in the sense that each message has an independent probability p, $0 < p < 1$, of getting delivered successfully. (As usual, we allow each process to send only one message per round.)

For this setting, devise an algorithm that terminates in a fixed number r of rounds, has probability at most ϵ of disagreement, and likewise has probability at most ϵ of violating the validity condition. Obtain the smallest ϵ you can.

5.4. For the setting described in the previous exercise, prove a lower bound on the size of the bound ϵ that can be obtained.

5.5. Prove Lemma 5.2.

5.6. Prove Lemma 5.3.

5.7. Prove carefully the first claims in the proof of Theorem 5.4, that is, that the *RandomAttack* algorithm correctly computes the *level* values, and correctly conveys the initial values and key.

5.8. For the *RandomAttack* algorithm, prove the stronger validity properties given at the end of Section 5.2.2. That is, prove

(a) If any process starts with 0, then 0 is the only possible decision value.

(b) For any adversary B for which all the initial values are 1,

$$Pr^B[\text{all processes decide } 1] \geq l\epsilon,$$

where l is the minimum level of any process at time r in B.

5.9. Generalize the randomized version of the coordinated attack problem to allow for probability ϵ of violating the validity condition as well as of violating the agreement condition. Adjust the *RandomAttack* algorithm so that it achieves the smallest possible ϵ for this modified problem statement. Analyze.

5.10. Extend the *RandomAttack* algorithm and its analysis to arbitrary (not necessarily complete) undirected graphs.

5.11. Prove Lemma 5.6.

5.12. Extend the lower bound result in Theorem 5.5 to arbitrary (not necessarily complete) undirected graphs.

5.13. What happens to the results of this chapter for the randomized setting, if the communication pattern determined by the adversary is not fixed in advance as we have assumed, but is determined on-line? More precisely, suppose that the adversary is an entity that is able to examine the entire execution up to the beginning of any round k, before deciding which round k messages will be delivered.

   (a) What bound ϵ on disagreement is guaranteed by the *RandomAttack* algorithm, when working against arbitrary on-line adversaries?

   (b) Can you prove an interesting lower bound on attainable values of ϵ?

Chapter 6

Distributed Consensus with Process Failures

In this chapter we continue the study of consensus problems in the synchronous model, which we began in Chapter 5. This time, we consider the case where processes, but not links, may fail. Of course, it is more sensible to talk about failure of physical "processors" than of logical "processes," but to stay consistent with the terminology elsewhere in the book, we use the term *process*. We investigate two failure models: the *stopping failure* model, where processes may simply stop without warning, and the *Byzantine failure* model, where faulty processes may exhibit completely unconstrained behavior. Stopping failures are intended to model unpredictable processor crashes. Byzantine failures are intended to model any arbitrary type of processor malfunction, including, for example, failures of individual components within the processors.

The term *Byzantine* was first used for this type of failure in a landmark paper by Lamport, Pease, and Shostak, in which a consensus problem is formulated in terms of *Byzantine generals*. As in the coordinated attack problem of Chapter 5, the Byzantine generals attempt to agree on whether or not to carry out an attack. This time, however, the generals must worry not about lost messengers, but about the possible traitorous behavior of some generals. The term *Byzantine* is intended as a pun—the battle scenario takes place in ancient Byzantium, and the behavior of some of the traitorous generals can only be described as "Byzantine."

In the particular consensus problem we consider in this chapter, which we call simply the *agreement problem*, the processes start with individual inputs from a particular value set V. All the nonfaulty processes are required to produce outputs from the same value set V, subject to simple agreement and validity conditions. (For validity, we assume that if all processes begin with the same value v, the only allowed decision value is v.)

The agreement problem is a simplified version of a problem that originally arose in the development of on-board aircraft control systems. In this problem, a collection of processors, each with access to a separate altimeter, and some of which may be faulty, attempt to agree on the airplane's altitude. Byzantine agreement algorithms have also been incorporated into the hardware of fault-tolerant multiprocessor systems; there, they are used to help a small collection of processors to carry out identical computations, agreeing on the results of every step. This redundancy allows the processors to tolerate the (Byzantine) failure of one processor. Byzantine agreement algorithms are also useful in processor fault diagnosis, where they can permit a collection of processors to agree on which of their number have failed (and should therefore be replaced or ignored).

In both of our failure models, we will need to assume limitations on the frequency of occurrence of process(or) failures. How should such limitations be expressed? In other work on analysis of systems with processor failures, these limitations often take the form of probability distributions governing the occurrences of failures. Here, instead of using probabilities, we simply assume that the number of failures is bounded in advance, by a fixed number f. This is a simple assumption to work with, since it avoids the complexities of reasoning about probabilistic failure occurrences. In practice, this assumption may be realistic in the sense that it may be unlikely that more than f failures will occur. However, we should keep in mind that the assumption is somewhat problematic: in most practical situations, if the number of failures is already large, then it is likely that more failures will occur. Assuming a bound on the number of failures implies that failures are *negatively correlated*, whereas in practice, failures are usually independent or positively correlated.

After defining the agreement problem, for both stopping and Byzantine failures, we present a series of algorithms. We then prove lower bounds on the number of processes needed to solve the problem for Byzantine failures, and on the number of rounds needed to solve the problem for either type of failure.

6.1 The Problem

We assume that the network is an n-node connected undirected graph with processes $1, \ldots, n$, where each process knows the entire graph. Each process starts with an input from a fixed value set V in a designated state component; we assume that, for each process, there is exactly one start state containing each input value. The goal is for the processes to eventually output decisions from the set V, by setting special *decision* state components to values in V. We use the same synchronous model that we have been using in Chapters 3–5, only this time we allow the possibility that a limited number (at most f) of processes might fail. In this chapter, we assume that the links are perfectly reliable—all the messages that are sent are delivered. We consider two kinds of process failures: stopping failures and Byzantine failures.

In the stopping failure model, at any point during the execution of the algorithm, a process might simply stop taking steps altogether. In particular, a process might stop *in the middle of a message-sending step*; that is, at the round in which the process stops, only a subset of the messages the process is supposed to send might actually be sent. In this case, we assume that *any subset* of the messages might be sent. A process might also stop after sending its messages for some round but before performing its transition for that round.

For the stopping failure model, the correctness conditions for the agreement problem are

Agreement: No two processes decide on different values.

Validity: If all processes start with the same initial value $v \in V$, then v is the only possible decision value.

Termination: All nonfaulty processes eventually decide.

In the Byzantine failure model, a process might fail not just by stopping, but by exhibiting arbitrary behavior. This means that it might start in an *arbitrary state*, not necessarily one of its start states; might send *arbitrary messages*, not necessarily those specified by its *msgs* function; and might perform *arbitrary state transitions*, not necessarily those specified by its *trans* function. (As a technical but convenient special case, we even allow for the possibility that a Byzantine process behaves completely correctly.) The only limitation on the behavior of a failed process is that it can only affect the system components over which it is supposed to have control, namely, its own outgoing messages and its own state. It cannot, for example, corrupt the state of another process.

For the Byzantine failure model, the agreement and validity conditions are slightly different from those for the stopping failure model:

Agreement: No two nonfaulty processes decide on different values.

Validity: If all nonfaulty processes start with the same initial value $v \in V$, then v is the only possible decision value for a nonfaulty process.

Termination: The termination condition is the same.

The modified conditions reflect the fact that in the Byzantine model, it is impossible to impose any limitations on what the faulty processes might start with or what they might decide. We refer to the agreement problem for the Byzantine failure model as the *Byzantine agreement problem.*

Relationship between the stopping and Byzantine agreement problems. It is not quite the case that an algorithm that solves the Byzantine agreement automatically solves the agreement problem for stopping failures; the difference is that in the stopping case, we require that all the processes that decide, *even those that subsequently fail,* must agree. If the agreement condition for the stopping failure case is replaced by the one for the Byzantine failure case, then the implication does hold. Alternatively, if all the nonfaulty processes in the Byzantine algorithm always decide at the same round, then the algorithm also works for stopping failures. The proofs are left as exercises.

Stronger validity condition for stopping failures. An alternative validity condition that is sometimes used for the stopping failure model is as follows.

Validity: Any decision value for any process is the initial value of some process.

It is easy to see that this condition implies the validity condition we have already stated. We will use this stronger condition in our definition of the k-agreement problem, a generalization of the agreement problem, in Chapter 7. In this chapter, we use the weaker condition we gave earlier; this slightly weakens our claims about algorithms and slightly strengthens our impossibility results. For the algorithms in this chapter, we will indicate explicitly whether or not this stronger validity condition is satisfied.

Complexity measures. For the time complexity, we count the number of rounds until all the nonfaulty processes decide. For the communication complexity, we count both the number of messages and number of bits of communication; in the stopping case, we base these counts on the messages sent by all processes, but in the Byzantine case, we only base it on the messages sent by nonfaulty processes. This is because there is no way to provide nontrivial bounds on the communication sent by faulty processes in the Byzantine model.

6.2   Algorithms for Stopping Failures

In this section, we present algorithms for agreement in the stopping failure model, for the special case of a complete n-node graph. We begin with a basic algorithm in which each process just repeatedly broadcasts the set of all values it has ever seen. We continue with some reduced-complexity versions of the basic algorithm, and finally, we present algorithms that use a strategy known as *exponential information gathering (EIG)*. Exponential information gathering algorithms, though costly and somewhat complicated, extend to less well-behaved fault models.

Conventions. In this and the following section, we use v_0 to denote a prespecified default value in the input set V. We also use b to denote an upper bound on the number of bits needed to represent any single value in V.

6.2.1 A Basic Algorithm

The agreement problem for stopping failures has a very simple algorithm, called *FloodSet*. Processes just propagate all the values in V that they have ever seen and use a simple decision rule at the end.

> ### *FloodSet* algorithm (informal):
>
> Each process maintains a variable W containing a subset of V. Initially, process i's variable W contains only i's initial value. For each of $f + 1$ rounds, each process broadcasts W, then adds all the elements of the received sets to W.
>
> After $f + 1$ rounds, process i applies the following decision rule. If W is a singleton set, then i decides on the unique element of W; otherwise, i decides on the default value v_0.

The code follows.

> ### *FloodSet* algorithm (formal):
>
> The message alphabet consists of subsets of V.
>
> ***states$_i$:***
> $rounds \in \mathbb{N}$, initially 0
> $decision \in V \cup \{unknown\}$, initially *unknown*
> $W \subseteq V$, initially the singleton set consisting of i's initial value
>
> ***msgs$_i$:***
> if $rounds \le f$ then send W to all other processes
>
> ***trans$_i$:***
> $rounds := rounds + 1$
> let X_j be the message from j, for each j from which a message arrives
> $W := W \cup \bigcup_j X_j$
> if $rounds = f + 1$ then
>   if $|W| = 1$ then $decision := v$, where $W = \{v\}$
>   else $decision := v_0$

In arguing the correctness of *FloodSet*, we use the notation $W_i(r)$ to denote the value of variable W at process i after r rounds. As usual, we use the subscript i to denote the instance of a state component belonging to process i. We say that a process is *active* after r rounds if it does not fail by the end of r rounds.

The first easy lemma says that if there is ever a round at which no process fails, then all the active processes have the same W at the end of that round.

Lemma 6.1 *If no process fails during a particular round r, $1 \leq r \leq f+1$, then $W_i(r) = W_j(r)$ for all i and j that are active after r rounds.*

Proof.   Suppose that no process fails at round r and let I be the set of processes that are active after r rounds (or equivalently, after $r-1$ rounds). Then, because every process in I sends its own W set to all other processes, at the end of round r, the W set of each process in I is exactly the set of values that are held by processes in I just before round r.   □

We next claim that if all the active processes have the same W sets after some particular round r, then the same is true after subsequent rounds.

Lemma 6.2 *Suppose that $W_i(r) = W_j(r)$ for all i and j that are active after r rounds. Then for any round r', $r \leq r' \leq f + 1$, the same holds, that is, $W_i(r') = W_j(r')$ for all i and j that are active after r' rounds.*

Proof.   The proof is left as an exercise.   □

The following lemma is crucial for the agreement property.

Lemma 6.3 *If processes i and j are both active after $f+1$ rounds, then $W_i = W_j$ at the end of round $f + 1$.*

Proof.   Since there are at most f faulty processes, there must be some round r, $1 \leq r \leq f+1$, at which no process fails. Lemma 6.1 implies that $W_i(r) = W_j(r)$ for all i and j that are active after r rounds. Then Lemma 6.2 implies that $W_i(f + 1) = W_j(f + 1)$ for all i and j that are active after $f + 1$ rounds.   □

Theorem 6.4 *FloodSet solves the agreement problem for stopping failures.*

Proof.   Termination is obvious, by the decision rule. For validity, suppose that all the initial values are equal to v. Then v is the only value that ever gets sent anywhere. Each set $W_i(f + 1)$ is nonempty, because it contains i's initial value. Therefore, each $W_i(f+1)$ must be exactly equal to $\{v\}$, so the decision rule says that v is the only possible decision.

For agreement, let i and j be any two processes that decide. Since decisions only occur at the end of round $f + 1$, it means that i and j are active after $f + 1$ rounds. Lemma 6.3 then implies that $W_i(f + 1) = W_j(f + 1)$. The decision rule then implies that i and j make the same decision. $\square$

Complexity analysis. *FloodSet* requires exactly $f + 1$ rounds until all non-faulty processes decide. The total number of messages is $O\left((f + 1)n^2\right)$. Each message contains a set of at most n elements (since each element must be the initial value of some process), so the number of bits per message is $O\left(nb\right)$. Thus, the total number of communication bits is $O\left((f + 1)n^3 b\right)$.

Alternative decision rule. The decision rule given for *FloodSet* is somewhat arbitrary. Since *FloodSet* guarantees that all nonfaulty processes obtain the same set W after $f + 1$ rounds, various other decision rules would also work correctly, as long as all the processes apply the same rule. For instance, if the value set V has a total ordering, then all processes could simply choose the minimum value in W. This alternative rule has the advantage that it guarantees the stronger validity condition mentioned near the end of Section 6.1. The decision rule given for *FloodSet* does not guarantee this stronger condition, because the default value v_0 might not be the initial value of any process.

Process versus communication failures. The *FloodSet* algorithm shows that the agreement problem is solvable for process stopping failures. This positive result should be contrasted with the impossibility results for the coordinated attack problem in a setting with communication failures. (See Theorem 5.1 and Exercise 5.1.)

6.2.2 Reducing the Communication

It is possible to reduce the amount of communication somewhat from the $O\left((f + 1)n^2\right)$ messages and $O\left((f + 1)n^3 b\right)$ bits used by *FloodSet*. For example, the number of messages can be reduced to $2n^2$ and the number of bits of communication to $O\left(n^2 b\right)$ by using the following simple idea. Notice that at the end, each process i only needs to know the exact elements of its set W_i if $|W_i| = 1$; otherwise, i needs to know only the fact that $|W_i| \geq 2$. So it is plausible that each process might need to broadcast *only the first two values* it sees, rather than all values. This idea is the basis for the following algorithm.

OptFloodSet algorithm:

The processes operate as in *FloodSet*, except that each process i broadcasts at most two values altogether. The first broadcast is at round 1, when i

broadcasts its initial value. The second broadcast is at the first round r, $2 \leq r \leq f + 1$, such that at the beginning of round r, i knows about some value v different from its initial value (if any such round exists). Then i broadcasts this new value v. (If there are two or more new values at this round, then any one of these may be selected for broadcast.)

As in *FloodSet*, process i decides v if its final set W_i is the singleton set $\{v\}$ and otherwise decides v_0.

Complexity analysis. The number of rounds for *OptFloodSet* is the same as for *FloodSet*, $f + 1$. The number of messages is at most $2n^2$, since each process sends at most two non-*null* messages to each other process. The number of bits of communication is $O\left(n^2 b\right)$.

We prove the correctness of *OptFloodSet* by relating it to *FloodSet* using a *simulation relation* (a similar strategy was used in Section 4.1.3 to prove correctness of *OptFloodMax* by relating it to *FloodMax*). This requires first filling in the details in the description of *OptFloodSet*, including explicit *rounds*, *decision*, and W variables as in *FloodSet*. We use the notation $W_i(r)$ and $OW_i(r)$, respectively, to denote the values of W_i after r rounds of *FloodSet* and *OptFloodSet*, respectively. The following lemma describes message propagation in *FloodSet*.

Lemma 6.5 *In FloodSet, suppose that i sends a round $r + 1$ message to j, and j receives and processes it. Then $W_i(r) \subseteq W_j(r + 1)$.*

Proof. The proof is left as an exercise. ◻

The key pruning property of *OptFloodSet* is captured by the following lemma.

Lemma 6.6 *In OptFloodSet, suppose that i sends a round $r + 1$ message to j, and j receives and processes it. Then*

1. *If $|OW_i(r)| = 1$, then $OW_i(r) \subseteq OW_j(r + 1)$.*

2. *If $|OW_i(r)| \geq 2$, then $|OW_j(r + 1)| \geq 2$.*

Moreover, the same two conclusions hold in case i does not fail in the first r rounds, and does not send a round $r + 1$ message to j, but just because Opt-FloodMax does not specify that any such message is supposed to be sent.

Proof. The proof is left as an exercise. ◻

Now we run *OptFloodSet* and *FloodSet* side by side, with the same inputs and same failure pattern. That is, the same processes fail at the same rounds in both executions. Moreover, if process i sends only some of its round r messages in one algorithm, then it sends its round r messages to the same processes in the other algorithm; more precisely, there is no j to which i sends a message at round r in one algorithm but fails to send one that it is supposed to send in the other algorithm. We give invariant assertions relating the states of the two algorithms.

Lemma 6.7 *After any number of rounds* r, $0 \leq r \leq f + 1$:

1. $OW_i(r) \subseteq W_i(r)$.

2. *If* $|W_i(r)| = 1$, *then* $OW_i(r) = W_i(r)$.

Proof. The proof is left as an exercise. □

Lemma 6.8 *After any number of rounds* r, $0 \leq r \leq f + 1$:

If $|W_i(r)| \geq 2$, *then* $|OW_i(r)| \geq 2$.

Proof. By induction. The basis case, $r = 0$, is true vacuously. Assume now that the lemma holds for r. We show that it holds for $r + 1$. Suppose that $|W_i(r + 1)| \geq 2$. If $|W_i(r)| \geq 2$, then by inductive hypothesis we have that $|OW_i(r)| \geq 2$, which implies that $|OW_i(r + 1)| \geq 2$, as needed.

So assume that $|W_i(r)| = 1$. Then Lemma 6.7 implies that $OW_i(r) = W_i(r)$. We consider two subcases.

1. $|W_j(r)| = 1$ for all j from which i receives a round $r + 1$ message in *FloodSet*.

   Then for all such j, we have by Lemma 6.7 that $OW_j(r) = W_j(r)$, so that $|OW_j(r)| = 1$. Lemma 6.6 implies that for all such j, $OW_j(r) \subseteq OW_i(r+1)$. It follows that $OW_i(r + 1) = W_i(r + 1)$, which is sufficient to prove the inductive step.

2. $|W_j(r)| \geq 2$ for some j from which i receives a round $r + 1$ message in *FloodSet*.

   Then by the inductive hypothesis, $|OW_j(r)| \geq 2$. Then Lemma 6.6 implies that $|OW_i(r + 1)| \geq 2$, as needed. □

Lemma 6.9 *After any number of rounds* r, $0 \leq r \leq f + 1$, *the rounds and decision variables have the same values in FloodSet and OptFloodSet.*

Proof Sketch. The interesting thing to show is that the same decision is made by any process i at round $f + 1$ in the two algorithms. This follows from Lemmas 6.7 and 6.8 for $r = f + 1$ and the decision rules of the two algorithms. □

Theorem 6.10 *OptFloodSet solves the agreement problem for stopping failures.*

Proof.   By Lemma 6.9 and Theorem 6.4 (the correctness theorem for *FloodSet*).

$\square$

Other ways to reduce communication complexity.   There are other ways to reduce the communication complexity of *FloodSet*. For example, recall that if V has a total ordering, the decision rule can be modified to simply choose the minimum value in W. Then it is possible to modify the *FloodSet* algorithm so that each node just remembers and relays the minimum value it has seen so far, rather than all values. This algorithm uses $O\left((f+1)n^2b\right)$ communication bits. It can be proved correct by a simulation relating it to *FloodSet* (with the modified decision rule). This algorithm satisfies the stronger validity condition of Section 6.1.

6.2.3   Exponential Information Gathering Algorithms

In this section, we present algorithms for agreement with stopping failures based on a strategy known as *exponential information gathering (EIG)*. In exponential information gathering algorithms, processes send and relay initial values for several rounds, recording the values they receive along various communication paths in a data structure called an *EIG tree*. At the end, they use a commonly agreed-upon decision rule based on the values recorded in their trees.

   EIG algorithms are generally costly for solving agreement with stopping failures, both in terms of the number of bits that are communicated and the amount of local storage used. The main reason we present this strategy here is that the same *EIG* tree data structure can be used for solving Byzantine agreement, as we show in Section 6.3.2. The stopping failure case provides a simple introduction to the use of this data structure. A second reason for presenting this strategy for stopping failures is that simple stopping failure *EIG* algorithms can easily be adapted to solve the agreement problem for a restricted form of the Byzantine failure model known as the *authenticated Byzantine failure* model.

   The basic data structure used by *EIG* algorithms is a labelled *EIG tree* $T = T_{n,f}$, whose paths from the root represent chains of processes along which initial values are propagated; all chains represented consist of distinct processes. The tree T has $f + 2$ levels, ranging from level 0 (the root) to level $f + 1$ (the leaves). Each node at level k, $0 \le k \le f$, has exactly $n-k$ children. Each node in T is labelled by a string of process indices as follows. The root is labelled by the empty string λ, and each node with label $i_1 \ldots i_k$ has exactly $n - k$ children with labels $i_1 \ldots i_k j$, where j ranges over all the elements of $\{1, \ldots, n\} - \{i_1, \ldots, i_k\}$. See Figure 6.1 for an illustration.

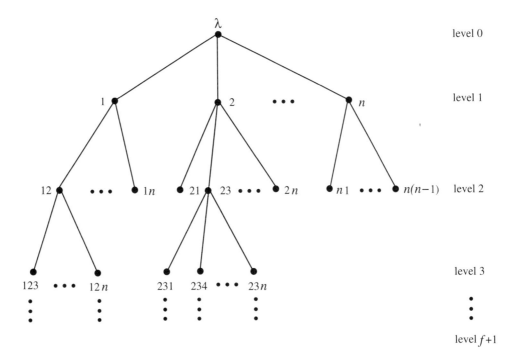

Figure 6.1: The *EIG* tree $T_{n,f}$.

In the *EIG* algorithm for stopping failures, which we call *EIGStop*, the processes simply relay values on all possible paths. Each process maintains a copy of the *EIG* tree $T = T_{n,f}$. The computation proceeds for exactly $f + 1$ rounds. In the course of the computation, the processes decorate the nodes of their trees with values in V or *null*, decorating all those at level k at the end of round k. The root of process i's tree gets decorated with i's input value. Also in process i's tree, if the node labelled by the string $i_1 \ldots i_k$, $1 \le k \le f + 1$, is decorated by a value $v \in V$, then it means that i_k has told i at round k that i_{k-1} has told i_k at round $k - 1$ that $\ldots$ that i_1 has told i_2 at round 1 that i_1's initial value is v. On the other hand, if the node labelled by the string $i_1 \ldots i_k$ is decorated by *null*, then it means that the chain of communication $i_1, i_2, \ldots, i_k, i$ has been broken by a failure. After $f + 1$ rounds, the processes use their individual decorated trees to decide on a value in V, based on a commonly agreed-upon decision rule (described below). A more detailed description of the algorithm follows.

In this algorithm description and in some others later on, it is convenient to pretend that each process i is able to send messages to itself in addition to the other processes; this can help to make the algorithm descriptions more uniform. These messages are technically not permitted in the model, but there is no harm in allowing them because the fictional transmissions could just be simulated by local computation.

EIGStop algorithm:

For every string x that occurs as a label of a node of T, each process has a variable $val(x)$. Variable $val(x)$ is used to hold the value with which the process decorates the node labelled x. Initially, each process i decorates the root of its tree with its own initial value, that is, it sets its $val(\lambda)$ to its initial value.

Round 1: Process i broadcasts $val(\lambda)$ to all processes, including i itself. Then process i records the incoming information:

1. If a message with value $v \in V$ arrives at i from j, then i sets its $val(j)$ to v.

2. If no message with a value in V arrives at i from j, then i sets $val(j)$ to *null*.

Round k, $2 \leq k \leq f+1$: Process i broadcasts all pairs (x, v), where x is a level $k-1$ label in T that does not contain index i, $v \in V$, and $v = val(x)$.[1] Then process i records the incoming information:

1. If xj is a level k node label in T, where x is a string of process indices and j is a single index, and a message saying that $val(x) = v \in V$ arrives at i from j, then i sets $val(xj)$ to v.

2. If xj is a level k node label and no message with a value in V for $val(x)$ arrives at i from j, then i sets $val(xj)$ to *null*.

At the end of $f + 1$ rounds, process i applies a decision rule. Namely, let W be the set of non-*null* *vals* that decorate nodes of i's tree. If W is a singleton set, then i decides on the unique element of W; otherwise, i decides on v_0.

It should not be hard to see that the trees get decorated with the values we indicated earlier. That is, process i's root gets decorated with i's input value. Also, if process i's node labelled by the string $i_1 \ldots i_k$, $1 \leq k \leq f+1$, is decorated by a value $v \in V$, then it must be that i_k has told i at round k that i_{k-1} has told

---

[1]In order to fit our formal model, in which only one message can be sent from i to each other process at each round, all the messages with the same destination are packaged together into one large message.

i_k at round $k-1$ that ... that i_1 has told i_2 at round 1 that i_1's initial value is v. Moreover, if process i's node labelled by the string $i_1 \ldots i_k$, $1 \le k \le f+1$, is decorated by *null*, then it must be that i_k does send a message to i at round k giving a value for $i_1, \ldots, i_{k-1}$.

Example 6.2.1 Execution of *EIGStop*

As an example of how the *EIGStop* algorithm executes, consider the case of three processes $(n = 3)$, one of which may be faulty $(f = 1)$. Then the protocol executes for 2 rounds, and the tree has 3 levels. The structure of the *EIG* tree $T_{3,1}$ is as in Figure 6.2.

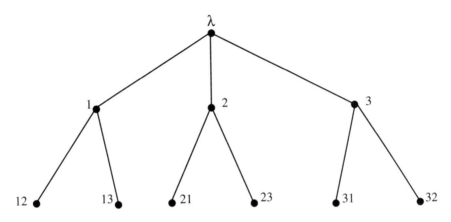

Figure 6.2: Structure of *EIG* tree $T_{3,1}$.

Suppose that processes 1, 2, and 3 have initial values 0, 0, and 1, respectively. Suppose that process 3 is faulty and that it fails after sending its round 1 message to 1 but not to 2. Then the three processes' trees get filled in as in Figure 6.3.

Note that process 2 does not discover that process 3's initial value is 1 until it hears this from process 1 at round 2.

To see that *EIGStop* works correctly, we first give two lemmas that relate the values in the various trees. The first lemma describes the initialization and the relationships between *vals* at different processes at adjacent levels in the trees.

Lemma 6.11 *After $f+1$ rounds of the EIGStop algorithm, the following hold:*

1. *$val(\lambda)_i$ is i's input value.*

2. *If xj is a node label and $val(xj)_i = v \in V$, then $val(x)_j = v$.*

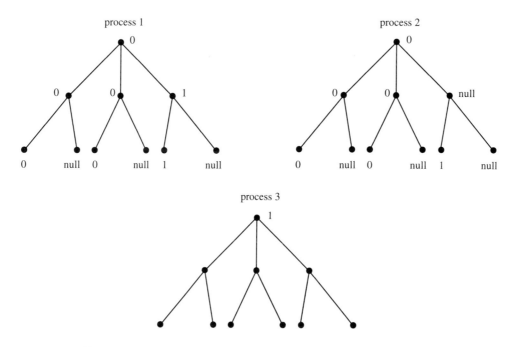

Figure 6.3: Execution of *EIGStop*; process 3 fails at round 1.

3. If xj is a node label and $val(xj)_i = null$, then either $val(x)_j = null$ or else j fails to send a message to i at round $|x| + 1$.

Proof.   The proof is left as an exercise.   □

The second lemma describes the relationship between *vals* at not-necessarily-adjacent levels in the trees. The first two conditions trace the origin of values appearing anywhere in the trees. The third condition is a technical one, asserting that any value v that appears in a tree must appear in that tree at some node whose label does not contain the index i. Loosely speaking, this means that the first time that process i learns a value, it is not as a result of propagating the value to itself.

Lemma 6.12 *After $f + 1$ rounds of the EIGStop algorithm, the following hold.*

1. *If y is a node label, $val(y)_i = v \in V$, and xj is a prefix of y, then $val(x)_j = v$.*

2. *If $v \in V$ appears in the set of vals at any process, then $v = val(\lambda)_i$ for some i.*

3. If $v \in V$ appears in the set of *vals* at process i, then there is some label y that does not contain i such that $v = val(y)_i$.

Proof. Part 1 follows from repeated use of part 2 of Lemma 6.11.

For part 2, suppose that $v = val(y)_i$. If $y = \lambda$, we are done. Otherwise, let j be the first index in y. Part 1 then implies that $v = val(\lambda)_j$.

For part 3, suppose to the contrary that v only appears as the *val* for labels containing i and let y be a shortest label such that $v = val(y)_i$. Then y has a prefix of the form xi. But then part 1 implies that $val(x)_i = v$, which contradicts the choice of y. □

The next lemma provides the key to the agreement property.

Lemma 6.13 *If processes i and j are both nonfaulty, then $W_i = W_j$.*

Proof. We may assume that $i \neq j$. We show inclusion both ways.

1. $W_i \subseteq W_j$.
   Suppose $v \in W_i$. Then Lemma 6.12 implies that $v = val(x)_i$ for some label x that does not contain i. We consider two cases:

   (a) $|x| \leq f$.
       Then $|xi| \leq f + 1$, so since string x does not contain index i, (non-faulty) process i relays value v to process j at round $|xi|$. This implies that $val(xi)_j = v$, so $v \in W_j$.

   (b) $|x| = f + 1$.
       Then because there are at most f faulty processes and all indices in x are distinct, there must be some nonfaulty process l whose index appears in x. Therefore, x has a prefix of the form yl, where y is a string. Then Lemma 6.12 implies that $val(y)_l = v$. Since process l is nonfaulty, it relays v to process j at round $|yl|$. Therefore, $val(yl)_j = v$, so again $v \in W_j$.

2. $W_j \subseteq W_i$.
   Symmetric to the previous case.

The two cases together imply the needed equality. □

Example 6.2.2   Cases in the proof of Lemma 6.13

Example 6.2.1 illustrates the two cases, (a) and (b), considered in the proof of Lemma 6.13. Process 1 first decorates its tree with a value of 1 at round 1, which is not the last round, so as in case (a), process

2 decorates its tree with 1 by round 2. In particular, $val(3)_1 = 1$, so $val(31)_2 = 1$.

On the other hand, process 2 first decorates its tree with a value of 1 at the last round, round 2, setting $val(31)_2 = 1$. This implies that some nonfaulty process index, in this case 1, must appear in the node label. Then as in case (b), the value 1 appears at node 31 in process 1's tree. That is, $val(31)_2 = 1$, so $val(31)_1 = 1$.

Theorem 6.14 *EIGStop solves the agreement problem for stopping failures.*

Proof.   Termination is obvious, by the decision rule.

For validity, suppose that all the initial values are equal to v. Then the only values that ever decorate any process's tree are v and *null*, by Lemma 6.12. Each set W_i is nonempty, since it contains i's initial value. Therefore, each W_i must be exactly equal to $\{v\}$, so the decision rule says that v is the only possible decision.

For agreement, let i and j be any two processes that decide. Since decisions only occur at the end, this means that i and j are nonfaulty. Then Lemma 6.13 implies that $W_i = W_j$. The decision rule then implies that i and j make the same decision.   □

Complexity analysis.   The number of rounds is $f + 1$, and the number of messages sent is $O\left((f+1)n^2\right)$. (This counts each combined message sent by any process to any other at any round as a single message.) The number of *bits* communicated is exponential in the number of failures: $O\left(n^{f+1}b\right)$.

Alternative decision rule.   Since *EIGStop* guarantees that the same set W of values appears in the trees of nonfaulty processes, various other decision rules would also work correctly. For instance, if the value set V has a total ordering, then all processes could simply choose the minimum value in W. As before, this has the advantage that it guarantees the stronger validity condition mentioned in Section 6.1.

It is possible to reduce the amount of communication in the *EIGStop* algorithm in much the same way as we did for *FloodSet*. As before, each process i only needs to know the exact elements of its set W_i in case $|W_i| = 1$. So again, it is plausible that the processes might need to broadcast only the first two values they learn about.

OptEIGStop algorithm:

The processes operate as in *EIGStop*, except that each process i broadcasts at most two values altogether. The first broadcast is at round 1, when i

broadcasts its initial value. The second broadcast is at the first round r, $2 \leq r \leq f + 1$, such that at the beginning of round r, i knows about some value v different from its initial value (if any such round exists). Then i broadcasts the new value v, together with the label of any level $r - 1$ node x that is decorated with v. (If there are two or more possible choices of (x, v), then any one of these may be selected for broadcast.)

As in *EIGStop*, let W be the set of non-*null* *val*s that decorate nodes of i's tree. If W is a singleton set, then i decides on the unique element of W; otherwise, i decides on v_0.

Complexity analysis. *OptEIGStop* uses $f + 1$ rounds. The number of messages is at most $2n^2$, since each process sends at most two non-*null* messages to each other process. The number of bits of communication is $O\left(n^2(b + (f + 1)\log n)\right)$: the value part of each messages uses $O(b)$ bits, while the label part uses $O((f + 1)\log n)$ bits.

The correctness of *OptEIGStop* can be proved by relating it to *EIGStop* using a simulation relation. The proof is similar to the proof of correctness of *OptFloodSet*. Alternatively, a correctness proof that relates *OptEIGStop* to *OptFloodSet* can be given. Details are left for exercises.

6.2.4 Byzantine Agreement with Authentication

Although the *EIG* algorithms described in this section are designed to tolerate stopping failures only, it happens that they can also tolerate some worse types of failures. They cannot cope with the full difficulty of the Byzantine fault model, where processes can exhibit arbitrary behavior. However, they can cope with an interesting restriction on the Byzantine fault model in which processes have the extra power to *authenticate* their communications, based on the use of *digital signatures*. A digital signature for process i is a transformation that i can apply to any of its outgoing messages in order to prove that the message really did originate at i. No other process is able to generate i's signature without i's cooperation. Digital signatures are a reasonable capability to assume in modern communication networks.

We do not provide a formal definition of the Byzantine model with authentication—in fact, we do not know of a nice formal definition—but just describe it informally. In this model, it is assumed that processes can use digital signatures to authenticate any of their outgoing messages. In the literature, it is usually assumed that the initial values originate from some common source, which also signs them; here, we assume that each nonfaulty process starts in an initial state containing a single input value signed by the source, while each faulty process starts in some state containing some set of input values signed by the source. Faulty processes are permitted to send arbitrary messages and perform arbitrary state transitions; the only limitation is that they are unable to generate signatures of nonfaulty processes or of the source.

The correctness conditions to be satisfied in this model are the usual termination and agreement conditions for Byzantine agreement, plus the following validity condition:

Validity: If all processes start with exactly one initial value $v \in V$, signed by the source, then v is the only possible decision value for a nonfaulty process.

It is not difficult to see that the *EIGStop* and *OptEIGStop* algorithms, modified so that all messages are signed and only correctly signed messages are accepted, solve the agreement problem for the authenticated Byzantine failure model. The proofs are similar to those given for the stopping failure model and are left as exercises.

6.3 Algorithms for Byzantine Failures

In this section, we present algorithms for Byzantine agreement, for the special case of an n-node complete graph. We begin with one that uses exponential information gathering. Then we show how an algorithm that solves Byzantine agreement for a binary value set, $V = \{0, 1\}$, can be used as a "subroutine" for solving Byzantine agreement for a general value set V. Finally, we describe a Byzantine agreement algorithm with reduced communication complexity.

A common property that all these algorithms have is that the number of processes they use is *more than three times* the number of failures, $n > 3f$. This situation is different from what we saw for the stopping failure case, where there were no special requirements on the relationship between n and f. This process bound reflects the added difficulty of the Byzantine fault model. In fact, we will see in Section 6.7 that this bound is inherent. This might seem surprising at first, because you might guess that $2f + 1$ processes could tolerate f Byzantine faults, using some sort of majority voting algorithm. (There is a standard fault-tolerance technique known as *triple-modular redundancy*, in which a task is triplicated and the majority result accepted; you might think that this method could be used to solve Byzantine agreement for one faulty process, but you will see that it cannot.)

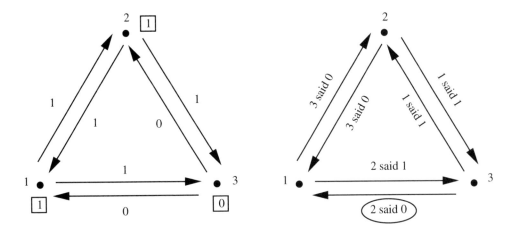

Figure 6.4: Execution α_1—false message is circled.

6.3.1 An Example

Before presenting the *EIG* Byzantine agreement algorithm, we give an idea of why the Byzantine agreement problem is more difficult than the agreement problem for stopping failures. Specifically, we give an example suggesting (though not proving) that three processes cannot solve Byzantine agreement, if there is the possibility that even one of them might be faulty.

Suppose that processes 1, 2, and 3 solve the Byzantine agreement problem, tolerating one fault. Suppose, for example, that they decide at the end of two rounds and that they operate in a particular, constrained manner: at the first round, each process simply broadcasts its initial value, while in the second round, each process reports to each other process what was told to it in the first round by the third process. Consider the following execution.

> *Execution α_1:*
> Processes 1 and 2 are nonfaulty and start with initial values of 1, while process 3 is faulty and starts with an initial value of 0. In the first round, all processes report their values truthfully. In the second round, processes 1 and 2 report truthfully what they heard in the first round, while process 3 tells 1 (falsely) that 2 sent 0 in round 1 and otherwise behaves truthfully. Figure 6.4 shows the interesting messages that are sent in α_1. In this execution, the validity condition requires that processes 1 and 2 both decide 1.

Now consider a second execution.

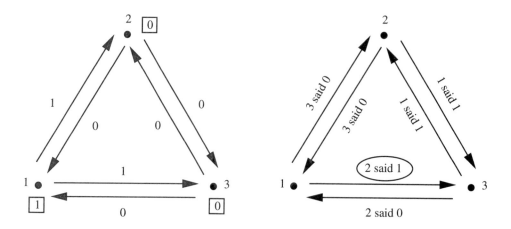

Figure 6.5: Execution α_2—false message is circled.

Execution α_2:
This is symmetric to α_1. This time, processes 2 and 3 are nonfaulty and start with initial values of 0, while process 1 is faulty and starts with an initial value of 1. In the first round, all processes report their values truthfully. In the second round, processes 2 and 3 report truthfully what they heard in the first round, while process 1 tells 3 (falsely) that 2 sent 1 in round 1 and otherwise behaves truthfully. Figure 6.5 shows the interesting messages that are sent in α_2. In this execution, the validity condition requires that processes 2 and 3 both decide 0.

To get a contradiction, consider a third execution.

Execution α_3:
Now suppose that processes 1 and 3 are nonfaulty and start with 1 and 0, respectively. Process 2 is faulty, telling 1 that its initial value is 1 and telling 3 that its initial value is 0. All processes behave truthfully in the second round. The situation is shown in Figure 6.6.

Notice that process 2 sends the same messages to 1 in α_3 as it does in α_1, and sends the same messages to 3 in α_3 as it does in α_2, in both rounds. In fact, it is easy to check that α_3 and α_1 are indistinguishable to process 1, $\alpha_3 \overset{1}{\sim} \alpha_1$, and similarly $\alpha_3 \overset{3}{\sim} \alpha_2$. Since process 1 decides 1 in α_1, it also does so in α_3, and since process 3 decides 0 in α_2, it also does so in α_3. But this violates the agreement condition for α_3, which contradicts the assumption that processes 1, 2, and 3 solve the Byzantine agreement problem. We have shown that no algorithm of this particularly simple form can solve Byzantine agreement.

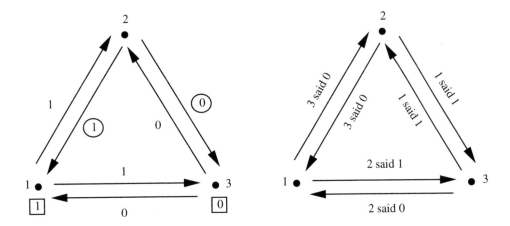

Figure 6.6: Execution α_3—conflicting messages are circled.

Note that process 1, for example, can tell that some process is faulty in α_3, since process 2 tells 1 that its value is 1, but process 3 tells 1 that 2 said its value is 0. The problem is that process 1 is unable to tell which of 2 and 3 is faulty.

This example does not constitute a proof that three processes cannot solve Byzantine agreement with the possibility of a single fault. This is because the argument presupposes that the algorithm uses only two rounds and sends particular types of messages. But it is possible to extend the example to more rounds and arbitrary types of messages. In fact, as we will see in Section 6.4, the ideas can be extended to show that $n > 3f$ processes are needed to solve Byzantine agreement in the presence of f faults.

6.3.2 EIG Algorithm for Byzantine Agreement

We now give an *EIG* algorithm for Byzantine agreement, which we call *EIG-Byz*. Unlike the *EIGStop* algorithm, *EIGByz* presupposes that the number of processes is large relative to the number of faults, in particular, that $n > 3f$. This is necessary because of the limitations described in Sections 6.3.1 and 6.4. Before you read about this algorithm, we suggest that you try to construct an algorithm of your own for a special case, say $n = 7$ and $f = 2$.

The *EIGByz* algorithm for n processes with f faults uses the same *EIG* tree data structure, $T_{n,f}$, that is used in *EIGStop*. Essentially the same propagation strategy is used as for *EIGStop*; the only difference is that a process that receives an "ill-formed" message corrects the information to make it look sensible. The decision rule is quite different, however—it is no longer the case that a process can trust all values that appear anywhere in its tree. Now processes must take some action to mask values that arrive in false messages.

EIGByz algorithm:

The processes propagate values for $f + 1$ rounds exactly as in the *EIGStop* algorithm, with the following exceptions. If a process i ever receives a message from another process j that is not of the specified form (e.g., it contains complete garbage or contains duplicate values for the same node in j's tree), then i "throws away" the message, that is, acts just as if process j did not send it anything at that round.

At the end of $f + 1$ rounds, process i adjusts its *val* assignment so that any *null* value is replaced by the default value v_0.

Then to determine its decision, process i works from the leaves up in its adjusted, decorated tree, decorating each node with an additional *newval*, as follows. For each leaf labelled x, $newval(x) := val(x)$. For each non-leaf node labelled x, $newval(x)$ is defined to be the *newval* held by a strict *majority* of the children of node x, that is, the element $v \in V$ such that $newval(xj) = v$ for a majority of the nodes of the form xj, provided that such a majority exists. If no majority exists, process i sets $newval(x) := v_0$. Process i's final decision is $newval(\lambda)$.

To show the correctness of *EIGByz*, we start with some preliminary assertions. The first says that all nonfaulty processes agree on the values relayed directly from nonfaulty processes.

Lemma 6.15 *After $f + 1$ rounds of the EIGByz algorithm, the following holds. If i, j, and k are all nonfaulty processes, with $i \neq j$, then $val(x)_i = val(x)_j$ for every label x ending in k.*

Proof.   If $k \notin \{i, j\}$, then the result follows from the fact that, since k is nonfaulty, it sends the same message to i and j at round $|x|$. If $k \in \{i, j\}$, then the result follows similarly from the convention by which each process relays values to itself.   □

The next lemma asserts that all nonfaulty processes agree on the *newvals* computed for nodes whose labels end with nonfaulty process indices.

Lemma 6.16 *After $f + 1$ rounds of the EIGByz algorithm, the following holds. Suppose that x is a label ending with the index of a nonfaulty process. Then there is a value $v \in V$ such that $val(x)_i = newval(x)_i = v$ for all nonfaulty processes i.*

Proof. By induction on the tree labels, working from the leaves up—that is, from those of length $f + 1$ down to those of length 1.

Basis: Suppose x is a leaf, that is, that $|x| = f + 1$. Then Lemma 6.15 implies that all nonfaulty processes i have the same $val(x)_i$; call this common value v. Then also $newval(x)_i = v$ for every nonfaulty process i, by the definition of *newval* for leaves. So v is the required value.

Inductive step: Suppose $|x| = r$, $1 \leq r \leq f$. Then Lemma 6.15 implies that all nonfaulty processes i have the same $val(x)_i$; call this value v. Therefore, every nonfaulty process l sends the same value v for x to all processes, at round $r + 1$, so $val(xl)_i = v$ for all nonfaulty i and l. Then the inductive hypothesis implies that also $newval(xl)_i = v$ for all nonfaulty processes i and l.

We now claim that a majority of the labels of children of node x end in nonfaulty process indices. This is true because the number of children of x is exactly $n - r \geq n - f$. Since we have assumed that $n > 3f$, this number must be strictly greater than $2f$. Since at most f of the children have labels ending in indices of faulty processes, we have the needed majority.

It follows that for any nonfaulty i, $newval(xl)_i = v$ for a majority of children xl of node x. Then the majority rule used in the algorithm implies that $newval(x)_i = v$ for all nonfaulty i. So v is the required value. $\square$

We now argue validity.

Lemma 6.17 *If all nonfaulty processes begin with the same initial value $v \in V$, then v is the only possible decision value for a nonfaulty process.*

Proof. If all nonfaulty processes begin with v, then all nonfaulty processes broadcast v at the first round, and therefore $val(j)_i = v$ for all nonfaulty processes i and j. Lemma 6.16 implies that $newval(j)_i = v$ for all nonfaulty i and j. Then the majority rule used in the algorithm implies that $newval(\lambda)_i = v$ for all nonfaulty i. Therefore, i's decision is v, as needed. $\square$

To show the agreement property, we need two more definitions. First, we say that a subset C of the nodes of a rooted tree is a *path covering* provided that every path from the root to a leaf contains at least one node in C.

Second, consider any execution α of the *EIGByz* algorithm. A tree node x is said to be *common* in α provided that at the end of $f + 1$ rounds in α, all the nonfaulty processes i have the same $newval(x)_i$. A set of tree nodes (e.g., a path covering) is said to be *common* in α if all the nodes in the set are common in α. Notice that Lemma 6.16 implies that if i is nonfaulty, then for every x, xi is a common node.

Lemma 6.18 *After $f + 1$ rounds of any execution α of EIGByz, there exists a path covering that is common in α.*

Proof. Let C be the set of nodes of the form xi, where i is nonfaulty. As observed just above, all nodes in C are common. To see why C is a path covering, consider any path from the root to a leaf. It contains exactly $f + 1$ non-root nodes, and each such node ends with a distinct process index, by construction of T. Since there are at most f faulty processes, there is some node on the path whose label ends in a nonfaulty process index. This node must be in C.   □

The following lemma shows how common nodes propagate up the tree.

Lemma 6.19 *After $f + 1$ rounds of EIGByz, the following holds. Let x be any node label in the EIG tree. If there is a common path covering of the subtree rooted at x, then x is common.*

Proof. By induction on tree labels, working from the leaves up.
Basis: Suppose that x is a leaf. Then the only path covering of x's subtree consists of the single node x itself. So x is common, as needed.
Inductive step: Suppose that $|x| = r$, $0 \le r \le f$. Suppose that there is a common path covering C of x's subtree. If x itself is in C, then x is common and we are done, so suppose $x \notin C$.
Consider *any* child xl of x. Since $x \notin C$, C induces a common path covering for the subtree rooted at xl. So by the inductive hypothesis, xl is common. Since xl was chosen to be an arbitrary child of x, all the children of x are common. Then the definition of $newval(x)$ implies that x is common.   □

As a simple consequence, we obtain

Lemma 6.20 *After $f + 1$ rounds of EIGByz, the root node λ is common.*

Proof. Immediate by Lemmas 6.18 and 6.19.   □

We now tie the pieces together in the main correctness theorem.

Theorem 6.21 *EIGByz solves the Byzantine agreement problem for n processes with f failures, if $n > 3f$.*

Proof. Termination is obvious. Validity follows from Lemma 6.17. Agreement follows from Lemma 6.20 and the decision rule.   □

Complexity analysis. The costs are the same as for the *EIGStop* algorithm: $f + 1$ rounds, $O\left((f + 1)n^2\right)$ messages, and $O\left(n^{f+1}b\right)$ bits of communication. In addition, there is the new requirement that the number of processes be large relative to the number of failures: $n > 3f$.

6.3.3 General Byzantine Agreement Using Binary Byzantine Agreement

In this subsection, we show how to use an algorithm that solves Byzantine agreement for inputs in $\{0, 1\}$ as a subroutine for solving general Byzantine agreement. The overhead is just 2 extra rounds, $2n^2$ extra messages, and $O\left(n^2b\right)$ bits of communication. This can lead to a substantial savings in the total number of bits that need to be communicated, since it is not necessary to send values in V, but only binary values, while executing the subroutine. This improvement, however, is not sufficient to reduce the number of bits of communication from exponential to polynomial in f.

We call the algorithm *TurpinCoan*, after its designers. The algorithm assumes that $n > 3f$. As earlier, we pretend that each process can send messages to itself as well as to the other processes.

> **TurpinCoan algorithm:**
>
> Each process has local variables x, y, z, and *vote*, where x is initialized to the process's input value and y, z, and *vote* are initialized arbitrarily.
>
> *Round 1:* Process i sends its value of x to all processes, including itself. If, in the set of messages received at this round, there are $\geq n - f$ copies of a particular value $v \in V$, then i sets $y := v$; otherwise $y := null$.
>
> *Round 2:* Process i sends its value of y to all processes, including itself. If, in the set of messages received at this round, there are $\geq n - f$ copies of a particular value in V, then i sets *vote* $:= 1$; otherwise *vote* $:= 0$. Also, i sets z equal to the non-*null* value that occurs most often among the messages received by i at this round, with ties broken arbitrarily; if all messages are *null*, then z remains undefined.
>
> *Round r, $r \geq 3$:* The processes run the binary Byzantine agreement subroutine using the values of *vote* as the input values. If process i decides 1 in the subroutine and if z is defined, then the final decision of the algorithm is z; otherwise it is the default value v_0.

A key fact about the *TurpinCoan* algorithm is

Lemma 6.22 *There is at most one value $v \in V$ that is sent in round 2 messages by nonfaulty processes.*

Proof. Suppose for the sake of contradiction that nonfaulty processes i and j send round 2 messages containing values v and w respectively, where $v, w \in V$, $v \neq w$. Then i receives at least $n - f$ round 1 messages containing v. Since there are at most f faulty processes, and nonfaulty processes send the same round 1 messages to all processes, it must be that j receives at least $n - 2f$ messages containing v. Since $n > 3f$, this means j receives at least $f + 1$ messages containing v.

But also, since j sends w in round 2, j receives at least $n - f$ round 1 messages containing w, for a total of at least $(f + 1) + (n - f) > n$ messages. But the total number of round 1 messages received by j is only n, so this is a contradiction.
□

Theorem 6.23 *The TurpinCoan algorithm solves general Byzantine agreement when given a binary Byzantine agreement algorithm as a subroutine, if $n > 3f$.*

Proof. Termination is easy to see.

To show validity, we must prove that if all nonfaulty processes start with the same initial value, v, then all nonfaulty processes decide v. So suppose that all nonfaulty processes start with v. Then all the $\geq n - f$ nonfaulty processes successfully broadcast round 1 messages containing v to all processes. So at round 1, all nonfaulty processes set their y variables to v. Then in round 2, each nonfaulty process receives at least $n - f$ messages containing v, which implies that it sets its z variable to v and its *vote* to 1. Since all the nonfaulty processes use input 1 for the binary Byzantine agreement subroutine, they all decide 1 in the subroutine, by the validity condition for the binary algorithm. This means that they all decide v in the main algorithm, which shows validity.

Finally, we show agreement. If the subroutine's decision value is 0, then v_0 is chosen as the final decision value by all nonfaulty processes and agreement holds by default.

So assume that the subroutine's decision value is 1. Then by the validity condition for the subroutine, some nonfaulty process i must begin the subroutine with $vote_i = 1$. This means that process i receives at least $n - f$ round 2 messages containing some particular value $v \in V$, so since there are at most f faulty processes, i receives at least $n - 2f$ round 2 messages containing v from nonfaulty processes. Then if j is any nonfaulty process, it must be that j also receives at least $n - 2f$ round 2 messages containing v from those same nonfaulty processes. By Lemma 6.22, no value in V other than v is sent by any nonfaulty process in round 2. So process j receives no more than f round 2 messages containing values in V other than v (and these must be from faulty processes). Since $n > 3f$, we have $n - 2f > f$, so v is the value that occurs most often in round 2 messages received by j. It follows that process j sets $z := v$ in round 2.

Since the subroutine's decision value is 1, this means that j decides v. Since this argument holds for any nonfaulty process j, agreement holds. $\qquad\square$

In the proof of the *TurpinCoan* algorithm, the limitation of f on the number of faulty processes is used to obtain claims about the similarity between the views of different processes in an execution. This sort of argument also appears in proofs for other consensus algorithms, for instance the *approximate agreement* algorithm in Section 7.2.

Complexity analysis. The number of rounds is $r + 2$, where r is the number of rounds used by the binary Byzantine agreement subroutine. The extra communication used by *TurpinCoan*, in addition to that used by the subroutine, is $2n^2$ messages, each of at most b bits, for a total of $O\left(n^2 b\right)$ bits.

6.3.4 Reducing the Communication Cost

Although the *TurpinCoan* algorithm can be used to reduce the bit communication complexity of Byzantine agreement somewhat, its cost is still exponential in the number f of failures. Algorithms that are polynomial in the number of failures are much more difficult to obtain in the Byzantine failure model than in the stopping failure model. In this section, we present one example; this algorithm is not optimal in terms of time complexity, but it is fairly simple and uses some interesting techniques. This algorithm is for the special case of Byzantine agreement on a value in $\{0, 1\}$; the results of Section 6.3.3 show how this algorithm can be used to obtain a polynomial algorithm for a general value domain.

The algorithm uses a mechanism known as *consistent broadcast* for all its communication. This mechanism is a way of ensuring a certain amount of coherence among the messages received by different processes. Using consistent broadcast, a process i can *broadcast* a message of the form (m, i, r) at round r, and the message can be *accepted* by any of the processes (including i itself) at any subsequent round. The consistent broadcast mechanism is required to satisfy the following three conditions:

1. If nonfaulty process i broadcasts message (m, i, r) in round r, then the message is accepted by all nonfaulty processes by round $r + 1$ (i.e., it is either accepted at round r or round $r + 1$).

2. If nonfaulty process i does not broadcast message (m, i, r) in round r, then (m, i, r) is never accepted by any nonfaulty process.

3. If any message (m, i, r) is accepted by any nonfaulty process j, say at round r', then it is accepted by all nonfaulty processes by round $r' + 1$.

The first condition says that nonfaulty processes' broadcasts are accepted quickly, while the second says that no messages are ever falsely attributed to nonfaulty processes. The third condition says that any message that is accepted by a nonfaulty process (whether from a faulty or nonfaulty sender) must also be accepted by every other nonfaulty process soon thereafter.

The consistent broadcast mechanism can be implemented easily.

ConsistentBroadcast algorithm:

In order to broadcast (m, i, r) at round r, process i sends a message (*"init"*, m, i, r) to all processes at round r. If process j receives an (*"init"*, m, i, r) message from process i at round r, it sends (*"echo"*, m, i, r) to all processes at round $r + 1$.

If, before any round $r' \geq r + 2$, process j has received (*"echo"*, m, i, r) messages from at least $f + 1$ processes, then j sends an (*"echo"*, m, i, r) message at round r' (if it has not already done so).

If, by the end of any round $r' \geq r+1$, process j has received (*"echo"*, m, i, r) messages from at least $n - f$ processes, then j accepts the communication at round r' (if it has not already done so).

Theorem 6.24 *The ConsistentBroadcast algorithm solves the consistent broadcast problem, if $n > 3f$.*

Proof.   We verify the three properties.

1. Suppose that nonfaulty process i broadcasts message (m, i, r) at round r. Then i sends (*"init"*, m, i, r) to all processes at round r, and each of the $\geq n - f$ nonfaulty processes sends (*"echo"*, m, i, r) to all processes at round $r + 1$. Then, by the end of round $r + 1$, each nonfaulty process receives (*"echo"*, m, i, r) messages from at least $n - f$ processes and so accepts the message.

2. If nonfaulty process i does not broadcast message (m, i, r) in round r, then it sends no (*"init"*, m, i, r) messages, so no nonfaulty process ever sends an (*"echo"*, m, i, r) message. Then no nonfaulty process ever accepts the message, because acceptance requires receipt of *echo* messages from at least $n - f > f$ processes.

3. Suppose message (m, i, r) is accepted by nonfaulty process j at round r'. Then j receives (*"echo"*, m, i, r) messages from at least $n - f$ processes by round r'. Among these $n - f$ processes, there are at least $n - 2f \geq f + 1$ nonfaulty processes. Since nonfaulty processes send the same messages to all processes, every nonfaulty process receives at least $f + 1$ (*"echo"*, m, i, r) messages by round r'. This implies that every nonfaulty process sends an (*"echo"*, m, i, r) message by round $r' + 1$, so that every process receives at least $n - f$ (*"echo"*, m, i, r) messages by round $r' + 1$. Therefore, the message is accepted by all nonfaulty processes by round $r' + 1$.

$\square$

Complexity analysis. The consistent broadcast of a single message uses $O(n^2)$ messages.

Now we describe a simple binary Byzantine agreement algorithm that uses consistent broadcast for all its communication. Called the *PolyByz algorithm*, it only sends around information about initial values of 1. It uses increasing thresholds for broadcasting messages.

> ### *PolyByz* algorithm:
>
> The algorithm operates in $f + 1$ stages, where each stage consists of two rounds. The messages that are sent (using consistent broadcast) are all of the form $(1, i, r)$, where i is a process index and r is an odd round number. That is, messages are only sent at the first rounds of stages, and the only information ever sent is just the value 1.
>
> The conditions under which process i broadcasts a message are as follows. At round 1, i broadcasts a message $(1, i, 1)$ exactly if i's initial value is 1. At round $2s - 1$, the first round of stage s, where $2 \leq s \leq f + 1$, i broadcasts a message $(1, i, 2s - 1)$ exactly if i has accepted messages from at least $f + s - 1$ different processes before round $2s - 1$ and i has not yet broadcast a message.
>
> At the end of $2(f + 1)$ rounds, process i decides on 1 exactly if i has accepted messages from at least $2f + 1$ different processes by the end of round $2(f + 1)$. Otherwise, i decides 0.

Theorem 6.25 *PolyByz solves the binary Byzantine agreement problem, if* $n > 3f$.

Proof. Termination is obvious.

For validity, there are two cases. First, if all nonfaulty processes start with initial value 1, then at least $n - f \geq 2f + 1$ processes broadcast at round 1. By property 1 of consistent broadcast, all nonfaulty processes accept these messages by round 2, so that each nonfaulty process accepts messages from at least $2f+1$ different processes by the end of round 2. This is sufficient to imply that each nonfaulty process decides 1.

On the other hand, if all nonfaulty processes start with initial value 0, then no nonfaulty process ever broadcasts. This is because the minimum number of acceptances needed to trigger a broadcast is $f+1$, which is impossible to achieve without a prior broadcast by a nonfaulty process. (We are using property 2 of consistent broadcast here.) This implies that each nonfaulty process decides 0.

Finally, we argue agreement. Suppose that nonfaulty process i decides 1; it is enough to show that every other nonfaulty process also decides 1. Since i decides 1, i must accept messages from at least $2f+1$ different processes by the end of round $2(f+1)$. Let I be the set of nonfaulty processes among these; then $|I| \geq f+1$.

If all the processes in I have initial values of 1, then they broadcast at round 1, and, by property 1 of consistent broadcast, all nonfaulty processes accept these messages by round 2. Then before round 3,[2] each nonfaulty process has accepted messages from at least $f+1$ different processes, which is enough to trigger it to broadcast at round 3; again by property 1 of consistent broadcast, all nonfaulty processes accept these messages by round 4. Thus, each nonfaulty process accepts messages from at least $n-f \geq 2f+1$ different processes by the end of round 4, and so decides 1, as needed.

On the other hand, suppose that one of the processes in I, say j, does not have an initial value of 1. Then it must be that j broadcasts at some round $2s-1$, where $2 \leq s \leq f+1$, which means that j accepts messages from at least $f+s-1$ different processes before round $2s-1$; moreover, none of these messages is from j itself. Then by property 3 of consistent broadcast, messages from all of these $f+s-1$ processes get accepted by all nonfaulty processes by the end of round $2s-1$, and, by property 1, the message broadcast by j gets accepted by all nonfaulty processes by the end of round $2s$. It follows that each nonfaulty process accepts messages from at least $(f+s-1)+1 = f-s$ different processes by the end of round $2s$.

Now there are two cases. If $s = f+1$, then each nonfaulty process accepts messages from at least $2f+1$ different processes by the end of round $2(f+1)$, which is enough to ensure that they all decide 1. On the other hand, if $s \leq f$, then every nonfaulty process accepts sufficiently many messages before round $2s+1$ to broadcast at round $2s+1$, if it has not done so already. Then by property 1 of consistent broadcast, all nonfaulty processes accept messages from

---

[2]We assume that $f \geq 1$, so that there actually is a round 3.

all the nonfaulty processes by the end of round $2s + 2$. Again, this is enough to ensure that they all decide 1, as needed. □

Complexity analysis. *PolyByz* requires $2f + 2$ rounds. There are at most n broadcasts, each requiring $O(n^2)$ messages; thus, the number of messages is $O(n^3)$. The number of bits in each message is $O(\log n)$, because messages contain process indices. Thus, the total bit complexity is just $O(n^3 \log n)$.

Relationship with the authenticated Byzantine failure model. Adding a consistent broadcast capability to the ordinary Byzantine model produces a model that is somewhat like the authenticated Byzantine failure model discussed informally in Section 6.2.4. However, the two are not exactly the same. For instance, consistent broadcast is just for broadcasting, not for sending individualized messages. More significantly, consistent broadcast does not prevent a process i from broadcasting a message saying (falsely) that a nonfaulty process j has previously sent a particular message; the nonfaulty processes will all accept this message, even though its contents represent a false claim. In the authenticated Byzantine failure model, the use of digital signatures allows processes to reject such messages immediately. However, even though the models are somewhat different, the consistent broadcast capability is strong enough that it can be used to implement, in the ordinary Byzantine model, some algorithms designed for the authenticated Byzantine failure model.

6.4 Number of Processes for Byzantine Agreement

We have presented algorithms to solve the agreement problem in a complete network graph, in the presence of stopping failures, and even in the presence of Byzantine failures. You have probably noticed that these algorithms are quite costly. For stopping failures, the best algorithm we gave was the *OptFloodSet* algorithm, which requires $f + 1$ rounds, $2n^2$ messages, and $O(n^2 b)$ bits of communication. For the Byzantine case, the *EIGByz* algorithm uses $f + 1$ rounds and an exponential amount of communication, while *PolyByz* uses $2(f+1)$ rounds and a polynomial amount of communication. Both Byzantine agreement algorithms also require $n > 3f$.

In the rest of this chapter, we show that these high costs are not accidental. First, in this section, we show that the $n > 3f$ restriction is needed for any solution to the Byzantine agreement problem. The next two sections contain related results: Section 6.5 describes exactly the amount of connectivity that is needed in an incomplete network graph in order for Byzantine agreement to

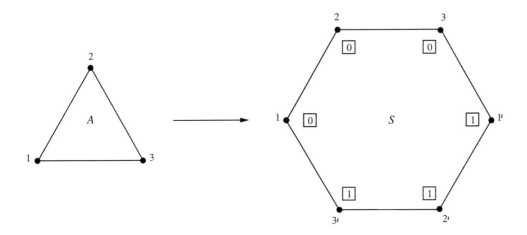

Figure 6.7: Combining two copies of A to get S.

be solvable, while Section 6.6 shows that the $n > 3f$ bound extends to weaker problem statements than Byzantine agreement. The final section of the chapter shows that the lower bound of $f + 1$ on the number of rounds is also necessary, even for the simple case of stopping failures.

In order to prove that $n \leq 3f$ processes cannot solve Byzantine agreement in the presence of f faults, we begin by showing the simplest special case: that three processes cannot solve Byzantine agreement with the possibility of one fault. This result is suggested by the example in Section 6.3.1, although that example does not constitute a proof. We then show the general result, for arbitrary n and f, $n \leq 3f$, by "reducing" the problem to the case of three versus one.

Lemma 6.26 *Three processes cannot solve Byzantine agreement in the presence of one fault.*

Proof.   By contradiction. Assume there is a three-process algorithm A that solves the Byzantine agreement problem for the three processes 1, 2, and 3, even if one of these three may be faulty. We construct a new system S using *two copies* of A and show that S must exhibit contradictory behavior. It follows that the assumed algorithm A cannot exist.

Specifically, we take two copies of each process in A and configure them into a single hexagonal system S. We start one copy each of processes 1, 2, and 3 (the unprimed copy) with input value 0, and the other (the primed copy) with input value 1. The arrangement is shown in Figure 6.7.

What is system S, formally? It is a synchronous system, based on a hexagonal network graph, within the general model of Chapter 2. Note that it is *not* a system that is supposed to solve the Byzantine agreement problem—we don't care what it does, in fact, only that it is a synchronous system of some kind. We will not consider any faulty process behavior in S.

Remember that in the systems we consider as solutions for the Byzantine agreement problem, we assume that the processes all "know" the entire network graph. For example, in A, process 1 knows the names 2 and 3 and presumes that there are exactly three nodes, named 1, 2, and 3, arranged in a triangle. In S, we do not assume that the processes know the entire (hexagonal) network graph, but rather that each process just has local names for its neighbors. For example, in S, process 1 knows that it has two neighbors, which it knows by the names 2 and 3, even though one of them is really $3'$. It does not know that there are duplicate copies of the nodes in the network. The situation is similar to the one considered in Chapter 4, where each process only had local knowledge of its portion of the network graph. In particular, notice that the network in S appears to each process just like the network in A.

System S is not required to exhibit any special type of behavior. However, note that S with any particular input assignment does exhibit *some* well-defined behavior. We will obtain a contradiction by showing that, for the particular input assignment indicated above, no such well-defined behavior is possible.

So suppose that the processes in S are started with the input values indicated in Figure 6.7, that is, the unprimed processes with 0 and the primed processes with 1; let α be the resulting execution of S.

We first consider execution α from the point of view of processes 2 and 3. To processes 2 and 3, it appears as if they are running in the triangle system A, in an execution α_1 in which process 1 is faulty. That is, α and α_1 are indistinguishable to processes 2 and 3, $\alpha \overset{2}{\sim} \alpha_1$ and $\alpha \overset{3}{\sim} \alpha_1$, according to the definition of "indistinguishable" in Section 2.4. See Figure 6.8. In α_1, process 1 exhibits a peculiar type of faulty behavior—it behaves like the combination of processes $1'$, $2'$, $3'$, and 1 in α. Although it is peculiar, it is an allowable behavior for a faulty process in A, under the assumptions for Byzantine faults.

Since α_1 is an execution of A in which only process 1 is faulty and processes 2 and 3 begin with input 0, and since A is assumed to solve Byzantine agreement, the correctness conditions for Byzantine agreement imply that eventually in α_1, processes 2 and 3 must decide 0. Since α is indistinguishable from α_1 to processes 2 and 3, both decide 0 in α as well.

Next consider execution α from the point of view of processes $1'$ and $2'$. To processes $1'$ and $2'$, it appears as if they are running in the triangle system A, in an execution α_2 in which process 3 is faulty. That is, $\alpha \overset{1'}{\sim} \alpha_2$ and $\alpha \overset{2'}{\sim} \alpha_2$.

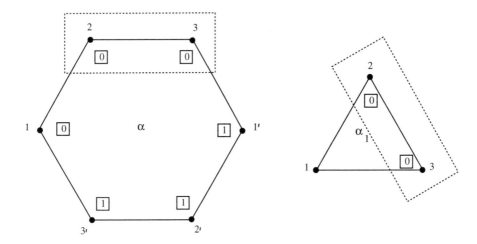

Figure 6.8: Executions α and α_1 are indistinguishable to processes 2 and 3.

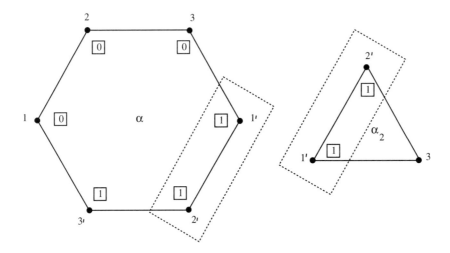

Figure 6.9: Executions α and α_2 are indistinguishable to processes $1'$ and $2'$.

See Figure 6.9. By the same argument as above, processes $1'$ and $2'$ eventually decide 1 in α.

Finally, consider execution α from the point of view of processes 3 and $1'$. To processes 3 and $1'$, it appears as if they are running in the triangle system A, in an execution α_3 in which process 2 is faulty. That is, $\alpha \overset{3}{\sim} \alpha_3$ and $\alpha \overset{1'}{\sim} \alpha_3$. See Figure 6.10. By the correctness conditions for Byzantine agreement, processes 3 and $1'$ must eventually decide in α_3, and their decisions must be the same. Because process 3 starts with input 0 and process $1'$ starts with input 1, there is

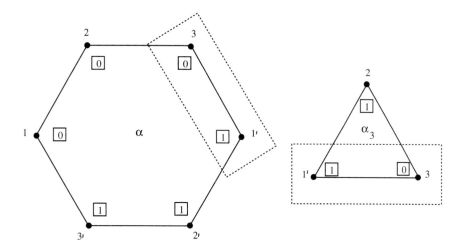

Figure 6.10: Executions α and α_3 are indistinguishable to processes 1 and 3.

no requirement about what value they agree upon, but the agreement condition implies that they agree. Therefore, they decide on the same value in α also.

But this is a contradiction, because we have already observed that in α, process 3 decides 0 and process $1'$ decides 1. $\qquad\square$

We now use Lemma 6.26 to show that Byzantine agreement is impossible with $n \leq 3f$ processes. We do this by showing how the existence of an $n \leq 3f$ process solution that can tolerate f Byzantine failures implies the existence of a three-process solution that can tolerate a single Byzantine failure, which contradicts Lemma 6.26.

Theorem 6.27 *There is no solution to the Byzantine agreement problem for n processes in the presence of f Byzantine failures, if $2 \leq n \leq 3f$.*

Proof. For the special case where $n = 2$, it is easy to see that the problem cannot be solved. Informally speaking, suppose that one process starts with 0 and the other with 1. Then each must allow for the possibility that the other is faulty and decide on its own value, in order to ensure the validity property. But if neither is faulty, this violates the agreement property. So we may assume that $n \geq 3$.

Assume for the sake of contradiction that there is a solution A for Byzantine agreement with $3 \leq n \leq 3f$. We show how to transform A into a solution B to Byzantine agreement for three processes, numbered 1, 2, and 3, tolerating one fault. Each of the three processes in B will simulate approximately one-third of the processes of A.

Specifically, we partition the processes of A into three nonempty subsets, I_1, I_2, and I_3, each of size at most f. We let each process i in B simulate the processes in I_i, as follows.

> **B:**
> Each process i keeps track of the states of all the processes in I_i, assigns its own initial value to every member of I_i, and simulates the steps of all the processes in I_i as well as the messages between pairs of processes in I_i. Messages from processes in I_i to processes in another subset are sent from process i to the process simulating that subset. If any simulated process in I_i decides on a value v, then i decides on the value v. (If there is more than one such value, then i can choose any such value.)

We show that B correctly solves Byzantine agreement for three processes. Designate the faulty processes of A to be exactly those that are simulated by faulty processes of B.[3] Fix any particular execution α of B with at most one faulty process and let α' be the simulated execution of A. Since each process of B simulates at most f processes of A, there are at most f faulty processes in α'. Since A is assumed to solve Byzantine agreement for n processes with at most f faults, the usual agreement, validity, and termination conditions for Byzantine agreement hold in α'.

We argue that these conditions carry over to α. For termination, let i be a nonfaulty process of B. Then i simulates at least one process, j, of A, and j must be nonfaulty since i is. The termination condition for α' implies that j must eventually decide; as soon as it does so, i decides (if it has not already done so).

For validity, if all nonfaulty processes of B begin with a value v then all the nonfaulty processes of A also begin with v. Validity for α' implies that v is the only decision value for a nonfaulty process in α'. Then v is the only decision value for a nonfaulty process in α.

For agreement, suppose i and j are nonfaulty processes of B. Then they simulate only nonfaulty processes of A. Agreement for α' implies that all of these simulated processes agree, so i and j also agree.

We conclude that B solves the Byzantine agreement problem for three processes, tolerating one fault. But this contradicts Lemma 6.26. $\square$

---

[3]We invoke the technicality that Byzantine faulty processes are allowed to behave completely correctly, in order to justify this classification.

6.5 Byzantine Agreement in General Graphs

So far in this chapter, we have considered agreement problems only in complete graphs. For complete graphs with n nodes, we showed in Sections 6.3 and 6.4 that Byzantine agreement can be solved if and only if $n > 3f$. In this section, we consider the problem of Byzantine agreement in general network graphs. We characterize exactly the graphs in which the problem is solvable.

First, if the network graph is a tree with at least three nodes, we cannot hope to solve the Byzantine agreement problem with even one faulty process, for any faulty process that is not a leaf could essentially "disconnect" the processes in one part of the tree from the processes in another. The nonfaulty processes in different components would not even be able to communicate reliably, much less reach agreement. Similarly, it should be plausible that if f nodes can disconnect the graph, then Byzantine agreement is impossible with f faulty processes.

To formalize this intuition, we use the following notion from graph theory. The *connectivity* of a graph G, $conn(G)$, is defined to be the minimum number of nodes whose removal results in either a disconnected graph or a trivial 1-node graph. Graph G is said to be *c-connected* if $conn(G) \geq c$.

Example 6.5.1 Connectivity

Any tree with at least two nodes has connectivity 1, and an n-node complete graph has connectivity $n - 1$. Figure 6.11 shows a graph with connectivity 2. If nodes 2 and 4 are removed, then we are left with two disconnected nodes, 1 and 3.

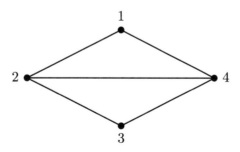

Figure 6.11: A graph G with $conn(G) = 2$.

We use a classical theorem of graph theory known as *Menger's Theorem*.

Theorem 6.28 (Menger's Theorem) *A graph G is c-connected if and only if every pair of nodes in G is connected by at least c node-disjoint paths.*

Now we can characterize those graphs in which it is possible to solve Byzantine agreement with a given number of faults. The characterization is in terms of both the number of nodes in the graph and the connectivity. The proof of the impossibility part of the characterization uses methods similar to those used in Section 6.4 to prove the lower bound for the number of faulty processes.

Theorem 6.29 *The Byzantine agreement problem can be solved in an n-node network graph G, tolerating f faults, if and only if both the following hold:*

1. $n > 3f$

2. $conn(G) > 2f$

Proof.   We have already shown, in Theorem 6.27, that $n > 3f$ processes are required to solve Byzantine agreement in a complete graph. It should not be hard to believe that in an arbitrary (not necessarily complete) network graph we still need $n > 3f$; this is because an algorithm for an incomplete graph with $n \leq 3f$ could also be run in an n-node complete graph.

We next show the *if* direction of the proof, namely, that Byzantine agreement is possible if $n > 3f$ and $conn(G) > 2f$. Since G is $2f + 1$-connected, Menger's Theorem, Theorem 6.28, implies that there are at least $2f+1$ node-disjoint paths between any two nodes in G. It is possible to implement reliable communication between any pair of nonfaulty processes, i and j, by having i send a message along $2f+1$ paths between itself and j. Since there are at most f faulty processes, the messages received by j along a majority of these paths must be correct.

Once we have reliable communication between all pairs of nonfaulty processes, we can solve Byzantine agreement just by simulating any algorithm that solves the problem in an n-node complete graph. The implementation given above for reliable communication is used in place of the point-to-point communication in the complete graph. Of course, there is an increase in complexity, but that is not the issue here—the algorithm still works correctly.

We now turn to the most interesting part of the proof, showing that Byzantine agreement can only be solved if $conn(G) > 2f$. We simplify matters by only arguing the case where $f = 1$; we leave the (similar) argument for larger values of f for an exercise.

So, assume there is a graph G with $conn(G) \leq 2$, in which Byzantine agreement can be solved in the presence of one fault, using algorithm A. Then there are two nodes in G that either disconnect G or reduce it to one node. But if they reduce it to one node, it means that G consists of only three nodes, and we already know that Byzantine agreement cannot be solved in a three-node graph in the presence of one fault. So we can assume that the two nodes disconnect G.

Then the picture must be something like Figure 6.11, except that nodes 1 and 3 might be replaced by arbitrary connected subgraphs and there might be several edges between each of processes 2 and 4 and each of the two connected subgraphs. (The link between 2 and 4 could also be missing, but this would only make things harder.) Again for simplicity, we just consider the case where 1 and 3 are single nodes. We construct a system S by combining two copies of A. We start one copy of each process with input value 0 and the other with input value 1, as shown in Figure 6.12. As in the proof of Lemma 6.26, S with the given input assignment does exhibit some well-defined behavior. Again, we will obtain a contradiction by showing that no such behavior is possible.

So suppose that the processes in S are started with the input values indicated in Figure 6.12, that is, the unprimed processes with 0 and the primed processes with 1; let α be the resulting execution of S.

We consider α from the point of view of processes 1, 2, and 3. To these processes, it appears as if they are running in system A, in an execution α_1 in which process 4 is faulty. See Figure 6.13. Then the correctness conditions for Byzantine agreement imply that eventually in α_1, processes 1, 2, and 3 must decide 0. Since α is indistinguishable from α_1 to processes 1, 2, and 3, all three must eventually decide 0 in α as well.

Next consider α from the point of view of processes $1'$, $2'$, and $3'$. To these three processes, it appears as if they are running in A, in an execution α_2 in which process 4 is faulty. See Figure 6.14. By the same argument, processes $1'$, $2'$, and $3'$ must eventually decide 1 in α.

Finally, consider execution α from the point of view of processes 3, 4, and $1'$. To these processes, it appears as if they are running in A, in an execution α_3 in which process 2 is faulty. See Figure 6.15. By the correctness conditions for Byzantine agreement, these three processes must eventually decide in α_3, and their decisions must be the same. Then the same is true in α.

But this is a contradiction, because we have already shown that process 3 must decide 0 and process $1'$ must decide 1 in α. It follows that we cannot solve Byzantine agreement in graphs G with $conn(G) \leq 2$ and $f = 1$.

In order to generalize the result to $f > 1$, we can use the same diagrams, with 2 and 4 replaced by sets I_2 and I_4 of at most f nodes each and 1 and 3 by arbitrary sets I_1 and I_3 of nodes. Removing all the nodes in I_2 and I_4 disconnects I_1 and I_3. The edges of Figure 6.11 can now be considered to represent bundles of edges between the different groups of nodes I_1, I_2, I_3, and I_4. $\qquad\square$

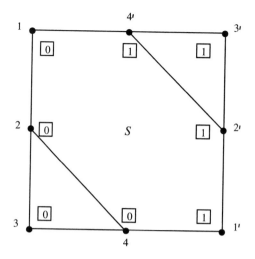

Figure 6.12: Combining two copies of A to get S.

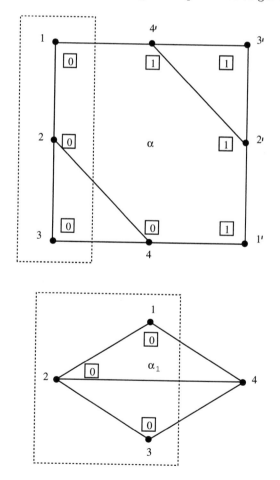

Figure 6.13: Executions α and α_1 are indistinguishable to processes 1, 2, and 3.

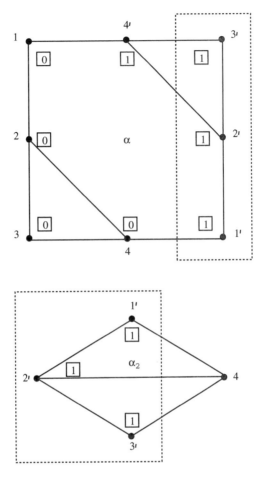

Figure 6.14: Executions α and α_2 are indistinguishable to processes $1'$, $2'$, and $3'$.

6.6 Weak Byzantine Agreement

The same general proof method that we used in Sections 6.4 and 6.5 to prove impossibility for Byzantine agreement with $n \leq 3f$ or $conn \leq 2f$ can also be used to prove impossibility for other consensus problems. As an example, in this section we show how this method can be used to prove impossibility for a weaker variant of the Byzantine agreement problem known as *weak Byzantine agreement*.

The only difference between the problem statement for weak Byzantine agreement and ordinary Byzantine agreement is in the validity condition. The validity condition for weak Byzantine agreement is

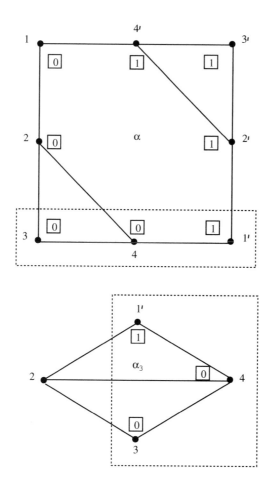

Figure 6.15: Executions α and α_3 are indistinguishable to processes 3, 4, and $1'$.

Validity: If there are no faulty processes and all processes start with the same initial value $v \in V$, then v is the only possible decision value.

In the ordinary Byzantine agreement problem, if all the nonfaulty processes start with the same initial value v, then they must all decide v *even if there are faulty processes*. In weak Byzantine agreement, they are required to decide v only in the case where there are no failures.

Since the new problem statement is weaker than the old one, the algorithms we have described for ordinary Byzantine agreement also work for weak Byzantine agreement. On the other hand, the impossibility results do not immediately carry over; it is plausible that more efficient algorithms might exist for weak Byzantine agreement. However, it turns out that (except for a tiny technicality) the limitations on the number of processes and the graph connectivity still hold. (The technicality is that now we need to assume that $n \geq 3$, because there is a trivial algorithm for weak Byzantine agreement for the special case where $n = 2$.)

Theorem 6.30 *Assume that $n \geq 3$. The weak Byzantine agreement problem can be solved in an n-node network graph G, tolerating f faults, if and only if both the following hold:*

1. $n > 3f$

2. $conn(G) > 2f$

Proof.   The *if* direction follows from the existence of protocols for ordinary Byzantine agreement, as claimed in Theorem 6.29. We give the proof that three processes cannot solve weak Byzantine agreement with one possible fault and leave the extension to $f > 1$ and the connectivity argument for exercises. For simplicity, we assume that $V = \{0, 1\}$.

Assume there is a three-process algorithm A that solves the weak Byzantine agreement problem for the three processes 1, 2, and 3, even if one is faulty. Let α_0 be the execution of A in which all three processes start with 0 and no failures occur. The termination and validity conditions then imply that all three processes eventually decide 0 in α_0; let r_0 be the smallest round number by which all processes decide. Likewise, let α_1 be the execution in which all processes start with 1 and no failures occur, so all processes eventually decide 1 in α_1. Let r_1 be the number of rounds required and choose $r \geq \max\{r_0, r_1, 1\}$.

We construct a new system S by pasting $2r$ copies of A into a ring with $6r$ processes, $3r$ in the "top half" and $3r$ in the "bottom half." We start all the processes in the top half with input value 0 and those in the bottom half with input value 1. The arrangement is shown in Figure 6.16. (This time, we have not bothered to include prime symbols or other distinguishing notation for the multiple copies of the same process of A.) Let α be the resulting execution of S.

By arguing as in the proof of Lemma 6.26, we can show that any two adjacent processes in S must decide on the same value in execution α; this is because it looks to the two processes as if they are in the triangle, interacting with a third process that is faulty. It follows that all processes in S must reach the *same* decision in α. Suppose (without loss of generality) that they all decide 1.

Now to get a contradiction, we argue that some process in the top half of S must decide 0. Let B be any "block" of $2r + 1$ consecutive processes in the top half of S; these all start with initial value 0 in α. Now, all the processes in B begin in the same state in α as the same-named processes do in α_0, and send the same messages at round 1. Thus, at round 1, all the processes in B

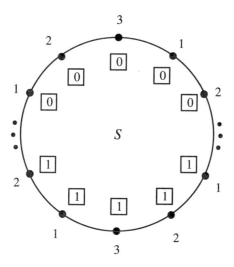

Figure 6.16: Combining $2r$ copies of A to get S.

except possibly for the one at each end receive the same messages in α as their namesakes do in α_0 and so remain in the same states and send the same messages at round 2, in the two executions. At round 2, all processes in B except the two at each end receive the same messages and remain in the same states, in the two executions. Continuing in this way, we see that at round k, $1 \leq k \leq r$, all processes in B except the k at each end receive the same messages and remain in the same states, in α and α_0. In other words, α and α_0 are indistinguishable to all processes in B except the k at each end, for k rounds. Informally speaking, this is because information does not have time to propagate to those processes from outside the block B.

In particular, α and α_0 are indistinguishable to the middle process, process i, of block B for r rounds. But since process i decides 0 by the end of round r in α_0, it also does so in α. This contradicts the fact that process i decides 1 in α.

$\square$

6.7 Number of Rounds with Stopping Failures

We complete this chapter by showing that the agreement problem cannot be solved in fewer than $f + 1$ rounds, either for Byzantine or stopping failures. In other words, there does not exist an agreement protocol, for either type of failure, in which all the nonfaulty processes decide by the end of f rounds.

We will proceed by assuming that an f-round agreement algorithm exists and obtaining a contradiction. It is convenient for us to impose some restrictions on the assumed algorithm, none of which causes any loss of generality. First, we assume that the network graph is completely connected; a fast algorithm for an incomplete graph could also be run in a complete graph, so there is certainly no loss of generality in this restriction. We also assume that all processes that decide do so exactly at the end of round f, then immediately halt. In this case, an algorithm for Byzantine agreement is necessarily an algorithm for stopping agreement (see the remark on the relationship between the two problems in Section 6.1). So, for the purpose of obtaining an impossibility result, we can restrict attention to the stopping agreement problem only. Also, we assume that every process sends a message to every other process at every round k, $1 \leq k \leq f$ (unless and until it fails). Finally, we restrict attention to the case where the value set $V = \{0, 1\}$.

As for the coordinated attack problem in Chapter 5, it is convenient to carry out the proof using the notion of a communication pattern, which is an indication of which processes send messages to which other processes at each round. Specializing the previous definition to the case of a complete graph, we define a *communication pattern* to be any subset of the set

$$\{(i, j, k) : 1 \leq i, j \leq n, i \neq j, 1 \leq k\}.$$

A communication pattern does not describe the contents of messages, but only which processes send to which others, at which rounds.

We consider three restrictions on communication patterns. First, because the algorithm we consider has f rounds, we consider only communication patterns in which all triples (i, j, k) have $k \leq f$. Second, because we are working with the stopping failure model, all the communication patterns that arise satisfy the following restriction: if any triple (i, j, k) is missing from the pattern, then so is every triple of the form (i, j', k'), where $k' > k$. That is, if process i fails to send any of its messages at round k, then it sends no messages at subsequent rounds. Third, because we consider executions with at most f failures, all the communication patterns that arise contain at most f faulty processes. (We define a process i to be *faulty* in a communication pattern if some triple of the form (i, j, k), $k \leq f$, is missing from the pattern.) We say (in the rest of this chapter only) that a communication pattern that satisfies these three restrictions is *good*.

Example 6.7.1 Good communication pattern

An example of a good communication pattern (for $n = f = 4$) is depicted in Figure 6.17. In this pattern, process 3 sends a message to process 4 but fails to send messages to processes 1 and 2 at round 1.

Thus, it must be that process 3 stops in round 1 and sends nothing in later rounds. Also, process 2 stops just at the end of round 2. Processes 1 and 4 are nonfaulty.

processes

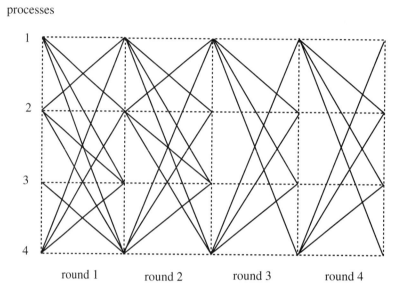

Figure 6.17: A good communication pattern.

Now we define a *run* to be a combination of

1. An assignment of input values to all the processes

2. A good communication pattern

(This is similar to what we called an adversary in Section 5.2.1.)

For a particular agreement algorithm A, each run ρ defines a corresponding execution, $exec(\rho)$, in a natural way. Namely, the initial states of the processes are defined by setting the input state components according to the input assignment given in ρ; the messages that are sent are determined from the communication pattern of ρ, using the message transition function of A applied to the prior state of the sender process; and states after the initial states are determined using the transition function of A. (But after any process fails to send a message, we stop applying its state-transition function.)

In order to give some intuition for the lower bound, we begin by proving the theorem for the special case where $f = 1$.

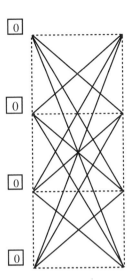

Figure 6.18: Run ρ_0—all inputs are 0, and there are no failures.

Theorem 6.31 *Suppose that $n \geq 3$. Then there is no n-process stopping agreement algorithm that tolerates one fault, in which all nonfaulty processes always decide by the end of round 1.*

Proof. Suppose, to obtain a contradiction, that there is such an algorithm, A; we assume that A satisfies all the restrictions listed at the beginning of this section.

The idea is to construct a chain of executions of A, each with at most one faulty process, such that (a) the first execution in the chain contains 0 as its unique decision value, (b) the last execution in the chain contains 1 as its unique decision value, and (c) any two consecutive executions in the chain are indistinguishable to some process that is nonfaulty in both. Then, since any two consecutive executions look the same to some nonfaulty process, say i, process i must make the same decision in both executions; therefore, the two executions must have the same unique decision value. It follows that *every* execution in the chain must have the same unique decision value, which contradicts the combination of properties (a) and (b).

We start the chain with the execution $exec(\rho_0)$ determined from the run ρ_0 in which all processes have input value 0 and no process is faulty. This run is depicted in Figure 6.18. By validity, the unique decision value in $exec(\rho_0)$ must be 0. Starting from execution $exec(\rho_0)$, we form the next execution by removing a single message—the one from process 1 to process 2. The result is depicted in Figure 6.19. This execution is indistinguishable from $exec(\rho_0)$ to every process

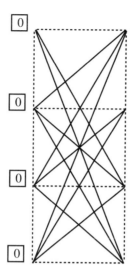

Figure 6.19: The result of removing one message from ρ_0.

except for 1 and 2. Since $n \geq 3$, there is at least one such process. This process is nonfaulty in both executions.

Next we remove the message from 1 to 3; this and the previous execution are indistinguishable to each process except for 1 and 3, and there is at least one such process. We continue in this manner, removing one message from process 1 at a time, in such a way that every two consecutive executions are indistinguishable to some nonfaulty process.

Once we have removed all the messages sent by 1, we continue by changing process 1's input value from 0 to 1. Of course, the resulting execution is indistinguishable from the previous one to every process except 1, since 1 sends no messages in either execution. Next, we replace process 1's messages one by one, and again every consecutive pair of executions is indistinguishable to some nonfaulty process. In this way, we end up with $exec(\rho_1)$, where ρ_1 is defined to be the run in which process 1 has input value 1, all the rest have input value 0, and there are no failures.

Next, we repeat this construction for process 2, first removing its messages one by one, then changing 2's input value from 0 to 1, and then replacing its messages. The resulting execution is $exec(\rho_2)$, where ρ_2 is the run in which processes 1 and 2 have input value 1, the others have input value 0, and there are no failures. Repeating this construction for processes $3, \ldots, n$, we end up with $exec(\rho_n)$, where ρ_n is the run in which all processes start with 1 and there are no failures.

So we have constructed a chain from $exec(\rho_0)$ to $exec(\rho_n)$ satisfying property (c). But validity implies that the unique decision value in $exec(\rho_0)$ is 0 and the unique decision value in $exec(\rho_n)$ is 1, which yields (a) and (b). So we have the needed chain, which gives a contradiction. □

Before moving to the general case, we will do one more preliminary case—the case where $f = 2$.

Theorem 6.32 *Suppose that $n \geq 4$. Then there is no n-process stopping agreement algorithm that tolerates two faults, in which all nonfaulty processes always decide by the end of round 2.*

Proof. Again suppose that there is such an algorithm. We construct a chain with the same properties (a), (b), (c) as in the previous proof, using a similar construction. For each i, $0 \leq i \leq n$, let ρ_i denote the (two-round) run in which processes $1, \ldots, i$ have input 0, processes $i + 1, \ldots, n$ have input 1, and there are no faults. The chain starts with $exec(\rho_0)$, ends with $exec(\rho_n)$, and passes through all the executions $exec(\rho_i)$ along the way.

Starting with $exec(\rho_0)$, we want to work toward killing process 1 at the beginning. When we were only dealing with one round, we could simply remove messages from process 1 one by one. Now there is no problem in removing process 1's round 2 messages one by one. But if we remove a round 1 message from 1 to some other process i in one step of the chain, it is no longer the case that the two consecutive executions must look the same to some nonfaulty process. This is because in round 2, i is able to tell all other processes whether or not it received a message from process 1 in round 1.

We solve this problem by using several steps to remove the round 1 message from 1 to i. In the intermediate executions that occur along the way, processes 1 and i are both faulty; this is permissible since $f = 2$. In particular, we start with an execution in which 1 sends a message to i at round 1 and i is nonfaulty. We remove round 2 messages sent by i, one by one, until we obtain an execution in which 1 sends to i at round 1 and i sends no messages at round 2. Next, we remove the round 1 message from 1 to i; the resulting execution is indistinguishable from the preceding one to all processes other than 1 and i. Then we replace round 2 messages sent by i one by one, until we obtain an execution in which 1 does not send to i at round 1 and i is nonfaulty. This achieves our goal of removing a round 1 message from 1 to i, while ensuring that each consecutive pair of executions are indistinguishable to some nonfaulty process.

In this way, we remove round 1 messages from 1 one by one until 1 sends no messages. Then we change process 1's input from 0 to 1 as before. We continue this procedure "in reverse," replacing process 1's round 1 messages one by one. Repeating this for processes $2, \ldots, n$ gives the needed chain.   □

We now prove the general theorem:

Theorem 6.33 *Suppose that $n \geq f + 2$. Then there is no n-process stopping-agreement algorithm that tolerates f faults, in which all nonfaulty processes always decide by the end of round f.*

The proofs of Theorems 6.31 and 6.32 contain the main ideas for the proof of Theorem 6.33. In the general proof, a longer chain is constructed, using f process failures. We proceed more formally than we did in the proofs of Theorems 6.31 and 6.32. We need some notation.

First, if ρ and ρ' are runs in both of which process i is nonfaulty, then we write $\rho \overset{i}{\sim} \rho'$ to mean that $exec(\rho) \overset{i}{\sim} exec(\rho')$—that is, the executions generated by runs ρ and ρ' are indistinguishable to process i. We write $\rho \sim \rho'$ if $\rho \overset{i}{\sim} \rho'$ for some process i that is nonfaulty in both ρ and ρ'. And we write $\rho \approx \rho'$ for the transitive closure of the $\sim$ relation.

Next, notice that all the communication patterns that occur in the chains in the proofs of Theorems 6.31 and 6.32 have a particularly simple form. We capture this form with the following definition. We define a good communication pattern to be *regular* if for every k, $0 \leq k \leq f$, there are at most k processes that fail (to send at least one message) by the end of k rounds. We say that a run or execution is *regular* if its communication pattern is regular.

Finally, if ρ is any run and $0 \leq k \leq f$, we define the run $f\!f(\rho, k)$—the variant of ρ that is *failure-free* after time k—to be the run that has the same input assignment as ρ, and whose communication pattern is the same as that of ρ for the first k rounds and contains no new failures thereafter. Here are some obvious facts involving $f\!f$ runs.

Lemma 6.34 *If ρ is a regular run, then*

  1. *For any k, $0 \leq k \leq f$, $f\!f(\rho, k)$ is regular.*

  2. *If ρ' is identical to ρ except that some process i that fails in ρ fails at a later round in ρ', then ρ' is regular.*

  3. *If no process fails at round $k + 1$, then $f\!f(\rho, k) = f\!f(\rho, k + 1)$.*

The heart of the proof of Theorem 6.33 is the following strong lemma, which says that it is possible to construct a chain between *any two* regular executions having the same input assignment.

Lemma 6.35 *Suppose that A is an n-process stopping agreement algorithm that tolerates f faults, in which all nonfaulty processes always decide by the end of round f. Let ρ and ρ' be two regular runs of A with the same input assignment. Then $\rho \approx \rho'$.*

Proof.   We show this by proving the following parameterized claim. The case where $k = 0$ immediately implies the lemma.

Claim 6.36 *Let k be an integer, $0 \le k \le f$. Let ρ and ρ' be two regular runs of A with the same input assignment and with identical communication patterns through k rounds. Then $\rho \approx \rho'$.*

Proof.   The proof of Claim 6.36 is by reverse induction on k, starting with $k = f$ and ending with $k = 0$.

Basis: $k = f$. This case is trivial because the assumption that ρ and ρ' have the same inputs and same communication patterns through f rounds implies that ρ and ρ' are identical.

Inductive step: $0 \le k \le f - 1$ and the claim is true for $k + 1$. In this case, it is enough to show that any regular run ρ satisfies $\rho \approx f\!f(\rho, k)$, because we can apply this result twice to obtain the required claim. So fix some regular run ρ. By Lemma 6.34, $f\!f(\rho, k)$ is regular.

By inductive hypothesis, $f\!f(\rho, k+1) \approx \rho$, so it is enough to show that $f\!f(\rho, k) \approx f\!f(\rho, k+1)$. If no process fails at round $k+1$ in ρ, then Lemma 6.34 implies that $f\!f(\rho, k) = f\!f(\rho, k+1)$ and we are done. So we assume that at least one process fails at round $k+1$ in ρ. Let I be the set of processes that do so.

Let ρ_0 be the run that is identical to $f\!f(\rho, k)$ except that all processes in I fail at the end of round $k+1$. Then Lemma 6.34, part 2 (applied to ρ), implies that ρ_0 is regular.

Since ρ_0 and $f\!f(\rho, k)$ are regular runs that are identical through $k+1$ rounds, we can apply the inductive hypothesis to show that $\rho_0 \approx f\!f(\rho, k)$. Therefore, to show that $f\!f(\rho, k) \approx f\!f(\rho, k+1)$, it is enough to show that $\rho_0 \approx f\!f(\rho, k+1)$.

Now we construct a chain of regular runs spanning from ρ_0 to $f\!f(\rho, k + 1)$. The only difference between ρ_0 and $f\!f(\rho, k + 1)$ is that some messages sent by processes in I at round $k+1$ in ρ_0 are missing in $f\!f(\rho, k + 1)$. So we remove those messages one at a time, while keeping the runs otherwise unchanged.

For instance, consider the removal of a message from i to j, where $i \in I$. Let σ be the run including the message and τ be the run without the message; we must argue that $\sigma \approx \tau$. If $k + 1 = f$, then σ and τ are indistinguishable to all processes except for i and j; since $n \ge f + 2$ and i is faulty, this must include at least one nonfaulty process. So $\sigma \approx \tau$, as needed.

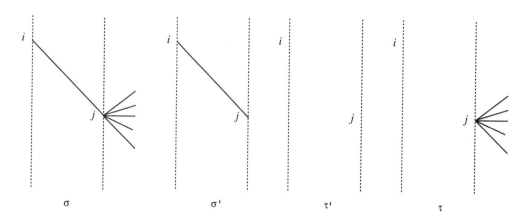

Figure 6.20: Removal of round $k + 1$ message from i to j, in proof of Claim 6.36.

On the other hand, if $k + 1 \leq f - 1$, then define σ' and τ' to be the same as σ and τ respectively, but with j failing just at the start of round $k + 2$ (if it has not previously failed). See Figure 6.20.

Both σ' and τ' are regular, since each of σ and τ involves at most $k+1 \leq f-1$ failures, and we only introduce one new failure for the new round $k + 2$. Then $\sigma \approx \sigma'$ and $\tau \approx \tau'$, by inductive hypothesis. And $\sigma' \approx \tau'$, because they are indistinguishable to all processes except for i and j. So again, $\sigma \approx \tau$.

This shows that the needed chain from ρ_0 to $\mathit{ff}(\rho, k + 1)$ can be constructed, so $\rho_0 \approx \mathit{ff}(\rho, k + 1)$, so $\rho \approx \mathit{ff}(\rho, k)$, as needed. $\square$

As we noted earlier, Claim 6.36 immediately implies Lemma 6.35.

Now we extend Lemma 6.35 to apply to different input assignments.

Lemma 6.37 *Suppose that A is an n-process stopping agreement algorithm that tolerates f faults, in which all nonfaulty processes always decide by the end of round f. If ρ and ρ' are two regular runs of A, then $\rho \approx \rho'$.*

Proof.   By Lemma 6.35, each run ρ is related to its failure-free version, that is, $\rho \approx \mathit{ff}(\rho, 0)$. So we can assume without loss of generality that ρ and ρ' in the statement of the lemma are both failure-free.

If ρ and ρ' have the same input assignment, then they are identical and there is nothing to prove.

Suppose that ρ and ρ' differ in the input of exactly one process i; say i has input 0 in ρ and input 1 in ρ'. Then define σ and σ' to be the runs that are identical to ρ and ρ', respectively, except that i fails right at the start. Then

Lemma 6.35 implies that $\rho \approx \sigma$ and $\rho' \approx \sigma'$. Also, $\sigma \approx \sigma'$, because σ and σ' are indistinguishable to all processes except for i. It follows that $\rho \approx \rho'$, as needed.

Finally, suppose that ρ and ρ' differ in the input of more than one process. Then we can construct a chain of failure-free runs, spanning from ρ to ρ', changing exactly one process's input at each step in the chain. The previous case applies to each step in this chain. So again, we obtain $\rho \approx \rho'$. $\qquad\square$

Using Lemma 6.37, it is easy to prove Theorem 6.33. We already know that all regular runs are related by chains; now we consider the decision values that arise in these runs. Assuming that $n > f$, the termination and agreement properties imply that for every run ρ, there is a unique decision value, $dec(\rho)$, that arises in $exec(\rho)$. The following lemma says that runs that are related by $\sim$ or $\approx$ necessarily give rise to the same decision values.

Lemma 6.38

1. *If $\rho \sim \rho'$, then $dec(\rho) = dec(\rho')$.*

2. *If $\rho \approx \rho'$, then $dec(\rho) = dec(\rho')$.*

Proof. For part 1, recall that $\rho \sim \rho'$ means that there is a process i that is nonfaulty in both ρ and ρ', such that $exec(\rho) \overset{i}{\sim} exec(\rho')$. This implies that process i decides on the same value in $exec(\rho)$ and $exec(\rho')$. Therefore, $dec(\rho) = dec(\rho')$.

Part 2 follows from part 1. $\qquad\square$

Proof (of Theorem 6.33). Suppose there is such an algorithm, A; we assume that A satisfies the restrictions listed at the beginning of the section.

Let ρ_0 be the run of A in which all processes start with 0 and there are no faults, and let ρ_1 be the run in which all processes start with 1 and there are no faults. Lemma 6.37 implies that $\rho_0 \approx \rho_1$. Then Lemma 6.38, part 2, implies that $dec(\rho) = dec(\rho')$. But the validity condition implies that $dec(\rho_0) = 0$ and $dec(\rho_1) = 1$, a contradiction. $\qquad\square$

Weaker validity condition. Notice that this impossibility proof still works if we weaken the validity condition to the one that we used in Section 6.6 for the weak Byzantine agreement problem. That is, we have shown that the weak Byzantine agreement problem also requires at least $f + 1$ rounds, under the assumption that $n \geq f + 2$.

6.8   Bibliographic Notes

Many of the ideas in this chapter originated in the two seminal papers by Pease, Shostak, and Lamport [237] and by Lamport, Shostak, and Pease [187]. These two papers contain upper and lower bounds of $3f + 1$ for the number of processes required for Byzantine agreement, plus an algorithm for agreement with authentication, all for the case of a completely connected graph. The presentation in the second paper is in terms of attacking generals rather than processes. It is the second paper that coined the term *Byzantine* for this fault model.

In more detail, these two papers define the Byzantine agreement problem and motivate it as an abstraction of a problem arising in the SIFT (Software-Implemented Fault Tolerance) aircraft control system [289]. The algorithms in [237] use an exponential data structure similar to an *EIG* tree; the Byzantine agreement algorithm is similar to *EIGByz*, while the algorithm using authentication is similar to *EIGStop*. The algorithms in [187] are very much the same but are formulated recursively. The impossibility proof for $n \leq 3f$ processes in [237] involves the explicit construction of detailed scenarios. The impossibility proof in [187] introduces the reduction to the case of three versus one that appears in the proof of Theorem 6.27.

Dolev and Strong [93] developed algorithms similar to *FloodSet* and *OptFloodSet* for Byzantine agreement in the case where authentication is available. Dolev [94] considered the Byzantine agreement problem in graphs that are not necessarily completely connected. He proved the connectivity bounds represented in Theorem 6.29, using explicit construction of scenarios. Dolev, Reischuk, and Strong [99] developed algorithms with "early stopping" for certain favorable communication patterns. Other early stopping algorithms were developed by Dwork and Moses [105] and by Halpern, Moses, and Waarts [145].

Bar-Noy, Dolev, Dwork, and Strong defined the *EIG* tree data structure and presented the *EIGByz* algorithm in essentially the form given in this book [39]. The *TurpinCoan* algorithm is from [279].

The first polynomial communication algorithm for Byzantine agreement was provided by Dolev and Strong [101]; it was subsequently improved by Dolev, Fischer, Fowler, Lynch, and Strong [96] to yield a time bound of $2f + 3$. Coan [82] developed a tradeoff algorithm, which decreased the number of rounds to $(1+\epsilon)f$, for any $\epsilon > 0$; the communication is polynomial, but the degree of the polynomial depends on ϵ. The consistent broadcast primitive and the *ConsistentBroadcast* algorithm are due to Srikanth and Toueg [269]. The *PolyByz* algorithm is based on algorithms by Srikanth and Toueg [269] and by Dolev et al. [96]. Subsequent research by Moses and Waarts [231], Berman and Garay [49], and Garay and Moses [133] has produced $f + 1$ round Byzantine agreement algorithms with polynomial communication; the last of these also achieves the $n = 3f + 1$ minimum bound on the number of processes. Unfortunately, these algorithms are complicated.

As already noted, the $n > 3f$ lower bound on the number of processes required for Byzantine agreement was originally proved in [237, 187], while the connectivity lower bound was originally proved in [94]. However, the proofs presented in this book were developed by Fischer, Lynch, and Merritt [122]. Menger's Theorem was originally proved by Menger [225] and appears in Harary's book [147].

The weak Byzantine agreement problem was defined by Lamport [178]. The lower bound result for the number of processes needed for weak Byzantine agreement is due to Lamport [178], but the proof given here is due to Fischer, Lynch, and Merritt [122].

The first lower bound result for the number of rounds required to reach agreement was proved by Fischer and Lynch [119], for the case of Byzantine failures. The result was subsequently extended by Dolev and Strong [93] and by DeMillo, Lynch, and Merritt [88] to the case of Byzantine failures with authentication. The extension to the case of stopping failures seems to have first been carried out by Merritt [226], using ideas of Dolev and Strong [101]. Another proof of this result was presented by Dwork and Moses [105]; their proof provides a finer analysis of the time requirements for different runs. Feldman and Micali [113] obtained a constant time randomized solution using "secret-sharing" techniques.

A paper by Fischer [117] surveys much of the early work on the agreement problem.

There has been a considerable amount of work at Draper Laboratories involving the design of fault-tolerant multiprocessors and processor fault-diagnosis algorithms, using Byzantine agreement [172, 173]. These designs have been used for safety-critical applications such as unmanned undersea vehicles, nuclear attack submarines, and nuclear power plant control.

6.9 Exercises

6.1. Prove that any algorithm that solves the Byzantine agreement problem also solves the stopping agreement problem, if the validity condition for stopping failures is modified to require only that nonfaulty processes agree.

6.2. Prove that any algorithm that solves the Byzantine agreement problem, and in which all nonfaulty processes always decide at the same round, also solves the stopping agreement problem.

6.3. Prove Lemma 6.2.

6.4. Trace the execution of the *FloodSet* algorithm for four processes and two failures, where the processes have initial values 1, 0, 0, and 0, respectively. Suppose that processes 1 and 2 are faulty, with process 1 failing in the first round after sending to 2 only and process 2 failing in the second round after sending to 1 and 3 but not 4.

6.5. Consider the *FloodSet* algorithm for f failures. Suppose that instead of running for $f + 1$ rounds, the algorithm runs for only f rounds, with the same decision rule. Describe a particular execution in which the correctness requirements are violated.

6.6. (a) Describe another alternative decision rule that works correctly for the *FloodSet* algorithm, besides the ones discussed in the text.

     (b) Give an exact characterization of the set of decision rules that work correctly.

6.7. Extend the *FloodSet* algorithm, its correctness proof, and its analysis to arbitrary (not necessarily complete) connected graphs.

6.8. Give code for *OptFloodSet*. Complete the proof given in the text by proving Lemmas 6.5, 6.6, and 6.7.

6.9. Consider the following simple algorithm for agreement with stopping failures, for a value domain V. Each process maintains a variable *min-val*, originally set to its own initial value. For each of $f+1$ rounds, the processes all broadcast their *min-vals*, then each resets its *min-val* to the minimum of its old *min-val* and all the values it receives in messages. At the end, the decision value is *min-val*. Give code for this algorithm, and prove (either directly or via a simulation proof) that it works correctly.

6.10. Trace the execution of the *EIGStop* algorithm for four processes and two failures, where the processes have initial values 1, 0, 0, and 0, respectively. Suppose that processes 1 and 2 are faulty, with process 1 failing in the first round after sending to 2 only, and process 2 failing in the second round after sending to 1 and 3 but not to 4.

6.11. Prove Lemma 6.11.

6.12. Prove Lemma 6.12, part 1.

6.13. Consider the *EIGStop* algorithm for f failures. Suppose that instead of running for $f + 1$ rounds, the algorithm only runs for f rounds, with the same decision rule. Describe a particular execution in which the correctness requirements are violated.

6.14. An alternative way to prove the correctness of *FloodSet* is by relating it to *EIGStop* by a simulation relation. In order to do this, it is convenient to first extend *EIGStop* by allowing each process i to broadcast all values at all rounds, not just values associated with nodes whose labels do not contain i. It must be argued that this extension does not affect correctness. Also, some details in the description of *EIGStop* must be filled in, for example, explicit *rounds* and *decision* variables, manipulated in the obvious ways. Then *FloodSet* and the modified *EIGStop* can be run side by side, starting with the same set of initial values, and with failures occurring at the same processes at exactly the same times.

Prove the correctness of *FloodSet* in this way. The heart of the proof should be the following simulation relation, which involves the states of both algorithms after the same number of rounds.

> **Assertion 6.9.1** *For any r, $0 \leq r \leq f + 1$, the following are true after r rounds.*
>
> *(a) The values of the rounds and decision variables are the same in the states of both algorithms.*
>
> *(b) For each i, the set W_i in FloodSet is equal to the set of vals that decorate nodes of i's tree in EIGStop.*

Be sure to include the statement and proof of any additional invariants of *EIGStop* that you need to establish the simulation.

6.15. Prove the correctness of *OptEIGStop*, in either of the following two ways:

(a) By a simulation of *EIGStop*, using a proof analogous to the simulation proof relating *OptFloodSet* to *FloodSet*.

(b) By relating it to *OptFloodSet*.

6.16. Prove the correctness of the *EIGStop* and *OptEIGStop* algorithms for the authenticated Byzantine failure model. Some key facts that can be used in the proof of *EIGStop* are expressed by the following assertion, analogous to the statement of Lemma 6.12:

Assertion 6.9.2 *After $f + 1$ rounds:*

(a) *If i and j are nonfaulty processes, $val(y)_i = v \in V$, and xj is a prefix of y, then $val(x)_j = v$.*

(b) *If v is in the set of vals at any nonfaulty process, then v is an initial value of some process.*

(c) *If i is a nonfaulty process, and $v \in V$ is in the set of vals at process i, then there is some label y that does not contain i such that $v = val(y)_i$.*

These facts follow from the properties of digital signatures.

6.17. *Research Question*: Define the authenticated Byzantine failure model formally and prove results about its power and limitations.

6.18. Give an example of an execution of *EIGStop* that shows that *EIGStop* does not solve the agreement problem for Byzantine faults.

6.19. Consider the *EIGByz* algorithm with seven processes and three rounds. Arbitrarily select two of the processes as faulty and provide random choices for the inputs of all processes and for the message values of the faulty processes. Calculate all the information produced in the execution and verify that the correctness conditions are satisfied.

6.20. In the *EIGByz* algorithm, show that not every node in the *EIG* tree need be common.

6.21. Consider the *EIGByz* algorithm. Construct explicit executions to show that the algorithm can give wrong results if it is run with

(a) Seven nodes, two faults, and two rounds.

(b) Six nodes, two faults, and three rounds.

6.22. The *TurpinCoan* algorithm uses the threshold $n - f$ at rounds 1 and 2. What other pairs of thresholds would also allow the algorithm to work correctly?

6.23. Suppose we consider the *TurpinCoan* algorithm with *two* sets of faulty processes, F and G, rather than just one. Each set has at most f processes. Processes in F behave correctly except that they can send incorrect messages during rounds 1 and 2. Processes in G are allowed to behave incorrectly during execution of the binary Byzantine agreement subroutine (and only then). What correctness conditions are guaranteed by the combined algorithm under these failure assumptions? Prove.

6.24. Now you may assume that $n > 4f$. Design an algorithm that uses a subroutine for binary Byzantine agreement and solves multivalued Byzantine agreement. The algorithm should improve on the *TurpinCoan* algorithm by only requiring one additional round rather than two.

6.25. Show that there is no upper bound on the time until a nonfaulty process might accept a message (m, i, r) in the *ConsistentBroadcast* algorithm. That is, for any t, produce an execution of *ConsistentBroadcast* in which some nonfaulty process accepts the message at a round $r' \geq r + t$.

6.26. Can you design an algorithm to implement the consistent broadcast mechanism in the Byzantine failure model, with $f \gg 1$ faults, having the additional property that no nonfaulty process ever accepts a message (m, i, r) strictly after round $r + 1$?

Either give such an algorithm and prove its correctness, or argue why no such algorithm exists.

6.27. Describe a worst-case execution of *PolyByz*, that is, one in which there is some nonfaulty process i such that the earliest round by which process i accepts messages from $2f + 1$ distinct processes is exactly round $2(f + 1)$.

6.28. A programmer at the Flaky Computer Corporation has modified his implementation of the *PolyByz* algorithm so that the acceptance threshold for each round of the form $2s - 1$ is $s - 1$ rather than $f + s - 1$, and the decision threshold is $f + 1$ rather than $2f + 1$. Is his modification correct? Prove or give a counterexample.

6.29. Design a polynomial communication algorithm for Byzantine agreement for a general input value set, without using a subroutine for binary Byzantine agreement. Your algorithm should use the consistent broadcast mechanism, but you might have to design a better implementation than the *ConsistentBroadcast* algorithm.

6.30. Design an algorithm for stopping agreement that satisfies the following *early stopping* property: If in an execution of the algorithm only $f' < f$ processes fail, then the time until all the nonfaulty processes decide is at most kf', for some constant k. Do the same for Byzantine agreement.

6.31. Design a protocol for four processes in a completely connected graph that tolerates *either* one Byzantine fault or three stopping faults. Try to minimize the number of rounds.

6.32. *Research Question*: Devise a *simple* $f+1$ round protocol solving Byzantine agreement, requiring only $3f+1$ processes and polynomial communication.

6.33. This exercise is designed to explore the construction in the proof of Lemma 6.26, which pastes together two triangle systems to yield a hexagon system.

   (a) Carefully describe an algorithm A for a three-process complete graph that solves the *no-fault agreement problem*, that is, the Byzantine agreement problem in the special case where no processes are faulty.

   (b) Now construct system S by pasting together two copies of your algorithm A, as in the proof of Lemma 6.26. Describe carefully the execution of S in which processes 1, 2, and 3 start with input 0, and $1'$, $2'$, and $3'$ start with input 1.

   (c) Does S solve the no-fault agreement problem (for the hexagon network)? Either prove that it does or give an execution that shows that it does not.

   (d) Does there exist a three-process algorithm A such that *arbitrarily many* copies of A can be pasted together into a ring, and the resulting ring will always solve the no-fault agreement problem?

6.34. What is the largest number of faulty processes that can be tolerated by Byzantine agreement algorithms that run in the following network graphs?

   (a) A ring of size n.

   (b) A three-dimensional cube, m nodes on a side, in which nodes are connected only to their neighbors in the three dimensions.

   (c) A complete bipartite graph with m nodes in each of its two components.

6.35. Give a more careful impossibility proof for Byzantine agreement when $n = 2$ and $f = 1$.

6.36. Analyze the time, number of messages, and number of communication bits for the Byzantine agreement algorithm for general graphs, described in the proof of Theorem 6.29. Can you improve on any of these?

6.37. Show carefully that the simplifications assumed in the proof of Theorem 6.29 to prove that Byzantine agreement is impossible with $f = 1$ and $conn(G) \leq 2$ are in fact justified. That is, show that the existence of an algorithm for the case where nodes 1 and 3 are replaced by arbitrary connected subgraphs implies the existence of an algorithm for the case where they are just single nodes.

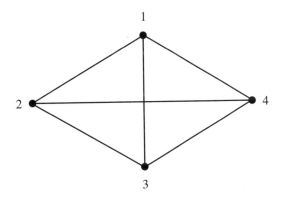

Figure 6.21: Network graph for Exercise 6.38.

6.38. Reconsider the proof that Byzantine agreement cannot be reached in the graph in Figure 6.11. Why does this proof fail to extend to the graph in Figure 6.21?

6.39. Prove that Byzantine agreement for f failures, where $f > 1$, cannot be solved in a graph G with $conn(G) \leq 2f$. This can be done either using the process grouping argument sketched at the end of the proof of Theorem 6.29, or else using a reduction similar to the one in Theorem 6.27.

6.40. Give a simple algorithm for weak Byzantine agreement in a network graph consisting of two nodes connected by a single link.

6.41. Complete the proof of Theorem 6.30, by showing impossibility

   (a) When $n \leq 3f$ and $f > 1$

   (b) When $conn(G) \leq 2f$

6.42. Consider the *Byzantine Firing Squad* problem, defined as follows. There are n processes in a fully connected network with no input values and with variable start times. That is, each process begins in a *quiescent* state containing no information and from which it sends only *null* messages. It does not change state until and unless it receives a special *wakeup* message from the outside or a non-*null* message from another process. A process does not know the current round number when it awakens. The model is similar to the one in Section 2.1, except that we do not assume here that all processes must receive *wakeup* messages—only some arbitrary subset of the processes. Also, we permit Byzantine faults.

The problem is for processes to issue *fire* signals, subject to the following conditions:

Agreement: If any nonfaulty process issues a *fire* signal at some round, then all nonfaulty processes issue a *fire* signal at that same round and no nonfaulty process issues a *fire* signal at any other round.

Validity: If all nonfaulty processes receive *wakeup* messages, then all nonfaulty processes eventually *fire*; if no nonfaulty process receives a *wakeup* message, then no nonfaulty process ever *fires*.

(a) Design an algorithm to solve the Byzantine Firing Squad problem for $n > 3f$.

(b) Prove that the problem cannot be solved if $n \leq 3f$.

6.43. State and give a direct proof of the special case of Theorem 6.33 for $f = 3$.

6.44. Does Lemma 6.37 still hold if the runs are not required to be regular? Give a proof or a counterexample.

6.45. In Section 6.7, it is shown that stopping agreement tolerating f faults cannot be solved in f rounds. The construction involves the construction of a long chain connecting the two runs in which all the processes are nonfaulty and have the same inputs. The chain, however, is only constructed implicitly.

(a) How long is the chain of runs?

(b) By how much can you shorten this chain using Byzantine faults rather than stopping faults?

6.46. *Research Question:* Obtain upper and lower bound results about the time required to solve the stopping agreement problem and/or the Byzantine agreement problem, in general (not necessarily complete) network graphs.

Chapter 7

More Consensus Problems

The past two chapters have been devoted to consensus problems—Chapter 5 to the coordinated attack problem and Chapter 6 to the agreement problem. In this chapter, we finish our study of synchronous distributed consensus by considering three other consensus problems: the *k-agreement problem*, the *approximate agreement problem*, and the *distributed database commit problem*. As in Chapter 6, we consider process failures only.

7.1 *k*-Agreement

The first problem we consider is the k-agreement problem, where k is some nonnegative integer. The k-agreement problem is a natural generalization of the ordinary agreement problem considered in Chapter 6. But now, instead of requiring that all processes decide on exactly the same value, we insist only that they limit their decisions to a small number, k, of distinct values.

The original motivation for this problem was purely mathematical—it is interesting to try to determine how the results of Chapter 6 change when the problem requirements are varied in this simple way. But it is possible to imagine practical situations in which such an algorithm could be useful. For example, consider the problem of allocating shareable resources, such as broadcast frequencies in a communication network. It might be desirable for a number of processes to agree on a small number of frequencies to use for the broadcast of a large amount of data (say, a videotape). Because the communication is by broadcast, any number of processes could receive the data using the same frequency. In order to minimize the total communication load, it is preferable to keep the number k of frequencies that are used small.

In this section, we prove exactly matching upper and lower bounds on the number of rounds required to solve the k-agreement problem, in a complete network graph and for the case of stopping failures only. These bounds are given in terms of n, the number of processes; f, the number of failures tolerated; and k, the allowed number of decision values.

7.1.1   The Problem

In the k-agreement problem, just as for the ordinary agreement problem, we assume that the network is an n-node connected undirected graph with processes $1, \ldots, n$, where each process knows the entire graph. Each process starts with an input from a fixed set V and is supposed to eventually output a decision from the set V. (Again, we assume that for each process, there is exactly one start state containing each input value.) We assume that at most f processes might fail. We consider *stopping failures* only. The required conditions are as follows.

Agreement: There is a subset W of V, $|W| = k$, such that all decision values are in W.

Validity: Any decision value for any process is the initial value of some process.

Termination: All nonfaulty processes eventually decide.

The agreement condition is the natural generalization of the agreement condition for the ordinary agreement problem. Notice that we use the stronger validity condition for stopping failures given near the end of Section 6.1 rather than the weaker one we used in most of Chapter 6; we need this stronger condition for the lower bound proof in Section 7.1.3. The ordinary agreement problem with the stronger validity condition is exactly the k-agreement problem for $k = 1$.

For the results we present in this section, we consider the special case of a complete network graph only. We also assume that V comes equipped with a total ordering.

As in Section 6.2.1, we define a process to be *active* after r rounds, $0 \leq r$, if it does not fail by the end of r rounds.

7.1.2   An Algorithm

We present a very simple algorithm, called *FloodMin*; in fact, it is exactly the algorithm sketched in Exercise 6.9, but it runs for a smaller number of rounds. As we claimed in Exercise 6.9, when this algorithm runs for $f + 1$ rounds, it guarantees ordinary stopping agreement. It turns out that it still guarantees k-agreement when it runs for only $\lfloor \frac{f}{k} \rfloor + 1$ rounds. Thus, roughly speaking, allowing k decision values rather than just one divides the running time by k.

FloodMin algorithm (informal):

Each process maintains a variable *min-val*, originally set to its own initial value. For each of $\lfloor \frac{f}{k} \rfloor + 1$ rounds, the processes all broadcast their *min-vals*, then each process resets its *min-val* to the minimum of its old *min-val* and all the values in its incoming messages. At the end, the decision value is *min-val*.

The code follows. (Compare its structure with that of *FloodSet* in Section 6.2.1.)

FloodMin algorithm (formal):

The message alphabet is V.

states$_i$:
rounds $\in \mathbb{N}$, initially 0
decision $\in V \cup \{unknown\}$, initially *unknown*
min-val $\in V$, initially i's initial value

msgs$_i$:
if *rounds* $\leq \lfloor \frac{f}{k} \rfloor$ then send *min-val* to all other processes

trans$_i$:
rounds := *rounds* + 1
let m_j be the message from j, for each j from which a message arrives
min-val := $\min(\{min\text{-}val\} \cup \{m_j : j \neq i\})$
if *rounds* $= \lfloor \frac{f}{k} \rfloor + 1$ then *decision* := *min-val*

We argue correctness; the proof is similar to that for the *FloodSet* algorithm in Section 6.2.1. Let $M(r)$ denote the set of *min-val* values of active processes after r rounds. We first observe that the set $M(r)$ can only decrease at successive times.

Lemma 7.1 $M(r) \subseteq M(r-1)$ *for all* r, $1 \leq r \leq \lfloor \frac{f}{k} \rfloor + 1$.

Proof. Suppose that $m \in M(r)$. Then m is the value of *min-val$_i$* after r rounds, for some process i that is active after r rounds. Then either $m = min\text{-}val_i$ just before round r or else m arrives at i in some round r message, say from j. But in this case, $min\text{-}val_j = m$ after $r-1$ rounds, and j must be active after $r-1$ rounds because it sends a message at round r. It follows that $m \in M(r-1)$. $\square$

Lemma 7.2 *Let* $d \in \mathbb{N}^+$. *If at most* $d-1$ *processes fail during a particular round* r, $1 \leq r \leq \lfloor \frac{f}{k} \rfloor + 1$, *then* $|M(r)| \leq d$, *that is, there are at most* d *different min-vals for active processes after round* r.

Proof. Suppose for the sake of contradiction that at most $d - 1$ processes fail during round r, yet $|M(r)| > d$. Let m be the maximum element of $M(r)$ and let $m' \neq m$ be any other element of $M(r)$. Then m' is an element of $M(r-1)$, by Lemma 7.1; let i be any process that is active and has $m' = min\text{-}val_i$ after $r - 1$ rounds. If i does not fail in round r, then every process receives a message containing m' from i at round r. But this cannot occur, because some active process has $m > m'$ as its $min\text{-}val$ after r rounds. It follows that i fails during round r.

But m' was chosen to be any arbitrary element of $M(r)$ other than the maximum, m. Thus, for every element $m' \neq m$ of $M(r)$, there is some process that is active, has its $min\text{-}val$ equal to m' after $r - 1$ rounds, and fails during round r. By assumption, there are at most $d - 1$ processes that fail at round r, so there can be at most $d - 1$ elements of $M(r)$ other than m. Therefore, $|M(r)| \leq d$; this is a contradiction. $\qquad\square$

Now we can prove the main correctness theorem.

Theorem 7.3 *The FloodMin algorithm solves the k-agreement problem for the stopping failure model.*

Proof. Termination and validity are straightforward. We prove the new agreement condition. Suppose, to obtain a contradiction, that the number of distinct decision values is greater than k in a particular execution having at most f failures. Then the number of $min\text{-}vals$ for active processes after $\lfloor \frac{f}{k} \rfloor + 1$ rounds is at least $k + 1$, that is, $|M(\lfloor \frac{f}{k} \rfloor + 1)| \geq k + 1$. By Lemma 7.1, $|M(r)| \geq k + 1$ for all r, $0 \leq r \leq \lfloor \frac{f}{k} \rfloor + 1$. Then Lemma 7.2 implies that at least k processes fail in each round r, $1 \leq r \leq \lfloor \frac{f}{k} \rfloor + 1$. This yields a total number of failures that is at least $(\lfloor \frac{f}{k} \rfloor + 1)k$. But this is strictly greater than f, which yields a contradiction. $\qquad\square$

Complexity analysis. The number of rounds is $\lfloor \frac{f}{k} \rfloor + 1$. The number of messages is at most $(\lfloor \frac{f}{k} \rfloor + 1)n^2$, and the number of message bits is at most $(\lfloor \frac{f}{k} \rfloor + 1)n^2 b$, where b is an upper bound on the number of bits needed to represent a single element of V.

7.1.3 Lower Bound*

In this section, we show that the upper bound of $\lfloor \frac{f}{k} \rfloor + 1$ is tight, by proving that it is also a lower bound, provided that $|V| \geq k + 1$. This gives an exact characterization of the speedup that is achievable by allowing k output values rather than just 1—essentially, the time is divided by k. As you might expect, the ideas of the proof are derived from those used for the proof of the lower bound for ordinary agreement, Theorem 6.33, but they are a good deal more advanced and more interesting. In fact, they take us into the realm of algebraic topology.

For the remainder of this section, fix A to be an n-process algorithm that solves the k-agreement problem, tolerating the stopping failure of at most f processes. Suppose that A halts in $r < \lfloor \frac{f}{k} \rfloor + 1$ rounds; that is, that $r \leq \lfloor \frac{f}{k} \rfloor$. In order to obtain a contradiction, we need the additional assumption that $n \geq f + k + 1$, which means that at least $k + 1$ processes never fail.

Without loss of generality, we may assume that all processes that decide do so exactly at the end of round r and immediately halt. We also assume that every process sends a message to every other process at every round k, $1 \leq k \leq r$ (until and unless it fails). Finally, we assume that the value domain V consists of exactly the $k + 1$ elements, $0, 1, \cdots, k$, since that is all we need to obtain a contradiction.

We obtain a contradiction by showing that in one of the executions of A (with at most f failures), there are $k + 1$ processes that choose $k + 1$ distinct values, thus violating k-agreement.

Overview. Recall the proof of Theorem 6.33, the $f + 1$ round lower bound for ordinary stopping agreement. It uses a *chain argument*, producing a chain of executions that spans from one in which 0 is the only allowable decision to one in which 1 is the only allowable decision. We would like to extend this proof to other values of k. Unfortunately, in the k-agreement problem, unlike in the ordinary agreement problem, the decision values in one execution do not determine the decision values in closely related executions. For example, if executions α and α' of an ordinary agreement algorithm are indistinguishable to nonfaulty process i, then not only must i's decision be the same in both, but also the decisions of all the other nonfaulty processes in both α and α' must be the same as i's decision. In a k-agreement algorithm, if α and α' are indistinguishable to i, then i's decision is still guaranteed to be the same in both, but now the decisions of the other processes are not determined. Even if α and α' are indistinguishable to $n - 1$ processes, the decision value of the remaining process is not determined.

The key idea we use is to construct a k-dimensional collection of executions rather than a (one-dimensional) chain. Adjacent executions in this collection are indistinguishable to designated nonfaulty processes. We call the k-dimensional structure used to organize these executions the *Bermuda Triangle* (because any hypothetical k-agreement algorithm vanishes somewhere in its interior).

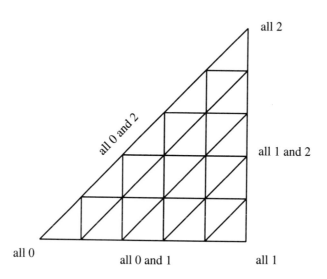

Figure 7.1: Bermuda Triangle for $k = 2$.

Example 7.1.1   Bermuda Triangle

Figure 7.1 is an example of a Bermuda Triangle, for the case where $k = 2$. It consists of a large triangle "triangulated" into a collection of "tiny triangles."

For $k > 2$, we need a k-dimensional version of a triangle. Fortunately, such a generalization already exists in the field of algebraic topology: it is called a k-dimensional *simplex*. For example, a one-dimensional simplex is just an edge, a two-dimensional simplex is a triangle, and a three-dimensional simplex is a tetrahedron. (Beyond three dimensions, the simplices are much harder to imagine.)

So, for an arbitrary k, we start with a k-dimensional simplex in k-dimensional Euclidean space. This simplex contains a number of *grid points*, which are the points in Euclidean space with integer coordinates. The *k-dimensional Bermuda Triangle*, B, is obtained by triangulating this simplex with respect to these grid points, obtaining a collection of tiny k-dimensional simplices.

The proof involves first assigning an execution to each vertex (grid point) of B. The executions in which all processes start with the same input in $\{0, \ldots, k\}$ and there are no failures get assigned to the $k + 1$ corner vertices of B. For instance, in the case where $k = 2$, we assign an execution in which all processes have input 0 to the lower left-hand corner, an execution in which all processes have input 1 to the lower right-hand corner, and an execution in which all processes have input 2 to the upper right-hand corner (see Figure 7.1). Moreover, for every vertex x on any face of B (of any dimension), the only inputs appearing in the execution assigned to x are those that appear in the executions assigned to the corners of the face. For instance, in the case where $k = 2$, all executions assigned to vertices on the lower edge have inputs chosen from $\{0, 1\}$.

Next, to each vertex in B, we assign the index of some process that is non-faulty in the execution assigned to that vertex. This process assignment is done in such a way that, for each tiny simplex T, there is a single execution α with at most f faults that is compatible with the executions and processes assigned to the corners of T in the following sense:

1. All the processes assigned to the corners of T are nonfaulty in α.

2. If execution α' and process i are assigned to some corner of T, then α and α' are indistinguishable to i.

This assignment of executions and processes to vertices of B has some nice properties. Suppose α and i are associated with vertex x. If x is a corner of B, then all processes start with the same input in α, so, by the validity condition, i must decide on this value in α. If x is on an external edge of B, then in α each process starts with one of the two input values that are associated with the corners of B at the two ends of the edge; the validity condition then implies that i must decide on one of these two values. More generally, if x is on any face (of any dimension) of B, then in α each process starts with one of the input values that are associated with the corners of the face; the validity condition then implies that i must decide on one of these values. Finally, if x is in the interior of B, then i is allowed to decide on any of the $k + 1$ values.

Our ability to assign executions and indices to the vertices in the manner just described depends on the fact that the number r of rounds in each execution is at most $\lfloor \frac{f}{k} \rfloor$, that is, that $f \geq rk$. This is because the executions are assigned using a k-dimensional generalization of the chain argument in the proof of Theorem 6.33. The construction uses r process failures for each of the k dimensions.

After having assigned executions and indices to vertices, we "color" each vertex with a "color" chosen from the set $\{0, \ldots, k\}$. Namely, we color a vertex x having associated execution α and associated process i with the color that corresponds to i's decision value in α. This coloring has the following properties:

1. The colors of the $k + 1$ corners of B are all different.

2. The color of each point on an external edge of B is the color of one of the corners at the endpoints of the edge.

3. More generally, the color of each point on any external face (of any dimension) of B is the color of one of the corners of the face.

It turns out that colorings of this k-simplex with exactly these properties have been studied in the field of algebraic topology, under the name *Sperner colorings*.

At this point, we can apply a remarkable combinatorial result first proved in 1928: *Sperner's Lemma* says that any Sperner coloring of a triangulated k-dimensional simplex must include at least one tiny simplex whose $k + 1$ corners are colored with all $k + 1$ distinct colors. In our case, this simplex corresponds to an execution with at most f faults, in which $k + 1$ processes choose $k + 1$ distinct values. But this contradicts the agreement condition for the k-agreement problem.

It follows that the hypothesized algorithm cannot exist, that is, there is no algorithm for the k-agreement problem tolerating f faults and halting in $r \leq \lfloor \frac{f}{k} \rfloor$ rounds. The rest of this subsection contains more details.

Definitions. We use the definition of a communication pattern from Section 6.7. Now, we redefine a *good* communication pattern to be one in which $k \leq r$ for all triples (i, j, k) and in which the missing triples are consistent with the stopping failure model. (That is, we use the first two conditions in the definition of a good communication pattern in Section 6.7, except that the upper bound for the number of rounds is now r instead of f. For the moment, we do not limit the number of failures.) Based on this new definition of a good communication pattern, we define a *run* and define $exec(\rho)$ for a run ρ in the same way as in Section 6.7. We also say that process i is *silent* after t rounds in a run if i sends no messages in any round numbered $t + 1$ or higher.

Bermuda Triangle. We begin with the k-simplex in k-dimensional Euclidean space whose corner vertices are the length k vectors $(0, \ldots, 0)$, $(N, 0, \ldots, 0)$, $(N, N, 0, \ldots, 0)$, ..., $(N, \ldots, N)$, where N is a huge integer to be defined shortly. The *Bermuda Triangle B* is this simplex, together with the following triangulation into *tiny simplices*. The vertices of B are the grid points contained in the simplex, that is, the points of the form $x = (x_1, \ldots, x_k)$, where the vector components are integers between 0 and N satisfying $x_1 \geq x_2 \geq \cdots \geq x_k$. The tiny simplices are defined as follows: pick any grid point and walk one step in the positive direction along each dimension, in any order. The $k + 1$ points visited by this walk define the vertices of a tiny simplex.

Example 7.1.2   Coordinates of vertices in the Bermuda Triangle

The two-dimensional Bermuda Triangle is illustrated in Figure 7.2.

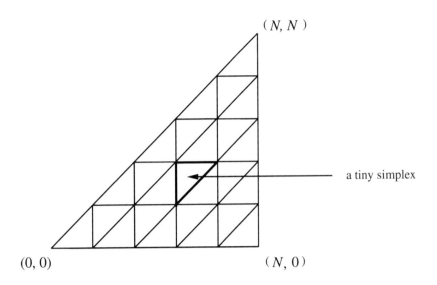

Figure 7.2: Two-dimensional Bermuda Triangle.

Labelling B with executions and runs. In this section, we describe how to assign executions to vertices of B (that is, to "label" the vertices with executions). We do this by first augmenting runs by attaching *tokens* to some of the (process, round number) pairs (i, t) in the runs. Such a token should be thought of as "giving permission" for process i to fail in round t or later. More than one token may be attached to the same pair (i, t).

More specifically, for any $l > 0$, we define an l-*run* to be a run augmented with exactly l tokens for each round number t, $1 \le t \le r$, in such a way that if some process i fails at some round t, then there is a token attached to some pair $(i, t'), t' \le t$. An l-run contains a total of lr tokens. We are really only interested in the two cases where $l = 1$ and $l = k$, that is, 1-runs and k-runs. We define a *failure-free l-run* to be an l-run in which there are no failures and in which all tokens are attached to pairs of the form $(1, t)$ (that is, only process 1 has permission to fail).

Since each augmented run is constructed from a run, each augmented run gives rise to an execution in an obvious way. We extend the notation $exec(\rho)$, which was previously defined for runs, to the case where ρ is an augmented run. In order to label the vertices of B with executions, we label them with k-runs.

We now define four operations on l-runs, each of which makes only minor changes. Each operation can only remove or add a single triple, change the value of a single process's input, or move a single token between processes with adjacent indices within the same round. These operations are very similar to the ones used in the proof of Theorem 6.33. The operations are defined as follows.

1. *remove*(i, j, t), where i and j are process indices and t is a round number, $1 \le t \le r$.

   This operation removes the triple (i, j, t) (which represents the round t message from i to j) if it is there, and has no effect otherwise. It can only be applied if i and j are both silent after t rounds and there is a token attached to some (i, t'), $t' \le t$.

2. *add*(i, j, t).

   This operation adds the triple (i, j, t) if it is not already there and has no effect otherwise. It can only be applied if i and j are both silent after t rounds and i is active after $t - 1$ rounds.

3. *change*(i, v).

   This operation changes process i's input value to v and has no effect if this input value is already v. It can only be applied if i is silent after 0 rounds and $(i, 1)$ has a token.

4. *move*(i, j, t).

   This operation moves a token from (i, t) to (j, t), where j is either $i + 1$ or $i - 1$. It can only be applied if (i, t) has a token and if all failures have permission from other tokens.

It should be obvious from the definitions that when any of these operations is applied to an l-run, the result is also an l-run.

Now, for any $v \in \{1, \ldots, k\}$, we can define a sequence *seq*(v) of *remove*, *add*, *change*, and *move* operations that can be applied to any failure-free 1-run ρ to transform it into the failure-free 1-run in which all processes have input v. In fact, the same sequence *seq*(v) can be used for all failure-free 1-runs ρ. This can be done using the methods in the proof of Theorem 6.33; the main difference is the explicit movement of the tokens giving permission to fail. In this construction, inputs of processes are changed to v one at a time, starting with process 1. As before, this construction uses r failures in r rounds.

It turns out that the sequences *seq*(v) can be constructed so that they are isomorphic for different v—that is, they are the same except for the choice of v. Now we can (finally) define the parameter N used in defining the size of B: N is simply the length of the sequence *seq*(v) (for any v).

We will use several sequences *seq*(v) to label the vertices of B. Recall that the elements of the value domain are $0, 1, \ldots, k$. For each $v \in \{0, 1, \ldots, k\}$, define τ_v to be the failure-free 1-run in which all processes' initial values are

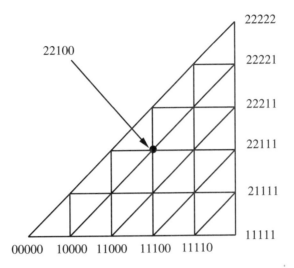

Figure 7.3: Labelling the Bermuda Triangle with k-runs.

equal to v. We will apply each sequence $seq(v)$, $1 \leq v \leq k$, to the failure-free 1-run τ_{v-1}, to generate a sequence of 1-runs to use as *preliminary labels* for the vertices along the edge of B in the vth dimension (the "v-axis"). Then the k-run we assign to each vertex x of B will be obtained by "merging" the k 1-runs that are preliminary labels of the projections of x on the k axes.

Example 7.1.3 Labelling Bermuda Triangle with k-runs

To give some intuition for how this merging works, we give a simplified diagram for the case where $k = 2$ (so $V = \{0, 1, 2\}$) and $n = 5$. See Figure 7.3.

The diagram does not depict all the vertices—only those labelled by failure-free k-runs. Thus, the only interesting information we need to provide is the vector of input values for each depicted vertex. The k-run labelling each corner of B is a failure-free k-run in which all inputs are equal and where the 0s appear at the lower left, the 1s at the lower right, and the 2s at the upper right. The chain along the horizontal axis is constructed by using $seq(1)$ to span from all 0s to all 1s, while the chain along the vertical axis is constructed using $seq(2)$ to span from all 1s to all 2s.

Note the pattern of inputs appearing in B. Along the horizontal axis, the processes' inputs are changed from 0 to 1 one at a time, starting from process 1. Along the vertical axis, the processes' inputs are changed from 1 to 2 one at a time, starting from process 1.

In the interior of B, changes take place in both directions at the same time. For example, consider the indicated interior vertex with input vector 22100. The vectors labelling its projections on the horizontal and vertical axes are 11100 and 22111, respectively. The vector 22100 can be changed into 22111 by changing the inputs of the last two processes from 0 to 1, moving horizontally in B. Similarly, the vector 11100 can be changed into 22100 by changing the inputs of the first two processes from 1 to 2, moving vertically in B. The vector labelling each node of B consists of values in $\{0, 1, 2\}$ occurring in nonincreasing order.

Now we give a formal definition for merging. The *merge* of the sequence $\sigma_1, \ldots, \sigma_k$ of 1-runs is the k-run ρ defined as follows:

1. Process i has the input value v in ρ, where v is the maximum value in $\{1, \ldots, k\}$ such that i has input value v in σ_v, or 0 if no such v exists.

2. A triple (i, j, t) is included in ρ exactly if it is included in all the σ_v, $1 \le v \le k$.

3. The number of tokens assigned to a pair (i, t) in ρ is the sum of the number of tokens assigned to the pair (i, t) in all the σ_v.

To motivate the first condition, we reconsider the way that the merge operation is to be used. Each σ_v will be obtained by applying some prefix of $seq(v)$ to τ_{v-1}. At some point in this sequence, the input value for process i is changed from $v - 1$ to v. If this has already happened in σ_v then let us say that process i has "converted" in dimension v. The first condition just chooses the largest v (if any) such that process i has converted in dimension v.

The second condition says that a message is missing in the new run ρ if and only if it is missing in any of the runs σ_v being merged. The third condition just accumulates the tokens. It is not hard to see that the merge of a sequence of 1-runs is in fact a k-run.

Now we put the pieces together and define the labelling of vertices of B with k-runs. Let $x = (x_1, \ldots, x_k)$ be an arbitrary vertex of B. For each $v \in \{1, \ldots, k\}$, let σ_v be the 1-run that results from applying the first x_v operations of $seq(v)$ to τ_{v-1}. Then the k-run labelling x is the merge of $\sigma_1, \ldots, \sigma_k$. Note that there are at most $rk \le f$ tokens in the merged run, and hence at most f failures. For the rest of this proof, we fix the labelling of B with k-runs (and executions).

We end this subsection by giving some close connections among the k-runs labelling the vertices of any single tiny simplex T in B. Let $y_0, \ldots, y_k$ be the vertices of T, in the order determined by the "walk" that generates T (as described in the definition of the Bermuda Triangle). Let $\rho_0, \ldots, \rho_k$ be the respective k-runs labelling these vertices.

The first lemma says that any process that is faulty in one of these k-runs must have a token in all of them.

Lemma 7.4 *If process i is faulty in some ρ_v, $0 \leq v \leq k$, then i has a token in every ρ_v.*

Proof Sketch. This is because the changes in each sequence *seq* are so gradual, in particular because movement of a token and removal of a triple occur in two separate steps. The detailed proof is left as an exercise. $\square$

The second lemma limits the number of total failures in all of the runs.

Lemma 7.5 *For any $v \in \{0, \ldots, k\}$, let F_v denote the set of processes that fail in ρ_v. Let $F = \cup_v F_v$. Then $|F| \leq rk \leq f$.*

Proof. Left as an exercise. The proof uses Lemma 7.4. $\square$

Finally, we consider labelling vertices of T with process indices. A *local process labelling* of T is an assignment of distinct process indices $i_0, \ldots, i_k$ to the vertices $y_0, \ldots, y_k$ of T in such a way that, for every v, i_v has no tokens in ρ_v. The final important property of the k-runs labelling the vertices of T is that if there is a local process labelling of T, then T is consistent with a single execution.

Lemma 7.6 *Let $i_0, \ldots, i_k$ be a local process labelling of T. Then there is a run ρ with at most f failures such that for all v, i_v is nonfaulty in ρ and $exec(\rho_v)$ and $exec(\rho)$ are indistinguishable to process i_v.*

Proof Sketch. We define ρ as follows. We define the initial value for each process i in ρ to be i's initial value from any one of the ρ_v. For $1 \leq t \leq r-1$, we include the triple (i, j, t) in ρ exactly if it is in all the ρ_v. Likewise, we include (i, j, r), where the recipient j is not one of the processes i_v, exactly if it is in all the ρ_v. Finally, (i, j, r), where $j = i_v$ (for a specific v) is included exactly if it is in ρ_v (for the same v).

We leave it as an exercise to show that ρ has all the needed properties: that it is indeed a run, that it has at most f failures, and that for each v, i_v is nonfaulty in ρ and $exec(\rho_v)$ and $exec(\rho)$ are indistinguishable to process i_v. The proof uses Lemma 7.5 to bound the number of failures. $\square$

Labelling B with process indices.   Recall that we are supposed to assign process indices to the vertices of B so that for each tiny simplex T, there is an execution that is compatible with the executions and processes labelling the vertices of T. Lemma 7.6 suggests a way of doing this: for each vertex of B, we pick a process that has no tokens in the corresponding k-run, in such a way that the processes chosen for the vertices of any tiny simplex are all distinct. Lemma 7.6 then implies the needed compatibility condition for each tiny simplex.

We define a *global process labelling* for B to be an assignment of processes to vertices of B such that for every vertex x, the process assigned to x has no tokens in the k-run labelling x, and such that for each tiny simplex T, all the processes assigned to vertices of T are distinct. A global process labelling for B yields a local process labelling for each tiny simplex of B.

We now construct a global process labelling for B. (Since the construction is technical, you might prefer to skip it on a first reading and proceed directly to Lemma 7.10.) We begin the construction by associating a set $live(\rho)$ of processes with each k-run ρ labelling a vertex of B and then choosing one process from each set $live(\rho)$. The sets $live(\rho)$ will satisfy the following properties:

1. Each set $live(\rho)$ consists of exactly $n - rk$ processes. (Since we have assumed that $n \geq f + k + 1$ and $f \geq rk$, this means that each set $live(\rho)$ contains at least $k + 1$ processes.)

2. The processes in $live(\rho)$ are chosen from among those that do not have tokens in ρ.

3. If ρ and ρ' are two k-runs labelling two vertices of the same tiny simplex in B, and if process $i \in live(\rho) \cap live(\rho')$, then i has the same rank in both sets.[1]

So fix some k-run ρ. It contains exactly rk tokens; let *tokens* be the multiset of process indices describing the number of tokens associated with each process. We "flatten" the multiset *tokens* to obtain a new multiset *newtokens* with the same number of tokens, but in which no more than one token is associated with any process. Also, any process that has a token in *tokens* also has a token in *newtokens*. The *Flatten* procedure works as follows:

Flatten **procedure:**

   newtokens := *tokens*
   while *newtokens* has a duplicate element do
       select such an element, say i

---

[1]The *rank* of an element i within a finite totally ordered set L is the number of elements of L that are less than or equal to i.

> if there exists $j < i$ such that $newtokens(j) = 0$, then
>> move a token from i to the largest such j
>> else move a token from i to the smallest $j > i$ such that $newtokens(j) = 0$

Then we define $live(\rho)$ to be all processes i such that $newtokens(i) = 0$.

It is easy to see that this definition of *live* satisfies the first two properties required above. To see the third property, fix a tiny simplex T, let $y_0, \ldots, y_k$ be the vertices of T, in the order determined by the walk that generates T, and let $\rho_0, \ldots, \rho_k$ be the respective k-runs labelling these vertices. First, we note that, when we walk the vertices of T in order, if process i ever acquires a token, then it always has tokens later in the walk.

Lemma 7.7 *Let $v < v' < v''$. If process i has no tokens in ρ_v but has a token in $\rho_{v'}$, then i has a token in $\rho_{v''}$.*

Proof.   Left as an exercise.   □

Now we can prove the third property for the *live* sets.

Lemma 7.8 *If $i \in live(\rho_v) \cap live(\rho_w)$, then i has the same rank in $live(\rho_v)$ and $live(\rho_w)$.*

Proof.   Assume without loss of generality that $v < w$. Since $i \in live(\rho_v)$ and $i \in live(\rho_w)$, i has no tokens in either ρ_v or ρ_w. Then Lemma 7.7 implies that i has no tokens in any of the runs $\rho_v, \ldots, \rho_w$.

Since token placements in adjacent k-runs differ by at most the movement of one token from one process to an adjacent process, and since i has no tokens in any of these runs, it follows that the total number of tokens on processes smaller than i is the same, say s, in all of the runs $\rho_v, \ldots, \rho_w$. Since $i \in live(\rho_v)$, the way the *Flatten* procedure works implies that $s < i$. (If $s \geq i$, then the tokens that start on processes smaller than i would "overflow" in the *Flatten* procedure so that one would end up on i.) Therefore, i is guaranteed to have the same rank, $i - s$, in $live(\rho_v)$ and $live(\rho_w)$.   □

Now we are ready to label the vertices of B with process indices. Let $x = (x_1, \ldots, x_k)$ be any vertex of B, and let ρ be its k-run; we choose a particular process index from the set $live(\rho)$. Namely, let $plane(x) = \sum_{i=1}^{k} x_i \pmod{k+1}$; we label x with the process having rank $plane(x)$ in $live(\rho)$. This choice is motivated by the following fact about B:

Lemma 7.9 *If x and y are distinct vertices of the same tiny simplex, then $plane(x) \neq plane(y)$.*

Now we obtain our goal:

Lemma 7.10 *This labelling of B with process indices is a global process labelling.*

Proof.   Because the index for each vertex x is chosen from the set $live(\rho)$, where ρ is the associated k-run, it must be that that index has no tokens in ρ. For any fixed tiny simplex T, Lemmas 7.8 and 7.9 together imply that the chosen indices are all distinct.   □

We summarize what we know about the labellings we have produced:

Lemma 7.11 *The given labellings of B with k-runs and processes have the following property. For every tiny simplex T with run labels $\rho_0, \dots, \rho_k$ and process labels $i_0, \dots, i_k$, there is a run ρ with at most f failures, such that for all v, i_v is nonfaulty in ρ and $exec(\rho_v)$ and $exec(\rho)$ are indistinguishable to process i_v.*

Proof.   This follows from Lemmas 7.6 and 7.10.   □

Sperner's Lemma.   We are nearly done! It remains only to state Sperner's Lemma (for the special case of the Bermuda Triangle) and to apply it to obtain a contradiction. This will yield the lower bound on the number of rounds required to solve k-agreement. A *Sperner coloring* of B assigns one of a set of $k+1$ colors to each vertex of B so that

1. The colors of the $k + 1$ corners of B are all different.

2. The color of each point on an external edge of B is the color of one of the corners at the endpoints of the edge.

3. More generally, the color of each interior point on an external face (of any dimension) of B is the color of one of the adjacent corners of B.

Sperner colorings have a remarkable property: there must be at least one tiny simplex whose $k + 1$ vertices are colored with all $k + 1$ colors.

Lemma 7.12 (Sperner's Lemma for B) *For any Sperner coloring of B, there is at least one tiny simplex in B whose $k+1$ corners are all colored with distinct colors.*

Now recall that A is the hypothesized k-agreement algorithm, assumed to tolerate f faults and halt in at most $\lfloor \frac{f}{k} \rfloor$ rounds. We define a coloring C_A of B as follows. Given a vertex x labelled with run ρ and process i, color x with process i's decision in the execution $exec(\rho)$ of A.

Lemma 7.13 *If A is an algorithm for k-agreement tolerating f faults and halting in $\lfloor \frac{f}{k} \rfloor$ rounds, then C_A is a Sperner coloring of B.*

Proof. By the validity condition of k-agreement. $\square$

Now we can prove the main theorem:

Theorem 7.14 *Suppose that $n \geq f+k+1$. Then there is no n-process algorithm for k-agreement that tolerates f faults, in which all nonfaulty processes always decide within $\lfloor \frac{f}{k} \rfloor$ rounds.*

Proof. Lemma 7.13 implies that C_A is a Sperner coloring, so Sperner's Lemma, Lemma 7.12, implies that there is a tiny simplex T, all of whose vertices are colored distinctly by C_A.

Suppose that T's k-run labels are $\rho_0, \ldots, \rho_k$ and its process labels are $i_0, \ldots, i_k$. By the definition of C_A, this means that all $k+1$ different decisions are produced by the $k+1$ processes i_v in their respective executions $exec(\rho_v)$. But Lemma 7.11 implies that there is a single run ρ with at most f failures, such that for all v, i_v is nonfaulty in ρ and $exec(\rho_v)$ and $exec(\rho)$ are indistinguishable to process i_v. But this implies that in ρ, the $k+1$ processes $i_0, \ldots, i_k$ decide on $k+1$ distinct values, violating the agreement condition for the k-agreement problem. $\square$

7.2 Approximate Agreement

Now we consider the *approximate agreement* problem in the presence of Byzantine failures. In this problem, the processes start with real-valued inputs and are supposed to eventually decide on real-valued outputs. They are permitted to send real-valued data in messages. Instead of having to agree exactly, as in the ordinary agreement problem, this time the requirement is just that they agree to within a small positive real-valued tolerance ϵ. More precisely, the requirements are

Agreement: The decision values of any pair of nonfaulty processes are within ϵ of each other.

Validity: Any decision value for a nonfaulty process is within the range of the initial values of the nonfaulty processes.

Termination: All nonfaulty processes eventually decide.

This problem arises, for example, in clock synchronization algorithms, where processes attempt to maintain clock values that are close but do not necessarily agree exactly. Many real distributed network algorithms work in the presence of approximately synchronized clocks, so approximate agreement on clock values is usually sufficient.

Here, we consider the approximate agreement problem in complete graphs only. One way of solving the problem is by using an ordinary Byzantine agreement algorithm as a subroutine. This solution assumes that $n > 3f$.

ByzApproxAgreement algorithm:

The processes run an ordinary Byzantine agreement algorithm to decide on a value for each process. All these algorithms run in parallel. In the algorithm for process i, i begins by sending its message to all processes in round 1, then all processes use the received values as their inputs in a Byzantine agreement algorithm. When these algorithms terminate, all nonfaulty processes have the same decision values for all processes. Each chooses the $\lfloor \frac{n}{2} \rfloor$th largest value in the multiset of decision values as its own final decision value.

To see that this works, note that if i is nonfaulty, then the validity condition for Byzantine agreement guarantees that the value obtained by all nonfaulty processes for i is i's actual input value. Since $n > 3f$, it follows that the middle value in the multiset must be in the range of the initial values of the nonfaulty processes.

Theorem 7.15 *ByzApproxAgreement solves the approximate agreement problem for an n-node complete graph, if $n > 3f$.*

Now we present a second solution, not using Byzantine agreement. The main reason we present this solution is that it has an easy extension to the asynchronous network model, which we present in Chapter 21. In contrast, the Byzantine agreement problem cannot be solved in asynchronous networks. The second solution also has the property that it sometimes terminates in fewer than the number of rounds required for Byzantine agreement, depending on how far apart the initial values of nonfaulty processes are. The algorithm is based on successive approximation. For simplicity, we describe a nonterminating version of the algorithm, then discuss termination separately. This algorithm again assumes that $n > 3f$.

We need a little notation and terminology: First, if U is a finite multiset of reals with at least $2f$ elements, and $u_1, \ldots, u_k$ is an ordering of the elements of U in nondecreasing order, then let *reduce*(U) denote the result of removing the f smallest and f largest elements from U, that is, the multiset consisting of $u_{f+1}, \ldots, u_{k-f}$. Also, if U is a nonempty finite multiset of reals, and $u_1, \ldots, u_k$ is again an ordering of the elements of U in nondecreasing order, then let $select(U)$ be the multiset consisting of $u_1, u_{f+1}, u_{2f+1}, \ldots$, that is, the smallest element of U and every fth element thereafter. Finally, if U is a nonempty finite multiset of reals, then $mean(U)$ is just the mean of the elements in U.

We also say that the *range* of a nonempty finite multiset of reals is the smallest interval containing all the elements, and the *width* of such a multiset is the size of the range interval.

The second solution is as follows:

ConvergeApproxAgreement algorithm:

Process i maintains a variable *val* containing its latest estimate. Initially, val_i contains i's initial value. At each round, process i does the following.

First, it broadcasts its *val* value to all processes, including itself.[2] Then it collects all the values it has received at that round into a multiset W; if i does not receive a value from some other process, it simply picks some arbitrary default value to assign to that process in the multiset, thus ensuring that $|W| = n$.

Then, process i sets *val* to $mean(select(reduce(W)))$. That is, process i throws out the f smallest and f largest elements of W. From what is left, i selects only the smallest element and every fth element thereafter. Finally, *val* is set to the average (mean) of the selected elements.

We claim that at any round, all the nonfaulty processes' *vals* are in the range of the nonfaulty processes' *vals* just prior to the round. Moreover, at each round, the width of the multiset of nonfaulty processes' *vals* is reduced by a factor of at least $\lfloor \frac{n-2f-1}{f} \rfloor + 1$. If $n > 3f$, this is greater than 1.

Lemma 7.16 *Suppose that* $val_i = v$ *just after round* r *of an execution of ConvergeApproxAgreement. Then* v *is in the range of the nonfaulty processes' vals just before round* r.

Proof. If W_i is the multiset collected by process i at round r, then there are at most f elements of W_i that are not values sent by nonfaulty processes. Then all the elements of $reduce(W_i)$ are in the range of nonfaulty processes' *vals* just prior to round r. It follows that the same is true for $mean(select(reduce(W_i)))$, which is the new value of val_i. $\qquad \square$

---

[2] As usual, sending to itself is simulated by a local transition.

Lemma 7.17 *Suppose that $val_i = v$ and $val_{i'} = v'$ just after round r of an execution of ConvergeApproxAgreement, where i and i' are both nonfaulty processes. Then*

$$|v - v'| \leq \frac{d}{\left\lfloor \frac{n-2f-1}{f} \right\rfloor + 1},$$

where d is the width of the range of the nonfaulty processes' vals just before round r.

Proof.   Let W_i and $W_{i'}$ be the respective multisets collected by processes i and i' in round r. Let S_i and $S_{i'}$ be the respective multisets $select(reduce(W_i))$ and $select(reduce(W_{i'}))$. Let $c = \lfloor \frac{n-2f-1}{f} \rfloor + 1$; note that c is exactly the number of elements in S_i and in $S_{i'}$. Let the elements of S_i be denoted by $u_1, \ldots, u_c$ and those of $S_{i'}$ by $u'_1, \ldots, u'_c$, both in nondecreasing order. We begin with a claim that says that the reduced multisets differ in at most f elements.

Claim 7.18 $|reduce(W_i) - reduce(W_{i'})| \leq f$.

Proof.   Since nonfaulty processes contribute the same value to both W_i and $W_{i'}$, we have that $|W_i - W_{i'}| \leq f$. We can show that removing a smallest element from both multisets does not increase the number of elements in the difference, and we can show the same for removing a largest element. Using these two facts f times apiece yields the result.   □

Claim 7.18 can be used to show

Claim 7.19 $u_j \leq u'_{j+1}$ and $u'_j \leq u_{j+1}$ for all j, $1 \leq j \leq c-1$.

Proof.   We show the first claim only; the second is symmetric. Note that u_j is the $((j-1)f + 1)$st smallest element of $reduce(W_i)$, and u'_{j+1} is the $(jf + 1)$st smallest element of $reduce(W_{i'})$. Since, by Claim 7.18, there are at most f elements of $reduce(W_{i'})$ that are not elements of $reduce(W_i)$, it must be that $u_j \leq u'_{j+1}$.   □

Now we finish the proof of Lemma 7.17 by calculating the required bound. We have that

$$
\begin{aligned}
|v - v'| &= |mean(S_i) - mean(S_{i'})| \\
&= \frac{1}{c}|(\Sigma_{j=1}^c (u_j - u'_j))| \\
&\leq \frac{1}{c}(\Sigma_{j=1}^c |u_j - u'_j|) \\
&= \frac{1}{c}(\Sigma_{j=1}^c (\max(u_j, u'_j) - \min(u_j, u'_j))).
\end{aligned}
$$

By Claim 7.19, $\max(u_j, u_j') \leq \min(u_{j+1}, u_{j+1}')$ for all j, $1 \leq j \leq c-1$, so this latter expression is less than or equal to

$$\frac{1}{c}(\Sigma_{j=1}^{c-1}(\min(u_{j+1}, u_{j+1}') - \min(u_j, u_j'))) + \frac{1}{c}(\max(u_c, u_c') - \min(u_c, u_c')),$$

which collapses to

$$\frac{1}{c}(\max(u_c, u_c') - \min(u_1, u_1')).$$

But all of the values u_c, u_c', u_1, and u_1' are in the range of the nonfaulty processes' *vals* just before round r, since all elements of $reduce(W_i)$ and $reduce(W_{i'})$ are in this range. So this last expression is less than or equal to $\frac{d}{c}$, as needed.

Termination. We convert *ConvergeApproxAgreement* to a terminating algorithm, that is, one in which all processes eventually decide. (In fact, all processes eventually halt.) Namely, each nonfaulty process uses the range of all the values it receives at round 1 to compute a round number by which it is sure that the *vals* of any two nonfaulty processes will be at most ϵ apart. Each process can do this because it knows the value of ϵ and the guaranteed rate of convergence, and furthermore, it knows that the range of values it receives at round 1 includes the initial values of all the nonfaulty processes. Different nonfaulty processes might compute different round numbers, however.

Any process i that reaches its computed round decides on its own current *val*. After doing this, process i broadcasts its *val* with a special *halting* tag and then halts. After any process j receives a *val* with a *halting* tag from i, it uses this *val* as its message from i, not only for the current round, but also for all future rounds (until j itself decides to halt, on the basis of j's own computed round number).

Although nonfaulty processes might compute different round numbers, it should be clear that the smallest such estimate is correct. Thus, at the time the first nonfaulty process halts, the range of *vals* is already sufficiently small. At subsequent rounds, the range of *vals* of nonfaulty processes never increases, although there is no guarantee that it continues to decrease.

Theorem 7.20 *ConvergeApproxAgreement, with termination added as above, solves the approximate agreement problem for an n-node complete graph, if $n > 3f$.*

Complexity analysis. There is no upper bound depending only on n, f, ϵ and the width of the multiset of nonfaulty processes' initial values, for the time for all nonfaulty processes to decide in the *ConvergeApproxAgreement* algorithm.

This is because faulty processes can send arbitrary values at round 1, which can cause the nonfaulty processes to compute arbitrarily large round numbers for termination.

The exercises discuss bounds on the number of processes and the connectivity needed to solve the approximate agreement problem. We will revisit this problem in Chapter 21, in the asynchronous network setting.

7.3 The Commit Problem

In this, the final section on distributed consensus problems in synchronous systems, we present some of the key ideas about the *distributed database commit* problem. As discussed in Section 5.1, the problem arises when a collection of processes participate in the processing of a database transaction. After this processing, each process arrives at an initial "opinion" about whether the transaction ought to be *committed* (i.e., its results made permanent and released for the use of other transactions) or *aborted* (i.e., its results discarded). A process will generally favor committing the transaction if all its local computation on behalf of that transaction has been successfully completed, and otherwise will favor aborting the transaction. The processes are supposed to communicate and eventually agree on one of the outcomes, *commit* or *abort*. If possible, the outcome should be *commit*.

Solutions to this problem have been designed for real distributed networks, in which there can be a combination of process and link failures. However, the results in Chapter 5 imply that there can be no solution in the case of unlimited link failures. Some limitation must therefore be assumed on message loss.

7.3.1 The Problem

We consider a simplified version of the commit problem, for networks in which there is no message loss, but only process failures. If you are interested in implementing the algorithms in this chapter in a real network, you will have to add other mechanisms, such as repeated retransmissions, to cope with lost messages. We allow any number of process stopping failures.

We assume that the input domain is $\{0, 1\}$, where 1 represents *commit* and 0 represents *abort*. We restrict attention here to the case where the network is a complete graph. The correctness conditions are

Agreement: No two processes decide on different values.

Validity:

1. If any process starts with 0, then 0 is the only possible decision value.

2. If all processes start with 1 and there are no failures, then 1 is the only possible decision value.

Termination: This comes in two flavors. The *weak termination condition* says that if there are no failures then all processes eventually decide. The *strong termination condition* (also known as the *non-blocking condition*) says that all nonfaulty processes eventually decide.

Commit algorithms that satisfy the strong termination condition are sometimes called *non-blocking commit algorithms*, while commit algorithms that satisfy the weak termination condition but not the strong one are sometimes called *blocking commit algorithms*.

Notice that our agreement condition is that *no two processes* decide on different values. Thus, we do not allow even a failed process to decide differently from other processes. We require this because, in practical uses of a commit protocol, a process might fail and later recover. Suppose, for example, that a process i decides *commit* before it fails, and that later, other processes decide *abort*. If process i recovers and retains its *commit* decision, then there would be an inconsistency.

The formal problem statement is similar to two others we have already considered: the coordinated attack problem in Section 5.1 and the agreement problem for stopping failures in Section 6.1. The most important difference between the commit problem and the coordinated attack problem is that we are here considering process failure and not link failure; there is also a difference in the validity condition. The important differences between the commit problem and the stopping agreement problem are, first, the particular choice of validity condition, and, second, the consideration of a weaker notion of termination. Results in Section 6.7 about the stopping agreement problem imply a lower bound of $n - 1$ on the number of rounds needed to solve the commit problem with the strong termination condition. (Note that the proof of Theorem 6.33 still works with the commit validity conditions.)

In the rest of this section, we give versions of two standard practical commit algorithms (for the simplified setting with only process faults). The first, *two-phase commit*, is a blocking algorithm, while the second, *three-phase commit*, is non-blocking. We then give a simple lower bound on the number of messages needed to solve the problem, even if only weak termination is required.

7.3.2   Two-Phase Commit

The best-known practical commit algorithm is *two-phase commit*; without any embellishments, this simple algorithm guarantees only weak termination.

TwoPhaseCommit algorithm:

The algorithm assumes a distinguished process, say process 1.

Round 1: All processes except for process 1 send their initial values to process 1, and any process whose initial value is 0 decides 0. Process 1 collects all these values, plus its own initial value, into a vector. If all positions in this vector are filled in with 1s, then process 1 decides 1. Otherwise—that is, if there is some position in the vector that contains 0 or else some position that is not filled in (because no message was received from the corresponding process)—process 1 decides 0.

Round 2: Process 1 broadcasts its decision to all the other processes. Any process other than process 1 that receives a message at round 2 and has not already decided at round 1 decides on the value it receives in that message.

See Figure 7.4 for an illustration of the communication pattern used in the failure-free runs of *TwoPhaseCommit*.[3]

Theorem 7.21 *TwoPhaseCommit solves the commit problem with the weak termination condition.*

Proof.   Agreement, validity, and weak termination are all easy to show.   □

However, *TwoPhaseCommit* does not satisfy the strong termination condition, that is, it is a blocking algorithm. This is because if process 1 fails before beginning its broadcast in round 2, then no nonfaulty process whose initial value is 1 ever decides. In practice, if process 1 fails, then the remaining processes usually carry out some sort of *termination protocol* among themselves and sometimes manage to decide. For example, if process 1 fails but some other process, i, has already decided 0 in round 1, then process i can inform the remaining nonfaulty processes that its decision is 0, and they can also safely decide 0. But the termination protocol cannot succeed in all cases. For example, suppose that all processes except for 1 start with input 1, but process 1 fails before sending any

---

[3]Our round designation does not correspond exactly to the usual designation of phases for the two-phase commit protocol. Usually, an extra round is added at the beginning, in which process 1 requests the *commit* or *abort* values from the other processes. Phase 1 then consists of this extra round plus our round 1. We do not need the extra round for our simplified model and problem statement.

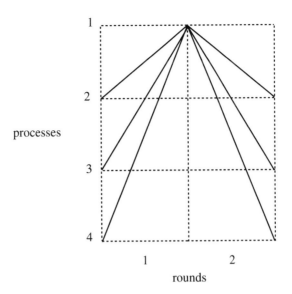

Figure 7.4: Communication pattern in *TwoPhaseCommit*.

messages. Then no other process ever learns process 1's initial value, so, because of the validity condition, no process can decide 1. On the other hand, no process can decide 0, since as far as any other process can tell, it might be that process 1 has already decided 1 just before failing, and the inconsistency would violate the agreement condition.

Complexity analysis. *TwoPhaseCommit* takes only two rounds. Recall that Theorem 6.33 gives a lower bound of $f + 1$ on the number of rounds for stopping agreement. The time bound for *TwoPhaseCommit* does not contradict this lower bound, because *TwoPhaseCommit* satisfies only the weak termination condition. The communication complexity, as measured by the worst-case number of non-*null* messages that are sent in any execution, is $2n - 2$; in particular, this number of messages is sent in a failure-free execution.

7.3.3 Three-Phase Commit

Now we describe the *ThreePhaseCommit algorithm*; this is an embellishment of the *TwoPhaseCommit* algorithm that guarantees strong termination.

The key is simply that process 1 does not decide 1 unless every process that has not yet failed is "ready" to decide 1. Making sure they are ready requires an extra round. We first describe and analyze the first three rounds of the algorithm. The rest of the algorithm, needed to obtain the non-blocking property, is described afterward.

ThreePhaseCommit algorithm, first three rounds:

Round 1: All processes except for 1 send their initial values to process 1, and any process whose initial value is 0 decides 0. Process 1 collects all these values, plus its own initial value, into a vector. If all positions in this vector are filled in with 1s, then process 1 becomes *ready* but does not yet decide. Otherwise—that is, if there is some position that contains 0 or else some position that is not filled in (because no message was received from the corresponding process)—process 1 decides 0.

Round 2: If process 1 has decided 0, then it broadcasts *decide*(0). If not, then process 1 broadcasts *ready*. Any process that receives *decide*(0) decides 0. Any process that receives *ready* becomes *ready*. Process 1 decides 1 if it has not already decided.

Round 3: If process 1 has decided 1, it broadcasts *decide*(1). Any process that receives *decide*(1) decides 1.

See Figure 7.5 for an illustration of the communication pattern used in the failure-free runs of *ThreePhaseCommit*.[4]

Before presenting the termination protocol, we analyze the situation after the first three rounds. We classify the states of each process (failed or not) into four exclusive and exhaustive categories:

1. *dec0:* Those in which the process has decided 0.

2. *dec1:* Those in which the process has decided 1.

3. *ready:* Those in which the process has not decided, but is *ready*.

4. *uncertain:* Those in which the process has not decided and is not *ready*.

The key properties of *ThreePhaseCommit* are expressed by the following lemma. It describes certain combinations of states that cannot coexist.

Lemma 7.22 *After three rounds of ThreePhaseCommit, the following are true:*

1. *If any process's state is in ready or dec1, then all processes' initial values are 1.*

---

[4]Again, our round designation does not correspond exactly to the usual designation of phases for the three-phase commit protocol. An extra request round is usually added at the beginning, as well as some explicit acknowledgments.

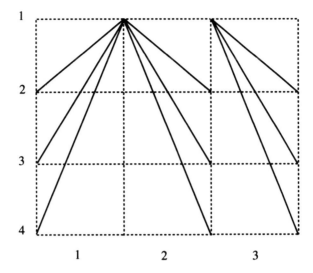

Figure 7.5: Communication pattern in *ThreePhaseCommit*.

2. *If any process's state is in dec0, then no process is in dec1, and no non-failed process is in ready.*

3. *If any process's state is in dec1, then no process is in dec0, and no non-failed process is in uncertain.*

Proof. Straightforward. The most interesting part of the proof is the proof of the third condition. For this, we note that process 1 can only decide 1 at the end of round 2, after it has already broadcast *ready* messages. This means that process 1 knows at the end of round 2 that each other process has either received and processed the *ready*, thereby entering the *ready* state, or else has failed. (The synchrony of the model is important here.) □

Now we can prove that most of the conditions of interest hold after the first three rounds.

Lemma 7.23 *After three rounds of ThreePhaseCommit, the following are true:*

1. *The agreement condition holds.*

2. *The validity condition holds.*

3. *If process 1 has not failed, then all non-failed processes have decided.*

Proof.   The agreement condition follows from Lemma 7.22, as does half of the validity condition—the half that says that if some process starts with 0, then 0 is the only possible decision value. The other half of the validity condition can be proved by inspection.

Finally, if process 1 has not failed, then we claim that every non-failed process has decided. This is because process 1 cannot be prevented from deciding by any actions of the other processes, and once 1 decides, it immediately broadcasts its decision to the other processes, who decide in the same way.   □

These three rounds alone are not enough to solve the non-blocking commit problem, however, because they do not guarantee strong termination. If process 1 does not fail, then every nonfaulty process decides, as noted in Lemma 7.23. But if process 1 fails, it is possible that the other processes might be left in an undecided state. To take care of this case, the remaining processes must execute a *termination protocol* after the first three rounds. The precise details can vary somewhat; we describe one possibility below.

ThreePhaseCommit, termination protocol:

Round 4: All (not yet failed) processes send their current status, either *dec0*, *dec1*, *ready*, or *uncertain*, to process 2. Process 2 collects all these status values, plus its own status, into a vector. Not all the positions in the vector need be filled in—process 2 just ignores those that are not. If the vector contains any *dec0* values and process 2 has not already decided, then process 2 decides 0. If the vector contains any *dec1* values and process 2 has not already decided, then process 2 decides 1. If all the filled-in positions in the vector contain the value *uncertain*, then process 2 decides 0. Otherwise—that is, if the only values in the vector are *uncertain* and *ready* and there is at least one *ready*—process 2 becomes *ready* but does not yet decide.

Round 5: In this and the next round, process 2 behaves similarly to process 1 in rounds 2 and 3. If process 2 has (ever) decided, then it broadcasts its decision, in a *decide* message. If not, then process 2 broadcasts *ready*. Any process that receives *decide(0)* or *decide(1)* and has not already decided, decides 0 or 1, as indicated. Any process that receives *ready* becomes *ready*. Process 2 decides 1 if it has not already decided.

Round 6: If process 2 has decided 1, it broadcasts *decide(1)*. Any process that receives *decide(1)*, and has not already decided, decides 1.

After round 6, the protocol then continues with three similar rounds coordinated by each of processes $3, \ldots, n$.

Theorem 7.24 *The complete ThreePhaseCommit algorithm, including the termination protocol, is a non-blocking commit algorithm.*

Proof Sketch. We first claim that the three properties listed in the statement of Lemma 7.22 hold after *any number* of rounds of the full *ThreePhaseCommit* algorithm, not just after three rounds as claimed. This can be shown by induction on the number of rounds.

Then, agreement and half of the validity condition—that if some process starts with 0, then 0 is the only possible decision value—follow from the extended Lemma 7.22, as before. The other half of the validity condition is true, because if there are no failures, all processes decide within the first three rounds.

We argue the strong termination property. If all processes fail, then this property is vacuously true. Otherwise, suppose that i is a nonfaulty process. Then during the time when i is the coordinator, every nonfaulty process decides. $\square$

Complexity analysis. *ThreePhaseCommit*, in the version presented here, requires $3n$ rounds. Even if we permit all the processes to fail, this is still much higher than the bound of approximately n rounds that is generally achieved by stopping agreement algorithms of the sort studied in Chapter 6. Of course, the stopping agreement algorithms yield a different validity condition, but it is possible to modify them slightly to achieve the commit validity condition. So why are algorithms like *ThreePhaseCommit* considered better in practice?

The main reason is that the *ThreePhaseCommit* algorithm can be tailored to yield low complexity in the failure-free case. If no processes fail, then all processes decide by round 3. Then it is possible to add a simple protocol whereby processes can detect that every process has decided and can then discontinue participation in the rest of the termination protocol. With this addition, the entire algorithm requires only a small constant number of rounds and only $O(n)$ messages.

7.3.4 Lower Bound on the Number of Messages

We close this chapter (and Part I) by considering the number of messages that must be sent in order to solve the commit problem. Recall that the *TwoPhaseCommit* algorithm uses $2n - 2$ messages in the failure-free case. *ThreePhaseCommit* uses somewhat more, but still $O(n)$ if the algorithm is modified to terminate early. In this section, we prove that it is not possible to do better than $2n - 2$ in the failure-free case, even if we are satisfied with a blocking algorithm.

Theorem 7.25 *Any algorithm that solves the commit problem, even with weak termination, uses at least $2n - 2$ messages in the failure-free execution in which all inputs are* 1.

For the rest of this section, we fix a particular commit algorithm A and let α_1 be the failure-free execution of A in which all inputs are 1. Our object is to show that α_1 must contain at least $2n - 2$ messages.

We again use the definition of a *communication pattern* from Section 6.7. This time, we use a communication pattern to describe the set of messages that are sent in a failure-free execution. (We do not assume, as we have done in the past, that all processes send to all other processes at every round.) From any failure-free execution α of A, we extract a communication pattern $patt(\alpha)$ in the obvious way.

We also use the definition of the ordering $\leq_\gamma$ for a communication pattern γ, given in Section 5.2.2, to capture the flow of information between various processes at various times. We say that process i *affects* process j in a communication pattern γ provided that $(i, 0) \leq_\gamma (j, k)$ for some k. The key idea in the lower bound is stated in the following lemma.

Lemma 7.26 *For every two processes i and j, i affects j in $patt(\alpha_1)$.*

Example 7.3.1   Lower bound for commit

> Before proving Lemma 7.26, we give an example to show why it is true. Suppose that α_1 (the failure-free execution of A with all inputs equal to 1) includes exactly the messages depicted in the left-hand diagram in Figure 7.6.
>
> By the validity and weak termination conditions, all processes must eventually decide 1 in α_1. Note that in $patt(\alpha_1)$, process 4 does not affect process 1; let us see what problems arise as a result. Consider an alternative execution α_1', which is the same as α_1 except that process 4's input is 0 and every process fails just after it first gets affected by process 4. Execution α_1' is depicted in the right-hand diagram in Figure 7.6; the failures are indicated by Xs. It is straightforward to show that $\alpha_1 \overset{1}{\sim} \alpha_1'$, which implies that process 1 also decides 1 in α_1'. But this violates the validity condition for α_1', yielding a contradiction.

The proof of Lemma 7.26 uses the same argument as in Example 7.3.1.

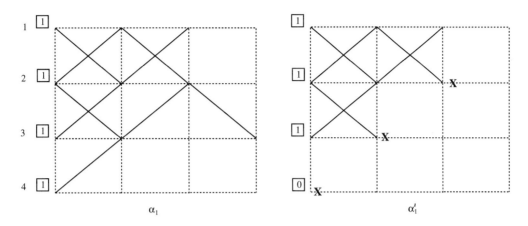

Figure 7.6: Messages sent in α_1 and α_1'.

Proof. By the validity and weak termination conditions, all processes must eventually decide 1 in α_1. Suppose that the lemma is false and fix two processes, i and j, such that i does not affect j in $patt(\alpha_1)$. By definition, it must be that $i \neq j$. Construct α_1' by changing process i's input to 0 and causing every process to fail just after it first gets affected by process i. Then $\alpha_1 \overset{j}{\sim} \alpha_1'$, so process j also decides 1 in α_1'. This violates the validity condition, yielding a contradiction. $\square$

In order to complete the proof of Theorem 7.25, we must simply show that the requirement that every process affect every other process implies that there must be at least $2n - 2$ total messages. We use a lemma about communication patterns:

Lemma 7.27 *Let γ be any communication pattern. If in γ, each of a set of $m \geq 1$ processes affects each of the n processes in the system, then there are at least $n + m - 2$ messages (triples) in γ.*

Proof. By induction on m.

Basis: $m = 1$. Let i be the single process that we have assumed affects each of the n processes. Since i affects all n processes, γ must contain some message to each of the $n - 1$ processes other than i. This is a total of at least $n - 1$ messages, as needed.

Inductive step: We assume the lemma holds for m and show it for $m + 1$. Let I be a set of $m + 1$ processes that affect all n processes in γ. Without loss of generality, we can assume that in round 1, at least one of the processes in I sends a message to some process. For if not, then we could remove all the initial rounds in which no process in I sends a message; in the remaining communication pattern, all processes in I would still affect all n processes. Let i be some process in I that sends a message at round 1 in γ.

Now consider the communication pattern γ', obtained from γ by removing a single round 1 message sent by i. Then all processes in $I - \{i\}$ affect all n processes in γ'. By induction, there are at least $n + m - 2$ messages in γ'. So γ contains at least $n + m - 1 = n + (m + 1) - 2$ messages, as needed. $\square$

Now we can complete the proof of Theorem 7.25.

Proof (of Theorem 7.25).   By Lemma 7.26, for every two processes i and j, i affects j in $patt(\alpha_1)$. Then Lemma 7.27 implies that there are at least $2n - 2$ messages in $patt(\alpha_1)$. $\square$

7.4   Bibliographic Notes

The k-agreement problem has usually been called the "k-set agreement problem" in the literature. The problem was first introduced by Chaudhuri in [73] as a natural extension of the previously well-studied ordinary agreement problem. The *FloodMin* algorithm is taken from the work of Chaudhuri, Herlihy, Lynch, and Tuttle [75] and is based on an algorithm originally designed by Chaudhuri [73]. The lower bound argument for k-agreement is taken from [75, 76, 77]. Background for the algebraic topology used in the lower bound argument appears in Spanier's classical book on algebraic topology [266]. Sperner's Lemma was originally developed by Sperner [267] and is discussed in [266].

The work on approximate agreement is taken from a paper by Dolev, Lynch, Pinter, Stark, and Weihl [98]. Other work on this problem has been done by Fekete [110, 111] and by Attiya, Lynch, and Shavit [24]. The material on the commit problem, as well as the *TwoPhaseCommit* and *ThreePhaseCommit* algorithms, is taken from a book by Bernstein, Hadzilacos, and Goodman on database theory [50]. That book goes much further than this one in discussing practical implementation issues for the protocols, including how to handle recovery of failed processes. The lower bound on the number of messages for commit is taken from work by Dwork and Skeen [106].

7.5   Exercises

7.1. If the *FloodMin* algorithm for k-agreement is run for only $\lfloor \frac{f}{k} \rfloor$ rounds instead of $\lfloor \frac{f}{k} \rfloor + 1$, what is the largest number of different decisions that can be reached by nonfaulty processes?

7.2. Give a good upper bound for the length of sequence $seq(v)$, in the proof of Theorem 7.14. In order to do this, you will need to describe an explicit construction for the sequence.

7.3. Prove that the merge of a sequence of 1-runs is in fact a k-run. This involves showing that the conditions required in the definition of a run are satisfied, as well as the conditions involving the tokens.

7.4. Prove Lemma 7.4.

7.5. Prove Lemma 7.5.

7.6. Prove Lemma 7.6.

7.7. Prove Lemma 7.7.

7.8. Let $n = 5$, $k = f = 2$, and $r = 1$.

    (a) Describe the Bermuda Triangle for these parameter values in detail, as well as its labelling with k-runs and process indices.

    (b) Consider the trivial algorithm A that works as follows: all processes exchange values once, and each chooses the minimum value it receives. Describe the Sperner coloring C_A.

    (c) Can you locate a particular tiny simplex in which three different values are decided upon, for algorithm A?

7.9. Fix any n and f, where $n > 3f$, any ϵ, any $w \in R^{\geq 0}$, and any $r \in \mathbb{N}$. Describe a particular execution of the *ConvergeApproxAgreement* algorithm with termination, for n, f, and ϵ, in which the multiset of nonfaulty processes' initial values has width at most w and in which termination takes more than r rounds.

7.10. *Research Question*: Modify *ConvergeApproxAgreement* so that the time until all processes decide is bounded above by a function of n, f, ϵ, and the width w of the multiset of nonfaulty processes' initial values.

7.11. Suppose that, instead of computing $mean(select(reduce(W)))$ in *ConvergeApproxAgreement*, the processes instead compute one of the following:

    (a) $mean(select(W))$

    (b) $mean(reduce(W))$

    (c) $mean(W)$

Does the algorithm still solve the approximate agreement problem? Why or why not?

7.12. Prove that the approximate agreement problem can be solved in a network graph G, tolerating f Byzantine faults, if and only if both of the following hold:

(a) $n > 3f$

(b) $conn(G) > 2f$

7.13. Design an approximate agreement algorithm for the case of stopping failures.

(a) Try to minimize the number of processes needed, relative to the number of faults.

(b) Try to minimize the number of rounds required.

7.14. Formulate a variant of the approximate agreement problem that uses a fixed number r of rounds and in which ϵ is not predetermined. Each process starts with a real value, as before. After r rounds, the processes should output their final values. The validity condition is the same as before. The object is now to ensure the best possible agreement, expressed as an upper bound on the ratio of the width of the nonfaulty processes' final values to the width of the nonfaulty processes' initial values.

(a) What ratio is achieved by the *ConvergeApproxAgreement* algorithm in this setting?

(b) Prove a lower bound on the achievable ratio, in terms of n, f, and r. (*Hint:* Use chain argument ideas similar to those used in the proof of Theorem 6.33. Your upper and lower bounds probably will not match.)

7.15. Write code for the complete *ThreePhaseCommit* algorithm (including the termination protocol).

7.16. Prove carefully that Lemma 7.22 extends to any number of rounds of *ThreePhaseCommit*.

7.17. Give a careful description of a modification to the *ThreePhaseCommit* algorithm that permits processes to decide and halt quickly in the failure-free case. Your algorithm should use a small constant number of rounds and $O(n)$ messages, in the failure-free case. Prove its correctness.

7.18. Design an algorithm in the style of the stopping agreement algorithms in Chapter 6 that solves the commit problem with strong termination. Try to minimize the number of rounds.

7.19. *Research Question*: Design an algorithm that solves the commit problem with strong termination. Can you simultaneously obtain a worst-case number of rounds that is $n + k$ for some constant k, a small constant number of rounds for deciding and halting in the failure-free case, and a low communication complexity in the failure-free case?

7.20. Fill in all the details of the proof of Lemma 7.26. Where does the proof fail if we do not force any processes to fail when we construct α'_1, but only change the initial value of process i from 1 to 0?

7.21. Design a non-blocking commit algorithm that uses the fewest messages you can manage, for failure-free runs. Can you prove that this number of messages is optimal?

Part II

Asynchronous Algorithms

The second part consists of Chapters 8–22 and is, in fact, the bulk of the book. These chapters make a major shift in computing paradigm, from the lock-step synchronous model studied in Chapters 2–7 to the *asynchronous model*, in which system components take steps at arbitrary speeds.

Like the synchronous model, the asynchronous model is not hard to describe. The subtleties mainly involve *liveness* conditions, for example, requiring that each component keep getting chances to take steps. It is, however, harder to program than the synchronous model because of the extra uncertainty in the order of events. The asynchronous model assumes less about time than is actually guaranteed by typical distributed systems. Thus, algorithms designed for the asynchronous model are general and portable, in that they are guaranteed to run correctly in networks with arbitrary timing behavior.

The first chapter in Part II, Chapter 8, presents a general model for asynchronous systems, the *input/output automaton model*. You can skip this chapter for now if you like and refer back to it as needed. The rest of Part II is divided into two subparts: Chapters 9–13 covering *asynchronous shared memory algorithms*, and Chapters 14–22, covering *asynchronous network algorithms*.

Chapter 8

Modelling II: Asynchronous System Model

The purpose of this chapter is to introduce a formal model for asynchronous computing, the *input/output (I/O) automaton* model. This is a very general model, suitable for describing almost any type of asynchronous concurrent system, including the two types we will study in this book: asynchronous shared memory systems and asynchronous network systems. By itself, the I/O automaton model has very little structure, which allows it to be used for modelling many different types of distributed systems. Additional structure must be added to the basic model to enable it to describe particular types of asynchronous systems. What the model does provide is a precise way of describing and reasoning about system components (e.g., processes or communication channels) that interact with each other and that operate at arbitrary relative speeds.

We begin with the definitions of an I/O automaton and its execution. We then define a *composition operation* by which I/O automata can be combined to form a larger automaton representing a concurrent system. We show that this composition operation has the nice properties that it should. Then we introduce the important notion of *fairness*, which specifies that all the components in a system get "fair" turns to perform steps every so often. Fairness represents a limitation on the arbitrary relative speeds of system components—it rules out the possibility that some components are permanently denied turns to take steps. We show how fairness interacts with the composition operation. The rest of the chapter describes some conventions for specifying problems to be solved by systems described as I/O automata, as well as some proof methods that are useful for showing that the systems do in fact solve the problems.

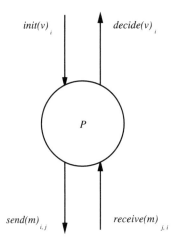

Figure 8.1: A process I/O automaton.

This chapter is intended to be used as a reference for methods of modelling asynchronous systems—not only the systems described in this book, but many others as well. You need not read this chapter carefully at this point. Instead, we suggest that you begin reading some of the later algorithm chapters, such as Chapters 10, 11, 12, and 15, returning to this chapter (as well as to Chapters 9 and 14) as needed, to supply the formal foundation.

8.1   I/O Automata

An I/O automaton models a distributed system component that can interact with other system components. It is a simple type of state machine in which the transitions are associated with named *actions*. The actions are classified as either *input, output,* or *internal*. The inputs and outputs are used for communication with the automaton's environment, while the internal actions are visible only to the automaton itself. The input actions are assumed not to be under the automaton's control—they just arrive from the outside—while the automaton itself specifies what output and internal actions should be performed.

An example of a typical I/O automaton is a process in an asynchronous distributed system. The interface of a typical process automaton with its environment is depicted in Figure 8.1. The automaton P_i is drawn as a circle, with incoming arrows labelled by input actions and outgoing arrows labelled by output actions. Internal actions are not shown. The depicted automaton receives inputs of the form $init(v)_i$ from the outside world, which are supposed to represent the receipt of an input value v. It conveys outputs of the form $decide(v)_i$,

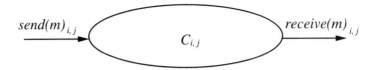

Figure 8.2: A channel I/O automaton.

which are supposed to represent a decision of v. In order to reach a decision, process P_i may want to communicate with other processes using a message system. Its interface to the message system consists of output actions of the form $send(m)_{i,j}$, which represents process P_i sending a message with contents m to process P_j, and input actions of the form $receive(m)_{j,i}$, which represents process P_i receiving a message with contents m from process P_j. When the automaton performs any of the indicated actions (or any internal action), it may also change state.

Another example of a typical I/O automaton is a FIFO message channel. A typical channel automaton, named $C_{i,j}$, is depicted in Figure 8.2. Its input actions are of the form $send(m)_{i,j}$, and its outputs are of the form $receive(m)_{i,j}$. In the usual way of describing a distributed system using I/O automata, a collection of process automata and channel automata are composed, matching outputs of one automaton with same-named inputs of other automata. Thus, a $send_{i,j}$ output performed by process P_i is identified with (i.e., performed together with) a $send_{i,j}$ input performed by channel $C_{i,j}$. The important thing to note is that the various actions are performed one at a time, in an unpredictable order. This is in contrast with synchronous systems, in which all the processes send messages at once and then all receive messages at once, at each round of computation.

Formally, the first thing that gets specified for an I/O automaton is its "signature," which is simply a description of its input, output, and internal actions. We assume a universal set of *actions*. A *signature* S is a triple consisting of three disjoint sets of actions: the *input actions*, $in(S)$, the *output actions*, $out(S)$, and the *internal actions*, $int(S)$. We define the *external actions*, $ext(S)$, to be $in(S) \cup out(S)$; the *locally controlled actions*, $local(S)$, to be $out(S) \cup int(S)$; and $acts(S)$ to be all the actions of S. The *external signature*, $extsig(S)$, is defined to be the signature $(in(S), out(S), \emptyset)$. We will often refer to the external signature as the *external interface*.

An *I/O automaton* A, which we also call simply an *automaton*, consists of five components:

- $sig(A)$, a signature

- $states(A)$, a (not necessarily finite) set of *states*

- $start(A)$, a nonempty subset of $states(A)$ known as the *start states* or *initial states*

- $trans(A)$, a *state-transition relation*, where $trans(A) \subseteq states(A) \times acts(sig(A)) \times states(A)$; this must have the property that for every state s and every input action π, there is a transition $(s, \pi, s') \in trans(A)$

- $tasks(A)$, a *task partition*, which is an equivalence relation on $local(sig(A))$ having at most countably many equivalence classes

We use $acts(A)$ as shorthand for $acts(sig(A))$, and similarly $in(A)$, and so on. We say that A is *closed* if it has no inputs, that is, if $in(A) = \emptyset$.

This definition looks somewhat similar to that of a *process* in the synchronous network model in Chapter 2. However, the signature allows for more general types of actions than just the message-sending and message-receipt actions modelled in the synchronous case. As for the set of process states in the synchronous network model, the set of states need not be finite. This generality is important, since it permits us to model systems that have unbounded data structures such as counters and unbounded length queues. As in the synchronous case, we allow multiple start states so that we can include some input information in the start states.

We call an element (s, π, s') of $trans(A)$ a *transition*, or *step*, of A. The transition (s, π, s') is called an *input transition*, *output transition*, and so on, based on whether the action π is an input action, output action, and so on. Unlike in the synchronous model, the transitions are not necessarily associated with the receipt of a collection of messages; they can be associated with arbitrary actions.

If for a particular state s and action π, A has some transition of the form (s, π, s'), then we say that π is *enabled* in s. Since every input action is required to be enabled in every state, automata are said to be *input-enabled*. The input-enabling assumption means that the automaton is not able to somehow "block" input actions from occurring. This assumption means, for example, that a process has to be prepared to cope in some way with *any* possible message value when a message arrives. We say that state s is *quiescent* if the only actions that are enabled in s are input actions.

You might think that the input-enabling property is too strong a restriction to impose on a general model, because many system components are designed to *expect* certain inputs only to occur at designated times. For example, an automaton designed to model a resource-allocation system (as studied in Chapter 11) might expect a user not to submit two requests in a row, before the system has granted the first request. However, there are other ways of modelling such restrictions on the environment, without requiring that the environment actually be barred from performing the input. For example, in the resource-allocation example, we might say that the environment is not expected to submit a second request before receiving a response to the first, but that we do not constrain the behavior of the system in the case of such an unexpected input. Or, we might require the system to detect the unexpected input and respond with an error message.

There are two major advantages of having the input-enabling property. First, a serious source of errors in the development of system components is the failure to specify what the component does in the face of unexpected inputs. Using a model that requires consideration of arbitrary inputs is helpful in eliminating such errors. And second, use of input-enabling makes the basic theory of the model work out nicely; in particular, input-enabling makes it reasonable to use simple notions of external behavior for an automaton, based on sequences of external actions. (Theorem 8.4 is an example of a basic result that fails if we do not assume input-enabling.)

The fifth component of the I/O automaton definition, the task partition *tasks*(*A*), should be thought of as an abstract description of "tasks," or "threads of control," within the automaton. This partition is used to define fairness conditions on an execution of the automaton—conditions that say that the automaton must continue, during its execution, to give fair turns to each of its tasks. This is useful for modelling a system component that performs more than one job—for example, participating in an ongoing algorithm while at the same time periodically reporting status information to its environment. It is also useful when several automata are composed to yield one larger automaton representing the entire system. The partition is then used to specify that the automata being composed all continue to take steps in the composed system. Another use of the partition is in modelling asynchronous shared memory algorithms, as you will see in Chapter 9. We will usually refer to the task-partition classes as just *tasks*.

We sometimes say that a task *C* is *enabled* in a state *s*; this is just a short way of saying that some action in *C* is enabled in *s*.

We give an example of a simple I/O automaton. Here and in most of our descriptions of I/O automata, the transition relation is described in a *precondition-effect* style. This style groups together all the transitions that involve each particular type of action into a single piece of code. The code specifies the conditions under which the action is permitted to occur, as a predicate on the pre-state *s*. Then it describes the changes that occur as a result of the action, in the form of a simple program that is applied to *s* to yield *s'*. The entire piece of code gets executed indivisibly, as a single transition. Grouping the transitions according to their actions tends to produce concise code, because the transitions involving each action typically involve only a small portion of the state.

Programs written in precondition-effect style normally use only very simple control structures. This tends to make the translation from programs to I/O automata transparent, which makes it easier to reason formally about the automata.

Example 8.1.1   Channel I/O automaton

As an example of an I/O automaton, consider a communication channel automaton $C_{i,j}$. Let M be a fixed message alphabet. First we give the signature, $sig(C_{i,j})$. Here and elsewhere, we use the convention that if we do not mention a signature component (usually, the internal actions), then that set of actions is empty.

Signature:

Input: Output:
    $send(m)_{i,j}, m \in M$ $receive(m)_{i,j}, m \in M$

The states, $states(C_{i,j})$, and the start states, $start(C_{i,j})$, are most conveniently described in terms of a list of state variables and their initial values. This is just as in the synchronous setting.

States:
queue, a FIFO queue of elements of M, initially empty

The transitions of $C_{i,j}$ are described by the following code:

Transitions:

$send(m)_{i,j}$ $receive(m)_{i,j}$
  Effect: Precondition:
    add m to *queue* m is first on *queue*
                 Effect:
                   remove first element of *queue*

This code should be self-explanatory: the *send* action is allowed to occur at any time and has the effect of adding the message to the end of *queue*, while the *receive* action can only occur when the message in question is at the front of *queue*, and has the effect of removing it.

The task partition, $tasks(C_{i,j})$, groups together all the *receive* actions into a single task. That is, the job of receiving (i.e., delivering) messages is thought of as a single task.

Tasks:
$\{receive(m)_{i,j} : m \in M\}$

Example 8.1.2   Process I/O automaton

As a second example of an I/O automaton, consider a process automaton P_i. This automaton has the external interface described below. Here, V is a fixed value set, *null* is a special value not in V, and f is a fixed function, $f : V^n \to V$.

Signature:

Input:
  $init(v)_i$, $v \in V$
  $receive(v)_{j,i}$, $v \in V$, $1 \leq j \leq n$, $j \neq i$

Output:
  $decide(v)_i$, $v \in V$
  $send(v)_{i,j}$, $v \in V$, $1 \leq j \leq n$, $j \neq i$

The states and start states are as follows:

States:
val, a vector indexed by $\{1, \dots, n\}$ of elements in $V \cup \{null\}$, all initially *null*

The transitions are as follows:

Transitions:

$init(v)_i$, $v \in V$
  Effect:
    $val(i) := v$

$send(v)_{i,j}$, $v \in V$
  Precondition:
    $val(i) = v$
  Effect:
    none

$receive(v)_{j,i}$, $v \in V$
  Effect:
    $val(j) := v$

$decide(v)_i$, $v \in V$
  Precondition:
    for all j, $1 \leq j \leq n$:
      $val(j) \neq null$
      $v = f(val(1), \dots, val(n))$
  Effect:
    none

Thus, the *init* action causes P_i to fill in the designated value in its own position in the *val* vector, while the *receive* action causes it to fill in another position. These values can be updated any number of times, by means of multiple *init* or *receive* actions. P_i is allowed to send its own value any number of times on any channel. P_i is also allowed to decide any number of times, based on new applications of f to its vector.

The task partition, $tasks(P_i)$, contains n tasks: one for all the $send_{i,j}$ actions for each $j \neq i$, and one for all the *decide* actions. Thus, sending on each channel is regarded as a single task, as is reporting decisions.

Tasks:
for every $j \neq i$:
  $\{send(v)_{i,j} : v \in V\}$
$\{decide(v)_i : v \in V\}$

Now we describe how an I/O automaton A executes. An *execution fragment* of A is either a finite sequence, $s_0, \pi_1, s_1, \pi_2, \ldots, \pi_r, s_r$, or an infinite sequence, $s_0, \pi_1, s_1, \pi_2, \ldots, \pi_r, s_r, \ldots$, of alternating states and actions of A such that $(s_k, \pi_{k+1}, s_{k+1})$ is a transition of A for every $k \geq 0$. Note that if the sequence is finite, it must end with a state. An execution fragment beginning with a start state is called an *execution*. We denote the set of executions of A by $execs(A)$. A state is said to be *reachable* in A if it is the final state of a finite execution of A.

If α is a finite execution fragment of A and α' is any execution fragment of A that begins with the last state of α, then we write $\alpha \cdot \alpha'$ to represent the sequence obtained by concatenating α and α', eliminating the duplicate occurrence of the last state of α. Clearly, $\alpha \cdot \alpha'$ is also an execution fragment of A.

Sometimes we will be interested in observing only the external behavior of an I/O automaton. Thus, the *trace* of an execution α of A, denoted by $trace(\alpha)$, is the subsequence of α consisting of all the external actions. We say that β is a *trace* of A if β is the trace of an execution of A. We denote the set of traces of A by $traces(A)$.

Example 8.1.3   Executions

The following are three executions of the automaton $C_{i,j}$ described in Example 8.1.1 (assuming that the message alphabet M is equal to the set $\{1, 2\}$). Here, we indicate the states by putting the sequences in *queue* in brackets; λ denotes the empty sequence.

$$[\lambda], send(1)_{i,j}, [1], receive(1)_{i,j}, [\lambda], send(2)_{i,j}, [2], receive(2)_{i,j}, [\lambda]$$

$$[\lambda], send(1)_{i,j}, [1], receive(1)_{i,j}, [\lambda], send(2)_{i,j}, [2]$$

$$[\lambda], send(1)_{i,j}, [1], send(1)_{i,j}, [11], send(1)_{i,j}, [111], \ldots$$

The last two are allowed even though they contain messages that are sent but never received. This is because we have (so far) placed no restrictions on executions saying that enabled actions must occur. In Section 8.3 we introduce fairness requirements, which allow us to express such restrictions.

8.2   Operations on Automata

In this section, we define the operation of *composition* and the operation of *hiding output actions* for I/O automata.

8.2.1 Composition

The composition operation allows an automaton representing a complex system to be constructed by composing automata representing individual system components. The composition identifies actions with the same name in different component automata. When any component automaton performs a step involving π, so do all component automata that have π in their signatures.

We impose certain restrictions on the automata that may be composed. First, since internal actions of an automaton A are intended to be unobservable by any other automaton B, we do not allow A to be composed with B unless the internal actions of A are disjoint from the actions of B. (Otherwise, A's performance of an internal action could force B to take a step.) Second, in order that the composition operation might satisfy nice properties (such as Theorem 8.4 below), we establish a convention that at most one component automaton "controls" the performance of any given action; that is, we do not allow A and B to be composed unless the sets of output actions of A and B are disjoint. Third, we do not preclude the possibility of composing a countably infinite collection of automata, but we do require in this case that each action must be an action of only finitely many of the component automata. This latter restriction is needed because otherwise Theorem 8.3 fails.

Why do we not simply rule out the composition of infinitely many automata? After all, physical computer systems consist of only finitely many components (computers, message channels, etc.). The reason for allowing infinite composition is that I/O automata are used to model *logical systems* as well as *physical systems*. A logical system can consist of a large number of logical components, intended to be implemented on a physical system with fewer components. In fact, some logical systems allow components to be created dynamically, during execution—possibly infinitely many components over the course of an infinite execution. (For example, database systems can allow the creation of new transaction instances while the system is executing.) The way to model component creation using I/O automata is to imagine that all possible components that might ever be created are actually present from the beginning but have special *wakeup* input actions that wake them up when they are supposed to be created. With this modelling trick, the ordinary composition operator is adequate for describing the way the dynamically created components interact with the rest of the system. But it is necessary to allow infinitely many components to be combined.

Formally, we define a countable collection $\{S_i\}_{i \in I}$ of signatures to be *compatible* if for all $i, j \in I$, $i \neq j$, all of the following hold:

1. $int(S_i) \cap acts(S_j) = \emptyset$

2. $out(S_i) \cap out(S_j) = \emptyset$

3. No action is contained in infinitely many sets $acts(S_i)$

We say that a collection of automata is *compatible* if their signatures are compatible.

When we compose a collection of automata, output actions of the components become output actions of the composition, internal actions of the components become internal actions of the composition, and actions that are inputs to some components but outputs of none become input actions of the composition. Formally, the *composition* $S = \prod_{i \in I} S_i$ of a countable compatible collection of signatures $\{S_i\}_{i \in I}$ is defined to be the signature with

- $out(S) = \cup_{i \in I} out(S_i)$

- $int(S) = \cup_{i \in I} int(S_i)$

- $in(S) = \cup_{i \in I} in(S_i) - \cup_{i \in I} out(S_i)$

Now the *composition* $A = \prod_{i \in I} A_i$ of a countable, compatible collection of I/O automata $\{A_i\}_{i \in I}$ can be defined. It is the automaton defined as follows:[1]

- $sig(A) = \prod_{i \in I} sig(A_i)$

- $states(A) = \prod_{i \in I} states(A_i)$

- $start(A) = \prod_{i \in I} start(A_i)$

- $trans(A)$ is the set of triples (s, π, s') such that, for all $i \in I$, if $\pi \in acts(A_i)$, then $(s_i, \pi, s_i') \in trans(A_i)$; otherwise $s_i = s_i'$

- $tasks(A) = \cup_{i \in I} tasks(A_i)$

Thus, the states and start states of the composition automaton are vectors of states and start states, respectively, of the component automata. The transitions of the composition are obtained by allowing all the component automata that have a particular action π in their signature to participate simultaneously in steps involving π, while all the other component automata do nothing. The task partition of the composition's locally controlled actions is formed by taking the union of the components' task partitions; that is, each equivalence class of each

---

[1]The Π notation in the definition of $start(A)$ and $states(A)$ refers to the ordinary Cartesian product, while the Π notation in the definition of $sig(A)$ refers to the composition operation just defined, for signatures. Also, we are here using the notation s_i to denote the *i*th component of the state vector s.

component automaton becomes an equivalence class of the composition. This means that the task structure of individual components is preserved when the components are composed. Notice that since the automata A_i are input-enabled, so is their composition. It follows that $\prod_{i \in I} A_i$ is actually an I/O automaton.

When I is a finite set, we sometimes use the infix operation symbol $\times$ to denote composition. For instance, if $I = \{1, \ldots, n\}$, we sometimes denote $\prod_{i \in I} A_i$ by $A_1 \times \cdots \times A_n$.

Notice that an action π that is an output of one component and an input of another is classified as an output action in the composition, not as an internal action. This is because we want to permit the possibility of further communication using π. For example, suppose that automaton A has π as an output action, while automata B and C both have π as input actions. Thus, π is essentially a broadcast action from A to both B and C in the composition $A \times B \times C$ of the three automata. We would like to be able to think about this composition in a modular way, first constructing $A \times B$, then composing the result with C. According to the way we have defined composition, $A \times B \times C$ is actually isomorphic to $(A \times B) \times C$, the result of first composing A and B, then composing the result with C. But if π were classified as internal in the composition $A \times B$, then we no longer would have this modularity: the composition $A \times B$ could not even be composed with C, since the first compatibility condition would be violated.

It is possible to "hide" actions that are used for communication between components, thereby preventing them from being used for further communication. This is done using the hiding operation defined in Section 8.2.2 in addition to the composition operation.

Example 8.2.1   Composition of automata

Consider a fixed index set $I = \{1, \ldots, n\}$ and let A be the composition of all the process automata P_i, $i \in I$, from Example 8.1.2 and all the channel automata $C_{i,j}$, $i, j \in I$, from Example 8.1.1. In order to compose them, we must assume that the message alphabet M for the channel automata contains the value set V for the process automata. Figure 8.3 depicts the "architecture" for the special case where $n = 3$.

The resulting composition is a single automaton representing a distributed system. The state of the system consists of a state for each process (each a vector of values, one per process), plus a state for each channel (each a queue of messages in transit). Each transition of the system involves one of the following:

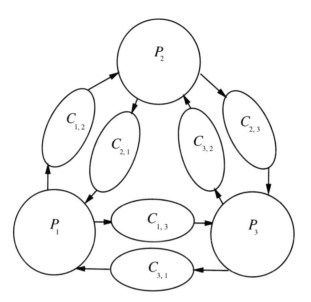

Figure 8.3: Composition of P_is and $C_{i,j}$s.

1. An $init(v)_i$ input action, which deposits a value in P_i's $val(i)$ variable, $val(i)_i{}^2$

2. A $send(v)_{i,j}$ output action, by which P_i's value $val(i)_i$ gets put into channel $C_{i,j}$

3. A $receive(v)_{i,j}$ output action, by which the first message in $C_{i,j}$ is removed and simultaneously placed into P_j's variable $val(i)_j$

4. A $decide(v)_i$ output action, by which P_i announces its current computed value

A sample trace of this composition, for $n = 2$, where the value set V is $\mathbb{N}$ and where f is addition, is

$$init(2)_1,\ init(1)_2,\ send(2)_{1,2},\ receive(2)_{1,2},\ send(1)_{2,1},$$
$$receive(1)_{2,1},\ init(4)_1,\ init(0)_2,\ decide(5)_1,\ decide(2)_2$$

In the unique system state that is reachable using this trace, P_1 has val vector $(4, 1)$ and P_2 has val vector $(2, 0)$, and both channels are empty. Of course, there are many other traces that can arise in executions of this composed system.

---

[2] As in the chapters on the synchronous model, we use the convention of subscripting a variable by the index of the process at which the variable resides.

We close this subsection with three basic results that relate the executions and traces of a composition to those of the component automata. The first says that an execution or trace of a composition "projects" to yield executions or traces of the component automata. Given an execution, $\alpha = s_0, \pi_1, s_1, \ldots,$ of A, let $\alpha | A_i$ be the sequence obtained by deleting each pair π_r, s_r for which π_r is not an action of A_i and replacing each remaining s_r by $(s_r)_i$, that is, automaton A_i's piece of the state s_r. Also, given a trace β of A (or, more generally, any sequence of actions), let $\beta | A_i$ be the subsequence of β consisting of all the actions of A_i in β. We also use the $|$ notation to represent the subsequence of a sequence β of actions consisting of all the actions in a given set in β.

Theorem 8.1 *Let $\{A_i\}_{i \in I}$ be a compatible collection of automata and let $A = \prod_{i \in I} A_i$.*

1. *If $\alpha \in execs(A)$, then $\alpha | A_i \in execs(A_i)$ for every $i \in I$.*

2. *If $\beta \in traces(A)$, then $\beta | A_i \in traces(A_i)$ for every $i \in I$.*

Proof. The proof is left as an exercise. $\qquad\qquad\qquad\qquad\qquad$ $\square$

The other two are converses of Theorem 8.1. The next theorem says that, under certain conditions, executions of component automata can be "pasted together" to form an execution of the composition.

Theorem 8.2 *Let $\{A_i\}_{i \in I}$ be a compatible collection of automata and let $A = \prod_{i \in I} A_i$. Suppose α_i is an execution of A_i for every $i \in I$, and suppose β is a sequence of actions in $ext(A)$ such that $\beta | A_i = trace(\alpha_i)$ for every $i \in I$. Then there is an execution α of A such that $\beta = trace(\alpha)$ and $\alpha_i = \alpha | A_i$ for every $i \in I$.*

Proof. The proof is left as an exercise. $\qquad\qquad\qquad\qquad\qquad$ $\square$

The final theorem says that traces of component automata can also be pasted together to form a trace of the composition.

Theorem 8.3 *Let $\{A_i\}_{i \in I}$ be a compatible collection of automata and let $A = \prod_{i \in I} A_i$. Suppose β is a sequence of actions in $ext(A)$. If $\beta | A_i \in traces(A_i)$ for every $i \in I$, then $\beta \in traces(A)$.*

Proof. The proof is left as an exercise. $\qquad\qquad\qquad\qquad\qquad$ $\square$

Theorem 8.3 implies that in order to show that a sequence is a trace of a system, it is enough to show that its projection on each individual system component is a trace of that component.

8.2.2   Hiding

We now define an operation that "hides" output actions of an I/O automaton by reclassifying them as internal actions. This prevents them from being used for further communication and means that they are no longer included in traces.

We first define the hiding operation for signatures: if S is a signature and $\Sigma \subseteq out(S)$, then $hide_\Sigma(S)$ is defined to be the new signature S', where $in(S') = in(S)$, $out(S') = out(S) - \Sigma$, and $int(S') = int(S) \cup \Sigma$.

The hiding operation for I/O automata is now easy to define: if A is an automaton and $\Phi \subseteq out(A)$, then $hide_\Phi(A)$ is the automaton A' obtained from A by replacing $sig(A)$ with $sig(A') = hide_\Phi(sig(A))$.

8.3   Fairness

In distributed systems, we are usually interested only in those executions of a composition in which all components get fair turns to perform steps. In this section, we define an appropriate notion of fairness for I/O automata.

Recall that each I/O automaton comes equipped with a partition of its locally controlled actions; each equivalence class in the partition represents some task that the automaton is supposed to perform. Our notion of fairness is that each task gets infinitely many opportunities to perform one of its actions.

Formally, an execution fragment α of an I/O automaton A is said to be *fair* if the following conditions hold for each class C of *tasks*(A):

1. If α is finite, then C is not enabled in the final state of α.

2. If α is infinite, then α contains either infinitely many events from C or infinitely many occurrences of states in which C is not enabled.

Here and elsewhere, we use the term *event* to denote the occurrence of an action in a sequence, for example, an execution or a trace.

We can understand the definition of fairness as saying that infinitely often, each task (i.e., equivalence class) C is given a turn. Whenever this happens, either an action of C gets performed or no action from C could possibly be performed since no such action is enabled. We can think of a finite fair execution as an execution at the end of which the automaton repeatedly gives turns to all the tasks in round-robin order, but never succeeds in performing any action since none are enabled in the final state.

We denote the set of fair executions of A by *fairexecs*(A). We say that β is a *fair trace* of A if β is the trace of a fair execution of A, and we denote the set of fair traces of A by *fairtraces*(A).

Example 8.3.1　Fairness

In Example 8.1.3, the first execution given is fair, because no *receive* action is enabled in its final state. The second is not fair, because it is finite and a *receive* action is enabled in the final state. The third is also not fair, because it is infinite, contains no *receive* events, and has *receive* actions enabled at every point after the first step.

Example 8.3.2　Fairness

To further illustrate the fairness definition, consider the following *Clock* I/O automaton, representing a discrete clock.

Clock automaton:

Signature:

Input:　　　　　　　Internal:
　request　　　　　　*tick*
Output:
　$clock(t)$, $t \in \mathbb{N}$

States:

$counter \in \mathbb{N}$, initially 0
flag, a Boolean, initially *false*

Transitions:

tick　　　　　　　　　　　　*clock(t)*
　Precondition:　　　　　　　　Precondition:
　　true　　　　　　　　　　　*flag = true*
　Effect:　　　　　　　　　　　*counter = t*
　　$counter := counter + 1$　　Effect:
　　　　　　　　　　　　　　　flag := false

request
　Effect:
　　flag := true

Tasks:

$\{tick\}$
$\{clock(t) : t \in \mathbb{N}\}$

The *Clock* automaton simply "ticks" forever, incrementing a counter. In addition, if a request arrives, *Clock* responds (in a separate step) with the current value of the counter. The following is the sequence of actions in a fair execution of *Clock*:

tick, tick, tick, ...

The following is the action sequence of an execution that is not fair:

tick, tick, tick

In fact, *Clock* has no finite fair executions, since *tick* is always enabled. The following is fair:

tick, tick, request, tick, tick, clock(4), tick, tick, . . . ,

since once *Clock* has responded to the single request, no further *clock* action is enabled. Finally, the following is not fair:

tick, tick, request, tick, tick, tick, . . . ,

because after the *request* event, the *clock* task remains enabled but no *clock* action ever occurs.

We can prove the following analogues to Theorems 8.1–8.3:

Theorem 8.4 *Let $\{A_i\}_{i \in I}$ be a compatible collection of automata and let $A = \prod_{i \in I} A_i$.*

1. *If $\alpha \in fairexecs(A)$, then $\alpha | A_i \in fairexecs(A_i)$ for every $i \in I$.*

2. *If $\beta \in fairtraces(A)$, then $\beta | A_i \in fairtraces(A_i)$ for every $i \in I$.*

Theorem 8.5 *Let $\{A_i\}_{i \in I}$ be a compatible collection of automata and let $A = \prod_{i \in I} A_i$. Suppose α_i is a fair execution of A_i for every $i \in I$, and suppose β is a sequence of actions in $ext(A)$ such that $\beta | A_i = trace(\alpha_i)$ for every $i \in I$. Then there is a fair execution α of A such that $\beta = trace(\alpha)$ and $\alpha_i = \alpha | A_i$ for every $i \in I$.*

Theorem 8.6 *Let $\{A_i\}_{i \in I}$ be a compatible collection of automata and let $A = \prod_{i \in I} A_i$. Suppose β is a sequence of actions in $ext(A)$. If $\beta | A_i \in fairtraces(A_i)$ for every $i \in I$, then $\beta \in fairtraces(A)$.*

Proofs.   The proofs are left as exercises.   □

Theorems 8.1–8.3 and Theorems 8.4–8.6 make it possible to reason in a modular way about the behavior of a distributed system modelled as a composition.

Example 8.3.3   Fairness

We consider the fair executions of the system of three processes and three channels in Example 8.2.1. In every fair execution, every message that is sent is eventually received. Also, in every fair execution containing at least one $init_i$ event for each i, each process sends infinitely many messages to each other process and each process performs infinitely many *decide* steps.

On the other hand, in every fair execution that does not contain at least one *init* event for each process, no process ever performs a *decide* step. Note that fairness imposes no requirements on the occurrence of *init* events—the number of $init_i$ events involving each P_i can be finite (possibly zero) or infinite.

We close this section with a theorem that says that every finite execution (or trace) can be extended to a fair execution (or trace).

Theorem 8.7 *Let A be any I/O automaton.*

1. *If α is a finite execution of A, then there is a fair execution of A that starts with α.*

2. *If β is a finite trace of A, then there is a fair trace of A that starts with β.*

3. *If α is a finite execution of A and β is any (finite or infinite) sequence of input actions of A, then there is a fair execution $\alpha \cdot \alpha'$ of A such that the sequence of input actions in α' is exactly β.*

4. *If β is a finite trace of A and β' is any (finite or infinite) sequence of input actions of A, then there is a fair execution $\alpha \cdot \alpha'$ of A such that $trace(\alpha) = \beta$ and such that the sequence of input actions in α' is exactly β'.*

Proof.   The proof is left as an exercise.   □

8.4   Inputs and Outputs for Problems

Problems to be solved by I/O automata normally have some type of input and output; we must model this somehow. In the synchronous model, we generally modelled such input and output in terms of special state variables, assuming that inputs are built into designated variables in the start states and that outputs appear in designated write-once variables. It is possible to do the same thing in the asynchronous setting. However, since I/O automata can have input and output actions, it is usually more natural to model inputs and outputs of systems directly, in terms of input and output actions.

8.5   Properties and Proof Methods

I/O automata can be used not only to describe asynchronous systems precisely, but also to formulate and prove precise claims about what the systems do. In this section, we describe some of the types of properties that are typically proved about asynchronous systems, as well as some of the methods that are typically used to prove them.

In our chapters on asynchronous algorithms, Chapters 10–13 and 15–22, we use the methods described here (plus some ad hoc arguments) to prove properties of asynchronous algorithms. Whether the arguments are done using one of the typical methods or not, they can all be made rigorous using I/O automata.

8.5.1   Invariant Assertions

The most fundamental type of property to be proved is an *invariant assertion*, or just *invariant*, for short. In this book, we define an invariant assertion of an automaton A to be any property that is true of all reachable states of A.

Invariants are typically proved by induction on the number of steps in an execution leading to the state in question. More generally, it is possible to prove invariants one (or a few) at a time, making use of the invariants previously proved when carrying out subsequent inductive proofs.

Recall that we also used invariant assertions to prove properties of synchronous algorithms. In the synchronous setting, invariants are proved about the system state after an arbitrary number of *rounds*. On the other hand, in the asynchronous setting, invariants are proved about the system state after an arbitrary number of *steps*. Since the granularity of the reasoning is much smaller for asynchronous algorithms, the arguments are typically longer, more detailed, and more difficult.

8.5.2   Trace Properties

An I/O automaton can be viewed as a "black box" from the point of view of a user. What the user sees is just the traces of the automaton's executions (or fair executions). Some of the properties to be proved about I/O automata are naturally formulated as properties of their traces or fair traces.

Formally, a *trace property* P consists of the following:

- $sig(P)$, a signature containing no internal actions

- $traces(P)$, a set of (finite or infinite) sequences of actions in $acts(sig(P))$

That is, a trace property specifies both an external interface and a set (in other words, a property) of sequences observed at that interface. We write $acts(P)$ as shorthand for $acts(sig(P))$, and similarly $in(P)$, and so on.

The statement that an I/O automaton A satisfies a trace property P can mean either of (at least) two different things:

1. $extsig(A) = sig(P)$ and $traces(A) \subseteq traces(P)$

2. $extsig(A) = sig(P)$ and $fairtraces(A) \subseteq traces(P)$

In either case, the intuitive idea is that every external behavior that can be produced by A is permitted by property P. Note that we do not require the opposite inclusion—that every trace of P can actually be exhibited by A. Nevertheless, the given inclusion statements are not trivial: the fact that A is input-enabled ensures that $fairtraces(A)$ (and so $traces(A)$) contains a response by A to each possible sequence of input actions. If $fairtraces(A) \subseteq traces(P)$, then all of the resulting sequences must be included in the property P.

Since there is some ambiguity in what we mean by an automaton "satisfying a trace property," we will say explicitly what we mean each time the issue arises.

Example 8.5.1 Automata and trace properties

Consider automata and trace properties with input set $\{0\}$ and output set $\{1, 2\}$. First suppose that $traces(P)$ is the set of sequences over $\{0, 1, 2\}$ that include at least one 1. Then $fairtraces(A) \subseteq traces(P)$ means that in every fair execution, A must output at least one 1. It is easy to design an I/O automaton for which this is the case—for example, it can include a task whose entire job is to output 1. The fairness condition is used to ensure that this task actually does get a chance to output 1. On the other hand, there does not exist any automaton A for which $traces(A) \subseteq traces(P)$, because $traces(A)$ always includes the empty string λ, which does not contain a 1.

Now suppose that $traces(P)$ is the set of sequences over $\{0, 1, 2\}$ that include at least one 0. In this case, there is no I/O automaton A (with the given external interface) for which $fairtraces(A) \subseteq traces(P)$, because $fairtraces(A)$ must contain some sequence that includes no inputs.

We define a composition operation for trace properties. Namely, we say that a countable collection $\{P_i\}_{i \in I}$ of trace properties is *compatible* if their signatures are compatible. Then the *composition* $P = \prod_{i \in I} P_i$ is the trace property such that

- $sig(P) = \prod_{i \in I} sig(P_i)$

- $traces(P)$ is the set of sequences β of external actions of P such that $\beta | acts(P_i) \in traces(P_i)$ for all $i \in I$

8.5.3　Safety and Liveness Properties

In this section, we define two important special types of trace properties—*safety properties* and *liveness properties*, give two basic results about these types of properties, and indicate how such properties can be proved.

Safety properties.　We say that a trace property P is a *trace safety property*, or a *safety property* for short, provided that P satisfies the following conditions.

1. $traces(P)$ is nonempty.

2. $traces(P)$ is *prefix-closed*, that is, if $\beta \in traces(P)$ and β' is a finite prefix of β, then $\beta' \in traces(P)$.

3. $traces(P)$ is *limit-closed*, that is, if $\beta_1, \beta_2, \ldots$ is an infinite sequence of finite sequences in $traces(P)$, and for each i, β_i is a prefix of β_{i+1}, then the unique sequence β that is the limit of the β_i under the successive extension ordering is also in $traces(P)$.

A safety property is often interpreted as saying that some particular "bad" thing never happens. We presume that, if something bad happens in a trace, then it happens as a result of some particular event in the trace; therefore, limit-closure is a reasonable condition to include in the definition. Also, if nothing bad happens in a trace, then nothing bad happens in any prefix of the trace; thus, prefix-closure is reasonable. Finally, nothing bad can happen before any events occur, that is, nothing bad happens in the empty sequence λ; therefore, nonemptiness is a reasonable condition.

Example 8.5.2　Trace safety property

　　Suppose $sig(P)$ consists of inputs $init(v)$, $v \in V$ and outputs $decide(v)$, $v \in V$. Suppose $traces(P)$ is the set of sequences of $init$ and $decide$ actions in which no $decide(v)$ occurs without a preceding $init(v)$ (for the same v). Then P is a safety property.

If P is a safety property, then the statement that $traces(A) \subseteq traces(P)$ is equivalent to the statement that $fairtraces(A) \subseteq traces(P)$, which is in turn equivalent to the statement that the finite traces of A are all in $traces(P)$. (We leave the proof as an exercise.) For a given automaton A, the simplest to prove of these three statements is usually that the finite traces of A are all in $traces(P)$. This is usually proved by induction on the length of a finite execution generating the given trace. The strategy is closely related to the strategy used to prove invariants. In fact, by adding a state variable to A to keep track of the trace that has been generated so far, the safety property P can be reformulated as an invariant about the automaton's state.

Liveness properties. We say that a trace property P is a *trace liveness property*, or a *liveness property* for short, provided that every finite sequence over $acts(P)$ has some extension in $traces(P)$.

A liveness property is often informally understood as saying that some particular "good" thing eventually happens (though the formal definition includes more complicated statements than this). We assume that no matter what has happened up to some point, it is still possible for the good occurrence to happen at some time in the future.

Example 8.5.3   Trace liveness property

Suppose $sig(P)$ consists of inputs $init(v), v \in V$ and outputs $decide(v)$, $v \in V$. Suppose $traces(P)$ is the set of sequences β of $init$ and $decide$ actions in which, for every $init$ event in β, there is some $decide$ event occurring later in β. Then P is a liveness property. The same is true for the condition that for every $init$ event in β, there are infinitely many $decide$ events occurring later in β.

One often wants to prove that $fairtraces(A) \subseteq traces(P)$ for some automaton A and liveness property P, that is, that the fair traces of A all satisfy some liveness property. Methods based on *temporal logic* work well in practice for proving such claims. A temporal logic consists of a logical language containing symbols for temporal notions like "eventually" and "always," plus a set of proof rules for describing and verifying properties of executions.

Another method for proving liveness claims, which we call the *progress function method*, is specially designed for proving that some particular goal is eventually reached. This method involves defining a "progress function" from states of the automaton to a well-founded set and showing that certain actions are guaranteed to continue to decrease the value of this function until the goal is reached. The progress function method can be formalized using temporal logic.

In this book, we prove liveness properties informally; however, all our liveness arguments can be formalized using temporal logic.

There are two simple theorems that describe basic connections between safety and liveness properties. The first says that there are no nontrivial trace properties that are both safety and liveness properties.

Theorem 8.8 *If P is both a safety property and a liveness property, then P is the set of all (finite and infinite) sequences of actions in $acts(P)$.*

Proof.   Suppose that P is both a safety and a liveness property and let β be an arbitrary sequence of elements of $acts(P)$. If β is finite, then since P is a liveness property, β has some extension β' in $traces(P)$. Then since P is a safety property—in particular, since $traces(P)$ is prefix-closed—it must be that $\beta \in traces(P)$. Thus, any finite sequence of elements of $acts(P)$ must be in $traces(P)$.

On the other hand, if β is infinite, then for each $i \geq 1$, define β_i to be the length i prefix of β. As shown in the previous paragraph, each β_i is in $traces(P)$. Therefore, since P is a safety property—in particular, since $traces(P)$ is limit-closed—it must be that $\beta \in traces(P)$.   □

The second theorem says that *every* trace property can be expressed as the intersection (or equivalently, the conjunction) of a safety property and a liveness property.

Theorem 8.9 *If P is an arbitrary trace property with $traces(P) \neq \emptyset$, then there exist a safety property S and a liveness property L such that*

1. $sig(S) = sig(L) = sig(P)$

2. $traces(P) = traces(S) \cap traces(L)$

Proof.   Let $traces(S)$ be the prefix- and limit-closure of $traces(P)$, that is, the smallest set of sequences over $acts(P)$ that is prefix-closed and limit-closed and contains $traces(P)$. Obviously, S is a safety property. Let

$traces(L) = traces(P)$
$\qquad \cup \{\beta : \beta \text{ is a finite sequence and no extension of } \beta \text{ is in } traces(P)\}$.

Then we claim that L is a liveness property. To see this, consider any finite sequence β of actions in $acts(P)$. If some extension of β is in $traces(P)$, then certainly that extension is in $traces(L)$ since $traces(P) \subseteq traces(L)$. On the other hand, if no extension of β is in $traces(P)$, then β is explicitly defined to be in

$traces(L)$. In either case, β has an extension in $traces(L)$, so that L is a liveness property.

Now we claim that $traces(P) = traces(S) \cap traces(L)$. It is obvious that $traces(P) \subseteq traces(S) \cap traces(L)$, since each of S and L is explicitly defined so that its traces include those of P. We must show that $traces(S) \cap traces(L) \subseteq traces(P)$. So suppose for the purpose of contradiction that $\beta \in traces(S) \cap traces(L)$ and $\beta \notin traces(P)$. Then by definition of L, β is a finite sequence having no extension in $traces(P)$. But $\beta \in traces(S)$, which is the prefix- and limit-closure of $traces(P)$; since β is a finite sequence, β must be a prefix of an element of $traces(P)$. This is a contradiction. $\square$

So far, we have only defined safety and liveness properties for traces. But analogous definitions can also be made for safety and liveness properties of executions, and the results are analogous to those for traces. In future chapters, we will often classify properties of executions as safety or liveness properties.

8.5.4 Compositional Reasoning

In order to prove properties of a composed system of automata, it is often helpful to reason about the component automata individually. In this section, we give some examples of this sort of "compositional" reasoning.

First, if $A = \prod_{i \in I} A_i$ and each A_i satisfies a trace property P_i, then it follows that A satisfies the product trace property $P = \prod_{i \in I} P_i$. Theorem 8.10 states this more precisely.

Theorem 8.10 *Let $\{A_i\}_{i \in I}$ be a compatible collection of automata and let $A = \prod_{i \in I} A_i$. Let $\{P_i\}_{i \in I}$ be a (compatible) collection of trace properties and let $P = \prod_{i \in I} P_i$.*

1. *If $extsig(A_i) = sig(P_i)$ and $traces(A_i) \subseteq traces(P_i)$ for every i, then $extsig(A) = sig(P)$ and $traces(A) \subseteq traces(P)$.*

2. *If $extsig(A_i) = sig(P_i)$ and $fairtraces(A_i) \subseteq traces(P_i)$ for every i, then $extsig(A) = sig(P)$ and $fairtraces(A) \subseteq traces(P)$.*

Proof Sketch. Part 1 can be shown using Theorem 8.1 (which says that every trace of the composed system A projects on each A_i to give a trace of A_i). Part 2 follows analogously from Theorem 8.4. $\square$

Example 8.5.4 Satisfying a product trace property

Consider the composed system of Example 8.2.1. Each process automaton P_i satisfies (in the sense of trace inclusion) a trace safety property that asserts that any $decide_i$ event has a preceding $init_i$ event. Also, each channel automaton $C_{i,j}$ satisfies a trace safety property that asserts that the sequence of messages in $receive_{i,j}$ events is a prefix of the sequence of messages in $send_{i,j}$ events.

Then it follows from Theorem 8.10 that the composed system satisfies the product trace safety property. This means that in any trace of the combined system, the following hold:

1. For every i, any $decide_i$ event has a preceding $init_i$ event.

2. For every i and j, $i \neq j$, the sequence of messages in $receive_{i,j}$ events is a prefix of the sequence of messages in $send_{i,j}$ events.

Second, suppose that we want to show that a particular sequence of actions is a trace of a composed system $A = \prod_{i \in I} A_i$. This typically arises if A is an abstract system used as a problem specification. Theorem 8.3 shows that, in order to do this, it is enough to show that the projection of the sequence on each of the system components is a trace of that component. Theorem 8.6 implies an analogous result for fair traces.

Third, consider the compositional proof of safety properties. Suppose we want to show that a composed system $A = \prod_{i \in I} A_i$ satisfies a safety property P. One strategy is to show that none of the components A_i is the first to violate P. This strategy is useful, for example, when we want to show that a pair of components observe a "handshake protocol" between them, alternating signals from one to the other. If we can show that neither component is the first to violate the handshake protocol, then we know that the protocol is observed.

Formally, we define the notion of an automaton "preserving" a safety property. Let A be an I/O automaton and let P be a safety property with $acts(P) \cap int(A) = \emptyset$ and $in(P) \cap out(A) = \emptyset$. We say that A preserves P if for every finite sequence β of actions that does not include any internal actions of A, and every $\pi \in out(A)$, the following holds. If $\beta | acts(P) \in traces(P)$ and $\beta\pi | A \in traces(A)$, then $\beta\pi | acts(P) \in traces(P)$. This says that A is not the first to violate P: as long as A's environment only provides inputs to A in such a way that the cumulative behavior satisfies P, then A will only perform outputs such that the cumulative behavior satisfies P.

The key fact about preservation of safety properties is that if all the components in a composed system preserve a safety property, then so does the entire system. Moreover, if the composed system is closed, then it actually satisfies the safety property.

Theorem 8.11 *Let $\{A_i\}_{i \in I}$ be a compatible collection of automata and let $A = \prod_{i \in I} A_i$. Let P be a safety property with $acts(P) \cap int(A) = \emptyset$ and $in(P) \cap out(A) = \emptyset$.*

1. If A_i preserves P for every $i \in I$, then A preserves P.

2. If A is a closed automaton, A preserves P, and $acts(P) \subseteq ext(A)$, then $traces(A)|acts(P) \subseteq traces(P)$.

3. If A is a closed automaton, A preserves P, and $acts(P) = ext(A)$, then $traces(A) \subseteq traces(P)$.

Proof.   The proof is left as an exercise.   □

Example 8.5.5   Automata preserving properties

Let A be an automaton with output a and input b, and B an automaton with output b and input a. We consider the safety property P such that $sig(P)$ has no inputs and has both a and b as outputs, and such that $traces(P)$ is the set of all finite and infinite sequences of alternating a's and b's, beginning with an a (plus the empty sequence λ). P represents a handshake protocol between A and B, with A initiating the handshake.

Suppose that A has one variable $turn$, with values in the set $\{a, b\}$, initialized at a. A's transitions are as follows.

Transitions:

a b
   Precondition: Effect:
       $turn = a$ $turn := a$
   Effect:
       $turn := b$

Thus, A can perform a at the beginning and again each time it receives a b input. If it receives two b inputs in a row before it has had a chance to respond with the next a, then A can only respond with one a.

Automaton B has one variable $turn$, with values in the set $\{a, b\}$, initialized at a, plus a Boolean variable $error$, initially *false*. B's transitions are as follows.

Transitions:

b a
   Precondition: Effect:
       $turn = b$ or $error = true$ if $error = false$ then
   Effect: if $turn = a$ then $turn := b$
       if $error = false$ then $turn := a$ else $error := true$

Thus, B can only perform b once each time it receives an a input, as long as its environment does not submit two a's in a row. If the environment does submit two a's in a row, then B sets an *error* flag, which allows it to output b's at any time.

Each of A and B preserves P. It follows from Theorem 8.11 that every trace of the composition $A \times B$ is in *traces(P)*.

8.5.5 Hierarchical Proofs

In this section, we describe an important proof strategy based on a hierarchy of automata. This hierarchy represents a series of descriptions of a system or algorithm, at different levels of abstraction. The process of moving through the series of abstractions, from the highest level to the lowest level, is known as *successive refinement*. The top level may be nothing more than a problem specification written in the form of an automaton. The next level is typically a very abstract representation of the system: it may be centralized rather than distributed, or have actions with large granularity, or have simple but inefficient data structures. Lower levels in the hierarchy look more and more like the actual system or algorithm that will be used in practice: they may be more distributed, have actions with small granularity, and contain optimizations. Because of all this extra detail, lower levels in the hierarchy are usually harder to understand than the higher levels. The best way to prove properties of the lower-level automata is by relating these automata to automata at higher levels in the hierarchy, rather than by carrying out direct proofs from scratch.

Chapters 4 and 6 contain examples of such a process of refinement for the synchronous setting. For example, in Chapter 6, we first presented an algorithm (*FloodSet*) for agreement in the face of stopping failures that was liberal in its use of communication. Then we presented an improved ("lower-level") version of the algorithm (*OptFloodSet*) in which many of the messages were pruned out; this yielded a smaller bound on communication. The improved algorithm was verified using a simulation relation relating the states of the two algorithms. The correctness proof involved showing, by induction on the number of rounds, that the simulation relation was preserved throughout the computation. Essentially, this strategy involved running the two algorithms side by side, with the same inputs and failure pattern, and observing similarities between the two executions.

How can we extend the simulation method to asynchronous systems? The asynchronous model allows much more freedom than does the synchronous model, both in the order in which components take steps and in the state changes that accompany each action. This makes it more difficult to determine which executions to compare. It turns out that it is enough to obtain a *one-way relationship* between the two algorithms, showing that for any execution of the lower-level automaton there is a "corresponding" execution of the higher-level automaton. We do this by defining a simulation relation between states of the two automata.

Specifically, let A and B be two I/O automata with the same external interface; we think of A as the lower-level automaton and B as the higher-level automaton. Suppose f is a binary relation over $states(A)$ and $states(B)$, that is, $f \subseteq states(A) \times states(B)$; we use the notation $u \in f(s)$ as an alternative way of writing $(s, u) \in f$. Then f is a *simulation relation* from A to B, provided that both of the following are true:

1. If $s \in start(A)$, then $f(s) \cap start(B) \neq \emptyset$.

2. If s is a reachable state of A, $u \in f(s)$ is a reachable state of B, and $(s, \pi, s') \in trans(A)$, then there is an execution fragment α of B starting with u and ending with some $u' \in f(s')$, such that $trace(\alpha) = trace(\pi)$.

The first condition, or *start condition*, asserts that any start state of A has some corresponding start state of B. The second condition, or *step condition*, asserts that any step of A, and any state of B corresponding to the initial state of the step, have a corresponding sequence of steps of B. This corresponding sequence can consist of one step, many steps, or even no steps, as long as the correspondence between the states is preserved and the external behavior is the same. A representation of the step correspondence, for the case where π is an external action, appears in Figure 8.4. The following theorem gives the key property of simulation relations:

Theorem 8.12 *If there is a simulation relation from A to B, then $traces(A) \subseteq traces(B)$.*

Proof. The proof is left as an exercise. ☐

In particular, Theorem 8.12 implies that any safety property that is satisfied by B is also satisfied by A: if P is a trace safety property, $extsig(A) = sig(P)$, and $traces(A) \subseteq traces(P)$, then also $extsig(B) = sig(P)$ and $traces(B) \subseteq traces(P)$. Proofs of correctness based on simulation relations are quite stylized—so stylized that they are amenable to computer assistance.

Example 8.5.6 Simulation proof

As a simple example of a simulation proof, we show that two channel automata compose to implement another channel automaton.

Let C be the communication channel given in Example 8.1.1. (We suppress the subscripts in this example.) Let A and B be automata

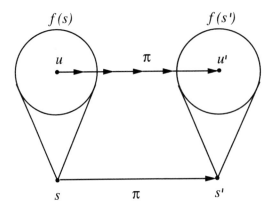

Figure 8.4: Step correspondence for a simulation relation.

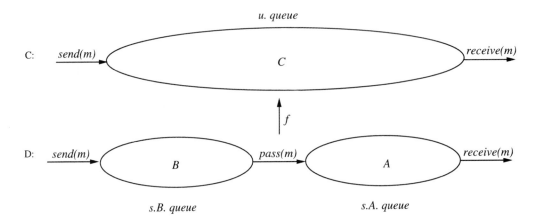

Figure 8.5: Simulation relation f from D to C.

that are the same as C except for some renaming of actions. Namely, the outputs of B are renamed as $pass(m)$ instead of $receive(m)$, and the inputs of A are renamed as $pass(m)$ instead of $send(m)$. Let D be the result of composing A and B and then hiding the $pass$ actions. Note that C and D have the same external interface.

We claim that $traces(D) \subseteq traces(C)$. To see this, we define a simulation relation f from D to C. See Figure 8.5.

Namely, if s is a state of D and u is a state of C, then we define $(s, u) \in f$, provided that the following holds (we use dot notation both to denote the value of a given variable in a state and to denote a given automaton in a composition):

u.*queue* is the concatenation of s.*A*.*queue* and s.*B*.*queue* (with s.*A*.*queue* coming first)

To see that f is in fact a simulation relation, we must check the two conditions in the definition. The start condition is trivial, because the initial states of A, B, and C are all the empty queue. For the step condition, suppose that s is a state of D, $u \in f(s)$ is a state of C, and $(s, \pi, s') \in trans(D)$. We consider cases, based on the type of action being performed.

1. $\pi = send(m)$.

   Let the corresponding execution fragment of C consist of a single $send(m)$ step. The given step in D adds m to the end of s.*B*.*queue*, while the step in C adds m to the end of u.*queue*. This preserves the state correspondence given by the definition of f.

2. $\pi = receive(m)$.

   Let the corresponding execution fragment of C consist of a single $receive(m)$ step. The given step in D removes m from the front of s.*A*.*queue*. The correspondence between s and u implies that m is also at the front of u.*queue*, which implies that the $receive(m)$ action is in fact enabled in u. Then the step in C removes m from the front of u.*queue*. Again, this preserves the state correspondence given by f.

3. $\pi = pass(m)$.

   Let the corresponding execution fragment of C consist of 0 steps. Since the step of D does not affect the concatenation of the two queues, the state correspondence is preserved.

It follows that f is a simulation relation. Since f is a simulation relation, Theorem 8.12 implies that $traces(D) \subseteq traces(C)$, as needed.

Simulations are sometimes also useful in helping to prove that liveness properties of B are satisfied by A. The idea is that a simulation relation from A to B actually implies more than just trace inclusion—it implies a close correspondence, involving both traces and states, between each execution of A and some execution of B. Such a strong correspondence, together with fairness assumptions for A, can sometimes be used to prove the needed liveness properties.

For example, here is one useful formal definition of a stronger correspondence between executions. Let A and B be two I/O automata with the same input and output actions. Let α and α' be executions of A and B, respectively, and let f

be a binary relation over $states(A)$ and $states(B)$. Then we say that α and α' *correspond* with respect to f, provided that there is a mapping g from indices (occurrences) of states in α to indices of states in α', satisfying the following properties:

1. g is monotone nondecreasing.

2. g exhausts all of α' (i.e., the supremum of the range of g is the supremum of the indices of states in α').

3. g-corresponding pairs of states are related by f.

4. Between successive g-corresponding pairs of states, the traces in α and α' are identical.

Then it is not hard to see that a simulation relation yields this type of correspondence between executions:

Theorem 8.13 *If f is a simulation relation from A to B, then for every execution α of A, there is an execution α' of B such that α and α' correspond with respect to f.*

Theorem 8.13 can be used to prove a liveness property for A, assuming a similar liveness property for B. We use this strategy, for example, in our proof sketch for a mutual exclusion algorithm (*TicketME*, Theorem 10.40) and our proof sketch for a data link protocol (*Stenning*, Lemma 22.2).

8.6   Complexity Measures

Even though the I/O automaton model is asynchronous, it has a natural notion of time complexity. For a given automaton A, we define upper time bounds for any subset of the equivalence classes in the task partition $tasks(A)$. Specifically, for any task C, we may define a bound $upper_C$, which can be either a positive real number or ∞. Then for any fair execution α of A, a real-valued time can be associated with every event of α, subject to the following conditions:

1. The times are monotone nondecreasing in α.

2. If α is infinite, then the times approach ∞.

3. From any point in α, a task C can be enabled for time at most $upper_C$ before some action in C must occur.

Roughly speaking, this imposes an upper bound of $upper_C$ on the time between successive chances by task C to perform a step. A fair execution with times associated in this way is called a *timed execution*.

Notice that, for a given set of $upper_C$ bounds, there are many ways that times can be associated with the events of α, that is, many timed executions. We measure the *time* until some designated event π in α by the supremum of the times that can be assigned to π in all such timed executions. Likewise, we measure the *time* between two events in α by the supremum of the differences between the times that can be assigned to those two events.

Example 8.6.1 Time analysis

Let α be any fair execution of the system of Example 8.2.1 in which all processes receive *init* inputs. We associate an upper bound of ℓ with each task of each process and an upper bound of d with the single task of each channel. Then the time from when the last process receives its first *init* input in α until all processes have performed a *decide* output is at most $\ell + d + \ell = d + 2\ell$. The reason is that it takes at most time ℓ for the last process that receives an *init* input to perform *send* events for all its neighbors. Then it takes at most time d for all of these messages to be delivered, and then at most time ℓ for each process to perform *decide*.

8.7 Indistinguishable Executions

We define a notion of indistinguishability that will be useful in some impossibility proofs. This is analogous to the notion of indistinguishability defined in Section 2.4 for executions of synchronous systems.

If α and α' are executions of two composed systems of automata, each containing automaton A, then we say that α and α' are *indistinguishable to A* provided that $\alpha|A = \alpha'|A$.

8.8 Randomization

As in synchronous systems, it is sometimes useful to allow components in asynchronous systems to make random choices based on some given probability distributions. In order to model such random choices, we augment the I/O automaton model to obtain a new *probabilistic I/O automaton* model. A probabilistic I/O automaton is just like an I/O automaton, except that the notion of a transition is modified: instead of being a triple (s, π, s'), it is a triple of the form (s, π, P), where P is a probability distribution over some subset of the set of states. (If a step does not involve a random choice, we model it using a trivial distribution P.) Every probabilistic I/O automaton A has a *nondeterministic version*, $\mathcal{N}(A)$, which is obtained by replacing each transition (s, π, P) by the set of transitions (s, π, s'), where s' is an element of the domain of P. Thus, $\mathcal{N}(A)$ simply replaces random choices with nondeterministic choices. $\mathcal{N}(A)$ is an ordinary I/O automaton.

An execution of probabilistic I/O automaton A is generated by means of a series of pairs of choices. In each pair, a nondeterministic choice is made first, to determine the next transition (s, π, P), and then a random choice is made, using P, to determine the next state. The only restriction on the choices is that the nondeterministic choice of the next transition must be "fair," in the sense that all the executions generated by all possible sequences of random choices are fair executions (in the usual sense) of the I/O automaton $\mathcal{N}(A)$.

As in the synchronous case, claims about what is computed by a randomized system are usually probabilistic. When a claim is made, the intention is generally that it is supposed to hold for all inputs and all fair patterns of nondeterministic choices. As in Chapter 5, a fictitious *adversary* is usually invented to describe these inputs and nondeterministic choices, and the automaton is required to behave well in competition with any adversary.

8.9   Bibliographic Notes

The I/O automaton model was originally developed in Tuttle's M.S. thesis [217]. The important features of the model are summarized in papers by Lynch and Tuttle [217, 218]. Descriptions and proofs of algorithms modelled as I/O automata are sprinkled throughout the research literature on distributed algorithms; some representative examples appear in the work of Afek et al. and Bloom [3, 4, 53]. An example of the use of I/O automata to model systems with dynamic process creation is the framework for modelling database concurrency control algorithms presented in the book *Atomic Transactions*, by Lynch, Merritt, Weihl, and Fekete [207]. The I/O automaton model has been influenced by many other models for concurrent systems, most notably the asynchronous shared memory model of Lynch and Fischer [216], the Actor model of Hewitt [7, 81], and the Communicating Sequential Processes model of Hoare [159].

The origins of the notion of invariant assertion are discussed in the Bibliographic Notes at the end of Chapter 2. The notion of trace property described here is adapted from the "schedule module" definition in [217, 218]. The notions of safety and liveness are adapted from work by Lamport [175] and by Alpern and Schneider [8]. Theorem 8.9 is adapted from [8].

A good reference for temporal logic is the book by Manna and Pnueli [219].

Lamport's work on Temporal Logic of Actions (TLA) contains a useful temporal logic framework [184], plus a well-developed methodology for using the framework to verify algorithms.

The strategy of showing that a sequence projects to give traces of all the components of a composed system A, in order to prove that the sequence is in fact a trace of the entire system A, is used in [207]. There, the system A is an abstract specification of a database system that executes all transactions serially. It is shown, by analyzing projections in this way, that certain sequences produced by database systems that execute the transactions concurrently are in fact traces of A. This is the key to the correctness of these database systems. The work on preservation of safety properties is derived from [218].

Simulation relations originate from many sources. They are a generalization of the notion of refinement mapping used by Lamport in [177]; they are an abstraction of the history variables of Owicki and Gries [235]; and they are very similar to the simulations of Park [236], the possibilities mappings of Lynch [203, 214] and of Lynch and Tuttle [217, 218], and the simulations of Jonsson [165]. The value of the simulation method for verifying safety properties of asynchronous systems is now well established. Many papers and books, for example, [217, 288, 69, 233, 214, 207, 189, 190], contain substantial examples of its use. A fair number of proofs using simulations have been carried out with computer assistance and checking. See work by Nipkow [233] and by Søgaard-Andersen, Garland, Guttag, Lynch, and Pogosyants [265] for representative examples, the former using the Isabelle Theorem Prover and the latter using the Larch Prover.

The modelling of randomized systems is derived from the work of Segala and Lynch [257].

General results about models for concurrent systems are well represented in the annual International Conference on Concurrency Theory (CONCUR).

8.10 Exercises

8.1. Consider the composition of the automata P_i and $C_{i,j}$, $1 \leq i, j \leq n$, in Example 8.2.1.

   (a) Describe all the states that arise in the unique execution arising from the trace given in that example (for $n = 2$).

   (b) Now let $n = 3$. Let m be any arbitrary natural number. Describe an execution in which m gets decided by all three processes. In your execution, the successive $init_1$ values should be some prefix of the sequence $0, 4, 8, 12, \ldots$, the successive $init_2$ values should be some prefix of $0, 2, 0, 2, \ldots$, and the successive $init_3$ values should be some prefix of $0, 1, 0, 1, \ldots$.

(c) Again let $n = 3$. This time, let m_1, m_2, and m_3 be three arbitrary natural numbers. Describe an execution in which m_i gets decided by P_i, $i \in \{1, 2, 3\}$. The successive $init$ values of the three processes should be as in (b), above.

8.2. Prove Theorems 8.1, 8.2, and 8.3. Where are the compatibility conditions used?

8.3. Prove Theorems 8.4, 8.5, and 8.6. Where are the compatibility conditions used? Where is the input-enabling condition used?

8.4. Consider the following two I/O automata. Note that they are not written using precondition-effect notation, but just using a brute force listing of all the components.

- Automaton A:
  $in(A) = int(A) = \emptyset$, $out(A) = \{go\}$,
  $states(A) = \{s, t\}$,
  $start(A) = \{s\}$,
  $trans(A) = \{(s, go, t)\}$, and
  $tasks(A) = \{\{go\}\}$.

- Automaton B:
  $in(B) = \{go\}$, $out(B) = \{ack\}$, $int(B) = \{increment\}$,
  $states(B) = \{on, off\} \times \mathbb{N}$,
  $start(B) = \{(on, 0)\}$,
  $trans(B)) = \{((on, i), increment, (on, i + 1)), i \in \mathbb{N}\} \cup$
  $\{((on, i), go, (off, i)), i \in \mathbb{N}\} \cup$
  $\{((off, i), go, (off, 0)), i \in \mathbb{N}\} \cup$
  $\{((off, i), ack, (off, i - 1)), i \in \mathbb{N} - \{0\}\}$, and
  $tasks(B) = \{\{increment\}, \{ack\}\}$.

For each of the three automata A, B, and $A \times B$, describe the sets of traces and fair traces.

8.5. (a) Define an I/O automaton A representing a reliable message channel that accepts and delivers messages from the union of two alphabets, M_1 and M_2. The message channel is supposed to preserve the order of messages from the same alphabet. Also, if a message from alphabet M_1 is sent prior to another message from alphabet M_2, then the corresponding deliveries must occur in the same order. However, if a message from M_1 is sent after a message from M_2, then the deliveries are permitted to occur in the opposite order. Your automaton should actually exhibit all of the allowable external behaviors. Be sure to give all the components of A: the signature, states, start states, steps, and tasks.

(b) For your automaton, give an example of each of the following: a fair execution, a fair trace, an execution that is not fair, and a trace that is not fair.

8.6. Describe a specific I/O automaton having no input actions, whose output actions are $\{0, 1, 2, \ldots\}$, and whose fair traces are exactly the sequences in set S, defined as follows. S consists of *all* the sequences of length 1 over the output set, that is, all the sequences consisting of exactly one nonnegative integer.

8.7. Prove Theorem 8.7.

8.8. Let A be any I/O automaton. Show that there is another I/O automaton B with only a single task, such that $fairtraces(B) \subseteq fairtraces(A)$. (You do not need to show $fairtraces(B) = fairtraces(A)$—inclusion is enough.)

8.9. Let A be any I/O automaton with a single task. Show that there is another I/O automaton B, also with a single task, that is "deterministic" in the sense that the following all hold:

(a) There is exactly one initial state.

(b) For every state s and every action π, there is at most one transition of the form (s, π, s').

(c) In every state, at most one locally controlled action is enabled.

Moreover, $fairtraces(B) \subseteq fairtraces(A)$. (You do not need to show $fairtraces(B) = fairtraces(A)$—inclusion is enough.)

8.10. State and prove a theorem that combines the results of Exercises 8.8 and 8.9.

8.11. Reconsider Exercises 8.8, 8.9, and 8.10 in the case where the equality $fairtraces(B) = fairtraces(A)$ is required. If these exercises can be solved with this stronger requirement, then solve them. Otherwise, show that they cannot be solved.

8.12. If P is a safety property, prove that the following three are equivalent statements about an I/O automaton A:

(a) $traces(A) \subseteq traces(P)$.

(b) $fairtraces(A) \subseteq traces(P)$.

(c) The finite traces of A are all in $traces(P)$.

8.13. Consider the following trace properties P; in each case, $sig(P)$ is the signature consisting of no inputs and outputs $\{1, 2\}$.

     (a) Suppose $traces(P)$ is the set of sequences over $\{1, 2\}$ in which there is no instance of a 1 followed immediately by a 2. Show that P is a safety property.

     (b) Suppose that $traces(P)$ is the set of sequences over $\{1, 2\}$ in which every occurrence of 1 is eventually followed by a 2. Show that P is a liveness property.

     (c) Suppose that $traces(P)$ is the set of sequences over $\{1, 2\}$ in which every occurrence of 1 is immediately followed by a 2. Show that P is neither a safety property nor a liveness property. Show explicitly how to express P as the intersection of a safety property and a liveness property.

8.14. Formulate careful definitions of safety and liveness properties for executions, analogous to those for traces. Prove the analogues of Theorems 8.8 and 8.9.

8.15. Prove Theorem 8.11.

8.16. Prove Theorem 8.12.

Part IIA

Asynchronous Shared Memory Algorithms

The next several chapters, Chapters 9–13, deal with algorithms for the *asynchronous shared memory model*, in which processes take steps asynchronously and communicate via shared memory.

The first chapter in this part, Chapter 9, simply presents our formal model for asynchronous shared memory systems. As before, skip it for now and use it as a reference. Chapter 10 deals with the fundamental problem of *mutual exclusion*, and Chapter 11 deals with the more general problem of *distributed resource allocation*. Chapter 12 contains fundamental results on *consensus* in fault-prone asynchronous systems. Finally, Chapter 13 contains a study of *atomic objects*—powerful abstract objects for programming distributed systems.

Chapter 9

Modelling III: Asynchronous Shared Memory Model

In this chapter, we give a formal model for asynchronous shared memory systems. This model is presented in terms of the general I/O automaton model for asynchronous systems that we defined in Chapter 8.

A shared memory system consists of a collection of communicating processes, as does a network system. But this time, instead of sending and receiving messages over communication channels, the processes perform instantaneous operations on shared variables.

9.1 Shared Memory Systems

Informally speaking, an *asynchronous shared memory system* consists of a finite collection of processes interacting with each other by means of a finite collection of shared variables. The variables are used only for communication among the processes in the system. However, so that the rest of the world can interact with the shared memory system, we also assume that each process has a *port*, on which it can interact with the outside world using input and output actions. The interactions are depicted in Figure 9.1.

We model a shared memory system using I/O automata, in fact, using just a single I/O automaton with its external interface consisting of the input and output actions on all the ports. It might seem more natural to use several automata, one per process and one per shared variable. However, that leads to some complications we would rather avoid in this book. For instance, if each process and each variable were an I/O automaton and we combined them using ordinary I/O automaton composition, then we would get a system in which an

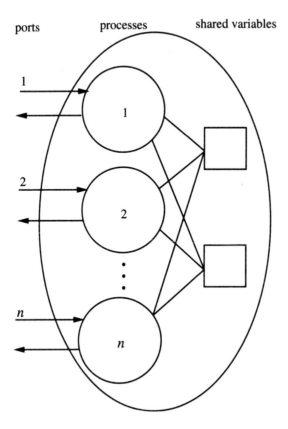

Figure 9.1: An asynchronous shared memory system.

operation by a process i on a shared variable x would be modelled by a pair of events—an invocation that is an output of process i and an input of variable x, followed by a response that is an output of variable x and an input of process i. But then the system would also have some executions in which these pairs of events are split. For instance, several operations could be invoked before the first of them returns. This kind of behavior does not occur in the shared memory systems that we are trying to model.

One way out of this difficulty would be to consider a restricted subset of all the possible executions—those in which invocations and corresponding responses occur consecutively. A second way out would be to model only the processes as I/O automata, but to model the shared variables as state machines of a different kind (with invocations and responses combined into single events); in this case, a new composition operation would have to be defined to allow combination of the process and variable automata into one I/O automaton. Since these approaches introduce their own complexities—restricted subsets of the set of executions, pairs of events, a new kind of state machine, or a new operation—we sidestep all these issues by just modelling the entire system as one big I/O automaton A. We capture the process and variable structure within automaton A by means of some locality restrictions on the events.

As in the synchronous network model, we assume that the processes in the system are indexed by $1, \ldots, n$. Suppose that each process i has an associated set of *states*, $states_i$, among which some are designated as *start states*, $start_i$. Also suppose that each shared variable x in the system has an associated set of *values*, $values_x$, among which some are designated as the *initial values*, $initial_x$. Then each state in $states(A)$ (the set of states of the system automaton A) consists of a state in $states_i$ for each process i, plus a value in $values_x$ for each shared variable x. Each state in $start(A)$ consists of a state in $start_i$ for each process i, plus a value in $initial_x$ for each shared variable x.

We assume that each action in $acts(A)$ is associated with one of the processes. In addition, some of the internal actions in $int(A)$ may be associated with a shared variable. The input actions and output actions associated with process i are used for interaction between process i and the outside world; we say they occur on *port i*. The internal actions of process i that do not have an associated shared variable are used for local computation, while the internal actions of i that are associated with shared variable x are used for performing operations on x.

The set $trans(A)$ of transitions has some locality restrictions, which model the process and shared variable structure of the system. First, consider an action π that is associated with process i but with no variable; as we noted above, π is used for local computation. Then only the state of i can be involved in any π step. That is, the set of π transitions can be generated from some set of triples of the form (s, π, s'), where $s, s' \in states_i$, by attaching any combination of states for the other processes and values for the shared variables to both s and s' (the same combination to both).

On the other hand, consider an action π that is associated with both a process i and a variable x; as we noted above, π is used by i to perform an operation on x. Then only the state of i and the value of x can be involved in any π step. That is, the set of π transitions can be generated from some set of triples of the form $((s, v), \pi, (s', v'))$, where $s, s' \in states_i$ and $v, v' \in values_x$, by attaching any combination of states for the other processes and values for the other shared variables. There is a technicality: if π is associated with process i and variable x, then whether or not π is enabled should depend only on the state of process i, although the resulting changes may also depend on the value of x. That is, if π is enabled when the state of i is s and the value of x is v, then π is also enabled when the state of i is s and when x has any other value v'.

The task partition $tasks(A)$ must be consistent with the process structure: that is, each equivalence class (task) should include locally controlled actions of only one process. In many cases that we will consider, there will be exactly one task per process—this makes sense, for example, if each process is a sequential program. In this case, the standard definition of fairness for I/O automata, given in Section 8.3, says that each process gets infinitely many chances to take steps. In the more general case, where there can be several tasks per process, the fairness definition says that each task gets infinitely many chances to take steps.

Example 9.1.1   Shared memory system

Let V be a fixed value set. Consider a shared memory system A consisting of n processes, numbered $1, \ldots, n$, and a single shared variable x with values in $V \cup \{unknown\}$, initially $unknown$. The inputs are of the form $init(v)_i$, where $v \in V$ and i is a process index. The outputs are of the form $decide(v)_i$. The internal actions are of the form $access_i$. All the actions with subscript i are associated with process i, and in addition, the $access$ actions are associated with variable x.

After process i receives an $init(v)_i$ input, it accesses x. If it finds $x = unknown$, then it writes its value v into x and decides v. If it finds $x = w$, where $w \in V$, then it does not write anything into x, but decides w.

Formally, each set $states_i$ consists of local variables.

States of i:
$status \in \{idle, access, decide, done\}$, initially $idle$
$input \in V \cup \{unknown\}$, initially $unknown$
$output \in V \cup \{unknown\}$, initially $unknown$

The transitions are

Transitions of i:

$init(v)_i$
    Effect:
        $input := v$
        if $status = idle$ then
            $status := access$

$access_i$
    Precondition:
        $status = access$
    Effect:
        if $x = unknown$ then $x := input$
        $output := x$
        $status := decide$

$decide(v)_i$
    Precondition:
        $status = decide$
        $output = v$
    Effect:
        $status := done$

There is one task per process, which contains all the *access* and *decide* actions for that process.

It is not hard to see that in every fair execution α of A, any process that receives an *init* input eventually performs a *decide* output. Moreover, every execution (fair or not, and with any number of *init* events occurring anywhere) satisfies the "agreement property" that no two processes decide on different values, and the "validity property" that every decision value is the initial value of some process.

We can formulate these correctness claims in terms of trace properties, according to the definition in Section 8.5.2. For example, let P be the trace property such that $sig(P) = extsig(A)$ and $traces(P)$ is the set of sequences β of actions in $acts(P)$ satisfying the following conditions:

1. For any i, if exactly one $init_i$ event appears in β, then exactly one $decide_i$ event appears in β.

2. For any i, if no $init_i$ event appears in β, then no $decide_i$ event appears in β.

3. (Agreement) If $decide(v)_i$ and $decide(w)_j$ both appear in β, then $v = w$.

4. (Validity) If a $decide(v)_i$ event appears in β, then some $init(v)_j$ event (for the same v) appears in β.

It is then possible to show that $fairtraces(A) \subseteq traces(P)$. The proof is left for an exercise.

9.2 Environment Model

Sometimes it is useful to model the environment of a system as an automaton also. This provides an easy way to describe assumptions about the environment's behavior. For instance, in Example 9.1.1, we might like to specify that the environment submits *exactly one* $init_i$ input for each i, or maybe *at least one* for each i. For shared memory systems that arise in practice, the environment can often be described as a collection of independent *user automata*, one per port.

Example 9.2.1   Environment model

We describe an environment for the shared memory system A described in Example 9.1.1. The environment is a single I/O automaton that is composed (using the composition operation for I/O automata defined in Section 8.2.1) of one *user automaton*, U_i, for each process index i. U_i's code is as follows.

U_i automaton:

Signature:

Input: Internal:
    $decide(v)_i$, $v \in V$ $dummy_i$
Output:
    $init(v)_i$, $v \in V$

States:

$status \in \{request, wait, done\}$, initially *request*
$decision \in V \cup \{unknown\}$, initially *unknown*
error, a Boolean, initially *false*

Transitions:

$init(v)_i$ $decide(v)_i$
    Precondition: Effect:
        $status = request$ or $error = true$ if $error = false$ then
    Effect: if $status = wait$ then
        if $error = false$ then $status := wait$ $decision := v$
                                                  $status := done$
$dummy_i$ else $error := true$
    Precondition:
        $error = true$
    Effect:
        none

Tasks:
All locally controlled actions are in one class.

Thus, U_i initially performs an $init_i$ action, then waits for a decision. If the shared memory system produces a decision without a preceding $init_i$ or produces two decisions, then U_i sets an *error* flag, which allows it to output any number of $init$s at any time. (The presence of the $dummy_i$ action allows it also to choose not to perform outputs.) Of course, the given shared memory system is not supposed to cause such errors.

The composition of the shared memory system A with all the U_i, $1 \leq i \leq n$, is depicted in Figure 9.2. This composition is quite well-behaved: in any fair execution of the composition, there is exactly one $init_i$ event and exactly one $decide_i$ event for each i. Moreover, the *decide* events satisfy appropriate agreement and validity conditions.

More formally, let Q be the trace property such that $sig(Q)$ consists of outputs $init(v)_i$ and $decide(v)_i$ for all i and v, and such that

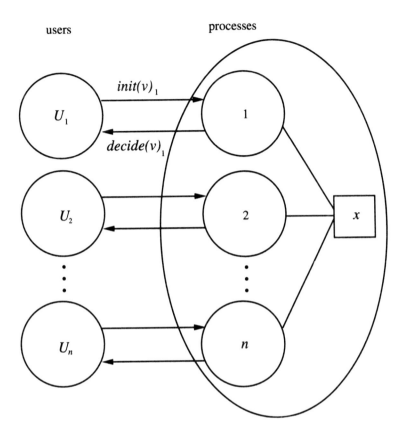

Figure 9.2: Users and shared memory system.

$traces(Q)$ is the set of sequences β of actions in $acts(Q)$ satisfying the following conditions:

1. For any i, β contains exactly one $init_i$ event followed by exactly one $decide_i$ event.

2. (Agreement) If $decide(v)_i$ and $decide(w)_j$ both appear in β, then $v = w$.

3. (Validity) If a $decide(v)_i$ event appears in β, then some $init(v)_j$ event (for the same v) appears in β.

Then it is possible to show that $fairtraces(A \times \prod_{1 \le i \le n} U_i) \subseteq traces(Q)$. The proof is left for an exercise.

9.3   Indistinguishable States

We define a notion of indistinguishability that will be useful in some impossibility proofs in Chapter 10.

Consider an n-process shared memory system A and a collection of users U_i, $1 \leq i \leq n$. Let s and s' be two states of the composed system $A \times \prod_{1 \leq i \leq n} U_i$. Then we say that s and s' are *indistinguishable* to process i if the state of process i, the state of U_i, and the values of all the shared variables are the same in s and s'. We write $s \overset{i}{\sim} s'$ to indicate that s and s' are indistinguishable to i.

9.4   Shared Variable Types

In the general definition we have given for shared memory systems, we have not restricted the types of operations a process may perform on a shared variable when it accesses the variable. That is, when a process i accesses a variable x, we have allowed arbitrary changes to the state of i and the value of x to occur, depending in arbitrary ways on the previous state of i and value of x. But in practice, shared variables normally support only a fixed set of operations, such as read and write operations, or a combined read-modify-write operation. In this subsection, we define the notion of a *variable type*, and say what it means for a shared memory system to observe type restrictions.[1]

A *variable type* consists of

- a set V of values

- an initial value $v_0 \in V$

- a set of *invocations*

- a set of *responses*

- a function $f : invocations \times V \to responses \times V$

The function f says what happens when a given invocation arrives at the variable and the variable has a given value; f describes the new value the variable takes on and the response that is returned. Note that a variable type is *not* an I/O automaton, even though some of its components look similar to I/O automaton components. Most importantly, in a variable type, the invocations and responses are thought of as occurring together as part of one function application, whereas

---

[1]The definition we use here requires the variable to behave deterministically. This could be generalized to allow nondeterminism, but we would rather avoid the complication here, since it is not needed for the results in this book.

in the I/O automaton model, inputs and outputs are separate actions (and other actions may occur between them).

Suppose we have a shared memory system A. What does it mean to say that shared variable x in system A is of a given variable type? It means, first, that the set $values_x$ must be equal to the set V of values of the type, and that the set $initial_x$ of initial values for x consists of just one element, v_0. Moreover, all the transitions involving x must be describable in terms of the invocations and responses allowed by the type. Namely, each action involving x must be associated with some invocation a of the variable type. Moreover, for each process i and each invocation a, the set of transitions involving i and a must be describable in the following form, where p is some predicate on $states_i$ and g is some relation, $g \subseteq states_i \times responses \times states_i$. (In the code, we use the notation $state_i$ to denote the state of process i.)

Transitions involving i and a
    Precondition:
        $p(state_i)$
    Effect:
        $(b, x) := f(a, x)$
        $state_i := $ any s such that $(state_i, b, s) \in g$

This code means that the determination that variable x is to be accessed by process i using invocation a is made according to predicate p (which just involves the state of i). If this access is to be performed, then the function f for the variable type is applied to the invocation a and the value of variable x to determine a response b and a new value for x. The response b is then used by process i to update its state, in some way allowed by relation g.

In the descriptions of shared memory algorithms in this book, transitions involving accesses to shared variables of particular types will not be written explicitly in terms of predicates p and relations g as above. However, theoretically, they could all be expressed in this style.

Example 9.4.1   Read/write shared variables (registers)

The most frequently used variable type in multiprocessors is one supporting only read and write operations. A variable of this type is known as a *read/write variable*, or a *read/write register*, or just a *register*.

A read/write register comes equipped with an arbitrary set V of values and an arbitrary initial value $v_0 \in V$. Its invocations are *read*

and $write(v), v \in V$. Its responses are $v \in V$ and ack.[2] Its function
f is defined by: $f(read, v) = (v, v)$ and $f(write(v), w) = (ack, v)$.

Note that variable x in the system of Example 9.1.1 cannot be
described as a read/write register, because there is no way that the
given accesses could be rewritten in the form given above. It is possible to rewrite the algorithm so that x is a register, for example,
by separating each access into a read and a write step. The resulting process code might look as follows. The *status* value *access* is
replaced by two new *status* values, *read* and *write*.

Transitions:

$init(v)_i$
    Effect:
        $input := v$
        if $status = idle$ then $status := read$

$read_i$
    Precondition:
        $status = read$
    Effect:
        if $x = unknown$ then
            $output := input$
            $status := write$
        else
            $output := x$
            $status := decide$

$write(v)_i$
    Precondition:
        $status = write$
        $v = input$
    Effect:
        $x := v$
        $status := decide$

$decide(v)_i$
    Precondition:
        $status = decide$
        $output = v$
    Effect:
        $status := done$

The task partition again groups together all locally controlled
actions of process i. Although this code is not explicitly written in
terms of a predicate p and a relation g, note that it could easily be
rewritten in this way. For instance, for the $read_i$ action, the predicate
p is simply "$status = read$," and the relation g is just the set of triples
$(s, b, s') \in states_i \times (V \cup \{unknown\}) \times states_i$ such that s' is obtained
from s by the code:

    if $b = unknown$ then
        $output := input$
        $status := write$
    else
        $output := b$
        $status := decide$

For the $write(v)_i$ action, the predicate p is simply "$status = write$
and $v = input$," and the relation g is just the set of triples $(s, b, s') \in$

---

[2]The invocations and responses will sometimes also include additional information such as
the name of the register. We mostly ignore such complications here.

$states_i \times (V \cup \{unknown\}) \times states_i$ such that s' is obtained from s by the code:

$status := decide$

So x is a read/write shared variable.

Notice that when we rewrite the algorithm in this way, the agreement condition mentioned in Example 9.1.1 is no longer guaranteed.

Example 9.4.2   Read-modify-write shared variables

Another important variable type allows the powerful *read-modify-write* operation. In one instantaneous read-modify-write operation on a shared variable x, a process i can do all of the following:

1. Read x.

2. Carry out some computation, possibly using the value of x, that modifies the state of i and determines a new value for x.

3. Write the new value to x.

It is not easy to implement a general read-modify-write operation using the usual primitives provided by multiprocessors. The shared memory model requires not only that each access to the variable be *indivisible*, but also that all the processes should get *fair* turns to perform such accesses. Implementing this fairness requires some sort of low-level arbitration mechanism.

As we have described it, it is not obvious that read-modify-write variables can be modelled in terms of variable types: the read-modify-write operation appears to involve two accesses to the variable rather than just one as required. One way to do this is to have a process that wishes to access the variable determine, based on its state, a function h to use as an invocation of the variable. The function h provides the information from the process's state that is needed to determine the transition, expressed in the form of a function to apply to the variable. The effect of the function h on the variable when it has value v is to change the variable's value to $h(v)$ and return the previous value v to the process. The process can then change its state, based on its old state and v.

Formally, a read-modify-write variable can have any set V of values and any $v_0 \in V$ as an initial value. Its invocations are all the functions h, where $h : V \rightarrow V$. Its responses are $v \in V$. Its function f is defined by $f(h, v) = (v, h(v))$. That is, it responds with the prior value and updates its value based on the submitted function.

For instance, in Example 9.1.1, the function submitted by a process to the variable is of the form h_v, where

$$h_v(x) = \begin{cases} v, & \text{if } x = unknown \\ x, & \text{otherwise} \end{cases}$$

The particular h_v submitted by a process uses the process's *input* as the value of v. A return value of *unknown* causes *output* to be set to the value of *input*, while a return value of $v \in V$ causes *output* to be set to v. In either case, *status* is appropriately modified.

Example 9.4.3   Other variable types

Many of the variable types used in shared memory multiprocessors include restricted forms of read-modify-write, plus basic operations such as read and write. Some popular restricted form of read-modify-write include *compare-and-swap*, *swap*, *test-and-set*, and *fetch-and-add* operations. These operations are defined as follows. Fix a set V and initial value v_0.

The invocations for *compare-and-swap* operations are of the form *compare-and-swap*(u, v), $u, v \in V$, and the responses are elements of V. The function f is defined for compare-and-swap invocations by

$$f(compare\text{-}and\text{-}swap(u, v), w) = \begin{cases} (w, v), & \text{if } u = w \\ (w, w), & \text{otherwise} \end{cases}$$

That is, if the variable's value is equal to the first argument, u, then the operation resets it to the second argument, v; otherwise, the operation does not change the value of the variable. In either case, the original value of the variable is returned.

The invocations for *swap* operations are of the form *swap*(u), $u \in V$, and the responses are elements of V. The function f is defined for swap invocations by

$$f(swap(u), v) = (v, u).$$

That is, the operation writes the input value u into the variable and returns the original variable value v.

The invocations for *test-and-set* operations are of the form *test-and-set*(u), $u \in V$, and the responses are elements of V. The function f is defined for test-and-set by

$$f(test\text{-}and\text{-}set(u), v) = (v, 1).$$

That is, the operation writes 1 into the variable and returns the original variable value v.

Finally, the invocations for *fetch-and-add* operations are of the form *fetch-and-add*(u), $u \in V$, and the responses are elements of V. The function f is defined for fetch-and-add by

$$f(\textit{fetch-and-add}(u), v) = (v, v + u).$$

That is, the operation adds the input value u to the variable value v and returns the original value v. (This operation requires that the set V support a notion of addition.)

We can define the *executions* of a variable type in a natural way, as finite sequences $v_0, a_1, b_1, v_1, a_2, b_2, v_2, \dots, v_r$ or infinite sequences $v_0, a_1, b_1, v_1, a_2, b_2, v_2,$ $\dots$. Here, the v's are values in V, v_0 is the initial value of the variable type, the a's are invocations, the b's are responses, and the quadruples $v_k, a_{k+1}, b_{k+1}, v_{k+1}$ satisfy the function of the type. (That is, $(b_{k+1}, v_{k+1}) = f(a_{k+1}, v_k)$.) Also, the *traces* of a type are the sequences of a's and b's that are derived from executions of the type.

Example 9.4.4   Trace of a read/write variable type

The following is a trace of a read/write variable type with $V = \mathbb{N}$ and $v_0 = 0$:

$$\textit{read}, 0, \textit{write}(8), \textit{ack}, \textit{read}, 8$$

We finish this section by defining a simple composition operation for variable types. This lets us regard a collection of separate variable types, each with its own operations, as a single variable type with several components, and with operations acting on the individual components.

We define a countable collection $\{\mathcal{T}_i\}_{i \in I}$ of variable types to be *compatible* if all their sets of invocations are disjoint, and likewise for all their sets of responses. Then the *composition* $\mathcal{T} = \prod_{i \in I} \mathcal{T}_i$ of a countable compatible collection of variable types is defined as follows:

- The set V is the Cartesian product of the value sets of the $\mathcal{T}_i$.

- The initial value v_0 consists of the initial values of the $\mathcal{T}_i$.

- The set of invocations is the union of the sets of invocations of the $\mathcal{T}_i$.

- The set of responses is the union of the sets of responses of the $\mathcal{T}_i$.

- The function f operates "componentwise." That is, consider $f(a, w)$, where a is an invocation of $\mathcal{T}_i$. Function f applies a to the ith component of w, using the function of $\mathcal{T}_i$, to obtain (b, v). It returns b and sets the ith component of w to v.

When I is a finite set, we sometimes use the infix operation symbol $\times$ to denote composition.

Example 9.4.5   Composition of variable types

We describe the composition of two read/write variable types $\mathcal{T}_x$ and $\mathcal{T}_y$. (You should think of x and y as the names of two registers.) Suppose the value sets are V_x and V_y, respectively, and the initial values are $v_{0,x}$ and $v_{0,y}$.

We can only compose these two types if they are compatible. So we disambiguate the invocations and responses of the two types by attaching the (literal) subscript x or y. Then the composed type $\mathcal{T}_x \times \mathcal{T}_y$ has $V_x \times V_y$ as its value set and the pair $(v_{0,x}, v_{0,y})$ as its initial value. Its invocations are $read_x$, $read_y$, $write(v)_x$, $v \in V_x$, and $write(v)_y$, $v \in V_y$. Its responses are v_x, $v \in V_x$, plus v_y, $v \in V_y$, plus ack_x and ack_y.

Now we consider the function f. Let $w = (v, v')$ be an arbitrary element of $V_x \times V_y$. Then f is defined for w by $f(read_x, w) = (v_x, w)$, $f(read_y, w) = (v'_y, w)$, $f(write(v'')_x, w) = (ack_x, (v'', v'))$, and $f(write(v'')_y, w) = (ack_y, (v, v''))$. Thus, a *read* returns the indicated component of the vector, while a *write* updates the indicated component.

9.5   Complexity Measures

In order to measure time complexity in asynchronous shared memory systems, we assume an upper bound of ℓ on process step time. Such an upper bound allows us to prove upper bounds on the time required for events of interest to occur (e.g., for a process that has received an $init_i$ input to produce a $decide_i$ output).

More precisely, we establish a *time complexity measure* for shared memory systems as a special case of the time complexity measure defined for general I/O automata in Section 8.6. That is, we define an upper bound of ℓ for each task C of each process; this imposes an upper bound of ℓ on the time between successive chances by task C to perform a step. We measure the *time* until some designated event π by the supremum of the times that can be assigned to π by time assignments that respect the upper bounds. Likewise, we measure the *time* between two events of interest by the supremum of the differences between the times that can be assigned to those two events.

Note that our time measure does not take into account any overhead due to contention among processes for accessing a common variable. In multiprocessor settings where such contention is an issue, the time measure must be modified accordingly.

Other interesting measures of complexity for shared memory systems include some static measures such as the number of shared variables and the size of their value sets.

9.6 Failures

The stopping failure of a process i in a shared memory system is modelled using an input action $stop_i$, which causes the stopping failure of all tasks of process i but does not affect any other processes. More precisely, a $stop_i$ event can change only the state of process i, although we do not constrain these state changes except for requiring that they permanently disable all the tasks of process i. We leave open the issue of whether later inputs to process i are ignored, or cause the same changes to the state of process i that they would if no $stop_i$ had occurred, or cause some other state changes. These distinctions do not matter, because the effects of such state changes could never be communicated to any other processes.

Figure 9.3 depicts the architecture for an asynchronous shared memory system with stopping failures.

9.7 Randomization

A probabilistic shared memory system is defined by specializing the general definition of a probabilistic I/O automaton in Section 8.8 to the case where the I/O automaton is a shared memory system.

9.8 Bibliographic Notes

There are no special references for the basic model described in this chapter. It is a garden-variety shared memory model, formulated within the I/O automaton framework. Another model for shared memory systems was defined by Lynch and Fischer [216]; in that model, processes communicate by means of instantaneous accesses to shared variables, but not by means of external events. Kruskal,

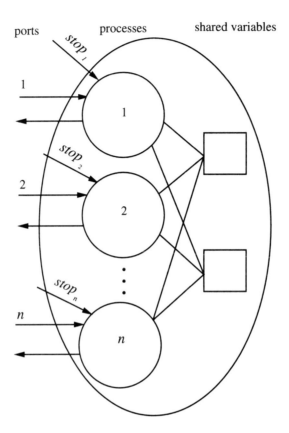

Figure 9.3: Architecture for asynchronous shared memory system with stopping failures.

Rudolph, and Snir [171] defined the various types of variables used in shared memory multiprocesssors.

Dwork, Herlihy, and Waarts [103] have suggested a time complexity measure that takes into account contention for shared memory access. The formal modelling of probabilistic shared memory systems is derived from work by Lynch, Saias, and Segala [208].

9.9 Exercises

9.1. Let A be the shared memory system described in Example 9.1.1.

  (a) Prove that $fairtraces(A) \subseteq traces(P)$, where P is the trace property described in Example 9.1.1.

  (b) Define an interesting trace safety property Q and show that the (not necessarily fair) traces of A satisfy it. That is, show $traces(A) \subseteq traces(Q)$. Your property should include mention of what can happen where there is more than one $init_i$ action for the same process i.

9.2. Prove that $fairtraces(A \times \prod_{1 \leq i \leq n} U_i) \subseteq traces(Q)$, where A is the shared memory system described in Example 9.1.1 and Q is the trace property described in Example 9.2.1.

One way to do this is to reformulate Q as the intersection of a safety property S and a liveness property L. S can include the agreement and validity condition, plus part of the first condition—that for each i, the subsequence of actions of i is some prefix of a sequence of the form $init_i$, $decide_i$. L can just say that at least one $init_i$ event and at least one $decide_i$ event occur, for each i. Show that each system component preserves S and use Theorem 8.11 to show that $traces(A \times \prod_{1 \leq i \leq n} U_i) \subseteq traces(S)$. (The fact that A preserves S could be argued from the fact that $traces(A) \subseteq traces(P)$.) Then use the fairness assumptions to show liveness.

9.3. Prove that the following is an invariant of the system $A \times \prod_{1 \leq i \leq n} U_i$ of Example 9.2.1: If $decision_{U_i} \neq unknown$ and $decision_{U_j} \neq unknown$, then $decision_{U_i} = decision_{U_j}$.[3] Do this in two alternative ways:

(a) Based on the fact that $traces(A \times \prod_{1 \leq i \leq n} U_i) \subseteq traces(S)$, proved in Exercise 9.2.

(b) Using the usual method for proving invariants—an induction on the length of an execution leading to a given system state.

9.4. Does the system described in Example 9.4.1, based on a read/write register, satisfy the same trace property P as the system in Example 9.1.1? If so, prove this. If not, then give a counterexample and then state and prove the strongest claims you can for the system's behavior.

9.5. *Research Question:* Define an alternative model for shared memory systems by using I/O automata to model processes only, and by defining a new type of state machine (similar to the model for variable types) for shared variables. Define an appropriate composition operation to combine "compatible" process and shared variable automata into a single I/O automaton to model the entire system. What modifications are needed to the results in subsequent chapters to fit them to your new definitions?

---

[3]We use the subscript notation to designate the variables belonging to particular automata.

Chapter 10

Mutual Exclusion

In this chapter, we begin the study of *asynchronous algorithms*. Asynchronous algorithms are generally quite different from synchronous algorithms, since they must cope with the uncertainty imposed by asynchrony as well as the uncertainty caused by distribution. In asynchronous networks, for example, process steps and message deliveries do not necessarily take place in lock-step synchrony; rather, they may happen in an arbitrary order.

Instead of moving immediately to the study of asynchronous network algorithms, we first study algorithms in the asynchronous shared memory setting. The main reason we do this is that the setting is somewhat simpler. But also, as you will see in Chapter 17, there are close connections between the asynchronous shared memory model and the asynchronous network model. For instance, it is possible to translate algorithms written for the asynchronous shared memory model into versions that can run in asynchronous networks. In this chapter and Chapter 11, we will not consider failures very much; asynchrony alone introduces enough interesting complications for now.

The problem we study here is the *mutual exclusion* problem, a problem of managing access to a single indivisible resource (e.g., a printer) that can only support one user at a time. Alternatively, it can be viewed as the problem of ensuring that certain portions of program code are executed within *critical regions*, where no two programs are permitted to be in critical regions at the same time. It is not known which users are going to request the resource nor when they will do so. This problem arises in both centralized and distributed operating systems.

We present several mutual exclusion algorithms for the read/write shared memory model, starting with an early algorithm by Dijkstra. Subsequent algorithms improve on Dijkstra's by guaranteeing fairness to the different users and by weakening the type of shared memory that is used. We then give a fundamental lower bound for the number of read/write shared variables that are needed to solve the problem. Finally, we give a collection of upper and lower bound results for the case where the shared memory consists of stronger, read-modify-write shared variables.

This chapter is quite long. The main reason for its length is that we are using it not just to present a collection of algorithms and impossibility results, but also to introduce many ideas that will be used in the rest of the book. These include techniques for modelling shared memory systems and their environments, statements of correctness conditions for asynchronous algorithms (including safety, progress, and fairness conditions), proof techniques for asynchronous algorithms (including operational, invariant assertion, and simulation relation proofs), ways of defining and analyzing time complexity for asynchronous algorithms, and techniques for proving lower bounds.

10.1 Asynchronous Shared Memory Model

Before we begin describing any algorithms, we describe the computation model we will use in this and the next three chapters. Here, we describe the model briefly and informally; a more complete, formal description appears in Chapter 9.

The system is modelled as a collection of processes and shared variables, with interactions as depicted in Figure 10.1. Each process i is a kind of state machine, with a set $states_i$ of states and a subset $start_i$ of $states_i$ indicating the start states, just as in the synchronous setting. However, now process i also has labelled *actions*, describing the activities in which it participates. These are classified as either *input*, *output*, or *internal* actions. In Figure 10.1, the arrows entering and leaving the process circles represent the input and output actions of the various processes. We further distinguish between two different kinds of internal actions: those that involve the shared memory and those that involve strictly local computation. If an action involves the shared memory, we assume that it only involves one shared variable.

Unlike in the synchronous setting, there is no message-generation function, since there are no messages in this model. All communication between the processes is via the shared memory.

There is a transition relation *trans* for the entire system, which is a set of (s, π, s') triples, where s and s' are *automaton states*, that is, combinations of states for all the processes and values for all the shared variables, and where π is the label of an input, output, or internal action. We call these combinations of process states and variable values "automaton states" because, in the formal model of Chapter 9, the entire system is modelled as a single automaton. The statement that $(s, \pi, s') \in$ *trans* says that from automaton state s it is possible to

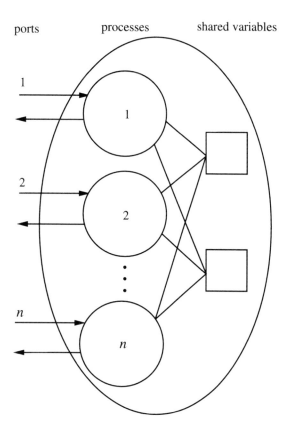

Figure 10.1: An asynchronous shared memory system.

go to automaton state s' as a result of performing action π. Note that *trans* is a *relation* rather than a function—for convenience, we allow our model to include nondeterminism.

We assume that input actions can always happen, that is, that the system is *input-enabled*. Formally, this means that for every automaton state s and input action π, there exists s' such that $(s, \pi, s') \in trans$. In contrast, output and internal steps might be enabled only in a subset of the states. The intuition behind the input-enabling property is that the input actions are controlled by an arbitrary external user, while the internal and output actions are controlled by the system itself.

The set of transitions has some "locality" restrictions. First, for any transition that does not involve the shared memory, only the state of the process that performs the action can be involved. On the other hand, for a transition that involves a process i and a shared variable x, only the state of process i and the value of variable x can be involved. We assume that the *enabling* of a shared memory action depends only on the process state and not on the value of the shared variable accessed. However, the resulting changes to the process state and the variable value may depend also on the variable value.

The shared variable steps are usually constrained further, to be executions of operations of particular types, such as *read* and *write*. A *read* step for variable x involves changing the process state, based on its previous state and the value in x; however, the value of variable x does not change. A *write* step involves writing a designated value to a shared variable, overwriting whatever was there before; it may also change the process state. We will mostly consider the model in which the variables are accessed using *read* and *write* operations, but we will also consider some more powerful operations such as read-modify-write.

The execution of an asynchronous shared memory system is very different from that of a synchronous system. This time, processes are assumed to take steps one at a time, in an *arbitrary* order rather than in synchronized rounds. This arbitrary order is the essence of the asynchronous model. An execution is formalized as an alternating sequence, $s_0, \pi_1, s_1, \ldots$, consisting of automaton states alternated with actions (each action belonging to a particular process), where successive (state, action, state) triples satisfy the transition relation. An execution may be a finite or an infinite sequence.

There is one important exception to the arbitrariness in the order of process steps. We do not want to allow a process to stop taking steps when it is supposed to be taking steps, that is, when the process is in a state in which some *locally controlled* action (i.e., a non-input action) is enabled. (Although input actions are always enabled, we do not assume that they ever occur.) This condition is a little tricky to state precisely.

For example, we might try to express it by saying: "If a process takes only finitely many steps, then its final state is one in which no locally controlled action is enabled." But this is not quite sufficient—we might want also to rule out some situations in which a process takes infinitely many steps, but after some point, all the remaining steps are input steps. We need to make sure that the process itself also gets turns to perform locally controlled actions.

So, we might try to express the needed condition by saying: "If a process takes only finitely many steps, then its final state is one in which no locally controlled action is enabled, and if a process takes infinitely many steps, then infinitely many of these steps are locally controlled steps." But again this is not quite right—consider the situation in which the process receives infinitely many inputs and performs no locally controlled actions, but in fact no locally controlled actions are enabled. That situation seems fine, since we could say that the process had "turns" to perform locally controlled steps, but simply had none that it "wanted" to perform.

We account for all these possibilities in the following definition. For each process i, we assume that one of the following holds:

1. The entire execution is finite, and in the final state no locally controlled action of process i is enabled.

2. The execution is infinite, and there are either infinitely many occurrences of locally controlled actions of i, or else infinitely many places where no such action is enabled.

We call this condition the *fairness condition* for this shared memory system. (In terms of the I/O automaton definitions in Chapter 8, this amounts to grouping all the locally controlled actions of one process into one task.)

10.2 The Problem

The mutual exclusion problem involves the allocation of a single, indivisible, nonshareable resource among n *users*, $U_1, \ldots, U_n$. The users can be thought of as application programs. The resource could be, for example, a printer or other output device that requires exclusive access in order to ensure that the output is sensible. Or it could be a database or other data structure that requires exclusive access in order to avoid interference among the operations of different users.

A user with access to the resource is modelled as being in a *critical region,* which is simply a designated subset of its states. When a user is not involved in any way with the resource, it is said to be in the *remainder region.* In order to gain admittance to its critical region, a user executes a *trying protocol,* and after it is done with the resource, it executes an (often trivial) *exit protocol.* This procedure can be repeated, so that each user follows a cycle, moving from its *remainder region* (R) to its *trying region* (T), then to its *critical region* (C), then to its *exit region* (E), and then back again to its remainder region. This cycle is shown in Figure 10.2.

We consider mutual exclusion algorithms within the shared memory model described above—see Figure 10.1 for the architecture. The shared memory system contains n processes, numbered $1, \ldots, n$, each corresponding to one user U_i. The inputs to process i are the try_i action, which models a request by user U_i for access to the resource, and the $exit_i$ action, which models an announcement by user U_i that it is done with the resource. The outputs of process i are $crit_i$, which models the granting of the resource to U_i, and rem_i, which tells U_i that it can continue with the rest of its work. The *try, crit, exit,* and *rem* actions

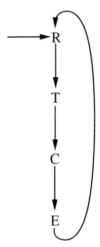

Figure 10.2: The cycle of regions of a single user.

are the only external actions of the shared memory system. The processes are responsible for performing the trying and exit protocols. Each process i acts as an "agent" on behalf of user U_i.

Each of the users U_i, $1 \leq i \leq n$, is modelled as a state machine (formally, an *I/O automaton*) that communicates with its agent process using the try_i, $crit_i$, $exit_i$, and rem_i actions. The external interface (formally, the *external signature*) of U_i is depicted in Figure 10.3.

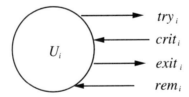

Figure 10.3: External interface of user U_i.

We think of each user U_i as executing some application program. The only thing that we assume about U_i is that it obeys the cyclic region protocol, that is, that U_i is not the first to violate the cyclic order of actions, try_i, $crit_i$, $exit_i$, ... (starting with try_i), between itself and its agent process. Formally, we define a sequence of try_i, $crit_i$, $exit_i$ and rem_i actions to be *well-formed* for user i if it is a prefix of the cyclically ordered sequence try_i, $crit_i$, $exit_i$, rem_i, try_i, ... Then we require that U_i *preserve* the *trace property* defined by the set of sequences that are well-formed for user i. (We use the definitions of *trace property* and *preserves* from Section 8.5.4.)

In executions of U_i that do observe the cyclic order of actions, we say that U_i is

- in its *remainder region* initially and in between any rem_i event and the following try_i event.

- in its *trying region* in between any try_i event and the following $crit_i$ event.

- in its *critical region* in between any $crit_i$ event and the following $exit_i$ event. During this time, U_i should be thought of as being free to use the resource (although we do not model the resource explicitly).

- in its *exit region* in between any $exit_i$ event and the following rem_i event.

Figure 10.4 depicts all the interactions in the system.

Now we can state what it means for a shared memory system A to *solve the mutual exclusion problem* for a given collection of users. Namely, the combination (formally, the composition) of A and the users must satisfy the following conditions:

Well-formedness: In any execution, and for any i, the subsequence describing the interaction between U_i and A is well-formed for i.

Mutual exclusion: There is no reachable system state (that is, a combination of an automaton state for A and states for all the U_i) in which more than one user is in the critical region C.

Progress: At any point in a *fair execution*

1. (Progress for the trying region) If at least one user is in T and no user is in C, then at some later point some user enters C.

2. (Progress for the exit region) If at least one user is in E, then at some later point some user enters R.

We say that a shared memory system A *solves the mutual exclusion problem* provided that it solves it for every collection of users.

Note that we have stated the correctness conditions in terms of the users' regions. Normally, the process states will also be classified according to their regions, and these regions will correspond exactly to the user regions. So we can equivalently state the correctness conditions in terms of process regions. We will talk interchangeably about user regions and process regions in the rest of this chapter.

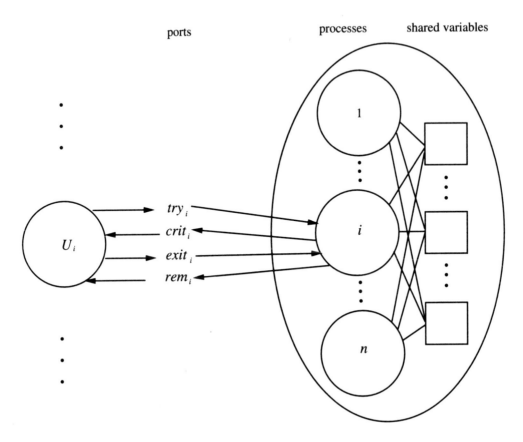

Figure 10.4: Interactions between components for the mutual exclusion problem.

Note that the progress condition assumes that the execution of the system is fair, that is, it assumes that all the processes (and users) continue taking steps. If we did not assume this, then it would not be reasonable to require that *crit* or *rem* outputs eventually be performed. On the other hand, we do not need to assume fairness in order to require that the system guarantee well-formedness or mutual exclusion. The difference is that the well-formedness and mutual exclusion conditions are *safety properties* (properties that say that particular "bad" things never happen), while the progress condition is a *liveness property* (a property that says that some "good" thing eventually happens).

Trace properties.   Still another equivalent way of presenting these correctness conditions is in terms of a *trace property*, as defined in Section 8.5.2. For example, we can define a trace property P, where $sig(P)$ has all the *try*, *crit*, *exit*, and *rem* actions as outputs, and *traces*(*P*) is the set of sequences *β* of these actions that satisfy the following three conditions:

1. *β* is well-formed for each *i*.

2. *β* does not contain two *crit* events without an intervening *exit* event.

3. At any point in *β*,

   (a) If some process's last event is *try* and no process's last event is *crit*, then there is a later *crit* event.

   (b) If some process's last event is *exit*, then there is a later *rem* event.

Then an equivalent restatement of the mutual exclusion problem is the requirement that, for all combinations *B* of *A* with users, *fairtraces*(*B*) ⊆ *traces*(*P*). (Recall that the external actions of *B* are just the *try*, *crit*, *exit*, and *rem* actions.) Trace property *P* could also be split into two parts, a safety property encompassing the well-formedness and mutual exclusion conditions, and a liveness property for the progress condition.

Shared responsibility for progress. According to the correctness conditions we have given, responsibility for the continuing progress of the entire system rests not only with the protocol, but with the users as well. If a user U_i gets the resource (by means of a $crit_i$ event) but never returns it (by means of an $exit_i$ event), then the entire system grinds to a halt. But if each user eventually returns the resource every time it receives it, then the progress condition implies that the entire system continues to make progress, repeatedly moving processes to new regions (unless all users remain in their remainder regions from some point on).

Lockout. The progress condition we have stated does not imply that any particular requesting user ever succeeds in reaching its critical region. Rather, it is a "global" notion of progress, saying only that *some* user reaches its critical region. For instance, the following scenario does not violate the progress condition: Starting from an initial state, user U_1 enters *T*. Then user U_2 cycles through its four regions infinitely many times, while U_1 remains in *T* and the rest of the processes remain in *R*. Our progress condition does not guarantee that U_1 ever reaches *C*.

Restricting process activity. There is one other constraint—a technical one—that we assume in this chapter: that a process within the shared memory system can have a locally controlled action enabled only when its user is in the trying or exit region. This says that a process can be actively engaged in executing the protocol only while it has active requests. This assumption is consistent with the view that each process is simply an agent for its corresponding user.

In practical settings, this assumption might or might not be reasonable. The mutual exclusion problem was first studied in the setting of a time-shared uniprocessor, where the users are logically independent processes sharing a single processor. In this setting, allowing a permanent process to manage access to the resource would cause extra context-switching, between the manager process and the user processes. In a true multiprocessor environment, it is possible to avoid the context-switching by using a dedicated processor to manage the resource. However, there will generally be many resources to be managed, and all the processors dedicated to managing resources would be unavailable for participation in other computational tasks.

Read/write shared variables.   For most of the chapter (except for Section 10.9), we assume that the shared variables are read/write variables, also known as *registers*.   In one step, a process can either read or write a single shared variable, but not both. Thus, the two actions involving process i and register x are

1. (*read*) Process i reads register x and uses the value read to modify the state of process i.

2. (*write*) Process i writes a value determined from process i's state to register x.

We finish this section with a simple lemma saying that processes cannot stop taking steps while they are in their trying or exit regions.

Lemma 10.1 *Let A be an algorithm that solves the mutual exclusion problem (for all collections of users). Let $U_1, \ldots, U_n$ be any particular collection of users, and let B be the combination of A and the given collection of users. Let s be a reachable state of B.*

If process i is in its trying or exit region in state s, then some locally controlled action of process i is enabled in s.

Proof.   Without loss of generality, we may assume that each of the users, $U_1, \ldots, U_n$, always returns the resource.

Let α be a finite execution of B ending in s, and suppose for the sake of contradiction that process i is in either its trying or exit region in state s, and no locally controlled action of process i is enabled in s. Then we claim that no events involving i occur in any execution of B that extends α, after the prefix α. This follows from the fact that enabling of locally controlled actions is determined only by the local process state, plus the fact that well-formedness prevents inputs to process i while process i is in T or E.

Now let α' be a fair execution of B that extends α, in which no *try* events occur after the prefix α. Repeated use of the progress assumption, plus the fact that the users always return the resource, imply that process i must eventually perform either a *crit$_i$* or a *rem$_i$* action. But this contradicts the fact that α' contains no further actions of i. □

10.3 Dijkstra's Mutual Exclusion Algorithm

The first mutual exclusion algorithm for the asynchronous read/write shared memory model was developed in 1965 by Edsger Dijkstra, based on a prior two-process solution by Dekker. This algorithm is not the most elegant or efficient algorithm now available, nor does it satisfy the strongest conditions. However, we present it anyway, for several reasons. First, it is the earliest example we can find of an algorithm that we would categorize as "distributed." Second, it contains several interesting algorithmic ideas. And third, it is a good example to use for illustrating some of the basic reasoning techniques for asynchronous shared memory algorithms.

10.3.1 The Algorithm

We begin by presenting code for the algorithm in a traditional "pseudocode" style, similar to that used in the original paper by Dijkstra. Although this code should make sense informally, it is probably not completely clear how it should be translated into an instance of our model. We call the algorithm *DijkstraME*.

***DijkstraME* algorithm:**

Shared variables:
$turn \in \{1, \dots, n\}$, initially arbitrary, writable and readable by all processes
for every i, $1 \leq i \leq n$:
    $flag(i) \in \{0, 1, 2\}$, initially 0, writable by process i and readable by all processes

Process i:

```
** Remainder region **

       try_i
L:     flag(i) := 1
       while turn ≠ i do
              if flag(turn) = 0 then turn := i
       flag(i) := 2
       for j ≠ i do
              if flag(j) = 2 then goto L
       crit_i

** Critical region **

       exit_i
       flag(i) := 0
       rem_i
```

The shared variables are *turn*, an integer in $\{1, \ldots, n\}$, and $flag(i), 1 \leq i \leq n$, one per process, each taking on values from $\{0, 1, 2\}$, initially 0. The *turn* variable is a *multi-writer/multi-reader* register, writable and readable by all processes. Each $flag(i)$ is a *single-writer/multi-reader* register, writable only by process i but readable by all processes.

In process i's first stage, it starts by setting its *flag* to 1 and then repeatedly checks the *turn* variable to see if *turn* = i. If not, and if the current owner of *turn* is seen not to be currently active, process i sets *turn* := i. Once having seen *turn* = i, process i moves on to the second stage.

In the second stage, process i again sets its *flag*, this time to 2, and then checks to see that no other process has its *flag* = 2. This check of other processes' *flags* can be done in any order. If the check completes successfully, process i goes to its critical region; otherwise, it returns to the first stage. Upon leaving the critical region, process i lowers its *flag* back to 0.

Before we can prove anything about *DijkstraME*, we need to understand it as an instance of our formal state machine model. It is not completely obvious how to translate the code into an automaton.

First, the state of each process should consist of the values of its local variables, as you would expect, plus some other information that is not represented explicitly in the code, including

- temporary variables needed to remember values just read from shared variables

- a program counter, to say where the process is in its code

- temporary variables introduced by the flow of control of the program (e.g., the for loop can introduce a set variable to keep track of the indices of processes that have already been checked successfully)

- a region designation, R, T, C, or E (R indicates the remainder region, T indicates the portion of the code from a try_i event until the next $crit_i$ event, C indicates the critical region, and E indicates the portion of the code from an $exit_i$ event until the next rem_i event)

The unique start state of each process should consist of specified initial values for local variables, arbitrary values for temporary variables, and the program counter and the region designation indicating the remainder region. The initial value for each shared variable is as specified.

The steps of the automaton should follow the code; however, there are some ambiguities in the code that need to be resolved in the automaton. Although the code describes the changes to the local and shared variables, it does not say explicitly what happens to the implicit variables (the temporaries, program counter, and region designation). For example, when a try_i action occurs, i's program counter should move to statement L in the code and i's region designation should become T. These changes must be described explicitly in the automaton.

The code also does not specify exactly which portions of the code comprise indivisible steps. However, it is essential to know this in order to reason carefully about the algorithm. For *DijkstraME*, the indivisible steps are the *try*, *crit*, *exit*, and *rem* steps at the user interface, plus individual writes to and reads from the shared variables, plus some local computation steps. There is at least one minor subtlety: the test for whether $flag(turn) = 0$ does not require two separate reads—since *turn* was just read in the previous line, a local copy of *turn* can be used.

We resolve all of these ambiguities by rewriting the *DijkstraME* code by hand, in the *precondition-effect* style used in Chapter 8. Rewriting in this way makes the code a good deal longer, but all the transitions are now described explicitly. For readability, we arrange the pieces of code for the different actions in approximately the order in which they are supposed to be executed; however, note that this order has no significance in the formal model—any action is allowed to occur at any time when it is enabled. The region designations R, T, C, and E are encoded into program counter values: R corresponds to *rem*; T corresponds to *set-flag-1*, *test-turn*, *test-flag*, *set-turn*, *set-flag-2*, *check*, and *leave-try*; C corresponds to *crit*; and E corresponds to *reset* and *leave-exit*. Note that each code fragment is performed indivisibly.

DijkstraME algorithm (rewritten):

Shared variables:
$turn \in \{1, \ldots, n\}$, initially arbitrary
for every i, $1 \leq i \leq n$:
   $flag(i) \in \{0, 1, 2\}$, initially 0

Actions of i:

Input:	Internal:
try_i	$set\text{-}flag\text{-}1_i$
$exit_i$	$test\text{-}turn_i$
Output:	$test\text{-}flag(j)_i$, $1 \leq j \leq n$, $j \neq i$
$crit_i$	$set\text{-}turn_i$
rem_i	$set\text{-}flag\text{-}2_i$
	$check(j)_i$, $1 \leq j \leq n$, $j \neq i$
	$reset_i$

States of i:
$pc \in \{rem, set\text{-}flag\text{-}1, test\text{-}turn, test\text{-}flag(j), set\text{-}turn, set\text{-}flag\text{-}2, check, leave\text{-}try, crit,$
   $reset, leave\text{-}exit\}$, initially rem
S, a set of process indices, initially $\emptyset$

Transitions of i:

try_i
   Effect:
      $pc := set\text{-}flag\text{-}1$

$set\text{-}flag\text{-}1_i$
   Precondition:
      $pc = set\text{-}flag\text{-}1$
   Effect:
      $flag(i) := 1$
      $pc := test\text{-}turn$

$test\text{-}turn_i$
   Precondition:
      $pc = test\text{-}turn$
   Effect:
      if $turn = i$ then $pc := set\text{-}flag\text{-}2$
      else $pc := test\text{-}flag(turn)$

$test\text{-}flag(j)_i$
   Precondition:
      $pc = test\text{-}flag(j)$
   Effect:
      if $flag(j) = 0$ then $pc := set\text{-}turn$
      else $pc := test\text{-}turn$

$set\text{-}turn_i$
   Precondition:
      $pc = set\text{-}turn$
   Effect:
      $turn := i$
      $pc := set\text{-}flag\text{-}2$

$set\text{-}flag\text{-}2_i$
   Precondition:
      $pc = set\text{-}flag\text{-}2$
   Effect:
      $flag(i) := 2$
      $S := \{i\}$
      $pc := check$

$check(j)_i$
   Precondition:
      $pc = check$
      $j \notin S$
   Effect:
      if $flag(j) = 2$ then
         $S := \emptyset$
         $pc := set\text{-}flag\text{-}1$
      else
         $S := S \cup \{j\}$
         if $|S| = n$ then $pc := leave\text{-}try$

$crit_i$
    Precondition:
        $pc = leave\text{-}try$
    Effect:
        $pc := crit$

$exit_i$
    Effect:
        $pc := reset$

$reset_i$
    Precondition:
        $pc = reset$
    Effect:
        $flag(i) := 0$
        $S := \emptyset$
        $pc := leave\text{-}exit$

rem_i
    Precondition:
        $pc = leave\text{-}exit$
    Effect:
        $pc := rem$

The translation should be mainly self-explanatory. Note that the new style makes it easy to express slight improvements; for instance, the $set\text{-}turn_i$ action can allow process i to go directly to the second stage, without retesting $turn$.

10.3.2 A Correctness Argument

In this section we sketch a correctness proof for $DijkstraME$. This will be a somewhat brute-force *operational* proof, that is, one that consists of ad hoc arguments about executions. In the following section, Section 10.3.3, we give an alternative, more stylized proof of the mutual exclusion condition using invariant assertions.

We give three lemmas showing that $DijkstraME$ satisfies its requirements.

Lemma 10.2 *DijkstraME guarantees well-formedness for each user.*

More precisely, we mean that in any execution of the combination (composition) of $DijkstraME$ and any collection of users, the subsequence describing the interaction between any U_i and $DijkstraME$ is well-formed for user i.

Proof. By inspection of the code, it is easy to check that $DijkstraME$ preserves well-formedness for each user. Since, by assumption, the users also preserve well-formedness, Theorem 8.11 implies that the system produces only well-formed sequences.   □

Lemma 10.3 *DijkstraME satisfies mutual exclusion.*

More precisely, we mean that in the combination of $DijkstraME$ and any collection of users, there is no reachable state in which more than one user is in the critical region C.

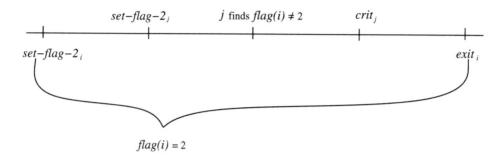

Figure 10.5: Order of events in the proof of Lemma 10.3.

Proof.   By contradiction. Assume that U_i and U_j, $i \neq j$, are simultaneously in region C in some reachable state. Consider an execution that leads to this state. By the code, both process i and process j perform *set-flag-2* steps before entering their critical regions. Consider the last such step for each process and assume, without loss of generality, that *set-flag-2_i* comes first. Then $flag(i)$ remains equal to 2 from that point until process i leaves C, which must be after process j enters C, by the assumption that they both end up in C simultaneously. So, $flag(i)$ has the value 2 throughout the interval from the *set-flag-2_j* event until process j enters C. See Figure 10.5. But, during this time, process j must test $flag(i)$ and find it unequal to 2, a contradiction.   □

Lemma 10.4 *DijkstraME guarantees progress.*

Proof.   The argument for the exit region is easy: If at any point in a fair execution, U_i is in the exit region, then process i keeps taking steps. After at most two more of these steps, process i will perform a *rem$_i$* action, sending U_i to its remainder region.

We consider the progress condition for the trying region. Suppose for the sake of contradiction that α is a fair execution that reaches a point where there is at least one user in T and no user in C, and suppose that after this point, no user ever enters C.

We begin by removing some complications. First, any process in E keeps taking steps, so after at most two steps, it must reach R. So, after some point in α, every process must be in T or R. Second, since there are only finitely many processes in the system, after some point in α, no new processes enter T. Thus, after some point in α, every process is in T or R, and no process ever again changes region. This implies that α has a suffix α_1 in which there is a fixed nonempty set of processes in T, continuing to take steps forever, and no region changes occur. Call these processes *contenders*.

Note that after at most a single step in α_1, each contender i ensures that *flag*$(i) \geq 1$, and it remains ≥ 1 for the rest of α_1. So we can assume, without loss of generality, that *flag*$(i) \geq 1$ for all contenders i throughout α_1.

Clearly, if *turn* is modified during α_1, it is changed to a contender's index. Moreover, we have the following claim.

Claim 10.5 *In α_1, turn eventually acquires a contender's index.*

Proof. Suppose not, that is, suppose the value of *turn* remains equal to the index of a non-contender throughout α_1. Consider any contender i.

If pc_i ever reaches *test-turn* (i.e., the beginning of the while loop in the original code), then we claim that i will set *turn* to i. This is because i first performs a *test-turn$_i$* and finds that *turn* equal to some $j \neq i$. Then it performs a *test-flag*$(j)_i$ and finds *flag*$(j) = 0$, since j is not a contender. Process i therefore performs *set-turn$_i$*, setting *turn* to i.

Now we show that i reaches *test-turn*. The only way it might not is if i succeeds in its *check*s of all the other processes' *flag*s (in the second stage of the original code) and proceeds to *leave-try*. But by assumption about α_1, we know that i does not reach C. So it must be that some *check* must fail, taking i back to *set-flag-1*, from which it proceeds to *test-turn*.

So, i reaches *test-turn* and thereafter sets *turn* := i. Since i is a contender, this is the needed contradiction. ☐

Once *turn* is set to a contender's index, it is always thereafter equal to *some* contender's index, although the value of *turn* may change to the index of different contenders. (This is because it is possible for several processes to be simultaneously at *set-turn*.) Then any later *test-turn* and subsequent *test-flag* yield *flag*$(turn) \geq 1$, since for all contenders i, *flag*$(i) \geq 1$. Thus, *turn* will not be changed as a result of these tests. Therefore, eventually *turn* stabilizes to a final (contender's) index. Let α_2 be a suffix of α_1 in which the value of *turn* is stabilized at some contender's index, say i.

Next we claim that in α_2, any contender $j \neq i$ eventually ends up with its program counter looping forever between *test-turn* and *test-flag*. (That is, it winds up looping forever in the while loop.) This is because if it ever reaches *check* (in the second stage), then, since it doesn't reach C, it must eventually return to *set-flag-1*. But then it is stuck looping forever, because *turn* = $i \neq j$ and *flag*$(i) \neq 0$ throughout α_2. So let α_3 be a suffix of α_2 in which all contenders other than i loop forever between *test-turn* and *test-flag*. Note that this means that all contenders other than i have their *flag* variables equal to 1 throughout α_3.

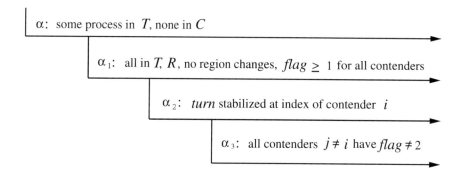

Figure 10.6: Successive suffixes in proof of Lemma 10.4.

We conclude the argument by claiming that in α_3, process i (the one whose index is in *turn*) has nothing to stand in the way of its reaching C. For example, if i performs *test-turn*, then i finds $turn = i$ and so proceeds to *set-flag-2*. Then, since no other process has $flag = 2$, process i succeeds in all its *check*s and enters C.

See Figure 10.6 for a depiction of the successive suffixes that appear in this proof.

Theorem 10.6 *DijkstraME solves the mutual exclusion problem.*

Although the arguments above are correct, they are rather intricate and ad hoc. It would be nice to have some more systematic ways of carrying out such proofs. In the following section, we give an alternative proof of the mutual exclusion condition, using invariant assertions. The progress condition could also be proved somewhat more systematically using temporal logic, but we do not do that in this book.

10.3.3   An Assertional Proof of the Mutual Exclusion Condition

In the synchronous network model, many of the neatest and most systematic proofs are based on invariant assertions about the state of the system after some number of rounds. In the asynchronous setting, there is no notion of round, but invariants can still be used. The method just has to be applied at a finer granularity, to verify claims about the system state after any number of individual process steps. Of course, it is usually harder to devise statements about the state of an asynchronous system after any number of steps than it is to devise statements about the state of a synchronous system after any number of rounds. And proving such statements is also usually more difficult. But the effort is generally worthwhile because of the insights that the invariants provide. Invariant assertions are the single most important formal tool for reasoning about the correctness of asynchronous algorithms.

We now give an assertional proof of the mutual exclusion condition for the *DijkstraME* algorithm.

Proof (of Lemma 10.3). To prove mutual exclusion, we must show

Assertion 10.3.1 *In any reachable system state,[1]* $|\{i : pc_i = crit\}| \leq 1$.

We would like to prove this assertion by induction on the number of steps in an execution. But, as usual, the given statement is not strong enough to prove alone in this way—we need some auxiliary invariants. We prove Assertion 10.3.1 as a consequence of the next two assertions.

Assertion 10.3.2 *In any reachable system state, if* $pc_i \in \{leave\text{-}try, crit, reset\}$, *then* $|S_i| = n$.

Assertion 10.3.3 *In any reachable system state, there do not exist* i *and* j, $i \neq j$, *such that* $i \in S_j$ *and* $j \in S_i$.

If both Assertions 10.3.2 and 10.3.3 are true, then Assertion 10.3.1 follows immediately: Assume, for contradiction, that in some reachable system state, there are two distinct processes, i and j, such that $pc_i = pc_j = crit$. Then by Assertion 10.3.2, $|S_i| = |S_j| = n$. But then $j \in S_i$ and $i \in S_j$, contradicting Assertion 10.3.3.

Assertion 10.3.2 can be proved easily by induction on the length of an execution. The basis is true vacuously, since all the processes are in R in the initial system state. The inductive step is a case analysis, considering all the types of actions one at a time. In this case, the only steps that could cause a violation are those that cause pc_i to enter the set of listed values and those that reset S_i to $\emptyset$, namely, $check_i$ and $reset_i$. In the case of a $check_i$, the only way the condition $pc_i \in \{leave\text{-}try, crit, reset\}$ could be true after the step is if $|S_i| = n$, which is just what we need. In the case of a $reset_i$, the process leaves the indicated set of values after the step, so the statement is true vacuously.

So it remains to prove Assertion 10.3.3. This uses two simple facts. The first one constrains where process i can be in its code when $S_i \neq \emptyset$.

Assertion 10.3.4 *In any reachable system state, if* $S_i \neq \emptyset$, *then* $pc_i \in \{check, leave\text{-}try, crit, reset\}$.

---

[1] Recall that a system state is a combination of states of the users and processes plus values of the shared variables.

This is also proved by a simple induction on the length of an execution. The basis is easy, since $S_i = \emptyset$ in the initial system state. For the inductive step, the only events that could cause a violation of this statement are events that cause S_i to become unequal to $\emptyset$ and events that cause pc_i to leave the set of listed values, that is, $set\text{-}flag\text{-}2_i$, $check_i$, and $reset_i$. But $set\text{-}flag\text{-}2_i$ sets $pc_i := check$. Also, when $check_i$ causes pc_i to leave the set of listed values, it also sets $S_i := \emptyset$. Finally, $reset$ sets $S_i := \emptyset$. Thus, all these events preserve the condition.

The second fact says that $flag(i) = 2$ when process i is at certain points in its code.

> **Assertion 10.3.5** *In any reachable system state, if $pc_i \in \{check,$ leave-try, crit, reset$\}$, then $flag(i) = 2$.*

This is also proved by an easy induction on the length of an execution. Putting these two facts together, we see the following:

> **Assertion 10.3.6** *In any reachable system state, if $S_i \neq \emptyset$, then $flag(i) = 2$.*

Now we can prove Assertion 10.3.3, again by induction on the length of an execution. The basis is easy because in the initial state, all sets S_i are empty. For the inductive step, the only event that could cause a violation is one that adds an element j to S_i for some i and j, $i \neq j$, that is, a $check(j)_i$ for some i and j, $i \neq j$. So consider the case where j gets added to S_i as a result of a $check(j)_i$ event. Then it must be that $flag(j) \neq 2$ when this event occurs. But then Assertion 10.3.6 implies that $S_j = \emptyset$, so $i \notin S_j$. Thus, this step cannot cause a violation. □

10.3.4 Running Time

In this section, we prove an upper bound on the time from any point in an execution when some process is in T and no one is in C, until someone enters C.

The first difficulty we face in proving such a bound is that it is not clear what this "time" should mean—unlike in the synchronous setting, there are no rounds to count. Instead, we just assume that each step occurs at some point in real time and that the execution begins at real time 0. We impose an upper bound of ℓ on the time between successive steps of each process (when these steps are enabled); recall that all the precondition-effect code for one action is assumed to comprise a single step. We also assume an upper bound of c on the maximum time that any user spends in the critical region. In terms of these assumed bounds, we can deduce upper bounds for the time required for interesting activity to occur.

Theorem 10.7 *In DijkstraME, suppose that at a particular time some user is in T and no user is in C. Then within time $O(\ell n)$, some user enters C.*

The constant involved in the big-O is independent of ℓ, c, and n. This proof is ad hoc and a little tricky, using ideas from the proof of the progress condition.

Proof. Suppose the lemma is false and consider an execution in which, at some point, process i is in T and no process is in C, and in which no process enters C for time at least $k\ell n$, for some particular large constant k. Constant k is chosen to be considerably bigger than the constants in the big-O terms in the following analysis.

First, it is easy to see that the time elapsed from the starting point of the analysis until there is no process either in C or E is at most $O(\ell)$.

Second, we claim that the additional time until process i performs a *test-turn$_i$* is at most $O(\ell n)$. This is because i can at worst spend this much time checking flags in the second stage before returning to *set-flag-1*. We know that it must return to *set-flag-1*, because otherwise it would go to C, which we have assumed does not happen this quickly.

Third, we claim that the additional time from when process i does *test-turn$_i$* until the value of *turn* is a contender index is at most $O(\ell)$. To see this, we need a rather annoying case analysis. If at the time i does *test-turn$_i$*, *turn* already holds a contender index, then we are done, so suppose that this is not the case; specifically, suppose that *turn* = j, where j is not a contender. Then within time $O(\ell)$ after this test, i performs a *test-flag(j)$_i$*. If process i finds *flag(j)* = 0, then i sets *turn* to i, which is the index of a contender, and we are again done. But if it finds *flag(j)* $\neq$ 0, then it must be that in between the *test-turn$_i$* and the *test-flag(j)$_i$*, process j entered the trying region and became a contender. If *turn* has not changed in the interim, then *turn* is equal to the index of a contender (j) and we are done. But if *turn* has changed in the interim, then it must have been set to the index of a contender. So again, we are done.

Fourth, after an additional time $O(\ell)$, a point is reached at which the value of *turn* has stabilized to the index of some particular contender, say j, and furthermore no process advances again to *set-turn* or *set-flag-2* (at least until time $k\ell n$ after the starting point of the analysis).

Fifth, we claim that by an additional time $O(\ell n)$, all contenders other than j will have their program counters in {*test-turn, test-flag*}. This is because otherwise they would reach C, which we have assumed does not happen this quickly.

Sixth and finally, within an additional time $O(\ell n)$, j must succeed in entering C. This contradicts the assumption that no process enters C within this amount of time.

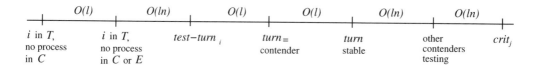

Figure 10.7: Order of events and time bounds in proof of Theorem 10.7.

The order of events in this proof, and the time bounds between them, are depicted in Figure 10.7.   □

10.4   Stronger Conditions for Mutual Exclusion Algorithms

Although the *DijkstraME* algorithm guarantees mutual exclusion and progress, there are other desirable conditions that it does not guarantee. It does not guarantee that the critical region is granted *fairly* to different users; for example, it allows one user to be repeatedly granted access to its critical region while other users trying to gain access are forever prevented from doing so. This situation is sometimes called *lockout* or *starvation*.

Note that the kind of fairness we are talking about here is different from that discussed up to this point. So far, we have been talking about fair execution of process steps (and user automata steps), whereas now we are talking about fair granting of the resource. In order to distinguish these two types of fairness, we will call the fair execution of process steps and user automata steps *low-level fairness*, and the fair granting of the resource *high-level fairness*. In practice, high-level fairness might not be critical; in many practical situations in which mutual exclusion is used, contention between users is sufficiently infrequent that a user can afford to wait until all conflicting users get their turns. The importance of high-level-fairness considerations depends on the amount of contention for the resource, as well as the criticality of individual user programs.

Another not-so-attractive property of Dijkstra's algorithm is that it uses a shared *multi-writer/multi-reader* register (*turn*). Such a variable is difficult and expensive to implement in many kinds of multiprocessor systems (as well as in nearly all message-passing systems). It would be better to design algorithms that use only *single-writer/multi-reader* registers, or even better, *single-writer/single-reader* registers.

Many mutual exclusion algorithms that improve upon *DijkstraME* in various ways have been designed. In the rest of this chapter, we shall look at a representative collection of these algorithms.

Before proceeding to the algorithms, we define carefully what it means for a mutual exclusion algorithm to guarantee high-level fairness. Depending upon the context in which the algorithm is used, different notions of high-level fairness may be appropriate; we define three notions. Each of these properties is stated for a particular mutual exclusion algorithm A composed with a particular collection $U_1, \ldots, U_n$ of users.

Lockout-freedom: In any low-level-fair execution, the following hold:

1. (Lockout-freedom for the trying region) If all users always return the resource, then any user that reaches T eventually enters C.

2. (Lockout-freedom for the exit region) Any user that reaches E eventually enters R.

Note that the lockout-freedom condition, like the basic well-formedness, mutual exclusion, and progress conditions, can be expressed as a trace property.

Time bound b: In any low-level-fair execution with associated times, the following hold:

1. (Time bound b for the trying region) If each user always returns the resource within time c of when it is granted, and the time between successive steps of each process in T or E is at most ℓ, then any user that reaches T enters C within time b.

2. (Time bound b for the exit region) If the time between successive steps of each process in T or E is at most ℓ, then any user that reaches E enters R within time b.

(Note that the value of b will typically be a function of ℓ and c.)

Number of bypasses a: Consider any interval of an execution starting when a process i has performed a locally controlled step in T, and throughout which it remains in T. During this interval, any other user j, $j \neq i$, can only enter C at most a times.

In the first two cases above, we have stated high-level-fairness conditions for the exit region that are similar to those for the trying region. However, in most algorithms, the exit regions are actually trivial.

We say that algorithm A is *lockout-free* provided that it guarantees lockout-freedom for all collections of users. We extend the other high-level-fairness definitions similarly. There are some simple implications among these fairness conditions:

Theorem 10.8 *Let A be a mutual exclusion algorithm, let $U_1, \dots, U_n$ be a collection of users, and let B be the composition of A with $U_1, \dots, U_n$. If B has any finite bypass bound and is lockout-free for the exit region, then B is lockout-free.*

Proof. Consider a low-level-fair execution of B in which all users always return the resource, and suppose that at some point in the execution, i is in T. Assume for the sake of contradiction that i never enters C.

Lemma 10.1 implies that eventually i must perform a locally controlled action in that trying region, if it has not already done so. Repeated use of the progress condition and of the assumption that users always return the resource together imply that infinitely many total region changes occur. But then some process other than i enters C an infinite number of times while i remains in T, which violates the bypass bound. □

Theorem 10.9 *Let A be a mutual exclusion algorithm, let $U_1, \dots, U_n$ be a collection of users, and let B be the composition of A with $U_1, \dots, U_n$. If B has any time bound b (for both the trying and the exit region), then B is lockout-free.*

Proof. Consider a low-level-fair execution of B in which all users always return the resource, and suppose that at some point in the execution, i is in T.

Associate times with the events in the execution in any monotone nondecreasing, unbounded way, so that the times for the steps of each process are at most ℓ and the times for all the critical regions are all at most c.

Since the algorithm satisfies the time bound b, i enters C in at most time b, so in particular, i eventually enters C, as needed for lockout-freedom. □

In the following sections, we will look at some protocols that satisfy some of these stronger high-level-fairness conditions.

10.5   Lockout-Free Mutual Exclusion Algorithms

The first improvements that we present are a trio of algorithms developed by Peterson, all of which guarantee lockout-freedom. The first algorithm is for two processes only, but it demonstrates most of the basic ideas. This algorithm is then extended to $n > 2$ processes in two ways: first, by using a version of the two-process algorithm in a series of $n - 1$ competitions, and second, by using a version of the two-process algorithm in a tournament to select a single winner.

10.5.1   A Two-Process Algorithm

We start with the two-process solution, which we call *Peterson2P*. Usually, we name the two processes in a two-process system processes 1 and 2. This time, for convenience, we count mod 2 and identify 2 with 0, that is, we call the two processes 0 and 1. If $i \in \{0, 1\}$, then we write $\bar{i}$ to indicate $1 - i$, the index of the other process. The code, in a traditional style, is given below.

Peterson2P algorithm:

Shared variables:
$turn \in \{0, 1\}$, initially arbitrary, writable and readable by all processes
for every $i \in \{0, 1\}$:
    $flag(i) \in \{0, 1\}$, initially 0, writable by i and readable by $\bar{i}$

Process i:

    ** Remainder region **

    try_i
    $flag(i) := 1$
    $turn := i$
    waitfor $flag(\bar{i}) = 0$ or $turn \neq i$
    $crit_i$

    ** Critical region **

    $exit_i$
    $flag(i) := 0$
    rem_i

In the *Peterson2P* algorithm, process i starts by setting its *flag* to 1, which is the same as the processes do in *DijkstraME*. But this time, process i immediately proceeds to set $turn := i$. It then waits to discover either that the other process's *flag* is 0, or else that $turn \neq i$. That is, either the other process is not currently involved in the competition at all, or else the *turn* variable has been reset by the other process since the most recent time when i set it. Thus (and slightly strangely), having the *turn* variable set to the index of the *other* process gives permission for i to enter its critical region.

How can this program be translated into a state machine in the formal model? As before, we need to introduce a program counter, temporary variables, and a region designation. An ambiguity in the code that needs to be resolved is the order in which process i checks the *flag* and the *turn* variables, in the waitfor statement. For correctness, it is necessary that both checks be done repeatedly; for simplicity, we assume that the checks are done alternately, though looser assumptions would also work.

We rewrite the algorithm in precondition-effect notation, in order to make it easier to carry out a proof. Here, the region designation R corresponds to *rem*; T corresponds to *set-flag*, *set-turn*, *check-flag*, *check-turn*, and *leave-try*; C corresponds to *crit*; and E corresponds to *reset* and *leave-exit*.

Peterson2P algorithm (rewritten):

Shared variables:
$turn \in \{0, 1\}$, initially arbitrary
for every $i \in \{0, 1\}$:
    $flag(i) \in \{0, 1\}$, initially 0

Actions of i:

Input:	Internal:
try_i	*set-flag*$_i$
$exit_i$	*set-turn*$_i$
Output:	*check-flag*$_i$
$crit_i$	*check-turn*$_i$
rem_i	*reset*$_i$

States of i:
$pc \in \{rem, \text{set-flag}, \text{set-turn}, \text{check-flag}, \text{check-turn}, \text{leave-try}, crit, reset, \text{leave-exit}\}$,
    initially *rem*

Transitions of i:

try_i
  Effect:
    $pc := \text{set-flag}$

set-flag$_i$
  Precondition:
    $pc := \text{set-flag}$
  Effect:
    $flag(i) := 1$
    $pc := \text{set-turn}$

set-turn$_i$
  Precondition:
    $pc = \text{set-turn}$
  Effect:
    $turn := i$
    $pc := \text{check-flag}$

check-flag$_i$
  Precondition:
    $pc = \text{check-flag}$
  Effect:
    if $flag(\bar{i}) = 0$ then
      $pc := \text{leave-try}$
    else
      $pc := \text{check-turn}$

check-turn$_i$
  Precondition:
    $pc = \text{check-turn}$
  Effect:
    if $turn \neq i$ then
      $pc := \text{leave-try}$
    else
      $pc := \text{check-flag}$

$crit_i$
  Precondition:
    $pc = leave\text{-}try$
  Effect:
    $pc := crit$

$exit_i$
  Effect:
    $pc := reset$

$reset_i$
  Precondition:
    $pc = reset$
  Effect:
    $flag(i) := 0$
    $pc := leave\text{-}exit$

rem_i
  Precondition:
    $pc = leave\text{-}exit$
  Effect:
    $pc := rem$

We now argue that the *Peterson2P* algorithm is correct. Well-formedness is easy to check.

Lemma 10.10 *Peterson2P satisfies mutual exclusion.*

Proof. We use an argument based on invariant assertions. It is easy to show by induction that

> **Assertion 10.5.1** *In any reachable system state, if* $flag(i) = 0$, *then* $pc_i \in \{leave\text{-}exit, rem, set\text{-}flag\}$.

Using Assertion 10.5.1, we can show by induction that

> **Assertion 10.5.2** *In any reachable system state, if* $pc_i \in \{leave\text{-}try, crit, reset\}$ *and* $pc_{\bar{i}} \in \{check\text{-}flag, check\text{-}turn, leave\text{-}try, crit, reset\}$, *then* $turn \neq i$.

That is, if i has won the competition, and if $\bar{i}$ is a competitor, then the *turn* variable is set favorably for i, that is, set to the value $\bar{i}$. In the inductive step of the proof of Assertion 10.5.2, the key events to check are

1. "Successful" $check\text{-}flag_i$ events, that is, those that cause pc_i to reach *leave-try*

2. "Successful" $check\text{-}turn_i$ events

3. $set\text{-}turn_{\bar{i}}$ events, which cause $pc_{\bar{i}}$ to take on the value $check\text{-}flag$

4. $set\text{-}turn_i$ events, which falsify the conclusion $turn \neq i$

When i does a successful *check-flag$_i$*, it must be that $flag(\bar{i}) = 0$, which implies by Assertion 10.5.1 that $pc_{\bar{i}} \notin \{$ *check-flag, check-turn, leave-try, crit, reset* $\}$, which makes the statement true vacuously. When i does a successful *check-turn$_i$*, it must be that $turn \neq i$, which suffices. When $\bar{i}$ does *set-turn$_{\bar{i}}$*, it explicitly sets $turn \neq i$, which suffices. Finally, when i does *set-turn$_i$*, then the resulting $pc_i =$ *check-flag*, which makes the statement true vacuously.

This proves Assertion 10.5.2. Now mutual exclusion follows easily: Suppose that both i and $\bar{i}$ are in C, in some reachable state. Then Assertion 10.5.2, applied twice—for i and $\bar{i}$—implies that both $turn \neq i$ and $turn \neq \bar{i}$. This is a contradiction.   □

Lemma 10.11 *Peterson2P guarantees progress.*

Proof.   Suppose for the sake of contradiction that α is a low-level-fair execution that reaches a point where at least one of the processes, say i, is in T and neither process is in C, and suppose that after this point, neither process ever enters C. We consider two cases. First, if $\bar{i}$ is in T sometime after the given point in α, then both processes must get stuck permanently in their *check* loops, since neither ever enters C. But this cannot happen, since $turn$ must stabilize to a value that is favorable to one of them.

On the other hand, suppose that $\bar{i}$ is never in T after the given point in α. In this case, we can show that $flag(\bar{i})$ eventually becomes and stays equal to 0, contradicting the assumption that i is stuck in its *check* loop.   □

Lemma 10.12 *Peterson2P is lockout-free.*

Proof.   The argument for the exit region is trivial; we consider the trying region. We show the stronger condition of two-bounded bypass and invoke Theorem 10.8.

Suppose the contrary, that is, that at some point in execution α, process i is in T after having performed *set-flag$_i$*, and thereafter, while i remains in T, process $\bar{i}$ enters C three times. Note that in each of the second and third times, it must be that $\bar{i}$ first sets $turn := \bar{i}$ and then sees $turn = i$; it cannot see $flag(i) = 0$, because $flag(i)$ remains at 1. This means that there are at least two occurrences of *set-turn$_i$* after the given point in α, because only i can set $turn$ to i. But *set-turn$_i$* is only performed once during one of i's trying regions. This is a contradiction.   □

So we have Theorem 10.13.

Theorem 10.13 *Peterson2P solves the mutual exclusion problem and guarantees lockout-freedom.*

Complexity analysis. As for the analysis of *DijkstraME*, let ℓ and c be upper bounds on process step time and critical section time, respectively. You might want to reread our discussion at the beginning of Section 10.3.4 to be sure you understand exactly what these bounds mean.

Theorem 10.14 *In Peterson2P, the time from when a particular process i enters T until it enters C is at most $c + O(\ell)$.*

Proof Sketch. Suppose the bound does not hold and consider an execution in which process i is in T at some point, but does not enter C for time at least $c + k\ell$ after that point, for some particular large constant k. The constant k is chosen to be considerably bigger than the constants in the big-O terms in the following analysis.

First, within time at most 3ℓ, process i performs *check-flag$_i$*. This can be seen by a case analysis, based on the various places where i might be in its trying region. Note that i cannot succeed in any of its *check*s during this time, because if it did, it would go to C within time $O(\ell)$, which we have assumed does not happen this quickly. Then when process i performs this *check-flag$_i$*, it must find *flag($\bar{i}$)* = 1, because otherwise i would reach C within time $O(\ell)$. So by Assertion 10.5.1, it must be that $pc_{\bar{i}} \in \{$ *set-turn, check-flag, check-turn, leave-try, crit, reset* $\}$ at that point.

Then we claim that either *crit$_i$* occurs within additional time $O(\ell)$ or *reset$_{\bar{i}}$* occurs within additional time $c + O(\ell)$. This is argued by a case analysis, based on the value of *turn* and where the processes are in their code; the key point is that the *turn* variable, once stabilized, will be set favorably to one of the processes. But the former case would again mean that i would reach C too soon, so the latter must hold, that is, *reset$_{\bar{i}}$* occurs within additional time $c + O(\ell)$.

Now i performs *check-flag$_i$* again, within additional time $O(\ell)$. Once again, it must find *flag($\bar{i}$)* = 1. This means that $\bar{i}$ has entered T again, after the *reset$_{\bar{i}}$*. Then either *turn* already has taken on the value $\bar{i}$, or will do so within additional time ℓ. Then within at most another time $O(\ell)$, process i finds conditions favorable for it to enter C. This contradicts the assumption that i does not enter C within this amount of time. Figure 10.8 shows the order of events in this proof and the time bounds between them. □

10.5.2 An *n*-Process Algorithm

For n processes, we can use the idea of the *Peterson2P* algorithm iteratively, in a series of $n - 1$ competitions at levels $1, 2, \ldots, n - 1$. At each successive competition, the algorithm ensures that there is at least one *loser*. Thus, all n

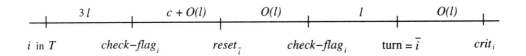

Figure 10.8: Order of events and time bounds in the proof of Theorem 10.14.

processes may compete in the level 1 competition, but at most $n - 1$ processes can win. In general, at most $n - k$ processes can win at level k. So at most one process can win at level $n - 1$, which yields the mutual exclusion condition.

The code is given below. Here we have reverted to our usual convention of numbering the processes $1, \ldots, n$. We call the algorithm *PetersonNP*.

PetersonNP algorithm:

Shared variables:
for every $k \in \{1, \ldots, n - 1\}$:
    $turn(k) \in \{1, \ldots, n\}$, initially arbitrary, writable and readable by all processes
for every i, $1 \leq i \leq n$:
    $flag(i) \in \{0, \ldots, n - 1\}$, initially 0, writable by i and readable by all $j \neq i$

Process i:

    ** Remainder region **

    try_i
    for $k = 1$ to $n - 1$ do
        $flag(i) := k$
        $turn(k) := i$
        waitfor $[\forall j \neq i : flag(j) < k]$ or $[turn(k) \neq i]$
    $crit_i$

    ** Critical region **

    $exit_i$
    $flag(i) := 0$
    rem_i

Process i engages in one competition for each level, $1 \leq k \leq n - 1$. Now each level k has its own *turn* variable, $turn(k)$. At each level k, process i behaves similarly to the way a process behaves in the *Peterson2P* algorithm: it sets $turn(k) := i$, then waits to discover either that all the other processes' *flag* variables are strictly less than k, or else that $turn(k) \neq i$. That is, either none of the other processes is currently involved in the level k competition, or else the $turn(k)$ variable has been reset by some other process since i most recently set it.

As before, there are some ambiguities in the code that need to be resolved. First, one of the conditions in the waitfor statement involves the *flag* variables for all the other processes. In our model, these variables cannot all be checked simultaneously. Rather, we intend that the variables be checked one at a time, and we regard the condition as satisfied if all the values seen during these checks are less than k. Second, we need to specify some conditions on the order in which process i checks the various *flag* variables and the $turn(k)$ variable, in the waitfor statement. For simplicity, we assume that process i cycles through the checks, in each cycle first checking all the *flag* variables in arbitrary order and then checking the $turn(k)$ variable.

The details appear below. The code is quite similar to that of *Peterson2P*. Note the use of the local variable *level* to keep track of which competition the process is engaged in (or is ready to engage in) and the use of S to keep track of processes that have been observed to have *flag* values smaller than k.

PetersonNP algorithm (rewritten):

Shared variables:
for every $k \in \{1, \dots, n-1\}$:
  $turn(k) \in \{1, \dots, n\}$, initially arbitrary
for every i, $1 \leq i \leq n$:
  $flag(i) \in \{0, \dots, n-1\}$, initially 0

Actions of i:

Input:	Internal:
try_i	$set\text{-}flag_i$
$exit_i$	$set\text{-}turn_i$
Output:	$check\text{-}flag(j)_i, 1 \leq j \leq n, j \neq i$
$crit_i$	$check\text{-}turn_i$
rem_i	$reset_i$

States of i:
$pc \in \{rem, set\text{-}flag, set\text{-}turn, check\text{-}flag, check\text{-}turn, leave\text{-}try, crit, reset, leave\text{-}exit\}$, initially *rem*
$level \in \{1, \dots, n-1\}$, initially 1
S, a set of process indices, initially $\emptyset$

Transitions of i:

try_i
    Effect:
        $pc := set\text{-}flag$

$set\text{-}flag_i$
    Precondition:
        $pc := set\text{-}flag$
    Effect:
        $flag(i) := level$
        $pc := set\text{-}turn$

$set\text{-}turn_i$
    Precondition:
        $pc = set\text{-}turn$
    Effect:
        $turn(level) := i$
        $S := \{i\}$
        $pc := check\text{-}flag$

$check\text{-}flag(j)_i$
    Precondition:
        $pc = check\text{-}flag$
        $j \notin S$
    Effect:
        if $flag(j) < level$ then
            $S := S \cup \{j\}$
            if $|S| = n$ then
                $S := \emptyset$
                if $level < n - 1$ then
                    $level := level + 1$
                    $pc := set\text{-}flag$
                else
                    $pc := leave\text{-}try$
        else
            $S := \emptyset$
            $pc := check\text{-}turn$

$check\text{-}turn_i$
    Precondition:
        $pc = check\text{-}turn$
    Effect:
        if $turn(level) \neq i$ then
            if $level < n - 1$ then
                 $level := level + 1$
                 $pc := set\text{-}flag$
            else
                $pc := leave\text{-}try$
        else
            $S := \{i\}$
            $pc := check\text{-}flag$

$crit_i$
    Precondition:
        $pc = leave\text{-}try$
    Effect:
        $pc := crit$

$exit_i$
    Effect:
        $pc := reset$

$reset_i$
    Precondition:
        $pc = reset$
    Effect:
        $flag(i) := 0$
        $level := 1$
        $pc := leave\text{-}exit$

rem_i
    Precondition:
        $pc = leave\text{-}exit$
    Effect:
        $pc := rem$

We now argue that *PetersonNP* is correct. Well-formedness is clear. For mutual exclusion, the key idea is that the level k competition only permits $n - k$ winners.

In any system state of *PetersonNP*, we say that a process i is a *winner* at level k provided that either $level_i > k$ or else $level_i = k$ and $pc_i \in \{leave\text{-}try, crit, reset\}$. (This latter condition will only arise for $k = n - 1$.) We also say that process i

is a *competitor* at level k, provided that it is either a winner at level k or else $level_i = k$ and $pc_i \in \{check\text{-}flag, check\text{-}turn\}$.

Lemma 10.15 *PetersonNP satisfies mutual exclusion.*

Proof. In order to prove mutual exclusion, we prove the following assertion, which is analogous to Assertion 10.5.2 for *Peterson2P*. An important difference is that now the assertion must deal with intermediate stages in the process of checking flags.

> **Assertion 10.5.3** *In any reachable system state of PetersonNP, the following are true:*
>
> 1. *If process i is a competitor at level k, if $pc_i = check\text{-}flag$, and if any process $j \neq i$ in S_i is a competitor at level k, then $turn(k) \neq i$.*
>
> 2. *If process i is a winner at level k and if any other process is a competitor at level k, then $turn(k) \neq i$.*

The proof, by induction as usual, is left as an exercise. Using Assertion 10.5.3, we prove

> **Assertion 10.5.4** *In any reachable system state of PetersonNP, if there is a competitor at level k, then the value of $turn(k)$ is the index of some competitor at level k.*

Again, the inductive proof is left as an exercise. Finally, we show the following, which directly implies the mutual exclusion condition.

> **Assertion 10.5.5** *In any reachable system state of PetersonNP, and for any k, $1 \leq k \leq n - 1$, there are at most $n - k$ winners at level k.*

The proof of Assertion 10.5.5 is also an induction, but not on the length of an execution. Rather, we use induction on the value of k.

Basis: $k = 1$. If the statement is false for $k = 1$, it means that all n processes are winners at level 1. Then Assertion 10.5.3 implies that the value of $turn(1)$ cannot be the index of any of the processes, a contradiction.

Inductive step: We assume the statement for k, $1 \leq k \leq n - 2$, and show it for $k + 1$. Suppose for the sake of contradiction that the statement is false for $k + 1$, that is, that there are strictly more than $n - (k + 1)$ winners at level $k + 1$; let W be the set of such winners. Every winner at level $k + 1$ is also a winner at level k, and by the inductive hypothesis, the number of winners at level k is at most $n - k$. It follows that W is also the set of winners at level k, and that $|W| = n - k \geq 2$.

Then Assertion 10.5.3 implies that the value of $turn(k + 1)$ cannot be the index of any of the processes in W. And Assertion 10.5.4 implies that the value of $turn(k+1)$ is the index of some competitor at level $k+1$. But every competitor at level $k + 1$ is a winner at level k, and so is in W. This is a contradiction. □

In order to prove progress, it is enough to prove lockout-freedom (see Exercise 10.6). And Theorem 10.9 implies that lockout-freedom is in turn implied by a time bound. A time bound for the exit region is trivial; the following theorem gives a time bound for the trying region. Warning: We do not claim that this bound is tight—we leave it as an exercise to try to tighten it—but any bound is enough to prove lockout-freedom.

Theorem 10.16 *In PetersonNP, the time from when a particular process i enters T until it enters C is at most $2^{n-1}c + O(2^n n\ell)$.*

Proof.   We prove the bound using a recurrence. Define $T(0)$ to be the maximum time from when a process enters T until it enters C. For k, $1 \leq k \leq n-1$, define $T(k)$ to be the maximum time from when a process becomes a winner at level k until it enters C. We want to bound $T(0)$.

By the code, we know that $T(n - 1) \leq \ell$, since only one step is needed to enter C after winning the final competition. In order to bound $T(0)$, we set up a recurrence for $T(k)$ in terms of $T(k + 1)$, where $0 \leq k \leq n - 2$.

Suppose process i has just won at level k if $k \geq 1$, or has just entered T if $k = 0$. Then within time 2ℓ, process i performs *set-turn$_i$*, setting $turn(k+1) := i$. Let π denote this *set-turn$_i$* event. We consider two cases.

First, if $turn(k + 1)$ gets set to some value other than i within time $T(k + 1) + c + (2n + 2)\ell$ after π, then i wins at level $k + 1$ within an additional time $n\ell$. Then within additional time $T(k+1)$, i enters C. In this case, the total time from π until i's entrance to C is at most $2T(k + 1) + c + (3n + 2)\ell$.

On the other hand, assume that $turn(k + 1)$ does not get set to any value other than i within time $T(k + 1) + c + (2n + 2)\ell$ after π. Then no process can set its *flag* to $k+1$ within time $T(k+1) + c + (2n+1)\ell$ after π. Let I be the set of processes $j \neq i$ for which $flag(j) \geq k + 1$ when π occurs. Then each process in I wins at level $k+1$ within time at most $n\ell$ after π (since it finds $turn(k+1)$ unequal to its index), then enters C within an additional time $T(k + 1)$, then leaves C within additional time c and performs *reset* within additional time ℓ. That is, within time $n\ell + T(k + 1) + c + \ell = T(k + 1) + c + (n + 1)\ell$ after π, all processes in I set their *flags* to 0.

Thus, within time $T(k+1) + c + (n+1)\ell$ after π, all processes $j \neq i$ for which $flag(j) \geq k+1$ when π occurs, set their $flags$ to 0. As we assumed above, for an additional time $n\ell$ after that, no process sets its $flag$ to $k+1$. That is sufficient time for process i to detect that all the $flag$ variables are less than $k+1$ and so to win at level $k+1$. That is, in this case, process i wins at level $k+1$ within time $T(k+1) + c + (2n+1)\ell$ after π. Again, within another $T(k+1)$, i enters C. In this case, the total time from π until i's entrance to C is at most $2T(k+1) + c + (2n+1)\ell$.

The worst-case time is thus at most 2ℓ plus the maximum of the times in the two cases above, that is, $2T(k+1) + c + (3n+4)\ell$. Thus, we need to solve the following recurrence for $T(0)$:

$$T(k) \leq 2T(k+1) + c + (3n+4)\ell, \text{ for } 0 \leq k \leq n-2$$
$$T(n-1) \leq \ell$$

Solving this recurrence yields the claimed time bound. (See the following subsection, Section 10.5.3, for a more detailed solution for a similar recurrence.)

□

We have

Theorem 10.17 *PetersonNP solves the mutual exclusion problem and is lockout-free.*

10.5.3 Tournament Algorithm

Another way to extend the basic *Peterson2P* algorithm to more processes is to use a version of the basic two-process algorithm as a building block in a *tournament*. For simplicity, we assume that n, the number of processes, is a power of 2. Once again, we number the processes starting with 0, as $0, \ldots, n-1$ rather than $1, \ldots, n$. Each process engages in a series of $\log n$ competitions in order to obtain the resource. You should think of these competitions as being arranged in a complete n-leaf binary *tournament tree*; the n leaves correspond left-to-right to the n processes $0, \ldots, n-1$.

We need some notation to name the various competitions, the roles played by the processes in all of the competitions, and the set of potential opponents that all the processes can have in all the competitions. For $0 \leq i \leq n-1$ and $1 \leq k \leq \log n$, we define the following notions.

- $comp(i, k)$, the *level k competition* of process i, is the string consisting of the high-order $\log n - k$ bits of the binary representation of i. In terms

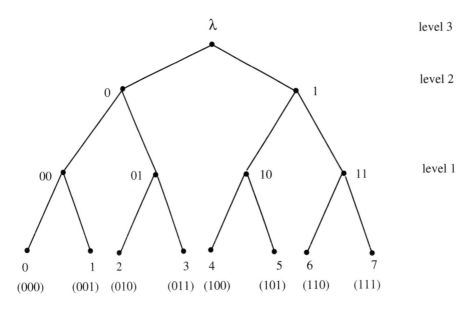

Figure 10.9: Names of competitions in the *Tournament* algorithm.

of the tournament tree, $comp(i, k)$ can be used as a name for the internal node that is the level k ancestor of i's leaf. In particular, the root is named by λ, the empty string.

- $role(i, k)$, the *role* of process i in the level k competition of process i, is the $(\log n - k + 1)$st bit of the binary representation of i. In terms of the tournament tree, $role(i, k)$ indicates whether i's leaf is a descendant of the left or right child of the node for competition $comp(i, k)$.

- $opponents(i, k)$, the *opponents* of process i in the level k competition of process i, is the set of process indices with the same high-order $\log n - k$ bits as i and the opposite $(\log n - k + 1)$st bit. In terms of the tournament tree, the processes in $opponents(i, k)$ are those whose leaves are descendants of the opposite child of node $comp(i, k)$, that is, of the child that is not an ancestor of i's leaf.

Example 10.5.1   Tournament tree

Figure 10.9 shows the tournament tree for $n = 8$. For example, note that $comp(5, 2) = 1$, $role(5, 2) = 0$ and $opponents(5, 2) = \{6, 7\}$.

We call the algorithm the *Tournament algorithm*.

Tournament **algorithm:**

Shared variables:

for every binary string x of length at most $\log n - 1$:

$turn(x) \in \{0,1\}$, initially arbitrary, writable and readable by exactly those
processes i for which x is a prefix of the binary representation of i

for every i, $0 \leq i \leq n - 1$:

$flag(i) \in \{0, \ldots, \log n\}$, initially 0, writable by i and readable by all $j \neq i$

Process i:

     ** Remainder region **

     try_i
     for $k = 1$ to $\log n$ do
        $flag(i) := k$
        $turn(comp(i,k)) := role(i,k)$
        waitfor $[\forall j \in opponents(i,k) : flag(j) < k]$ or $[turn(comp(i,k)) \neq role(i,k)]$
     $crit_i$

     ** Critical region **

     $exit_i$
     $flag(i) := 0$
     rem_i

This code is very much like that of the *PetersonNP* algorithm. The main difference is that in each competition, the process only checks the flags of its opponents in that competition. As in *PetersonNP*, we assume that a process checks its opponents in any order, one at a time. The testing must alternate in some systematic way; for example, it can be done in a cycle where all the *flags* are first tested, and then *turn*. We only sketch the correctness arguments for the *Tournament* algorithm briefly, since the ideas are so similar to those for the *PetersonNP* and *Peterson2P* algorithms.

First, the algorithm should be rewritten in precondition-effect style, making explicit the program counters and the variables that accumulate the sets of processes whose flags have already been checked. Then notions such as "winner at level k" and "competitor at level k" must be defined for the *Tournament* algorithm, analogously to the way they were defined for *PetersonNP*.

Lemma 10.18 *The Tournament algorithm satisfies mutual exclusion.*

Proof Sketch.   The proof uses the same ideas as the invariant assertion proofs of the *Peterson2P* and *PetersonNP* algorithms. This time, the key invariant is

> **Assertion 10.5.6** *In any reachable system state of the Tournament algorithm, and for any k, $1 \leq k \leq \log n$, at most one process from any subtree rooted at level k is a winner at level k.*

This follows immediately from an invariant analogous to the second part of Assertion 10.5.3.

> **Assertion 10.5.7** *If process i is a winner at level k and if any level-k opponent of i is a competitor at level k, then $turn(comp(i,k)) \neq role(i,k)$.*

As for the second part of Assertion 10.5.3, we cannot prove Assertion 10.5.7 directly by induction. We must strengthen it as before to include some information about what happens inside the waitfor loop, after the process has discovered that some of its opponents have *flag* variables with values that are strictly less than k. We leave this strengthening and the inductive proof as an exercise for the reader. $\square$

In order to show progress and lockout-freedom, we prove a time bound.

Theorem 10.19 *In the Tournament algorithm, the time from when a particular process i enters T until it enters C is at most $(n-1)c + O\left(n^2 \ell\right)$.*

Proof.   The proof is like the proof of Theorem 10.16. Define $T(0)$ to be the maximum time from when a process enters T until it enters C. For k, $1 \leq k \leq \log n$, define $T(k)$ to be the maximum time from when a process wins at level k until it enters C. We want to bound $T(0)$. By the code, we know that $T(\log n) \leq \ell$, since only one step is needed to enter C after winning the final competition. We bound $T(k)$ in terms of $T(k+1)$, where $0 \leq k \leq \log n - 1$.

Suppose process i has just won at level k if $k \geq 1$, or has just entered T if $k = 0$. Let x denote $comp(i, k+1)$. Then, within time 2ℓ, process i sets the $turn(x)$ variable to $role(i, k+1)$. Let π denote this event; we consider two cases.

First, if $turn(x)$ gets changed within time $T(k+1) + c + (2^{k+1} + 4)\ell$ after π, then i wins at level $k+1$ within an additional time $(2^k + 1)\ell$. Then, within additional time $T(k+1)$, i enters C. In this case, the total time from π until i's entrance to C is at most $2T(k+1) + c + (2^{k+1} + 2^k + 5)\ell$.

On the other hand, assume that $turn(x)$ does not get changed within time $T(k+1) + c + (2^{k+1} + 4)\ell$ after π. Then no level $k+1$ opponent of i can set its *flag* to $k+1$ within time $T(k+1) + c + (2^{k+1} + 3)\ell$ after π. If j is a level

$k + 1$ opponent of i for which $flag(j) \geq k + 1$ when π occurs, then within time $(2^k + 1)\ell + T(k + 1) + c + \ell = T(k + 1) + c + (2^k + 2)\ell$ after π, process j sets its *flag* to 0.

Thus, within time $T(k + 1) + c + (2^k + 2)\ell$ after π, all level $k + 1$ opponents j of i for which $flag(j) \geq k + 1$ when π occurs, set their *flags* to 0. As we assumed above, for an additional time $(2^k + 1)\ell$ after that, no process sets its *flag* to $k + 1$. That is sufficient time for process i to detect that all its level $k + 1$ opponents' *flag* variables are less than $k + 1$, and so to win at level $k + 1$. That is, in this case, process i wins at level $k + 1$ within time $T(k + 1) + c + (2^{k+1} + 3)\ell$ after π. Within another $T(k + 1)$, i enters C. In this case, the total time from π until i's entrance to C is at most $2T(k + 1) + c + (2^{k+1} + 3)\ell$.

The worst-case time is thus at most 2ℓ plus the maximum of the times in the two cases above, that is, $2T(k + 1) + c + (2^{k+1} + 2^k + 7)\ell$. Thus, we need to solve the following recurrence for $T(0)$:

$$T(k) \leq 2T(k + 1) + c + (2^{k+1} + 2^k + 7)\ell, \text{ for } 0 \leq k \leq \log n - 1$$
$$T(\log n) \leq \ell.$$

Choose some constant a such that $(2^{k+1} + 2^k + 7) \leq a \cdot 2^k$. Then we have

$$
\begin{aligned}
T(0) &\leq 2T(1) + 2^0 c + a 2^0 \ell \\
&\leq 2^2 T(2) + (2^0 + 2^1)c + a(2^0 + 2^2)\ell \\
&\leq 2^3 T(3) + (2^0 + 2^1 + 2^2)c + a(2^0 + 2^2 + 2^4)\ell \\
&\qquad\vdots \\
&\leq 2^k T(k) + (2^0 + 2^1 + \ldots + 2^{k-1})c + a(2^0 + 2^2 + \ldots + 2^{2k-2})\ell \\
&\qquad\vdots \\
&\leq 2^{\log n} T(\log n) + (2^0 + 2^1 + \ldots + 2^{\log n - 1})c + a(2^0 + 2^2 + \ldots 2^{2(\log n - 1)})\ell \\
&\leq (n - 1)c + n\ell + O\left(n^2 \ell\right) \\
&= (n - 1)c + O\left(n^2 \ell\right).
\end{aligned}
$$

$\square$

Theorem 10.20 *The Tournament algorithm solves the mutual exclusion problem and is lockout-free.*

Bounded bypass. The *Tournament* algorithm does *not* guarantee any bound on the number of bypasses. To see this, consider an execution in which process 0 enters the tournament at its leaf and takes steps with intervening times exactly equal to the assumed upper bound ℓ. Meanwhile, process $n-1$ enters the tournament at its leaf, going much faster. Process $n-1$ can reach the top and win, and in fact it can repeat this arbitrarily many times, before process 0 even wins at level 1. This is possible because we have not assumed any lower bound on process step times.

Note that there is no contradiction between unbounded bypass and a time upper bound. No process is locked out for very long—the unbounded bypasses only occur because some processes operate very fast.

10.6 An Algorithm Using Single-Writer Shared Registers

The mutual exclusion algorithms we have studied so far use multi-writer shared registers (the *turn* variables) as well as single-writer shared registers (the *flag* variables). Because multi-writer registers are often difficult to implement, it is worth investigating algorithms that use only single-writer shared registers. In this section and the next, we present two such algorithms.

The algorithm in this section solves the mutual exclusion problem (including the progress condition, as usual), but does not guarantee any high-level-fairness condition. Its shared registers are all binary. The algorithm in Section 10.7 is also lockout-free, but it has the disadvantage of using unbounded size variables.

We call the first algorithm *BurnsME*, after Burns, its inventor.

BurnsME algorithm:

Shared variables:
for every i, $1 \leq i \leq n$:
   $flag(i) \in \{0, 1\}$, initially 0, writable by i and readable by all $j \neq i$

Process i:

    ** Remainder region **

    try_i
L: $flag(i) := 0$
    for j, $1 \leq j \leq i-1$ do
        if $flag(j) = 1$ then goto L
    $flag(i) := 1$
    for j, $1 \leq j \leq i-1$ do
        if $flag(j) = 1$ then goto L
M: for j, $i+1 \leq j \leq n$ do
        if $flag(j) = 1$ then goto M

$crit_i$

** Critical region **

$exit_i$
$flag(i) := 0$
rem_i

The *flag* values used in *BurnsME* are 0 and 1 instead of 0, 1, and 2 as in *DijkstraME*. Each process executes three for loops. The first two loops involve checking the *flag*s of all processes with smaller indices, while the third loop involves checking the *flag*s of all processes with larger indices. If process i passes all the tests in all three loops, it proceeds to its critical region.

Lemma 10.21 *The BurnsME algorithm satisfies mutual exclusion.*

Proof. The proof is similar to the first (operational) proof that *DijkstraME* satisfies mutual exclusion (see Lemma 10.3). The main difference is that now the *flag* variables are set to 1, whereas in *DijkstraME* they are set to 2.

Thus, if processes i and j are simultaneously in C, then assume that i sets its *flag* to 1 first. Then $flag(i)$ keeps the value 1 until process i leaves C. But after j sets $flag(j)$ to 1, j must check that $flag(i) = 0$ before j can enter C. (If $i < j$, then this is done in the second for loop, while if $i > j$, then it is done in the third for loop.) This check must occur during the interval when the value of $flag(i) = 1$, which yields a contradiction. □

Note that the first for loop in the code is not needed for the mutual exclusion condition.

Lemma 10.22 *BurnsME guarantees progress.*

Proof. The argument for the exit region is easy. For the trying region, we assume for the sake of contradiction that α is a low-level-fair execution that reaches a point where there is at least one process in T and no process in C, and that after this point, no process ever enters C. Arguing similarly to the way we did in the proof of Lemma 10.4, we can assume without loss of generality that every process is in T or R and that no process changes region, in α. Let the *contenders* be the processes in T.

Now we partition the contenders into two sets: those that ever reach label M and those that never do. Call the first set P and the second set Q. There must be some point in α by which all the processes in P have already reached label M; note that they never thereafter drop back to any point in the code prior to label M. Let α_1 be a suffix of α in which all processes in P are in the final for loop, after label M.

We claim that there is at least one process in P. Specifically, the process with the smallest index among all the contenders is not blocked from reaching label M.

Let i be the largest index of a process in P. We claim that eventually in α_1, any process $j \in Q$ such that $j > i$ has $flag(j)$ set permanently to 0. This is because each time j executes one of the first two for loops, it discovers the presence of a smaller index contender and returns to L. Whenever it does this, it sets $flag(j) := 0$, and once it has done this, it can never progress far enough to set $flag(j) := 1$. So let α_2 be a suffix of α_1 in which all processes in Q with indices $> i$ always have their $flags$ equal to 0.

Now in α_2, there is nothing to stop process i from reaching C: every larger-index process j has $flag(j) = 0$, so i will complete the third for loop successfully. Thus, i enters C, which is a contradiction.   □

Theorem 10.23 *BurnsME solves the mutual exclusion problem.*

10.7 The Bakery Algorithm

In this section we present the *Bakery algorithm* for mutual exclusion. It works somewhat the way a bakery does, where customers draw tickets when they enter and are served in the order of their ticket numbers.

The *Bakery* algorithm only uses single-writer/multi-reader shared registers. In fact, it also works using a weaker form of register known as a *safe register*, in which the registers are allowed to provide arbitrary responses to reads that are performed concurrently with writes.

The *Bakery* algorithm guarantees lockout-freedom and a good time bound. It does not exactly guarantee bounded bypass, but rather guarantees a related condition—it is "FIFO after a wait-free doorway" (to be defined below). An unattractive property of the *Bakery* algorithm is that it uses unbounded size registers.

The code follows. We remark that the code given here can be simplified if we are only interested in the usual sort of registers (and not weaker types of registers such as safe registers). We leave this simplification for an exercise.

Bakery algorithm:

Shared variables:
for every i, $1 \leq i \leq n$:
    $choosing(i) \in \{0, 1\}$, initially 0, writable by i and readable by all $j \neq i$
    $number(i) \in \mathbb{N}$, initially 0, writable by i and readable by all $j \neq i$

Process i:

    ** Remainder region **

    try_i
    $choosing(i) := 1$
    $number(i) := 1 + \max_{j \neq i} number(j)$
    $choosing(i) := 0$
    for $j \neq i$ do
        waitfor $choosing(j) = 0$
        waitfor $number(j) = 0$ or $(number(i), i) < (number(j), j)$
    $crit_i$

    ** Critical region **

    $exit_i$
    $number(i) := 0$
    rem_i

In the *Bakery* algorithm, the first part of the trying region, until the point where process i sets $choosing(i) := 0$, is designated as the *doorway*. While in the doorway, process i chooses a *number* that is greater than all the numbers that it reads for the other processes. It reads the other processes' *numbers* one at a time, in any order, then writes its own *number*. While it is reading and choosing numbers, i makes sure that $choosing(i) = 1$, as a signal to the other processes.

Note that it is possible for two processes to be in the doorway at the same time, which can cause them to choose the same number. To break such ties, processes compare not just their *numbers*, but their (*number*, *index*) pairs. This comparison is done lexicographically, thus breaking ties in favor of the process with the smaller index.

In the rest of the trying region, the process waits for the other processes to finish choosing and also waits for its (*number*, *index*) pair to become the lowest.

To prove correctness, let D denote the doorway (i.e., the set of process states in which the process is in the doorway), and let $T - D$ denote the rest of the trying region. Well-formedness is easy to see. To show the mutual exclusion condition, we use a lemma.

Lemma 10.24 *In any reachable system state of the Bakery algorithm, and for any processes i and j, $i \neq j$, the following is true. If i is in C and j is in $(T - D) \cup C$, then $(number(i), i) < (number(j), j)$.*

We give an operational proof, since it can be extended more easily to the safe register case.

Proof. Fix some point s in an execution in which i is in C and j is in $(T - D) \cup C$. (Formally, s is an occurrence of a system state.) Call the values of $number(i)$ and $number(j)$ at point s the *correct* values of these variables.

Process i must read $choosing(j) = 0$ in its first waitfor loop, prior to entering C. Let π denote this reading event; thus, π precedes s. When π occurs, j is not in the "choosing region" (i.e., the portion of the doorway after setting $choosing(j) := 1$). But since j is in $(T - D) \cup C$ at point s, j must pass through the choosing region at some point. There are two cases to consider.

1. j enters the choosing region after π. Then the correct $number(i)$ is chosen before j starts choosing, ensuring that j sees the correct $number(i)$ when it chooses. Therefore, at point s, we have $number(j) > number(i)$, which suffices.

2. j leaves the choosing region before π. Then whenever i reads j's number in its second waitfor loop, it gets the correct $number(j)$ But since i decides to enter C anyhow, it must be that $(number(i), i) < (number(j), j)$. This again suffices.

$\square$

Lemma 10.25 *The Bakery algorithm satisfies mutual exclusion.*

Proof. Suppose that, in some reachable state, two processes, i and j, are both in C. Then by Lemma 10.24 applied twice, we must have both $(number(i), i) < (number(j), j)$ and $(number(j), j) < (number(i), i)$. This is a contradiction. $\square$

Lemma 10.26 *The Bakery algorithm guarantees progress.*

Proof. The exit region is easy, as usual. For the trying region, we again argue by contradiction. Suppose that progress is not guaranteed. Then eventually a point is reached after which all processes are in T or R, and no new region changes occur. By the code, all of the processes in T eventually complete the doorway and reach $T - D$. Then the process with the lowest $(number, index)$ pair is not blocked from reaching C. $\square$

Lemma 10.27 *The Bakery algorithm guarantees lockout-freedom.*

Proof. Consider a particular process i in T and suppose it never reaches C. Process i eventually completes the doorway and reaches $T - D$. Thereafter, any new process that enters the doorway sees i's latest *number* and so chooses a higher number. Thus, since i doesn't reach C, none of these new processes reach C either, since each is blocked by the test of *number(i)* in its second wait loop.

But repeated use of Lemma 10.26 implies that there must be continuing progress, including infinitely many *crit* events, which contradicts the fact that all new entrants to the trying region are blocked. □

Theorem 10.28 *The Bakery algorithm solves the mutual exclusion problem and is lockout-free.*

Complexity analysis. An upper bound for the time from when a process i enters the trying region until it enters the critical region is $(n - 1)c + O\left(n^2\ell\right)$. This is not so easy to show; we just give a brief sketch and leave the details for an exercise.

First, it only takes time $O\left(n\ell\right)$ for process i to complete the doorway; we must bound the length of the time interval I that i spends in $T - D$. Let P be the set of other processes already in T at the moment i enters $T - D$. Then only processes in P can enter C before i does, and each of these can only do so once. It follows that the total time within interval I during which some process is in C is at most $(n - 1)c$, and that the total time within interval I during which some process is in the doorway is at most $O\left(n^2\ell\right)$.

It remains to bound the *residual time* within interval I, that is, the total time within I during which no process is either in C or in the doorway. We bound the residual time by considering the progress of processes in $P \cup \{i\}$. During the residual time, note that none of these processes is ever blocked in its first waitfor loop, since all the *choosing* variables are 0. Moreover, some process in $P \cup \{i\}$ will not be blocked at any step of its second waitfor loop either, and so, within residual time $O\left(n\ell\right)$, will enter C. After it finishes, some other process in $P \cup \{i\}$ will not be blocked, and so, within an additional residual time $O\left(n\ell\right)$, will enter C, and so on. This continues until i enters C, for a total residual time of $O\left(n^2\ell\right)$.

FIFO after a wait-free doorway. The *Bakery* algorithm guarantees a high-level-fairness condition that is somewhat stronger than lockout-freedom. Namely, if process i completes the doorway before j enters T, then j cannot enter C before i does. Note that the algorithm is not actually FIFO based on the time of entry to T, or even the first locally controlled step in T. For example, process 1 could enter and set *choosing*(1) := 1; then process 2 could enter, choose a number, and complete the doorway; then process 1 could choose its number. In this case, process 1 would choose a larger number than process 2's, allowing 2 to precede it into C.

It would not be useful just to claim that an algorithm was "FIFO after a doorway," because there are no constraints on where the doorway might end. (If the doorway ended right at the entrance to C, then this claim is completely trivial.) However, the doorway in the *Bakery* algorithm has an interesting property: it is *wait-free*, which means that a process is guaranteed eventually to complete it, if that process continues to take steps, regardless of whether any other processes continue to do so.

Thus, the property of being "FIFO after a wait-free doorway," which is a nontrivial and interesting high-level-fairness condition, is satisfied by the *Bakery* algorithm.

10.8   Lower Bound on the Number of Registers

We have presented several mutual exclusion algorithms that use read/write shared memory. All guarantee the basic conditions of mutual exclusion and progress, and most also guarantee some sort of high-level-fairness condition: lockout-freedom, a time bound, or a bypass bound. One thing that all the algorithms have in common, though, is that they all use at least n shared variables.

In this section, we show that this is not an accident: it turns out that the mutual exclusion problem cannot be solved at all with fewer than n read/write shared variables! This is so even if we only require the basic conditions—mutual exclusion and progress; no high-level-fairness requirements are needed for proving this lower bound. Also, the impossibility result holds regardless of the size of the shared variables (as measured by the number of values they can take on)—they can be as small as a single bit or even unbounded in size. This result represents a fundamental limitation on the power of shared memory systems.

We need two definitions. First, as in Section 9.3, we say that two system states, s and s', are *indistinguishable* to process i, written as $s \overset{i}{\sim} s'$, if the state of process i, the state of U_i, and the values of all the shared variables are the same in s and s'. Second, we define a system state s to be *idle* if all processes are in their remainder regions in s.

In the proof, we consider a fixed collection of user automata. Namely, we assume that each user U_i is the most nondeterministic possible—that it is able to perform its *try* and *exit* outputs at any time, subject only to the well-formedness condition. Restricting attention to this collection of users does not cause any loss of generality, because the algorithm is supposed to work for all collections of users. We leave it for an exercise to show that, for each i, there is in fact a single I/O automaton U_i that exhibits exactly the allowable nondeterminism.

10.8.1 Basic Facts

The proof uses two basic facts. The first is that a process running on its own from an idle state can reach its critical region.

Lemma 10.29 *Suppose that an algorithm A solves the mutual exclusion problem (that is, guarantees well-formedness, mutual exclusion, and progress) for $n \geq 2$ processes, using only read/write shared variables. Suppose that s is a reachable idle system state and let i be any process.*

Then there is an execution fragment[2] starting from state s and involving steps of process i only, in which process i reaches C.

Proof. This follows from the progress condition. (Formally, the progress condition is applied to a low-level-fair execution containing s in which i enters T after the occurrence of s.) □

As an easy consequence, we have that a process running on its own from a system state that *appears to be* an idle state can reach C.

Lemma 10.30 *Suppose A solves the mutual exclusion problem for $n \geq 2$ processes, using only read/write shared variables. Let s and s' be reachable system states that are indistinguishable to process i and suppose that s' is an idle state.*

Then there is an execution fragment starting from state s and involving steps of process i only, in which process i reaches C.

The second basic fact is that any process that reaches C on its own must write something in shared memory before doing so.

Lemma 10.31 *Suppose A solves the mutual exclusion problem for $n \geq 2$ processes, using only read/write shared variables. Suppose that s is a reachable system state in which process i is in the remainder region. Suppose that process i reaches C in an execution fragment starting from s that involves steps of i only. Then, along the way, i must write some shared variable.*

---

[2]This is just an execution that starts in an arbitrary state, not necessarily an initial state of the algorithm.

Proof. Let α_1 be any finite execution fragment that starts from state s, involves steps of i only, and ends with process i in C. Suppose for the sake of contradiction that α_1 does not include any write to a shared variable. Let s' denote the state at the end of α_1. Since process i does not write any shared variable, the only differences between s and s' are in the states of process i and user U_i. So $s \overset{j}{\sim} s'$ for every $j \neq i$.

Repeated use of the progress condition implies that there is an execution fragment starting from s and not including any steps of process i, in which some process reaches C. Since $s \overset{j}{\sim} s'$ for every $j \neq i$, there is also such an execution fragment starting from s'.

But this easily yields a counterexample execution α. Execution α begins with a finite execution fragment leading to reachable state s, then continues with α_1, thus letting i into C with no shared variable writes. It finishes by letting another process go to C without any steps of i, starting from s'. This violates the mutual exclusion condition, because two processes are in C at the end of α. ☐

10.8.2   Single-Writer Shared Variables

If the shared variables are constrained to be single-writer/multi-reader read/write registers (like the variables used in the *BurnsME* and *Bakery* algorithms), then Lemmas 10.29 and 10.31 immediately imply the lower bound:

Theorem 10.32 *If algorithm A solves the mutual exclusion problem for $n \geq 2$ processes, using only single-writer/multi-reader read/write shared variables, then A must use at least n shared variables.*

Proof. Consider any process i. By Lemma 10.29, i can reach C on its own, starting from an initial (idle) system state of A. Then Lemma 10.31 implies that i must write some shared variable along the way. Since this holds for every process i, and since each shared variable has only a single writer, there must be at least n shared variables. ☐

10.8.3   Multi-Writer Shared Variables

But notice that even the algorithms that we have presented that use multi-writer registers (like the *DijkstraME* and *Peterson* algorithms) require at least n variables. In this subsection, we extend Theorem 10.32 to the case of multi-writer registers. That is, we prove:

Theorem 10.33 *If algorithm A solves the mutual exclusion problem for $n \geq 2$ processes, using only read/write shared variables, then A must use at least n shared variables.*

To give the intuition for the proof, we start by proving two special cases. We first show impossibility for two processes and one variable, then for three processes and two variables. Afterward, we extend the ideas to the general case.

Two processes and one variable. We use the following definition many times in the proofs: we say that process i *covers* shared variable x in system state s provided that in state s, process i is enabled to write to x. (That is, process i can write to x in its next step.)

Theorem 10.34 *There is no algorithm that solves the mutual exclusion problem for two processes using only one read/write shared variable.*

Proof. Suppose for the sake of contradiction that there is such an algorithm, A, using a single shared register x. Let s be an initial (idle) system state. We construct an execution of A that violates mutual exclusion.

Lemmas 10.29 and 10.31 imply that there is an execution involving process 1 only, starting from state s, that causes process 1 to enter C and to write the single shared variable x before doing so. Just before process 1 writes x, it covers x. Let α_1 be the prefix of this execution up to the first point where process 1 covers x and let s' denote the final state of α_1. Note that $s \overset{2}{\sim} s'$, since process 1 does not write anything to shared memory during α_1. Then Lemma 10.30 implies that process 2 can reach C on its own, starting from state s'.

The counterexample execution α begins with α_1, thus bringing process 1 to state s', where it covers x. It then continues by letting process 2 reach C, running on its own from s'. Next, we resume process 1, allowing it to write x, thereby overwriting anything process 2 might have written on its way to C. This eliminates all traces of process 2's execution. So process 1 can continue to run just as it does in its solo execution and reach C. But this puts both processes in C, which contradicts the mutual exclusion requirement.

Execution α is depicted in Figure 10.10. It "splices" several steps of process 2 into an execution involving process 1 only. $\square$

Three processes and two variables. Now we show impossibility for three processes and two variables.

Theorem 10.35 *There is no algorithm that solves the mutual exclusion problem for three processes using only two read/write shared variables.*

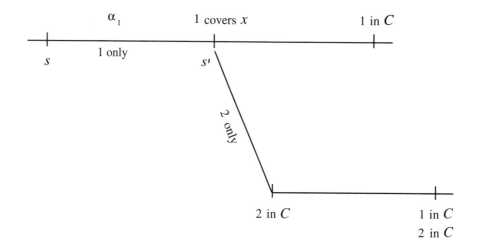

Figure 10.10: Execution α for proof of Theorem 10.34.

Proof. Suppose for the sake of contradiction that there is such an algorithm, A, using shared registers x and y. Let s be an initial system state. We construct an execution of A that violates mutual exclusion.

We will use the following strategy. Starting from s, we will maneuver processes 1 and 2 only, to a point where each covers one of the two variables x and y; moreover, the resulting state, s', will be indistinguishable to process 3 from a reachable idle state. Then we run process 3 on its own from state s' until it reaches C; Lemma 10.30 implies that this is possible.

Next, we let each of processes 1 and 2 take one step. Since each covers one of the two shared variables, they can thereby eliminate all traces of process 3's execution. Then we let processes 1 and 2 continue to take steps; since they have eliminated all evidence of process 3, they can run as if process 3 had never entered its trying region. Thus, by the progress condition, either 1 or 2 will eventually reach C. But this yields two processes in C, contradicting the mutual exclusion condition.

It remains to show how to maneuver processes 1 and 2 to cover the two shared variables while appearing to process 3 to still be in R. We do this as follows (see Figure 10.11).

First, we construct execution α_1 by running process 1 alone from s until it first covers a shared variable. Then we extend α_1 to α_2 by continuing to run process 1 alone until it enters C, then E, then R, then T once again, and again covers some shared variable. We extend α_2 to α_3 in the same way. Let the final states of α_1, α_2, and α_3 be s_1, s_2, and s_3, respectively.

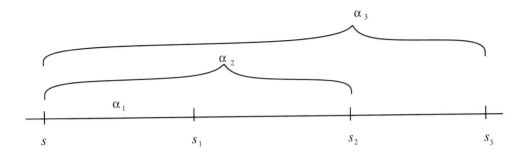

Figure 10.11: Process 1 runs alone.

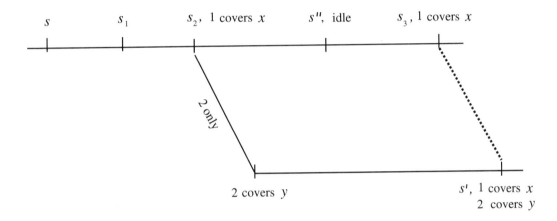

Figure 10.12: Construction of α.

Since there are only two shared variables, in two of the three states s_1, s_2, and s_3, process 1 must cover the *same variable*. To be specific, suppose that in s_2 and s_3, process 1 covers variable x. (The same argument holds for all the other cases.)

Now consider what happens if we run process 2 alone, starting from state s_2. We claim that process 2 can enter C; this follows from Lemma 10.30, because state s_2 is indistinguishable to process 2 from the last preceding state in α in which process 1 is in R. Moreover, we claim that along the way process 2 must write the other shared variable y. For otherwise, process 2 could reach C, then process 1 could take one step, overwriting whatever process 2 wrote to variable x and thus eliminating all traces of 2, and then process 1 could continue and violate mutual exclusion.

Now we construct a counterexample execution α (see Figure 10.12). Execution α begins with α_2, thus bringing process 1 to a point where it covers x. It then continues by letting process 2 run just until the first point where it covers y. At this point, we have processes 1 and 2 covering variables x and y respectively. But we are not yet done, because we still need the resulting state to be indistinguishable to process 3 from some idle state. (In the situation we have so far, process 2 might have written x since it last left R, which could be detectable by process 3.)

So we continue; from the point where process 2 covers y, we resume process 1. It can first write x, thereby eliminating all traces of process 2. Then process 1 can continue to run just as it does in its solo execution and reach a point that looks to it like the point after α_3, where it again covers x. This completes the construction of α; let s' be the final state of α.

We claim that α has all the properties we want. It is easy to see that processes 1 and 2 cover variables x and y respectively, in state s'. It remains to show that s' is indistinguishable to process 3 from a reachable idle state. Let s'' be the last idle state occurring in α_3. Then the only differences between s'' and s_3 are in the state of process 1 and user U_1, while the only differences between s' and s_3 are in the states of process 2 and user U_2. It follows that $s' \overset{3}{\sim} s''$, as needed. □

The general case. The proof for the general case is a natural extension of the proofs for the two special cases, using induction on the number of variables. We need one more basic fact—a strengthened version of Lemma 10.31. It says that a process must not only write *some* variable on the way to C, it must in fact write a variable that is not covered by another process. We have already used this idea, within the proof of Theorem 10.35.

Lemma 10.36 *Suppose A solves the mutual exclusion problem for $n \geq 2$ processes, using only read/write shared variables. Suppose that s is a reachable system state in which process i is in the remainder region. Suppose that process i reaches C in an execution fragment starting from s that involves steps of i only. Then, along the way, i must write some shared variable that is not covered by any other process in s.*

Proof Sketch. The proof is similar to that of Lemma 10.31. The main difference is that now we must ensure that the execution fragment involving the other processes begins with a single step of each process that covers a shared variable, thus overwriting that variable. This allows the other processes to eliminate all traces of i's computation. A detailed proof is left for an exercise. □

We can now prove the main lemma. For any k, $1 \leq k \leq n$, we say that one system state is *k-reachable* from another if it is reachable using steps of processes $1, \ldots, k$ only.

Lemma 10.37 *Suppose A solves the mutual exclusion problem for $n \geq 2$ processes, using only read/write shared variables. Assume that there are exactly $n-1$ shared variables. Let s be any reachable idle system state. Suppose $1 \leq k \leq n-1$. Then there are two system states, s' and s'', each k-reachable from s, satisfying the following properties:*

1. *k distinct variables are covered by processes $1, \ldots, k$ in s'.*

2. *s'' is an idle state.*

3. *$s' \overset{i}{\sim} s''$ for all i, $k+1 \leq i \leq n$.*

Proof. By induction on k.

Basis: $k = 1$. We run process 1 alone from s until it first covers a shared variable; Lemmas 10.29 and 10.31 imply that it is possible to do this. Defining s' to be the resulting state and $s'' = s$ gives the needed properties.

Inductive step: Suppose the lemma holds for k, where $1 \leq k \leq n-2$; we prove it for $k+1$. Using the inductive hypothesis, we obtain a state t_1 that is k-reachable from s and in which processes $1, \ldots, k$ cover k distinct variables; however, t_1 is indistinguishable to processes $k+1, \ldots, n$ from some idle state that is also k-reachable from s. Next, we let each of processes $1, \ldots, k$ take one step from t_1, thereby writing the variable that it covers. Then we let all of $1, \ldots, k$ proceed to R, resulting in a new reachable idle state u_1.

Now we apply the inductive hypothesis again to obtain a state t_2 that is k-reachable from u_1 and in which processes $1, \ldots, k$ cover k distinct variables, yet which is indistinguishable to processes $k+1, \ldots, n$ from an idle state that is k-reachable from u_1. Again let processes $1, \ldots, k$ write their covered variables and return to an idle state u_2.

We repeat this procedure a total of $\binom{n-1}{k}+1$ times, yielding "covering states" $t_1, \ldots, t_{\binom{n-1}{k}+1}$. Now, by the Pigeonhole Principle, among these $\binom{n-1}{k}+1$ covering states, there must be two in which processes $1, \ldots, k$ cover the same set of k shared variables; call this set X. Let s_1 be the first of these two covering states and s_2 the second. Also, let s_1' be the idle state that was constructed to correspond to s_1, and likewise s_2' for s_2. Thus, $s_1 \overset{i}{\sim} s_1'$ and $s_2 \overset{i}{\sim} s_2'$ for all i, $k+1 \leq i \leq n$.

Now consider what happens if we run process $k+1$ alone from system state s_1. Since $s_1 \overset{k+1}{\sim} s_1'$ and s_1' is a reachable idle state, Lemma 10.30 implies that process $k+1$ can eventually enter C. Along the way, by Lemma 10.36, it must write to some variable x not in X.

Now we are ready to define the two needed states, s' and s'', both $k+1$-reachable from the original state s. (See Figure 10.13.) First, to define s' (the

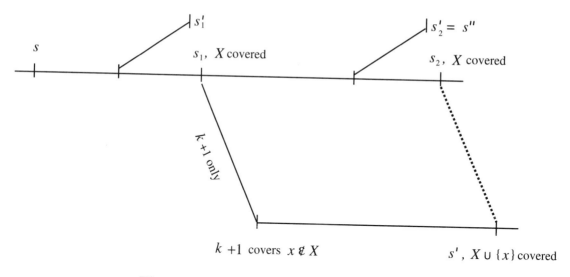

Figure 10.13: Construction for the general case.

state in which $k + 1$ variables are covered), run process $k + 1$ from s_1 just until it first covers a shared variable not in X. Then resume processes $1, \ldots, k$, letting them first write the covered variables, and then proceed to the point corresponding to s_2, where they cover X again. Let s' be the resulting state. Note that s' is the same as s_2, except for the state of process $k + 1$. To define s'' (the idle state), we simply let $s'' = s_2'$.

We claim that s' and s'' have all the required properties. First, note that only processes $1, \ldots, k + 1$ are involved in the construction (including the uses of the inductive hypothesis); so s' and s'' are both $k + 1$–reachable from s. Also, it should be easy to see that $k + 1$ variables are covered in s': the k variables in X plus the new variable x covered by process $k + 1$. Furthermore, $s'' = s_2'$ is an idle state by the definition of s_2'.

It remains only to show that s' and s'' are indistinguishable to all processes i, $k + 2 \leq i \leq n$. But the definition of s_2 and s_2' implies that s_2 and $s'' = s_2'$ are indistinguishable to all processes i, $k + 1 \leq i \leq n$. And we have already noted that s_2 and s' are indistinguishable to all processes except $k + 1$. Putting these two facts together implies the needed condition.   □

Now Theorem 10.33 follows:

Proof (of Theorem 10.33).   Suppose for the sake of contradiction that algorithm A solves the mutual exclusion problem for $n \geq 2$ processes using at most $n - 1$ read/write shared variables. Without loss of generality, we may assume that A has exactly $n - 1$ shared variables.

Let s be any initial system state of A. Then Lemma 10.37 implies that there are two system states, s' and s'', each $n-1$–reachable from s, such that all of the $n-1$ shared variables are covered by processes $1, \ldots, n-1$ in s', s'' is an idle state, and $s' \overset{n}{\sim} s''$. Lemma 10.30 implies that there is an execution fragment starting from s' and involving steps of process n only, in which process n reaches C. Lemma 10.36 implies that in this execution fragment, process n must write some shared variable that is not covered in s'. But all the $n-1$ variables are covered in s', so this is a contradiction. $\qquad\square$

We emphasize again that Theorem 10.33 holds regardless of the size of the shared variables: they can even be unbounded in size. Moreover, no high-level-fairness assumption is needed; the progress condition is the only liveness assumption that is needed for this impossibility result.

10.9 Mutual Exclusion Using Read-Modify-Write Shared Variables

In this final section, we consider mutual exclusion using *read-modify-write* shared memory. That is, a process is able, in one instantaneous step, to access a shared variable and to use the variable value and the process state to determine a new variable value and a new process state. A formal definition appears in Section 9.4.

You might think that considering the mutual exclusion problem in the read-modify-write model is a trivial exercise, because this model is so powerful. The read-modify-write model provides fair exclusive access to each shared variable—each process gets fair turns to access the variable, and when it does so, it can perform an arbitrary computation before the variable is released. This is very close to what is required of a fair mutual exclusion algorithm, namely, fair exclusive access to the critical region. It almost seems as though we are assuming a solution to the very problem we are trying to solve.

Indeed, having such a powerful form of shared memory does simplify the situation considerably, but it does not make all the difficulties disappear. Along with a collection of algorithms, we shall present some nontrivial lower bound results.

We consider the basic mutual exclusion problem first, then consider what happens when we add a high-level-fairness requirement—bounded bypass or lockout-freedom.

For the rest of this section, we assume that the shared memory system only contains a *single* shared variable. This does not cause any loss of generality in the read-modify-write model, because several read-modify-write variables could be combined into a single multipart read-modify-write variable, anyway. Contrast this with the situation for the read/write model, for which we have shown that the existence of a solution to the mutual exclusion problem is quite sensitive to the number of read/write shared variables.

10.9.1 The Basic Problem

To see how different the read-modify-write model is from the read/write model, consider the following trivial one-variable algorithm, *TrivialME*. In this algorithm, the shared variable x has value 1 exactly if the resource has been granted to some process. Any process in the trying region simply tests x until it discovers $x = 0$, at which time it immediately sets $x := 1$. Upon exiting, a process resets $x := 0$. It is straightforward to see that the *TrivialME* algorithm solves the mutual exclusion problem.

TrivialME algorithm:

Shared variables:
$x \in \{0, 1\}$, initially 0

Actions of i:

Input: Internal:
  try_i $test_i$
  $exit_i$ $reset_i$
Output:
  $crit_i$
  rem_i

States of i:
$pc \in \{rem, test, leave\text{-}try, crit, reset, leave\text{-}exit\}$, initially rem

Transitions of i:

try_i
  Effect:
    $pc := test$

$test_i$
  Precondition:
    $pc = test$
  Effect:
    if $x = 0$ then
      $x := 1$
      $pc := leave\text{-}try$

$crit_i$
  Precondition:
    $pc = leave\text{-}try$
  Effect:
    $pc := crit$

$exit_i$
  Effect:
    $pc := reset$

$reset_i$
   Precondition:
     $pc = reset$
   Effect:
     $x := 0$
     $pc := leave\text{-}exit$

rem_i
   Precondition:
     $pc = leave\text{-}exit$
   Effect:
     $pc := rem$

Theorem 10.38 *TrivialME solves the mutual exclusion problem.*

10.9.2   Bounded Bypass

The *TrivialME* algorithm does not guarantee any high-level-fairness conditions. However, we can easily obtain very strong high-level-fairness conditions, even a FIFO condition (based on the first locally controlled step each process takes in its trying region), still just using a single shared variable. For example, we have the *QueueME* algorithm.

QueueME algorithm (informal):

The processes maintain a queue of process indices, initially empty, in the shared variable. A process that enters T adds its index to the end of the queue; a process that finds itself at the beginning of the queue goes to C; and when a process leaves C, it deletes itself from the queue.

Expressing this more formally in precondition-effect notation, we have the following.

QueueME algorithm (formal):

Shared variables:
queue, a FIFO queue of process indices, initially empty

Actions of i:

Input:	Internal:
try_i	$enter_i$
$exit_i$	$test_i$
Output:	$reset_i$
$crit_i$	
rem_i	

States of i:
$pc \in \{rem, enter, test, leave\text{-}try, crit, reset, leave\text{-}exit\}$, initially rem

Transitions of i:

try_i
    Effect:
        $pc := enter$

$enter_i$
    Precondition:
        $pc = enter$
    Effect:
        add i to *queue*
        if i is first on *queue* then
          $pc := leave\text{-}try$
        else $pc := test$

$test_i$
    Precondition:
        $pc = test$
    Effect:
        if i is first on *queue* then
          $pc := leave\text{-}try$

$crit_i$
    Precondition:
        $pc = leave\text{-}try$
    Effect:
        $pc = crit$

$exit_i$
    Effect:
        $pc := reset$

$reset_i$
    Precondition:
        $pc = reset$
    Effect:
        remove first element of *queue*
        $pc := leave\text{-}exit$

rem_i
    Precondition:
        $pc = leave\text{-}exit$
    Effect:
        $pc := rem$

It should be easy to see that *QueueME* guarantees well-formedness, mutual exclusion, and progress. Moreover, it satisfies the high-level-fairness condition that entry to the critical region is FIFO with respect to the first locally controlled action in the trying region (the *enter* action). This implies that *QueueME* guarantees bounded bypass (with a bound of 1).

Theorem 10.39 *QueueME solves the mutual exclusion problem and guarantees bounded bypass.*

The *QueueME* algorithm is simple and is also fast, at least according to our time measure, but it does have the problem that the shared variable is very large. There are $n! + (n - 1)! + \ldots$ different queues consisting of at most n distinct indices, so the variable must be able to assume that many different values. This requires $\Omega(n \log n)$ bits. It would be better to reduce the size of the shared variable, not just in order to save shared memory, but also because it is not so reasonable to assume instantaneous access to such a large variable. An interesting question is how large the shared variable must be in order to guarantee high-level fairness. Can we solve the problem with a variable that takes on a number of values that is linear in n? What about a constant number of values?

It is not very hard to achieve the same type of FIFO behavior as the *QueueME* algorithm, using a shared variable with only n^2 values ($2 \log n$ bits). For example, we may use an algorithm based on issuing "tickets" to the critical region.

TicketME algorithm (informal):

The shared variable holds a pair (*next*, *granted*), of values in $\{0, \ldots, n-1\}$, initially $(0, 0)$. The *next* component represents the next "ticket" to the critical region that is to be issued to a process, while the *granted* component represents the last "ticket" that has been granted permission to enter the critical region. When a process enters the trying region, it "takes a ticket," that is, it copies and increments the *next* component. If a process's ticket is equal to the *granted* component, it goes to the critical region. When a process exits, it increments the *granted* component modulo n.

Now we present the algorithm in the more formal precondition-effect style.

TicketME algorithm (formal):

Shared variables:
(*next*, *granted*), a pair of elements of $\{0, \ldots, n-1\}$, initially $(0, 0)$

Actions of i:
Input: Internal:
   try$_i$ *enter*$_i$
   exit$_i$ *test*$_i$
Output: *reset*$_i$
   crit$_i$
   rem$_i$

States of i:
$pc \in \{rem, enter, test, leave\text{-}try, crit, reset, leave\text{-}exit\}$, initially *rem*
$ticket \in \{0, \ldots, n-1\} \cup \{null\}$, initially *null*

Transitions of i:

try$_i$
  Effect:
     $pc := enter$

enter$_i$
  Precondition:
    $pc = enter$
  Effect:
     $ticket := next$
     $next := next + 1 \bmod n$
     if $ticket = granted$ then
       $pc := leave\text{-}try$
     else $pc := test$

test_i
    Precondition:
        $pc = test$
    Effect:
        if $ticket = granted$ then
            $pc := leave\text{-}try$

crit_i
    Precondition:
        $pc = leave\text{-}try$
    Effect:
        $pc = crit$

exit_i
    Effect:
        $pc := reset$

reset_i
    Precondition:
        $pc = reset$
    Effect:
        $granted := granted + 1 \bmod n$
        $ticket := null$
        $pc := leave\text{-}exit$

rem_i
    Precondition:
        $pc = leave\text{-}exit$
    Effect:
        $pc := rem$

TicketME satisfies the same correctness conditions as *QueueME*, including being FIFO with respect to the first locally controlled action in the trying region. The proof of the following theorem appears in Section 10.9.4.

Theorem 10.40 *TicketME solves the mutual exclusion problem and guarantees bounded bypass, using n^2 values of shared memory.*

Can we do better than n^2? The following theorem gives a simple lower bound of n on the number of shared variable values required to solve bounded bypass mutual exclusion.

Theorem 10.41 *Let A be an n-process mutual exclusion algorithm guaranteeing bounded bypass, using a single read-modify-write shared variable. Then the number of distinct values the variable can take on is at least n.*

Proof. Suppose that A is an n-process mutual exclusion algorithm guaranteeing bounded bypass, with a bypass bound of a. Assume again (as in Section 10.8), without loss of generality, that the users U_i are the most nondeterministic possible. We proceed by contradiction: we construct an execution in which some process is bypassed more than a times.

We start by defining a sequence of finite executions, $\alpha_1, \alpha_2, \ldots, \alpha_n$, each an extension of the previous one. Execution α_1 is obtained by letting process 1 run alone from an initial system state until it enters C. (The progress condition implies that this is possible.) To obtain α_2, we extend α_1 by letting process 2 enter the trying region and take one locally controlled step. Obviously, process 2 must remain in its trying region after α_2, in order to avoid violating the mutual exclusion condition. Then execution α_i, for $3 \le i \le n$, is constructed in a similar way to α_2: starting at the end of α_{i-1}, we let process i enter the trying region and take one locally controlled step. Each process i, $3 \le i \le n$, also remains in its trying region.

Define s_i to be the system state and v_i the value of the shared variable after α_i, $1 \le i \le n$. We claim that $v_i \ne v_j$ for $1 \le i, j \le n$, $i \ne j$, which implies the result.

So assume the contrary, that is, that $v_i = v_j$ for some particular i and j, $i \ne j$, and assume without loss of generality that $i < j$. Then $s_i \overset{k}{\sim} s_j$ for every process k, $1 \le k \le i$. (That is, the system states after α_i and α_j include the same states for processes and users $1, \dots, i$, and the same value of the shared variable.)

Now, there is some low-level-fair execution that extends α_i, involving only processes $1, \dots, i$, that causes some process to enter C infinitely many times. This follows from the progress assumption (which only applies in low-level-fair executions). The same steps can be applied after α_j, again yielding an execution in which the same process enters C infinitely many times. Note that this new execution is *not* low-level fair: processes $i + 1, \dots, j$ do not perform any steps in the portion of the execution after α_j, even though they are all in T. But this does not matter: low-level fairness is not required for a violation of the bypass bound. Just running a sufficiently large portion of this execution is enough to cause process j to be bypassed more than a times by some other process, which is the needed contradiction.

The construction is illustrated in Figure 10.14. □

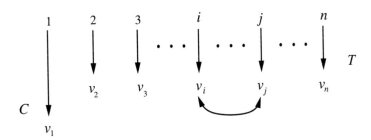

Figure 10.14: Construction of execution for the proof of Theorem 10.41.

Is this lower bound tight, or can it be raised, say to $\Omega(n^2)$? It turns out that it cannot—there is a *counterexample algorithm* (i.e., an algorithm that is not of much interest on its own, that is neither practical nor elegant, but that does serve to demonstrate a counterexample to an impossibility conjecture) that only requires $O(n)$ values. In fact, the algorithm only needs $n + k$ values, for a small constant k. We call this algorithm the *BufferMainME algorithm*, for reasons that will become apparent in a moment.

BufferMainME algorithm:

The basic idea of the *BufferMainME* algorithm is as follows. The trying region is divided into two pieces, called the *buffer* region and the *main* region. When processes enter the trying region, they go into the buffer; no order information is maintained among the processes in the buffer. At some time, when the main region is empty, all processes in the buffer go to the main region, thereby emptying the buffer. From the main region, processes go one at a time, in an arbitrary order, to the critical region.

Implementing this idea requires some communication mechanisms, so that processes can discover when they should change regions. For a first cut at an implementation, suppose that in addition to the usual "agent" processes $1, \ldots, n$, we allow a dedicated *supervisor* process that is always allowed to take steps. We will design a solution that centralizes system control in the supervisor process: the supervisor keeps track of when processes should change regions and informs them accordingly. Afterward, we will describe how to remove the need for the special supervisor process.

Using the supervisor process, we have the following strategy. First, let the variable have two components, one for a *count* $\in \{0, \ldots, n\}$ and one for a *message* chosen from a designated finite set of control messages. This is a total of kn values for some constant k, but we can optimize this to $n + k$ by using a priority scheme to allow reuse of the variable for different types of communication.

The supervisor maintains local variables *buffer-count* and *main-count*, counts of the numbers of processes that it has heard about that are in the buffer and main regions. When a process enters the trying region, it increments the *count* component of the shared variable to inform the supervisor that some new process has entered and then waits in the buffer. The supervisor, whenever it sees a non-zero *count* in the shared variable, absorbs the count into its local *buffer-count* and resets the *count* component of the variable to 0.

The supervisor can figure out when to move the processes in the buffer to the main region, that is, after its *main-count* is 0. It moves them, one at a time, by putting *enter-main* messages in the *message* component of the shared variable. The supervisor stops moving processes from the buffer to the main region when it sees that its *buffer-count* and the *count* in the variable are both equal to 0. Then the supervisor moves processes from the main region to the critical region, by putting *enter-crit* messages in the *message* component of the shared variables.

The control messages that are used are

- *enter-main*: The supervisor places this into the *message* component of the shared variable to move a process from the buffer to the main region. The first process in the buffer that sees this message picks it up and proceeds to the main region.

- *ack-main*: A process that picks up an *enter-main* message from the shared variable leaves this in its place as an acknowledgment to the supervisor. The supervisor picks this up.

- *enter-crit*: The supervisor places this into the *message* component of the shared variable to move a process from the main region to the critical region. The first process in the main region that sees this message picks it up and proceeds to the critical region.

- *ack-crit*: A process that picks up an *enter-crit* message from the shared variable leaves this in its place as an acknowledgment to the supervisor.

- *done*: A process exiting the critical region places this into the *message* component of the shared variable to announce that it is done.

Now we outline how we can avoid the two separate components in the shared variable. Note that the variable is being used for two purposes: recording the number of newly entered processes and communicating control messages. We will now "time-share" the variable, allowing it to serve both purposes, but not at the same time. The variable will at any point have a value that is *either* a count or a control message, but not both.

Note that, in the algorithm described so far, control-message communication proceeds according to a single sequential "thread of control," as depicted in Figure 10.15.

Suppose that this thread were to be interrupted by a newly entering process i overwriting a control message with a count (of 1, announcing its own arrival). Then (because there are only finitely many processes that can enter the system), the system would eventually reach a stable state. The supervisor would eventually absorb all count information in the shared variable, making the *count* in the variable permanently equal to 0. At this

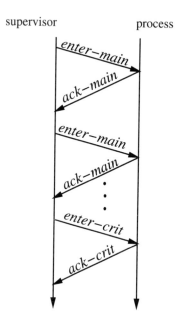

Figure 10.15: A thread of control for the bounded bypass mutual exclusion algorithm.

point, it would be possible for process i to put the overwritten message back in the variable, allowing the thread of control to resume.

More specifically, the following occurs. When process i enters the trying region and sees a control message in the shared variable, it remembers the message and replaces it with a count of 1. Process i holds the message until it sees that the *count* is 0, and then overwrites the 0 with the remembered message. The result is a mutual exclusion algorithm with bounded bypass that uses $n + 6$ values of the shared variable, assuming the availability of a dedicated supervisor process.

Now we modify this algorithm so that it works in the model we have been studying—that is, without a dedicated supervisor process. The idea is to allow the processes to cooperate in a distributed simulation of the supervisor. (The simulation has to be distributed, since there is no process that is guaranteed to be available at all times.) The processes simply take turns performing the simulation; in particular, whenever a process is in the critical region, it will be the process responsible for the supervisor simulation.

The main difficulty of this simulation is that a process leaving C must pass the responsibility for the supervisor simulation on to the next process to enter C. This involves communicating all the state information needed by the supervisor (in particular, *buffer-count* and *main-count*) to the next process. We must use the shared variable for this new type of communication, as well as for the other two types of communication we have already discussed; again, we time-share. Note that the new state communication does not go on at the same time as the control-message communication, so there is no interference here. Moreover, interference between the counts of newly arrived processes and the communication of state information can be managed in the same way as the interference between the counts and the control messages.

One last detail: Sometimes, when a process leaves C, there will be no other process to which it can pass responsibility for the supervisor simulation. In such a case, it means that there is no other process in the trying region. But then there is no interesting information in the supervisor state, anyway, so the process can just abandon responsibility, leaving a special indicator in the shared variable.

Theorem 10.42 *The BufferMainME algorithm solves the mutual exclusion problem, guaranteeing bounded bypass, using a single read-modify-write shared variable with only $n + k$ values (for some small constant k).*

10.9.3 Lockout-Freedom

The lower bound of Theorem 10.41 only holds when the high-level-fairness requirement is bounded bypass. For the weaker requirement of lockout-freedom, the proof does not work. The problem is that lockout-freedom is a property of low-level-fair executions, and the bad execution constructed in the proof was not fair to processes $i + 1, \dots, j$. In fact, the result of Theorem 10.41 does not hold for lockout-freedom. We have another counterexample algorithm, this one with a surprisingly small bound. We call this one the *Executive algorithm*.

Executive algorithm:

The idea of the algorithm is as follows. As in the *BufferMainME* algorithm, each incoming process increments a *count* in the shared variable, but this time the *count* is only allowed to take on values $0, \dots, \frac{n}{2}$ before wrapping back around to 0. The *count* is absorbed by a (simulated) supervisor, as before.

When the *count* wraps around to 0, a group of $\frac{n}{2} + 1$ processes is temporarily "hidden" from the rest of the system; the resulting system state is indistinguishable to all the other processes from the state just before they all entered. If these hidden processes take no further steps, the rest of the system will proceed as if the hidden processes were still in R. However, in a low-level-fair execution, the hidden processes will take further steps and so can make their presence known.

To make sure that the processes do not remain hidden, we designate the process that performs the transition from $\frac{n}{2}$ to 0 as the *executive*, and give it responsibility for the hidden processes. The executive sends special *sleep* messages to (an arbitrary set of) $\frac{n}{2}$ processes in the buffer, to put them to sleep for a while. Then, having removed $\frac{n}{2}$ processes from the competition, the executive reenters the system, incrementing the *count* on its own behalf once again. Now, with $\frac{n}{2}$ processes sleeping, the algorithm runs exactly like the *BufferMainME* algorithm; the shared variable cannot overflow now, because there are at most $\frac{n}{2}$ remaining active processes and the count in the variable is allowed to reach $\frac{n}{2}$. In particular, a second concurrent executive cannot be created. According to the behavior of the *BufferMainME* algorithm, the executive eventually reaches C.

When the executive reaches C, it takes care of the sleepers by sending them *wakeup* messages and telling the supervisor about them. Again, we must time-share the variable for these new types of communication, now with a slightly more complicated priority scheme.

Theorem 10.43 *The Executive algorithm solves the mutual exclusion problem, guaranteeing lockout-freedom, using a single read-modify-write shared variable with only $\frac{n}{2} + k$ values (for some small constant k).*

We finish this subsection with a lower bound of approximately $\sqrt{n}$ on the number of values needed for lockout-free mutual exclusion. This bound is not tight with respect to the $\frac{n}{2} + k$ upper bound, but the proof does contain an interesting method of constructing bad low-level-fair executions.

Theorem 10.44 *Let $k \geq 2$. Let A be any system of $n \geq \frac{k^2 - k}{2} + 1$ processes solving the mutual exclusion problem and guaranteeing lockout-freedom, using a single read-modify-write shared variable. Then the number of distinct values the variable can take on in reachable states of A is at least k.*

Proof.   Again, we assume that the users are the most nondeterministic possible. We proceed by induction on k.

Basis: $k = 2$. Then the inequality says that $n \geq 2$. It is easy to show that the variable must take on at least two values, since otherwise the processes could not communicate. The formal argument is similar to the one used for Lemma 10.31.

Inductive step: Assume now that the result holds for $k \geq 2$; we show that it holds for $k + 1$. Suppose $n \geq \frac{(k+1)^2 - (k+1)}{2} + 1$, and suppose for contradiction that the number of values of the shared variable is strictly less than $k + 1$. By the inductive hypothesis, it follows that the number of values is at least k, so it must be exactly k. We now construct a bad execution to derive a contradiction.

We define finite execution α_1 by running process 1 alone until it enters C; let the resulting system state be s_1. Then we extend α_1 to α_2 by running process 2 just until a system state s_2 is reached in which the shared variable has a value that process 2 can cause to recur infinitely many times by running on its own from state s_2. Such a state must exist since the variable can assume only finitely many values. Likewise, we define α_i, for $3 \leq i \leq n$, by running process i after α_{i-1} until a system state s_i is reached in which the variable has a value that process i can cause to recur infinitely many times by running on its own from state s_i. Let v_i be the value of the variable in system state s_i, for all i, $1 \leq i \leq n$. Since there are only k values that are taken on by the shared variable, the Pigeonhole Principle implies that there must be two processes, i and j, where $n - k \leq i < j \leq n$, such that $v_i = v_j$. Fix these i and j. Note that $s_i \overset{m}{\sim} s_j$ for all processes m, $1 \leq m \leq i$.

Now, processes $1, \ldots, i$ constitute a system with at least $\frac{k^2 - k}{2} + 1$ processes, solving the mutual exclusion problem with lockout-freedom. So, by the inductive hypothesis, they must use all k values of shared memory. In fact, we can sharpen this claim: for every system state s that is i-reachable[3] from system state s_i, and every value v of shared memory, there must be a system state that is i-reachable from s in which the value of the shared variable is v. (If not, then we could use any idle state that is i-reachable from s as an initial state for a system involving processes $1, \ldots, i$, in which the variable takes on fewer than k values. This contradicts the inductive hypothesis.) Using this sharpened claim, we can produce a low-level-fair execution of processes $1, \ldots, i$ that extends α_i and in which all k values of the shared variable recur infinitely many times.

Now we construct the bad execution α as follows. It begins with α_j, which brings processes $1, \ldots, j$ into the system and brings the system state to s_j and the variable value to $v_j = v_i$. Next, run processes $1, \ldots, i$ as described above, but from state s_j instead of s_i; again, these processes cause each of the k values of the shared variable to recur infinitely often.

Now recall that from its local state in s_m, each process m, $i + 1 \leq m \leq j$ is able to cause the value of the variable in state s_m to recur infinitely often. So we splice into the main execution of processes $1, \ldots, i$ some steps of processes $i + 1, \ldots, j$ as follows: each time the shared variable is set in the main execution

---

[3]As in Section 10.8, we define this to mean that the state s is reachable using steps of processes $1, \ldots, i$ only.

to some value v_m, $i + 1 \leq m \leq j$, we run process m for just enough steps (but at least one step) to let it return the value of the shared variable to v_m. These insertions yield an infinite execution that is fair to *all* processes and that locks out all processes m, $i + 1 \leq m \leq j$.   □

The key idea to remember in the proof of Theorem 10.44 is the construction of bad low-level-fair executions by splicing together execution fragments. Also, note that Theorem 10.44 implies what might at first seem to be a paradox. Namely, there is a nontrivial inherent cost to solving lockout-free mutual exclusion, even though our model already contains something very close to what is needed—fair exclusive access to a shared variable for arbitrary computation.

Note that there is a gap between the upper bound of Theorem 10.43 and the lower bound of Theorem 10.44. Closing this gap is a research question.

10.9.4 A Simulation Proof

We close this section by outlining a correctness proof for the *TicketME* algorithm presented in the previous section. Our proof uses the simulation method described in Section 8.5.5. We have already used the simulation method to show correctness of several algorithms—for example, *OptFloodSet*—in the synchronous model; however, this is our first interesting use of this method for asynchronous algorithms.

We would like to prove that the *TicketME* algorithm guarantees the same correctness conditions as the *QueueME* algorithm: well-formedness, mutual exclusion, progress, and FIFO behavior with respect to the first locally controlled event in T. Showing this would imply Theorem 10.40. It turns out that a good way to understand the *TicketME* algorithm is to relate it, not to *QueueME*, but to a new *InfiniteTicketME algorithm* that is just like *TicketME* except that it uses an infinite sequence of tickets rather than counting modulo n. Then *TicketME* can be seen as a reduced-complexity version of *InfiniteTicketME*. Here are the modifications to *TicketME* needed to obtain the new *InfiniteTicketME* algorithm:

InfiniteTicketME algorithm:

Shared variables:
$(next, granted) \in \mathbb{N} \times \mathbb{N}$, initially $(0, 0)$

Actions of i:
As for *TicketME*.

States of i:
$ticket \in \mathbb{N} \cup \{null\}$, initially *null*

Transitions of i:

$enter_i$
    Precondition:
        $pc = enter$
    Effect:
        $ticket := next$
        $next := next + 1$
        if $ticket = granted$ then
          $pc := leave\text{-}try$
        else $pc := test$

$reset_i$
    Precondition:
        $pc = reset$
    Effect:
        $granted := granted + 1$
        $ticket := null$
        $pc := leave\text{-}exit$

It is easy to show that *InfiniteTicketME* satisfies all the properties claimed for *TicketME*, since only one ticket is granted at a time and tickets are never reused. Then we can show the correctness of *TicketME* by relating it formally to *InfiniteTicketME*, using the method of simulations. The idea is to run the two algorithms side by side, proving that certain strong relationships hold between the two executions.

Some invariants for *InfiniteTicketME* are useful. (These would naturally be proved anyway in the course of verifying the algorithm's properties.)

Lemma 10.45 *In any reachable system state of InfiniteTicketME, the following are true:*

1. *A process i has a non-null ticket exactly if $pc_i \in \{test, leave\text{-}try, crit, reset\}$.*

2. *The non-null ticket values are exactly the integers in the interval $[granted, next)$, and each is held by exactly one process.*

3. *$granted \leq next \leq granted + n$.*

4. *If $pc_i \in \{leave\text{-}try, crit, exit\}$, then $ticket_i = granted$.*

The next step is to define a simulation relation f between the system states of *TicketME* and *InfiniteTicketME* when the two algorithms are combined with the same collection of users. This correspondence is simple: we define $(s, u) \in f$ (alternatively written as $u \in f(s)$) provided that the two states are identical except that the various corresponding ticket components are only required to be the same modulo n. We use dot notation below to indicate the value of a given variable in a given state.

1. All user states are identical in s and u.

2. For every i, $s.pc_i = u.pc_i$.

3. $s.granted = u.granted \bmod n$.

4. $s.next = u.next \bmod n$.

5. For every i, $s.ticket_i = u.ticket_i \bmod n$.

We show that f is a simulation relation. More precisely, we define T and I to be the *TicketME* and *InfiniteTicketME* systems, respectively, each modified slightly so that all the actions are classified as external. We show that f is a simulation relation from T to I. The two conditions that we need to show are

1. If s is an initial state of T, then $f(s)$ contains an initial state of I.

2. If s is a reachable state of T, $u \in f(s)$ is a reachable state of I, and (s, π, s') is a transition of T, then there is a step (u, π, u') of I, where $u' \in f(s')$.

Lemma 10.46 *f is a simulation relation from T to I.*

Proof.   The two conditions given above are straightforward to prove. For the first condition, that is, the start condition, a start state s of T consists of the unique start state of the *TicketME* algorithm and arbitrary start states for the users. It is easy to see that the unique start state of the *InfiniteTicketME* algorithm, together with the same start states for the users, is in $f(s)$.

The second condition, that is, the step condition, is proved by a case analysis, according to the type of action being performed. Any locally controlled actions of the users are mimicked exactly. For each locally controlled action of the algorithm, the existence of a step (s, π, s') in T immediately implies that the same action π is enabled in the corresponding state of I, because the enabling conditions are based only on the pc values. Also, in every case, the new state u' is uniquely determined by the definition of *InfiniteTicketME*. The only remaining thing to show, then, is that $u' \in f(s')$.

But this is also easy. The only interesting case is an action of the form $test_i$, where a process i makes a decision, based on whether $ticket_i = granted$, about whether it should proceed to C. We must verify that the two algorithms do not make different decisions. Because *TicketME* only uses ticket values $0, \dots, n - 1$ and corresponding values in s and u are the same modulo n, the only way that the decisions could be different is if equality holds in *TicketME* but not in *InfiniteTicketME*. That is, the danger is that incrementing ticket values modulo

n might be blurring distinctions that are important in determining the behavior of *InfiniteTicketME*.

But this turns out not to be a problem. Suppose that $s.ticket_i = s.granted$. Then the fact that $u \in f(s)$ implies that $u.ticket_i = u.granted \bmod n$. The invariants proved in Lemma 10.45 imply that $u.granted \leq u.ticket_i < u.next$ and $u.next \leq u.granted + n$. Therefore, $u.granted \leq u.ticket_i < u.granted + n$. So it must be that $u.ticket_i = u.granted$, as needed. $\qquad\square$

How does Lemma 10.46 help to prove the correctness of *TicketME?*

Proof Sketch (of Theorem 10.40). Lemma 10.46 and Theorem 8.12 imply that $traces(T) \subseteq traces(I)$. The well-formedness, mutual exclusion, and FIFO conditions can all be expressed as properties of traces (when all the actions are included, as they are here). So the fact that these three conditions hold for I implies that they also hold for T. This implies that *TicketME* guarantees the well-formedness, mutual exclusion, and FIFO conditions.

But this does not prove that *TicketME* guarantees progress. The progress condition is different from the other three conditions in that it is supposed to hold only for the *fair* executions of an algorithm. To show that this condition carries over from *InfiniteTicketME* to *TicketME*, we would like to know that $fairtraces(T) \subseteq fairtraces(I)$. It turns out that the simulation relation f can also be used to help prove this inclusion.

The key idea is that a simulation relation actually implies more than just inclusion of sets of traces—it really establishes a close correspondence between *executions* of the two algorithms. See Section 8.5.5 for a formal definition of such a correspondence. In the present situation, Theorem 8.13 of Section 8.5.5 implies that for any execution α of T, there is an execution α' of I that corresponds to it in the following very strong sense:

1. The sequences of actions in α and α' are identical.

2. States in the same position in α and α' are related by f.

We obtain such a strong correspondence here because all actions of T and I are external.

Now we argue that $fairtraces(T) \subseteq fairtraces(I)$. Let $\beta \in fairtraces(T)$ and let α be any fair execution of T such that $\beta = trace(\alpha)$. Then, by Theorem 8.13, there is a corresponding execution α' of I satisfying the two conditions enumerated above. In particular, the traces of α and α' are the same, so that $\beta = trace(\alpha')$. We claim that α' is a fair execution of I.

There are two ways in which it might fail to be fair. First, there might be some process i that is enabled (to take a locally controlled step) from some point on in α', yet no such step occurs after that point in α'. Then the strong correspondence implies that process i is also enabled from the same point on in α, but no such step occurs after that point in α. This violates the fairness of α, a contradiction. Second, there might be some user task that is enabled from some point on in α', yet no step of that task occurs after that point in α'. Again, the correspondence implies that the same thing happens in α, violating the fairness of α.

It follows that α' is a fair execution of I, which implies that $\beta \in fairtraces(I)$. Thus, $fairtraces(T) \subseteq fairtraces(I)$. Since the progress condition can be expressed as a property of fair traces (when all the actions are included, as they are here), this implies that the progress condition carries over from *Infinite-TicketME* to *TicketME*. $\qquad\Box$

10.10   Bibliographic Notes

The *DijkstraME* algorithm appeared in a short note by Dijkstra [90]. It extended a previous two-process algorithm by Dekker to an arbitrary number of processes. Before these results, it was not even clear that the problem could be solved with only read/write shared memory. The assertional proof that *DijkstraME* satisfies the mutual exclusion condition is adapted from a paper by Goldman and Lynch on shared memory modelling [141]. Dijkstra's original note was followed by a series of replies, by Knuth, de Bruijn, and Eisenberg and McGuire [168, 86, 108], each improving on the prior solutions by adding new high-level-fairness conditions and/or better performance properties.

The *Peterson2P* and *PetersonNP* algorithms were designed by Peterson [238]. The *Tournament* algorithm is based on a combination of the ideas of *Peterson2P* and those of the tournament protocol of Peterson and Fischer [242]. Our *Tournament* algorithm is simpler and easier to prove correct than the tournament algorithm in [242]; however, it has the disadvantage that it uses multi-writer variables, while the original requires only single-writer variables.

The *BurnsME* algorithm is due to Burns [60], and the *Bakery* algorithm to Lamport [174]. A later paper by Lamport [180] contains additional improved mutual exclusion algorithms. The lower bound on the number of registers required for solving the mutual exclusion problem is due to Burns and Lynch [63].

The *TicketME* algorithm is due to Fischer, Lynch, Burns, and Borodin [120, 121]. The results on bounded bypass and lockout-free mutual exclusion with read-modify-write shared memory all appear in a paper by Burns, Fischer, Jackson, Lynch, and Peterson [62]. These results build on earlier work by Cremers and Hibbard [84]; in particular, the *BufferMainME* algorithm is based closely on an algorithm of [84]. Another result in [62], not discussed in this chapter, says that lockout-free mutual exclusion requires at least $\frac{n}{2}$ values of shared memory, if the special assumption is made that processes have only a single remainder state. (That is, they cannot retain any memory of prior executions of the algorithm.) Cremers and Hibbard [85] also designed an $n + k$ algorithm to achieve FIFO access to the critical region, using read-modify-write shared memory.

A good source for information about temporal logic, which can be used to formalize the liveness proofs in this chapter and elsewhere in this book, is the book by Manna and Pnueli [219].

The k-exclusion problem considered in Exercise 10.13 was first defined by Fischer, Lynch, Burns, and Borodin [120] and later studied by Shavit [261]. A book by Raynal [249] contains descriptions of many mutual exclusion algorithms, for both the asynchronous shared memory and asynchronous network models. Mutual exclusion is also discussed in books by Ben-Ari [45] and by Peterson and Silberschatz [262].

10.11 Exercises

10.1. Consider yet another way of defining the mutual exclusion problem, this one in terms of the traces of the shared memory system A alone, rather than in terms of the combination of A and the users. That is, define a trace property Q such that $traces(Q)$ is the set of sequences β of *try, crit, exit,* and *rem* actions that satisfy the following three conditions:

(a) In β, the system is not the first to violate well-formedness, for any i.

(b) If β is well-formed for every i, then β does not contain two *crit* events without an intervening *exit* event.

(c) If β is well-formed for every i, then the following hold:

i. If at some point in β, some process's last event is *try* and no process's last event is *crit*, then there is a later *crit* event.

ii. If at some point in β, some process's last event is *exit*, then there is a later *rem* event.

Prove that if $fairtraces(A) \subseteq traces(Q)$, then A combined with any collection of users satisfies the definition of the mutual exclusion problem given in Section 10.2.

10.2. Describe a fair execution of the *DijkstraME* algorithm in which a particular process is locked out.

10.3. Show that the second phase of the *DijkstraME* algorithm (where the *flag* is raised to 2 and the other processes' *flags* are tested) is needed to solve the problem correctly.

10.4. Fill in more details in the inductive proof of mutual exclusion, for the *DijkstraME* algorithm.

10.5. Consider the timing analysis for *DijkstraME*, for the time from a point where some user is in T and no user is in C until a point where some user enters C.

    (a) Refine the analysis to express the bound in the form $k_1 n\ell + k_2\ell$, where k_1 and k_2 are particular constants. Try to make k_1 and k_2 as small as possible.

    (b) Construct an execution of *DijkstraME* in which the bound is as large as you can make it; try to match your computed upper bound.

10.6. The lockout-freedom condition makes sense for those algorithms that guarantee well-formedness, but not necessarily mutual exclusion or progress. Prove carefully that if an algorithm guarantees well-formedness and is lockout-free (for all collections of users), then it also guarantees progress (for all collections of users).

10.7. Modify the processes in the *Peterson2P* algorithm so that they do not necessarily perform *check-flag* and *check-turn* in strict alternation, but according to some looser discipline. Make sure your resulting algorithm is still a lockout-free mutual exclusion algorithm. Prove the correctness of your modified algorithm and analyze its time complexity.

10.8. Design a lockout-free mutual exclusion algorithm for two processes that uses only *single-writer*/multi-reader read/write registers. Prove the correctness of your algorithm, preferably using invariant assertions. (*Hint:* If you get stuck, you might want to consider the two-process solution in [242]. You're on your own for the invariant proof, though.)

10.9. Prove Assertion 10.5.3.

10.10. Prove Assertion 10.5.4.

10.11. Reconsider the time bound proved in Theorem 10.16, for the *PetersonNP* algorithm. Is it tight? Either exhibit an execution in which the exponential behavior described there is actually realized, or else give a finer analysis with a smaller complexity bound.

10.12. Does the *PetersonNP* algorithm guarantee bounded bypass? Prove that it does or give a counterexample.

10.13. Modify the *PetersonNP* algorithm to yield a solution to the *k-exclusion problem*, $2 \leq k \leq n$. This problem allows k processes to coexist inside the critical region at the same time. Formally, the mutual exclusion condition is modified to forbid more than k users to be in C at once. The progress condition for the trying region is also modified, to say that if there is at least one user in T and at most $k - 1$ users are in C, then some user eventually enters C. Prove that your algorithm works correctly. State carefully the high-level-fairness conditions that your algorithm satisfies.

10.14. (a) Rewrite the *Tournament* algorithm in precondition-effects form.

 (b) In terms of this rewrite, define the notions of "winner" and "competitor" carefully.

 (c) Prove Assertion 10.5.7. (*Hint:* Strengthen it to include some information about what happens when a process is inside the waitfor loop, after the process has discovered that some of its opponents have *flag* variables strictly less than k. Then prove the strengthened invariant together with the original one by induction.)

 (d) Complete the proof that the *Tournament* algorithm guarantees mutual exclusion.

10.15. Show how the *Tournament* algorithm can be adapted for use with n processes, where n is not a power of 2. What happens to the time complexity?

10.16. *Research Question*: Devise a variant of the *Tournament* protocol that uses single-writer/multi-reader registers rather than multi-writer/multi-reader registers. Provide a complete correctness proof and analysis.

10.17. What happens to the behavior of the *BurnsME* algorithm if the second for loop is removed? Either prove that it still solves the mutual exclusion problem or exhibit a counterexample execution.

10.18. Give an assertional proof showing that the *BurnsME* algorithm satisfies the mutual exclusion condition. To do this, you should rewrite the algorithm in precondition-effect form and define explicit variables to keep track of checked processes within the for loops.

10.19. Exhibit a low-level-fair execution of the *BurnsME* algorithm in which some process is locked out.

10.20. Carry out a time analysis for the progress condition, for the *BurnsME* algorithm. That is, assume that c and ℓ are upper bounds on critical region time and process step time, and consider the time from when there is some process in T and no process in C until some process enters C.

   (a) Prove an upper bound for this time.

   (b) Exhibit a particular execution in which this time is as large as possible.

   Try to get your bounds in (a) and (b) to be as close as possible.

10.21. Describe an execution of the *Bakery* algorithm in which the values taken on by the *number* registers are unbounded.

10.22. Why does the *Bakery* algorithm fail if the integers are replaced by the integers mod b, for some very large value of b? Describe a specific counterexample execution.

10.23. Rewrite the *Bakery* algorithm in precondition-effect form. While doing this, try to generalize the algorithm slightly by allowing as much nondeterminism in the order of actions as you can. (The precondition-effect notation generally makes it easier to express such nondeterminism than does the usual flow-of-control notation.) Give an assertional proof of the mutual exclusion condition for the generalized algorithm.

10.24. Prove that the *Bakery* algorithm works correctly even in the following much weaker model. Suppose that reads and writes are no longer instantaneous, but have duration. Suppose that the shared registers are only guaranteed to be *safe*, that is, to yield the correct value only in the absence of concurrent reading and writing. In the event that a read overlaps any write, any value might be returned by the read.

10.25. Does Burns's mutual exclusion algorithm work if the shared registers are all safe registers (as defined in Exercise 10.24)? Why or why not?

10.26. Suppose that the *Bakery* algorithm only needs to work for the case of instantaneous-access shared memory, not the more general model with safe registers. Give a simplified version of the algorithm that guarantees the same mutual exclusion and high-level-fairness conditions as the original *Bakery* algorithm. Prove your claims.

10.27. Fill in the details for the complexity analysis of the *Bakery* algorithm, sketched at the end of Section 10.7.

10.28. Give explicit code for a particular user automaton U_i that exhibits all the nondeterminism allowed for user i—it should be able to perform its try_i and $exit_i$ actions at any time, or never perform them, subject only to the well-formedness condition. Your automaton should have the property that for any other user automaton V_i for i, $fairtraces(V_i) \subseteq fairtraces(U_i)$.

10.29. Give a careful proof for Lemma 10.36.

10.30. *Research Question*: How are the results in Section 10.8 affected if, instead of the mutual exclusion problem, we consider:

  (a) The k-exclusion problem, $2 \le k \le n$, as defined in Exercise 10.13.

  (b) A weaker version of the k-exclusion problem, which uses the modified mutual exclusion condition as above, but retains the original progress condition.

10.31. Programmers at the Flaky Computer Corporation have designed the following algorithm for n-process mutual exclusion. They claim that their algorithm guarantees mutual exclusion and progress, but do not claim any high-level-fairness conditions.

A:

Shared variables:
$x \in \{1, \ldots, n\}$, initially arbitrary
$y \in \{0, 1\}$, initially 0

Process i:

```
        ** Remainder region **

        try_i
L:      x := i
        if y ≠ 0 then goto L
        y := 1
        if x ≠ i then goto L
        crit_i

        ** Critical region **

        exit_i
        y := 0
        rem_i
```

Does this protocol satisfy the two claimed conditions? Either prove that it does or give explicit counterexample executions to show that it doesn't.

10.32. *Research Question*: Consider a generalization of the progress condition to the *k-concurrent progress* condition, which only requires progress if there are never more than k users concurrently outside of R:

> **k-concurrent progress:** In any *fair execution* in which there are never more than k users outside of R at once:
>
> (a) (k-concurrent progress for the trying region) If at least one user is in T and no user is in C, then at some later point some user enters C.
>
> (b) (k-concurrent progress for the exit region) If at least one user is in E, then at some later point some user enters R.

Give the best upper and lower bounds you can on the number of shared read/write variables needed to achieve well-formedness, mutual exclusion, and k-concurrent progress.

10.33. Design a good mutual exclusion algorithm for a read/write shared memory model that is a little different from the model used in this chapter. In this new model, there is one extra process besides the usual "agent" processes $1, \dots, n$: a *supervisor process*, which is always permitted to take steps. The model should use single-writer/multi-reader shared variables. Prove your algorithm's correctness and analyze its complexity.

10.34. Prove all the claimed properties for the *QueueME* algorithm. You should begin by identifying and proving key system invariants and then use these to prove the mutual exclusion condition. Progress can then be proved using an argument by contradiction, as usual. The FIFO condition can use an ad hoc operational argument. In particular, your proofs should yield Theorem 10.39.

10.35. In the *Bakery* algorithm, it is not possible to reduce the unbounded ticket values by counting modulo any integer; however, this trick works for the *TicketME* algorithm. Explain the reasons for this difference.

10.36. Consider the *BufferMainME* algorithm.

(a) Write precondition-effect code for the supervisor and "agent" processes, for the version of the algorithm with a supervisor. Prove that the algorithm works correctly.

(b) Do the same for the final version of the algorithm, without a supervisor. (*Hint:* You might try to relate this to the version with a supervisor, using a simulation proof.)

10.37. Design a new algorithm that solves mutual exclusion using a single read-modify-write shared variable, and is FIFO (with respect to the first locally controlled step in the trying region). Try to minimize the number of values taken on by the shared variable. You may assume a dedicated supervisor process. (*Hint:* $n + k$ is achievable, for a small constant k.)

10.38. Show that the *Executive* algorithm does not guarantee bounded bypass.

10.39. *Research Question:* Write code for the *Executive* algorithm and argue its correctness. Can its proof be based formally on the correctness of the *BufferMainME* algorithm? Can a simulation proof be used?

10.40. Give upper bounds on the time from when a process enters T until it enters C, in

 (a) The *BufferMainME* algorithm
 (b) The *Executive* algorithm

 Your analysis should be based on the underlying I/O automata rather than the code. You will probably find it convenient to write precondition-effect code for the algorithms.

10.41. Why doesn't the idea of the *Executive* algorithm generalize to allow the variable to have only $\frac{n}{3}$ values?

10.42. *Research Question:* Close the gap between the upper and lower bound results in Theorems 10.43 and 10.44. (*Hint:* A partial result appears in [62].)

10.43. Carry out all the details of the proof of Lemma 10.46.

10.44. *Research Question:* Redo all the proofs of liveness conditions (progress and lockout-freedom) in this chapter using a formal temporal logic.

Chapter 11

Resource Allocation

In Chapter 10, we considered the *mutual exclusion problem*, an abstract resource-allocation problem involving access by concurrent users to a single unshareable resource. In this chapter, we generalize the problem to include many resources instead of just one. This generalization is useful for modelling application programs that require several resources for their execution, for example, a printer plus a database plus a network port.

There are more general types of resource-allocation problems than those we consider here. For instance:

1. We do not consider (except in some general definitions and some exercises) the possibility that a user might be willing to accept alternative combinations of resources. For example, a user might request "some printer" rather than a specific printer.

2. We do not consider the possibility that resources might be shared. For example, individual data objects in a database can be thought of as resources to be allocated to database transactions. In this case, some sharing is typically permitted; for example, two transactions that need only to read an object can be allowed concurrent access to the object.

We begin by defining our generalized resource-allocation problem, including the *Dining Philosophers problem* as an interesting special case. We then give several typical solutions. Our last solution is a randomized protocol—our first example of a randomized protocol for the asynchronous setting.

11.1   The Problem

In this section, we begin by giving some ways of specifying conflict relationships among users. Then we describe how to use such specifications to define resource-allocation problems. Finally, we define the Dining Philosophers problem.

11.1.1   Explicit Resource Specifications and Exclusion Specifications

There are two different ways of looking at the mutual exclusion problem: as the problem of allocating an explicitly represented resource or as the problem of ensuring that only one user at a time is in its critical region. We can also look at generalized resource-allocation problems in these two ways. Thus, we define both *explicit resource specifications* and *exclusion specifications* as alternative ways of describing conflict relationships among users.

An *explicit resource specification* $\mathcal{R}$ for n users consists of

1. A universal finite set R of objects known as *resources*

2. For every i, $1 \leq i \leq n$, a set $R_i \subseteq R$

The intention is that the resources in R_i should be those that user U_i needs to perform its work. We say that two users U_i and U_j *conflict* with respect to a given explicit resource specification if they require some common resource, that is, if $R_i \cap R_j \neq \emptyset$.

Example 11.1.1   Explicit resource specification

Consider an explicit resource specification for four users, $U_1, \ldots, U_4$. The set R of resources is $\{r(1), r(2), r(3), r(4)\}$. The resource requirements for the four users are

$$
\begin{array}{rcl}
U_1 & : & \{r(1), r(2)\} \\
U_2 & : & \{r(1), r(3)\} \\
U_3 & : & \{r(2), r(4)\} \\
U_4 & : & \{r(3), r(4)\}
\end{array}
$$

Thus, U_1 needs exclusive possession of resources $r(1)$ and $r(2)$ to perform its work, and so on. Users U_1 and U_2 conflict, as do U_1 and U_3, U_2 and U_4, and U_3 and U_4.

On the other hand, an *exclusion specification* does not mention resources at all. Rather, the specification is given in terms of a collection $\mathcal{E}$ of "bad sets" of user indices. A "bad set" is a set of indices of users that are not allowed to perform their work simultaneously. There is one restriction on exclusion specifications: the collection of bad sets is required to be closed under superset. That is, if a particular bad set E of users belongs to an exclusion specification $\mathcal{E}$, then any superset of E also belongs to $\mathcal{E}$.

Example 11.1.2   Exclusion specification

The mutual exclusion condition can be described by the exclusion specification $\mathcal{E} = \{E \subseteq \{1, \ldots, n\} : |E| > 1\}$.

Example 11.1.3   Another exclusion specification

The k-exclusion condition (in which the number of users in the critical region at any time is constrained to be at most k) can be defined by the exclusion specification $\mathcal{E} = \{E \subseteq \{1, \ldots, n\} : |E| > k\}$. The k-exclusion condition is introduced in Exercise 10.13.

Example 11.1.4   Still another exclusion specification

For $n = 4$, consider the exclusion specification $\mathcal{E}$ consisting of the two-element sets $\{1, 2\}$, $\{1, 3\}$, $\{2, 4\}$, and $\{3, 4\}$, plus all the sets that contain these two-element sets. In this exclusion specification, note that user U_1 does not exclude user U_4, and U_2 does not exclude U_3. This means that U_1 and U_4 can perform their work simultaneously, as can U_2 and U_3.

Note that any explicit resource specification gives rise to an exclusion specification that is equivalent in that it permits the same combinations of users to execute simultaneously. This exclusion specification consists of exactly those sets of users with no intersections among their resource requirements.

Example 11.1.5   Corresponding specifications

The exclusion specification that corresponds to the explicit resource specification in Example 11.1.1 consists of the two-element sets $\{1, 2\}$, $\{1, 3\}$, $\{2, 4\}$, and $\{3, 4\}$, plus all the sets that contain these two-element sets.

However, it is not the case that every exclusion specification has a corresponding explicit resource specification. We leave this for an exercise.

11.1.2   Resource-Allocation Problem

We now describe how to incorporate explicit resource specifications and exclusion specifications into resource-allocation problems to be solved by shared memory systems. To be specific, consider a fixed exclusion specification $\mathcal{E}$ (which could be derived from an explicit resource specification).

The architecture is exactly the same as we used for the mutual exclusion problem in Chapter 10—a combination of user automata and a shared memory system automaton (see Figure 10.4). Again, users cycle through their *remainder* (R), *trying* (T), *critical* (C), and *exit* (E) regions, as depicted in Figure 10.2. A sequence of interactions between U_i and the shared memory system is *well-formed* for user i if it respects this cyclic order.

The well-formedness condition on the composed system is as before.

Well-formedness: In any execution, and for any i, the subsequence describing the interaction between U_i and A is well-formed for i.

The mutual exclusion condition is now replaced by the more general exclusion condition.

Exclusion: There is no reachable system state in which the set of users in their critical regions is a set in $\mathcal{E}$.

The progress condition is as before.

Progress: At any point in a *fair execution*,

1. (Progress for the trying region) If at least one user is in T and no user is in C, then at some later point some user enters C.

2. (Progress for the exit region) If at least one user is in E, then at some later point some user enters R.

We say that a shared memory system A *solves the general resource-allocation problem* for a given collection of users provided that, in combination with those users, it satisfies the well-formedness, exclusion, and progress conditions. We say that A *solves the general resource-allocation problem* provided that it solves it for every collection of users.

The progress condition for the trying region is weaker than one might like in the present setting. For general resource-allocation problems, we would like also to say that users that do not conflict with each other should not prevent each other from entering the critical region, even if they hold onto the resources forever. We do not know a good way of stating such a condition, for arbitrary exclusion specifications. However, for explicit resource specifications, we can at least state the following condition.

Independent progress: At any point in a *fair execution*,

1. (Independent progress for the trying region) If U_i is in T and all conflicting users are in R, then at some later point either U_i enters C or some conflicting user enters T.

2. (Independent progress for the exit region) If U_i is in E and all conflicting users are in R, then at some later point either U_i enters R or some conflicting user enters T.

For high-level-fairness conditions, the same lockout-freedom and time bound conditions that we defined for the mutual exclusion problem also make sense for the general resource-allocation problem. We will not discuss the bounded bypass condition here. Some simple relationships among these properties are as follows. (Compare with Theorem 10.9 and Execise 10.6.)

Lemma 11.1

1. *If a general resource-allocation algorithm has any time bound b, then it is lockout-free.*

2. *If an algorithm in the model of this chapter guarantees well-formedness and lockout-freedom, then it also guarantees progress.*

Proof. The proof is left as an exercise. □

Trace properties. As we did for similar properties in Chapter 10, we can express the well-formedness, exclusion, progress, independent progress, and lockout-freedom conditions equivalently in terms of trace properties. Each of these trace properties P has a signature consisting of *try*, *crit*, *exit*, and *rem* outputs (and no inputs). The external actions of the combined system are also exactly these actions, and the requirement in each case is that the fair traces of the combined system are all in *traces*(P).

Restricting process activity. As in Chapter 10, we assume in this chapter that a process within the shared memory system can have a locally controlled action enabled only when its user is in the trying or exit region. Thus, the processes can only be actively engaged in executing the protocol while there are active requests.

11.1.3 Dining Philosophers Problem

The *Dining Philosophers problem*, one of the best-known problems in distributed computing theory, is a simple special case of our general resource-allocation problem. It is usually formulated in terms of an explicit resource specification.

Traditionally, the problem is described in terms of the following informal scenario. There are n philosophers (users) seated around a table, usually thinking (i.e., in R). Between each pair of philosophers is a single fork (resource). From time to time, any philosopher might become hungry (i.e., enter T) and attempt to eat (i.e., to enter C). In order to eat, the philosopher needs exclusive use of the two adjacent forks. After eating, the philosopher relinquishes the two forks (i.e., performs an exit protocol E) and resumes thinking (R).

For each philosopher p_i, we label the forks to the right (counterclockwise) and left (clockwise) by $f(i)$ and $f(i+1)$, respectively. (As usual, addition is modulo n, identifying n with 0.) See Figure 11.1 for the arrangement of philosophers and forks for $n = 5$.

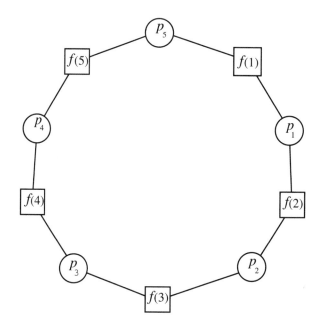

Figure 11.1: Dining Philosophers problem ($n = 5$).

In our formal model, there is one user and one agent process for each philosopher. As usual, the user decides when to request and return the resources, and the agent process performs the algorithm.

The exclusion specification for n dining philosophers consists of the two-element sets $\{\{i, i+1\} : 1 \leq i \leq n\}$ together with all sets containing them.

11.1.4   Restricted Form of Solutions

All the solutions we consider in this chapter are of a particular form: there is exactly one read-modify-write shared variable associated with each resource, accessible only by the processes whose users require the corresponding resource.

The architecture for solutions to the Dining Philosophers problem in this restricted form is depicted in Figure 11.2. Notice that the diagram is very similar to the one in Figure 11.1; the new diagram includes the users U_i and relabels the processes by their indices. The shared variables correspond exactly to the forks $f(1), \ldots, f(5)$. Note that each process i accesses fork variables $f(i)$ and $f(i+1)$.

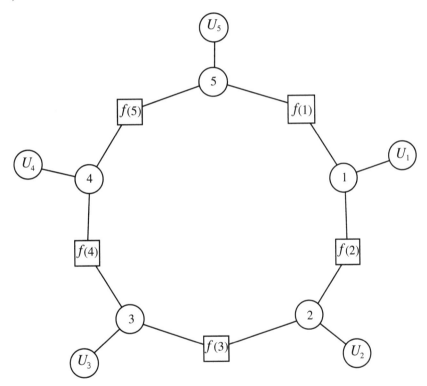

Figure 11.2: Dining Philosophers problem, with user automata.

11.2   Nonexistence of Symmetric Dining Philosophers Algorithms

An interesting class of candidate Dining Philosophers algorithms is the class of symmetric algorithms. An algorithm in the given framework is said to be *symmetric* if all processes are identical and may only refer to their accessible fork variables by the local names $f(left)$ and $f(right)$, and if all the shared variables have the same initial values. As for the leader-election problem in Chapter 3, it is not hard to see that the Dining Philosophers problem cannot be solved in the symmetric case. The argument is essentially the same as the one for Theorem 3.1:

Theorem 11.2 *There is no symmetric solution to the Dining Philosophers problem.*

Proof. Assume for the purpose of contradiction that there is a symmetric algorithm for n processes, say A. Consider an execution α of A that begins with all processes in the same process state and all shared variables with the same initial value. Execution α then proceeds "round robin," where processes take corresponding steps in order, $1, \ldots, n, 1, \ldots$, starting with a *try* step for each process. Moreover, all nondeterministic choices are resolved in the same way.

For example, when a try_1 action occurs, a *try* action will also occur for each other process, and the local state changes associated with this action will be the same as those for process 1. For another example, if process 1 accesses its left variable, then all the other processes also access their left variables, and the state changes and variable value changes are the same as those for process 1.

Then it is straightforward to show, by induction on the number r of round-robin "rounds," that all processes are again in the same state and all variables have the same value, after r rounds. But the progress property says that some process eventually enters C. This implies that all other processes also enter C at the same round. But this is a contradiction to the exclusion property. □

For example, consider the following simple symmetric algorithm.

WrongDP algorithm (informal):

Each process, upon entering the trying region, waits first for its right fork and then for its left fork. After getting both forks, it goes to C. When a process exits C, it puts down both forks before returning to R.

The formal code follows; *right* and *left* are local names used by process i to denote the indices i and $i + 1$ (for its two forks), respectively.

WrongDP algorithm (formal):

Shared variables:
for every i, $1 \leq i \leq n$:
  $f(i)$, a Boolean, initially *false*, accessible by processes i and $i - 1$

Actions of i:

Input: Internal:
   try_i *test-right$_i$*
   $exit_i$ *test-left$_i$*
Output: *reset-right$_i$*
   $crit_i$ *reset-left$_i$*
   rem_i

States of i:

$pc \in \{rem, \textit{test-right}, \textit{test-left}, \textit{leave-try}, crit, \textit{reset-right}, \textit{reset-left}, \textit{leave-exit}\}$, initially *rem*

Transitions of i:

try_i
   Effect:
      $pc := \textit{test-right}$

test-right$_i$
   Precondition:
      $pc = \textit{test-right}$
   Effect:
      if $f(right) = false$ then
         $f(right) := true$
         $pc := \textit{test-left}$

test-left$_i$
   Precondition:
      $pc = \textit{test-left}$
   Effect:
      if $f(left) = false$ then
         $f(left) := true$
         $pc := \textit{leave-try}$

$crit_i$
   Precondition:
      $pc = \textit{leave-try}$
   Effect:
      $pc := crit$

$exit_i$
   Effect:
      $pc := \textit{reset-right}$

reset-right$_i$
   Precondition:
      $pc = \textit{reset-right}$
   Effect:
      $f(right) := false$
      $pc := \textit{reset-left}$

reset-left$_i$
   Precondition:
      $pc = \textit{reset-left}$
   Effect:
      $f(left) := false$
      $pc := \textit{leave-exit}$

rem_i
   Precondition:
      $pc = \textit{leave-exit}$
   Effect:
      $pc := rem$

Since the *WrongDP* algorithm is symmetric, Theorem 11.2 implies that it does not solve the Dining Philosophers problem. But it is interesting to see what goes wrong. It should be clear that *WrongDP* does guarantee well-formedness and does satisfy the exclusion condition; this latter is because the code ensures that a process that reaches C has explicitly "obtained" both its adjacent forks.

The progress property, however, fails. Consider an execution in which all of the processes enter their trying regions, one after the other. Next, all of the processes grab their right forks. At this point, each process is ready to try to obtain its left fork. But since all forks have already been picked up, no process can do so. The system is now deadlocked—there is no way that any further progress can be made.

Theorem 11.2 implies that it is necessary to break the symmetry of a ring network in order to solve the Dining Philosophers problem. There are several ways of doing this. The processes could use different programs, or the same program but different initial states or unique identifiers. Or, the variables could be initialized differently. Or, we could use randomization. In the rest of this chapter, we will illustrate some of these approaches.

11.3   Right-Left Dining Philosophers Algorithm

In this section, we present a (correct) Dining Philosophers algorithm that we call the *RightLeftDP algorithm*. In addition to satisfying the basic required properties, this algorithm also guarantees lockout-freedom. It also has a good worst-case time bound: a constant, independent of the size of the ring. The way the *RightLeftDP* algorithm breaks symmetry is by having processes classified into two categories, which we call "right" and "left." The two types of processes execute slightly different programs, with their category indicating which adjacent fork to seek first.

11.3.1   Waiting Chains

The constant-time bound property is especially notable. It is certainly desirable, in a distributed system, to have time performance that is independent of the size of the system. But how can such a small time bound be achieved?

The *RightLeftDP* algorithm is one of a general class of algorithms in which processes proceed sequentially, waiting first for one fork and then for the other. In such algorithms, we must be careful about the order in which the forks are sought. For example, if all processes seek their right forks first, then there is the possibility of deadlock as in the *WrongDP* algorithm. There are other orders that do not admit the possibility of deadlock but still allow for executions with very poor time performance. In particular, some orders can lead to the establishment of long *waiting chains* of processes, each waiting for a resource held by the process ahead of it in the chain.

Example 11.3.1   Waiting chain

Consider a five-node ring. Suppose that an algorithm in this ring has an execution in which the following events occur, in the indicated order:

Process 5 obtains both forks.
Process 4 obtains its right fork, then waits for its left fork.
Process 3 obtains its right fork, then waits for its left fork.
Process 2 obtains its right fork, then waits for its left fork.

This yields a chain in which process 2 is waiting for a fork held by 3, which is waiting for a fork held by 4, which is in turn waiting for a fork held by 5. This is a waiting chain of length 3. See Figure 11.3.

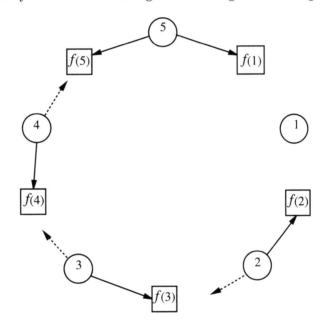

Figure 11.3: A waiting chain. Solid arrows indicate possession of the fork, while dotted arrows indicate waiting.

The same example, for arbitrary $n \geq 3$, yields a waiting chain of length $n - 2$.

Notice that the processes in a waiting chain *must* enter the critical region sequentially. Thus, for any algorithm of this general type, the worst-case time for a trying process to enter the critical region is at least proportional to the maximum length of a waiting chain that can be produced. In order to obtain a small time bound, then, we must guarantee a small bound on the maximum length of a waiting chain. In fact, the maximum length of the waiting chain produced by *RightLeftDP* is 3.

11.3.2   The Basic Algorithm

In the *RightLeftDP* algorithm, the shared variable associated with each fork contains a FIFO queue of process indices, of length at most 2. This queue is designed to hold the indices of processes wanting the fork, in the order in which they begin trying to get it. Since there are only two processes that can request each fork, a length 2 queue suffices.

For simplicity, we assume here that the number of processes in the ring is even. There is a simple modification, left for an exercise, that works in the case of an odd number of processes.

> ### *RightLeftDP* algorithm (n even):
>
> There are two different programs: one for the processes with odd indices and one for those with even indices. The basic strategy is very simple: odd-numbered processes seek their right fork first and even-numbered processes seek their left fork first. A process seeks a fork by putting its index at the end of that fork's queue. The process obtains the fork when its index reaches the front of that fork's queue. When a process exits C, it returns both forks by removing its index from their queues before entering R.

We give the code for a process with an odd index i in precondition-effect style. The code for even i is symmetric.

RightLeftDP algorithm (even n, odd i):

Shared variables:
for every i, $1 \leq i \leq n$:
  $f(i)$, a queue of process indices of length at most 2, initially empty,
    accessible by processes i and $i - 1$

Actions of i:

Input:	Internal:
try_i	*test-right*
$exit_i$	*test-left*
Output:	*reset-right*
$crit_i$	*reset-left*
rem_i	

States of i:
$pc \in \{rem, test\text{-}right, test\text{-}left, leave\text{-}try, crit, reset\text{-}right, reset\text{-}left, leave\text{-}exit\}$, initially rem

Transitions of i:

try_i
    Effect:
        $pc := test\text{-}right$

$test\text{-}right_i$
    Precondition:
        $pc = test\text{-}right$
    Effect:
        if i is not on $f(i).queue$ then
            add i to $f(i).queue$
        if i is first on $f(i).queue$ then
            $pc := test\text{-}left$

$test\text{-}left_i$
    Precondition:
        $pc = test\text{-}left$
    Effect:
        if i is not on $f(i+1).queue$ then
            add i to $f(i+1).queue$
        if i is first on $f(i+1).queue$ then
            $pc := leave\text{-}try$

$crit_i$
    Precondition:
        $pc = leave\text{-}try$
    Effect:
        $pc := crit$

$exit_i$
    Effect:
        $pc := reset\text{-}right$

$reset\text{-}right_i$
    Precondition:
        $pc = reset\text{-}right$
    Effect:
        remove i from $f(i).queue$
        $pc := reset\text{-}left$

$reset\text{-}left_i$
    Precondition:
        $pc = reset\text{-}left$
    Effect:
        remove i from $f(i+1).queue$
        $pc := leave\text{-}exit$

rem_i
    Precondition:
        $pc = leave\text{-}exit$
    Effect:
        $pc := rem$

Now we argue correctness. The well-formedness condition is obvious. The exclusion condition should be easy to see, because the code ensures that a process that reaches C is first on the queues of both of its forks. We will prove an explicit upper bound on the time for any trying process to reach the critical region. A small upper bound (independent of n) for the exit region is easy to see. In view of Lemma 11.1, these bounds are sufficient to imply lockout-freedom, which in turn is sufficient to imply progress.

For the time bound, we assume as before that ℓ is an upper bound on the step time for each process, and c is an upper bound on the time any user spends in the critical region.

Lemma 11.3 *In RightLeftDP, the time from when a particular process i enters T until it enters C is at most $3c + 18\ell$.*

Proof.   The key idea is that a fork between two processes is either the first fork for both or the second fork for both. This implies (for the case we are assuming, where n is even) that the maximum length of a waiting chain is at most 2.

Define T to be the maximum time from when any process i enters the trying region until that process enters the critical region. Our goal is to bound T. As an auxiliary quantity, we define S to be the maximum time from when any process i obtains its first fork until that process enters the critical region. Formally, we say that process i obtains its first fork at the event where i becomes first on the queue for that fork. (This could be either a step of i or a step of the neighbor with which i shares the fork.)

We start by bounding T in terms of S. Consider a process i entering the trying region. Within time ℓ, it performs a *test* event π to try to get its first fork. If it obtains the fork immediately, then within additional time S, process i enters the critical region. This is a total time of at most $\ell + S$.

Otherwise, the neighbor with which i shares the fork, say j, has the fork when π occurs. As mentioned above, this fork must also be j's first fork. Hence the additional time until j releases this fork is at most $S + c + \ell$ (enough time for j to reach the critical region, leave the critical region, and release its first fork). At the instant j releases the fork, process i obtains it; this is because of the way "obtaining a fork" is defined, and because of the fact that process i puts its index on the queue in event π. Then, within additional time S, i reaches the critical region. It follows that in this case process i enters the critical region after a total of at most $\ell + (S + c + \ell) + S = c + 2\ell + 2S$ time.

We conclude that

$$T \leq \max\{\ell + S,\ c + 2\ell + 2S\} = c + 2\ell + 2S. \tag{11.1}$$

Next we bound S. Consider a process i that has just obtained its first fork (i.e., has become first on the queue for that fork). Within time ℓ, it discovers this fact, and within an additional time ℓ, it performs a *test* action on its second fork. If it obtains this second fork immediately, then, within an additional time ℓ, it goes to the critical region, for a total time of at most 3ℓ.

Otherwise, the neighbor with which i shares the fork has it, and it is also the neighbor's second fork. The time until the neighbor releases the second fork is at most $2\ell + c + 2\ell$ (enough time for the neighbor to discover that it has the fork, reach the critical region, leave the critical region, and release the two forks). From the point after the neighbor releases the fork, it is at most time ℓ until process i discovers it and an additional time ℓ until process i enters the critical region. It follows that in this case process i enters the critical region after at most $2\ell + (2\ell + c + 2\ell) + 2\ell = c + 8\ell$ time.

We conclude that

$$S \leq \max\{3\ell, \ c + 8\ell\} = c + 8\ell. \tag{11.2}$$

Combining Equations 11.1 and 11.2 yields

$$T \leq 3c + 18\ell.$$

$\square$

Since it is easy to see that the algorithm also satisfies the independent progress condition, we obtain

Theorem 11.4 *The RightLeftDP algorithm solves the Dining Philosophers problem and guarantees lockout-freedom, independent progress, a time bound of $3c + 18\ell$ for the trying region, and a time bound of 3ℓ for the exit region.*

So, the *RightLeftDP* algorithm breaks symmetry by distinguishing the odd- and even-numbered processes. Depending on the environment in which this algorithm is to be run, it might or might not be reasonable to assume that processes have this knowledge. For instance, if it is to be run in a distributed network (as we consider in Chapter 17), then an additional protocol may be needed for determining this parity information and communicating it to all the processes.

11.3.3 A Generalization

We describe a straightforward way to generalize the strategy in the *RightLeftDP* algorithm to an arbitrary resource-allocation problem, given by an arbitrary explicit resource specification. The generalization still has the virtue of having a time bound that is independent of the number of processes. However, the bound is not very small—there is still room for performance improvement.

We continue to assume that each resource has an associated shared variable, shared by all processes that require that resource. As in *RightLeftDP*, we assume that the variable contains a FIFO queue to record who is waiting for the resource. As in *RightLeftDP*, each process waits for its required resources one at a time. To avoid deadlock, however, we assume that the resources are totally ordered and allow each process to obtain its needed resources in order, according to this total ordering—smallest to largest. This strategy is known as *hierarchical resource allocation*.

It is not hard to see that hierarchical resource allocation guarantees progress. Roughly speaking, if process i waits for a resource held by process j, then j could only be delayed by waiting for a resource that is strictly larger (in the resource ordering) than the one for which i is waiting; since there are only finitely many processes, the one that holds the largest resource is not blocked. The FIFO nature of the queues also prevents lockout.

Although hierarchical resource allocation guarantees progress and lockout-freedom, the time performance of this strategy is not very good, in general. The only upper limit on the length of waiting chains is the total number n of processes, leading to time performance that is at least proportional to n. For instance, the chain described in Example 11.3.1 can be produced by a hierarchical resource-allocation algorithm in which the total order of resources is just the numerical order, $f(1), f(2), f(3), f(4), f(5)$.

What we would like is a "good" total ordering of resources, one that produces as small a time bound as possible. A reasonable strategy is to try to minimize the length of the waiting chains that are produced.

Suppose we are given a particular explicit resource specification $\mathcal{R}$, with universal resource set R and individual process resource requirements R_i. To construct a good total ordering, we first construct the *resource graph* for this specification. The nodes of this graph represent the resources, and there is an edge from one node to another exactly if there is some process that uses both associated resources.

Example 11.3.2   Resource graph

> For the Dining Philosophers problem with six nodes, the resource
> graph is as in Figure 11.4.

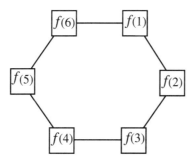

Figure 11.4: Resource graph for Dining Philosophers $(n = 6)$.

Next, we *color* the nodes of the graph in such a way that adjacent nodes have different colors. We try to minimize the number of colors used. (We do not consider the problem of how to obtain a small number of colors. Actually obtaining the minimum number is an NP-complete problem, but for our purposes here, a small number of colors will do. For example, a greedy algorithm can be used to color the graph with no more than $d + 1$ colors, where d is an upper bound on the degree of any node in the graph.)

Example 11.3.3 Coloring of resource graph

The resource graph of Figure 11.4 can be colored with only two colors, for example, by coloring the odd-numbered resources with color 1 and the even-numbered resources with color 2.

Now we totally order the colors in an arbitrary way. This induces a *partial* order on the resources, where $r(i) < r(j)$ if and only if the color of $r(i)$ is ordered ahead of the color of $r(j)$. Although this is only a partial order, note that it totally orders the resources needed by any single process. Since we seek a total ordering of all the resources, we simply complete the partial order to a total order in an arbitrary way (that is, we use a *topological sort* of the partial order).

Example 11.3.4 Partial order of resources

The coloring in Example 11.3.3 induces the partial order on resources depicted in Figure 11.5. "Smaller" resources appear at the top of the diagram.

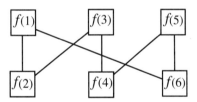

Figure 11.5: Partial ordering on resources.

Now we can describe the algorithm.

Coloring algorithm:

Each process seeks its resources in increasing order according to the total ordering constructed above, based on coloring. A process seeks a resource by putting its index at the end of that resource's queue. The process obtains the resource when its index reaches the front of that resource's queue. When a process exits C, it returns all of its resources by removing its index from their queues.

Since any two resources needed by the same process are ordered with respect to each other (i.e., are colored differently), an equivalent description of *Coloring* is that every process seeks its resources in increasing order according to the partial ordering. Notice that, in the special case of the Dining Philosophers problem for an even-sized ring, the *Coloring* algorithm reduces to the *RightLeftDP* algorithm.

In the *Coloring* algorithm, the maximum length of a waiting chain is at most equal to the number of distinct colors. This is because if a process i waits for a resource held by a process j, then j may be waiting only for a resource of a "larger" color.

The interesting property to verify for the *Coloring* algorithm is a time bound that is independent of the total numbers of processes and resources. As usual, we let ℓ be an upper bound on process step time and c an upper bound on critical region time. Also let k be the total number of colors used to color the resources and let m be the maximum number of processes that require any single resource. We show that the worst-case time bound is $O(m^k c + km^k \ell)$. We can interpret this as saying that the time depends only on "local" parameters, since the number of colors and the number of users per resource need not depend on the size of the system. If m and k are small relative to n (the total number of processes in the system), then this bound represents an improvement over the hierarchical resource-allocation strategy using an arbitrary total order; this is because the general strategy admits waiting chains of length nearly n. But note that this bound is not as small as one might like—instead of being proportional to the maximum length of a waiting chain, that is, proportional to k, it is exponential in k.

Lemma 11.5 *Let k be the number of colors and let m be an upper bound on the number of users for a single resource, in an instance of the Coloring algorithm. Then the time from when any particular process i enters T until it enters C is $O(m^k c + km^k \ell)$.*

Proof Sketch. Suppose the colors are exactly the integers $1, \dots, k$. Define $T(i,j)$, where $1 \le i \le k$ and $1 \le j \le m$, to be the worst-case time from when a process reaches any position $\le j$ on the queue for a resource of any color $\ge i$, until it reaches its critical region. We wish to bound T, the worse-case time from entry to the trying region until entry to the critical region. From when a process enters the trying region, it is at most time ℓ until its index is placed on some resource queue. Thus,

$$T \le \ell + T(1, m).$$

We bound the $T(i,j)$ by setting up recurrence equations as we did for the *RightLeftDP* algorithm. The base case is when a process is first on the queue for a resource with the highest color:

$$T(k,1) \le 2\ell$$

This allows time for the process to discover it is first on the queue and then to go to the critical region.

Another case is when a process is first on the queue for a resource with some color other than the highest:

$$T(i, 1) \leq \max\left(2\ell, 2\ell + T(i+1, m)\right) = 2\ell + T(i+1, m) \text{ for every } i, 1 \leq i < k$$

This gives the process time to discover it is first on the queue and then either proceed to the critical region or get on another queue, necessarily of a higher-colored resource.

The last case is when a process is in some position other than the first, on some queue.

$$T(i, j) \leq T(i, j-1) + c + k\ell + T(i, 1) \text{ for every } j, 1 < j \leq m$$

This allows time for the predecessor of the process on the queue to reach its critical region, then finish the critical region, then release all of its $\leq k$ resources (which will move the original process to the first position on the given queue), and then time for the process, now in position 1, to reach the critical region.

Solving these inequalities yields the claimed bound. For all $i, 1 \leq i \leq k$, we obtain that

$$T(i, m) \leq (m-1)(c + k\ell) + mT(i, 1).$$

Thus,

$$T(i, m) \leq m(c + (k+2)\ell) + mT(i+1, m) \text{ for every } i, 1 \leq i < k,$$

and

$$T(k, m) \leq m(c + (k+2)\ell).$$

So

$$T(1, m) \leq (c + (k+2)\ell) \sum_{i=1}^{k} m^i$$
$$= O\left(m^k(c + (k+2)\ell)\right).$$

Thus,

$$T = O\left(m^k(c + (k+2)\ell)\right) = O\left(m^k c + km^k \ell\right).$$

$\square$

Theorem 11.6 *The Coloring algorithm solves the resource-allocation problem and guarantees lockout-freedom, independent progress, a time bound of $O(m^k c + km^k \ell)$ for the trying region, and a time bound of $O(k\ell)$ for the exit region.*

It turns out that there are some executions of the *Coloring* algorithm with time performance that is close to this exponential bound. We leave it as an exercise for you to find such executions. Of course, it would be nice to cut down the time bound from exponential to linear in the number of colors, but that would require a different algorithm.

11.4 Randomized Dining Philosophers Algorithm*

The final algorithm we present is a *randomized* Dining Philosophers algorithm that guarantees exclusion (with certainty) and ensures progress with probability 1. We call this algorithm *LehmannRabin* after its inventors. In this algorithm, all processes are identical; the symmetry is broken by the use of randomization.

We have several points we hope to make by presenting this algorithm. First, it demonstrates that randomized algorithms can be used in the asynchronous setting as well as the synchronous setting, and that they sometimes can accomplish things that cannot be accomplished by nonrandomized algorithms. For example, the *LehmannRabin* algorithm can solve the Dining Philosophers problem even though the processes are identical, whereas Theorem 11.2 implies that this cannot be done by any nonrandomized algorithm. Actually, we should be careful when we say that this algorithm "solves the Dining Philosophers problem": the correctness conditions satisfied are not exactly those specified earlier, in that the progress condition only holds with probability 1, and not with absolute certainty.

Second, we show how meaningful probabilistic claims can be made for randomized asynchronous systems. It is not obvious how to do this, because a randomized algorithm does not by itself give rise to a probability distribution on executions. For instance, the order in which processes take steps in an asynchronous algorithm is rather arbitrary, not determined randomly. This order must be determined somehow in order to define a probability distribution.

Third, we demonstrate a Markov-style analysis technique for proving probabilistic time bound properties. Such properties can in turn be used to prove probabilistic liveness properties.

11.4.1 The Algorithm*

Because the processes are identical, they are assumed to know their forks by local names. As before, we assume that each process knows its forks by the local names $f(right)$ and $f(left)$. We use the notation

$$\bar{j} = \begin{cases} left, & \text{if } j = right \\ right, & \text{if } j = left \end{cases}$$

Also, the statement *first := random* here means that *first* is set either to *right* or *left*, each with probability $\frac{1}{2}$. An informal description follows.

LehmannRabin algorithm:

Shared variables:
for every i, $1 \leq i \leq n$:
    $f(i)$, a Boolean, initially *false*, accessible by processes i and $i-1$

Process i:

    ** Remainder region **

    try_i
    do forever
        first := random
        wait until $f(\mathit{first}) = \mathit{false}$
        $f(\mathit{first}) := \mathit{true}$
        if $f(\overline{\mathit{first}}) = \mathit{false}$ then
            $f(\overline{\mathit{first}}) := \mathit{true}$
            goto L
        else $f(\mathit{first}) := \mathit{false}$
L:
    $crit_i$

    ** Critical region **

    $exit_i$
    put down both forks
    rem_i

Thus, a trying process i executes a loop, in each iteration attempting to obtain both of its forks. In each iteration, it chooses a first fork randomly and waits as long as necessary to obtain it. After obtaining its first fork, it does not wait indefinitely for the second fork. Rather, it just checks once to see if the second fork is available. If it is, then process i obtains it and proceeds to C. If not, then process i gives up on this iteration, puts its first fork down, and proceeds to try again in the next iteration.

To resolve ambiguities, we give the precondition-effect code.

LehmannRabin algorithm (rewritten):

Shared variables:
for every i, $1 \leq i \leq n$:
    $f(i)$, a Boolean, initially *false*

Actions of i:

Input: Internal:
  try_i $flip_i$
  $exit_i$ $wait_i$
Output: $second_i$
  $crit_i$ $drop_i$
  rem_i $reset$-$right_i$
                 $reset$-$left_i$

States of i:

$pc \in \{rem, flip, wait, second, drop, leave$-$try, crit, reset$-$right, reset$-$left, leave$-$exit\}$, initially rem
$first \in \{right, left\}$, initially arbitrary

Transitions of i:

try_i
    Effect:
        $pc := flip$

$flip_i$
    Precondition:
        $pc := flip$
    Effect:
        $first := random$
        $pc := wait$

$wait_i$
    Precondition:
        $pc = wait$
    Effect:
        if $f(first) = false$ then
            $f(first) := true$
            $pc := second$

$second_i$
    Precondition:
        $pc = second$
    Effect:
        if $f(\overline{first}) = false$ then
            $f(\overline{first}) := true$
            $pc := leave$-try
        else $pc := drop$

$drop_i$
    Precondition:
        $pc = drop$
    Effect:
        $f(first) := false$
        $pc := flip$

$crit_i$
    Precondition:
        $pc = leave$-try
    Effect:
        $pc := crit$

$exit_i$
    Effect:
        $pc := reset$-$right$

$reset$-$right_i$
    Precondition:
        $pc = reset$-$right$
    Effect:
        $f(right) := false$
        $pc := reset$-$left$

reset-left$_i$
    Precondition:
        pc = reset-left
    Effect:
        f(left) := false
        pc := leave-exit

rem$_i$
    Precondition:
        pc = leave-exit
    Effect:
        pc := rem

Formally, the object described by this code is a *probabilistic I/O automaton*, as defined in Section 8.8. The random choice steps are exactly the *flip* steps; instead of a new state, each of these steps has a probability distribution containing two possible next states, each with probability $\frac{1}{2}$. Note that system execution proceeds by means of a combination of *nondeterministic choices* and *probabilistic choices*. The nondeterministic choices determine which process takes the next step and thereby determine what the next step is, whereas the probabilistic choices determine the new state for *flip* steps.

11.4.2 Correctness*

It is easy to see that the *LehmannRabin* algorithm guarantees well-formedness, exclusion, and independent progress; there is no probability involved in any of these claims. Formally, they are claims about the *nondeterministic version* of the system, as defined in Section 8.8. However the progress condition is not guaranteed with certainty.

Example 11.4.1   **Execution of *LehmannRabin* that does not make progress**

> Consider an execution α of *LehmannRabin* in which the processes take steps in round-robin order and always make the same random choices. Note that α is a fair execution (of the nondeterministic version of the system). In α, no process ever reaches C.

The interesting thing to prove about the *LehmannRabin* algorithm is that it guarantees progress with probability 1. Actually, rather than just proving progress with probability 1, we will prove a stronger *probabilistic time bound* claim, of the form $\mathcal{T} \xrightarrow{t}{}_{p} \mathcal{C}$. Informally speaking, this means that from any reachable state in which some process is in T, with probability at least p and within time t, some process is in C. The probability 1 progress condition can then be proved by repeated application of this claim.

In order to make claims about the probability of certain events, we need a probability distribution on executions. As described so far, the system includes nondeterministic choices—that is, which process takes the next step—as well as probabilistic choices. The nondeterministic choices must be resolved in order to obtain a purely probabilistic system. In fact, we would like to claim that the system has the desired property regardless of how the nondeterministic choices are resolved.

It is useful to imagine that the nondeterministic choices are under the control of an *adversary*. We allow the adversary to select arbitrary processes, as long as it allows fair turns to each process that is in its trying or exit region. In fact, since we are proving probabilistic time bound statements, we allow the adversary to choose not only which process takes the next step, but also the time at which that step occurs. The time decisions are subject to an upper bound of ℓ on process step time and an upper bound of c on critical region time, plus the requirement that, if the execution is infinite, the time must pass to infinity. To obtain the strongest result, we want to allow the adversary to be as powerful as possible; thus, we assume that, when making its decisions about who takes the next step and when, it has *complete knowledge* of the past execution, including information about process states and past random choices.

Formally, an adversary $\mathcal{A}$ is a function mapping finite executions to (process, time) pairs, indicating the next process to take a step and the time at which the step is to be taken. For each particular sequence D of random draws, there is a unique timed execution $exec(\mathcal{A}, D)$ generated by adversary $\mathcal{A}$ with random choices given by D. The adversary is restricted so that all timed executions in $exec(\mathcal{A}, D)$ have the fairness and timing properties described in the previous paragraph.

A fixed adversary $\mathcal{A}$ determines a probability distribution on the set of timed executions of the algorithm. Since each random choice is just "right" or "left," each with probability $\frac{1}{2}$, there is a probability associated with each (measurable set of) sequences of draws. This probability distribution on the sequences D induces a probability distribution on the timed executions $exec(\mathcal{A}, D)$.

We need one more notion for the proof. If $\mathcal{U}$ and $\mathcal{U}'$ are sets of states, then we write $\mathcal{U} \xrightarrow[p]{t} \mathcal{U}'$ to mean the following. For every adversary $\mathcal{A}$, if the algorithm is started in a state in $\mathcal{U}$, then in the probability distribution of executions determined by $\mathcal{A}$, the probability that a state in $\mathcal{U}'$ is reached within time t is at least p. Such statements can be combined. For example:

Lemma 11.7

1. *If $\mathcal{U} \xrightarrow[p]{t} \mathcal{U}'$ and $\mathcal{U}' \xrightarrow[p']{t'} \mathcal{U}''$, then $\mathcal{U} \xrightarrow[pp']{t+t'} \mathcal{U}''$.*

2. *If $\mathcal{U} \xrightarrow[p]{t} \mathcal{U}'$, then $\mathcal{U} \cup \mathcal{U}'' \xrightarrow[p]{t} \mathcal{U}' \cup \mathcal{U}''$.*

Now we have enough machinery to prove the progress property. One technicality: It happens that some of the constructions in our proof only work for the case where n, the size of the ring, is at least 3. So we assume this from now on in the chapter and leave as an exercise the (simpler) case where $n = 2$.

Define

- $\mathcal{T}$ to be the set of reachable states of *LehmannRabin* in which some process is in T

- $\mathcal{C}$ to be the set of reachable states in which some process is in C

We show that $\mathcal{T} \xrightarrow[\frac{1}{16}]{14\ell} \mathcal{C}$. That is, from any reachable state in which some process is in T, with probability at least $\frac{1}{16}$, some process will be in C within time 14ℓ. We prove this claim by five auxiliary claims, expressed by Lemmas 11.8–11.12, using the general rules expressed in Lemma 11.7.

Some shorthand is useful for classifying process states. We let F, W, S, D, and L denote the sets of process states where $pc = \textit{flip}$, *wait*, *second*, *drop*, and *leave-try*, respectively; these five sets of states partition the trying region T. We further subdivide the W, S, and D states according to the value of *first*: $\overrightarrow{W}$, $\overrightarrow{S}$, and $\overrightarrow{D}$ denote the subsets of W, S, and D, respectively, in which *first = right*, while $\overleftarrow{W}$, $\overleftarrow{S}$, and $\overleftarrow{D}$ denote the subsets of W, S, and D, respectively, in which *first = left*. We use the notation $\overrightarrow{*}$ to denote $\overrightarrow{W} \cup \overrightarrow{S} \cup \overrightarrow{D}$ and analogously for $\overleftarrow{*}$. Now we define the sets of system states that we will need in the auxiliary claims.

Define

- $\mathcal{L}$ to be the set of reachable states in which some process is in L (i.e., at *leave-try*)

- $\mathcal{RT}$ to be the subset of $\mathcal{T}$ consisting of states in which all processes are either in the remainder or trying region

- $\mathcal{F}$ to be the subset of $\mathcal{RT}$ consisting of states in which some process is in F (i.e., at *flip*)

- $\mathcal{G}$ to be the subset of $\mathcal{RT}$ consisting of states in which there is a process i such that one of the following holds:

    - $i \in \overleftarrow{W} \cup \overleftarrow{S}$ and $i - 1 \in \overrightarrow{*} \cup R \cup F$
    - $i \in \overrightarrow{W} \cup \overrightarrow{S}$ and $i + 1 \in \overleftarrow{*} \cup R \cup F$

The first three sets above should be self-explanatory. The last set, $\mathcal{G}$, is the set of "good" states, in which two processes are in a situation where, with high likelihood, one will soon obtain both its forks. The two situations allowed by $\mathcal{G}$ are depicted in Figure 11.6. A rough intuition is that in a good configuration, two neighboring processes have a high probability of having a common second fork. If they have a common second fork, then whichever accesses it first will get it and succeed in reaching C.

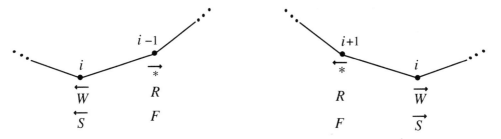

Figure 11.6: Good states of the *LehmannRabin* algorithm.

Then we will show the following claims:

- $\mathcal{T} \xrightarrow[1]{3\ell} \mathcal{RT} \cup \mathcal{C}$

- $\mathcal{RT} \xrightarrow[1]{3\ell} \mathcal{F} \cup \mathcal{L}$

- $\mathcal{F} \xrightarrow[\frac{1}{4}]{2\ell} \mathcal{G} \cup \mathcal{L}$

- $\mathcal{G} \xrightarrow[\frac{1}{4}]{5\ell} \mathcal{L}$

- $\mathcal{L} \xrightarrow[1]{\ell} \mathcal{C}$

Lemma 11.7 then allows these claims to be combined to yield the needed conclusion, $\mathcal{T} \xrightarrow[\frac{1}{16}]{14\ell} \mathcal{C}$.

We begin by proving the three probability 1 claims, since they are the easiest. In fact, they are actually true with certainty, not just with probability 1.

Lemma 11.8 $\mathcal{L} \xrightarrow[1]{\ell} \mathcal{C}$

Proof. If a process is at *leave-trying*, then within time ℓ, that same process will take a step and enter C.   □

Lemma 11.9 $\mathcal{T} \xrightarrow[1]{3\ell} \mathcal{RT} \cup \mathcal{C}$

Proof. If any process is initially in C or enters C within time 3ℓ, then we are done, so assume that this is not the case. Then all processes are in $R \cup T \cup E$ for time at least 3ℓ, and no process enters E during this time (because no process is in C). But any processes that are initially in E return to R within time 3ℓ. This forces all the processes into $R \cup T$ within time 3ℓ, as needed. $\qquad\square$

Lemma 11.10 $\mathcal{RT} \xrightarrow[1]{3\ell} \mathcal{F} \cup \mathcal{L}$

Proof. If any process is initially in $F \cup L$ or enters L within time 3ℓ, then we are done, so assume that this is not the case. Then no process enters C within time 3ℓ, so all the system states occurring within time 3ℓ are in $\mathcal{RT}$. Then, if any process enters F within 3ℓ time units, it places the system in $\mathcal{F}$ and we are done, so assume also that this is not the case. This implies, in particular, that no process enters the trying region within 3ℓ time units.

By elimination, all processes are initially in $R \cup W \cup S \cup D$. But if any is initially in $S \cup D$, or reaches $S \cup D$ within time ℓ, then within an additional time 2ℓ, it goes to $F \cup L$, which is a contradiction. So the only possibility is that all processes are initially in $R \cup W$ and (since $\mathcal{RT} \subseteq \mathcal{T}$), some process is in W. Moreover, no process reaches $S \cup D$ within time ℓ. Note that this implies that no fork is initially held by any process.

Because some process is in W, we know that some process must take a step within time ℓ. Let i be the first process to take a step. If i is initially in R, then it enters the trying region, a contradiction. On the other hand, if i is initially in W, then, since no fork is held, i immediately obtains its first fork. But this puts i in S, again a contradiction. $\qquad\square$

So far, we have avoided any arguments about probabilities. The remaining two claims involve such arguments. The first of these shows why, from an arbitrary state where some process is flipping, with probability at least $\frac{1}{4}$, either a good state is soon reached or else some process soon reaches *leave-try*.

Lemma 11.11 $\mathcal{F} \xrightarrow[\frac{1}{4}]{2\ell} \mathcal{G} \cup \mathcal{L}$

Proof. If any process is initially in L, then we are done, so assume that this is not the case. Let i be any process that is initially in F. Then one of the following must hold initially.

    1. $i - 1 \in \overrightarrow{\ast} \cup R \cup F$.

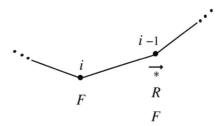

Figure 11.7: Initial state for Case 1 of proof of Lemma 11.11.

See Figure 11.7. Then with probability $\frac{1}{4}$, i's next random choice is *left* and $i-1$'s next random choice is *right*. So assume this.

Then within time ℓ, i flips, putting itself in state $\overleftarrow{W}$ because i's next random choice was *left*. There are two cases:

(a) In the meantime, $i-1$ does not access the shared fork. Then we claim that $i-1$'s state must still be in the set $\overrightarrow{*} \cup R \cup F$; this is argued by an examination of the possible transitions out of this set of states, using the fact that $i-1$'s next random choice is *right*. This brings the system state into $\mathcal{G}$, which suffices.

(b) In the meantime, $i-1$ does access the shared fork. Then consider the first time it does so. At that time, the shared fork must be $i-1$'s second fork (In the cases $\overrightarrow{D}$, R, and F, this is because of the fact that $i-1$'s next random choice is *right*.) Then $i-1$ obtains its second fork and goes to L, which suffices.

2. $i+1 \in \overleftarrow{*} \cup R \cup F$.

See Figure 11.8. This is symmetric with the previous case.

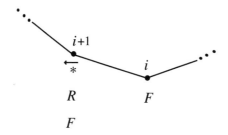

Figure 11.8: Initial state for Case 2.

3. $i-1 \in \overleftarrow{*}$ and $i+1 \in \overrightarrow{*}$.

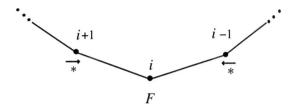

Figure 11.9: Initial state for Case 3.

See Figure 11.9.

This is the interesting case, because the situation looks nothing at all like what is supposed to happen in a good state. But because we are working in a ring, the fact that the situation around i is unfavorable implies that elsewhere in the ring, there must be some other process j such that $j + 1 \in \overleftarrow{*}$ and $j \in \overrightarrow{*} \cup R \cup F$. (We leave it as a simple exercise to show this.) See Figure 11.10. Then things look much better around process j.

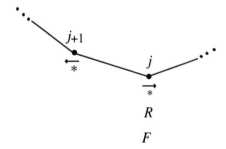

Figure 11.10: Elsewhere in the ring.

If $j + 1 \in \overleftarrow{W} \cup \overleftarrow{S}$, then the initial state is already in $\mathcal{G}$, and we are done.

The only other possibility is that $j + 1 \in \overleftarrow{D}$ and $j \in \overrightarrow{*} \cup R \cup F$. But in this case, with probability $\frac{1}{4}$, $j + 1$'s next random choice is *left* and j's next random choice is *right*; assume this. Then within time 2ℓ, process $j + 1$ takes two steps, which puts it in $\overleftarrow{W}$. This means that the resulting system state is in $\mathcal{G}$, unless in the meantime, j has moved out of the set $\overrightarrow{*} \cup R \cup F$. But if it has, then j has obtained its second fork and gone to L, which suffices.

□

The final lemma shows why a good state is good: from a good state, with probability at least $\frac{1}{4}$, some process soon reaches L.

Lemma 11.12 $\mathcal{G} \xrightarrow[\frac{1}{4}]{5\ell} \mathcal{L}$

Proof. Because the initial state is in $\mathcal{G}$, it is in $\mathcal{RT}$, and (at least) one of the two conditions indicated in the definition of $\mathcal{G}$ holds. Assume without loss of generality that the first holds, that is, that there is a process i such that $i \in \overleftarrow{W} \cup \overleftarrow{S}$ and $i - 1 \in \overrightarrow{*} \cup R \cup F$. The argument for the second condition is symmetric.

We use three preliminary claims. Their statements do not involve probability explicitly; rather, they involve it implicitly by referring to the values of certain future random choices. The first one bounds the amount of time a process can remain waiting for its first fork, if a neighbor is favorably oriented.

Claim 11.13 *If $i + 1 \in R \cup T$ with next random choice left, and $i \in \overleftarrow{W}$, then within time 4ℓ either $i \in \overleftarrow{S}$ or $i + 1 \in L$.*

See Figure 11.11.

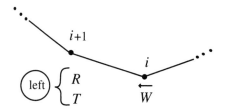

Figure 11.11: Situation for Claim 11.13.

Proof. This is a (somewhat tedious) argument by cases, based on the state of process $i + 1$.

1. $i + 1 \in L$.

   Then we are done.

2. $i + 1 \in \overleftarrow{*} \cup R \cup F$.

   Then, initially, $i + 1$ does not hold the shared fork. Within time ℓ, i checks the shared fork. If in the meantime $i + 1$ has not accessed it, then i obtains it and goes to $\overleftarrow{S}$, as needed.

   Suppose, on the other hand, that $i + 1$ has accessed the shared fork in the meantime and consider the first such time. Because of $i + 1$'s state, the shared fork must be $i + 1$'s second fork. (In the cases $\overleftarrow{D}$, R, and F, this is because of the fact that $i + 1$'s next random choice is *left*.) Since $i + 1$ obtains this fork, it succeeds in reaching L, as needed. Note that the time for this case is at most ℓ.

3. $i + 1 \in \overrightarrow{D}$.

Then within time ℓ, $i + 1$ drops its fork, which then puts the two processes in a configuration where $i+1 \in F$, with next random choice *left*, and $i \in \overleftarrow{W}$. (Process i must still be in $\overleftarrow{W}$ because it cannot obtain its first fork until process $i + 1$ drops it.) The resulting state then fits the previous case, so, within an additional time ℓ, either $i \in \overleftarrow{S}$ or $i + 1 \in L$. The time for this case is thus at most 2ℓ.

4. $i + 1 \in \overrightarrow{S}$.

Then within time ℓ, $i + 1$ checks its left fork and either goes immediately to L, which satisfies the condition, or goes to $\overrightarrow{D}$, which reduces to the previous case. The time for this case is thus at most 3ℓ.

5. $i + 1 \in \overrightarrow{W}$.

Then within time ℓ, both i and $i + 1$ check their shared fork. Whichever checks it first gets it. If the first one is i, then we have $i \in \overleftarrow{S}$, as needed. If not, then we get $i + 1 \in \overrightarrow{S}$, which reduces to the previous case. The time for this case is thus at most 4ℓ.

$\square$

The second claim bounds the time from when a process is ready to test its second resource and a neighbor is favorably oriented, until someone reaches L.

Claim 11.14 *Suppose that* $i \in \overleftarrow{S}$ *and either* $i-1 \in \overrightarrow{W} \cup \overrightarrow{S}$ *or* $i-1 \in \overrightarrow{D} \cup R \cup F$ *with next random choice right. Then within time* ℓ, *some process is in* L.

See Figure 11.12.

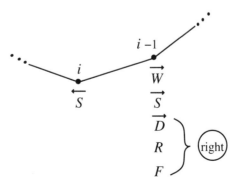

Figure 11.12: Situation for Claim 11.14.

Proof. Within time ℓ, i checks the shared fork; it obtains it and goes to L unless $i - 1$ has obtained it in the meantime. But if $i - 1$ has obtained it, then i has gone to L, since the shared fork must be $i - 1$'s second fork.   □

The final claim combines the previous two. It bounds the time from when a process i is waiting for its first fork and *both* neighbors are favorably oriented, until someone reaches L.

Claim 11.15 *If $i + 1 \in R \cup T$ with next random choice left, $i \in \overleftarrow{W}$, and $i - 1 \in \overrightarrow{*} \cup R \cup F$ with next random choice right, then within time 5ℓ, some process is in L.*

See Figure 11.13.

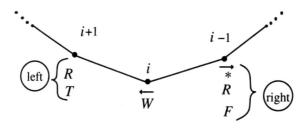

Figure 11.13: Situation for Claim 11.15.

Proof. Claim 11.13 implies that within time 4ℓ, either i reaches $\overleftarrow{S}$ or $i + 1$ reaches L. In the latter case, we are done, so assume that i reaches $\overleftarrow{S}$.

If, in the meantime, $i - 1$ has reached L, we are done, so assume that it has not. Then $i - 1$ must still be in $\overrightarrow{*} \cup R \cup F$. Moreover, if $i - 1$ is still in $\overrightarrow{D} \cup R \cup F$, then $i - 1$'s next random choice is still *right*. So then Claim 11.14 implies that in at most additional time ℓ, some process reaches L.   □

Now we return to the proof of Lemma 11.12. Recall that we have assumed that there is a process i such that $i \in \overleftarrow{W} \cup \overleftarrow{S}$ and $i - 1 \in \overrightarrow{*} \cup R \cup F$. See the first diagram in Figure 11.6. If $i \in \overleftarrow{W}$, then the result follows from Claim 11.15—the probability of $\frac{1}{4}$ arises because that is the probability that $i + 1$'s next random choice is *left* and $i - 1$'s next random choice is *right*. On the other hand, if $i \in \overleftarrow{S}$, then the result follows from Claim 11.14—the probability of $\frac{1}{2}$ arises because that is the probability that $i - 1$'s next random choice is *right*.

Thus we have:

Theorem 11.16 *For $n \geq 3$, the LehmannRabin algorithm satisfies the property that $\mathcal{T} \xrightarrow[\frac{1}{16}]{14\ell} \mathcal{C}$.*

We can apply Theorem 11.16 repeatedly to show that with probability 1, eventually someone reaches the critical region. We leave this for an exercise.

Theorem 11.17 *The LehmannRabin algorithm guarantees well-formedness, mutual exclusion, and independent progress. It also guarantees progress with probability 1.*

11.5 Bibliographic Notes

The Dining Philosophers problem was originally defined by Dijkstra [91], who devised an algorithm for an asynchronous shared memory model containing a globally shared semaphore variable. The *RightLeftDP* algorithm seems to be folklore; its generalization to the *Coloring* algorithm is due to Lynch [213].

The *LehmannRabin* algorithm was designed by Lehmann and Rabin [192]. An informal proof sketch appears in [192], but it is not clear how to formalize that sketch. The proof presented here was developed by Lynch, Saias, and Segala [208], following an earlier proof in a similar style by Pnueli and Zuck [244]. Lehmann and Rabin [192] gave a modification of the *LehmannRabin* algorithm that also guarantees lockout-freedom with high probability.

All of the algorithms in this chapter use shared variables. There has also been a considerable amount of work on resource-allocation problems in the asynchronous network model; see Chapter 20. For example, Chandy and Misra [67] present a solution for a general resource-allocation problem in asynchronous networks, together with an extension to a more dynamic version of the problem in which the resource requirements of processes can change over time. Also, Choy and Singh [80] and Awerbuch and Saks [37] present resource-allocation algorithms for asynchronous networks; their algorithms have good time complexity.

11.6 Exercises

11.1. Show that not every exclusion specification has an equivalent explicit resource specification.

11.2. It is possible to generalize the definition of an explicit resource specification to allow for alternative resource possibilities. Namely, for each i, the specification includes a description of resource requirements, in the form of a monotone Boolean formula (i.e., one involving only $\wedge$'s and $\vee$'s) over the set $\mathcal{R}$. A formula $f(R_1, R_2, \dots, R_k)$ specifies a collection of "acceptable" sets of resources in the obvious way: a set S of resources is acceptable if assigning *true* to all of the resources in S and *false* to all of the others causes the formula $f(R_1, R_2, \dots, R_k)$ to evaluate to *true*. The meaning of the formula is that the acceptable sets of resources are those sets whose exclusive possession authorizes the user to enter the critical region.

(a) Give a generalized explicit resource specification that is suitable for describing the k-exclusion problem, as defined in Chapter 10, Exercise 10.30.

(b) Show that any generalized explicit resource specification has an equivalent exclusion specification.

(c) Show that any exclusion specification has an equivalent generalized resource specification.

11.3. Prove Lemma 11.1.

11.4. *Research Question*: Define a notion of independent progress that is appropriate for resource-allocation problems expressed in terms of general exclusion conditions.

11.5. Generalize Theorem 11.2 to apply to a larger class of resource-allocation problems than just the Dining Philosophers problem. Try to obtain the largest class of resource-allocation problems you can.

11.6. Is the time upper bound on the *RightLeftDP* algorithm tight? Exhibit an execution whose time is as close to the computed bound of $3c + 18\ell$ as you can get.

11.7. Modify the *RightLeftDP* algorithm so that it works for a ring with an odd number of processes. Obtain an upper bound for the time complexity of the modified algorithm. The bound should be independent of n.

11.8. Construct an execution of the *Coloring* resource-allocation algorithm that has time complexity as close to the computed upper bound of $O\left(m^k c + k m^k \ell\right)$ as you can get.

11.9. *Research Question*: Construct a new algorithm for the general resource-allocation problem of this chapter, for the model in which there is one read-modify-write variable associated with each resource, accessible only by the processes that require the resource. Your new algorithm should have a much better time performance than the *Coloring* algorithm.

Extend your algorithm to apply to more types of resource-allocation problems, such as the two described in the introduction to this chapter.

11.10. Show that there exists an adversary for the *LehmannRabin* randomized Dining Philosophers algorithm for which the probability of locking out a particular process is non-zero. What is the highest probability you can achieve?

11.11. Prove the claim, made in Case 3 of the proof of Lemma 11.11, that there must be some process j such that $j + 1 \in \overleftarrow{*}$ and $j \in \overrightarrow{*} \cup R \cup F$.

11.12. Use Theorem 11.16 to prove the following, for the *LehmannRabin* algorithm:

(a) From any state in which some process is in T, with probability 1, some process eventually reaches C.

(b) From any state in which some process is in T, and for any $t \geq 0$, with probability $f(t)$, some process reaches C within time t. (You get to define f—try to make it as small as possible.)

11.13. Consider the *LehmannRabin* algorithm for the special case where $n = 2$. For this case, state and prove an interesting claim of the form $T \xrightarrow[p]{t} C$.

11.14. A novice programmer at the Flaky Computer Corporation, upon learning about the *LehmannRabin* algorithm, has proposed to improve its time performance by removing the wait for the first fork. Now instead of waiting for its first fork, a process simply tests it just as it does for its second fork. If the fork is unavailable, then the process goes back to the beginning and flips again.

Explain patiently to the programmer what is wrong with his algorithm.

11.15. *Research Question*: Can you generalize the idea of the *LehmannRabin* algorithm to more general resource-allocation problems than just the Dining Philosophers problem, while preserving the properties of exclusion, independent progress, and progress with probability 1?

Chapter 12

Consensus

In this chapter, we introduce another complication into our study of the asynchronous shared memory model: the possibility of failures. We only consider faulty processes, not faulty memory. In fact, we only consider the simplest type of process failure: *stopping failure*, whereby a process just stops without warning.

The problem we study in this chapter is one of *consensus*. We have already considered consensus problems extensively in the setting of synchronous message-passing systems, in Chapters 5, 6, and 7. For the case of process failures, we have shown that basic consensus problems are solvable, not only for stopping failures, but also for less well-behaved Byzantine failures. However, we gave several results showing that the costs of solutions, measured in terms of the number of processes and the amount of time required, are necessarily large.

Perhaps surprisingly, the situation turns out to be very different in the asynchronous setting, at least for read/write shared memory. Namely, we present a fundamental impossibility result, saying that a basic consensus problem *cannot be solved at all* in the asynchronous read/write shared memory setting, even if it is known that at most one process will fail. The same result holds, as you will see in Chapters 17 and 21, for the asynchronous network setting, and the reasons are essentially the same.

The impossibility of consensus is considered to be one of the most fundamental results of the theory of distributed computing. It has practical implications for any distributed application in which some type of agreement is required. For example, processes in a database system may need to agree on whether a transaction commits or aborts. Processes in a communication system may need to agree on whether or not a message has been received. Processes in a control system may need to agree on whether or not a particular other process is faulty. Then the impossibility result implies that there is no purely asynchronous algorithm that reaches the needed agreement and tolerates any failures at all.

This means that, in practice, designers must go outside the asynchronous model in order to solve such problems, for example, relying on timing information or being willing to settle for only probabilistic correctness.

12.1   The Problem

We define a particular consensus problem in the shared memory setting. Our presentation is informal, but it can be formalized in terms of the model defined in Chapter 9. Chapter 10 contains a similar informal presentation for the mutual exclusion problem, plus some guidelines showing how it can be formalized. You may find it useful to skim Sections 10.1 and 10.2 now.

The architecture we use here is essentially the same one we used in Chapters 9–11, with processes interacting with the environment via ports and communicating with each other via shared variables. See Figure 10.1, for example. We assume that $n \geq 2$, where n is the number of ports. The entire assembly of processes and variables is modelled as a single I/O automaton. We model the users as automata U_i also, as we did in Chapters 10 and 11. See Example 9.2.1 for one collection of users for the agreement problem. We assume a fixed value set V, $|V| \geq 2$, for the inputs and decisions.

This time, we assume that the external interface of each user U_i consists of output actions $init(v)_i$, where $v \in V$ is an input value for the shared memory system, and input actions $decide(v)_i$ inputs, where $v \in V$ is a decision value. The external interface of the shared memory system includes all the input actions $init(v)_i$, where $v \in V$ is an input value and i is a port name (i.e., process index), and all the output actions $decide(v)_i$, where $v \in V$ is a decision value and i is a port name. Thus, we are assuming that the inputs for the problem arrive from the users in input actions. (Note that most of the research papers in this area assume that the initial values appear in designated variables in the initial process states, while decisions are written into designated state variables. The formulation we use is more consistent with the style we are using elsewhere in the book.) Each user automaton must satisfy one restriction: it can only perform at most one $init_i$ event in an execution; that is, we assume that each process receives at most one input.

It is easy to formalize all of this in terms of I/O automata, as in Chapters 10 and 11. We assume in this chapter that there is exactly one task per process; in light of Exercise 8.8, this is not a significant restriction.

We assume that the processes are subject to *stopping failures*, by which we mean that they might simply stop without warning. Formally, we model this by including special $stop_i$ input actions, one for each process, in the external interface (external signature) of the shared memory system. A $stop_i$ event has

ports   processes   shared variables

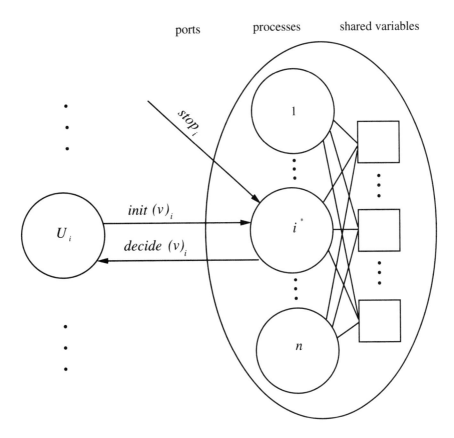

Figure 12.1: Shared memory system for the agreement problem.

the effect of disabling any future locally controlled actions of process i. The $stop_i$ actions are not considered to be part of the external interfaces of the user automata; they just arrive from some unspecified external environment (see Section 9.6). The complete architecture is depicted in Figure 12.1. With this method of modelling failures, and according to the formal definitions in Chapter 8, the *fair executions* of the system are those in which each process that does not fail, as well as each user task, gets infinitely many opportunities to perform locally controlled steps. We say that an execution of the system is *failure-free* if it contains no *stop* events.

We say that a sequence of $init_i$ and $decide_i$ actions is *well-formed* for user i, provided that it is some prefix of a sequence of the form $init(v)_i$, $decide(w)_i$ (i.e., the empty sequence, just an $init(v)_i$, or a two-action sequence $init(v)_i$, $decide(w)_i$). In particular, it does not contain repeated inputs at port i, nor repeated decisions at port i, nor does it contain any decision without a preceding input. Our assumptions about the user automata imply that each U_i preserves well-formedness (according to the definition of "preserves" in Section 8.5.4).

We require the following properties of any execution, fair or not, of the combined system.

Well-formedness: For any i, the interactions between U_i and the system are well-formed for i.

Agreement: All decision values are identical.

Validity: If all *init* actions that occur contain the same value v, then v is the only possible decision value.

Notice that the agreement and validity conditions are analogous to the corresponding conditions in Section 6.1, for the stopping agreement problem in the synchronous model; the main difference is in the input/output conventions.

We also need some kind of termination condition. The most basic requirement is the following, for failure-free executions.

Failure-free termination: In any fair failure-free execution in which *init* events occur on all ports, a *decide* event occurs on each port.

We say that a shared memory system A *solves the agreement problem* for a particular collection of users U_i if it guarantees the well-formedness, agreement, validity, and failure-free termination conditions for the users U_i. We say that it *solves the agreement problem* if it solves the agreement problem for all collections of users.

We also consider some stronger termination conditions involving fault-tolerance. The strongest condition we consider is the following, for executions in which any number of processes might fail:

Wait-free termination: In any fair execution in which *init* events occur on all ports, a *decide* event occurs on every non-failing port (i.e., every port i on which no $stop_i$ event occurs).

That is, any process that does not fail eventually decides, regardless of the failures of any of the other processes. This condition is analogous to the termination condition given in Section 6.1, for the stopping agreement problem in the synchronous setting. This condition is called *wait-freedom* because it implies that no process can ever be blocked, waiting indefinitely for help from any other process.

Note that we have stated the wait-freedom condition to assume that inputs arrive on all ports. We could have stated it equivalently to assume only that an input arrives at port i. We leave it as an exercise for you to show that this reformulation is in fact equivalent to our original statement.

Because the main impossibility result of this chapter involves only a single process failure rather than arbitrary process failures, we need yet another termination condition.

f-failure termination, $0 \leq f \leq n$: In any fair execution in which *init* events occur on all ports, if there are *stop* events on at most f ports, then a *decide* event occurs on every non-failing port.

It should be easy to see that the failure-free termination and wait-free termination conditions are the special cases of the f-failure termination condition where f is equal to 0 and n, respectively. The *single-failure termination* condition is the special case where $f = 1$.

Lemma 12.1 *Let A be an algorithm in the given architecture and U_i, $1 \leq i \leq n$, be a collection of users.*

1. *If A guarantees wait-free termination for the users U_i, then A guarantees f-failure termination for the U_i for any f, $0 \leq f \leq n$.*

2. *If A guarantees f-failure termination condition for the U_i for any f, $0 \leq f \leq n$, then A guarantees failure-free termination.*

We say that a shared memory system *guarantees wait-free termination, guarantees f-failure termination*, and so on, provided that it guarantees the corresponding condition for all collections of users.

Trace properties. As we did in Chapters 10 and 11, we can express the correctness conditions of this chapter equivalently in terms of trace properties. Each of these trace properties P has a signature consisting of $init(v)_i$ and $decide(v)_i$ outputs and $stop_i$ inputs. The external actions of the combined system are also exactly these actions, and the requirement in each case is that the fair traces of the combined system are all in $traces(P)$.

Synchronous termination conditions. The wait-free termination condition is similar to the termination condition used for the stopping agreement problem in the *synchronous* model, in Section 6.1, as well as to the strong termination condition used for the commit problem in Section 7.3. The failure-free termination condition is similar to the weak termination condition of Section 7.3.

In most of this chapter, we will consider the case of read/write shared memory, since that is the case in which the impossibility results hold. We allow the variables to be multi-writer/multi-reader registers. Near the end of the chapter, in Sections 12.3 and 12.4, we briefly consider other variable types.

12.2   Agreement Using Read/Write Shared Memory

Throughout this section, we suppose that A is an algorithm in the read/write shared memory model that solves the agreement problem and guarantees 1-failure termination. Our objective is to reach a contradiction, showing that such an A cannot exist.

We first make some simplifying restrictions on A, all without loss of generality, and then present some needed terminology. Next, we prove a result about the input values. Then, because the proof is easier, we show that the agreement problem is unsolvable in the read/write shared memory model, if the very strong *wait-free termination* condition is required. Finally, we show the main result—that not even a single fault can be tolerated.

12.2.1   Restrictions

For simplicity, and without loss of generality, we make the following four assumptions: First, we assume that the value set V is just $\{0, 1\}$. Second, we consider A in combination with a particular collection of users, trivial automata, each of which generates a single (arbitrary) *init* event and does nothing else.

Third, we assume that A is "deterministic," in the sense that the automaton has a unique initial state; that from any automaton state, any process has at most one locally controlled step; and that for any automaton state and any *init* input, there is a unique resulting automaton state. This does not restrict generality, because if we are given a nondeterministic solution, we could simply prune out all but one of the alternatives in each case. (This notion of determinism is similar to the one described in Exercise 8.9.)

Finally, we assume that every non-failed process always has a locally controlled step enabled, even after it decides. This does not restrict generality because we can always include dummy internal steps.

12.2.2   Terminology

We define an *initialization* to be an execution of the combination of A and the users consisting exactly of n *init* steps, one for each port, in order of index. Thus, the trace of an initialization has the form

$$init(v_1)_1, init(v_2)_2, \ldots, init(v_n)_n$$

where $v_1, \ldots, v_n \in V$. We define an execution α to be *input-first* provided that it begins with an initialization. Our proofs involve only input-first executions.

We define a finite execution α to be *0-valent* if 0 is the only value that appears in a *decide* event in α or in any execution that extends α; moreover, we insist that the value 0 actually does occur in some such decide event. After a 0-valent execution, the algorithm is already committed to 0 as the only decision value, even though no actual *decide*(0) event might yet have occurred. Similarly, α is 1-*valent* if the only such value is 1. We say that α is *univalent* if it is either 0-valent or 1-valent, and *bivalent* if each value appears in some extension. Figure 12.2 depicts a bivalent execution.

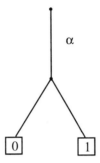

Figure 12.2: Bivalent execution α.

The following lemma says that this classification is exhaustive, in the absence of failures. That is, there are no finite failure-free executions after which *no* decision is possible.

Lemma 12.2 *Each finite failure-free execution α of A is either univalent or bivalent.*

Proof. Any such α can be extended to a fair failure-free execution α'. Then the failure-free termination condition guaranteed by A implies that in α', all processes eventually decide. $\qquad\square$

If α is a finite failure-free execution and i is any process, then define *extension*(α, i) to be the execution obtained by extending execution α by a single step of i. The fact that this is well-defined depends on two of the restrictions we made above: that every non-failed process always has a locally controlled step enabled and that the system is deterministic. This notation is extended to sequences of process indices in the obvious way, for example, *extension*$(\alpha, ij) = extension(extension(\alpha, i), j)$.

12.2.3 Bivalent Initializations

We begin by showing that A must have a *bivalent initialization*. This means that the final decision value cannot be determined just from the inputs. In contrast, if the algorithm is not required to tolerate any faults, then there are simple agreement algorithms in which the final value is completely determined by the inputs. We leave the discovery of such algorithms for an exercise.

Lemma 12.3 *A has a bivalent initialization.*

Proof.   Suppose not; then all the initializations are univalent. Note that the initialization α_0 consisting of all 0s must be 0-valent, by the validity condition. Similarly, the initialization α_1 consisting of all 1s must be 1-valent.

Now we construct a *chain* of initializations, spanning from α_0 to α_1.[1] At each step of the chain, we simply change the initial value of a single process from 0 to 1; thus, any two consecutive initializations in the chain differ only in the input to one process. By assumption, every initialization in the chain is univalent, so there must be two consecutive initializations in the chain, say α and α', such that α is 0-valent and α' is 1-valent. Suppose that they differ in the initial value of process i.

Now consider any fair execution that extends α and in which i fails immediately after the initialization (i.e., the next action is $stop_i$), but in which none of the other processes ever fails. Then all processes other than i must eventually decide, by the 1-failure termination condition. Since α is 0-valent, this decision must be 0.

Now we claim that it is possible to extend α' in the same way and still obtain a decision of 0. This is because α and α' are identical except for the initial value of i, and i fails immediately after the initialization in both extensions; thus, the rest of the processes can behave in exactly the same way after α' as after α. See Figure 12.3.

But this contradicts the assumption that α' is 1-valent.   □

12.2.4   Impossibility for Wait-Free Termination

Now we can prove the first (simpler) impossibility result—the one for wait-free termination. Namely, we suppose in this subsection that algorithm A has the wait-free termination property, which is stronger than the 1-failure termination property we have already assumed. We use the wait-free termination property to obtain a contradiction.

The contradiction is based on pinpointing a way in which a decision might be made. In particular, we define a *decider* execution α to be a finite failure-free input-first execution satisfying the following conditions:

---

[1] This chain construction is similar to the constructions used in the proof of Theorem 6.33, the lower bound on the number of rounds needed for agreement in the synchronous setting.

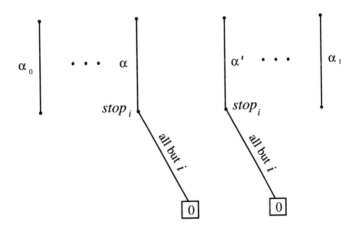

Figure 12.3: Construction for Lemma 12.3.

1. α is bivalent.

2. For every i, $extension(\alpha, i)$ is univalent.

Thus, after a decider execution, no decision has yet been determined, but any additional (non-*stop*) process step will determine the decision. We prove that A (with the wait-free termination property) must have a decider execution.

Lemma 12.4 *A has a decider execution.*

Proof. Suppose the contrary: that any bivalent failure-free input-first execution has a one-step bivalent failure-free extension.

Then starting with a bivalent initialization (whose existence is guaranteed by Lemma 12.3), we can produce an infinite failure-free input-first execution α, all of whose finite prefixes are bivalent. Thus, in α, no process ever decides. The construction is simple: at each stage, we start with a bivalent failure-free input-first execution, and we extend it by one step to another bivalent failure-free execution. Our assumption at the beginning of this proof says that we can do this.

Since α is infinite, it must contain infinitely many steps for some process, say i. We claim that i must decide in α, which yields a contradiction.

To see this, modify α by inserting a $stop_j$ event for each process j that only takes finitely many steps, right after its last step in α. Call the modified execution α'. Then α' is a fair execution in which process i does not fail. The wait-free termination condition then implies that i must decide in α'. But α and α' look identical to process i, so i decides in α also. This is the contradiction needed to prove this lemma. ☐

Now we can obtain the contradiction that we need to prove the impossibility
result for wait-free termination.

Lemma 12.5 *A does not exist.*

Proof.   By Lemma 12.4, we may fix some decider execution α. Since α is
bivalent, there exist two processes, say i and j, such that after α, a step of i
leads to a 0-valent execution and a step of j leads to a 1-valent execution. That
is, *extension*(α, i) is 0-valent and *extension*(α, j) is 1-valent. Obviously, $i \neq j$.
See Figure 12.4.

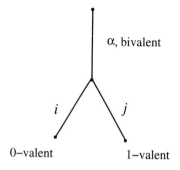

Figure 12.4: Execution α is a decider; *extension*(α, i) is 0-valent, and *extension*(α, j)
is 1-valent.

We complete the proof with a case analysis, getting a contradiction for each
possibility.

1. Process i's step is a read step.

   Consider extending *extension*(α, j) in such a way that no process fails,
   process i takes no further steps, and each process except for i takes infinitely many steps. This looks to every process except i like a fair execution in which process i fails immediately and no other process fails.
   Thus, by the wait-free termination condition (in fact, 1-failure termination
   is enough here), all processes except i must eventually decide, and since
   extension(α, j) is 1-valent, they must decide 1.

   Now, note that the states after α and *extension*(α, i) are indistinguishable
   to every process except i, in the sense defined in Section 9.3. This is
   because i's step is just a read, so the only thing it changes is the state of
   process i. So we can take the same suffix that we previously ran after α,
   beginning with the step of j, and run it after *extension*(α, i). In this case
   also, all processes except i decide 1, which contradicts the assumption that
   extension(α, i) is 0-valent. See Figure 12.5.

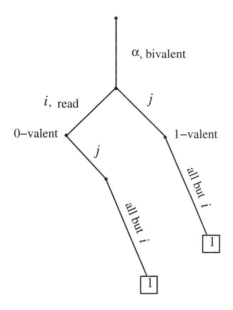

Figure 12.5: Construction for Case 1.

2. Process j's step is a read step.

   This case is symmetric to Case 1, and the same argument applies.

3. Process i's step and process j's step are both writes.

   We distinguish two subcases.

   (a) Processes i and j write to different variables.

   Consider two executions that extend α, one by allowing first i to take its step and then j, and the other allowing first j, then i. Since the two steps involve different processes and different variables, the system state is the same after either execution. See Figure 12.6.

   But then we have a common system state that can be reached after either a 0-valent or a 1-valent execution. If we run all the processes from this state with no failures, they are required to decide. However, either decision yields a contradiction. For instance, if a decision of 0 is reached, then we have a decision of 0 in an execution extending a 1-valent prefix.

   (b) Processes i and j write to the same variable.

   As in Case 1, we can run all processes but i after $extension(\alpha, j)$ until they decide 1. This time, note that the states after $extension(\alpha, j)$

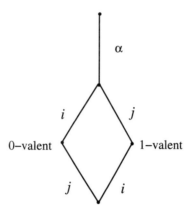

Figure 12.6: Construction for Case 3(a).

and *extension*(α, ij) are indistinguishable to every process except for
i. This is because the step of j overwrites the value written by i, so
the only memory of i's step is in the state of process i. So we can take
the same suffix that we previously ran after *extension*(α, j) and run it
after *extension*(α, ij). In this case also, all processes except i decide
1, which contradicts the 0-valence of *extension*(α, i). See Figure 12.7.

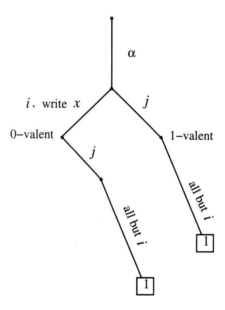

Figure 12.7: Construction for Case 3(b).

So, we have contradictions in all possible cases, and thus we conclude that no such algorithm A can exist. □

We have proved the first impossibility theorem:

Theorem 12.6 *For $n \geq 2$, there is no algorithm in the read/write shared memory model that solves the agreement problem and guarantees wait-free termination.*

12.2.5 Impossibility for Single-Failure Termination

Notice that the proof of Theorem 12.6 in the previous section does not work for the case where we only assume 1-failure termination. The problem is in the proof of Lemma 12.4, where we use the wait-free termination condition to assert that process i must decide in a fair execution in which it does not fail. In this section, we strengthen Theorem 12.6 to obtain the corresponding result for systems with 1-failure termination.

This time, the proof is based on the following lemma, which says that a bivalent execution can be extended to allow a given process to take a step, while still maintaining bivalence.

Lemma 12.7 *If α is a bivalent failure-free input-first execution of A, and i is any process, then there is a failure-free extension α' of α such that extension(α', i) is bivalent.*

See Figure 12.8.

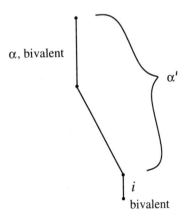

Figure 12.8: Maintaining bivalence while allowing process i to take a step.

At this point, you might prefer to skip ahead to the proof of Theorem 12.8, to see how Lemma 12.7 implies the impossibility result, before delving into the more technical proof of the lemma.

Proof.   We prove this lemma by contradiction. Suppose that the lemma is false. Then there must be some bivalent failure-free input-first execution α of A and some process i such that for every failure-free extension α' of α, $extension(\alpha', i)$ is univalent. This implies, in particular, that $extension(\alpha, i)$ is univalent; suppose without loss of generality that it is 0-valent.

Since α is bivalent, there is some extension α'' of α containing a decision of 1. We may assume without loss of generality that α'' is failure-free, since otherwise we could simply eliminate any *stop* actions without affecting the decision. Then it must be that $extension(\alpha'', i)$ is 1-valent. We consider what happens if i takes a step at each point along the "path" from α to α''. See Figure 12.9.

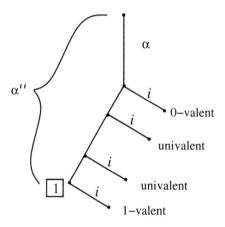

Figure 12.9: Process i's step leads to univalence.

At the beginning of the path, i's step yields 0-valence, while at the end, it yields 1-valence. At each intermediate point, it yields univalence. Therefore, it must be that there are two consecutive points in the path such that at the first of these points, i's step yields 0-valence, while at the second, i's step yields 1-valence. Let α' be the execution up to the first point. See Figure 12.10.

Suppose that j is the process that takes the intervening step. We claim that $j \neq i$. This is true because if $j = i$, then we have a situation where one step of i leads to 0-valence while two steps of i lead to 1-valence; since the processes are deterministic, this gives a 0-valent execution with a 1-valent extension, which is nonsense.

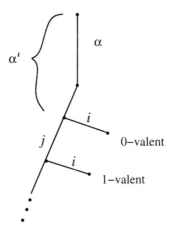

Figure 12.10: Two consecutive points where i yields different valences.

We finish with a case analysis similar to the one in the proof of Lemma 12.5, obtaining a contradiction for each case.

1. Process i's step is a read step.

    Then we claim that the states after $extension(\alpha', ji)$ and $extension(\alpha', ij)$ are indistinguishable to every process except for i. This is because the steps of i involved in these two extensions are both read steps, which do not affect anything except the state of process i.

    Consider extending $extension(\alpha', ij)$ in such a way that i takes no further steps and every other process takes infinitely many steps. By the 1-failure termination condition, all processes except i must eventually decide, and since $extension(\alpha', i)$ is 0-valent, they must decide 0. By the indistinguishability claim just above, we can take the same suffix that we previously ran after $extension(\alpha', ij)$ and run it after $extension(\alpha', ji)$. In this case also, the processes decide 0, which contradicts the 1-valence of $extension(\alpha', ji)$. See Figure 12.11.

2. Process j's step is a read step.

    The argument is similar to that for Case 1. This time, the states after $extension(\alpha', i)$ and $extension(\alpha', ji)$ are indistinguishable to all processes except j. We can let all processes except j run after $extension(\alpha', i)$, forcing them eventually to decide 0. Then we can run them in the same way after $extension(\alpha', ji)$. They again decide 0, contradicting the 1-valence of $extension(\alpha', ji)$.

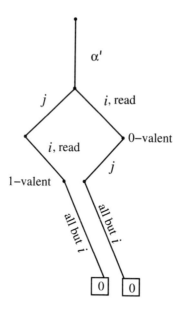

Figure 12.11: Construction for Case 1.

3. Process i's step and process j's step are both writes.

   (a) Processes i and j write to different variables.

   In this case we get the same sort of commutative scenario as in Case 3(a) of the proof of Lemma 12.5; see Figure 12.6. This implies the same contradiction as in that proof.

   (b) Processes i and j write to the same variable.

   In this case, the states after *extension*(α', i) and *extension*(α', ji) are indistinguishable to all processes except for j, because i's step overwrites j's step. Running all processes except for j after *extension*(α', i) and *extension*(α', ji) yields the same contradiction as before. See Figure 12.12.

$\square$

We can now prove the main theorem.

Theorem 12.8 *For $n \geq 2$, there is no algorithm in the read/write shared memory model that solves the agreement problem and guarantees 1-failure termination.*

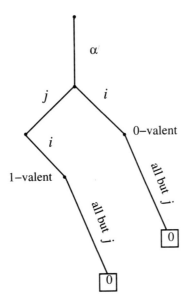

Figure 12.12: Construction for Case 3(b).

Proof.   We use Lemma 12.7 to construct a fair failure-free input-first execution in which no process ever decides. This contradicts the failure-free termination requirement.

The construction begins with a bivalent initialization, whose existence is guaranteed by Lemma 12.3. Then we repeatedly extend the current execution, including at least one step of process 1 in the first extension, then at least one step of 2 in the second extension, and so on, in round-robin order, all while maintaining bivalence and avoiding failures. Lemma 12.7 implies that each extension step is possible.

The resulting execution is fair, because each process takes infinitely many steps. However, no process ever reaches a decision, which gives the needed contradiction. □

12.3   Agreement Using Read-Modify-Write Shared Memory

In contrast to the situation for read/write shared memory, it is very easy to solve the agreement problem, guaranteeing wait-free termination, using read-modify-write shared memory. In fact, a single read-modify-write shared variable is enough.

RMWAgreement algorithm:

The shared variable begins with the value *unknown*. Each process accesses the variable. If it sees the value *unknown*, then it changes the value to its own initial value and decides on this value. On the other hand, if it sees a value $v \in V$, then it does not change the value written in the variable but instead accepts the previously written value as its decision value.

The precondition-effect code for process i of the *RMWAgreement* algorithm is the same as the code in Example 9.1.1, with the addition of some code for handling failures. Namely, the state contains an additional component *stopped*, a set of processes, initially empty. There is a new *stop$_i$* action, which puts i into *stopped*. The *access$_i$* and *decide$_i$* actions have the additional precondition that $i \notin stopped$, and the *init$_i$* action only makes its changes if $i \notin stopped$.

Theorem 12.9 *The RMWAgreement algorithm solves the agreement problem and guarantees wait-free termination.*

Proof.   Straightforward. Wait-free termination follows, because each process i, after receiving an *init$_i$* input, is immediately enabled to perform an *access$_i$* and then a *decide$_i$*. Agreement and validity follow, because the first process to perform an *access* establishes the common decision value.   □

12.4   Other Types of Shared Memory

The agreement problem can also be considered using shared memory of other variable types besides read/write and read-modify-write. For example, we can consider variables with operations such as *swap*, *test-and-set*, *fetch-and-add*, and *compare-and-swap*. These operations are defined in Example 9.4.3. Among the known results are the following theorems:

Theorem 12.10 *The agreement problem for any n can be solved with wait-free termination, using a single shared variable that allows compare-and-swap operations only.*

Theorem 12.11 *If $n \geq 3$, then the agreement problem cannot be solved with wait-free termination using shared variables that allow any combination of swap, test-and-set, fetch-and-add, read, and write operations.*

Proofs.   The proofs are left for exercises.   □

12.5 Computability in Asynchronous Shared Memory Systems*

The agreement problem is only one example of a "decision problem" that can be considered in the asynchronous shared memory model with stopping failures. In this section, we define the general notion of a decision problem, give some examples, and state (without proof) some typical computability results.

Our definition of a decision problem is based on the preliminary definition of a decision mapping. A *decision mapping* D specifies, for each length n vector w of inputs over some fixed value set V, a nonempty set $D(w)$ of allowable length n vectors of decisions. The vector w represents the inputs of processes $1, \dots, n$, in order of process index, and, similarly, each vector in $D(w)$ represents the decisions of processes $1, \dots, n$, also in order of process index.

We use a decision mapping D in the formulation of a problem to be solved by an asynchronous shared memory system. The external interface of the shared memory system consists of $init(v)_i$, $decide(v)_i$, and $stop_i$ actions, just as for the agreement problem. The well-formedness condition and the various termination conditions are defined in exactly the same way as for the agreement problem. However, in place of the agreement and validity conditions used in the agreement problem, we require only the single validity condition:

Validity: In any execution in which *init* events occur on all ports, it is possible to complete the vector of decisions that are reached by the processes to a vector in $D(w)$, where w is the given input vector.

Example 12.5.1   The agreement problem as a decision problem

The agreement problem is an example of a decision problem, based on the decision mapping D, defined as follows. For any vector $w = v_1, \dots, v_n$ of inputs in V, the set $D(w)$ of allowable vectors of decisions is defined by

1. If $v_1 = v_2 = \dots = v_n = v$, then $D(w)$ contains the single vector $x_1, \dots, x_n$ such that $x_1 = x_2 = \dots = x_n = v$.

2. If $v_i \neq v_j$ for some i and j, then $D(w)$ consists of exactly those vectors $x_1, \dots, x_n$ such that $x_1 = x_2 = \dots = x_n$.

It is easy to see that the decision problem based on D is the same as the agreement problem. (One apparent difference is that the definition of a general decision problem only mentions executions in which *init* inputs arrive on all ports, whereas the definition of the agreement problem involves other executions as well. But this is not an important difference, because any finite execution can be extended to one in which inputs arrive everywhere.)

Two other important examples of decision problems are the k-agreement problem and the approximate agreement problem, both of which we studied in the synchronous network model in Chapter 7. In the *k-agreement* problem, where k is any positive integer, the agreement and validity conditions of the agreement problem are replaced with the following:

Agreement: In any execution, there is a subset W of V, $|W| = k$, such that all decision values are in W.

Validity: In any execution, any decision value for any process is the initial value of some process.

The agreement condition is weaker than that for ordinary agreement in that it permits k decision values rather than only one. The validity condition is a slight strengthening of the validity condition for ordinary agreement. It is easy to formalize the k-agreement problem as a decision problem. The following can be shown, though we omit the proofs here and leave them for exercises:

Theorem 12.12 *The k-agreement problem is solvable with $k - 1$-failure termination in the asynchronous read/write shared memory model using single-writer/ multi-reader registers.*

Theorem 12.13 *The k-agreement problem is not solvable with k-failure termination in the asynchronous shared memory model with multi-writer/multi-reader registers.*

In the *approximate agreement* problem, the set V of values is the set of real numbers, and processes are permitted to send real-valued data in messages. Now instead of having to agree exactly, as in the agreement problem, the requirement is that the processes agree approximately, to within a small positive tolerance ϵ. That is, the agreement and validity conditions of the agreement problem are replaced with the following:

Agreement: In any execution, any two decision values are within ϵ of each other.

Validity: In any execution, any decision value is within the range of the initial values.

Again, it is easy to formalize this problem as a decision problem.

Theorem 12.14 *The approximate agreement problem is solvable with wait-free termination, in the asynchronous read/write shared memory model using single-writer/multi-reader registers.*

Proof. The proof is left as an exercise. □

We close this chapter with a theorem that gives some conditions that imply that a decision problem cannot be solved with 1-failure termination. This theorem generalizes Theorem 12.8.

For any set of length n vectors of elements of V, we define a graph. The vertices of this graph are the vectors of length n, and the edges are the pairs of vectors that differ in exactly one position.

Theorem 12.15 *Let D be a decision mapping whose associated decision problem is solvable with 1-failure termination, in the read/write shared memory model. Then there must be a decision mapping D' with $D'(w) \subseteq D(w)$ for all w, such that both of the following hold:*

1. *If input vectors w and w' differ in exactly one position, then there exist $y \in D'(w)$ and $y' \in D'(w')$ such that y and y' differ in at most one position.*

2. *For each w, the graph defined by $D'(w)$ is connected.*

We leave the proof of Theorem 12.15 for an exercise; it uses ideas similar to those used in the proof of Theorem 12.8.

12.6 Bibliographic Notes

The first result in the literature about the impossibility of agreement in fault-prone systems was proved by Fischer, Lynch, and Paterson [123]. This result was proved for the asynchronous message-passing setting, for the case of 1-failure termination. Later, this result and its proof were extended to the asynchronous shared memory setting, a slightly stronger model, by Loui and Abu-Amara [199]. (See Chapter 17 for relationships between the asynchronous shared memory and asynchronous network models.) The result about the impossibility of wait-free agreement was proved by Loui and Abu-Amara [199] and independently by Herlihy [150]. The presentation in this chapter follows the proofs of [199].

The results about agreement using other types of shared variables besides read/write variables are due to Herlihy [150]. Herlihy's paper not only classifies which types of variables are capable of solving the agreement problem, but also determines which types can "implement" which other types.

The problem of k-agreement was originally posed by Chaudhuri [73], in the setting of asynchronous networks. Chaudhuri proved that k-agreement can be solved with $k - 1$–failure termination, but the question of whether it can be solved with k-failure termination remained open for several years. The (negative) answer to this question appeared simultaneously in papers by Herlihy and Shavit [152], by Borowsky and Gafni [55], and by Saks and Zaharoglou [253]. Herlihy and Shavit presented their result in the context of a topological characterization of the problems that can be solved in fault-prone asynchronous read/write shared memory systems. They developed that characterization further in [151]. The characterization includes consideration of restricted sets of input vectors rather than just the complete sets considered in this book.

The problem of approximate agreement in asynchronous systems was originally defined by Dolev, Lynch, Pinter, Stark, and Weihl [98]. Their work was carried out in the asynchronous network model. Attiya, Lynch, and Shavit [24] developed a wait-free asynchronous shared memory algorithm for approximate agreement.

Biran, Moran, and Zaks [51] characterized the decision problems that can be solved in the asynchronous read/write shared memory setting with 1-failure termination, based on an earlier impossibility result by Moran and Wolfstahl [230]. The characterization includes consideration of restricted sets of input vectors. Theorem 12.15 follows from results in these two papers. These results were originally proved for the asynchronous network setting, but the proofs extend to the asynchronous read/write shared memory setting.

Chor, Israeli, and Li [78], Abrahamson [2], and Aspnes and Herlihy [16], among others, gave randomized solutions to the agreement problem, using read/write shared memory.

12.7 Exercises

12.1. Prove that the stronger form of the wait-free termination condition in which inputs need only arrive at port i is equivalent to the given formulation. More specifically, show how to modify a given algorithm A that guarantees well-formedness, agreement, validity, and wait-free termination, so that the modified version guarantees the same conditions but with the stronger wait-free termination condition.

12.2. Describe an algorithm that solves the agreement problem (without any fault-tolerance requirements) in the read/write shared memory model and

   (a) in which there exists a bivalent initialization.

(b) in which all initializations are univalent.

12.3. True or false?

(a) If A is a (non-fault-tolerant) agreement protocol in the read/write shared memory model that satisfies the restrictions in Section 12.1 and that has a bivalent initialization, then A must have a decider execution.

(b) If A is as in part (a) and is a two-process protocol, then A must have a decider execution.

12.4. Show that Theorem 12.8 still holds if we weaken the problem requirements by replacing the validity condition with the following weaker condition: There exist two input-first executions, α_0 and α_1, such that 0 is decided by some process in α_0 and 1 is decided by some process in α_1.

12.5. Reconsider the agreement problem using read/write shared memory. This time consider a more constrained fault model than general stopping failures, in which processes can only fail at the very beginning of computation. (That is, all *stop* events precede all other events.) Can the agreement problem be solved in this model, guaranteeing

(a) 1-failure termination?

(b) wait-free termination?

In each case, give either an algorithm or an impossibility proof.

12.6. Prove that any agreement protocol in the read-modify-write shared memory model that guarantees 1-failure termination must have a bivalent initialization.

12.7. Suppose we are given a single variable x of any variable type, having the following properties, for some a and b and some $v \neq v_0$:

(a) $f(a, v_0) = (b, v)$.

(b) For every $w \neq v_0$, there exist $c \neq b$ and some $w' \neq v_0$ such that $f(a, w) = (c, w')$.

(See Section 9.4 for the general notation we use for variable types.)

Give a solution to the agreement problem, guaranteeing wait-free termination, that uses just this variable x plus read/write shared variables.

12.8. Prove Theorem 12.10.

12.9. Show that for $n \geq 3$, the n-process agreement problem with wait-free termination cannot be solved using any number of shared variables, where each is of a type that is *interfering*, in the following sense. If a and b are invocations of the variable type, then, letting $f_2(a, v)$ denote the second projection of $f(a, v)$ (i.e., the new value of the variable), at least one of the following holds:

(a) (a and b commute) $f_2(a, f_2(b, v)) = f_2(b, f_2(a, v))$ for all $v \in V$

(b) (a overwrites b) $f_2(a, f_2(b, v)) = f_2(a, v)$ for all $v \in V$

(c) (b overwrites a) $f_2(b, f_2(a, v)) = f_2(b, v)$ for all $v \in V$

We use notation from Section 9.4.

12.10. Use the result of Exercise 12.9 to prove Theorem 12.11.

12.11. Express the following formally as decision problems by giving the decision mappings:

(a) The k-agreement problem

(b) The approximate agreement problem

12.12. Prove Theorem 12.12.

12.13. Prove Theorem 12.13. (*Warning:* This is very hard.)

12.14. Consider the approximate agreement problem for $n = 2$ processes. Give a wait-free algorithm for this problem in the asynchronous shared memory model with single-writer/multi-reader registers. Prove its correctness and analyze its time complexity.

12.15. Generalize the result of Exercise 12.14 to an arbitrary number n of processes. That is, prove Theorem 12.14.

12.16. An experienced software designer at the Flaky Computer Corporation has come up with a clever idea for solving the agreement problem of this chapter, for any number of stopping failures, for $V = \{0, 1\}$. Her idea is to regard 0 and 1 as real numbers and to use a wait-free solution to the approximate agreement problem as a "subroutine." Once the processes obtain their answers for the approximate agreement subroutine, they can simply round them off to the nearer of 0 or 1 to obtain their final decisions.

Explain what is wrong with her idea.

12.17. Consider the two-process wait-free approximate agreement algorithm you designed for Exercise 12.14. (We are assuming that your algorithm is "deterministic," as defined in Section 12.2.1.) For any input vector (v_1, v_2), define $D'(v_1, v_2)$ to be the set of decision vectors that are actually attained in input-first executions in which process 1 has input v_1 and process 2 has input v_2.

    (a) Describe the set $D'(0, 1)$ and its associated graph, as defined just before Theorem 12.15.

    (b) Consider the failure-free infinite execution in which processes 1 and 2 first receive inputs 0 and 1, respectively, and then alternate steps $1, 2, 1, \ldots$. For each input-first prefix α of this execution, describe the set of decision vectors that are actually attained in extensions of α.

    (c) Describe $D'(v_1, v_2)$, for every input vector (v_1, v_2).

    (d) Show that for each (v_1, v_2), the graph defined by $D'(v_1, v_2)$ is connected.

12.18. Prove Theorem 12.15. (*Hint:* Fix any algorithm A that solves D with 1-failure termination, in the read/write shared memory model. For any input vector w, define $D'(w)$ to be the set of decision vectors that are actually attained in input-first executions of A with input vector w. For part 1, use an argument like the one for Lemma 12.3. For part 2, argue by contradiction, using an argument like the one for Theorem 12.8. This time, after each finite failure-free input-first execution, consider whether the set of attainable decision vectors is connected or disconnected. Use an analogue to Lemma 12.7 that says that any "disconnected" α can be extended to another "disconnected" α', while allowing any given process i to take a step.)

12.19. Use Theorem 12.15 to prove Theorem 12.8.

12.20. Use Theorem 12.15 to prove that some other decision problems besides ordinary agreement cannot be solved in asynchronous read/write shared memory systems with 1-failure termination. Define as many interesting problems as you can for which impossibility can be proved in this way.

12.21. Extend the conditions in Theorem 12.15 to a general characterization of the decision problems that can be solved in asynchronous read/write shared memory systems with 1-failure termination. (*Warning:* This is very hard.)

Chapter 13

Atomic Objects

In this chapter, our last on the asynchronous shared memory model, we introduce *atomic objects*. An atomic object of a particular type is very much like an ordinary shared variable of that same type. The difference is that an atomic object can be accessed concurrently by several processes, whereas accesses to a shared variable are assumed to occur indivisibly. Even though accesses are concurrent, an atomic object ensures that the processes obtain responses that make it *look like the accesses occur one at a time, in some sequential order that is consistent with the order of invocations and responses*. Atomic objects are also sometimes called *linearizable objects*.

In addition to the atomicity property, most atomic objects that have been studied satisfy interesting fault-tolerance conditions. The strongest of these is the *wait-free termination* condition, which says that any invocation on a non-failing port eventually obtains a response. This property can be weakened to require such responses only if all the failures are confined to a designated set I of ports or to a certain number f of ports. The only types of failures we consider in this chapter are stopping failures.

Atomic objects have been suggested as building blocks for the construction of multiprocessor systems. The idea is that you should begin with basic atomic objects, such as single-writer/single-reader read/write atomic objects, which are simple enough to be provided by hardware. Then starting from these basic atomic objects, you could build successively more powerful atomic objects. The resulting system organization would be simple, modular, and provably correct. The problem, as yet unresolved, is to build atomic objects that provide sufficiently fast responses to be useful in practice.

Atomic objects are indisputably useful, however, as building blocks for asynchronous network systems. There are many distributed network algorithms that are designed to provide the user with something that looks like a centralized, coherent shared memory. Formally, many of these can be viewed as distributed implementations of atomic objects. We will see some examples of this phenomenon later, in Sections 17.1 and 18.3.3.

In Section 13.1, we provide the formal framework for the study of atomic objects. That is, we define atomic objects and give their basic properties, in particular, results about their relationship to shared variables of the same type and results indicating how they can be used in system construction.

Then in the rest of the chapter, we give algorithms for implementing particular types of atomic objects in terms of other types of atomic objects (or, equivalently, in terms of shared variables). The types of atomic objects we consider are read/write objects, read-modify-write objects, and snapshot objects. The results we present are only examples—there are many more such results in the research literature, and there is still much more research to be done.

13.1   Definitions and Basic Results

We first define atomic objects and their basic properties, then give a construction of a canonical wait-free atomic object of a given type, and then prove some basic results about composing atomic objects and about substituting them for shared variables in shared memory systems. These results can be used to justify the hierarchical construction of atomic objects from other atomic objects.

Many of the notions in this section are rather subtle. They are important, however, not only for the results in this chapter, but also for material involving fault-tolerance in Chapters 17 and 21. So we will go slowly here and present the ideas somewhat more formally than usual. On a first reading, you might want to skip the proofs and only read the definitions and results. In fact, you might want to start by reading only the definitions in Section 13.1.1, then skipping forward to Section 13.2 and referring back to this section as necessary.

13.1.1   Atomic Object Definition

The definition of an atomic object is based on the definition of a variable type from Section 9.4. You should reread that section now. In particular, recall that a variable type consists of a set V of values, an initial value v_0, a set of *invocations*, a set of *responses*, and a function $f : invocations \times V \rightarrow responses \times V$. This function f specifies the response and new value that result when a particular invocation is made on a variable with a particular value.

Also recall that the *executions* of a variable type are the finite sequences v_0, a_1, b_1, v_1, a_2, b_2, v_2, $\ldots$, v_r and infinite sequences v_0, a_1, b_1, v_1, a_2, b_2, v_2, $\ldots$, where the a's and b's are invocations and responses, respectively, and adjacent quadruples are consistent with f. Also, the *traces* of a variable type are the sequences of a's and b's that are derived from executions of the type.

If $\mathcal{T}$ is a variable type, then we define an *atomic object* A of type $\mathcal{T}$ to be an I/O automaton (using the general definition of an I/O automaton from Chapter 8) satisfying a collection of properties that we describe in the next few pages. In particular, it must have a particular type of external interface (external signature) and must satisfy certain "well-formedness," "atomicity," and liveness conditions.

We begin by describing the external interface. We assume that A is accessed through n *ports*, numbered $1, \ldots, n$. Associated with each port i, A has some input actions of the form a_i, where a is an invocation of the variable type, and some output actions of the form b_i, where b is a response of the variable type. If a_i is an input action, it means that a is an allowable invocation on port i, while if b_i is an output action, it means that b is an allowable response on port i. We assume a technical condition: if a_i is an input on port i and if $f(a, v) = (b, w)$ for some v and w, then b_i should be an output on port i. That is, if invocation a is allowed on port i, then all possible responses to a are also allowed on port i.

In addition, since we will consider the resiliency of atomic objects to stopping failures, we assume that there is an input $stop_i$ for each port i. The external interface is depicted in Figure 13.1.

Example 13.1.1 Read/write atomic object external interface

We describe an external interface for a *1-writer/2-reader* atomic object for domain V. The object has three ports, which we label by 1, 2, and 3. Port 1 is a *write* port, supporting *write* operations only, while ports 2 and 3 are *read* ports, supporting *read* operations only. More precisely, associated with port 1 there are input actions of the form $write(v)_1$ for all $v \in V$ and a single output action ack_1. Associated with port 2 there is a single input action $read_2$ and output actions of the form v_2 for all $v \in V$, and analogously for port 3. There are also $stop_1$, $stop_2$, and $stop_3$ input actions, associated with ports 1, 2, and 3, respectively. The external interface is depicted in Figure 13.2.

Next, we describe the required behavior of an atomic object automaton A of a particular variable type $\mathcal{T}$. As in Chapters 10–12, we assume that A is composed with a collection of user automata U_i, one for each port. The outputs of U_i are assumed to be the invocations of A on port i, and the inputs of U_i are assumed to be the responses of A on port i. The $stop_i$ action is not part of the signature of U_i; it is assumed to be generated not by U_i, but by some unspecified external source.

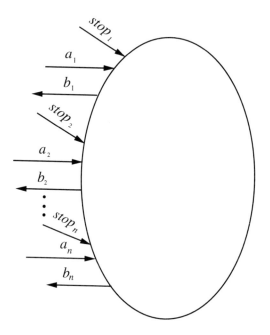

Figure 13.1: External interface of an atomic object.

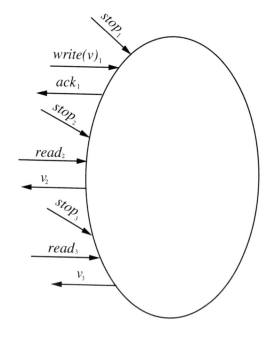

Figure 13.2: External interface of a 1-writer/2-reader read/write atomic object.

The only other property we assume for U_i is that it preserve a "well-formedness" condition, defined as follows. Define a sequence of external actions of user U_i to be *well-formed* for user i provided that it consists of alternating invocations and responses, starting with an invocation. We assume that each U_i *preserves* well-formedness for i (according to the formal definition of "preserves" in Section 8.5.4). That is, we assume that the invocations of operations on each port are strictly sequential, each waiting for a response to the previous invocation. Note that this sequentiality requirement only refers to individual ports; we allow concurrency among the invocations on different ports.[1] Throughout this chapter, we use the notation U to represent the composition of the separate user automata U_i, $U = \prod U_i$.

We require that $A \times U$, the combined system consisting of A and U, satisfy several properties. First, there is a well-formedness condition similar to the ones used in Chapters 10, 11, and 12.

Well-formedness: In any execution of $A \times U$ and for any i, the interactions between U_i and A are well-formed for i.

Since we have already assumed that the users preserve well-formedness, this amounts to saying that A also preserves well-formedness. This says that in the combined system $A \times U$, invocations and responses alternate on each port, starting with an invocation.

The next condition is the hardest one to understand. It describes the apparent atomicity of the operations, for a particular variable type $\mathcal{T}$. Note that a trace of $\mathcal{T}$ describes the correct responses to a sequence of invocations when *all* the operations are executed sequentially, that is, where each invocation after the first waits for a response to the previous invocation. The atomicity condition says that each trace produced by the combined system—which permits concurrent invocations of operations on different ports—"looks like" some trace of $\mathcal{T}$.

The way of saying this formally is a little more complicated than you might expect, since we want a condition that makes sense even for executions of $A \times U$ in which some of the invocations—the last ones on some ports—are *incomplete*, that is, have no responses. So we stipulate that each execution looks as if the operations that are completed *and some of the incomplete ones* are performed instantaneously at some points in their intervals.

In order to define atomicity for the system $A \times U$, we first give a more basic definition, of atomicity for a sequence of user actions. Namely, suppose that β is a (finite or infinite) sequence of external actions of $A \times U$ that is well-formed

---

[1]In practice, you might want also to allow concurrent access on individual ports. This would require some extensions to the theory presented in this chapter; we avoid these complications so that we can present the basic ideas reasonably simply.

for every i (that is, for every i, $\beta|ext(U_i)$ is well-formed for i). We say that β *satisfies the atomicity property* for $\mathcal{T}$ provided that it is possible to do all of the following:

1. For each completed operation π, to insert a *serialization point* $*_\pi$ somewhere between π's invocation and response in β.

2. To select a subset Φ of the incomplete operations.

3. For each operation $\pi \in \Phi$, to select a response.

4. For each operation $\pi \in \Phi$, to insert a *serialization point* $*_\pi$ somewhere after π's invocation in β.

These operations and responses should be selected, and these serialization points inserted, so that the sequence of invocations and responses constructed as follows is a trace of the underlying variable type $\mathcal{T}$:

> For each completed operation π, move the invocation and response events appearing in β (in that order) to the serialization point $*_\pi$. (That is, "shrink" the interval of operation π to its serialization point.) Also, for each operation $\pi \in \Phi$, put the invocation appearing in β, followed by the selected response, at $*_\pi$. Finally, remove all invocations of incomplete operations $\pi \notin \Phi$.

Notice that the atomicity condition only depends on the invocation and response events—it does not mention the *stop* events. We can easily extend this definition to executions of A and of $A \times U$. Namely, suppose that α is any such execution that is well-formed for every i (that is, for every i, $\alpha|ext(U_i)$ is well-formed for i). Then we say that α *satisfies the atomicity property* for $\mathcal{T}$ provided that its sequence of external actions, $trace(\alpha)$, satisfies the atomicity property for $\mathcal{T}$.

Example 13.1.2   Executions with serialization points

Figure 13.3 illustrates some executions of a single-writer/single-reader read/write object with domain $V = \mathbb{N}$ and initial value $v_0 = 0$ that satisfy the atomicity property for the read/write register variable type. The serialization points are indicated by stars. Suppose that ports 1 and 2 are used for writing and reading, respectively.

In (a), a *read* operation that returns 0 and a *write*(8) operation overlap and the serialization point for the *read* is placed before that of the *write*(8). Then if the operation intervals are shrunk to their serialization points, the sequence of invocations and responses is $read_2, 0_2,$

$write(8)_1, ack_1$. This is a trace of the variable type. (See Example 9.4.4.)

In (b), the same operation intervals are assigned serialization points in the opposite order. The resulting sequence of invocations and responses is then $write(8)_1, ack_1, read_2, 8_2$, again a trace of the variable type.

Each of the executions in (c) and (d) includes an incomplete $write(8)$ operation. In each case, a serialization point is assigned to the $write(8)$, because its result is seen by a *read* operation. For (c), the result of shrinking the operation intervals is $write(8)_1, ack_1, read_2, 8_2$, whereas for (d), the sequence is $read_2, 0_2, write(8)_1, ack_1, read_2, 8_2$. Both are traces of the variable type. (Again, see Example 9.4.4.)

In (e), there are infinitely many *read* operations that return 0, and consequently the incomplete $write(8)$ cannot be assigned a serialization point.

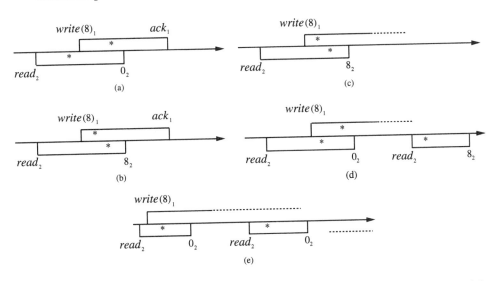

Figure 13.3: Executions of a single-writer/single-reader read/write object satisfying the atomicity property.

Example 13.1.3 Executions with no serialization points

Figure 13.4 illustrates some executions of a single-writer/single-reader read/write object that do not satisfy the atomicity property. In (a), there is no way to insert serialization points to explain the occurrence of a read that returns 8 followed by a read that returns 8. In (b),

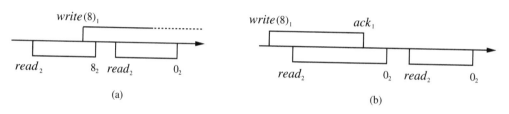

Figure 13.4: Executions of a single-writer/single-reader read/write object that do not satisfy the atomicity property.

there is no way to explain the occurrence of a read that returns 0, after the completion of a write of 8.

Now we are (finally) ready to define the atomicity condition for the combined system $A \times U$.

Atomicity: Let α be a (finite or infinite) execution of $A \times U$ that is well-formed for every i. Then α satisfies the atomicity property (as defined just before Example 13.1.2).

We can also express the atomicity condition in terms of a trace property (see the definition of a trace property in Section 8.5.2). Namely, define the trace property P so that its signature $sig(P)$ is the external interface of $A \times U$ and its trace set $traces(P)$ is exactly the set of sequences that satisfy both of the following:

1. Well-formedness for every i

2. The atomicity property for $\mathcal{T}$

(For convenience, we include the *stop* actions in the signature of P, even though they are not mentioned in the well-formedness and atomicity conditions.) The interesting thing about P is that it is a safety property, as defined in Section 8.5.3. That is, $traces(P)$ is nonempty, prefix-closed, and limit-closed. This is not obvious, because the atomicity property has a rather complicated definition, involving the existence of appropriate placements of serialization points and selections of operations and responses.

Theorem 13.1 P *(the trace property defined above, expressing the combination of well-formedness and atomicity) is a safety property.*

The proof of Theorem 13.1 uses *König's Lemma*, a basic combinatorial lemma about infinite trees:

Lemma 13.2 (König's Lemma) *If G is an infinite tree in which each node has only finitely many children, then G has an infinite path from the root.*

Proof Sketch (of Theorem 13.1). Nonemptiness is clear, since $\lambda \in traces(P)$.

For prefix-closure, suppose that $\beta \in traces(P)$ and let β' be a finite prefix of β. Since $\beta \in traces(P)$, it is possible to select a set Φ of incomplete operations, a set of responses for the operations in Φ, and a set of serialization points that together demonstrate the correctness of β. We show how to make such selections for β'.

Let γ denote the sequence obtained from β by inserting the selected serialization points. Let γ' be the prefix of γ ending with the last element of β'. Then γ' includes serialization points for all the complete operations in β' and some subset of the incomplete operations in β'. Choose Φ', the set of incomplete operations for β', to consist of those incomplete operations in β' that have serialization points in γ'. Choose a response for each operation $\pi \in \Phi'$ as follows: If π is incomplete in β, that is, if $\pi \in \Phi$, then choose the same response that is chosen for π in β. Otherwise choose the response that actually appears in β. Then it is not hard to see that the chosen set Φ', its chosen responses, and the serialization points in γ' together demonstrate the correctness of β'. This shows prefix-closure.

Finally, we show limit-closure. Consider an infinite sequence β and suppose that all finite prefixes of β are in $traces(P)$. We use König's Lemma.

The tree G that we construct in order to apply König's Lemma describes the possible placements of serialization points in β. Each node of G is labelled by a finite prefix of β, with serialization points inserted for some subset of the operations that are invoked in β. We only include labels that are "correct" in the sense that they satisfy the following three conditions:

1. Every completed operation has exactly one serialization point, and that serializaton point occurs between the operation's invocation and response.

2. Every incomplete operation has at most one serialization point, and that serialization point occurs after the operation's invocation.

3. Every response to an operation π is exactly the response that is calculated for π using the function of the given variable type $\mathcal{T}$ at the serialization points. (Start with the initial value v_0 and apply the function once for each serialization point, in order, with the corresponding invocation as the first argument. The response that is calculated for π is the response obtained when the function is applied for the serialization point $*_\pi$.)

Furthermore, in G,

1. The label of the root is λ.

2. The label of each non-root node is an extension of the label of its parent.

3. The label of each non-root node ends with an element of β.

4. The label of each non-root node contains exactly one more element of β than does the label of its parent node (and possibly some more serialization points).

Thus, at each branch point in G, a decision is made about which serialization points to insert, in which order, between two particular symbols in β. By considering the prefix-closure construction above, we can see that G can be constructed so that *every* finite prefix β' of β, with every "correct" assignment of serialization points prior to the last symbol of β', appears as the label of some node of G.

Now we apply König's Lemma to the tree G. First, it is easy to see that each node of G has only finitely many children. This is because only operations that have already been invoked can have their serialization points inserted and there are only finitely many places to insert these serialization points.

Second, we claim that G contains arbitrarily long paths from the root. This is because every finite prefix β' of the infinite sequence β is in $traces(P)$, which means that β' has an appropriate assignment of serialization points. This assignment yields a corresponding path in G of length $|\beta'|$.

Since G contains arbitrarily long paths from the root, it is infinite. Then König's Lemma (Lemma 13.2) implies that G contains an infinite path from the root. The node labels on this path yield a correct selection of serialization points (and consequently, of incomplete operations and responses) for the entire sequence β.   □

Having defined the safety properties for atomic objects—well-formedness and atomicity—we now turn to liveness properties. The liveness properties we consider are termination conditions similar to those we gave for the agreement problem, in Section 12.1. The simplest requirement is for *failure-free* executions, that is, those executions in which no *stop* event occurs.

Failure-free termination: In any fair failure-free execution of $A \times U$, every invocation has a response.

With this one liveness property, we can define "atomic objects." Namely, we say that A is an *atomic object* of variable type $\mathcal{T}$ if it guarantees the well-formedness condition, the atomicity condition for $\mathcal{T}$, and the failure-free termination condition, for all collections of users.

Note that if we wanted to consider only the failure-free case, then we could simplify the statement of the atomicity condition, because there would never be any need to consider incomplete operations. The reason we have given the more complicated statement of the atomicity condition is that we shall also consider failures.

As for the mutual exclusion problem in Section 10.2, it is possible to reformulate the entire definition of an atomic object equivalently in terms of a trace property P. This time, $sig(P)$ includes all the external interface actions of the atomic object, including the *stop* actions as well as the invocation and response actions, and $traces(P)$ expresses well-formedness, atomicity, and failure-free termination. Then an automaton A with the right interface is an atomic object of type $\mathcal{T}$ exactly if, for all collections of users, $fairtraces(A \times U) \subseteq traces(P)$.

We also consider some stronger termination conditions involving fault-tolerance.

Wait-free termination: In any fair execution of $A \times U$, every invocation on a non-failing port has a response.

That is, any port on which no failure occurs provides responses for all invocations, regardless of the failures that occur on any of the other ports. We generalize this property to describe termination in the presence of any number of failures.

f-failure termination, $0 \le f \le n$: In any fair execution of $A \times U$ in which *stop* events occur on at most f ports, every invocation on a non-failing port has a response.

Failure-free termination and wait-free termination are the special cases of the f-failure termination condition where f is equal to 0 and n, respectively. A further generalization allows us to talk about the failure of any particular set of ports.

I-failure termination, $I \subseteq \{1, \dots, n\}$: In every fair execution of $A \times U$ in which the only *stop* events occur on ports in I, every invocation on a non-failing port has a response.

Thus, f-failure termination is the same as I-failure termination for all sets I of ports of size at most f. We say that A *guarantees wait-free termination*, *guarantees I-failure termination*, and so on, provided that it guarantees the corresponding condition for all collections of users.

We close this section with a simple example of a shared memory system that is an atomic object.

Example 13.1.4   A read/increment atomic object

We define the *read/increment* variable type to have $\mathbb{N}$ as its domain, 0 as its initial value, and *read* and *increment* as its operations.

Let A be a shared memory system with n processes in which each port i supports both *read* and *increment* operations. A has n shared read/write registers $x(i)$, $1 \le i \le n$, each with domain $\mathbb{N}$ and initial value 0. Shared variable $x(i)$ is writable by process i and readable by all processes.

When an *increment$_i$* input occurs on port i, process i simply increments its own shared variable, $x(i)$. It can do this using only a *write* operation, by remembering the value of $x(i)$ in its local state. When a *read$_i$* occurs on port i, process i reads all the shared variables $x(j)$ one at a time, in any order, and returns the sum.

Then it is not hard to see that A is a read/increment atomic object and that it guarantees wait-free termination. For example, to see the atomicity condition, consider any execution of $A \times U$. Let Φ be the set of incomplete *increment* operations for which a *write* occurs on a shared variable. For each *increment* operation π that is either completed or is in Φ, place the serialization point $*_\pi$ at the point of the *write*.

Now, note that any completed (high-level) *read* operation π returns a value v that is *no less than* the sum of all the $x(i)$'s when the *read* is invoked and *no greater than* the sum of all the $x(i)$'s when the *read* completes. Since each *increment* operation only increases this sum by 1, there must be some point within π's interval at which the sum of the $x(i)$'s is exactly equal to the return value v. We place the serialization point $*_\pi$ at this point. These choices allow the shrinking needed to show atomicity.

13.1.2   A Canonical Wait-Free Atomic Object Automaton

In this subsection we give an example of an atomic object automaton C for a given variable type $\mathcal{T}$ and given external interface. Automaton C guarantees wait-free termination. C is highly nondeterministic and is sometimes regarded as a "canonical wait-free atomic object automaton" for the given type and external interface. It can be used to help show that other automata are wait-free atomic objects.

C automaton (informal):

C maintains an internal copy of a shared variable of type $\mathcal{T}$, initialized to the initial value v_0. It also has two buffers, *inv-buffer* for pending invocations and *resp-buffer* for pending responses, both initially empty.

Finally, it keeps track of the ports on which a *stop* action has occurred, in a set *stopped*, initially empty.

When an invocation arrives, C simply records it in *inv-buffer*. At any time, C can remove any pending invocation from *inv-buffer* and perform the requested operation on the internal copy of the shared variable. When it does this, it puts the resulting response in *resp-buffer*. Also at any time, C can remove any pending response from *resp-buffer* and convey the response to the user.

A $stop_i$ event just adds i to *stopped*, which enables a special $dummy_i$ action having no effect. It does not, however, disable the other locally controlled actions involving i. All the locally controlled actions involving each port i, including the $dummy_i$ action, are grouped into one task. This means that after a $stop_i$, actions involving i are permitted (but not required) to cease.

More precisely,

C automaton (formal):

Signature:

Input:
    a_i's as in the given external interface
    $stop_i$, $1 \leq i \leq n$
Output:
    b_i's as in the given external interface

Internal:
    $perform(a)_i$, a_i in the external interface,
    $1 \leq i \leq n$
    $dummy_i$, $1 \leq i \leq n$

States:

val, a value in V, initially v_0
inv-buffer, a set of pairs (i, a), for a_i in the external interface
resp-buffer, a set of pairs (i, b), for b_i in the external interface
stopped $\subseteq \{1, \ldots, n\}$, initially empty

Transitions:

a_i
    Effect:
        inv-buffer := *inv-buffer* $\cup \{(i, a)\}$

$perform(a)_i$
    Precondition:
        $(i, a) \in$ *inv-buffer*
    Effect:
        inv-buffer := *inv-buffer* $- \{(i, a)\}$
        $(b, val) := f(a, val)$
        resp-buffer := *resp-buffer* $\cup \{(i, b)\}$

b_i
  Precondition:
   $(i, b) \in resp\text{-}buffer$
  Effect:
   $resp\text{-}buffer := resp\text{-}buffer - \{(i, b)\}$

$stop_i$
  Effect:
   $stopped := stopped \cup \{i\}$

$dummy_i$
  Precondition:
   $i \in stopped$
  Effect:
   none

Tasks:
for every i:
 $\{perform(a)_i : a_i \text{ is an input}\} \cup \{b_i : b_i \text{ is an output}\} \cup \{dummy_i\}$

Theorem 13.3 *C is an atomic object with the given type and external interface, guaranteeing wait-free termination (for all collections of users).*

Proof Sketch. Well-formedness is straightforward. To see wait-freedom, consider any fair execution α of $C \times U$ and suppose that there are no failures on port i in α. Then the $dummy_i$ action is never enabled in α. The fairness of α then implies that every invocation on port i triggers a $perform_i$ event and a subsequent response.

It remains to show atomicity. Consider any execution α of $C \times U$. Let Φ be the set of incomplete operations for which a *perform* occurs in α. Assign a serialization point $*_\pi$ to each operation π that is either completed in α or is in Φ: place $*_\pi$ at the point of the *perform*. Also, for each $\pi \in \Phi$, select the response returned by the *perform* as the response for the operation. These choices allow the shrinking needed to show atomicity.   □

C can be used to help verify that other automata are also wait-free atomic objects, as follows:

Theorem 13.4 *Suppose that A is an I/O automaton with the same external interface as C. Suppose that fairtraces$(A \times U) \subseteq$ fairtraces$(C \times U)$ for every composition U of user automata. Then A is an atomic object guaranteeing wait-free termination.*

Proof Sketch. Follows from Theorem 13.3. For the well-formedness and atomicity, we use the fact that the combination of these two conditions is a safety property (Theorem 13.1), plus the fact that every finite trace can be extended to a fair trace (Theorem 8.7). The wait-freedom condition follows immediately from the definitions.   □

We also have a converse to Theorem 13.4, which says that every fair trace that is allowed for a wait-free atomic object is actually generated by C:

Theorem 13.5 *Suppose that A is an I/O automaton with the same external interface as C. Suppose that A is an atomic object guaranteeing wait-free termination. Then fairtraces$(A \times U) \subseteq$ fairtraces$(C \times U)$, for every composition U of user automata.*

Proof. The proof is left as an exercise. □

13.1.3 Composition of Atomic Objects

In this subsection, we give a theorem that says that the composition of atomic objects (using ordinary I/O automaton composition, defined in Section 8.2.1) is also an atomic object. Recall the definitions of *compatible* variable types and *composition* of variable types from the end of Section 9.4.

Theorem 13.6 *Let $\{A_j\}_{j \in J}$ be a countable collection of atomic objects having compatible variable types $\{\mathcal{T}_j\}_{j \in J}$ and all having the same set of ports $\{1, \dots, n\}$. Then the composition $A = \prod_{j \in J} A_j$ is an atomic object having variable type $\mathcal{T} = \prod_{j \in J} \mathcal{T}_j$ and having ports $\{1, \dots, n\}$.*
Furthermore, if every A_j guarantees I-failure termination (for all collections of users), then so does A.

In atomic object A, port i handles all the invocations and responses that are handled on port i of any of the A_j. According to the definition of composition, the state of A has a piece for each A_j. The invocations and responses that are derived from A_j only involve the piece of the state of A associated with A_j. The $stop_i$ actions, however, affect all parts of the state. We leave the proof of Theorem 13.6 for an exercise.

13.1.4 Atomic Objects versus Shared Variables

The definition of an atomic object says that its traces "look like" traces of a sequentially accessed shared variable of the underlying type. What good is this?

The most important fact about atomic objects, from the point of view of system construction, is that it is possible to substitute them for shared variables in a shared memory system. This permits modular construction of systems: it is possible first to design a shared memory system and then to replace the shared variables by arbitrary atomic objects of the given types. Under certain circumstances, the resulting system "behaves in the same way" as the original shared memory system, as far as the users can tell.

In this section, we describe this substitution technique. First we give some technical conditions on the original shared memory system that are required for the replacement to work correctly. Next, we give the substitution construction. Finally, we define the sense in which the resulting system behaves in the same way as the original system and prove that, with the given conditions, the resulting system really does behave in the same way. Although the basic ideas are reasonably simple, there are a few details that have to be handled carefully in order to make the substitution technique work out right.

We begin with A, an arbitrary algorithm in the shared memory model of Chapter 9. We assume that A interacts with user automata U_i, $1 \leq i \leq n$. We permit each process i of A to have any number of tasks. We also include $stop_i$ actions, as discussed in Section 9.6, and assume that each $stop_i$ event permanently disables all the tasks of process i.

Now for the technical conditions we mentioned above. Consider A in combination with any collection of user automata U_i. We assume that for each port i, there is a function $turn_i$ that, for any finite execution α of the combined system, yields either the value $system$ or $user$. This is supposed to indicate whose turn it is to take the next step, after α. Specifically, we require that if $turn_i(\alpha) = system$, then U_i has no $output\ step$ enabled in its state after α, while if $turn_i(\alpha) = user$, then process i of A has no $output\ or\ internal\ step$, that is, no locally controlled step, enabled in its state after α.

For example, all the mutual exclusion algorithms in Chapter 10 and all the resource-allocation algorithms in Chapter 11 satisfy these conditions (if we add the $stop$ actions). In those cases, $turn_i(\alpha) = system$ for any α after which U_i is in the trying or exit region, and $turn_i(\alpha) = user$ if U_i is in the critical or remainder region. In fact, the required conditions are implied by the restriction on process activity assumed near the end of Section 10.2 and at the end of Section 11.1.2.

For consensus algorithms, as studied in Chapter 12, we may define $turn_i(\alpha) = system$ for any α that contains an $init_i$ event, and $turn_i(\alpha) = user$ otherwise. Then to satisfy the conditions we need here, we would have to add a restriction, namely, that process i cannot do anything before an $init_i$ occurs. This condition is satisfied by the only algorithm in Chapter 12, $RMWAgreement$.

Now we give the substitution. Suppose that for each shared variable x of A, we are given an atomic object automaton B_x of the same type and the appropriate external interface. That is, B_x has ports $1, \ldots, n$, one for each process of A. On each port, it allows all invocations and responses that are used by process i in its interactions with shared variable x in algorithm A. It also has $stop_i$ inputs, one for each port, as usual.

Then we define $Trans(A)$, the transformed version of A that uses the atomic objects B_x in place of its shared variables, to be the following automaton:

$Trans(A)$ automaton:

$Trans(A)$ is a composition of I/O automata, one for each process i and one for each shared variable x of algorithm A. For each variable x, the automaton is the atomic object automaton B_x. For each process i, the automaton is P_i, defined as follows.

The inputs of P_i are the inputs of A on port i plus the responses of each B_x on port i plus the $stop_i$ action. The outputs of P_i are the outputs of A on port i plus the invocations for each B_x on port i.

P_i's steps simulate those of process i of A directly, with the following exceptions: When process i of A performs an access to shared variable x, P_i instead issues the appropriate invocation to B_x. After it does this, it suspends its activity, awaiting a response by B_x to the invocation. When a response arrives, P_i resumes simulating process i of A as usual. There is a task of P_i corresponding to each task of process i of A.

If a $stop_i$ event occurs, all tasks of P_i are thereafter disabled.

Example 13.1.5 A and $Trans(A)$

Consider a two-process shared memory system A that is supposed to solve some sort of consensus problem, using two read/write shared variables, x and y. We assume that process 1 writes x and reads y, and process 2 writes y and reads x. The interface between each U_i and A consists of actions of the form $init(v)_i$, which are outputs of U_i and inputs of A, and actions of the form $decide(v)_i$, which are outputs of A and inputs of U_i. In addition, $stop_i$, $i \in \{1, 2\}$ is an input of A. The architecture of this system is depicted in Figure 13.5, part (a).

The architecture of the transformed system $Trans(A)$ is depicted in part (b). Note the external interfaces of the automata B_x and B_y. For example, B_x has inputs $write(v)_1$ and $read_2$ and outputs ack_1 and v_2.[2] B_x also has inputs $stop_1$ and $stop_2$, which are *identified with* the $stop_1$ input to P_1 and the $stop_2$ input to P_2, respectively. This means, for example, that $stop_1$ simultaneously disables all tasks of P_1 and also has whatever effect $stop_1$ has on the implementation B_x.

---

[2]For the purpose of disambiguation, such invocation and response actions could also be subscripted with the name of the object, here x and y. We avoid this detail in this example since there happens to be no ambiguity here.

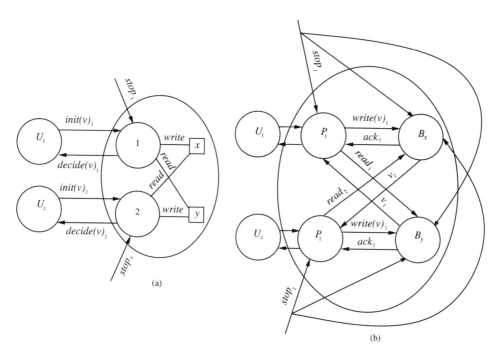

Figure 13.5: Transformation of a shared memory system to include atomic objects.

Now we give a theorem describing what is preserved by transformation *Trans*. Theorem 13.7 first describes conditions that hold for any execution α of A. Execution α does not have to be fair for these conditions to hold. These conditions say that α looks to the users like an execution α' of A. Moreover, the same *stop* events occur in α and α', although we allow for the possibility that the *stop* events could occur in different positions in the two executions.

Theorem 13.7 then goes on to identify some conditions under which the simulated execution α' of the A system is guaranteed to be a *fair* execution. As you would expect, one of the conditions is that α' is itself a fair execution of the *Trans*(A) system. But this is not enough—we also need to make sure that the object automata B_x do not cause processing to stop. So we include two other conditions that together ensure that this does not happen, namely, that all the failures that occur in α are confined to a particular set I of ports and that all the object automata B_x can tolerate failures on I (formally, they guarantee I-failure termination).

Theorem 13.7 *Suppose that α is any execution of the system Trans(A) $\times$ U. Then there is an execution α' of $A \times U$ such that the following conditions hold:*

    1. α and α' are indistinguishable[3] to U.

    2. For each i, a $stop_i$ occurs in α exactly if a $stop_i$ occurs in α'.

Moreover, if α is a fair execution, if every i for which $stop_i$ appears in α is in I, and if every B_x guarantees I-failure termination (for all collections of users), then α' is also a fair execution.

Proof Sketch. We modify α to get α' as follows. First, since each B_x is an atomic object, we can insert a serialization point $*_\pi$ in α between the invocation and response of each completed operation π on B_x and also after the invocation of each of a subset Φ of the incomplete operations on B_x. We also obtain responses for all the operations in Φ. These serialization points and responses can be guaranteed to satisfy the "shrinking" property described in the atomicity condition.

    Next, we move the invocation and response events for each completed operation π on B_x so that they are adjacent and occur exactly at $*_\pi$. Also, for each incomplete operation π in Φ—that is, each incomplete operation that has been assigned a serialization point—we place the invocation, together with the newly manufactured response, at $*_\pi$. And for each incomplete operation that is not in Φ—that is, each incomplete operation that has not been assigned a serialization point—we simply remove the invocation event. There is one additional technicality: if any $stop_i$ event in α occurs after an invocation by process i and before the serialization point to which the invocation is moved, then that $stop_i$ event is also moved to the serialization point, just after the invocation and response. We move, add, and remove events in this way for all shared variables x.

    We claim that it is possible to move all the events that we have moved in this construction without changing the order of events of any P_i (with one technical exception: a response to P_i by some B_x may be moved ahead of a $stop_i$). This follows from two facts. First, by construction, P_i performs no locally controlled actions while it is waiting for a response to an invocation. And second, while P_i is waiting for a response, it is the *system's turn* to take steps. This means that U_i will not perform any output steps, so P_i will receive no inputs.

    Similarly, we claim that we can add the responses we have added and remove the invocations we have removed in this construction without otherwise affecting the behavior of P_i. This is because if P_i performs an incomplete operation in α, it does not do anything after that operation. It does not matter if P_i stops just before issuing the invocation, while waiting for a response, or just after receiving the response.

---

[3]We use the definition of *indistinguishable* given in Section 8.7.

Since we have not changed anything significant by this motion, addition, and removal of events, we can simply fill in the states of the processes P_i as in α. (A technical exception: A response to P_i moved before a $stop_i$ might cause a different change in the state of P_i than it did in α.) The result is a new execution, α_1, also of the system $Trans(A) \times U$. Moreover, it is clear that α and α_1 are indistinguishable to U and have $stop$ events for the same ports.

Now, α_1 is an execution of $Trans(A) \times U$, which is not exactly what we need; rather, we need an execution of the system $A \times U$. But notice that in α_1, all the invocations and responses for the object automata B_x occur in consecutive matching pairs. So we replace those pairs by instantaneous accesses to the corresponding shared variables and thereby obtain an execution α' of the system $A \times U$. Then α and α' are indistinguishable to U and have $stop$ events for the same ports. This proves the first half of the theorem.

For the second half, suppose that α is a *fair* execution of $Trans(A) \times U$, that $I \subseteq \{1, \ldots, n\}$, that every i for which $stop_i$ appears in α is in I, and that each B_x guarantees I-failure termination. Then the only $stop_i$ inputs received by any B_x must be for ports $i \in I$. Thus, since every B_x guarantees I-failure termination, it must be that every B_x provides responses for every invocation by a process P_i for which no $stop_i$ event occurs in α. This fact, combined with the fairness assumption for processes P_i, is enough to imply that α' is a fair execution of $A \times U$. $\square$

Thus, Theorem 13.7 implies that any algorithm for the shared memory model (with some simple restrictions) can be transformed to work with atomic objects instead of shared variables and that the users cannot tell the difference.

We give as a corollary the special case of Theorem 13.7 where the atomic objects B_x all guarantee wait-free termination. In this case, we can conclude that α' is fair just by assuming that α is fair.

Corollary 13.8 *Suppose that all the B_x guarantee wait-free termination. Suppose that α is any fair execution of $Trans(A) \times U$. Then there is a fair execution α' of $A \times U$ such that the following conditions hold:*

1. *α and α' are indistinguishable to U.*

2. *For each i, a $stop_i$ occurs in α exactly if a $stop_i$ occurs in α'.*

Proof.   Immediate from Theorem 13.7, letting $I = \{1, \ldots, n\}$. $\square$

In the special case where A is itself an atomic object, Theorem 13.7 implies that $Trans(A)$ is also an atomic object. Including failure considerations, we obtain the following corollary.

Corollary 13.9 *Suppose that A and all the B_x's are atomic objects guaranteeing I-failure termination. Then $Trans(A)$ is also an atomic object guaranteeing I-failure termination.*

Proof. First let α be any execution of $Trans(A)$ and a collection of users U_i. Then Theorem 13.7 yields an execution α' of $A \times U$ such that α and α' are indistinguishable to U. Since A is an atomic object, α' satisfies the well-formedness and atomicity properties. Since both of these are properties of the external interface of U, and α and α' are indistinguishable to U, α also satisfies the well-formedness and atomicity properties.

It remains to consider the I-failure termination condition. Let α be any fair execution of $Trans(A)$ and a collection of users U_i such that every i for which $stop_i$ appears in α is in I. Since all the B_x guarantee I-failure termination, Theorem 13.7 yields a fair execution α' of $A \times U$, such that α and α' are indistinguishable to U and α and α' contain *stop* events for the same set of ports. Thus, every i for which $stop_i$ appears in α' is in I.

Now consider any invocation in α on a port i for which no $stop_i$ event occurs in α—that is, on a non-failing port. Since α and α' are indistinguishable to U, the same invocation appears in α'. Because A guarantees I-failure termination, there is a corresponding response event in α'. Then, since α and α' are indistinguishable to U, this response also appears in α. This is enough to show I-failure termination. $\qquad\square$

Hierarchical construction of shared memory systems.   In the special case where each atomic object B_x is itself a shared memory system, we claim that $Trans(A)$ can also be viewed as a shared memory system. Namely, each process i of $Trans(A)$ (viewed as a shared memory system) is a combination of process P_i of $Trans(A)$ and the processes indexed by i in all of the shared memory systems B_x. This combination is not exactly an I/O automaton composition, because the processes in the B_x's are not I/O automata. However, the combination is easy to describe: the state set of process i of $Trans(A)$ is just the Cartesian product of the state set of P_i and the state sets of all the processes indexed by i in all the B_x's, and likewise for the start states. The actions associated with process i of $Trans(A)$ are just the actions of all the component processes i, and similarly for the tasks.

The situation is depicted in Figure 13.6. Part (a) shows $Trans(A)$, including the shared memory systems B_x plugged in for all the shared variables x of A. (For simplicity, we have not drawn the *stop* input arrows.) All the shaded processes are associated with port 1. Part (b) shows the same system as in part (a), with

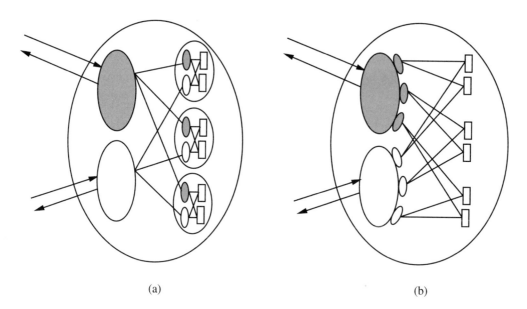

(a)   (b)

Figure 13.6: Hierarchical construction of a shared memory system.

the processes that are to be combined grouped together. Thus, all the shaded processes from part (a) are now combined into a single process 1 in part (b).

By the definition of *Trans(A)*, the effect of a *stop$_i$* event in the system of part (a) is to immediately stop all tasks of all the processes associated with port i—the tasks of P_i as well as the tasks of all the processes i of the B_x's. This is the same as saying that *stop$_i$* stops all tasks of the composed process i in the system of part (b), which is just what *stop$_i$* is supposed to do when that system is regarded as a shared memory system.

Hierarchical construction of atomic objects.   Finally, consider the very special case where shared memory system A is an atomic object guaranteeing I-failure termination and each atomic object B_x is a shared memory system that guarantees I-failure termination. Then Corollary 13.9 and the previous paragraph imply that *Trans(A)* is an atomic object guaranteeing I-failure termination and also that it is a shared memory system. This observation says that two successive layers of atomic object implementations in the shared memory model can be collapsed into one.

13.1.5 A Sufficient Condition for Showing Atomicity

Before presenting specific atomic object constructions, we give a sufficient condition for showing that a shared memory system guarantees the atomicity condition. This lemma enables us to avoid reasoning explicitly about incomplete operations in many of our proofs that objects are atomic.

For this lemma, we suppose that A is a shared memory system with an external interface appropriate for an atomic object for variable type $\mathcal{T}$. Also, we suppose that U_i, $1 \leq i \leq n$, is any collection of users for A; as usual, $U = \prod U_i$.

Lemma 13.10 *Suppose that the combined system $A \times U$ guarantees well-formedness and failure-free termination. Suppose that every (finite or infinite) execution α of $A \times U$ containing no incomplete operations satisfies the atomicity property. Then the same is true for every execution of $A \times U$, including those with incomplete operations.*

Proof. Let α be an arbitrary finite or infinite execution of the combined system $A \times U$, possibly containing incomplete operations. We must show that α satisfies the atomicity property, that is, that $\alpha|ext(U)$ satisfies the atomicity property.

If α is finite, then the handling of *stop* events in a shared memory system implies that there is a finite failure-free execution α_1, obtained by removing the *stop* events from α (and possibly modifying some state changes associated with inputs at ports on which a *stop* has occurred), such that $\alpha_1|ext(U) = \alpha|ext(U)$. By basic properties of I/O automata (in particular, Theorem 8.7), α_1 can be extended to a fair failure-free execution α_2 of $A \times U$. Since A guarantees failure-free termination, every operation in α_2 is completed. Then, by assumption, α_2 satisfies the atomicity property, that is, $\alpha_2|ext(U)$ satisfies the atomicity property. But $\alpha_1|ext(U)$ is a prefix of $\alpha_2|ext(U)$. Since, by Theorem 13.1, atomicity combined with well-formedness is a safety property and hence is prefix-closed, it follows that $\alpha_1|ext(U)$ satisfies the atomicity property. Since $\alpha|ext(U) = \alpha_1|ext(U)$, we have that $\alpha|ext(U)$ satisfies the atomicity property, as needed.

On the other hand, suppose that α is infinite. By what we have just proved, any finite prefix α_1 of α has the property that $\alpha_1|ext(U)$ satisfies the atomicity property. But $\alpha|ext(U)$ is just the limit of the sequences of the form $\alpha_1|ext(U)$. Since, by Theorem 13.1, atomicity combined with well-formedness is a safety property and hence is limit-closed, it follows that $\alpha|ext(U)$ satisfies the atomicity property, as needed. □

13.2   Implementing Read-Modify-Write Atomic Objects in Terms of Read/Write Variables

We consider the problem of implementing a read-modify-write atomic object in the shared memory model with read/write shared variables. (See Section 9.4 for the definition of a read-modify-write variable type.) To be specific, we fix an arbitrary n and suppose that the read-modify-write object being implemented has n ports, each of which can support arbitrary update functions as inputs.

If all we require is an atomic object and we are not concerned about tolerating failures, then there are simple solutions. For instance,

> ### *RMWfromRW* algorithm:
>
> The latest value of the read-modify-write variable corresponding to the object being implemented is kept in a read/write shared variable x. Using a set of read/write shared variables different from x, the processes perform the trying part of a lockout-free mutual exclusion algorithm (for example, *PetersonNP* from Section 10.5.2) whenever they want to perform operations on the atomic object. When a process i enters the critical region of the mutual exclusion algorithm, it obtains exclusive access to x. Then process i performs its *read-modify-write* operation using a *read* step followed by a separate *write* step. After completing these steps, process i performs the exit part of the mutual exclusion algorithm.

However, this algorithm is not fault-tolerant: a process might fail while it is in its critical region, thereby preventing any other process from accessing the simulated read-modify-write variable. In fact, this limitation is not an accident. We give an impossibility result, even for the case where only a single failure is to be tolerated.

Theorem 13.11 *There does not exist a shared memory system using read/write shared variables that implements a read-modify-write atomic object and guarantees 1-failure termination.*

Proof.   Suppose for the sake of contradiction that there is such a system, say B. Let A be the *RMWAgreement* algorithm for agreement in the read-modify-write shared memory model, given in Section 12.3. By Theorem 12.9, A guarantees wait-free termination and hence guarantees 1-failure termination (as defined for agreement algorithms in Section 12.1). Now we apply the transformation of Section 13.1.4 to A, using B in place of the single shared read-modify-write variable of A. Let *Trans*(A) denote the resulting system.

Claim 13.12 *Trans(A) solves the agreement problem of Chapter 12 and guarantees 1-failure termination.*

Proof. The proof of this is similar to that of Corollary 13.9. First let α be any execution of *Trans(A)* and a collection of users U_i. Then Theorem 13.7 yields an execution α' of $A \times U$ such that α and α' are indistinguishable to U. Since A solves the agreement problem, α' satisfies the well-formedness, agreement, and validity properties. Then since α and α' are indistinguishable to U, α also satisfies the well-formedness, agreement, and validity properties.

It remains to consider the 1-failure termination condition. Let α be any fair execution of *Trans(A)* and a collection of users U_i, in which *init* events occur on all ports and in which there is a *stop* event for at most one port. Since B guarantees 1-failure termination, Theorem 13.7 yields a fair execution α' of $A \times U$ such that α and α' are indistinguishable to U and contain *stop* events for the same set of ports. Thus, *init* events occur on all ports in α', and there is a *stop* event for at most one port in α'.

Now consider any port i with no *stop$_i$* event in α. Since α and α' contain *stop* events for the same ports, there is also no *stop$_i$* event in α'. Because A guarantees 1-failure termination, there is a *decide$_i$* event in α'. Then, since α and α' are indistinguishable to U, this *decide$_i$* also appears in α. This is enough to show 1-failure termination. $\qquad\square$

However, by the paragraph at the end of Section 13.1, *Trans(A)* is itself a shared memory system in the read/write shared memory model. But then *Trans(A)* contradicts Theorem 12.8, the impossibility of agreement with 1-failure termination in the read/write shared memory model.

13.3 Atomic Snapshots of Shared Memory

In the rest of this chapter, we consider the implementation of particular types of atomic objects in terms of other types of atomic objects, or, equivalently, in terms of shared variables. This section is devoted to snapshot atomic objects, and the next is devoted to read/write atomic objects.

In the read/write shared memory model, it would be useful for a process to be able to take an *instantaneous snapshot* of the entire state of shared memory. Of course, the read/write model does not directly provide this capability—it only permits reads on individual shared variables.

In this section, we consider the implementation of such a snapshot. We formulate the problem as that of implementing a particular type of atomic object called a *snaphot* atomic object, using the read/write shared memory model. The variable type underlying a snapshot atomic object has as its domain V the set of vectors of some fixed length over a more basic domain W. The operations are of two kinds: writes to individual vector components, which we call *update operations*, and reads of the entire vector, which we call *snap operations*. A snapshot atomic object can simplify the task of programming a read/write system by allowing the processes to view the entire shared memory as a vector accessible by these powerful operations.

We start with a description of the problem, then give a simple solution that uses read/write shared variables of unbounded size. Then we show how the construction can be modified to work with bounded-size shared variables. Section 13.4.5 contains an application of snapshot atomic objects in the implementation of read/write atomic objects.

13.3.1   The Problem

We first define the variable type $\mathcal{T}$ to which the snapshot atomic object will correspond; we call this a *snapshot variable type*.

The definition begins with an underlying domain W with initial value w_0. The domain V of $\mathcal{T}$ is then the set of vectors of elements of W of a fixed length m. The initial value v_0 is the vector in which every component has the value w_0. There are invocations of the form $update(i, w)$, where $1 \leq i \leq m$ and $w \in W$, with response ack, and an invocation $snap$, with responses $v \in V$. An $update(i, w)$ invocation causes component i of the current vector to be set to the value w and triggers an ack response. A $snap$ invocation causes no change to the vector but triggers a response containing the current value of the entire vector.

Next we define the external interface that we will consider. We assume that there are exactly $n = m + p$ ports, where m is the fixed length of the vectors and p is some arbitrary positive integer. The first m ports are the *update* ports, and the remaining p ports are the *snap* ports. On each port i, $1 \leq i \leq m$, we permit only invocations of the form $update(i, w)$—that is, only *updates* to the ith vector component are handled on port i. We sometimes abbreviate the redundant notation $update(i, w)_i$, which indicates an invocation of $update(i, w)$ on port i, as simply $update(w)_i$. On each port i, $m + 1 \leq i \leq n$, we permit only *snap* invocations. See Figure 13.7.

Notice that we are considering a special case of the general problem, where *updates* to each vector component arrive only at a single designated port and hence arrive sequentially. It is also possible to consider a more general case, where many ports allow *updates* to the same vector component. Of course, we

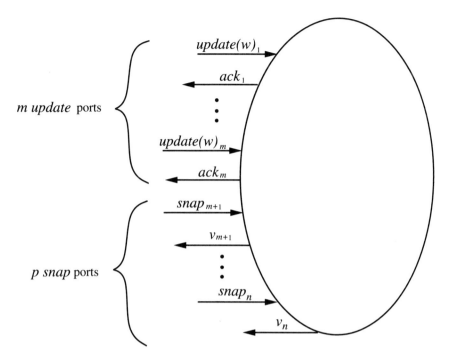

Figure 13.7: External interface of a snapshot atomic object (*stop* actions not depicted).

could also consider the case where *update* and *snap* operations are allowed to occur on the same port.

We consider implementing the atomic object corresponding to this variable type and external interface using a shared memory system with n processes, one per port. We assume that all the shared variables are 1-writer/n-reader read/write shared variables. The implementations we describe guarantee wait-free termination.

13.3.2 An Algorithm with Unbounded Variables

The *UnboundedSnapshot algorithm* uses m 1-writer/n-reader read/write shared variables $x(i)$, $1 \le i \le m$. Each variable $x(i)$ can be written by process i (the one connected to port i, which is the port for $update(i, w)$ operations) and can be read by all processes. The architecture appears in Figure 13.8. Each variable $x(i)$ holds values each of which consists of an element of W plus some additional values needed by the algorithm. One of these additional values is an unbounded integer "tag."

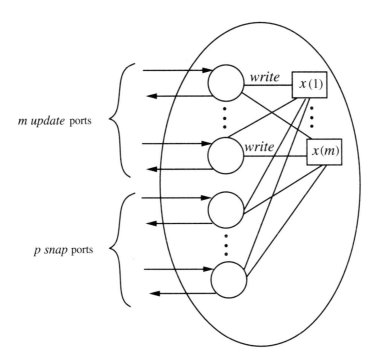

Figure 13.8: Architecture for *UnboundedSnapshot* algorithm.

In the *UnboundedSnapshot* algorithm, each process i writes the values that it receives in *update*$_i$ invocations into the shared variable $x(i)$. A process performing a *snap* operation must somehow obtain consistent values from all the shared variables, that is, values that appear to have coexisted in the shared memory at some moment in time. The way it does this is based on two simple observations.

Observation 1: Suppose that whenever a process i performs an *update*$(w)_i$ operation, it writes not only the value w into $x(i)$, but also a "tag" that uniquely identifies the *update*. Then, if a process j that is attempting to perform a *snap* operation reads all the shared variables twice, with the second set of *read*s starting after the first set of *read*s is finished, and if it finds the tag in each variable $x(i)$ to be the same in the first and second set of *read*s, then the common vector of values returned in the two sets of *read*s is in fact a vector that appears in shared memory at some point during the interval of the *snap* operation. In particular, this vector is the vector of values at any point after the completion of the first set of *read*s and before the start of the second set.

Observation 1 suggests the following simple algorithm. Each process i performing an *update*(w) operation writes v into $x(i)$, along with a unique local tag, obtained by starting with 1 for the first *update* at i and incrementing for each successive *update* at i.

Each process j performing a *snap* repeatedly performs a set of *reads*, one per shared variable, until two consecutive sets of *reads* are "consistent," that is, they return identical tags for every $x(i)$. When this happens, the vector of values returned by the second set of *reads* (which must be the same as that returned by the first set of *reads*) is returned as the response to the *snap* operation.

It is easy to see that whenever this simple algorithm completes an operation, the response is always "correct," that is, it satisfies the well-formedness and atomicity conditions. However, it fails to guarantee even failure-free termination: a *snap* may never return, even in the absence of process failures, if new *update* operations keep getting invoked while the *snap* is active. A way out of this difficulty is provided by

Observation 2: If process j, while performing repeated sets of *reads* on behalf of a *snap*, ever sees the same variable $x(i)$ with four different tags—say tag_1, tag_2, tag_3, and tag_4—then it knows that some $update_i$ operation is completely contained within the interval of the current *snap*. In particular, the $update_i$ operation that writes tag_3 must be totally contained within the current *snap*.

To see why this is so, we argue first that the *update* that writes tag_3 must begin after the beginning of the *snap*. This is because it begins after the end of the *update* that writes tag_2, and the end of the *update* that writes tag_2 must happen after the beginning of the *snap* interval (since the *snap* sees tag_1).

Second, we argue that the *update* that writes tag_3 must end before the end of the *snap*. This is because it ends before the beginning of the *update* that writes tag_4, and the *snap* sees tag_4.

Observations 1 and 2 suggest the *UnboundedSnapshot* algorithm. It extends the simple algorithm above so that before an *update* process i writes to $x(i)$, it first executes its own *embedded-snap* subroutine, which is just like a *snap*. Then, when it writes its value and tag in $x(i)$, it also places the result of its *embedded-snap* in $x(i)$. A *snap* that fails to discover two sets of *reads* with identical tags despite many repeated attempts can use the result of an *embedded-snap* as a default snapshot value. A more careful description follows. In this description, each shared variable is a record with several fields; we use dot notation to indicate the fields.

UnboundedSnapshot algorithm:

Each shared variable $x(i)$, $1 \le i \le m$, is writable by process i and readable by all processes. It contains the following fields:

$val \in W$, initially w_0
$tag \in \mathbb{N}$, initially 0
$view$, a vector indexed by $\{1, \ldots, m\}$ of elements of W, initially identically w_0

When a $snap_j$ input occurs on port j, $m + 1 \leq j \leq n$, process j behaves as follows. It repeatedly performs sets of $reads$, where a set consists of m $reads$, one $read$ of each shared variable $x(i)$, $1 \leq i \leq m$, in any order. It does this until one of the following happens:

1. Two sets of $reads$ return the same $x(i).tag$ for every i.
   In this case, the $snap$ returns the vector of values $x(i).val$, $1 \leq i \leq m$, returned by the second set of $reads$. (This is the same as the vector returned by the first set of $reads$.)

2. For some i, four distinct values of $x(i).tag$ have been seen.
   In this case, the $snap$ returns the vector of values in $x(i).view$ associated with the third of the four values of $x(i).tag$.

When an $update(w)_i$ input occurs, process i behaves as follows. First, it performs an *embedded-snap*. This involves exactly the same work as is performed by a $snap$, except that the vector determined is recorded locally by process i instead of being returned to the user. Second, process i performs a single *write* to $x(i)$, setting the three fields of $x(i)$ as follows:

1. $x(i).val := w$

2. $x(i).tag$ is set to the smallest unused tag at i.

3. $x(i).view$ is set to the vector returned by the *embedded-snap*.

Finally, process i outputs ack_i.

Theorem 13.13 *The UnboundedSnapshot algorithm is a snapshot atomic object guaranteeing wait-free termination.*

Proof.   The well-formedness condition is clear. Wait-free termination is also easy to see: the key is that every $snap$ and every *embedded-snap* must terminate after performing at most $3m + 1$ sets of $reads$. This is because after $3m + 1$ sets of $reads$, there must either be two consecutive sets with no changes or else some variable $x(i)$ with at least four different tags. In either of these two cases, the operation terminates.

It remains to show the atomicity condition. Fix any execution α of the *UnboundedSnapshot* algorithm plus users. In view of Lemma 13.10, we may assume without loss of generality that α contains no incomplete operations. We describe how to insert serialization points for all operations.

We insert the serialization point for each *update* operation at the point at which its *write* occurs. The insertion of serialization points for *snap* operations is a little more complicated. To describe this insertion, we find it helpful to assign serialization points not just to the *snap* operations but also to the *embedded-snap* operations.

First, consider any *snap* or *embedded-snap* that terminates by finding two consistent sets of *reads*. For each such operation, we insert the serialization point anywhere between the end of the first of its two sets of *reads* and the beginning of its second.

Second, consider those *snap* and *embedded-snap* operations that terminate by finding four different tags in the same variable. We insert serialization points for these operations one by one, in the order of their response events. For each such operation π, note that the vector it returns is the result of an *embedded-snap* ϕ whose interval is totally contained within the interval of operation π. Note that this operation ϕ has already been assigned a serialization point, since it completes earlier than π. We insert the serialization point for π at the same place as that for ϕ.

It is easy to see that all the serialization points are within the required intervals. For the *update* operations and for the *snap* and *embedded-snap* operations that terminate by finding two consistent sets of *reads*, this is obvious. For the *snap* and *embedded-snap* operations that terminate by finding four distinct tags, this can be argued by induction on the number of response events for such operations in α.

It remains to show that the result of shrinking the operation intervals to their respective serialization points is a trace of the underlying snapshot variable type. For this, first note that after any finite prefix α' of α, there is a unique vector in V resulting from the *write* events in α'. Call this the *correct vector* after α'. It is enough to show that every *snap* operation returns the correct vector after the prefix of α up to the operation's serialization point. More strongly, we argue that every *snap* and *embedded-snap* operation returns the correct vector for its serialization point.

This is clear for the operations that terminate by finding two consistent sets of *reads*. For the other *snap* and *embedded-snap* operations, we argue this by induction on the number of response events for such operations in α. $\qquad\square$

Complexity analysis. The *UnboundedSnapshot* algorithm uses m shared variables, each of which can take on an unbounded set of values. Even if the underlying domain W is finite, the variables are still unbounded because of the unbounded *tags*. For time complexity, a non-failing process executing a *snap* performs at most $3m + 1$ sets of *read*s, or at most $(3m + 1)m$ shared memory accesses, for a total time that is $O\left(m^2\ell\right)$, where ℓ is an upper bound on process step time. A non-failing process executing an *update* also performs $O\left(m^2\right)$ shared memory accesses, for a total time that is $O\left(m^2\ell\right)$; this is because of its *embedded-snap* operation.

13.3.3 An Algorithm with Bounded Variables*

The main problem with the *UnboundedSnapshot* algorithm is that it uses unbounded-size shared variables to store the unbounded tags. In this subsection, we sketch an improved algorithm called *BoundedSnapshot*, which replaces the unbounded tags with bounded data. In order to achieve this improvement in efficiency, the *BoundedSnapshot* algorithm uses some mechanisms that are more complicated than simple tags.

Note that the unbounded tags are used in the *UnboundedSnapshot* algorithm only for the purpose of allowing processes performing *snap* and *embedded-snap* operations to detect when new *update* operations have taken place. This information could, however, be communicated using a less powerful mechanism than a tag, in particular, using a combination of *handshake bits* and a *toggle bit*.

The handshake bits work as follows. There are now $n + m$ shared variables: variables $x(i), 1 \leq i \leq m$ as in the *UnboundedSnapshot* algorithm, plus new variables $y(j), 1 \leq j \leq n$. Each variable $x(i)$ is writable by update process i and readable by all processes, as before. Each variable $y(j)$, $1 \leq j \leq m$, is writable by update process j (specifically, by the *embedded-snap* part of update process j) and is readable by all update processes, and each variable $y(j)$, $m + 1 \leq j \leq n$, is writable by *snap* process j and readable by all update processes. Note that, unlike in the *UnboundedSnapshot* algorithm, the execution of the *snap* and *embedded-snap* operations in *BoundedSnapshot* involve writing to shared memory.

For each update process i, $1 \leq i \leq m$, there are n pairs of *handshake bits*, one pair per process j. The pair of bits for (i, j) allow process i to tell process j about new updates by process i and also allow process j to acknowledge that it has seen this information. Specifically, $x(i)$ contains a length n vector *comm* of bits, where the element $comm(j)$ in variable $x(i)$—which we denote by $x(i).comm(j)$—is used by process i to communicate with process j about new updates by process i. And $y(j)$ contains a length m vector *ack* of bits, where the element $ack(i)$ in variable $y(j)$—which we denote by $y(j).ack(i)$—is used by process j to acknowledge that it has seen new updates by process i. Thus, the pair of handshake bits for (i, j) are $x(i).comm(j)$ and $y(j).ack(i)$.

The way these handshake bits are used is roughly as follows. When a process i executes an *update(w)*, it begins by reading all the handshake bits $y(j).ack(i)$. Then it performs its *write* to $x(i)$; when it does this, it writes the value w and embedded snap response *view*, as it does in *UnboundedSnapshot*, and in addition writes the handshake bits in *comm*. In particular, for each j, it sets the bit $comm(j)$ to be *unequal* to the value of $y(j).ack(i)$ read at the beginning of the operation.

A process j performing a *snap* or *embedded-snap* repeatedly tries to perform two sets of *read*s, looking for the situation where nothing has changed in between the two sets of *read*s. But this time, changes are detected using the handshake bits rather than integer-valued tags. Specifically, before each attempt to find two consistent sets of *read*s, process j first reads all the handshake bits $x(i).comm(j)$ and sets each handshake bit $y(j).ack(i)$ *equal* to the value of $x(i).comm(j)$ just read. (Thus, the *update* operations attempt to set the handshake bits *unequal* and the *snap* and *embedded-snap* operations attempt to set them *equal.*) Process j looks for changes to the handshake bits $comm(j)$ in between its two sets of *read*s; if it finds such changes on $2m + 1$ separate attempts, then it knows it has seen the results of four separate *update* operations by the same process i and can adopt the vector *view* produced by the third of these operations.

The handshake protocol described so far is simple and is "sound" in the sense that every time a process performing a *snap* or *embedded-snap* detects a change, a new update has in fact occurred. However, it turns out that the handshake is not sufficient to discover every update—it is possible for two consecutive updates by a process i not to be distinguished by some other process j. Consider, for example, the following situation.

Example 13.3.1 Insufficiency of handshake bits

Suppose that at some point during an execution, $x(i).comm(j) = 0$ and $y(j).ack(i) = 1$, that is, the handshake bits used to tell j about i's updates are unequal. Then the following events may occur, in the indicated order. (The actions involving the two processes i and j appear in separate columns.)

$update(w_1)_i$
i reads $y(j).ack(i) = 1$
i writes w_1 and sets $x(i).comm(j) := 0$
ack_i
$update(w_2)_i$
i reads $y(j).ack(i) = 1$
   $snap_j$
   j reads $x(i).comm(j) = 0$
   j sets $y(j).ack(i) := 0$
   j reads $x(i).comm(j) = 0$
i writes w_2 and sets $x(i).comm(j) := 0$
ack_i
   j reads $x(i).comm(j) = 0$ and decides that no updates have
     occurred since its previous *read* of $x(i)$

In this sequence of events, process j performs three *reads* of $x(i).comm(j)$. The first of these is just a preliminary test; the second and third are part of an attempt to find two consistent sets of *reads*. Here, process j determines as a result of its second and third *reads* that no updates have occurred in between. This is erroneous.

To overcome this problem, we augment the handshake protocol with a second mechanism: each $x(i)$ contains an additional *toggle* bit that is flipped by process i during each of its *write* steps. This ensures that each *update* changes the value of the shared variable $x(i)$. In a bit more detail, the protocol works as follows:

BoundedSnapshot algorithm:

Each shared variable $x(i)$, $1 \le i \le m$, is writable by process i and readable by all processes. It contains the following fields:

  val $\in W$, initially w_0
  comm, a vector indexed by $\{1, \dots, n\}$ of $\{0, 1\}$, initially identically 0
  toggle $\in \{0, 1\}$, initially 0
  view, a vector indexed by $\{1, \dots, m\}$ of elements of W, initially identically w_0

Also, each shared variable $y(j)$, $1 \le j \le n$, is writable by process j and readable by processes i, $1 \le i \le m$. It contains the following field:

  ack, a vector indexed by $\{1, \dots, m\}$ of $\{0, 1\}$, initially identically 0

When a $snap_j$ input occurs on port j, $m + 1 \le j \le n$, process j behaves as follows. It repeatedly attempts to obtain two sets of *reads* that look "consistent." Specifically, in each attempt, process j first reads all the relevant handshake bits $x(i).comm(j)$, for all i, $1 \le i \le m$, in any order. Then for each i, process j sets $y(j).ack(i)$ to be equal to the value read in

$x(i).comm(j)$; it does this in a single *write* step. Then process j performs two complete sets of *reads*, the first set finishing before the second set begins. If for every i, $x(i).comm(j)$ and $x(i).toggle$ are identical in the two *reads* of $x(i)$, and, moreover, the common value of $comm(j)$ is the same one that process j read at the beginning of this attempt, then the *snap* returns the vector of values $x(i).val$ obtained in the final set of *reads*. Otherwise, process j records which variables $x(i)$ have changed.

If process j ever records on three separate attempts that the same $x(i)$ has changed, then consider the second of these three attempts. The $snap_j$ operation returns the vector of values in $x(i).view$ obtained in the final *read* of $x(i)$ at that attempt. (It is guaranteed that this vector was written in the course of an *update* operation whose interval is completely contained within the interval of the given $snap_j$.)

When an $update(w)_i$ input occurs on port i, $1 \leq i \leq m$, process i behaves as follows. First, it reads all the relevant handshake bits $y(j).ack(i)$, $1 \leq j \leq n$. Second, it performs an *embedded-snap*, which is the same as a *snap* except that the vector determined is not returned to the user. Third, process i performs a single *write* to $x(i)$, setting the four fields of $x(i)$ as follows:

1. $x(i).val := w$

2. For each j, $x(i).comm(j)$ is set unequal to the value of $y(j).ack(i)$ obtained in the initial *read* of $y(j)$.

3. $x(i).toggle$ is set unequal to its previous value.

4. $x(i).view$ is set to the vector returned by the *embedded-snap*.

Finally, process i outputs ack_i.

Theorem 13.14 *The BoundedSnapshot algorithm is a snapshot atomic object guaranteeing wait-free termination.*

Proof Sketch. Well-formedness and wait-freedom are easy to see, as in the proof of Theorem 13.13 for the *UnboundedSnapshot* algorithm. It remains to show the atomicity condition. The argument is similar to that for *Unbounded-Snapshot*.

Again, we fix execution α and (in view of Lemma 13.10) assume without loss of generality that α contains no incomplete operations. The serialization points are inserted exactly as for the *UnboundedSnapshot* algorithm. For example, for a *snap* or *embedded-snap* operation that terminates by finding two consistent sets of *reads*, we select any point between the end of the first of these two sets and the beginning of the second. As before, it is easy to see that the serialization points occur within the required intervals. It remains to show that the result of shrinking the operation intervals to their respective serialization points is a trace of the snapshot variable type. As before, it is enough to show that every completed *snap* and *embedded-snap* operation returns the correct vector after the prefix of α up to the serialization point.

This time, it is not so easy to show this property for *snap* and *embedded-snap* operations that terminate by finding two consistent sets of *reads*. To show this, it is enough to prove the following claim.

Claim 13.15 *If a snap or embedded-snap terminates by finding two consistent sets of reads, then the following is true for all i. No write event by process i occurs between the read of $x(i)$ in the first set and the read of $x(i)$ in the second set.*

Proof.   By contradiction, using a somewhat detailed operational argument. Suppose that a *snap* on port j terminates by finding two consistent sets of *reads*, yet a *write* event by process i occurs between π_1, the *read* of $x(i)$ in the first set, and π_2, the *read* of $x(i)$ in the second set. (The argument is the same for an *embedded-snap*.) Let ϕ be the last such *write*, that is, the last *write* of $x(i)$ prior to π_2.

By the fact that the two sets of reads are consistent, the values of $x(i).comm(j)$ read in π_1 and π_2 are equal and, moreover, are the same as the value last written in $y(j).ack(i)$ before π_1 (as part of process j's successful attempt to find the consistent sets of *reads*). Let b denote this common value and let π_0 denote this last *write* event. Also by consistency, the values of $x(i).toggle$ read in π_1 and π_2 are equal. Let t denote this common value.

Since ϕ is the last *write* of $x(i)$ prior to π_2, it must be that it sets $x(i).comm(j) := b$ and $x(i).toggle := t$. The *update* operation containing ϕ must contain an earlier *read* event ψ of $y(j)$. By the way *update* operations behave, the value of $y(j).ack(i)$ read by ψ must be $\bar{b}$. (We are using the bar notation here to denote bit complementation.) This implies that ψ must precede π_0.

Thus, the order of the various *read* and *write* events must be the following. (Again, the actions involving the two processes i and j appear in separate columns.)

ψ: A *read* by i sees $y(j).ack(i) = \bar{b}$.
  π_0: A *write* by j sets $y(j).ack(i) := b$.
  π_1: A *read* by j sees $x(i).comm(j) = b$ and $x(i).toggle = t$.
ϕ: A *write* by i sets $x(i).comm(j) := b$ and $x(i).toggle := t$.
  π_2: A *read* by j sees $x(i).comm(j) = b$ and $x(i).toggle = t$.

But note that the *read* event ψ is part of the same *update* operation as the *write* event ϕ. This implies that the two read events π_1 and π_2 must be returning results written by two consecutive *writes* by process i. However, the *toggle* bits returned by π_1 and π_2 are identical, which contradicts the way the *toggle* bits are managed. □

This shows Claim 13.15, which implies that every *snap* or *embedded-snap* operation that terminates by finding two consistent sets of *reads* in fact returns the correct vector after the prefix of α up to the serialization point. For the other *snap* and *embedded-snap* operations, the needed property is argued, as for *UnboundedSnapshot*, by induction on the number of response events for such operations in α.

Complexity analysis. The *BoundedSnapshot* algorithm uses $n + m$ shared variables. Each variable $x(i)$ takes on $|W|^{m+1}2^{n+1}$ values, and each variable $y(j)$ takes on 2^m values. For time complexity, a non-failing process executing a *snap* makes at most $2m + 1$ attempts to find two consistent sets of *reads*. For each attempt, there are at most $4m$ shared memory accesses, for a total time that is $O\left(m^2\ell\right)$. The same bound holds for an *update*.

Using snapshots in programming read/write shared memory systems. Snapshot shared variables represent a powerful type of shared memory. For example, using a single snapshot shared variable, it is possible to simplify considerably the *Bakery* mutual exclusion algorithm of Section 10.7. We leave this for an exercise.

Using the techniques of Section 13.1.4 and a snapshot algorithm such as the ones in this section, an algorithm A that uses snapshot shared variables can be transformed into an algorithm that uses only single-writer/multi-reader read/write shared variables. This transformation requires some simple restrictions on A, as discussed in Section 13.1.4. (Also, technically, the snapshot atomic objects used in the transformation have one port corresponding to each process of A; process i of A might submit both *update* and *snap* operations on the same port i. But there is no problem in modifying the snapshot atomic object external interface and implementations to permit this.)

Read/update/snap variables. A useful variation on a snapshot shared variable, which only supports *update* and *snap* operations, is a read/update/snap shared variable, which supports *read* operations on individual locations in the shared vector in addition to *snap* operations returning the entire vector. Of course, a model using read/update/snap shared variables has no more power than a model using only snapshot variables, because a *read* can be implemented using a *snap*. However, the use of read/update/snap shared variables can allow more efficient programming, because it is possible to implement a read/update/snap atomic object so that the *reads* are very fast. We leave this for an exercise.

13.4   Read/Write Atomic Objects

Read/write shared variables (registers) are among the most basic building blocks used in shared memory multiprocessors. In this section, we consider the implementation of powerful multi-writer/multi-reader registers in terms of less powerful registers, such as single-writer/single-reader registers. More precisely, we consider the problem of implementing multi-writer/multi-reader read/write atomic objects using single-writer/single-reader shared variables.

13.4.1   The Problem

Fix a domain V and initial value $v_0 \in V$.

In Example 13.1.1, we described an external interface for a 1-writer/2-reader read/write atomic object for domain V. In general, an m-writer/p-reader read/write atomic object for domain V has an analogous external interface, where ports $1, \ldots, m$ are *write* ports and ports $m + 1, \ldots, m + p$ are *read* ports. We again let $n = m + p$.

Since we consider the implementation of read/write atomic objects in terms of read/write shared variables, we need a way of distinguishing the high-level read and write operations that are submitted by the users at the ports from the low-level read and write operations that are performed on the read/write shared variables. We use the convention of capitalizing the names of the high-level operations. Thus, associated with port i, $1 \le i \le m$, there are $WRITE(v)_i$ inputs, $v \in V$, and ACK_i outputs, and associated with port j, $m + 1 \le j \le n$, there are $READ_j$ inputs and v_j outputs, $v \in V$. (We don't attempt to capitalize the values in V.) There are also $STOP_i$ inputs, $1 \le i \le n$.

We consider implementing such an m-writer/p-reader atomic object, where $n = m + p$, using a shared memory system with n processes, one per port. We assume that all the shared variables in this system are read/write shared variables, but the numbers of readers and writers will vary in the different algorithms we present. All the implementations we describe guarantee wait-free termination.

13.4.2   Another Lemma for Showing Atomicity

We begin with a technical lemma that is useful for showing that a sequence β of actions of a read/write atomic object external interface satisfies the atomicity property for read/write objects. This lemma lists four conditions involving a partial order on operations in β. If an ordering satisfying these four conditions exists, it is guaranteed that there is some way to insert serialization points so as to satisfy the atomicity property. When reasoning about algorithms, it is often easier to show the existence of such a partial order than it is to explicitly define the serialization points.

Lemma 13.16 *Let β be a (finite or infinite) sequence of actions of a read/write atomic object external interface. Suppose that β is well-formed for each i, and contains no incomplete operations. Let Π be the set of all operations in β.*

Suppose that $\prec$ is an irreflexive partial ordering of all the operations in Π, satisfying the following properties:

1. *For any operation $\pi \in \Pi$, there are only finitely many operations ϕ such that $\phi \prec \pi$.*

2. *If the response event for π precedes the invocation event for ϕ in β, then it cannot be the case that $\phi \prec \pi$.*

3. *If π is a WRITE operation in Π and ϕ is any operation in Π, then either $\pi \prec \phi$ or $\phi \prec \pi$.*

4. *The value returned by each READ operation is the value written by the last preceding WRITE operation according to $\prec$ (or v_0, if there is no such WRITE).*

Then β satisfies the atomicity property.

Condition 1 is a technical one, ruling out funny orderings in which infinitely many operations precede some particular other operation. Condition 2 says that the $\prec$ ordering must be consistent with the order of invocations and responses by the users. Condition 3 says that $\prec$ totally orders all the *WRITE* operations and orders all the *READ* operations with respect to the *WRITE* operations. Condition 4 says that the responses to *READ*s are consistent with $\prec$.

Proof. We describe how to insert a serialization point $*_\pi$ for every operation $\pi \in \Pi$. Namely, we insert each serialization point $*_\pi$ immediately after the latest of the invocations for π and for all the operations ϕ such that $\phi \prec \pi$. Condition 1 implies that this position is well-defined. We order $*$'s that are thereby placed contiguously in any way that is consistent with the ordering $\prec$ on the associated operations; that is, if π and ϕ are two operations whose $*$'s are placed contiguously, and if $\phi \prec \pi$, then $*_\phi$ precedes $*_\pi$.

We claim that the total order of the serialization points is consistent with $\prec$; that is, for any operations π and ϕ in Π, if $\phi \prec \pi$, then $*_\phi$ precedes $*_\psi$. To see this, assume that $\phi \prec \pi$. By construction, $*_\phi$ is placed after the latest of the invocations for ϕ and for all the operations that precede ϕ in the $\prec$ order. And $*_\pi$ is placed after the latest of the invocations for π and for all the operations that precede π in the $\prec$ order. But since $\phi \prec \pi$, it follows that any operation that precedes ϕ in $\prec$ also precedes π in $\prec$. Since a tie would be broken by ordering $*_\phi$ before $*_\pi$, it follows that $*_\phi$ precedes $*_\pi$, as claimed.

Next, we claim that these serialization points are within the required intervals. To see this, consider any operation $\pi \in \Pi$. By construction, the serialization point $*_\pi$ for π must appear after the invocation for π. We show that $*_\pi$ appears before the response for π. Suppose for the sake of contradiction that it appears after the response for π. Then, by construction, this means that the response for π must precede (in β) the invocation for some operation ϕ, where $\phi \prec \pi$. But this contradicts Condition 2.

It remains to show that the result of shrinking the operation intervals to their serialization points is a trace of the underlying read/write variable type. This means that each *READ* operation π returns the value of the *WRITE* whose serialization point is the last one before $*_\pi$ (or v_0, if there is no such *WRITE*).

But Condition 3 says that $\prec$ orders all the *WRITE* operations in Π with respect to all operations in Π. And by Condition 4 for *READ* operations, the value returned by any *READ* operation π is the value written by the last preceding *WRITE* operation according to $\prec$ (or v_0, if there is no such *WRITE*). Since the total order of the serialization points is consistent with $\prec$, it follows that π returns the required value.

$\square$

In this rest of this section, we use Lemma 13.16 to show that objects guarantee the atomicity condition.

13.4.3 An Algorithm with Unbounded Variables

Our first algorithm is the *VitanyiAwerbuch algorithm*, which implements m-writer/p-reader read/write atomic objects using single-writer/single-reader registers. (Recall that $n = m+p$.) This algorithm is simple but has the disadvantage that the shared variables are unbounded in size.

> ### *VitanyiAwerbuch* algorithm:
>
> The algorithm uses n^2 shared variables, which we can imagine to be arranged in an $n \times n$ matrix X, as depicted in Figure 13.9. The variables are named $x(i,j)$: $1 \le i, j \le n$. Each variable $x(i,j)$ is readable only by process i and writable only by process j; thus, each process i can read all the variables in row i and can write all the variables in column i of X.
>
> Each shared register $x(i,j)$ has the following fields:

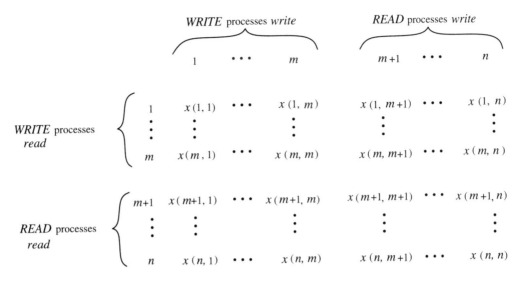

Figure 13.9: Matrix X of shared registers used in the *VitanyiAwerbuch* algorithm.

$val \in V$, initially v_0
$tag \in \mathbb{N}$, initially 0
$index \in \{1, \ldots, m\}$, initially arbitrary

We use the abbreviation *tagpair* for the pair $(tag, index)$. We order *tagpairs* lexicographically.

When a $WRITE(v)_i$ input occurs, process i behaves as follows. First, it reads all the variables $x(i, j)$, $1 \leq j \leq n$ (in any order). Let k be the greatest *tag* it finds. Next, process i performs a single *write* to each $x(j, i)$, $1 \leq j \leq n$, setting the three fields of $x(j, i)$ as follows:

1. $x(j, i).val := v$
2. $x(j, i).tag := k + 1$
3. $x(j, i).index := i$

Finally, process i outputs ACK_i.

When a $READ_i$ input occurs, process i behaves as follows. First, it reads all the variables $x(i, j)$, $1 \leq j \leq n$ (in any order). Let (v, k, j) be any $(val, tag, index)$ triple it finds with maximum $tagpair = (tag, index)$. Next, process i performs a single *write* to each $x(j, i)$, $1 \leq j \leq n$, setting the three fields of $x(j, i)$ as follows:

1. $x(j, i).val := v$
2. $x(j, i).tag := k$

3. $x(j, i).index := j$

(That is, it *propagates* the best information it has read to all the variables it can write.) Finally, process i outputs v_i (i.e., outputs value v on port i).

Theorem 13.17 *The VitanyiAwerbuch algorithm is a read/write atomic object guaranteeing wait-free termination.*

In order to prove the correctness of the *VitanyiAwerbuch* algorithm, we could proceed as in the proofs for the snapshot algorithms, explicitly inserting serialization points and then showing that the atomicity property is satisfied. However, for the *VitanyiAwerbuch* algorithm, it is not easy to see (as it is for the earlier algorithms) exactly where the serialization points ought to be placed. A more natural proof strategy here is to establish a partial order of operations based on the *tagpair* values, and then show that this partial order satisfies the conditions of Lemma 13.16.

Proof.   Well-formedness and wait-free termination are easy to see. For atomicity, we use Lemma 13.16.

Let α be any execution of the *VitanyiAwerbuch* algorithm. In view of Lemma 13.10, we may assume without loss of generality that α contains no incomplete operations. We begin with a simple claim.

Claim 13.18 *For any variable $x(i, j)$, the tagpair $=$ (tag, index) values are monotone nondecreasing in α.*

Proof.   Fix i and j. Note that variable $x(i, j)$ is written only by process j and that, by well-formedness, all operations by j must occur sequentially. Also, after any number of complete operations by j, all the variables in the jth column contain the same *tagpair*.

Each time j performs an operation, it starts by reading all variables in the jth row, including the "diagonal" variable $x(j, j)$. The *tagpair* that it writes is then chosen to be at least as large as the *tagpair* that it finds in $x(j, j)$. But this is the same as the *tagpair* in $x(i, j)$ prior to the operation. So the *tagpair* in $x(i, j)$ after the operation is at least as large as before the operation. This is enough to show the claim.   □

Next, define Π to be the set of operations occurring in α. For every (*WRITE* or *READ*) operation $\pi \in \Pi$, we define $tagpair(\pi)$ to be the unique *tagpair* value that it writes.

Claim 13.19 *All $tagpair(\pi)$ values for distinct WRITE operations in α are distinct.*

Proof. For *WRITE* operations on different ports this is certainly true, since the *index* fields of the *tagpairs* are different.

So consider operations on the same port; by well-formedness, these operations occur sequentially. Let π and ϕ be two *WRITE* operations on port i and assume without loss of generality that π precedes ϕ. Then π completes writing to all the variables in the ith column before ϕ begins reading the variables in the ith row. In particular, ϕ sees, in the "diagonal" variable $x(i,i)$, a *tagpair* written by π or a later operation. By Claim 13.18, this *tagpair* is at least as large as that of π. Then ϕ chooses a larger, and hence a different, *tagpair* for itself. $\square$

Now we define a partial ordering on operations in Π. Namely, we say that $\pi \prec \phi$ exactly if either of the following applies:

1. $tagpair(\pi) < tagpair(\phi)$

2. $tagpair(\pi) = tagpair(\phi)$, π is a *WRITE* and ϕ is a *READ*

It is enough to verify that this satisfies the four conditions needed for Lemma 13.16 (where $\beta = trace(\alpha) = \alpha | ext(A \times U)$).

1. For any operation $\pi \in \Pi$, there are only finitely many operations ϕ such that $\phi \prec \pi$.

   Suppose for the sake of contradiction that operation π has infinitely many $\prec$ predecessors. Claim 13.19 implies that it cannot have infinitely many predecessors that are *WRITE* operations, so it must have infinitely many predecessors that are *READ* operations. Without loss of generality, we may assume that π is a *WRITE*.

   Then there must be infinitely many *READ* operations with the same *tagpair*, t, where t is smaller than $tagpair(\pi)$. But the fact that π completes in α implies that $tagpair(\pi)$ eventually gets written to some variable in each row. After this happens, Claim 13.18 implies that any *READ* operation that is subsequently invoked is guaranteed to see, and thus to obtain, a *tagpair* that is $\geq tagpair(\pi) > t$. This contradicts the existence of infinitely many *READ* operations with *tagpair* t.

2. If the response event for π precedes the invocation event for ϕ in β, then it cannot be the case that $\phi \prec \pi$.

   Suppose that π's response precedes the invocation of ϕ. When π completes, its *tagpair* has been written to all its column variables. Thus by Claim 13.18, when ϕ reads its row variables, it reads a *tagpair* that is at least as large as $tagpair(\pi)$. Therefore, $tagpair(\phi)$ is chosen to be at least as large as $tagpair(\pi)$. Moreover, if ϕ is a *WRITE* operation, then $tagpair(\phi)$ is chosen to be strictly greater than $tagpair(\pi)$.

Since $tagpair(\pi) \leq tagpair(\phi)$, the only way we could have $\phi \prec \pi$ is if $tagpair(\pi) = tagpair(\phi)$, π is a *READ* operation and ϕ is a *WRITE* operation. But this is not possible, because if ϕ is a *WRITE*, then, as noted above, we have $tagpair(\phi) > tagpair(\pi)$. So it is not the case that $\phi \prec \pi$.

3. If π is a *WRITE* operation in Π and ϕ is any operation in Π, then either $\pi \prec \phi$ or $\phi \prec \pi$.

   By Claim 13.19, all *WRITE* operations obtain distinct *tagpairs*. This implies that all of the *WRITEs* are totally ordered and also that each *READ* is ordered with respect to all the *WRITEs*.

4. The value returned by each *READ* operation is the value written by the last preceding *WRITE* operation according to $\prec$ (or v_0, if there is no such *WRITE*).

   Let π be a *READ* operation. The value v returned by π is just the value that π finds associated with the largest *tagpair*, t, among the variables in its row; this t also becomes the *tagpair* of π. There are two cases:

   (a) Value v has been written by some *WRITE* operation ϕ with *tagpair* t.

       In this case, the ordering definition ensures that ϕ is the last *WRITE* preceding π in the $\prec$ order, as needed.

   (b) $v = v_0$ and $t = 0$.

       In this case, the ordering definition ensures that there are no *WRITEs* preceding π in the $\prec$ order, as needed.

Complexity analysis. The *VitanyiAwerbuch* algorithm uses n^2 shared variables, each of unbounded size, even if the underlying domain V is finite. Each *READ* and each *WRITE* that completes involves $4n$ shared memory accesses, for a total time complexity that is $O(n\ell)$.

13.4.4　A Bounded Algorithm for Two Writers

Like the *UnboundedSnapshot* algorithm, the *VitanyiAwerbuch* algorithm has the disadvantage that it uses unbounded-size shared variables to store unbounded tags. Many alternative algorithms have been designed that use only bounded data, but unfortunately, most are rather complicated (as well as too inefficient

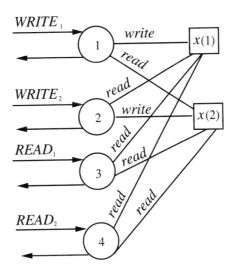

Figure 13.10: Architecture for the *Bloom* algorithm with two readers.

to be practical). In this section, we present only one very simple algorithm, for a special case.

Namely, we describe the *Bloom algorithm* for implementing a 2-writer/p-reader read/write atomic object using two 1-writer/$p + 1$–reader registers, $x(1)$ and $x(2)$. (Now $n = 2 + p$.) Each $x(i)$ is writable by *WRITE* process i and readable by all the other processes. Figure 13.10 depicts the architecture for the special case of two readers. The algorithm is simple but does not have an apparent generalization to more writers.

Bloom algorithm:

The algorithm uses two shared variables, $x(1)$ and $x(2)$, where $x(i)$ is writable by process i and readable by all other processes. Here let $\bar{i}$ denote 2 if $i = 1$, and 1 if $i = 2$. Register $x(i)$ has the following fields:

$val \in V$, initially v_0
$tag \in \{0, 1\}$, initially 0

When a $WRITE(v)_i$ occurs on port i, $i \in \{1, 2\}$, process i behaves as follows. First, it reads $x(\bar{i})$; let b be the tag it finds there. Then it writes $x(i)$, setting the fields as follows:

1. $x(i).val := v$

2. $x(i).tag := b + i \bmod 2$

Finally, it outputs ACK_i.

Thus, when a *WRITE* process i performs a *WRITE*, it not only writes the new value into its variable, but it also attempts to make the sum of the *tags* in the two variables equal to its own index, modulo 2. That is, process 1 always tries to make the *tags* in the two variables unequal, while process 2 tries to make them equal.

When a $READ_i$ occurs on port i, $3 \leq i \leq n$, process i behaves as follows. First, it reads both registers; let b be the sum modulo 2 of the two *tags* that it finds there. Then it rereads register $x(1)$ if $b = 1$ and register $x(2)$ if $b = 0$, and returns the *val* that it finds there.

Thus, all *READ* processes behave in exactly the same way. Each *READ* process reads both registers to determine whether they contain equal or unequal tags. If the tags are equal, the process obtains its return value from $x(2)$, and otherwise from $x(1)$.

Theorem 13.20 *The Bloom algorithm is a read/write atomic object guaranteeing wait-free termination.*

Once again, in order to prove correctness, we could proceed by explicitly inserting serialization points and then showing that the atomicity property is satisfied. However, this time we use an interesting strategy based on a combination of Lemma 13.16 and a simulation proof, as defined in Section 8.5.5. We first define a variant of the *Bloom* algorithm, *IntegerBloom*, which uses integer-valued *tags* instead of bits. We show that *IntegerBloom* is correct, using Lemma 13.16. Then we show that *Bloom* is correct by using a simulation relation from *Bloom* to *IntegerBloom*.

IntegerBloom algorithm:

The algorithm uses two shared variables, $x(1)$ and $x(2)$, where $x(i)$ is writable by process i and readable by all other processes. Register $x(i)$ has the following fields:

> $val \in V$, initially v_0
> $tag \in \mathbb{N}$, initially 0 for $i = 1$ and 1 for $i = 2$

When a $WRITE(v)_i$ occurs on port i, $i \in \{1, 2\}$, process i behaves as follows. First, it reads $x(\bar{i})$; let t be the *tag* it finds there. Then it writes $x(i)$, setting the fields as follows:

1. $x(i).val := v$

2. $x(i).tag := t + 1$

Finally, it outputs ACK_i.

When a $READ_i$ occurs on port i, $3 \le i \le n$, process i behaves as follows. First, it reads both registers; let t_1 and t_2 be the respective *tags* it finds there. Then there are two cases: If $|t_1 - t_2| \le 1$, then process i rereads the register holding the greater *tag* and returns the *val* that it finds there. (This register must be uniquely defined, because, as we state in Lemma 13.21 below, the *tags* in $x(1)$ are always even and the *tags* in $x(2)$ are always odd.) Otherwise—that is, if $|t_1 - t_2| > 1$—process i nondeterministically chooses either register to reread and returns the *val* that it finds there.

The following lemma gives some basic properties of *IntegerBloom*. It is easy to prove.

Lemma 13.21 *In any reachable state of IntegerBloom, the following are true:*

1. $x(1).tag$ *is even.*

2. $x(2).tag$ *is odd.*

3. $|x(1).tag - x(2).tag| \le 1$.

Theorem 13.22 *The IntegerBloom algorithm is a read/write atomic object guaranteeing wait-free termination.*

Proof. Similar to the proof of Theorem 13.17. Well-formedness and wait-free termination are easy to see. For atomicity, we use Lemma 13.16. Let α be any execution of the *IntegerBloom* algorithm. As before, we assume without loss of generality that α contains no incomplete operations.

Claim 13.23 *For each variable $x(i)$, the tag values are monotone nondecreasing in α.*

Let Π denote the set of operations occurring in α. For every $WRITE$ operation π in Π, we define $tag(\pi)$ to be the *tag* value written by π in its *write* step.

Now we define a partial ordering on operations in Π. First, we order the $WRITE$ operations by their *tag* values. If two $WRITE$ operations have the same *tag*, then they must belong to the same writer, and we order them in the order in which they occur. Next, we order each $READ$ operation in Π just after the $WRITE$ whose value it obtains (or before all the $WRITE$s, if there is no such $WRITE$).

It is enough to verify that this satisfies the four conditions needed for Lemma 13.16 (where $\beta = trace(\alpha) = \alpha|ext(A \times U)$). Conditions 3 and 4 are immediate, so all we must show are Conditions 1 and 2. For these, the following is useful:

Claim 13.24 *If the write step of WRITE operation π precedes the invocation of WRITE operation ϕ, then $\pi \prec \phi$.*

Proof. If π and ϕ occur on the same port, then Claim 13.23 implies that $tag(\pi) \leq tag(\phi)$, and the definition of $\prec$ implies that $\pi \prec \phi$. On the other hand, if π and ϕ occur on different ports, then ϕ reads the result of either π or a later *WRITE* on π's port. By Claim 13.23, the *tag* read by ϕ is greater than or equal to $tag(\pi)$. Therefore, $tag(\pi) < tag(\phi)$, so again $\pi \prec \phi$.   □

Claim 13.25 *If the write step of WRITE operation π precedes the invocation of READ operation ϕ, then $\pi \prec \phi$.*

Proof. We must show that ϕ returns the result of π or of some other *WRITE* ψ with $\pi \prec \psi$. Let $t = tag(\pi)$ and suppose that π occurs on port i.

When ϕ is invoked, Claim 13.23 implies that $x(i).tag \geq t$, and Lemma 13.21 implies that $|x(1).tag - x(2).tag| \leq 1$. Therefore, when ϕ is invoked, $x(\bar{i}).tag \geq t - 1$. By the definition of $\prec$ and Claim 13.23, the only problem is if ϕ returns the value of some *WRITE* with $tag = t - 1$. So suppose this is the case.

Then ϕ must see $x(\bar{i}).tag = t - 1$ on either its first or its second *read*, and again on its third *read*. If ϕ sees $x(i).tag = t$ on either its first or second *read*, then the combination of *tags* $t - 1$ and t causes ϕ to choose to reread register $x(i)$ rather than register $x(\bar{i})$, a contradiction. So it must be that ϕ sees $x(i).tag > t$. But Lemma 13.21 implies that by the time ϕ sees $x(i).tag > t$, it must also be the case that $x(\bar{i}) > t - 1$. This means that ϕ cannot see $x(\bar{i}) = t - 1$ on its third *read*, again a contradiction.

Using Claims 13.24 and 13.25, Condition 1 is easy to show; we leave this for an exercise.

For Condition 2, suppose that the response event for π precedes the invocation for ϕ in β. If π is a *WRITE*, then Claims 13.24 and 13.25 imply that $\pi \prec \phi$. So suppose that π is a *READ*. Suppose for the sake of contradiction that $\phi \prec \pi$.

If ϕ is a *WRITE*, then clearly π cannot return the result of ϕ, since ϕ does not perform its *write* step until after ϕ has completed. So the only problem is if π returns the result of some *WRITE* ψ, where $\phi \prec \psi$. But in this case, the *write* step within ψ precedes the end of π and so precedes the invocation of ϕ. But then Claim 13.24 implies that $\psi \prec \phi$, a contradiction.

On the other hand, if ϕ is a *READ*, then the assumption that $\phi \prec \pi$ implies that there must be some *WRITE* operation ψ such that $\phi \prec \psi$ and π obtains the result of ψ. Since π obtains the result of ψ, it must be that the *write* step within ψ precedes the end of π and so precedes the invocation of ϕ. But then Claim 13.25 implies that $\psi \prec \phi$, again a contradiction.   □

Now we show the correspondence between the *Bloom* and *IntegerBloom* algorithms, using a simulation relation. The general strategy is described in Section 8.5.5 and is used in other proofs in Example 8.5.6 and in Section 10.9.4.

The correspondence between the two algorithms turns out (strangely enough) to be that the $\{0, 1\}$-valued *tag*s used in the *Bloom* algorithm are the *second-lowest-order* bits of the integer-valued *tag*s in the *IntegerBloom* algorithm.

Example 13.4.1 Bits versus integers in the *Bloom* algorithm

Consider an execution of *IntegerBloom* in which *WRITE* operations alternate on ports 1 and 2, beginning with port 1; each *WRITE* begins only after the previous one has completed. Then each *WRITE* produces a successively larger *tag*. The *tag* values in the two registers, written in binary notation, are shown in Figure 13.11. Initially, $x(1)$ and $x(2)$ start with *tag*s 0 and 1, respectively. The first *WRITE*$_1$ sets $x(1).tag := 2$, and then a *WRITE*$_2$ sets $x(2).tag := 3$, and so on.

In the corresponding execution of *Bloom*, the *tag* values in the two registers are as shown in Figure 13.12. Initially, both registers start with $tag = 0$. Each *WRITE*$_1$ sets $x(1).tag$ to be unequal to $x(2).tag$, while each *WRITE*$_2$ sets $x(2).tag$ to be equal to $x(1).tag$.

Notice that in each case, the *tag* in the *Bloom* execution is just the second-lowest-order bit of the corresponding *tag* in the *IntegerBloom* execution.

It turns out that the correspondence illustrated in Example 13.4.1 holds in all executions of the two algorithms. If s and u are states of the *Bloom* and *IntegerBloom* systems (algorithms plus users), respectively, then we define $(s, u) \in f$ (or $u \in f(s)$), provided that all state components are identical, except that wherever u has an integer-valued *tag*, t, s has a bit-valued *tag* whose value is the second-lowest-order bit of t.

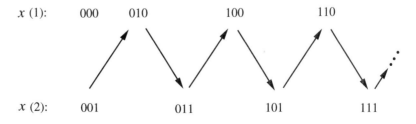

Figure 13.11: Successive *tag* values in the two registers, in the *IntegerBloom* algorithm.

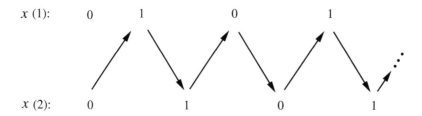

x (1):   0   1   0   1

x (2):   0   1   0   1

Figure 13.12: Successive *tag* values in the two registers, in the *Bloom* algorithm.

Lemma 13.26 f *is a simulation relation from Bloom to IntegerBloom.*

Proof Sketch.   Since the unique initial states of the two algorithms are related by f, the start condition of the simulation definition is straightforward. The interesting thing to show is the step condition. It is enough to show that for any step (s, π, s') of *Bloom* and any $u \in f(s)$, where s and u are reachable states, there is a corresponding step (u, ϕ, u') of *IntegerBloom*, where $u' \in f(s')$ and ϕ is "almost" the same as π. Specifically, ϕ is the same as π except that it can involve an integer value, whereas π involves the second-lowest-order bit. We consider cases, based on π. If π is an invocation or response event, then the arguments are straightforward. The interesting steps are the *write* steps within the *WRITE* operations and the third *read* steps within the *READ* operations.

So suppose that (s, π, s') is a step of *Bloom* in which process 1 writes $x(1)$ as part of a $WRITE_1$ operation. Then process 1 sets $x(1).tag$ to be unequal to the value b that it remembers reading from $x(2).tag$. That is, $s'.x(1).tag \neq b$. In the corresponding state u of *IntegerBloom*, process i remembers reading an integer-valued *tag* t from $x(2).tag$; since $u \in f(s)$, it must be that b is the second-lowest-order bit of t. Let u' be the unique state that results in *IntegerBloom*. Then $u'.x(1).tag = t + 1$. To see that $u' \in f(s')$, we need to show that the second-lowest-order bit of $u'.x(1).tag$ is equal to $s'.x(1).tag$, that is, that the second-lowest-order bit of $t + 1$ is unequal to b. But this follows from the fact that t is odd (by Lemma 13.21) and the fact that b is the second-lowest-order bit of t.

The argument for the case where (s, π, s') is a step in which process 2 writes $x(2)$ is similar.

Now suppose that (s, π, s') is a step of *Bloom* at which process i performs the third *read* step within a *READ*. The key claim is that *IntegerBloom* permits process i to read the same register, $x(1)$ or $x(2)$. Suppose that, in state s, the *tags* that process i of *Bloom* remembers reading in $x(1)$ and $x(2)$ are b_1 and b_2, respectively; likewise, suppose that in state u, the *tags* that process i of *IntegerBloom* remembers reading in $x(1)$ and $x(2)$ are t_1 and t_2, respectively.

Since $u \in f(s)$, we know that b_1 is the second-lowest-order bit of t_1 and b_2 is the second-lowest-order bit of t_2. There are three cases.

1. $t_1 = t_2 + 1$.
   Then Lemma 13.21 implies that the second-lowest-order bits of t_1 and t_2 are unequal. In this case, both *Bloom* and *IntegerBloom* read from register $x(1)$.

2. $t_2 = t_1 + 1$.
   Then Lemma 13.21 implies that the second-lowest-order bits of t_1 and t_2 are equal. In this case, both *Bloom* and *IntegerBloom* read from register $x(2)$.

3. $t_1 \neq t_2 + 1$ and $t_2 \neq t_1 + 1$.
   Then Lemma 13.21 implies that $|t_1 - t_2| > 1$. In this case, *IntegerBloom* permits *either* register to be read.

$\square$

Now we can prove Theorem 13.20, which asserts the correctness of the *Bloom* algorithm.

Proof (of Theorem 13.20). Lemma 13.26 and Theorem 8.12 imply that every trace of the *Bloom* system is a trace of the *IntegerBloom* system. (Recall that traces here include invocation and response events on ports, plus the *stop* events.) Theorem 13.22 implies that the well-formedness and atomicity conditions hold for *IntegerBloom*. Since the well-formedness and atomicity conditions are expressible as properties of traces, they carry over to the *Bloom* algorithm. Wait-free termination is easy to see. $\square$

Complexity analysis. The *Bloom* algorithm uses two shared variables, each of which can take on $2|V|$ values. Each operation requires only a constant number of shared memory accesses, or time $O(\ell)$.

13.4.5 An Algorithm Using Snapshots

In this final subsection, we give an implementation, *SnapshotRegister*, of a wait-free m-writer/p-reader read/write atomic object using a snapshot shared variable. (Again, let $n = m + p$.) Combining *SnapshotRegister* with the implementations of snapshot atomic objects in Section 13.3, using Corollary 13.9, yields implementations of wait-free m-writer/p-reader atomic objects using 1-writer/n-reader shared registers.

The snapshot shared variable used by *SnapshotRegister* has unbounded size, even if the underlying domain V for the read/write atomic object being implemented is bounded. It is possible, though quite difficult, to modify the *Snapshot-Register* algorithm to use a bounded snapshot shared variable.

SnapshotRegister algorithm:

The algorithm uses a single shared variable x, which is a snapshot object based on a length m vector. The domain W for each component of x consists of pairs (val, tag), where $val \in V$ and $tag \in \mathbb{N}$; the initial value w_0 is $(v_0, 0)$.

Each *WRITE* process i, $1 \leq i \leq m$, performs $update(i, w)$ and $snap$ operations on x, while each *READ* process i, $m + 1 \leq i \leq n$, performs only $snap$ operations on x.

When a $READ_i$ input occurs on port i, $m + 1 \leq i \leq n$, process i behaves as follows. First, it performs a $snap$ operation on x, thereby determining a vector u. Let j be the index, $1 \leq j \leq m$, such that the pair $(u(j).tag, j)$ is largest, in the lexicographic ordering of pairs. Then process i returns the associated value $u(j).val$.

When a $WRITE(v)_i$ input occurs on port i, $1 \leq i \leq m$, process i behaves as follows. First, it performs a $snap$ operation on x, thereby determining a vector u. As above, let j be the index, $1 \leq j \leq m$, such that the pair $(u(j).tag, j)$ is largest, in the lexicographic ordering of pairs. Then process i performs an $update(i, (v, u(j).tag + 1))$. Finally, process i outputs ACK_i.

The *SnapshotRegister* algorithm is somewhat similar to the *VitanyiAwerbuch* algorithm, but it is simpler because of the extra power provided by the snapshot shared memory.

Theorem 13.27 *The SnapshotRegister algorithm is a read/write atomic object guaranteeing wait-free termination.*

Proof Sketch.   This is similar to the proofs for *VitanyiAwerbuch* and *Integer-Bloom*, using Lemma 13.16, but simpler. We leave it as an exercise.   □

Complexity analysis.   The *SnapshotRegister* algorithm uses one snapshot shared variable, which is of unbounded size, even if the underlying domain V is finite. Each operation requires only a constant number of shared memory accesses, for a total time that is $O(\ell)$.

Hierarchical construction. Theorem 13.27 and any wait-free implementation of the snapshot atomic object together yield a wait-free implementation of an m-writer/p-reader read/write atomic object using 1-writer/$m + p$-reader shared registers. The proof is based on Corollary 13.9. (Technically, in order to apply Corollary 13.9, we need a snapshot atomic object with only $n = m + p$ ports, one per process—for example, *WRITE* process i should perform both its *update* and *snap* operations on the same port. There is no problem modifying the snapshot atomic object external interface and implementations to permit this.)

Generalizations. There are several interesting generalizations of the *Snapshot-Register* algorithm that also work correctly. First, during a *WRITE$_i$*, if $i = j$— that is, if process i itself has the largest *tag* pair—then i may optionally use the same *tag* that it previously had. Second, it it possible to use nonnegative real-valued *tag*s rather than integer-valued *tag*s. Then the *tag* chosen by a writer i can be any real number that is strictly greater than the largest *tag* it sees. Once again, if i itself has the greatest *tag* pair, then it can reuse its previous *tag*. Both of these generalizations are useful for proving the correctness of other implementations of read/write atomic objects using a snapshot shared variable.

13.5 Bibliographic Notes

The idea of an "atomic object" appears to have originated with the work of Lamport [181, 182] on read/write atomic objects. Herlihy and Wing [153] extended the notion of atomicity to arbitrary variable types and renamed it *linearizability*. König's Lemma was originally proved by König [170]; a proof appears in Knuth's book [169]. The canonical wait-free atomic object automaton is derived from the work of Merritt, described in [3]. The connection between atomic objects and shared variables is derived from work by Lamport and Schneider [186] and by Goldman and Yelick [139]. The impossibility of implementing read-modify-write atomic objects using read/write objects is due to Herlihy [150].

The idea of a snapshot atomic object is due to Afek, Attiya, Dolev, Gafni, Merritt, and Shavit [3] and to Anderson [11, 12], inspired by the work of Chandy and Lamport on consistent global snapshots in distributed networks [68]. The snapshot atomic object implementations presented here, both *UnboundedSnapshot* and *BoundedSnapshot*, are due to Afek, et al. The handshake strategy used in the *BoundedSnapshot* protocol is due to Peterson [240]. A more recent atomic snapshot algorithm, requiring only $O(n\ell \log n)$ time rather than quadratic time, has been developed by Attiya and Rachman [26].

Many algorithms have been designed for implementing read/write atomic objects in terms of simpler kinds of read/write registers. The *VitanyiAwerbuch* algorithm appears in a paper by Vitanyi and Awerbuch [283]; that paper also contains an algorithm using bounded shared variables, but that algorithm is incorrect. The *Bloom* algorithm is due to Bloom [53], and the *SnapshotRegister* algorithm is derived from work by Gawlick, Lynch, and Shavit [135]. Bounded algorithms for implementing single-writer/multi-reader atomic objects using single-writer/single-reader registers have been designed by Singh, Anderson, and Gouda [263] and Haldar and Vidyasankar [144]. Bounded algorithms for implementing multi-writer/multi-reader atomic objects using single-writer/multi-reader registers have been designed by Peterson and Burns [241]; Schaffer [254]; Israeli and Li [162]; Li, Tromp, and Vitanyi [196]; and Dolev and Shavit [100]. In particular, Schaffer's algorithm corrects errors in Peterson and Burns's algorithm. Gawlick, Lynch, and Shavit [135] describe an implementation of multi-writer/multi-reader atomic objects using a bounded snapshot variable and prove the correctness of this algorithm by a simulation proof, relating it to the generalized version of the *SnapshotRegister* algorithm. Several of these constructions use a notion of "bounded timestamping." Bounded timestamping algorithms have been given by Israeli and Li [162]; Dolev and Shavit [100]; Gawlick, Lynch, and Shavit [135]; Israeli and Pinchasov [163]; Dwork and Waarts [107]; and Dwork, Herlihy, Plotkin, and Waarts [102].

Attiya and Welch have compared the costs of implementing read/write atomic objects with those of implementing read/write objects with slightly weaker consistency requirements [28]. Their work is carried out in the asynchronous network model.

13.6 Exercises

13.1. Define the external interface for a 2-writer/1-reader atomic object and give several interesting examples of sequences for this external interface that satisfy the atomicity property, as well as sequences that do not satisfy the atomicity property. Be sure to include both finite and infinite sequences, as well as sequences that contain incomplete operations.

13.2. Consider a read-modify-write atomic object whose domain V is the set of integers and whose initial value is 0. (See Section 9.4 for the definition of a read-modify-write variable type—recall that the return value for a read-modify-write shared variable is the value of the variable prior to the operation.)

The object has two ports: port 1 supports *increment* operations (which add 1 to the value in the object) only and port 2 supports *decrement* operations (which subtract 1) only. Which of the following sequences satisfy the atomicity property?

(a) $increment_1, decrement_2, 0_1, 0_2$

(b) $increment_1, decrement_2, -1_1, 0_2$

(c) $increment_1, decrement_2, 0_1, 1_2$

(d) $decrement_2, increment_1, 0_1, increment_1, 1_1, increment_1, 2_1, increment_1,$ $3_1, \ldots$

(e) $decrement_2, increment_1, 0_1, increment_1, 0_1, increment_1, 1_1, increment_1,$ $2_1, \ldots$

13.3. Fill in some more details in the proof of Theorem 13.1. In particular, show in more detail than we have in the text that there are arbitrarily long paths from the root and that an infinite path yields a correct selection for the entire sequence β.

13.4. Generalize the definition of a variable type to allow finitely many initial values rather than just one and to allow finite nondeterministic choice rather than just a function. Generalize Theorem 13.1 and its proof to this new setting. What happens if we allow infinite nondeterminism?

13.5. Suppose that we modify Example 13.1.4 so that the system supports *decrement* operations as well as *read* and *increment* operations. The algorithm is the same as before, with the following addition: when a *decrement$_i$* input occurs on port i, process i decrements $x(i)$.

Is the resulting system a read/increment/decrement atomic object? Either prove that it is or give a counterexample execution.

13.6. Prove Theorem 13.4.

13.7. Prove Theorem 13.5.

13.8. Prove Theorem 13.6.

13.9. Show that Theorem 13.7 is false if we do not include the special assumption about A's *turn* function.

13.10. Give a formal description, using precondition-effect notation, of the *RMW-fromRW* algorithm. Your description should be modular in that it should represent the mutual exclusion component as a separate automaton, combined with the main portion of the *RMWfromRW* algorithm using I/O automaton composition. Prove that your algorithm works correctly (assuming the correctness properties of the mutual exclusion component).

13.11. Consider a modification of the *UnboundedSnapshot* algorithm in which each *snap* and *embedded-snap* looks for three different tags for some $x(i)$ rather than four as described. Is the modified algorithm still correct? Either prove that it is or give a counterexample execution.

13.12. Consider a modification of the *UnboundedSnapshot* algorithm in which process i increments $x(i).tag$ when it performs a *snap* operation, as well as when it performs an *update* operation. (The $x(i).val$ and $x(i).view$ components are not changed, and the *embedded-snap* operation is not modified in any way.)

Is the modified algorithm still correct? Either prove that it is or give a counterexample execution.

13.13. *Research Question*: Can you give an alternative proof of correctness for the *UnboundedSnapshot* algorithm, based on a formal relationship with the appropriate canonical wait-free atomic object automaton?

13.14. Design a modification of the *BoundedSnapshot* algorithm that eliminates the *toggle* bits. In your algorithm, a *snap* process should determine the consistency of two sets of *reads*, based not only on the handshake bits but also on the *val* fields. Prove that your algorithm is correct.

13.15. *Research Question*: Design a more efficient implementation of a wait-free snapshot atomic object than the *BoundedSnapshot* algorithm, also using bounded-size single-writer/multi-reader read/write shared variables. Can you design one that terminates in linear rather than quadratic time in the number of processes?

13.16. *Research Question*: Design a good implementation of a snapshot atomic object that allows updates to the same vector component to occur on several ports (and hence, concurrently).

13.17. Give a simplified version of the *Bakery* algorithm of Section 10.7 that uses snapshot shared variables. Prove its correctness.

13.18. State carefully and prove a result asserting the impossibility of solving the agreement problem with 1-failure termination using snapshot atomic objects.

13.19. Give an efficient implementation of a read/update/snap atomic object, using single-writer/multi-reader read/write shared variables. Prove its correctness and analyze its complexity.

13.20. Give a simplified version of the *Bakery* algorithm of Section 10.7 that uses read/update/snap shared variables. Try to make your algorithm as simple and efficient as you can. Prove its correctness and analyze its complexity. In your complexity analysis, consider the cost of implementing the read/update/snap variables in terms of an underlying model based on single-writer/multi-reader read/write shared variables, as described in Exercise 13.19.

13.21. Generalize Lemma 13.16 to handle arbitrary variable types rather than just read/write types.

13.22. Is the "propagation phase" of the *READ* protocol in the *VitanyiAwerbuch* algorithm needed? Either prove that the algorithm works without it or exhibit a counterexample.

13.23. Give an alternative correctness proof for the *VitanyiAwerbuch* algorithm, based on explicitly inserting serialization points into an arbitrary execution in which all operations complete, and then showing that the atomicity property is satisfied.

13.24. Design a simplified version of the *VitanyiAwerbuch* algorithm for the setting where the read/write shared variables are single-writer/multi-reader variables. Is the propagation phase of the *READ* protocol needed? Prove correctness and analyze complexity.

13.25. Prove that the third *read* within the *READ* protocol in the *Bloom* algorithm is necessary. That is, give an incorrect execution of the modified algorithm in which each *READ* simply returns the value already read (in the first or second *read*) from the appropriate register.

13.26. Near the end of the description of the *IntegerBloom* algorithm, it is specified that if $|t_1 - t_2| > 1$, then process i nondeterministically chooses either register to reread. Give a particular execution in which this case arises.

13.27. Prove that Condition 1 of Lemma 13.16 holds, in the proof of Theorem 13.22.

13.28. Fill in the details in the proof of Lemma 13.26. This requires writing precondition-effect code for the *Bloom* and *IntegerBloom* algorithms.

13.29. *Research Question*: Try to extend the *Bloom* algorithm to more than two writers.

13.30. Prove Theorem 13.27.

13.31. Give example executions to show that the *SnapshotRegister* algorithm is *not* correctly serialized by serialization points placed in either of the following two ways:

   (a) For a *READ*: at the point of its *snap* operation; for a *WRITE*: at the point of its *update* operation.

   (b) For every operation: at the point of its *snap* operation.

13.32. Describe a single algorithm that generalizes the *SnapshotRegister* algorithm in *both* of the two ways described at the end of Section 13.4.5. That is, a *WRITE* process whose own *tag* is the largest is allowed (though not forced) to reuse its *tag*, and real-value *tags* are permitted. Try to make your algorithm as nondeterministic as possible.

13.33. Design an algorithm to implement an m-writer/p-reader read/write atomic object with domain V and initial value v_0, using a snapshot shared variable. Unlike the *SnapshotRegister* algorithm, your snapshot variable should be of *bounded* size, in the case where V is finite. (*Warning:* This is very hard.)

13.34. *Research Question*: Use Lemma 13.16 to prove the correctness of some of the other atomic register implementations in the research literature.

13.35. *Research Question*: Design *efficient and simple* implementations of multi-writer/multi-reader read/write atomic objects using bounded-size single-writer/single-reader registers.

13.36. *Research Question*: Design a hierarchy of atomic objects that are efficient and simple enough to be used as the basis for the development of a practical multiprocessor system.

Part IIB

Asynchronous Network Algorithms

Chapters 14–22 deal with algorithms for the *asynchronous network model*, in which processes take steps asynchronously and communicate by exchanging messages. The ideas in these chapters build in many interesting ways on ideas presented in Parts I and IIA.

As usual, we begin with a chapter containing our formal model, Chapter 14. We follow this with Chapter 15, which contains a survey of basic algorithms for asynchronous networks, all programmed directly in terms of the model. Since some of these algorithms turn out to be quite complicated, we proceed, in Chapters 16–19, to introduce four techniques for simplifying the programming of asynchronous networks. The first technique, described in Chapter 16, is the introduction of a *synchronizer*. The second technique, described in Chapter 17, is the simulation of the asynchronous shared memory model by the asynchronous network model. The third technique, described in Chapter 18, is the assignment of consistent *logical times* to events in an asynchronous distributed network. Chapter 19 contains our fourth technique, the monitoring of asynchronous network algorithms while they run.

We then return to the study of specific problems in the asynchronous network setting. Chapter 20 studies the problem of *resource allocation* in asynchronous networks. Chapter 21 considers the problem of computing in an asynchronous network in the presence of failures. Finally, Chapter 22 considers the *data link problem*, a problem of implementing reliable communication in an unreliable network.

Chapter 14

Modelling IV: Asynchronous Network Model

In this chapter, we change the computing paradigm once again, this time switching from asynchronous shared memory systems to asynchronous networks. An asynchronous network consists of a collection of processes communicating by means of a communication subsystem. In the version of this model that is most frequently encountered, this communication is *point-to-point*, using *send* and *receive* actions. Other versions of the model allow *broadcast* actions, by which a process can send a message to all processes in the network (including itself), or *multicast* actions, by which a process can send a message to a subset of the processes. Special cases of the multicast model are also possible, for example, one that allows a combination of broadcast and point-to-point communication. In each case, various types of faulty behavior of the network, including message loss and duplication, can be considered.

The chapter contains three main sections, treating send/receive systems, broadcast systems, and multicast systems, respectively.

14.1 Send/Receive Systems

As in the synchronous network model defined in Chapter 2, we start with an n-node directed graph $G = (V, E)$. As before, we use the notation $out\text{-}nbrs_i$ and $in\text{-}nbrs_i$ to denote the outgoing and incoming neighbors of node i in the digraph, $distance(i, j)$ for the length of the shortest directed path from i to j in G, and $diam$ for the maximum distance from any node to any other.

As in the synchronous network model, we associate *processes* with the nodes of G and allow them to communicate over *channels* associated with directed edges. However, unlike in the synchronous model, there are no synchronous rounds of communication: now we allow asynchrony in both the process steps and the communication. To describe this asynchrony, we model the processes and the channels as I/O automata. Let M be a fixed message alphabet.

14.1.1   Processes

The process associated with each node i is modelled as an I/O automaton, P_i. P_i usually has some input and output actions by which it communicates with an external user; this allows us to express problems to be solved by asynchronous networks in terms of traces at the "user interface." In addition, P_i has outputs of the form $send(m)_{i,j}$, where j is an outgoing neighbor of i and m is a message (that is, an element of M), and inputs of the form $receive(m)_{j,i}$, where j is an incoming neighbor of i. Except for these external interface restrictions, P_i can be an arbitrary I/O automaton. (For specific results, we might sometimes want to impose additional restrictions on P_i, such as limiting the number of tasks or the number of states.) See Example 8.1.2 for an example of a process I/O automaton.

We consider two kinds of faulty behavior on the part of node processes: *stopping failure* and *Byzantine failure*. The stopping failure of P_i is modelled by including in the external interface of P_i a $stop_i$ input action, the effect of which is to permanently disable all tasks of P_i. (We do not constrain the state changes caused by a $stop_i$, nor the state changes caused by subsequent input actions. It is not important to constrain these state changes, because their effects could never be seen outside P_i, anyway.) The Byzantine failure of P_i is modelled by allowing P_i to be replaced by an arbitrary I/O automaton having the same external interface.

14.1.2   Send/Receive Channels

The channel associated with each directed edge (i, j) of G is modelled as an I/O automaton $C_{i,j}$. Its external interface consists of inputs of the form $send(m)_{i,j}$ and outputs of the form $receive(m)_{i,j}$, where $m \in M$. In general, except for this external interface specification, the channel could be an arbitrary I/O automaton. However, interesting communication channels have restrictions on their external behavior, for example, that any message that is received must in fact have been sent at some earlier time. The needed restrictions on the external behavior of a channel can generally be expressed in terms of a trace property P, as defined in Section 8.5.2. The allowable channels are those I/O automata whose external signature is $sig(P)$ and whose fair traces are in $traces(P)$.

There are two ways in which such a trace property P is commonly specified: by listing a collection of *axioms* or by giving a particular I/O automaton whose external interface is $sig(P)$ and whose fair traces are exactly $traces(P)$. An advantage of listing axioms is that this makes it easier to define a variety of channels, each of which satisfies a different subset of the axioms. On the other hand, an advantage of giving an explicit I/O automaton is that in this case, the entire system consisting of the processes and the most general allowable channels is described as a composition of I/O automata, which is itself another I/O automaton. This allows us to use the proof methods that have been developed for automata. For example, this provides us with a notion of "state" for the entire system, both processes and channels, which we can use in invariant assertion and simulation proofs.

Sometimes it may be necessary to do some rather annoying programming to specify the desired trace property as an I/O automaton; this is especially so when the trace property involves complicated *liveness constraints*. This often leads to a *mixed strategy* wherein the safety properties are described in terms of a basic automaton (which provides the machinery needed to support invariant and simulation proofs), while the liveness properties are described using special liveness axioms. The complete trace property P then has its traces defined to be exactly those traces of the basic automaton that satisfy the liveness axioms.

In the rest of this subsection, we describe some particular send/receive channels that we will use in Chapters 15–22.

Reliable FIFO channel. The communication channel that is most frequently assumed in the research literature and that we will use most frequently here is a *reliable FIFO channel*. The behaviors allowed for such a channel are easily specified as the fair traces of an I/O automaton with the appropriate external interface, whose state is a queue of messages. The $send(m)_{i,j}$ action adds m to the end of the queue. The $receive(m)_{i,j}$ action is enabled if m is first on the queue, and its effect is to remove the first message from the queue. The task partition puts all the locally controlled actions in a single class. A formal definition of this automaton has already been given, in Example 8.1.1.

This automaton is not only a specification of the allowable behavior for reliable FIFO channels, it is itself an example of a reliable FIFO channel. We call it the *universal reliable FIFO channel* with the given external interface.

Now we give an alternative specification, using axioms, of the allowed behavior for a reliable FIFO channel. Namely, we define a trace property P with $sig(P)$ equal to the given signature and $traces(P)$ equal to the set of sequences β of actions in $sig(P)$ that satisfy the following condition.

There exists a function *cause* mapping each *receive* event in β to a preceding *send* event in β such that

1. For every *receive* event π, π and $cause(\pi)$ contain the same message argument.

2. *cause* is surjective (onto).

3. *cause* is injective (one-to-one).

4. *cause* preserves order, that is, there do not exist *receive* events π_1 and π_2 with π_1 preceding π_2 in β and $cause(\pi_2)$ preceding $cause(\pi_1)$ in β.

The *cause* function is a device for identifying which *send* event "causes" each *receive* event. Condition 1 says that only correct messages are delivered; Condition 2 says that messages are not lost; Condition 3 says that they are not duplicated; and Condition 4 says that they are not reordered.

Notice that (for this particular trace property P) the *cause* function for each sequence in $traces(P)$ is unique.

Reliable reordering channel. Another type of channel that is often considered guarantees delivery of all messages, each exactly once, but does not necessarily preserve their order. The behaviors allowed for this type of channel are not so easily specified using an I/O automaton, so we instead use axioms. Namely, the specification is exactly the same as the axiomatic specification P for the reliable FIFO channel, given above, except that Condition 4 for the *cause* function is dropped.

An alternative, equivalent specification can be given using the mixed strategy mentioned above—using a basic I/O automaton A to describe the safety properties and additional axioms to describe liveness. This basic automaton A is as follows. (Here, $\cup$ and $\in$ are multiset operations.)

A automaton:

Signature:

Input: Output:
    $send(m)_{i,j}$, $m \in M$ $receive(m)_{i,j}$, $m \in M$

States:

in-transit, a multiset of elements of M, initially empty

Transitions:

$send(m)_{i,j}$
  Effect:
    $in\text{-}transit := in\text{-}transit \cup \{m\}$

$receive(m)_{i,j}$
  Precondition:
    $m \in in\text{-}transit$
  Effect:
    remove one copy of m from $in\text{-}transit$

Tasks:
Arbitrary.

The task partition does not matter, because we are not using it here. Using automaton A, we define a trace property P. The signature is the same as $sig(A)$, and $traces(P)$ is the set of traces of (not necessarily fair) executions α of A that satisfy the following condition.

> If at any point in α and for any $m \in M$ we have $m \in in\text{-}transit$, then at some later point in α, a $receive(m)$ event occurs.

Channels with failures.   We can also consider send/receive channels in which some failures occur. In this book, the only kinds of channel failures we discuss are message loss and duplication.

A channel permitting arbitrary loss but no duplication, or arbitrary duplication but no loss, or arbitrary duplication and loss, can be specified in the same way as reliable reordering channels, using the *cause* function. All we need to do is to omit Condition 2 and/or Condition 3, as appropriate.

However, often we want to assume a *limited amount* of message loss and/or duplication. For example, when we consider message loss, we generally do not want to consider the case where *all* messages are lost, because in this case nothing can be guaranteed ever to happen. A typical condition restricting message loss is one that says that a message that is sent infinitely many times must be received infinitely many times. To say this formally, we use the following condition on the *cause* function.

Strong loss limitation (SLL): If there are infinitely many $send(m)$ events in β (for any particular m), then there are infinitely many $send(m)$ events in the range of the *cause* function.

Notice that this says that infinitely many *different send* events succeed in having their messages delivered. This condition is not satisfied, for example, by a

sequence in which there are infinitely many *receive* events, all caused by the
same *send* event.

Another typical condition restricting message loss is one that does not mention any particular m, but just says that infinitely many *send*s cause *receive*s of infinitely many messages.

Weak loss limitation (WLL): If there are infinitely many *send* events in β, then the range of the *cause* function is infinite.

For duplication, we might want to limit the number of copies of each message to be finite or to be bounded by some particular number k. For example,

Finite duplication: The *cause* function maps only finitely many *receive* events to any particular *send* event.

So far, we have described all the channels with failures using axioms. We now use the mixed strategy to specify two such channels.

Example 14.1.1   A lossy FIFO channel

We define a channel that allows limited loss, finite duplication, and no reordering. (This channel will be used in Section 22.3, in the description of the Alternating Bit communication protocol.) The automaton is as follows.

A automaton:

Signature:
As usual.

States:
queue, a FIFO queue of elements of M, initially empty

Transitions:

$send(m)_{i,j}$
    Effect:
        add any finite number of copies
          of m to *queue*

$receive(m)_{i,j}$
    Precondition:
        m is first on *queue*
    Effect:
        remove first element of *queue*

Tasks:
Arbitrary.

The definition of automaton A guarantees that the channel does not reorder messages and only delivers finitely many copies of any message. However, we need to impose two extra liveness conditions.

1. If, at any point, *queue* is nonempty, then at some later point, a *receive* event occurs.

2. If there are infinitely many *send* events, then infinitely many of them succeed in putting (at least one copy of) their messages on the *queue*.

The combination of A and the liveness conditions are used to define a trace property as before. This trace property implies that if there are infinitely many *send* events, then infinitely many of those have corresponding *receive* events, that is, it implies the weak loss limitation (WLL) condition.

Example 14.1.2   A lossy reordering channel

We define a channel that allows limited loss, finite duplication, and reordering. (This channel will be used in Section 22.2, in the description of Stenning's communication protocol.) The automaton is as follows.

A automaton:

Signature:
As usual.

States:
in-transit, a multiset of elements of M, initially empty

Transitions:

$send(m)_{i,j}$
    Effect:
        add any finite number of copies
          of m to *in-transit*

$receive(m)_{i,j}$
    Precondition:
        $m \in in\text{-}transit$
    Effect:
        remove one copy of m from *in-transit*

Tasks:
Arbitrary.

We add two liveness conditions.

1. If, at any point, *in-transit* is nonempty, then at some later point, a *receive* event occurs.

2. If there are infinitely many *send* events, then infinitely many of them succeed in putting (at least one copy of) their messages in *in-transit*.

As in Example 14.1.1, the resulting trace property implies that if there are infinitely many *send* events, then infinitely many of them have corresponding *receive* events, that is, it implies the WLL condition.

Note that every trace allowed by the specification in Example 14.1.1 is also allowed by this specification. However, there are some traces allowed by this specification that are not allowed by the previous one.

14.1.3   Asynchronous Send/Receive Systems

An *asynchronous send/receive network system* for directed graph G is obtained by composing the process and channel I/O automata, using ordinary I/O automaton composition. An example of the architecture for such a system appears in Figure 8.3. The composition definition allows for the right interactions among the components; for example, when process P_i performs a $send(m)_{i,j}$ output action, a simultaneous $send(m)_{i,j}$ input action is performed by channel $C_{i,j}$. Appropriate state changes occur in both components.

Sometimes it is convenient to model the users of a send/receive system as another I/O automaton, U. U's external actions are just the actions of the processes at their user interface. The user automaton U is often described as the composition of a collection of user automata U_i, one for each node i of the underlying graph. In this case, U_i's external actions are the same as the actions of P_i at the user interface. (If stopping failures are considered, the *stop* actions are not included among the actions of the users.)

14.1.4   Properties of Send/Receive Systems with Reliable FIFO Channels

We give a basic theorem about asynchronous send/receive network systems with universal reliable FIFO channels, for use in Chapters 18 and 19. It identifies circumstances under which the events of a fair trace can be reordered to yield another fair trace. (Note that, according to the formal definition of I/O automaton composition, the traces include the *send* and *receive* events, as well as the events at the user interface.)   What is required is that the reordering should respect certain basic dependencies: the dependency of a *receive* event on the corresponding *send* event (with respect to the uniquely determined *cause* function) and the (possible) dependency of any event on all preceding events at the same node process.

Fix any asynchronous send/receive system A with universal reliable FIFO channels. Let β be any trace of A. We define an irreflexive partial order $\rightarrow_\beta$ on the events in β as follows. If π and ϕ are two events in β, with π preceding ϕ, then we say that $\pi \rightarrow_\beta \phi$, or ϕ *depends on* π, provided that one of the following holds:

1. π and ϕ are events of the same process P_i.

2. π is of the form $send(m)_{i,j}$, and ϕ is the corresponding $receive(m)_{i,j}$ event.

3. π and ϕ are related by a chain of relationships of types 1 and 2.

Theorem 14.1 *Let A be an asynchronous send/receive system with universal reliable FIFO channels, and let β be a fair trace of A. Let γ be a sequence obtained by reordering the events in β while preserving the $\rightarrow_\beta$ ordering. Then γ is also a fair trace of A.*

Proof. Theorem 8.4 implies that $\beta|P_i \in fairtraces(P_i)$ for every i. Since $\gamma|P_i = \beta|P_i$ for every i, it follows that $\gamma|P_i \in fairtraces(P_i)$ for every i.

Theorem 8.4 also implies that $\beta|C_{i,j} \in fairtraces(C_{i,j})$ for every i and j. Since $\gamma|C_{i,j}$ has the same set of events as $\beta|C_{i,j}$, and the reordering preserves the order of events at P_i, the order of events at P_j, and the ordering of *receive* events after their corresponding *send* events, it follows that $\gamma|C_{i,j} \in fairtraces(C_{i,j})$.

Theorem 8.6 then implies that $\gamma \in fairtraces(A)$. $\qquad\square$

Theorem 14.1 has a corollary that says that certain reorderings of fair executions are also fair executions.

Corollary 14.2 *Let A be an asynchronous send/receive system with universal reliable FIFO channels, and let α be a fair execution of A. Let γ be a sequence that is obtained by reordering the events in $\beta = trace(\alpha)$ while preserving the $\rightarrow_\beta$ ordering. Then there is a fair execution α' of A such that $trace(\alpha') = \gamma$ and such that α and α' are indistinguishable[1] to every process P_i.*

Proof Sketch. Theorem 14.1 implies that $\gamma \in fairtraces(A)$. Theorems 8.4 and 8.5 can then be used to show the existence of the needed α'. $\qquad\square$

The execution α' whose existence is guaranteed by Corollary 14.2 cannot be distinguished from the original execution α by the processes in system A (even if they combine their information). This means that the processes do not know the total ordering of events in an execution; they cannot determine the order of events at different processes if those events are not related by the message and process dependencies described by the partial order $\rightarrow_\beta$.

---

[1] This uses the formal definition of "indistinguishable" from Section 8.7.

14.1.5   Complexity Measures

We measure communication complexity in terms of the number of messages that are sent and/or the number that are received. We can also take into account the number of bits in the messages.

For measuring time complexity, we use a special case of the general time complexity measure defined for I/O automata in Section 8.6. That is, we associate an upper bound of ℓ with each task of each process; this imposes an upper bound of ℓ on the time between successive chances for that task to perform a step. We also need assumptions about the time for delivery of messages. For the special case of universal reliable FIFO channels, we usually associate an upper bound of d with the single task consisting of the *receive* actions of each channel; this imposes an upper bound of d on the delivery time for the *oldest* message in the channel. Thus, our usual time complexity measure takes into account the costs of pileups of messages in channels—the kth message on a channel's queue is guaranteed to be delivered within time kd.

We sometimes also make a less realistic but simpler assumption about message delivery time: an upper bound of d on the delivery time for *each* message in a channel, regardless of pileups. This assumption is *not* expressible just by associating time bounds with tasks (but it makes sense nonetheless). Also, we can extend the channel time bound assumptions to non-universal FIFO channels, in the obvious way.

14.2   Broadcast Systems

A broadcast system consists of a set of *processes* numbered $1, \ldots, n$, plus a single *broadcast channel* to model the broadcast communication subsystem. Again, let M be a fixed message alphabet.

14.2.1   Processes

Process i in a broadcast system is modelled as an I/O automaton P_i. As for processes in send/receive network systems, P_i usually has some input and output actions by which it communicates with an external user. In addition, P_i has outputs of the form $bcast(m)_i$, where $m \in M$, and inputs (as before) of the form $receive(m)_{j,i}$, where $m \in M$. Except for these external interface restrictions, P_i can be an arbitrary I/O automaton. See Figure 14.1.

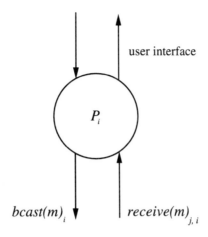

user interface

P_i

$bcast(m)_i$ $receive(m)_{j,i}$

Figure 14.1: A process I/O automaton for an asynchronous broadcast system.

14.2.2 Broadcast Channel

A broadcast channel is modelled as a single I/O automaton. Its external interface consists of inputs of the form $bcast(m)_i$ and outputs of the form $receive(m)_{i,j}$, where $m \in M$. In this book, we consider only reliable broadcast channels, but it is possible also to define other types of broadcast channels that exhibit various forms of failure.

Reliable broadcast channels. A *reliable broadcast channel* delivers every message that is broadcast, to every process, including the sender. We make one assumption about the ordering of the message deliveries: that the delivery order is FIFO between each particular pair of processes. The allowed behaviors for such a channel are easily specified as the fair traces of a single I/O automaton B that maintains a separate queue for each ordered pair of processes.

B automaton:

Signature:

Input: Output:
    $bcast(m)_i$, $m \in M$, $1 \le i \le n$ $receive(m)_{i,j}$, $m \in M$, $1 \le i,j \le n$

States:
for every i,j, $1 \le i,j \le n$:
    $queue(i,j)$, a FIFO queue of elements of M, initially empty

Transitions:

$bcast(m)_i$

    Effect:

        for all j do

            add m to $queue(i, j)$

$receive(m)_{i,j}$

    Precondition:

        m is first on $queue(i, j)$

    Effect:

        remove first element of $queue(i, j)$

Tasks:

for every i, j:

   $\{receive(m)_{i,j} : m \in M\}$

We call B the *universal reliable broadcast channel* with the given external interface.

14.2.3   Asynchronous Broadcast Systems

An asynchronous broadcast system is obtained by composing the process and broadcast channel I/O automata.

14.2.4   Properties of Broadcast Systems with Reliable Broadcast Channels

The definitions and results in Section 14.1.4 can be modified for broadcast systems with universal reliable broadcast channels. The relevant dependencies now are the dependency of a *receive* event on the corresponding *bcast* event and the (possible) dependency of any event on all preceding events at the same node process.

Fix any asynchronous broadcast system A with a universal reliable broadcast channel. Let β be any trace of A. We define an irreflexive partial order on the events in β as follows. If π and ϕ are two events in β, with π preceding ϕ, then we say that $\pi \rightarrow_\beta \phi$, or ϕ *depends on* π, provided that one of the following holds:

1. π and ϕ are events of the same process P_i.

2. π is of the form $bcast(m)_i$, and ϕ is a corresponding $receive(m)_{i,j}$ event.

3. π and ϕ are related by a chain of relationships of types 1 and 2.

Theorem 14.3 *Let A be an asynchronous broadcast system with a universal reliable broadcast channel and let β be a fair trace of A. Let γ be a sequence obtained by reordering the events in β while preserving the $\rightarrow_\beta$ ordering. Then γ is also a fair trace of A.*

Proof. The proof is left as an exercise. □

Corollary 14.4 *Let A be an asynchronous broadcast system with a universal reliable broadcast channel and let α be a fair execution of A. Let γ be a sequence obtained by reordering the events in $\beta = trace(\alpha)$, while preserving the $\rightarrow_\beta$ ordering. Then there is a fair execution α' of A such that $trace(\alpha') = \gamma$ and such that α and α' are indistinguishable to every process P_i.*

Proof. The proof is left as an exercise. □

14.2.5 Complexity Measures

We can measure communication complexity either in terms of the number of *bcast* events or the number of *receive* events.

For measuring time complexity, we use a special case of the time complexity measure for I/O automata. Namely, we associate an upper bound of ℓ with each task of each process. And for the special case of a universal reliable broadcast channel, we usually associate an upper bound of d with each task; this imposes an upper bound of d on the delivery time for the *oldest* message in transit from each P_i to each P_j. Thus, we again take into account the costs of pileups of messages.

Again, we occasionally make the stronger assumption of an upper bound of d on the delivery time for *each* message and extend the channel time bound assumptions to non-universal reliable broadcast channels.

14.3 Multicast Systems

Send/receive and broadcast systems are both generalized by *multicast systems*, which allow each process to send a message to a subset of the processes in the network. A multicast system contains a set of *processes* numbered $1, \ldots, n$, plus a single *multicast channel* to model the multicast communication subsystem. The system is parameterized by a set $\mathcal{I}$ of pairs of the form (i, I), where i is a process index and I is a set of process indices. Each such pair (i, I) indicates that process i can use set I as a destination set for multicasts. Again, M is a fixed message alphabet.

14.3.1 Processes

We again use an I/O automaton P_i. In addition to some actions at the user interface, P_i has outputs of the form $mcast(m)_{i,I}$, where m is a message and

$(i, I) \in \mathcal{I}$, and inputs of the form $receive(m)_{j,i}$. Except for these external interface restrictions, P_i can be an arbitrary I/O automaton.

14.3.2   Multicast Channel

A multicast channel is modelled as a single I/O automaton. Its external interface consists of inputs of the form $mcast(m)_{i,I}$, $(i, I) \in \mathcal{I}$, and outputs of the form $receive(m)_{i,j}$. We consider only reliable multicast channels.

Reliable multicast channels.   The allowed behaviors for a *reliable multicast channel* with set $\mathcal{I}$ of pairs are easily specified as the set of fair traces of the following I/O automaton B.

B automaton:

Signature:

Input: Output:
  $mcast(m)_{i,I}$, $m \in M$, $(i, I) \in \mathcal{I}$ $receive(m)_{i,j}$, $m \in M$, $1 \le i, j \le n$

States:
for every i, j, $1 \le i, j \le n$:
  $queue(i, j)$, a FIFO queue of elements of M, initially empty

Transitions:

$mcast(m)_{i,I}$ $receive(m)_{i,j}$
  Effect: Precondition:
      for all $j \in I$ do m is first on $queue(i, j)$
        add m to $queue(i, j)$ Effect:
                                                        remove first element of $queue(i, j)$

Tasks:
for every i, j:
  $\{receive(m)_{i,j} : m \in M\}$

We call B the *universal* reliable multicast channel with the given external interface.

An interesting special case of a reliable multicast channel is one in which the allowable destination sets are exactly the singleton sets and the set $\{1, \ldots, n\}$ of all processes. This channel supports a combination of point-to-point and broadcast communication. Note that the FIFO order is guaranteed even between broadcast and point-to-point messages.

14.3.3 Asynchronous Multicast Systems

An asynchronous multicast system is obtained by composing the process and multicast channel I/O automata. It is straightforward to extend the definitions and results in Section 14.1.4 to multicast systems based on universal reliable multicast channels. Likewise, the complexity measures for broadcast systems can be extended to multicast systems.

14.4 Bibliographic Notes

In general, we use no special source for the modelling of asynchronous send/receive, broadcast, and multicast networks; similar material appears in many papers on distributed algorithms and on formal verification of network protocols. The use of a *cause* function to describe the explicit connection between message sending and receiving events is derived from the work of Fekete, Lynch, Mansour, and Spinelli [112] and Afek, Attiya, Fekete, Fischer, Lynch, Mansour, Wang, and Zuck [4].

Our modelling of broadcast and multicast channels only includes basic correctness and complexity properties. There has been much work on the implementation and use of broadcast and multicast channels with stronger properties, including stronger ordering requirements and fault-tolerance properties. Hadzilacos and Toueg's paper [143] gives a good overview.

14.5 Exercises

14.1. Let P be the trace property defined in Section 14.1.2 to describe the allowable behaviors for a reliable FIFO send/receive channel. Prove that $traces(P)$ is exactly equal to the set of fair traces of the universal reliable FIFO channel automaton with the same external interface.

14.2. Let A be any I/O automaton that implements a universal reliable FIFO send/receive channel B—that is, A has the same external signature as B and $fairtraces(A) \subseteq fairtraces(B)$. Prove that in fact $fairtraces(A) = fairtraces(B)$. (In this sense, any reliable FIFO channel must be universal.)

14.3. Consider an alternative trace property Q as a specification for the allowable behavior of a reliable FIFO send/receive channel. Q is the same as P, only it does not require that $cause(\pi)$ precede π. Prove that for every I/O automaton A with the appropriate external interface, $fairtraces(A) \subseteq traces(Q)$ if and only if $fairtraces(A) \subseteq traces(P)$.

14.4. Give a careful description of a send/receive channel C that can lose messages, but not duplicate or reorder them, as an explicit I/O automaton. Suppose that C is even permitted to lose all of its messages. However, C should exhibit *all* the possible traces that satisfy this condition—for example, it should not be *required* to lose messages. Define a simulation relation (as defined in Section 8.5.5) from the universal reliable FIFO send/receive channel of Section 14.1.2 to C, and prove that it actually is a simulation relation.

14.5. (a) Prove that the two given specifications for the allowable behaviors of a reliable reordering send/receive channel are equivalent.

    (b) Can the allowable behaviors for a reliable reordering send/receive channel be equivalently defined by an I/O automaton? That is, does there exist an I/O automaton with the appropriate external signature whose fair traces are exactly the specified sequences of actions?

14.6. (Channel multiplexing) It is possible to use a single "real" send/receive channel to implement two or more "logical" send/receive channels, each needed for a separate algorithm or a separate piece of one algorithm. Formally, suppose that P_1 and P_2 are trace properties describing the correctness requirements for two separate channels, with disjoint message alphabets M_1 and M_2. Then the product trace property $P_1 \times P_2$ (see Section 8.5.2 for the definition of the product of trace properties) can be regarded as the specification for another channel, guaranteeing both sets of requirements.

As an example, let P_1 and P_2 describe the allowed behaviors for reliable FIFO channels, for message alphabets M_1 and M_2, respectively. Let P descibe the allowed behaviors for a reliable FIFO channel for message alphabet $M = M_1 \cup M_2$.

    (a) Prove that $traces(P) \subseteq traces(P_1 \times P_2)$.

       This implies that any I/O automaton A that implements P (in the sense that $extsig(A) = sig(P)$ and $fairtraces(A) \subseteq traces(P)$) in fact implements both channels P_1 and P_2 (in the sense that $extsig(A) = sig(P_1 \times P_2)$ and $fairtraces(A) \subseteq traces(P_1 \times P_2)$).

    (b) Show that $traces(P) \neq traces(P_1 \times P_2)$.

       This says that P's behavior is more constrained than is needed in order to implement the two channels P_1 and P_2.

14.7. Repeat Exercise 14.6, but in place of reliable FIFO send/receive channels, consider channels that allow arbitrary reordering, strong loss limitation (SLL), and

(a) no duplication

(b) finite duplication

(c) arbitrary duplication

14.8. Prove that the FIFO assumption for reliable send/receive channels is not necessary. Specifically, show how to transform any send/receive system A based on reliable FIFO channels into a send/receive system $T(A)$ based on reliable reordering channels that looks the same to the environment, in the following sense. For every fair execution α of $T(A)$ there is a fair execution α' of A that projects to give the same sequence of actions at the user interface. Be sure to state your result precisely.

14.9. Prove that the FIFO assumption for reliable broadcast channels is not necessary. That is, show that a system A with this assumption can be transformed into a system $T(A)$ without this assumption that looks the same to the environment. Be sure to state your result precisely.

14.10. Strengthen Theorem 14.1 so that it includes a claim about what is preserved at the user interface.

14.11. Prove Theorem 14.3.

14.12. Prove Corollary 14.4.

Chapter 15

Basic Asynchronous Network Algorithms

In this chapter, we describe a collection of algorithms for solving some basic problems—leader election, constructing an arbitrary spanning tree, broadcast and convergecast, breadth-first search, finding shortest paths, and constructing a minimum spanning tree—in the asynchronous network model with reliable FIFO send/receive channels. The problems are, for the most part, the same ones considered in the synchronous network model in Chapter 4. As before, these problems are motivated by the need to select a process to take charge of a network computation and by the need to build structures suitable for supporting efficient communication. We do not consider faults in this chapter.

All the algorithms in this chapter are constructed by direct programming of the "bare" asynchronous network model. It will not take long for us to see that this model is much more difficult to program than the synchronous network model. This will lead us to seek ways of simplifying and systematizing the programming task. In the four chapters following this one, Chapters 16–19, we introduce four such simplification techniques: *synchronizers*, *simulating shared memory*, *logical time*, and *runtime monitoring*.

15.1 Leader Election in a Ring

We considered the problem of leader election in a synchronous ring in Chapter 3. For the asynchronous version of the problem, the underlying digraph is again a ring of n processes, numbered 1 to n in the clockwise direction. As before, we often count mod n, allowing 0 to be another name for process n, and so on. The ring can be either unidirectional or bidirectional. Figure 15.1 shows

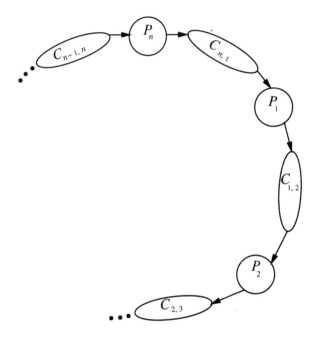

Figure 15.1: Architecture for unidirectional ring network.

the architecture for an asynchronous unidirectional ring network, including both processes and channels.

Now processes and channels are modelled as I/O automata. As in the synchronous setting, processes do not know their indices, nor those of their neighbors, but use local, relative names. This allows arbitrary processes to be arranged into a ring in an arbitrary order. Besides the *send* and *receive* actions by which process automaton P_i interacts with its channels, P_i has a *leader$_i$* output action by which it can announce its election as leader. We assume, here and throughout the rest of the chapter, that the channels are reliable FIFO send/ receive channels. We also assume here that the processes have UIDs. The problem is for exactly one process eventually to produce a *leader* output.

15.1.1   The LCR Algorithm

The *LCR* algorithm described in Section 3.3 can easily be adapted to run in an asynchronous network. Recall that in the *LCR* algorithm, each process sends its identifier around the ring. When a process receives an incoming identifier, it compares that identifier to its own. If the incoming identifier is greater than its own, it keeps passing the identifier; if it is less than its own, it discards the incoming identifier; if it is equal to its own, the process outputs *leader*.

The same idea still works in an asynchronous network; the main difference is that now each process's *send* buffer must be able to hold any number (up to n) of messages instead of just a single one. The reason for the difference is that the asynchrony can cause pileups of UIDs at nodes. We call the modified algorithm *AsynchLCR*.

In the following code, we use $AsynchLCR_i$ as an alternative name for process P_i in the *AsynchLCR* algorithm. When we discuss the algorithm, we use the two names, $AsynchLCR_i$ and P_i, as convenient; we also sometimes denote this process simply as "process i." We use similar conventions elsewhere.

$AsynchLCR_i$ automaton:

Signature:

Input:
    $receive(v)_{i-1,i}$, v a UID

Output:
    $send(v)_{i,i+1}$, v a UID
    $leader_i$

States:
u, a UID, initially i's UID
send, a FIFO queue of UIDs, initially containing only i's UID
status, with values in $\{unknown, chosen, reported\}$, initially *unknown*

Transitions:

$send(v)_{i,i+1}$
    Precondition:
        v is first on *send*
    Effect:
        remove first element of *send*

$receive(v)_{i-1,i}$
    Effect:
        case
            $v > u$: add v to *send*
            $v = u$: *status* := *chosen*
            $v < u$: do nothing
        endcase

$leader_i$
    Precondition:
        status = *chosen*
    Effect:
        status := *reported*

Tasks:
$\{send(v)_{i,i+1} : v$ a UID$\}$
$\{leader_i\}$

The transitions should be self-explanatory. Process i is responsible for performing two tasks: sending messages to process $i + 1$ and announcing itself as the leader. Thus, it has two tasks, one for all its *send* actions and one for its *leader* action. The behavior of the *AsynchLCR* is essentially the same as that of *LCR*, but possibly "skewed" in time.

In order to prove that *AsynchLCR* solves the leader-election problem, we use invariant assertions as we did for the synchronous *LCR* algorithm. Invariant assertion proofs work for asynchronous networks just as well as for synchronous networks; the main difference is that now the method must be applied at a finer granularity, to reason about individual events rather than about rounds.

Technically, in order to use invariant assertion proofs, we must know the structure of the state of each channel automaton. Thus, for convenience, we assume that the channels $C_{i,i+1}$ are all *universal* FIFO reliable channels as defined in Section 14.1.2. Then we know that the state of each $C_{i,i+1}$ consists of a single *queue* component, which we refer to as $queue_{i,i+1}$. This assumption does not restrict the generality of the results, because an algorithm that works correctly with universal reliable FIFO channels must also work with arbitrary reliable FIFO channels. We will make the same assumption in all of our correctness proofs for send/receive systems with reliable FIFO channels.

Let $i_{\max}$ denote the index of the process with the maximum UID, and let $u_{\max}$ denote its UID. Here, as in the synchronous case, we must show two things:

1. No process other than $i_{\max}$ ever performs a *leader* output.

2. Process $i_{\max}$ eventually performs a *leader* output.

The first of these two conditions is a safety property while the second is a liveness property.

Lemma 15.1 *No process other than i_{max} ever performs a leader output.*

Proof. We use an invariant similar to Assertion 3.3.3 for the synchronous case. Recall that Assertion 3.3.3 said that no UID v could reach any *send* queue between $i_{\max}$ and v's original home i. Now, because the *AsynchLCR* algorithm includes channel automata, we need a slightly stronger assertion that involves the UIDs in the channel states as well as the UIDs in the process states. As usual, we subscript process state components by the index of the process; we also subscript channel state components by the two indices of the channel.

Assertion 15.1.1 *The following are true in any reachable state:*

1. If $i \neq i_{max}$ and $j \in [i_{max}, i)$, then u_i does not appear in $send_j$.

2. *If* $i \neq i_{max}$ *and* $j \in [i_{max}, i)$, *then* u_i *does not appear in* $queue_{j,j+1}$.

Assertion 15.1.1 is proved by induction on the number of steps in a finite execution leading to the given state. The proof is generally similar to that of Assertion 3.3.3. This time, we proceed by case analysis based on the individual *send*, *receive*, and *leader* events. The key case is that of a $receive(v)_{j-1,j}$ event where $j = i_{\max}$; for this case, we must argue that if $v = u_i$ where $i \neq i_{\max}$, then v gets discarded.

Assertion 15.1.1 can be used to prove Assertion 15.1.2.

> **Assertion 15.1.2** *The following is true in any reachable state: If* $i \neq i_{max}$ *then* $status_i = unknown$.

Then it is easy to see that no process other than $i_{\max}$ ever performs a *leader$_i$* output, since the precondition of this action is never satisfied. ☐

Now we turn to the liveness property. Notice that this needs the hypothesis that the execution of *AsynchLCR* is *fair*. This formal notion means that the processes and channels continue to perform their work.

Lemma 15.2 *In any fair execution, process* i_{max} *eventually performs a leader output.*

Proof. The proof of this property for *AsynchLCR* is quite different from the proof of the corresponding result, Lemma 3.2, for the synchronous *LCR* algorithm. Recall that in the synchronous case, we used a very strong invariant assertion, Assertion 3.3.2, which described exactly where the maximum UID had travelled after any number r of rounds. Now we have no notion of round. Also, it is impossible to characterize precisely what happens in the computation, since the asynchrony introduces so much uncertainty. So we must use a different method.

Our proof is based on establishing intermediate milestones toward the main goal of electing a leader. In particular, we show inductively on r, for $0 \leq r \leq n - 1$, that *eventually* $u_{\max}$ appears in the buffer $send_{i_{\max}+r}$. Using this claim for $r = n - 1$, we show that eventually $u_{\max}$ is placed in channel $C_{i_{\max}-1,i_{\max}}$, that thereafter eventually $u_{\max}$ is received by process $i_{\max}$, and that thereafter eventually process $i_{\max}$ performs a *leader* output. The fairness properties of the process and channel I/O automata are used to prove all these eventuality claims.

For example, consider a state s in a fair execution α in which any UID v appears at the head of the $send_i$ buffer. We argue that eventually $send(v)_i$ occurs. If not, then examination of the transitions of process *AsynchLCR$_i$* shows that v remains at the head of the $send_i$ buffer forever. This implies that the $send_i$

task stays enabled forever, so by fairness, some $send_i$ event must subsequently occur. But since v is the message at the head of the $send_i$ buffer, this means that $send(v)_i$ must eventually occur.

Also, if v appears in the kth position on the $send_i$ buffer, for any value of $k \geq 1$, we can show that eventually $send(v)_i$ occurs. This follows by induction on k, with the basis case, $k = 1$, given just above. For the inductive step, we note that a UID v in position $k > 1$ eventually reaches position $k - 1$, when the head of the buffer gets removed, and then the inductive hypothesis implies that $send(v)_i$ eventually occurs.

Similar arguments can be made for the UIDs in the channels.   □

Putting these arguments together, we obtain

Theorem 15.3 *AsynchLCR solves the leader-election problem.*

We next consider the complexity of the *AsynchLCR* algorithm. The number of messages is $O(n^2)$, just as for the synchronous *LCR* algorithm. Recall that the time bound for *LCR* is n rounds. For the time analysis of *AsynchLCR*, we assume an upper bound of ℓ for each task of each process, and an upper bound of d on the time to deliver the oldest message in each channel queue.

A naive analysis gives an $O(n^2(\ell + d))$ time bound, by integrating time bounds into the eventuality argument in the proof of Lemma 15.2. Namely, note that the maximum length of any process *send* buffer or any channel *queue* is n. Therefore, it takes at most $n\ell$ time for a UID in a process *send* buffer to get placed in the adjacent channel, and at most nd time for a UID in a channel *queue* to get received by the next process. The overall time complexity is therefore $O(n^2(\ell + d))$.

However, it is possible to carry out a more refined analysis, yielding an upper bound that is only $O(n(\ell + d))$. The point is that although some *send* buffers and *queues* can reach size n, this cannot happen everywhere. In order for a pileup to form, some UIDs must travel *faster* than the worst-case upper bound in order to overtake others. The overall time turns out to be no worse than if the UIDs had all travelled at the same speed. We show:

Lemma 15.4 *In any fair execution, for any r, $0 \leq r \leq n - 1$, and for any i, the following are true:*

1. *By time $r(\ell + d)$, UID u_i either reaches the $send_{i+r}$ buffer or is deleted.*

2. *By time $r(\ell + d) + \ell$, UID u_i either reaches $queue_{i+r,i+r+1}$ or is deleted.*

Proof.   By induction on r.

Basis: $r = 0$. UID u_i starts out in $send_i$, and within time ℓ is placed in $queue_{i,i+1}$, as needed.

Inductive step: Suppose that the claim holds for $r - 1$ and prove it for r. Fix any i. For Part 1, suppose that u_i is not deleted by time $r(\ell + d)$. Then the inductive hypothesis implies that by time $t = (r - 1)(\ell + d) + \ell$, UID u_i reaches $queue_{i+r-1,i+r}$.

Claim 15.5 *If u_i is not delivered to process $i + r$ by time t, then u_i reaches the head of $queue_{i+r-1,i+r}$ by time t.*

Proof.   Suppose for the sake of contradiction that u_i is not delivered to process $i + r$ by time t and also does not reach the head of $queue_{i+r-1,i+r}$ by time t. Then it must be that some other UID, u_j, is ahead of u_i on $queue_{i+r-1,i+r}$ at time t. This is a pileup, where u_i has overtaken u_j; since u_i has not yet travelled distance r around the ring, it follows that u_j has not yet travelled distance $r - 1$ around the ring.

However, the inductive hypothesis implies that u_j either reaches $send_{j+r-1}$ (i.e., travels at least distance $r - 1$) or is deleted, by time $(r-1)(\ell+d) < t$. This implies that u_j cannot still be in $queue_{i+r-1,i+r}$ at time t, which is a contradiction. $\square$

Thus, either u_i is delivered to process $i + r$ by time t, or else u_i reaches the head of $queue_{i+r-1,i+r}$ by time t. In this latter case, within an additional time d, u_i is delivered to process $i + r$. In either case, u_i is delivered to process $i + r$ by time $t + d = r(\ell + d)$ and placed in the $send_{i+r}$ buffer, as needed.

The proof for Part 2 is similar.

Theorem 15.6 *The time until a leader event occurs in any fair execution of AsynchLCR is at most $n(\ell + d)) + \ell$, or $O\left(n(\ell + d)\right)$.*

Proof.   Lemma 15.4 for $r = n-1$ implies that UID u_{max} reaches $queue_{i_{max}-1,i_{max}}$ by time $(n-1)(\ell+d)+\ell$, and the same argument used in the proof of Lemma 15.4 implies that it reaches the first position on that queue by that time. Then within an additional time d, u_{max} is delivered to process i_{max}, which then performs a *leader* output within an additional time ℓ. The total is $n(\ell + d) + \ell$, as claimed. $\square$

Wakeups.   We can modify the input/output conventions for the leader-election problem so that the inputs (here, the UIDs) arrive at the processes in special *wakeup*$(v)_i$ messages from an external user U, instead of originating in the start states. The correctness conditions would then be modified to assume that exactly one *wakeup*$(v)_i$ occurs for each i. Then the *AsynchLCR* algorithm can easily be modified to satisfy the new correctness conditions: each process P_i simply delays performing any locally controlled actions until after it receives its *wakeup*. If P_i receives any messages before receiving its *wakeup*, then it buffers those messages in a new *receive* buffer and processes them after receiving the *wakeup*.

A similar modification can be made to the other leader-election algorithms later in this section. More generally, any distributed problem that is formulated with inputs in the start states can be reformulated to allow the inputs to arrive in *wakeup* messages. Using the same strategy described above, we can modify any algorithm that solves the original problem so that it satisfies the new correctness conditions.

15.1.2 The HS Algorithm

Recall the synchronous *HS* algorithm of Section 3.4, in which each process sends exploratory messages in both directions, for successively doubled distances. It is straightforward to see that this algorithm, suitably rewritten in terms of process I/O automata, still works correctly in the asynchronous network model. Its communication complexity is $O(n \log n)$, as before. We leave the determination of an upper bound on the time complexity for an exercise.

15.1.3 The Peterson Leader-Election Algorithm

The *HS* algorithm (in both its synchronous and asynchronous versions) requires only $O(n \log n)$ messages and uses bidirectional communication. In this subsection, we present the *PetersonLeader algorithm*, which achieves $O(n \log n)$ communication complexity using only unidirectional communication. This algorithm does not rely on knowledge of n, the number of nodes in the ring. It uses comparisons of UIDs only. It elects an arbitrary process as the leader, not necessarily the process with the maximum or minimum UID. The $O(n \log n)$ communication complexity has only a small constant factor (approximately 2).

PetersonLeader algorithm (informal):

While the algorithm is executing, each process is designated as being either in *active* mode or *relay* mode; all processes are initially active. The active processes carry out the "real work" of the algorithm; the relay processes just pass messages along. An execution of the *PetersonLeader* algorithm is divided into (asynchronously determined) *phases*. In each phase, the number of active processes is reduced by a factor of at least 2, so there are at most $\log n$ phases.

In the first phase of the algorithm, each process i sends its UID two steps clockwise. Then process i compares its own UID to those of its two predecessors in the counterclockwise direction. If the counterclockwise neighbor's UID is the highest of the three, that is, if $u_{i-1} > u_{i-2}$ and $u_{i-1} > u_i$, then process i remains active, adopting the UID u_{i-1} of its counterclockwise neighbor as a new "temporary UID." On the other hand, if one of the other two UIDs is the highest of the three, then process i simply becomes a relay for the remainder of the execution.

Each subsequent phase proceeds in much the same way. Each active process i now sends its temporary UID to the next and second-next active processes in the clockwise direction, and waits to learn the temporary UIDs from its two active predecessors in the counterclockwise direction. Now if the first active predecessor's UID is the largest of the three UIDs, process i remains active, adopting that predecessor's UID as its new temporary UID. On the other hand, if one of the two other UIDs is the largest of the three, then process i becomes a relay.

Also, if at any phase, a process i sees that the temporary UID it receives from its immediate active predecessor is the same as its own temporary UID, then i knows that it is the only active process left. In this case, process i elects itself as the leader.

It should be clear that in any phase in which there is more than one active process, at least one process will discover a combination of UIDs that allows it to remains active at the next phase. Moreover, at most half of the active processes can survive a given phase, since every process that remains active must have an immediate active predecessor that becomes a relay.

PetersonLeader$_i$ automaton (formal):

Signature:

Input:
    $receive(v)_{i-1,i}$, v a UID
Output:
    $send(v)_{i,i+1}$, v a UID
    $leader_i$

Internal:
    get-second-uid$_i$
    get-third-uid$_i$
    advance-phase$_i$
    become-relay$_i$
    relay$_i$

States:
$mode \in \{active, relay\}$, initially $active$
$status \in \{unknown, chosen, reported\}$, initially $unknown$
$uid(j)$, $j \in \{1, 2, 3\}$, each a UID or $null$; initially $uid(1) = i$'s UID, $uid(2) = uid(3) = null$

send, a FIFO queue of UIDs, initially containing i's UID
receive, a FIFO queue of UIDs, initially empty

Transitions:

get-second-uid$_i$
  Precondition:
      $mode = active$
      receive is nonempty
      $uid(2) = null$
  Effect:
      $uid(2) :=$ first element of *receive*
      remove first element of *receive*
      add $uid(2)$ to *send*
      if $uid(2) = uid(1)$ then $status := chosen$

get-third-uid$_i$
  Precondition:
      $mode = active$
      receive is nonempty
      $uid(2) \neq null$
      $uid(3) = null$
  Effect:
      $uid(3) :=$ first element of *receive*
      remove first element of *receive*

advance-phase$_i$
  Precondition:
      $mode = active$
      $uid(3) \neq null$
      $uid(2) > max\{uid(1), uid(3)\}$
  Effect:
      $uid(1) := uid(2)$
      $uid(2) := null$
      $uid(3) := null$
      add $uid(1)$ to *send*

become-relay$_i$
  Precondition:
      $mode = active$
      $uid(3) \neq null$
      $uid(2) \leq max\{uid(1), uid(3)\}$
  Effect:
      $mode := relay$

relay$_i$
  Precondition:
      $mode = relay$
      receive is nonempty
  Effect:
      move first element of *receive*
        to *send*

leader$_i$
  Precondition:
      $status = chosen$
  Effect:
      $status := reported$

send(v)$_i$
  Precondition:
      v is first on *send*
  Effect:
      remove first element of *send*

receive$_i$(v)
  Effect:
      add v to *receive*

Tasks:
$\{send(v)_{i,i+1} : v$ is a UID$\}$
$\{get\text{-}second\text{-}uid_i, get\text{-}third\text{-}uid_i, advance\text{-}phase_i, become\text{-}relay_i, relay_i\}$
$\{leader_i\}$

Theorem 15.7 *PetersonLeader solves the leader-election problem.*

Now we analyze the complexity. As stated above, the number of active processes is at least halved in each phase, until only one active process remains. This means that the total number of phases until a leader is elected is at most $\lfloor \log n \rfloor + 1$. During each phase, each process (either active or relay) sends at most two messages. Thus, at most $2n(\lfloor \log n \rfloor + 1)$ messages are sent in any execution of the algorithm. This is $O(n \log n)$, with a much better constant factor than in the *HS* algorithm.

For the time complexity, it is not hard to prove a naive upper bound of $O(n \log n(\ell + d))$. This is because there are $O(\log n)$ phases, and we can show that, for any p, the first p phases are completed within time $O(pn(\ell + d))$. (In each phase, each UID travels distance $O(n)$ around the ring. It takes time at most $\ell + d$ for a message to travel from one node to the next, provided that it is not blocked by a pileup. The same method we used in the proof of Lemma 15.4 can be used to argue that pileups cannot hurt the worst-case bound.)

A more refined analysis yields an upper bound of $O(n(\ell + d))$:

Theorem 15.8 *The time until a leader event occurs in any fair execution of PetersonLeader is $O(n(\ell + d))$.*

We only sketch the main ideas here, leaving the proof for a somewhat intricate exercise.

Proof Sketch. First, we can ignore pileups, since arguments such as those for Lemma 15.4 can be used to show that they do not affect the worst-case bound. The following claim is useful for the analysis.

Claim 15.9 *If processes i and j are distinct processes that are both active at phase p, then there must be some process k that is strictly after i and strictly before j in the clockwise direction, and such that process k is active at phase $p - 1$.*

The time complexity is proportional to the length of a certain chain of messages, ending with the message at the final phase p that causes the leader, i_p, to become *chosen*. The UID in that message originates at i_p itself at phase p and so travels a total distance of n at phase p. Process i_p starts this UID on its way when it enters phase p, which is just after i_p receives its $uid(3)$ at phase $p - 1$. This $uid(3)$ in turn originates at i_p's second predecessor that is active at phase $p - 1$, i_{p-1}, when i_{p-1} enters phase $p - 1$. By Claim 15.9, there is some process other than i_p that reaches phase $p - 1$, which implies that the greatest possible distance this UID can travel at phase $p - 1$ is n.

We continue tracing the chain backward. Process i_{p-1} enters phase $p - 1$ when it receives its $uid(3)$ at phase $p - 2$. This $uid(3)$ originates at i_{p-1}'s second predecessor that is active at phase $p - 2$, i_{p-2}, when i_{p-2} enters phase $p - 2$. Claim 15.9 can be used to show that i_{p-2} is no further back from i_{p-1} than i_{p-1}'s first predecessor that is active at phase $p - 1$. Continuing backward, we define $i_{p-3}, \ldots, i_1$, where each i_{q-1} is no further back from i_q than i_q's first predecessor that is active at phase q.

Now, using Claim 15.9 repeatedly, it is possible to show that the total length of the chain from i_{p-1} backward to i_1 is at most n. This implies that the total length of the chain is $3n$, which translates into a time bound of $O\left(n(\ell + d)\right)$. $\square$

15.1.4   A Lower Bound on Communication Complexity

We have just described two asynchronous network leader-election algorithms, *PetersonLeader* and the asynchronous version of *HS*, that have communication complexity $O\left(n \log n\right)$. In this section, we argue that the problem also has a lower bound of $\Omega(n \log n)$. Throughout this section we assume, without loss of generality, that the channels are universal reliable FIFO channels.

Recall that we have already given two $\Omega(n \log n)$ lower bound results for leader election in the synchronous setting, Theorems 3.9 and 3.11. Theorem 3.9 gives a lower bound for algorithms that are *comparison based*; it allows bidirectional communication and allows processes to know the number of nodes in the network. This result can be carried over directly to the asynchronous setting, since the synchronous model can be formulated as a restriction of the asynchronous model.

Theorem 15.10 *Let A be a comparison-based algorithm that elects a leader in asynchronous ring networks of size n, where communication is bidirectional and n is known to the processes. Then there is a fair execution of A in which $\Omega(n \log n)$ messages are sent by the time the leader is elected.*

Theorem 3.11 gives a lower bound for algorithms that can use UIDs in arbitrary ways but that have a fixed time bound and a large space of identifiers. Again, it allows bidirectional communication and allows processes to know the number of nodes. We also carry over a version of this result to the asynchronous setting:

Theorem 15.11 *Let A be any (not necessarily comparison-based) algorithm that elects a leader in asynchronous rings of size n, where the space of UIDs is infinite, communication is bidirectional, and n is known to the processes.*

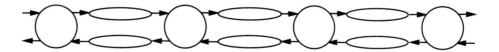

Figure 15.2: A line of automata.

Then there is a fair execution of A in which $\Omega(n \log n)$ messages are sent by the time the leader is elected.

Proof Sketch. If there is any fair execution of A in which more than $n \log n$ messages are sent by the time the leader is elected, then we are done, so assume that this is not the case. We "restrict" A to yield a synchronous algorithm S in which some message is sent at every round. Since at most $n \log n$ messages are sent in any fair execution of A by the time the leader is elected, this means that the number of rounds required for S to elect a leader is at most $n \log n$. Since the UID space is infinite, Theorem 3.11 applies to show that there is an execution of S in which $\Omega(n \log n)$ messages are sent by the time the leader is elected. This can be converted into a fair execution of A in which $\Omega(n \log n)$ messages are sent by the time the leader is elected. $\qquad \square$

Since Theorem 3.11 appears in a starred section of this book, we present an alternative, more elementary, lower bound proof for non-comparison-based algorithms. This proof is quite different from those of Theorems 3.9 and 3.11 in that it is based on asynchrony and on the assumption that the processes do not know the size of the ring.

Theorem 15.12 *Let A be any (not necessarily comparison-based) algorithm that elects a leader in rings of arbitrary size, where the space of UIDs is infinite, communication is bidirectional, and the ring size is unknown to the processes. Then there is a fair execution of A in which $\Omega(n \log n)$ messages are sent.*

The proof requires a few preliminary definitions. Assume that we have a universal infinite set $\mathcal{P}$ of process automata. All processes in $\mathcal{P}$ are assumed to be identical except for UIDs; also, they are assumed to know their neighbors only by local names, say "right" and "left."

Our main interest is in seeing how a collection of process automata from $\mathcal{P}$ behave when they are arranged in a ring; however, it is also useful to see how they behave when arranged in a straight line, as depicted in Figure 15.2. We define a *line* to be a linear composition (using I/O automaton composition) of distinct process automata from $\mathcal{P}$, with intervening reliable FIFO send/receive channels in both directions.

We say that two lines are *disjoint* if they contain no common process automaton, that is, no common UID. If L and M are two disjoint lines of automata, we define $join(L, M)$ to be the line consisting of L concatenated with M, with new reliable FIFO send/receive channels inserted between the rightmost process of L and the leftmost process of M. The *join* operator is associative, so we can extend it to apply to any number of lines. If L is any line of automata, we define $ring(L)$ to be the ring consisting of L wrapped around, with new reliable FIFO send/receive channels inserted in both directions between the rightmost and leftmost processes of L. Each process's right neighbor in the line becomes its clockwise neighbor in the ring. The *ring* and *join* operations are depicted in Figure 15.3. (We now represent the channels as just arrows rather than ovals.)

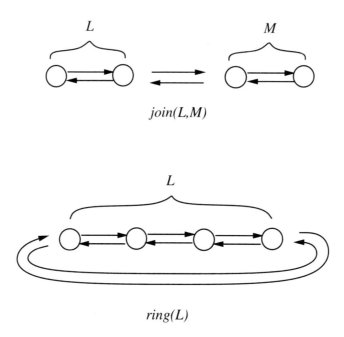

Figure 15.3: The *join* and *ring* operations.

If α is an execution of a line or ring, we define $C(\alpha)$ to be the number of messages sent in α. If R is a ring, we define $C(R)$ to be $sup\{C(\alpha) : \alpha$ is an execution of $R\}$, that is, the supremum of the number of messages that are sent in any execution of R. For a line, we consider the number of messages that can be sent when the line operates "in isolation," with no messages arriving at the end processes from the line's environment. Thus, if L is a line, we define $C(L)$ to be $sup\{C(\alpha) : \alpha$ is an input-free execution of $L\}$, that is, the supremum of the number of messages that are sent in any execution of L without any messages arriving at its endpoints from outside the line.

We say that a state s of a ring is *silent* if there is no execution fragment starting from s in which any new message is sent. We say that a state s of a line is *silent* if there is no input-free execution fragment starting from s in which any new message is sent. Note that if a ring or line is in a silent state, it does *not* mean that no further activity is possible—it just means that no further message-sending events can occur. It is still possible for processes to receive messages and perform internal steps and *leader* outputs.

We begin with a preliminary lemma.

Lemma 15.13 *There is an infinite set of process automata in $\mathcal{P}$, each of which can send at least one message without first receiving any message.*

Proof. We show something stronger: that all except possibly one process automaton in $\mathcal{P}$ can send at least one message without first receiving any message.

Suppose, to obtain a contradiction, that there are two processes in $\mathcal{P}$, say processes i and j, such that neither can send a message without first receiving one. Then consider the three rings R_1, R_2, and R_3 shown in Figure 15.4. (Now, for simplicity, we do not depict the channel automata at all.)

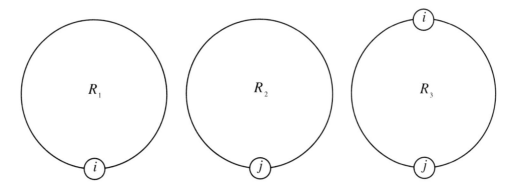

Figure 15.4: Rings R_1, R_2, and R_3 in the proof of Lemma 15.13.

Since neither i nor j can send a message unless it first receives one, no messages are ever sent in any execution of any of the three rings. Thus, the processes i and j proceed independently, performing local computation and *leader* actions, but never any communication actions. Since R_1 solves the leader-election problem, i must eventually perform a *leader* output in any fair execution of R_1. Likewise, since R_2 solves the leader-election problem, j must eventually perform a *leader* output in any fair execution of R_2. Now consider any fair execution α

of R_3. Because there is no communication, α is indistinguishable by process i from some fair execution of R_1 (using the formal notion of "indistinguishability" defined in Section 8.7), so i eventually performs a *leader* output in α. Likewise, α is indistinguishable by process j from some fair execution of R_2, so j eventually performs a *leader* output in α. But this causes two leaders to be elected in R_3, a contradiction.

We have shown that there cannot be two processes, i and j, in $\mathcal{P}$, neither of which can send a message without first receiving one. That is, there is at most one process in $\mathcal{P}$ that cannot send a message before receiving one. Since $\mathcal{P}$ is an infinite set, removing one process leaves an infinite set of processes, each of which can send a message without first receiving one.   ☐

The proof of Theorem 15.12 uses the following key lemma.

Lemma 15.14 *For every $r \geq 0$, there is an infinite collection of pairwise-disjoint lines, $\mathcal{L}_r$, such that for every $L \in \mathcal{L}_r$, it is the case that $|L| = 2^r$ and $C(L) \geq r2^{r-2}$.*

Proof.   By induction on r.

Basis: $r = 0$. Let $\mathcal{L}_0$ be the set of all single-node lines corresponding to all the processes in $\mathcal{P}$. The claim is trivial.

Basis: $r = 1$. Let $\mathcal{L}_1$ be any infinite collection of disjoint two-node lines composed of processes each of which can send a message without first receiving one. The existence of this collection is implied by Lemma 15.13. Then if L is any line from $\mathcal{L}_1$, there must be an input-free execution of L in which at least one message is sent: simply let one of the two processes send a message without first receiving one. This suffices.

Inductive step: Assume that $r \geq 2$ and the lemma is true for $r - 1$, that is, that there is an infinite collection of pairwise-disjoint lines, $\mathcal{L}_{r-1}$, such that for every $L \in \mathcal{L}_{r-1}$, it is the case that $|L| = 2^{r-1}$ and $C(L) \geq (r - 1)2^{r-3}$. Let $n = 2^r$.

Let L, M, and N be any three lines from $\mathcal{L}_{r-1}$. We consider the six possible joins of two of these three lines: $join(L, M)$, $join(M, L)$, $join(L, N)$, $join(N, L)$, $join(M, N)$, and $join(N, M)$. We show the following claim.

Claim 15.15 *At least one of these six lines has an input-free execution in which at least $\frac{n}{4} \log n = r2^{r-2}$ messages are sent.*

The lemma then follows from Claim 15.15, because infinitely many sets of three lines can be chosen from $\mathcal{L}_{r-1}$ without reusing any processes.

Proof (of Claim 15.15). Assume the contrary, that none of these six lines can be made to send as many as $\frac{n}{4} \log n$ messages. By the inductive hypothesis, there is a finite input-free execution α_L of L for which $C(\alpha_L) \geq (r-1)2^{r-3} = \frac{n}{8} \log \frac{n}{2}$. We can assume without loss of generality that the final state of α_L is silent, since otherwise α_L could be extended to a longer finite execution in which more messages are generated. (This extension cannot go on indefinitely, since we know that L alone cannot send as many as $\frac{n}{4} \log n$ messages.) Similarly, we obtain finite input-free executions α_M of M and α_N of N with the same properties.

Now we construct a finite execution $\alpha_{L,M}$ of the line $join(L, M)$. Execution $\alpha_{L,M}$ starts by running α_L on L and and α_M on M, delaying all messages sent on the channels connecting the lines L and M. In this prefix of $\alpha_{L,M}$, at least $2(\frac{n}{8}) \log \frac{n}{2} = \frac{n}{4}(\log n - 1)$ messages are sent.

Next, $\alpha_{L,M}$ continues to a silent state. Note that, however this happens, the number of additional messages that are sent in the extension must be strictly less than $\frac{n}{4}$, because otherwise the total number of messages in $\alpha_{L,M}$ would be at least $\frac{n}{4} \log n$, contradicting our assumption.

The particular way in which we make this extension is to allow only the $\frac{n}{4} - 1$ processes of L and the $\frac{n}{4} - 1$ processes of M that are closest to the junction of L and M to take steps after α_L and α_M, until the system reaches a state from which none of these processes can send any more messages. We claim that the resulting state of $join(L, M)$ must be silent. For if not, then a series of at least $\frac{n}{4} - 1$ messages must have been sent after the initial α_L and α_M, conveying information about the junction to a process at distance $\frac{n}{4}$ from the junction and enabling that process to send yet another message. (Convince yourself of this.) But this is a total of at least $\frac{n}{4}$ additional messages in the extension of α_L and α_M, which is impossible. So the indicated state of $join(L, M)$ must be silent.

Informally speaking, after $\alpha_{L,M}$, information about the junction of lines L and M has not reached either the midpoint of L or the midpoint of M. Only the $\frac{n}{4}$ processes on either side of the junction can know about the junction, and the two processes at distance exactly $\frac{n}{4}$ from the junction cannot send any new messages as a result of this knowledge. Figure 15.5 depicts the junction of L and M, for the case where $n = 16$.

In a similar way, we define finite executions $\alpha_{M,L}$, $\alpha_{L,N}$, and so on.

Now we combine the lines L, M, and N into several different rings to obtain a contradiction. First define R_1 to be $ring(join(L, M, N))$, as depicted in Figure 15.6. Define a fair execution α_1 of R_1, as follows. Execution α_1 begins with α_L, α_M, and α_N, thus making the three separate lines L, M, and N silent. Then α_1 continues as in $\alpha_{L,M}$, $\alpha_{M,N}$, and $\alpha_{N,L}$. Since the processes that learn about each junction extend at most halfway into each of the adjacent lines, there

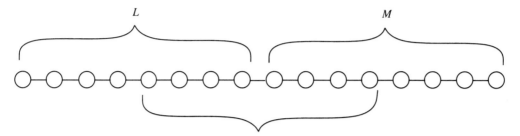

Only these processes can know about *join*

Figure 15.5: $\alpha_{L,M}$

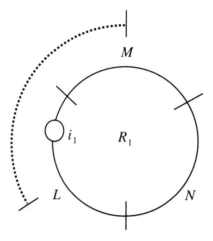

Figure 15.6: $R_1 = ring(join(L, M, N))$.

is no interference among these three extensions. Furthermore, after these three extensions, the entire ring is silent. Then α_1 continues in any fair manner. The correctness conditions imply that some leader, say i_1, is elected in α_1. We may assume without loss of generality that process i_1 is between the midpoint of L and the midpoint of M, as depicted in Figure 15.6.

Next we define $R_2 = ring(join(L, N, M))$, and define a fair execution α_2 of R_2 analogous to α_1 (this time using α_L, α_M, α_N, $\alpha_{L,N}$, $\alpha_{N,M}$, and $\alpha_{M,L}$). Then some leader, say i_2, is elected in α_2 (see Figure 15.7).

Next define $R_3 = ring(join(M, N))$, and define a fair execution α_3 of R_3 (using α_M, α_N, $\alpha_{M,N}$, and $\alpha_{N,M}$). Again, some leader, say i_3, must be elected

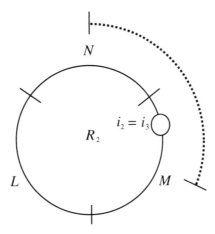

Figure 15.7: $R_2 = ring(join(L, N, M))$.

in α_3 (see Figure 15.8). We claim that i_3 must be in the lower half of R_3 as it is drawn in Figure 15.8, that is, somewhere between the midpoint of N and the midpoint of M, moving clockwise. For if i_3 were in the upper half of R_3, then α_1 and α_3 would be indistinguishable to process i_3, so i_3 would also be elected in α_1. But then two distinct processes, i_1 and i_3, would be elected in α_1, a contradiction. (Processes i_1 and i_3 are distinct because i_1 is between the midpoints of L and M, while i_3 is between the midpoints of M and N.)

Since i_3 is in the lower half of R_3, α_2 and α_3 are indistinguishable to i_3; hence, i_3 is also elected in R_2. Note that i_3 is between the midpoint of N and the midpoint of M in R_2. Since only one leader can be elected in α_2, we have $i_2 = i_3$. See Figure 15.7.

Finally, we define $R_4 = ring(join(L, N))$ and define a fair execution α_4 of R_4 (using α_L, α_N, $\alpha_{L,N}$, and $\alpha_{N,L}$). See Figure 15.9. We claim that no leader can be elected in α_4. For if a leader were elected from the top half of R_4, then that leader would also be elected in α_2, yielding two leaders in α_2. And if a leader were elected from the bottom half of R_4, then that leader would also be elected in α_1, yielding two leaders in α_1. Either way is a contradiction.

But the fact that no leader is elected in α_4 violates the problem requirements, which yields the contradiction needed to prove the claim. $\qquad\square$

The lemma now follows immediately from Claim 15.15, as described just before the proof of the claim.

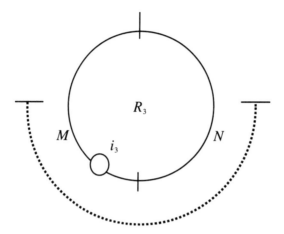

Figure 15.8: $R_3 = ring(join(M, N))$.

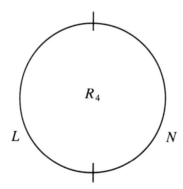

Figure 15.9: $R_4 = ring(join(L, N))$.

Now using Lemma 15.14, it is easy to complete the proof of Theorem 15.12.

Proof (of Theorem 15.12).   First suppose that n is a power of 2, say $n = 2^r$. Let L be any line in $\mathcal{L}_r$. Lemma 15.14 implies that $|L| = n$ and $C(L) \geq \frac{n}{4} \log n$. Let α be an input-free execution of L such that $C(\alpha) \geq \frac{n}{4} \log n$. Define $R = ring(L)$, that is, paste L into a ring. Define an execution α' of R that behaves exactly like α on L, delaying all messages across the junction between the endpoints of L until after at least $\frac{n}{4} \log n$ messages have been sent. Then $C(\alpha') \geq \frac{n}{4} \log n$, which proves that $C(R) \geq \frac{n}{4} \log n$.

We leave the argument for values of n that are non-powers of 2 for an exercise.

$\square$

Note the crucial parts played in the proof of Theorem 15.12 by the asynchrony and the unknown ring size.

15.2 Leader Election in an Arbitrary Network

So far in this chapter, we have considered algorithms for electing a leader in an asynchronous ring network. Now we will consider the leader-election problem in networks based on more general graphs. We assume in this section that the underlying graph is undirected, that is, that there is bidirectional communication on all the edges, and that it is connected. Processes are assumed to be identical except for UIDs.

Recall the *FloodMax* algorithm for synchronous networks from Section 4.1.2. It requires that processes know *diam*, the diameter of the network. In that algorithm, every process maintains a record of the maximum UID it has seen so far, initially its own. At each synchronous round, the process sends this maximum on all its channels. The algorithm terminates after *diam* rounds; the unique process that has its own UID as its known maximum then announces itself as the leader.

The *FloodMax* algorithm does not extend directly to the asynchronous setting, because there are no rounds in the asynchronous model. However, it is possible to simulate the rounds asynchronously. We simply require each process that sends a round r message to tag that message with its round number r. The recipient waits to receive round r messages from all its neighbors before performing its round r transition. By simulating *diam* rounds, the algorithm can terminate correctly.

In the synchronous setting, we described an optimization of *FloodMax* called *OptFloodMax*, in which each process only sends messages when it has new information, that is, when its maximum UID has just changed. It is not clear now to simulate this optimized version in an asynchronous network. If we simply tag messages with round numbers as for *FloodMax*, then a process that does not hear from all its neighbors at a round r cannot determine when it has received all its incoming messages for round r, so it cannot tell when it can perform its round r transition. We can, of course, add dummy messages between pairs of neighbors that do not otherwise communicate, but that destroys the optimization.

Alternatively, we can simulate *OptFloodMax* purely asynchronously—whenever a process obtains a new maximum UID, it sends that UID to its neighbors at some later time. This strategy will indeed eventually propagate the maximum to all processes. But there is a problem: now the processes have no way of knowing when to stop.

Many different solutions can be developed for the leader-election problem in general asynchronous networks, using many of the techniques that we will develop in the following sections and chapters. Some such techniques include

1. Asynchronous broadcast and convergecast, based on breadth-first search (Section 15.3).

2. Convergecast using a spanning tree (Section 15.5).

3. Using a synchronizer to simulate a synchronous algorithm (Section 16.5.1).

4. Using a consistent global snapshot to detect termination of an asynchronous algorithm (Section 19.2.3).

15.3   Spanning Tree Construction, Broadcast and Convergecast

Among the most fundamental tasks to be performed in an asynchronous network are the construction of a spanning tree for the network rooted at a given source node i_0 and the use of such a tree for performing broadcast and convergecast communication. In this section, we describe protocols for these tasks. We again assume that the underlying graph $G = (V, E)$ is undirected and connected. The processes do not need to know the size or diameter of the network. No UIDs are needed.

For the spanning tree problem, the requirement is that each process in the network should eventually report, via a *parent* output action, the name of its parent in a spanning tree of the graph G. Recall that in Section 4.2, we described a synchronous algorithm, *SynchBFS*, that constructs a *breadth-first* spanning tree rooted at i_0. The *SynchBFS* algorithm searches the graph synchronously starting from i_0, allowing each non-source process i to report as its parent the first neighbor from which it hears. This algorithm can be run in the asynchronous setting and is still guaranteed to produce a spanning tree, though not necessarily a breadth-first spanning tree. The code for the asynchronous algorithm follows.

AsynchSpanningTree$_i$ **automaton:**

Signature:

Input:
    receive("search")$_{j,i}$, $j \in nbrs$

Output:
    send("search")$_{i,j}$, $j \in nbrs$
    parent(j)$_i$, $j \in nbrs$

States:
parent ∈ *nbrs* ∪ {*null*}, initially *null*
reported, a Boolean, initially *false*
for every j ∈ *nbrs*:
    send(j) ∈ {*search, null*}, initially *search* if $i = i_0$, else *null*

Transitions:

send("search")$_{i,j}$
    Precondition:
        send(j) = *search*
    Effect:
        send(j) := *null*

receive("search")$_{j,i}$
    Effect:
        if $i \neq i_0$ and *parent* = *null* then
            parent := j
            for all k ∈ *nbrs* − {j} do
                send(k) := *search*

parent(j)$_i$
    Precondition:
        parent = j
        reported = *false*
    Effect:
        reported := *true*

Tasks:
{*parent*(j)$_i$: j ∈ *nbrs*}
for every j ∈ *nbrs*:
    {*send*("search")$_{i,j}$}

Theorem 15.16 *The AsynchSpanningTree algorithm constructs a spanning tree.*

Proof Sketch.   A key assertion for the proof is

> **Assertion 15.3.1** *In any reachable state, the edges defined by all the parent variables form a spanning tree of a subgraph of G, containing i_0; moreover, if there is a message in any channel $C_{i,j}$ then i is in this spanning tree.*

This is proved by induction, as usual. To show the liveness condition—that each node eventually gets included in the spanning tree—we use another invariant:

> **Assertion 15.3.2** *In any reachable state, if $i = i_0$ or parent$_i \neq$ null, and if j ∈ nbrs$_i$ − {i_0}, then either parent$_j \neq$ null or $C_{i,j}$ contains a search message or send(j)$_i$ contains a search message.*

We can then argue that for any $i \neq i_0$, we have *parent$_i \neq$ null* within time *distance*(i_0, i) · ($\ell + d$), which implies the liveness condition.   □

Complexity analysis.   In any fair execution of *AsynchSpanningTree*, the total number of messages is $O\left(|E|\right)$, and all the processes except i_0 produce *parent* outputs within time $diam(\ell + d) + \ell$. (Pileups are not an issue here, because only one message is ever sent on each channel.)

Note that the paths that are produced by the *AsynchSpanningTree* algorithm might be longer than the diameter of the network. This is because, in an asynchronous network, messages can sometimes travel faster on longer paths than on shorter ones. Nevertheless, the time to produce the tree is still bounded in terms of the diameter, because the time for each process to receive its first *search* message is no greater than the time for a message to travel to it from i_0 along a shortest path.

Message broadcast.   As for *SynchBFS*, it is easy to augment the *AsynchSpanningTree* algorithm to implement message broadcast from the source i_0. The message need only be piggybacked on all *search* messages during the formation of the spanning tree. The communication complexity of this broadcast is thus $O\left(|E|\right)$ and the time for it is $O\left(diam(\ell + d)\right)$.

Child pointers.   It is also easy to augment the *AsynchSpanningTree* algorithm so that parents learn who their children are. Since communication is here assumed to be bidirectional, all that is needed is for each recipient of a *search* message to respond directly with either a *parent* or *non-parent* message, as appropriate.

A precomputed spanning tree with child pointers can be used for *broadcasting* messages from process i_0 to all the other processes in the network. Each message is sent by i_0 to all its children, then forwarded from parents to children until it reaches the leaves of the tree. The total number of messages is only $O\left(n\right)$ per broadcast, and the time complexity is $O\left(h(\ell + d)\right)$, where h is the height of the spanning tree. There is an interesting *timing anomaly*: if the tree is produced using the *AsynchSpanningTree* algorithm, then the time complexity of the broadcast is $O\left(n(\ell + d)\right)$; it is not necessarily $O\left(diam(\ell + d)\right)$, even though the *AsynchSpanningTree* algorithm itself takes time bounded by the diameter. This is because the height of the tree that is produced by *AsynchSpanningTree* may be bigger than the diameter.

A precomputed spanning tree with child pointers can also be used for *convergecasting* information from all the processes in the tree to i_0. This works in the same way as it does in the synchronous setting: Each leaf process sends its information to its parent. Each internal process other than i_0 waits until it receives information from all its children, then combines this information with its own and sends the result to its parent. Finally, i_0 waits until it receives information from all its children, then combines this information with its own to produce the final result. The number of messages is $O(n)$, and the time is $O(h(\ell + d))$. As in the synchronous setting, this scheme can be used for the computation of a function based on distributed inputs.

A combination of a broadcast and a convergecast can be used to allow i_0 to send a message to all the other processes and to receive an acknowledgment that all processes have received it. Each leaf simply initiates a convergecast when it receives the broadcast message. The total number of messages is again $O(n)$, and the time is again $O(h(\ell + d))$.

We can also allow i_0 to broadcast a message and receive acknowledgments from all processes while a spanning tree is being constructed. Let W be the set of values that can be broadcast. The set M of messages is $\{(\text{"bcast"}, w) : w \in W\} \cup \{\text{"ack"}\}$.

$AsynchBcastAck_i$ automaton:

Signature:

Input:
    $receive(m)_{j,i}$, $m \in M$, $j \in nbrs$

Internal:
    $report_i$

Output:
    $send(m)_{i,j}$, $m \in M$, $j \in nbrs$

States:

$val \in W \cup \{null\}$, initially the value to be broadcast if $i = i_0$, else *null*
$parent \in nbrs \cup \{null\}$, initially *null*
reported, a Boolean, initially *false*
acked, a subset of *nbrs*, initially $\emptyset$
for every $j \in nbrs$:
    $send(j)$, a FIFO queue of messages in M; if $i = i_0$ then this initially contains the
        single element $(\text{"bcast"}, w)$, where $w \in W$ is the value to be broadcast; otherwise
        this is empty

Transitions:

$send(m)_{i,j}$
    Precondition:
        m is first on $send(j)$
    Effect:
        remove first element of $send(j)$

$receive(\text{"bcast"}, w)_{j,i}$
    Effect:
        if $val = null$ then
            $val := w$
            $parent := j$
            for all $k \in nbrs - \{j\}$ do
                add $(\text{"bcast"}, w)$ to $send(k)$
        else add "ack" to $send(j)$

receive("*ack*")$_{j,i}$
   Effect:
      acked := *acked* ∪ {*j*}

report$_i$ (for *i* ≠ *i*$_0$)
   Precondition:
      parent ≠ *null*
      acked = *nbrs* − {*parent*}
      reported = *false*
   Effect:
      add "*ack*" to *send*(*parent*)
      reported := *true*

report$_i$ (for *i* = *i*$_0$)
   Precondition:
      acked = *nbrs*
      reported = *false*
   Effect:
      reported := *true*

Tasks:
{*report*$_i$}
for every *j* ∈ *nbrs*:
   {*send*(*m*)$_{i,j}$: *m* ∈ *M*}

Complexity analysis. The total communication is $O(|E|)$, and the time is $O(n(\ell + d))$. The upper bound on time depends on n instead of *diam* because of the timing anomaly described above—the broadcast might travel fast along a long path, and the subsequent acknowledgments might travel slowly when they return along the same path. In Chapter 16, we will see how to obtain an algorithm whose time complexity depends only on *diam*.

Garbage collection. If the tree in *AsynchBcastAck* is only needed for sending and acknowledging one message, each process can delete all of the information about the algorithm after it performs its *report* action and sends out its *ack*s. We leave this modification and its correctness proof as an exercise.

Application to leader election. Asynchronous broadcast and convergecast can be used to solve the leader-election problem in arbitrary graphs without any distinguished source node and without the processes having any knowledge of the number of nodes or the diameter of the network. Now the processes need UIDs. We simply allow *every* node to initiate a broadcast-convergecast in order to discover the maximum UID in the network. The node that finds that the maximum is equal to its own UID elects itself as leader. This algorithm uses $O(n|E|)$ messages. We leave the time complexity for an exercise.

We finish this section by noting a close connection between two fundamental problems, in a connected, undirected graph network with only local knowledge, without any distinguished nodes, but with UIDs:

1. Finding an (unrooted) spanning tree for the graph

2. Electing a leader node

First, if we are given an unrooted spanning tree, then it is possible to elect a leader as follows. The idea is the same as we discussed for the synchronous case, at the end of Section 4.4.

STtoLeader algorithm:

The algorithm uses a convergecast of *elect* messages starting from the leaves of the tree. Each leaf node is initially enabled to send an *elect* message to its unique neighbor. Any node that receives *elect* messages from all but one of its neighbors is enabled to send an *elect* message to its remaining neighbor.

In the end, there are two possibilities: either some particular process receives *elect* messages along all of its channels before it has sent out an *elect* message, or *elect* messages are sent on some particular edge in both directions. In the first case, the process at which the *elect* messages converge elects itself as the leader. In the second case, one of the two processes adjacent to this edge, say the one with the larger UID, elects itself as the leader.

Theorem 15.17 *The STtoLeader algorithm elects a leader in a connected undirected graph network with a spanning tree in which the processes have only local knowledge and have UIDs.*

Complexity analysis. The *STtoLeader* algorithm uses only at most n messages and takes time only $O(n(\ell + d))$.

Conversely, if a leader is given, then we have already shown how to construct a spanning tree, using *AsynchSpanningTree*. This requires $O(|E|)$ messages and $O(diam(\ell + d))$ time. So, modulo the (reasonably small) costs of these two basic algorithms, the problems of leader election and finding an arbitrary spanning tree are equivalent.

15.4 Breadth-First Search and Shortest Paths

Now we reconsider the problem of breadth-first search (BFS) that we considered in Section 4.2 and the problem of finding shortest paths that we considered in Section 4.3, this time in asynchronous networks. Now we assume that the underlying graph $G = (V, E)$ is a connected undirected graph and that there is a distinguished source node i_0. For the shortest paths problem, we also assume that each undirected edge $(i, j) \in E$ has a nonnegative real-valued *weight*, *weight*(i, j), known at both endpoint processes. We assume that the processes do not know the size or diameter of the network and that there are no UIDs.

For breadth-first search, the problem is for each process in the network eventually to report, via a *parent* output action, the name of its parent in a breadth-first spanning tree. Recall that in the synchronous case, this can be accomplished by the simple *SynchBFS* algorithm. The asynchronous version of *SynchBFS* is the *AsynchSpanningTree* algorithm of Section 15.3; this is guaranteed to produce a spanning tree but not necessarily a breadth-first spanning tree.

It is possible to modify *AsynchSpanningTree* so that processes correct erroneous *parent* designations. That is, if process i initially identifies one of its neighbors, say j, as its parent, and later obtains information from another neighbor, say k, along a shorter path, then process i can change its *parent* designation to k. In this case, process i must inform its other neighbors about its correction, so that they might also correct their *parent* designations. The code appears below.

AsynchBFS$_i$ automaton:

Signature:

Input:
    $receive(m)_{j,i}$, $m \in \mathbb{N}$, $j \in nbrs$

Output:
    $send(m)_{i,j}$, $m \in \mathbb{N}$, $j \in nbrs$

States:
$dist \in \mathbb{N} \cup \{\infty\}$, initially 0 if $i = i_0$, ∞ otherwise
$parent \in nbrs \cup \{null\}$, initially *null*
for every $j \in nbrs$:
    $send(j)$, a FIFO queue of elements of $\mathbb{N}$, initially containing the single element 0 if $i = i_0$,
        else empty

Transitions:

$send(m)_{i,j}$
    Precondition:
        m is first on $send(j)$
    Effect:
        remove first element of $send(j)$

$receive(m)_{j,i}$
    Effect:
        if $m + 1 < dist$ then
            $dist := m + 1$
            $parent := j$
            for all $k \in nbrs - \{j\}$ do
                add $dist$ to $send(k)$

Tasks:
for every $j \in nbrs$:
    $\{send(m)_{i,j} : m \in \mathbb{N}\}$

Theorem 15.18 *In any fair execution of the AsynchBFS algorithm, the system eventually stabilizes to a state in which the parent variables represent a breadth-first spanning tree.*

Proof Sketch.   We first prove

> **Assertion 15.4.1** *The following are true in any reachable state.*
>
> 1. *For every process $i \neq i_0$, $dist_i$ is the length of some path p from i_0 to i in G in which the precedessor of i is $parent_i$.*
>
> 2. *For every message m in channel $C_{i,j}$, m is the length of some path p from i_0 to i.*

This implies that each process i always has correct information about *some* path from i_0 to i. But in order to show the liveness property—that each process eventually obtains information about a shortest path—we need another invariant that implies that information about shortest paths is "conserved."

> **Assertion 15.4.2** *The following is true in any reachable state. For every pair of neighbors i and j, either $dist_j \leq dist_i + 1$, or else either $send(j)_i$ or $C_{i,j}$ contains the value $dist_i$.*

We can then argue that for any i, we have $dist_i = distance(i_0, i)$ within time $distance(i_0, i) \cdot n(\ell + d)$; this argument can be made by induction on $distance(i_0, i)$. (We are taking pileups into account here.) This is enough to prove the liveness requirement.   □

Complexity analysis.   The number of messages sent in an execution of *Asynch-BFS* is $O(n|E|)$; this is because each node can acquire at most n different estimates of its distance from i_0, each of which causes a constant number of messages to traverse its incident edges. The time until the system reaches a stable state is $O(diam \cdot n(\ell + d))$; this is because the length of a shortest path from i_0 to any node is at most *diam*, and at most n messages are ever in any channel. (Again, we are taking pileups into account.)

Termination.   A problem with *AsynchBFS* is that there is no way for a process to know when there are no further corrections for it to make. (This would be true even if the size of the network were known.) Thus, the algorithm is technically not a solution to the BFS problem, because it never produces the required *parent* outputs. It is possible to augment *AsynchBFS* to produce the outputs by adding acknowledgments for all messages, convergecasting the acknowledgments back to i_0 as in *AsynchBcastAck*. This enables i_0 to learn when the system has reached a stable state and then to broadcast a signal to all the processes to perform their *parent* outputs.

This convergecast is a bit complicated, because, unlike for *AsynchBcastAck*, a process i may need to participate many times. Each time process i obtains a new *dist* estimate from a neighbor j and sends out corrections to all of its other neighbors, it waits for corresponding acknowledgments from all those neighbors before sending an acknowledgment to j. Bookkeeping is needed to keep the different sets of acknowledgments separate. We leave this for an exercise.

Known diameter.   If *diam* is known, then *AsynchBFS* can be improved somewhat by only allowing distance estimates that are less than or equal to *diam*. With this modification, each node can only acquire at most *diam* different estimates of its distance from i_0, leading to communication complexity $O\left(diam|E|\right)$ and time complexity $O\left(diam^2(\ell + d)\right)$. Adding termination as above keeps the same complexity bounds.

We now give another solution; this one does produce the needed *parent* outputs. It does not require any knowledge of the size or diameter of the network graph. This solution has smaller communication complexity than any of the versions of *AsynchBFS* but has higher time complexity than the version of *AsynchBFS* with known *diam*.

LayeredBFS algorithm:

The BFS tree is constructed in *layers*, where each layer k consists of the nodes at depth k in the tree. The layers are constructed in a series of phases, one per layer, all coordinated by process i_0.

In the first phase, process i_0 sends *search* messages to all of its neighbors and waits to receive acknowledgments. A process that receives a *search* message at phase 1 sends a positive acknowledgment. This enables all the processes at depth 1 in the tree to determine their parent, namely i_0, and, of course, i_0 knows its children. This constructs layer 1.

Inductively, we assume that k phases have been completed and that the first k layers have been constructed: each process at depth at most k knows its parent in the BFS tree, and each process at depth at most $k - 1$ knows its children. Moreover, the source i_0 knows that all of this has been accomplished. To construct the $k + 1$st layer in phase $k + 1$, process i_0 broadcasts a *newphase* message along all the edges of the spanning tree constructed so far, intended for the depth k processes.

Upon receiving a *newphase* message, each depth k process sends out *search* messages to all its neighbors except its *parent* and waits to receive acknowledgments. When a non-i_0 process receives its first *search* message in an execution, it designates the sender as its *parent* and returns a positive acknowledgment. When a non-i_0 process receives a subsequent *search* message, it returns a negative acknowledgment. When i_0 receives any *search* message, it returns a negative acknowledgment. When a depth k process has received acknowledgments for all its *search* messages, it designates the processes that have sent positive acknowledgments as its children.

Then the depth k processes convergecast the information that they have completed the determination of their children back to i_0, along the edges of the depth k spanning tree. They also convergecast a bit, saying whether any depth $k+1$ nodes have been found. Process i_0 terminates the algorithm after a phase at which no new nodes are discovered.

Theorem 15.19 *The LayeredBFS algorithm produces a breadth-first spanning tree.*

Complexity analysis. The *LayeredBFS* algorithm uses $O(|E| + n \cdot diam)$ messages. There are a total of $O(|E|)$ *search* and acknowledgment messages because each edge is explored at most once in each direction. Also, at every phase, each tree edge is traversed at most once by *newphase* and convergecast messages; since there at most $diam + 1$ phases, this yields a total of at most $O(n \cdot diam)$ such messages. Each phase takes time $O(diam(\ell + d))$, so the time complexity is $O\left(diam^2(\ell + d)\right)$.

The *AsynchBFS* algorithm with known *diam* and the *LayeredBFS* algorithm illustrate a trade-off between communication and time complexity. This trade-off is further illustrated by the following hybrid of the *AsynchBFS* and *LayeredBFS* algorithms. The *HybridBFS* algorithm uses a parameter m, $1 \le m \le diam$. If $m = 1$, then *HybridBFS* is the same as *LayeredBFS*, while if $m = diam$, *HybridBFS* is similar to *AsynchBFS* with known *diam*. For intermediate values of m, the communication and time complexity measures are between those of *LayeredBFS* and *AsynchBFS* with known *diam*.

HybridBFS algorithm:

The algorithm works in *phases*. In each phase, m layers in the BFS tree are determined (rather than just one as in *LayeredBFS*). In each phase, the next m layers are explored asynchronously, with corrections as in *Asynch-BFS*. Acknowledgments are convergecast back to process i_0. By the time a convergecast is completed, process i_0 knows that all the processes in the layers being explored in the current phase have stabilized to their correct distance estimates.

Complexity analysis. The *HybridBFS* algorithm has communication complexity $O\left(m|E| + \frac{n \cdot diam}{m}\right)$. There are a total of $O\left(m|E|\right)$ *search* and acknowledgment messages because each edge only carries information about at most m different distance estimates. Also, at every phase, each tree edge is traversed at most once by *newphase* and convergecast messages; since there at most $O\left(\frac{diam}{m}\right)$ phases, this yields at most $O\left(\frac{n \cdot diam}{m}\right)$ such messages. Each phase takes time $O\left(diam(\ell + d) + m^2(\ell + d)\right)$. (The m^2 term results from the possibility of a pileup of m messages in a single channel.) Thus, the total time complexity is $O\left(\frac{diam^2}{m}(l + d) + diam \cdot m(\ell + d)\right)$.

We have given three algorithms to solve the BFS problem: the *AsynchBFS* algorithm (with termination), the *LayeredBFS* algorithm, and the *HybridBFS* algorithm. For a simple comparison among the three, we consider the version of *AsynchBFS* with termination and in which *diam* is known. We neglect the local processing time ℓ and also neglect the effects of pileups in the links, using d as an upper bound for the delivery of each message in a channel. We obtain

	Messages	Time
AsynchBFS:	$O\left(diam|E|\right)$	$O\left(diam \cdot d\right)$
LayeredBFS:	$O\left(|E| + n \cdot diam\right)$	$O\left(diam^2 d\right)$
HybridBFS:	$O\left(m|E| + \frac{n \cdot diam}{m}\right)$	$O\left(\frac{diam^2}{m}d\right)$

Now we turn to the problem of finding shortest paths in an asynchronous network based on a weighted undirected graph. The problem is for each process in the network to determine and output its parent in a shortest paths tree from the source node i_0, as well as its distance from i_0. The problem of breadth-first search is just the special case of the shortest paths problem when all the weights are 1.

Recall that in the synchronous setting, the *BellmanFord* algorithm solves the problem of finding shortest paths. Even though this algorithm is synchronous, it must correct erroneous estimates of its distance. The *BellmanFord* algorithm can be run asynchronously, using the following code, which is the natural generalization of the code for *AsynchBFS*. The *AsynchBellmanFord algorithm* was the algorithm used to establish routes in the ARPANET between 1969 and 1980.

AsynchBellmanFord$_i$ automaton:

Signature:

Input:
  $receive(w)_{j,i}$, $w \in R^{\geq 0}$, $j \in nbrs$
Output:
  $send(w)_{i,j}$, $w \in R^{\geq 0}$, $j \in nbrs$

States:
$dist \in R^{\geq 0} \cup \{\infty\}$, initially 0 if $i = i_0$, ∞ otherwise
$parent \in nbrs \cup \{null\}$, initially *null*
for every $j \in nbrs$:
  $send(j)$, a FIFO queue of elements of $R^{\geq 0}$, initially containing the single element 0 if $i = i_0$,
  else empty

Transitions:

$send(w)_{i,j}$
  Precondition:
    w is first on $send(j)$
  Effect:
    remove first element of $send(j)$

$receive(w)_{j,i}$
  Effect:
    if $w + weight(j,i) < dist$ then
      $dist := w + weight(j,i)$
      $parent := j$
      for all $k \in nbrs - \{j\}$ do
        add $dist$ to $send(k)$

Tasks:
for every $j \in nbrs$:
  $\{send(w)_{i,j} : w \in R^{\geq 0}\}$

Theorem 15.20 *In any fair execution of the AsynchBellmanFord algorithm, the system eventually stabilizes to a state in which the parent variables represent a shortest paths tree rooted at i_0, and in which the dist variables contain the correct distances of the nodes from i_0.*

A problem for *AsynchBellmanFord*, as for *AsynchBFS*, is that there is no way for a process to know when it has no further corrections to make. Thus, the algorithm is not strictly correct, because it never produces the required outputs. We can augment *AsynchBellmanFord* with a convergecast of acknowledgments, in the same way that we did for *AsynchBFS*, and thus obtain the needed outputs.

The complexity analysis of *AsynchBellmanFord* is interesting, mainly because the worst-case message and time complexities are extremely bad—then are both *exponential* in n. For comparison, recall that the synchronous *BellmanFord* algorithm requires only $(n-1)|E|$ messages and $n-1$ rounds, while the *AsynchBFS* algorithm (without known diameter and without termination) requires only $O\left(n|E|\right)$ messages and $O\left(diam \cdot n(\ell + d)\right)$ time.

Theorem 15.21 *Let n be any even number, $n \geq 4$. Then there is a weighted graph G with n nodes, in which the AsynchBellmanFord algorithm sends at least $\Omega(c^n)$ messages and takes at least $\Omega(c^n d)$ time to stabilize in the worst case, for some constant $c > 1$. (We may take $c = 2^{\frac{1}{2}}$.)*

Proof.   We assume that the channels are universal FIFO reliable channels. Let $k = \frac{n-2}{2}$. Let G be the weighted graph depicted in Figure 15.10. Most of the edges in graph G have weight 0; the only edges with non-zero weights are the right-facing sloped edges, and they have weights that are successively decreasing powers of 2.

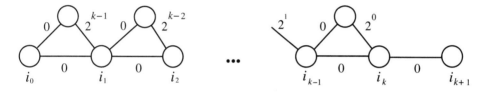

Figure 15.10: Bad weighted graph for the *AsynchBellmanFord* algorithm.

We claim that the possible finite *dist* estimates that process i_k can take on during an execution of *AsynchBellmanFord* on graph G are exactly the numbers in the set $\{2^k - 1, 2^k - 2, \dots, 3, 2, 1, 0\}$. Each of these can be generated by the flow of messages along a particular path from i_0 to i_k. In fact, we claim that it is possible to force i_k to take on all of these estimates in order, from the largest to the smallest, in the *same execution*, as follows.

Suppose that the messages on the upper paths propagate very fast, thus giving i_k the estimate $2^k - 1$. Next, the message from i_{k-1} to i_k along the lower path arrives at i_k, giving i_k the new estimate $2^k - 2$. Next, the message from i_{k-2} to i_{k-1} along the lower path arrives at i_{k-1}, causing i_{k-1} to reduce its estimate by 2, from $2^k - 2$ to $2^k - 4$. Process i_{k-1} then sends this reduced estimate on both paths to i_k. Once again, suppose that the messages on the upper path travel faster, so process i_k next obtains an estimate of $2^k - 3$, and afterward $2^k - 4$.

Next, the message from i_{k-3} to i_{k-2} along the lower path arrives at i_{k-2}, causing i_{k-2} to reduce its estimate. Continuing in this way, we can cause process i_k to obtain all of the estimates, $2^k - 1, \dots, 0$, in order.

It is possible to run the system in such a way that all the processes, and all the channels except for $C_{i_k,i_{k+1}}$, operate very quickly. This results in a queue of 2^k messages in $C_{i_k,i_{k+1}}$, which is $\Omega(2^{\frac{n}{2}})$ messages, or $\Omega(c^n)$ messages. Moreover, if all these messages take the maximum time to get delivered, then the time complexity is $\Omega(c^n d)$, as needed. $\qquad\square$

We next consider upper bounds on complexity for *AsynchBellmanFord*. The number of messages sent on any channel $C_{i,j}$ is proportional to the number of different estimates that the sending process, i, obtains. The number of such estimates is certainly no greater than the number of distinct simple paths from i_0 to i in the graph, which is $O(n^n)$. (Actually, it is smaller, but we leave the improvement for an exercise.) Thus, the total communication complexity is $O(n^n|E|)$. An upper bound on the time complexity is $O(n^{n+1}(\ell + d))$, using the bound of n^n on the number of messages in one channel.

Notice how heavily the time bounds depend on the pileups in the message channels. If we adopt the simpler assumption, sometimes made in the theoretical research literature, that any message takes at most time d from sending until receipt (and if we ignore local processing time), then the time bound for *Asynch-BellmanFord* can be calculated as only $O(nd)$. This is certainly not a realistic analysis for this algorithm.

15.5 Minimum Spanning Tree

For the last section in the chapter, we return to the problem of constructing a minimum-weight spanning tree of a network based on an arbitrary connected undirected graph. In Section 4.4, we gave an algorithm, *SynchGHS*, to solve this problem in the synchronous setting; now we show how to modify this algorithm so that it can be used in the asynchronous setting. The resulting algorithm, which we call *GHS* after its discoverers, Gallager, Humblet, and Spira, is one of the best-known algorithms in distributed computing theory. It is a carefully engineered, complex algorithm that has been considered interesting enough to serve as a case study for algorithm verification methods.

We suggest that you reread Section 4.4 at this point; it contains the underlying theory on which the *GHS* algorithm is based, plus the *SynchGHS* algorithm, which contains many of the ideas needed for *GHS*.

15.5.1 Problem Statement

As before, we assume that the underlying graph $G = (V, E)$ is connected and undirected, and we assume that the edges have associated weights. We want the processes to cooperate to construct a minimum-weight spanning tree (MST) for the graph G, that is, a tree spanning the vertices of G whose total edge weight is less than or equal to that of every other spanning tree for G.

We assume that processes have UIDs and that the weight of each edge is known to the processes associated with the incident vertices. We make one technical assumption: we assume that all the edge weights are unique. The same argument that we gave at the end of Section 4.4 shows that this uniqueness assumption is not significant—ties among edges with the same weights can be broken using the adjacent process UIDs. We assume that the processes have only local knowledge of the graph; in particular, they do not know the number of nodes or the diameter.

We assume that the processes are initially *quiescent*, that is, that no locally controlled actions are enabled in their start states. We assume that each process has a *wakeup* input action by which the environment signals it to begin executing an MST algorithm. We allow any number of processes to receive *wakeup* inputs during the course of an execution; thus, the algorithm must work regardless of the number of processes that initiate computation and regardless of when they do so. Note that we assume only that processes' start states are quiescent; we permit a process to awaken when it receives any sort of input—a *wakeup* or a message from another process.[1] The output of the algorithm is the set of edges comprising an MST, in particular, every process is required to output the set of edges adjacent to it that are in the MST.

15.5.2   The Synchronous Algorithm: Review

Recall that the *SynchGHS* algorithm is based on two fundamental properties of MSTs, given by Lemmas 4.3 and 4.4. These properties are used to justify a strategy in which, at any intermediate state, the algorithm has constructed a spanning forest all of whose edges are in the MST. Then each of an arbitrary subset of the components of the spanning forest may independently determine its own minimum-weight outgoing edge (MWOE), knowing that all such edges found must be included in the unique MST.

The *SynchGHS* algorithm works in "levels." The level 0 spanning forest consists of individual nodes and no edges. Given the level k spanning forest, the algorithm constructs the level $k + 1$ spanning forest by allowing *all* components in the level k spanning forest to determine their MWOEs and then combining all the components along these edges. It follows that each level k component contains at least 2^k nodes.

The determination of the MWOE for a component is managed by a distinguished leader node of the component, whose UID is used as a component

---

[1]The assumptions we are making here about *wakeup* messages are different from those we made at the end of Section 15.1.1. There, we assumed that *wakeup* messages arrived at *all* processes.

identifier. The leader broadcasts a request to determine the MWOE along the component edges, then the processes engage in a query protocol to learn which of their neighbors are in the same or different components, and then the processes convergecast their information back to the leader. The combination of components involves communication from the leader to the process adjacent to the MWOE. Using careful bookkeeping, the processes can ensure that the communication complexity is kept to $O(n \log n + |E|)$ and the number of rounds to $O(n \log n)$.

If we try to run *SynchGHS* in an asynchronous network, some difficulties arise. For instance,

Difficulty 1: In *SynchGHS*, when a process i queries a neighbor j to see if j is in the same component of the current spanning forest, it knows that j is up to the same level of the construction. Therefore, if process j has a distinct component identifier, then it must be the case that j is not in the same component. But in the asynchronous setting, a situation could arise whereby process j is actually in the same component as i but has not yet learned this (because a message containing the latest component identifier has not yet reached it).

Difficulty 2: The *SynchGHS* algorithm achieves a message cost of $O(n \log n + |E|)$, based on the fact that the levels are kept synchronized. Each level k component has at least 2^k nodes, which implies that the total number of levels is at most $\log n$. In the asynchronous setting, there is a danger of constructing the components in an unbalanced way, leading to many more messages. The number of messages sent by a component to find its MWOE will be at least proportional to the number of nodes in the component. We must avoid the situation where a large component repeatedly discovers that its MWOE leads to a single-node component and combines with that single node (as in Figure 15.11), for this could require $\Omega(n^2)$ messages.

Difficulty 3: In *SynchGHS*, the levels remain synchronized, whereas in the asynchronous setting, some components could advance to higher levels than others. It is not clear what type of interference might occur as a result of concurrent searches for MWOEs by adjacent components at different levels.

These difficulties require careful consideration in adapting the *SynchGHS* algorithm to the asynchronous setting.

15.5.3 The GHS Algorithm: Outline

The *GHS* algorithm follows the *SynchGHS* algorithm quite closely. In particular, it achieves the same communication complexity, $O(n \log n + |E|)$, and a corresponding time bound, $O(n \log n(\ell + d))$.

In the *GHS* algorithm, processes form themselves into components, which

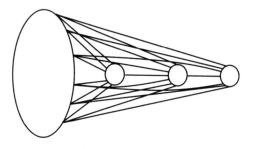

Figure 15.11: A large component might grow by one node at a time.

combine to form larger components. The initial components are just the individual nodes. Each component has a distinguished leader node, as well as a spanning tree that is a subgraph of the MST.

Within any component, the processes cooperate in an algorithm to find the MWOE for the entire component. This involves a broadcast originating at the leader, asking each process in the component to determine its own minimum-weight edge that leads outside the component. Information about all these edges is convergecast back to the leader, who can determine the MWOE for the entire component. This MWOE will be included in the MST.

Once the MWOE is found, a message is sent out over that edge to the component on the other side. The two components may then combine into a new, larger component. In this case, the entire procedure is repeated for the new component. Enough combinations are carried out so that, eventually, all the nodes in the graph are included in a single component, whose spanning tree is the needed MST.

There are several problems that need to be addressed in making this algorithm work correctly. First, how does a process i know which of its edges lead outside its current component? Certainly, we need some way of naming components so that two processes can use the names to determine whether they are in the same component. But this issue is more complicated than this: it may be, as described in Difficulty 1 above, that an adjacent process j with a different component name is in fact in the same component as the querying process i, but has not yet learned this fact because of communication delays. Some sort of synchronization is needed, to ensure that process j does not respond that it is in a different component unless it has current information about its component name.

The second problem, described in Difficulty 2 above, involves an excessive number of messages that might be produced by an unbalanced combination of components. In order to cope with this difficulty, we will try to keep the sizes of components that are combined roughly equal. More precisely, we will associate a *level* with each component, as we do in *SynchGHS*. As in *SynchGHS*, all the initial single-node components will have *level* = 0, and the number of nodes in a level k component will be at least 2^k. A level $k + 1$ component will only be formed by combining exactly two level k components, thereby preserving the size requirement. This strategy departs slightly from that used in *SynchGHS*: in *SynchGHS*, an arbitrary number of level k components can be combined to yield a level $k + 1$ component.

As it turns out, these *levels* will not only be useful in keeping the combinations balanced—they also provide some identifying information that can help processes determine if they are in the same component.

The third problem, described in Difficulty 3, is that some components can advance to higher levels than others, leading to possible interference between concurrent searches for MWOEs by adjacent components at different levels. Some synchronization will be required to prevent such interference.

15.5.4 In More Detail

The *GHS* algorithm combines components in two different ways, which we call *merging* and *absorbing*.

merge: This combining operation is applied to two components, C and C', where *level*(C), the *level* of C, is the same as *level*(C') and where C and C' have a common MWOE. The result of the *merge* is a new component containing all the nodes and edges of C and C' plus the common MWOE. The new component is assigned *level* = $k + 1$.

absorb: This combining operation is applied to two components, C and C', where *level*(C) < *level*(C') and the MWOE of C leads to a node in C'. The result of the *absorb* is a new component containing all the nodes and edges of C and C', plus the MWOE of C. The new component is assigned the same *level* as C'. In fact, we prefer not to think of the *absorb* as actually producing a "new component," but rather as just adding C to the already existing C'.

The *absorb* operation is useful for the case where some processes lag behind others. Suppose that a large group of nodes are formed into a large component, C', with a high *level* by a series of *merge* operations, while some other small components lag behind with lower *levels*. If one of the small components, C, discovers that its MWOE leads to C', then C can be absorbed into C' without obtaining any information about the MWOE of C'. This will be an inexpensive operation.

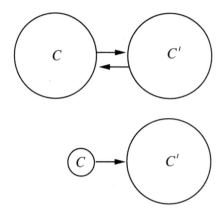

Figure 15.12: Merging and absorbing.

These two combining strategies are illustrated roughly by Figure 15.12. Note that the fact that $level(C) < level(C')$ in an *absorb* operation does not imply that C has fewer nodes than C'; the illustration is meant only to suggest the "typical" case.

The *merge* and *absorb* operations manipulate the *levels* in a way that handles Difficulty 2; in particular, they guarantee that any level k component has at least 2^k nodes. We now argue that the *merge* and *absorb* operations are sufficient to combine all components into an MST for the entire graph.

Lemma 15.22 *Suppose that we start from an initial situation in which each component consists of a single node with level $= 0$, and apply any allowable finite sequence of merge and absorb operations. Then after this sequence of operations, either there is only one component, or else some merge or absorb operation is enabled.*

Proof.   Suppose that there is more than one component after a sequence of *merge* and *absorb* operations. We show that there is some applicable operation.

We consider the "component digraph" G', whose nodes are the current components and whose directed edges correspond to the MWOEs; each edge is directed away from the component for which it is the MWOE. Lemma 4.5 implies that in any weakly connected portion of G', there is a unique cycle of length 2. This says that there are two components, C and C', whose MWOEs point to each other. But it is easy to see that in this case, the two MWOEs must be the same edge of the original graph G.

Now we claim that C and C' can be combined, using either a *merge* or an *absorb* operation. For if $level(C) = level(C')$, then a *merge* operation is enabled, whereas if C and C' have different *levels*, then the one with the smaller *level* can be absorbed into the one with the larger *level*. □

Now we consider in more detail how the MWOE is found for a given component. This involves each process i in the component determining its own minimum-weight edge (if any) that is outgoing from the component, $mwoe(i)$, and then all the processes sending their information to a leader node, who selects the one with the minimum weight overall. This requires some additional machinery. First, we need a mechanism for selecting the leader process for each component. And second, we need a way for a process to determine whether a given edge is outgoing from the component.

To help in these tasks, for every component of level 1 or greater, we identify a specific edge that we call its *core* edge. This edge is defined in terms of the series of *merge* and *absorb* operations that are used to construct the component.

- After a *merge* operation, the *core* is the common MWOE of the two original components.

- After an *absorb* operation, the *core* is the *core* of the original component with the larger level number.

Thus, the *core* of a component is the edge along which the last *merge* that was used in the formation of the component took place.

For a component of level 1 or greater, we use the pair consisting of the *core* (technically, the weight of the core) and the *level* as a component identifier. This makes sense because the weights of edges are assumed to be unique. We also designate one of the endpoints of the *core* edge—for instance, the one with the higher UID—as the leader. For a level 0 component, the unique node is, of course, the leader.

Now suppose that process i wishes to determine whether its edge to neighboring process j is outgoing from i's current component. If process j's current component identifier is the same as that of i, then process i is certain that j is in the same component as itself. However, if j's component identifier is different from that of i, then it is still possible that i and j are in the same component but that j has not yet received notification of the current component identifier. There is one special case that can be resolved: if j's component identifier is different from that of i, and j's latest known *level* is at least as high as that of i, then it is certain that j cannot be in the same component as i. This is so because, in the course of an execution, a node can only have at most one component identifier for each *level*, and because, when i is actively searching for its outgoing edges, it is certain that i's component identifier is up-to-date.

Thus, if i and j have the same component identifiers, j responds that it is in the same component. Also, if i and j have different component identifiers and the *level* of j is at least as great as that of i, then j responds that it is in a different component. The only remaining case is where the *level* of j is strictly smaller than that of i; in this case, process j simply delays answering i until its own *level* rises to become at least as great as that of i. This handles Difficulty 1.

However, notice that we now have to reconsider the progress argument, since this new delay could conceivably cause progress to be blocked. The fact that some processes in a component can be delayed in finding their minimum-weight outgoing edges means that the component as a whole can be delayed in finding its MWOE; we must consider whether this can cause the system to reach a state in which no further *merge* or *absorb* operations can be performed.

To see that this cannot happen, we use essentially the same progress argument as before, but this time we consider only those components with the current lowest *level*, say k. All the processes in these components must succeed in their individual minimum-weight outgoing edge determinations, so these components must succeed in determining their MWOEs. If any of the level k components finds that its MWOE leads to a higher-level component, then an *absorb* operation is possible. On the other hand, if every level k component finds that its MWOE leads to another level k component, then Lemma 4.5 implies that we must have a length 2 cycle involving level k components, and a *merge* operation is possible. Thus, even with the new type of delay, the algorithm must make progress until the complete MST is found.

Thus, we have seen how each process determine its own minimum-weight outgoing edge (if any). Then, as described above, the leader of the component determines the MWOE for the component via a broadcast and convergecast, selecting the edge with the overall minimum weight.

We must still consider Difficulty 3: the possible interference between concurrent searches for MWOEs by adjacent components at different levels. In particular, we consider what happens if a lower-level component C gets absorbed into a higher-level component C' while C' is involved in determining its own MWOE. Suppose that the MWOE of C connects node i of C and node j of C'. See Figure 15.13.

There are two cases to consider. First, suppose that process j has not yet determined its minimum-weight edge outgoing from the component at the time the *absorb* occurs. In this case, the algorithm searches for the MWOE of the combined component in C as well as in C'. The fact that j has not yet determined $mwoe(j)$ means that it is not too late to include C in the search.

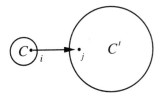

Figure 15.13: Component C is absorbed into C', while C' is searching for its MWOE.

On the other hand, suppose that process j has already determined $mwoe(j)$ at the time the *absorb* occurs. In this case, we claim that $mwoe(j) \neq (i, j)$, that is, the minimum-weight edge for j cannot possibly be the same as the MWOE for C. This is because the fact that $mwoe(j)$ has already been determined implies that it leads to a component with a *level* at least as great as that of C'. (A technical point: The fact that the *level* told to j by the other endpoint of $mwoe(j)$ was at least as great as the *level* of C' implies that it is still at least as great, because the *level* known by a process cannot decrease.) However, since C is absorbed into C', we know that $level(C)$ is strictly smaller than $level(C')$. So $mwoe(j) \neq (i, j)$, as claimed. This implies that the weight of $mwoe(j)$ is strictly less than the weight of (i, j).

Then we claim that the MWOE for the combined component cannot possibly be adjacent to a node in C. This is true because (i, j) is the MWOE for fragment C, so there can be no edges leading out of C with smaller cost than (i, j), and so no edges leading out of C with smaller cost than the already discovered $mwoe(j)$. Thus, if $mwoe(j)$ has already been determined at the time of the *absorb*, the algorithm need not search for the MWOE of the combined component in C. This is fortunate, since it might already be too late to search there—process j might have already reported its minimum-weight edge, and component C' might be in the process of deciding on an overall MWOE without knowing about the newly absorbed nodes.

15.5.5 Specific Messages

We now give a little more detail about the specific messages that are sent in the *GHS* algorithm. The messages are of the following types:

- *initiate*. An *initiate* message is broadcast throughout a component, starting at the leader, along the edges of the component's spanning tree. Normally,[2] it triggers processes to start trying to find their *mwoes*. It also carries the component identifier (*core* and *level*).

---

[2] There is an exceptional case, which we will mention below.

- *report.* A *report* message convergecasts information about minimum-weight edges back toward the leader.

- *test.* A process i sends a *test* message to a neighbor j to try to ascertain whether or not j is in the same component as i. This is part of the procedure by which process i searches for its own *mwoe*.

- *accept* and *reject.* These are sent in response to *test* messages. They tell the testing node whether the responding node is in a different component (*accept*) or the same component (*reject*).

- *changeroot.* A *changeroot* message is sent from the leader of a component toward the component process that is adjacent to the component's MWOE, after the MWOE has been determined. It is used to tell that process to attempt to combine with the component at the other end of the MWOE.

- *connect.* A *connect* message is sent across the MWOE of a component C when that component attempts to combine with another component. A *merge* operation occurs when *connect* messages have been sent both ways along the same edge. An *absorb* operation occurs when a *connect* message has been sent one way along an edge that leads to a process at a higher level than the sender.

In the *test-accept-reject* protocol, there is some bookkeeping that the testing process i must do in order to keep the communication complexity low; this is similar to the bookkeeping described earlier for *SynchGHS*. Namely, process i maintains a list of its incident edges in increasing order of weight. It classifies these incident edges into three categories:

- *branch* edges are those that have already been determined to be part of the MST.

- *rejected* edges are those that have already been determined not to be part of the MST, because they lead to other nodes within the same component.

- *basic* edges are all the others. These are the edges that process i cannot yet classify as being in or out of the MST.

Initially, all the edges are classified as *basic*.

When process i searches for its minimum-weight outgoing edge, it only needs to send *test* messages along *basic* edges. It tests the *basic* edges sequentially, lowest weight to highest. For each *basic* edge, process i sends a *test* message containing the component identifier (*core* and *level*) of its component C. The recipient j of a *test* message checks to see if its own latest known component identifier is the same as that of the sender i. If so, it responds with a *reject* message. When i receives the *reject* message, it reclassifies the edge as a *rejected* edge. Also, if the recipient j's *core* is different from that of i and its *level* is at least as great as that of i, then j responds with an *accept* message. (This does not cause i to reclassify the edge.) Finally, if j's *core* is different from that of i and its *level* is strictly smaller than that of i, process j simply delays responding until such time as it is able to send back a *reject* or *accept*, according to the rules above.

Note that it is possible for i to receive an *accept* message for edge (i, j), but for edge (i, j) not to be the one eventually identified as the MWOE for the entire component C. In this case, the same edge (i, j) may be retested by i in subsequent searches. Process i only reclassifies an edge as a *branch* edge when it actually discovers that the edge is part of the MST, for example, when process i receives a *changeroot* message referring to that edge or receives a *connect* message over the edge.

When two *connect* messages cross on a single edge, a *merge* operation occurs. Then the common edge is identified as the new *core*, the *level* is increased by one, and the endpoint with the larger UID is chosen as the new leader. The new leader then broadcasts *initiate* messages to begin looking for the MWOE of the new component formed by the *merge*. When a *connect* message is received by a process from a lower *level* component, an *absorb* operation occurs. The recipient process knows whether or not it has already found its *mwoe* and thus knows whether it needs to trigger a search in the newly absorbed component. In either case, it will broadcast an *initiate* message to that component to tell the processes in that component the latest component identifier.[3]

Note that each process is able to perform its output as soon as it no longer classifies any of its incident edges as *basic*; the output is simply the set of *branch* edges.

Theorem 15.23 *The GHS algorithm solves the MST problem in an arbitrary connected undirected weighted graph network.*

15.5.6 Complexity Analysis

The communication complexity analysis is similar to that for *SynchGHS*, giving the same bound of $O(n \log n + |E|)$. We divide the messages into two sets, resulting separately in the $O(n \log n)$ term and the $O(|E|)$ term. The $O(|E|)$ counts the *test* messages that lead to rejection, plus the *reject* messages, on all

---

[3]This is the exceptional case mentioned earlier.

edges. This is a total of $O\left(|E|\right)$, because each edge is rejected at most once: after a *reject* message is received on an edge by a process i, i never again tests that edge.

All the other messages—the *test-accept* pairs that enable a process to accept an edge as its *mwoe*, the *initiate* and *report* messages that are used for broadcast and convergecast, and the *changeroot* and *connect* messages that are used after a component has determined its MWOE—are charged to the task of finding the MWOE for a specific component (i.e., for a specific *core* and *level*). In this task for one component, these messages can be associated with nodes in such a way that there is at most one of each of these types of messages associated with each node. (In particular, each process sends at most one successful *test* message.) Thus, the number of messages charged to one component C is $O\left(|C|\right)$, where we are using $|C|$ to denote the number of nodes in component C. The total number of messages is, therefore, proportional to

$$\sum_C |C|.$$

Organizing the components according to their *levels*, we rewrite this expression as

$$\sum_{k:0\leq k\leq \log n}\left(\sum_{C:level(C)=k} |C|\right).$$

For each *level* k, the inner sum is at most n, because no node ever appears in more than one component with *level* $= k$. Therefore, this expression is at most equal to

$$\sum_0^{\log n} n = O\left(n\log n\right).$$

It follows that the overall communication complexity of the algorithm is $O(n\log n + |E|)$, as claimed.

For the time complexity, it is convenient to include a preliminary protocol to awaken all the processes as quickly as possible. Then it can be shown by induction on k that the time for all the processes to reach level at least k is $O\left(kn(\ell+d)\right)$. Thus, the total time is $O\left(n\log n(\ell+d)\right)$.

Lower bound. Note that the communication complexity must be $\Omega(n\log n)$, at least for *some* graphs. For example, if the communication complexity of MST in rings were less than this, then it would be possible to combine a communication-efficient MST algorithm with the *STtoLeader* algorithm to obtain a leader-election algorithm whose communication complexity is also less than this. But this would contradict Theorem 15.12, which says that $\Omega(n \log n)$ messages are necessary for leader election in rings of size n.

15.5.7 Proving Correctness for the GHS Algorithm

The *GHS* algorithm is the first one in this book for which we have not at least outlined a correctness proof. There is a good reason for this: at the present time, no simple proof is known. The algorithm has been proved correct, at least four times, by a variety of methods, but none of the proofs is sufficiently nicely organized to be outlined in a few pages.

One approach that works is the usual invariant assertion approach. Here, this involves collecting a rather large number of invariants, describing all the different tasks performed by the algorithm. For instance, there are invariants describing the correct operation of the broadcast and convergecast tasks, invariants describing the *test-accept-reject* protocol, and invariants describing the *changeroot-connect* protocol. All of these invariants can be proved together by a huge inductive argument. Such a proof involves a large number of cases and a large amount of tedious detail, but is, in principle, quite straightforward.

But such a brute-force proof does not seem to take full advantage of the modularity that is present in the algorithm. For instance, the algorithm appears to be decomposable into separate tasks such as broadcast-convergecast and testing, yet this decomposition is not expressed formally (e.g., using the I/O automaton composition operation). So it is not clear how we could carry out the correctness proofs for the various tasks separately and then combine the results.

Also, the brute-force invariant assertion proof does not take much advantage of high-level intuition about the algorithm. Note that much of our discussion of the algorithm has involved high-level notions such as graphs, components, levels, and MWOEs, rather than low-level concepts such as messages and local variables. It seems that a good proof ought to proceed, as far as possible, in terms of the high-level notions. In fact, a second approach that works is to give a high-level description of the algorithm, as an automaton that manipulates graphs, components, and so on, and to prove this correct using invariants. Then it is possible to prove that the detailed algorithm correctly simulates the high-level description. The formal correspondence between the low-level and high-level algorithms is a *simulation relation*, as defined in Section 8.5.5. For examples of simulation proofs, see the proof of the *InfiniteTicketME* mutual exclusion algorithm in Section 10.9.4 and the proofs of the *SimpleSynch* and *SafeSynch* synchronizer algorithms in Chapter 16. The proofs for synchronizer algorithms demonstrate especially nicely how some complex asynchronous network algorithms can be decomposed in two ways: using I/O automaton composition for separating the reasoning about separate tasks and using simulation relations to allow reasoning at the highest possible level of abstraction.

Another approach to proving the correctness of *GHS* is to try to relate its behavior formally to that of the synchronous version of the algorithm, *Synch-GHS*. Informally speaking, the correspondence seems very close. Note that this relationship cannot be a simple simulation relation, because in the asynchronous algorithm, different portions of the network can be far out of synchronization, as determined by the current *levels*. Whatever correspondence is used must allow some reordering of activities that happen in different places in the network.

We regard it as an interesting open problem to find a nicely decomposed proof of correctness for the *GHS* algorithm. It would be acceptable to modify the algorithm slightly to obtain the modularity, as long as the modifications do not affect the important algorithmic ideas or the complexity.

In Chapters 16–22, you will see a variety of asynchronous network algorithms, decomposed using a variety of methods. We hope that the complications of algorithms such as *GHS* have convinced you that it is important to find such decompositions.

15.5.8   A Simpler "Synchronous" Strategy

Note that the *GHS* algorithm has many complications that do not arise in the *SynchGHS* algorithm; most of these are the result of the fact that different portions of the network can be far out of synchronization, as determined by the current *levels*. One way of avoiding these complications is to try to simulate *SynchGHS* as closely as possible, keeping the *levels* of nearby processes close to each other.

> ### *SimpleMST* algorithm:
>
> The algorithm is again based on combining components, where each component has an associated *level*. The initial components are just the individual nodes, each with *level* = 0. Now level k components can only be combined into level $k + 1$ components, using the same general strategy as in *SynchGHS*.
>
> Each process i maintains a *local-level* variable, which keeps track of the latest *level* process i knows for its component. Initially, the *local-level* is 0, and when process i learns about its membership in a new component with *level* = k, i raises its *local-level* to k.
>
> The key idea is that a process i with *local-level* = k tries not to participate in the algorithm for finding its level k component's MWOE until all the processes in the network have *local-levels* at least equal to k. Actually

achieving this would require expensive global synchronization. But in fact, a weaker local synchronization is enough: each process only waits to learn that all of its *neighbors* in the underlying graph have *local-levels* at least k. So that all processes can discover this, each process sends a message on each of its incident edges each time its *local-level* increases.

The *SimpleMST* algorithm has the same time complexity upper bound as *GHS*, namely, $O(n \log n(\ell + d))$, and, of course, it is much simpler than *GHS*. The communication complexity is worse, however, because of the synchronization messages used at every level: now it is $O(|E| \log n)$.

15.5.9 Application to Leader Election

An MST algorithm can be used to solve the leader-election problem in an arbitrary connected undirected weighted graph with UIDs. Namely, after establishing an MST, the processes participate in the *STtoLeader* protocol to select the leader.

Note that the processes do not need to know when the MST algorithm has completed its execution throughout the network; it is enough for each process i to wait until it is finished locally, that is, has output its set of incident edges in the MST. If process i receives a message that is part of the *STtoLeader* algorithm before it has performed its output for the MST protocol, it simply delays the message until it is done with MST. The idea is the same as in the general strategy for handling input arrivals in *wakeup* messages, described at the end of Section 15.1.1.

If the *GHS* algorithm is used for establishing the MST, the total number of messages to elect a leader is $O(n \log n + |E|)$ and the total time is $O(n \log n(\ell + d))$.

15.6 Bibliographic Notes

The *AsynchLCR* and the asynchronous version of the *HS* algorithm, like the synchronous versions of these algorithms, are derived from the papers by LeLann [191], Chang and Roberts [71], and Hirschberg and Sinclair [156]. The *Peterson-Leader* algorithm was developed by Peterson and appears in [239]. Another unidirectional algorithm that achieves $O(n \log n)$ communication complexity was developed by Dolev, Klawe, and Rodeh [97]. The smallest upper bound currently known for the communication complexity for leader election in an asynchronous ring is $1.271 n \log n + O(n)$, by Higham and Przytycka [155].

The observations at the beginning of Section 15.1.4, indicating how the synchronous lower bound results for the communication complexity of leader election carry over to the asynchronous setting, are due to Gafni [129]. The direct proof of the lower bound for the asynchronous setting is due to Burns [61].

Afek and Gafni [6] have developed complexity bounds for leader election in complete asynchronous networks.

The key ideas for the simple spanning tree, broadcast, and convergecast algorithms appear to have originated in papers by Segall [258] and by Chang [72]. The *AsynchBFS* and *AsynchBellmanFord* algorithms are based on the sequential shortest paths algorithm of Bellman and Ford [43, 125]. The *AsynchBellmanFord* algorithm is essentially the algorithm used to establish routes in the ARPANET between 1969 and 1980 [223]. The termination protocol described for *AsynchBFS* and *AsynchBellmanFord* in this chapter is based on the work of Dijkstra and Scholten on termination detection for "diffusing computations" [92]; we present this work in Section 19.1. The *LayeredBFS* and its m-layer version are inspired by the work of Gallager [131]; these results were later improved by Awerbuch and Gallager [33]. Another interesting shortest paths algorithm was designed by Gabow [128].

The *GHS* protocol was developed by Gallager, Humblet, and Spira [130]. The code in their paper is of a slightly different style from the precondition-effect code of this book; a version more in the style of this book appears in Welch's Ph.D. thesis [287]. There have been several papers published with correctness proofs for the *GHS* algorithm or variants of it. Welch, Lamport, and Lynch [288] proved correctness using simulation methods. Chou and Gafni [79] verified a slightly modified version of the algorithm, using a correspondence with the synchronous algorithm. Stomp and de Roever [87] and Janssen and Zwiers [164] also carried out proofs. Awerbuch [31] developed an $O(nd)$ time, $O(n \log n)$ message MST algorithm. Garay, Kutten, and Peleg [132] developed an $O((diam + \sqrt{n})d)$ time algorithm. Awerbuch, Goldreich, Peleg, and Vainish [34] proved a lower bound result that says that the number of messages needed to establish a minimum spanning tree is $\Omega(|E|)$; this result assumes that the messages are of bounded length. The *SimpleMST* algorithm is due to Awerbuch.

Humblet [160] designed an asynchronous distributed algorithm for finding a minimum spanning tree in a directed graph network.

15.7   Exercises

15.1. Give an alternative proof of correctness for the *AsynchLCR* algorithm, based on relating it formally to the synchronous *LCR* algorithm.

15.2. Give precondition-effect code for the modification of *AsynchLCR*, described at the end of Section 15.1.1, which includes *wakeup* inputs and *receive* buffers.

15.3. For the asynchronous version of the *HS* algorithm:

(a) Give precondition-effect code.

(b) Prove the correctness of the algorithm, based on the code.

(c) Analyze its time complexity, assuming the usual upper bounds of ℓ for each task of each process and d on delivery time for the *oldest* message in any channel.

(d) Analyze its time complexity, assuming an upper bound of d on the delivery time for an *arbitrary* message and neglecting local processing time.

15.4. Consider the *PetersonLeader* algorithm in a ring with $n = 15$ nodes, in which the UIDs for processes $P_1, \dots, P_{16}$ are, respectively, 25, 3, 6, 15, 19, 8, 7, 14, 4, 22, 21, 18, 24, 1, 10, 23. Which process is elected as leader?

15.5. Design a version of the *PetersonLeader* algorithm for the synchronous network model described in Chapters 2 and 3. The processes in your algorithm may know n. Strive to make your algorithm as simple (to write and to understand) as possible, while keeping the unidirectionality and the $O(n \log n)$ communication complexity. Analyze the time (number of rounds) complexity of your algorithm.

15.6. Give a careful proof of the $O(n(\ell + d))$ upper bound for the time complexity of the *PetersonLeader* algorithm.

15.7. Design a version of the *PetersonLeader* leader-election algorithm for rings with bidirectional communication. In the new version of the algorithm, the UIDs remaining in contention do not need to precess around the ring, but can stay where they originate; each process simply collects the UIDs from its two active neighbors at each phase. Give precondition-effect code for your algorithm. Analyze its message and time complexity.

15.8. Extend the *AsynchLCR* algorithm, the asynchronous *HS* algorithm, and the *PetersonLeader* algorithm so that the non-leaders also announce that they are not the leader, via *non-leader$_i$* output actions. Analyze the communication and time complexities of the resulting algorithms.

15.9. Fill in the details of the proof sketch for Theorem 15.11.

15.10. Give a careful argument to justify the statement made in the inductive step of the proof of Claim 15.15, that the state after $\alpha_{L,M}$ is silent.

15.11. Extend the proof of Theorem 15.12 so that it applies to rings whose sizes are not powers of 2. What is the best lower bound you can obtain in this way?

15.12. Consider the problem of leader election in networks based on bidirectional *line graphs*; such a graph consists of n processes numbered $1, \dots, n$, arranged in a line, with bidirectional edges between each pair of neighbors. Assume that each process knows its neighbors by the local names "right" and "left," with the orientation consistent along the line. Assume that each process knows whether or not it is an endpoint. Assume that the processes have no knowledge of n.

   (a) Give a leader-election algorithm for such networks that uses a small number of messages.

   (b) Why does this result not contradict the lower bound in Lemma 15.14?

15.13. Consider the asynchronous simulation of *OptFloodMax* described in Section 15.2, in which the processes do not know when to terminate.

   (a) Write precondition-effect code for the asynchronous simulation.

   (b) For an arbitrary graph G and UID assignment, compare the maximum number of messages sent in your simulation to the maximum number sent in the synchronous *OptFloodMax* algorithm.

15.14. Fill in the details of the proof of Theorem 15.16.

15.15. Give a careful proof of correctness for *AsynchBcastAck*.

15.16. Write precondition-effect code for a modification of *AsynchBcastAck* in which each process garbage-collects all information about the algorithm after performing a *report* action and sending out its *acks*. Prove its correctness and analyze its complexity.

15.17. Design an algorithm for broadcast and acknowledgment in asynchronous networks, in which the time complexity depends on the diameter of the network rather than the total number of nodes.

15.18. Extend the spanning tree, broadcast, and convergecast algorithms in Section 15.3 to the case where the network is based on a strongly connected directed graph. Analyze the complexity of your algorithms.

15.19. Give a careful description and complexity analysis for the leader-election strategy given just after the description of *AsynchBcastAck*. Analyze the time complexity under two different assumptions: the usual upper bound of d on delivery of the oldest message in each channel and an upper bound of d on the delivery of an arbitrary message in each channel. In the latter case, you may ignore local processing time.

15.20. Describe in detail an algorithm that allows a distinguished process i_0 in an asynchronous network based on an arbitrary connected undirected graph G to calculate the number of nodes in G. Sketch a correctness proof.

15.21. Fill in the details of the proof of Theorem 15.18.

15.22. For the *AsynchBFS* algorithm,

(a) Produce an execution that uses as many messages as you can manage; try to achieve the given upper bound of $O\left(n|E|\right)$.

(b) Produce an execution that takes the longest time that you can manage until a stable state is reached; try to achieve the given upper bound of $O\left(diam \cdot n(\ell + d)\right)$.

15.23. Write precondition-effect code for the modification of *AsynchBFS* in which processes produce *parent* outputs, by means of an acknowledgment protocol. Do not assume any knowledge of the size or diameter of the network graph.

Prove the correctness of your protocol and analyze its complexity. (*Hint:* The communication complexity should be the same as for the basic *Asynch-BFS* algorithm. The time complexity becomes bigger because of the timing anomaly discussed for *AsynchSpanningTree* and *AsynchBcastAck*.)

15.24. Repeat Exercise 15.23 for the modification of *AsynchBFS* in which *diam* is known and in which processes produce *parent* outputs.

15.25. Write precondition-effect code for *LayeredBFS* and prove its correctness.

15.26. Give a detailed description of the *HybridBFS* algorithm, either using precondition-effect code or using very precise English. Prove correctness.

15.27. Design an efficient algorithm that allows a distinguished process i_0 in an asynchronous network based on an arbitrary connected undirected graph G to determine the maximum distance k from i_0 to the furthest node in the network. Analyze its message and time complexity.

15.28. Give an upper bound for the time complexity of the *AsynchBellmanFord* shortest paths algorithm. It should be as tight as you can make it.

15.29. Write precondition-effect code for a modification of *AsynchBellmanFord* in which processes produce parent and distance outputs, by means of an acknowledgment protocol. Prove the correctness of your protocol and analyze its complexity.

15.30. Design an algorithm to find the shortest paths from a fixed source node i_0 to all other nodes in the network. Your algorithm should have a much better time bound than the *AsynchBellmanFord* algorithm, say, $O\left(n(\ell + d)\right)$.

15.31. Extend the breadth-first search and shortest paths algorithms in Section 15.4 to the case where the network is based on a strongly connected directed graph. Analyze the complexity of your algorithms.

15.32. Give complete precondition-effect code for the *GHS* minimum spanning tree algorithm.

15.33. Consider the *GHS* minimum spanning tree algorithm.

   (a) State and prove carefully an upper bound on the time from when the first process awakens until the last process announces its results. You may assume that a preliminary protocol is used to awaken all the nodes as quickly as possible.

   (b) How tight is the upper bound you proved in (a)? That is, describe a particular execution of the algorithm that takes time that is as close as you can get to your upper bound.

15.34. Describe an execution of *GHS* in which a *reject* message arrives at process i along channel $C_{j,i}$, in response to a previous *test* message by i, at a time when i classifies edge (i, j) as a *branch* edge. Argue that the algorithm handles this case correctly.

15.35. Suppose that, at some point in an execution of the *GHS* algorithm, a process i in a component C sends a *connect* message over some edge (i, j), directed toward a component C' having the same *level* as C. Argue that component C eventually either gets merged with C' or else absorbed into some component that includes C'.

15.36. *Research Question*: Compare the operation of the *GHS* minimum spanning tree algorithm to that of *SynchGHS*. For example, what is the relationship between the components produced in the two cases? (It may be possible to exploit such a connection in a formal proof of correctness for *GHS*.)

15.37. *Research Question*: Find a nice, simple proof of correctness for the *GHS* algorithm as described in this chapter and in [130]. If it helps, you may modify the algorithm slightly, as long as you retain the same basic algorithmic ideas and the same message and time complexity.

15.38. For the *SimpleMST* algorithm,

    (a) Write precondition-effect code.

    (b) Prove correctness.

15.39. *Research Question*: Find an MST algorithm with approximately $O\,(diam \cdot d)$ time complexity and with all messages of size $O\,(\log n)$.

15.40. Give a formal description of the leader-election strategy described in Section 15.5.9, as a composition of I/O automata that produce an MST and I/O automata that use an MST to elect a leader. Describe the interactions between these two sets of automata carefully, identifying what actions are used for communication between the two sets of automata and identifying exactly what behavior each set of automata requires of the other set.

15.41. Consider a network based on a *line graph*, as described in Exercise 15.12. That is, the graph consists of n processes numbered $1, \ldots, n$, arranged in a line, with bidirectional edges between each pair of neighbors. Each process knows its neighbors by the local names "right" and "left," with the orientation consistent along the line. Each process knows whether or not it is an endpoint. Processes do not know n.

Assume that each process i initially has a very large integer value v_i, and that it can hold in memory only a constant number of such values at any time. Design an algorithm to sort the values among the processes, that is, to cause each process i to return one output value o_i, where the multiset of outputs is equal to the multiset of inputs and $o_1 \leq o_2 \leq \ldots \leq o_n$. Try to design the most efficient algorithm you can, both in terms of the number of messages and in terms of the time. Prove your claims.

15.42. Consider an asynchronous connected undirected network of arbitrary topology in which each process has a UID. Assume that each process i initially receives as input some integer value v_i. Design an algorithm that will cause each process to return the sum of all the inputs in the network. Try to keep the communication complexity, as measured in terms of the number of messages, low. Prove your claims.

15.43. Consider a "banking system" in which each process in a network keeps a number indicating an amount of money. We assume, for simplicity, that there are no external deposits or withdrawals, but messages travel between processes at arbitrary times, containing money that is being "transferred" from one location to another. The channels preserve FIFO order.

Design a distributed network algorithm that allows each process to decide on (that is, to output) its own balance, so that the total of all the balances is the correct amount of money in the system. Assume that the execution of this algorithm is triggered by signals arriving from the outside, at one or more of the system locations. (These signals could happen at any time and could happen at different times at different locations.)

Your algorithm should not halt or delay transfers "unnecessarily." Give a convincing argument that your algorithm works correctly.

15.44. Design a version of the *LubyMIS* algorithm of Section 4.5 that works in asynchronous networks. Give a careful statement of what your algorithm guarantees and prove it.

Chapter 16

Synchronizers

In Chapter 15, we gave several examples of distributed algorithms programmed directly on the "bare" asynchronous network model. As should be apparent by now, this model has so much uncertainty that it is very difficult to program directly. It is, therefore, desirable to have simpler models that can be programmed more easily and whose programs can be translated into programs for the general asynchronous network model.

We have already presented two models that are simpler than the asynchronous network model—the *synchronous network model* and the *asynchronous shared memory model*—and have given many examples of algorithms for these two models. In this chapter, we show how algorithms for the synchronous network model can be transformed into algorithms for the asynchronous network model, while in Chapter 17, we show how asynchronous shared memory algorithms can be transformed into asynchronous network algorithms. These transformations enable algorithms for the two simpler models to be run in asynchronous networks.

The idea of transforming synchronous network algorithms into asynchronous algorithms has already been suggested by some of the algorithms that appear in Chapter 15, namely, the simulation of *FloodMax* using round numbers on all messages in Section 15.2 and the *SimpleMST* algorithm in Section 15.5.8.

The strategy of transforming synchronous to asynchronous network algorithms works only for non-fault-tolerant algorithms. In fact, such a transformation cannot work for fault-tolerant algorithms because, as we will show in Chapter 21, the capabilities for fault-tolerance are fundamentally different in synchronous and asynchronous networks.

We formulate the transformation from the synchronous network model to the asynchronous network model in terms of a system module called a (local) *synchronizer*. We then describe several distributed implementations of the synchronizer. All of these implementations involve synchronizing the system *at every synchronous round*; this is necessary because the transformations are designed to work for arbitrary synchronous algorithms. The ability to synchronize less frequently (as, for example, in the *SimpleMST* algorithm) depends on special properties of the algorithm that ensure that it still works correctly if it is allowed to exhibit arbitrary interleavings of process steps between synchronization points.

Our presentation of the synchronizer implementations turns out to be a very good example of modular decomposition of distributed algorithms. We use several algorithm decomposition techniques, most of which are described in Chapter 8. We begin with a "global" specification of correctness in terms of I/O automata. Then we define a local synchronizer abstractly and show that it implements the global specification; this requires techniques based on partial orders of events. Next we describe several alternative ways of implementing the local synchronizer; each could be shown to do so using the simulation method of Section 8.5.5. However, most of these implementations can take advantage of additional decomposition steps. Thus, we define another system module known as a *safe synchronizer*, show how it can be used to implement the local synchronizer, and then develop several distributed algorithms as implementations of the safe synchronizer. The entire development is a good illustration of the power of decomposition methods in enabling simple description (and proofs) of complicated distributed algorithms.

We close the chapter with a contrasting lower bound on the time overhead required to run a synchronous network algorithm in an asynchronous network, if the synchronization requirements are very strong.

16.1 The Problem

In this section, we describe the problem to be solved by a synchronizer. The starting point is the synchronous network model, with a collection of synchronous processes running at the nodes of an undirected graph $G = (V, E)$, communicating by messages sent over the edges. In the formulation of that model in Chapter 2, each process i is presented as a kind of state machine, with message-generation and transition functions. Here, we deviate from the earlier development by instead representing each process i as a "user process" I/O automaton U_i.[1]

Let M be the fixed message alphabet used in the synchronous system. We define a *tagged message* to be a pair (m, i), where $m \in M$ and $1 \le i \le n$.

The user automaton U_i has output actions of the form *user-send*$(T, r)_i$, where

---

[1] We are referring to these processes here as "user processes" because they are users of the synchronizer system, which is the main system component we are now studying.

T is a set of tagged messages and $r \in \mathbb{N}^+$, by which it sends messages to its neighbors. The tag in a tagged message indicates the message destination, and the r argument represents the round number. If U_i does not have any messages to send at round r, then it performs $user\text{-}send(\emptyset, r)_i$. U_i also has input actions of the form $user\text{-}receive(T, r)_i$, where T is a set of tagged messages and $r \in \mathbb{N}^+$, by which it receives messages from its neighbors. Here, a tag indicates the message source and r is again the round number. U_i may also have other external actions by which it interacts with the outside world. We now model inputs and outputs of the user automata using input actions and output actions rather than encoding them in the states (as we did in Chapter 2).

Example 16.1.1   *user-send* and *user-receive* actions

> Suppose that $n = 4$. Then $user\text{-}send(\{(m_1, 1), (m_2, 2)\}, 3)_4$ indicates that at round 3, user U_4 sends message m_1 to user U_1 and message m_2 to user U_2, and sends no other messages. Also, $user\text{-}receive(\{(m_1, 1), (m_2, 2)\}, 3)_4$ indicates that at round 3, U_4 receives message m_1 from U_1 and message m_2 from U_2, and receives no other messages.

U_i is expected to preserve the *well-formedness* condition that the $user\text{-}send_i$ and $user\text{-}receive_i$ actions alternate, starting with a $user\text{-}send_i$ action, and that successive pairs of actions occur in order of rounds. That is, the sequence of such actions is a prefix of an infinite sequence of the form

$$user\text{-}send(T_1, 1)_i, user\text{-}receive(T'_1, 1)_i, user\text{-}send(T_2, 2)_i, user\text{-}receive(T'_2, 2)_i,$$
$$user\text{-}send(T_3, 3), \dots .$$

There is one other condition—a liveness condition—that U_i is required to satisfy: in any well-formed fair execution, U_i must eventually perform a $user\text{-}send_i$ for each round r such that $user\text{-}receive_i$ events for all previous rounds have already occurred. That is, the users continue sending messages for infinitely many rounds, as long as the system keeps responding.

We describe the rest of the system as a *global synchronizer, GlobSynch*. Its job is, at each round, to collect all the messages that are sent by user automata at that round in *user-send* actions and to deliver them to all the user automata in *user-receive* actions. It synchronizes globally, after all the *user-send* events and before all the *user-receive* events of each round. See Figure 16.1 for a picture of the combination of user and *GlobSynch* automata, that is, the *GlobSynch system*. Notice that *user-send* actions are input actions of *GlobSynch*, while *user-receive* actions are output actions of *GlobSynch*.

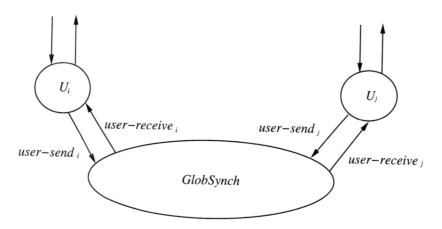

Figure 16.1: Architecture for the *GlobSynch* system.

GlobSynch can easily be described as an I/O automaton.

GlobSynch automaton:

Signature:

Input:

    user-send$(T, r)_i$, T a set of tagged messages, $r \in \mathbb{N}^+$, $1 \leq i \leq n$

Output:

    user-receive$(T, r)_i$, T a set of tagged messages, $r \in \mathbb{N}^+$, $1 \leq i \leq n$

States:

tray, an array indexed by $\{1, \ldots, n\} \times \mathbb{N}^+$ of sets of tagged messages, initially all $\emptyset$

user-sent, *user-rcvd*, each an array indexed by $\{1, \ldots, n\} \times \mathbb{N}^+$ of Booleans, initially all *false*

Transitions:

user-send$(T, r)_i$
    Effect:
        user-sent$(i, r) :=$ *true*
        for all $j \neq i$ do
            tray$(j, r) :=$ *tray*$(j, r) \cup \{(m, i) | (m, j) \in T\}$

user-receive$(T, r)_i$
    Precondition:
        for all j
            user-sent$(j, r) =$ *true*
        user-rcvd$(i, r) =$ *false*
        $T =$ *tray*(i, r)
    Effect:
        user-rcvd$(i, r) :=$ *true*

Tasks:

for every i, r:

    $\{$*user-receive*$(T, r)_i : T$ a set of tagged messages$\}$

In this code, *tray*(i, r) is designed to hold the messages to U_i that are submitted by all its neighbors; these messages are tagged with their senders' indices.

The *user-sent* and *user-rcvd* components just keep track of whether *user-send* and *user-receive* events have occurred.

It should not be hard to see that any algorithm in the synchronous network model of Chapter 2 can be described in this new style—as a composition of user automata U_i and the *GlobSynch* automaton. We leave this for an exercise.

The synchronizer problem is to "implement" the *GlobSynch* automaton with an asynchronous network algorithm, with one process P_i at each node i of the underlying graph G and a reliable FIFO send/receive channel $C_{i,j}$ in each direction on each edge (i, j) of G. This implementation should ensure that the individual user automata U_i cannot tell the difference between running in the implementation system (i.e., user automata plus the distributed algorithm) and running in the *GlobSynch* system. That is, we want to ensure that if α is any fair execution of the implementation system, then there is a fair execution α' of the specification system such that for each i, α is indistinguishable from α' to U_i.[2]

Note that we do not require that the relative order of events at different users be preserved, but only the view of each individual user. We will return to this issue in Section 16.6.

16.2 The Local Synchronizer

All of the synchronizer implementations we describe are "local," in the sense that they only involve synchronization among neighbors in the network rather than among arbitrary nodes. The advantage of using only local synchronization is the potential for savings in communication and time complexity. In this section, we define a local variant of *GlobSynch* that we call *LocSynch*; the algorithms will be presented as implementations of *LocSynch*.

LocSynch is nearly identical to *GlobSynch*. The only difference is in the *user-receive* transitions, which are now described by

---

LocSynch automaton:

Transitions:
$user\text{-}receive(T, r)_i$
    Precondition:
        for all $j \in nbrs \cup \{i\}$
            $user\text{-}sent(j, r) = true$
        $user\text{-}rcvd(i, r) = false$
        $T = tray(i, r)$
    Effect:
        $user\text{-}rcvd(i, r) := true$

---

[2] This uses the definition of "indistinguishable" from Section 8.7, which says that the two executions project to give identical executions of U_i.

Thus, in *LocSynch*, round r messages can be sent to U_i as soon as round r messages have been received from all its neighbors and from U_i itself; it is not necessary to wait for messages from all users in the entire network.

Lemma 16.1 *If α is any fair execution of the LocSynch system (i.e., users plus LocSynch), then there is a fair execution α' of the GlobSynch system that is indistinguishable from α to each U_i.*

We cannot use simulation techniques to prove this correspondence as we did, for example, in the proof of *TicketME* in Section 10.9. This is because the relative order of external actions that happen at different nodes is sometimes different in the two systems. Rather, we use a method based on *partial orders* of events.

Proof Sketch. Let L and G denote the *LocSynch* and *GlobSynch* systems, respectively, modified slightly by reclassifying all the internal actions of the user automata as outputs. (Thus, the external actions of each system are exactly all the actions of the user automata.) Certain events of L "depend on" other events: a *user-receive* event depends on *user-send* events for the same round at the same or neighboring nodes, and any event at a user automaton may depend on any preceding event at the same automaton. If β is any trace of L, then we define an irreflexive partial order $\rightarrow_\beta$ on the events of β as follows. (This is similar to the dependency relations defined in Sections 14.1.4 and 14.2.4.) If π and ϕ are two events in β, with π preceding ϕ, then we say that $\pi \rightarrow_\beta \phi$, or ϕ *depends on* π, provided that one of the following holds:

1. π and ϕ are events of the same user U_i.

2. $\pi = user\text{-}send(T, r)_i$ and $\phi = user\text{-}receive(T', r)_j$, where $j \in nbrs_i$.

3. π and ϕ are related by a chain of relationships of types 1 and 2.

The key property of these relations is the following claim. It says that the $\rightarrow_\beta$ relations capture enough about the dependencies in the trace to ensure that any reordering that preserves these dependencies is still a fair trace. (This claim is similar to Theorems 14.1 and 14.3.)

Claim 16.2 *If β is a fair trace of L and γ is a sequence obtained by reordering the events in β while preserving the $\rightarrow_\beta$ ordering, then γ is also a fair trace of L.*

Given Claim 16.2, to prove the lemma, we start with any fair execution α of L and let $\beta = trace(\alpha)$. We reorder the events of β to get a new trace γ in which the rounds "line up" globally: we do this by explicitly putting all the *user-send* events for a particular round r before all the *user-receive* events for the same round r. This new ordering requirement is consistent with the dependency requirements in $\rightarrow_\beta$, since they never require the reverse order, even when they are applied transitively. By Claim 16.2, γ is also a fair trace of L. But, in addition, since all the *user-send* events for each round r precede all the *user-receive* events for the same round r, it is not hard to show that γ is a trace of G. To complete the proof, we fill in the states in γ to get an execution of G, filling in the user states as in α. Formally, this filling in can be done using general theorems about I/O automaton composition, in particular, Theorems 8.4 and 8.5. □

A simple example of a distributed algorithm that implements *LocSynch* is as follows.

SimpleSynch algorithm (informal):

For any round r, after receiving an input of the form *user-send*$(T, r)_i$, process *SimpleSynch*$_i$ first sends a message to each neighbor *SimpleSynch*$_j$, containing the round number r and any messages from U_i to U_j that appear in T. When *SimpleSynch*$_i$ has received a round r message from each of its neighbors, it outputs *user-receive*$(T', r)_i$, where T' is the set of messages received, each tagged with its sender.

More formally, *SimpleSynch*$_i$ is the following automaton.

SimpleSynch$_i$ automaton (formal):

Signature:

Input:
    user-send$(T, r)_i$, T a set of tagged messages, $r \in \mathbb{N}^+$
    receive$(N, r)_{j,i}$, N a set of messages, $r \in \mathbb{N}^+$, $j \in nbrs$
Output:
    user-receive$(T, r)_i$, T a set of tagged messages, $r \in \mathbb{N}^+$
    send$(N, r)_{i,j}$, N a set of messages, $r \in \mathbb{N}^+$, $j \in nbrs$

States:

user-sent, *user-rcvd*, each a vector indexed by $\mathbb{N}^+$ of Booleans, initially all *false*
pkt-sent, *pkt-rcvd*, each an array indexed by $nbrs \times \mathbb{N}^+$ of Booleans, initially all *false*
outbox, an array indexed by $nbrs \times \mathbb{N}^+$ of sets of messages, initially all $\emptyset$
inbox, a vector indexed by $\mathbb{N}^+$ of sets of tagged messages, initially all $\emptyset$

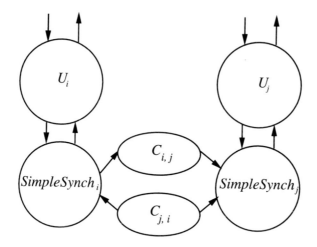

Figure 16.2: Architecture for the *SimpleSynch* system.

Transitions:

$user\text{-}send(T,r)_i$
  Effect:
    $user\text{-}sent(r) := true$
    for all $j \in nbrs$ do
      $outbox(j,r) := \{m|(m,j) \in T\}$

$send(N,r)_{i,j}$
  Precondition:
    $user\text{-}sent(r) = true$
    $pkt\text{-}sent(j,r) = false$
    $N = outbox(j,r)$
  Effect:
    $pkt\text{-}sent(j,r) := true$

$receive(N,r)_{j,i}$
  Effect:
    $inbox(r) := inbox(r) \cup \{(m,j)|m \in N\}$
    $pkt\text{-}rcvd(j,r) := true$

$user\text{-}receive(T,r)_i$
  Precondition:
    $user\text{-}sent(r) = true$
    for all $j \in nbrs$
      $pkt\text{-}rcvd(j,r) = true$
    $T = inbox(r)$
    $user\text{-}rcvd(r) = false$
  Effect:
    $user\text{-}rcvd(r) := true$

Tasks:

for every r:
  $\{user\text{-}receive(T,r)_i : T$ a set of tagged messages$\}$
for every $j \in nbrs$ and every r:
  $\{send(N,r)_{i,j} : N$ a set of messages$\}$

The *SimpleSynch* system is obtained by composing the *SimpleSynch$_i$* processes, reliable FIFO send/receive channels $C_{i,j}$ for all the edges, and the users. See Figure 16.2.

Lemma 16.3 *If α is any fair execution of the SimpleSynch system, then there is a fair execution α' of the LocSynch system that is indistinguishable from α to each U_i.*

Proof Sketch. This time, unlike in the proof of Lemma 16.1, there is no reordering of events at different users, and the correspondence can be proved using simulation methods. Let S and L denote the *SimpleSynch* and *LocSynch* systems, respectively, each modified slightly so that the actions that are classified as external are exactly all the actions of the user automata. (That is, the internal actions of the users are reclassified as outputs and the *send* and *receive* actions are "hidden"—reclassified as internal.) If s and u are states of S and L, respectively, then we define $(s, u) \in f$ exactly if all of the following hold:

1. All user states are identical in s and u.

2. $u.user\text{-}sent(i, r) = s.user\text{-}sent(r)_i$

3. $u.user\text{-}rcvd(i, r) = s.user\text{-}rcvd(r)_i$

4. $u.tray(i, r) = \bigcup_{j \neq i}\{(m, j) : m \in s.outbox(i, r)_j\}$

To prove that f is a simulation relation, we need the following invariant assertion for S.

> **Assertion 16.2.1** *In any reachable state of the SimpleSynch system, if $pkt\text{-}rcvd(j, r)_i = true$, then*
>
> 1. $user\text{-}sent(r)_j = true$
> 2. $\{m : (m, j) \in inbox(r)_i\} = outbox(i, r)_j$

The proof of this invariant uses other intermediate invariants, involving the correctness of the messages in transit. (As before, we assume that the channels are universal reliable FIFO channels in the statement and proof of such invariants.) Given Assertion 16.2.1, the proof that f is a simulation relation is straightforward; the only interesting case is *user-receive*, which uses Assertion 16.2.1 in its proof. We leave the details of the invariant and simulation proofs as an exercise.

The existence of a simulation relation implies that every trace of S is a trace of L. (Recall that the actions that are included in these traces are exactly the actions of the user automata.) But we need more—in particular, we need to know that the fairness conditions of S imply the fairness conditions of L. We prove that $fairtraces(S) \subseteq fairtraces(L)$, then apply general composition theorems about I/O automata (Theorems 8.4 and 8.5) to fill in the user states and obtain the needed relationship between executions.

To prove fair trace inclusion, we use the fact that a simulation relation guarantees more than just trace inclusion—it also guarantees a close correspondence between executions, as defined in Section 8.5.5. Let $\beta \in fairtraces(S)$ and let α be any fair execution of S with $\beta = trace(\alpha)$. Then Theorem 8.13 implies that there is an execution α' of L that corresponds to α, with respect to f. We claim that α' is a fair execution of L.

There are two ways in which it might fail to be fair. First, there might be some user task that is enabled from some point on in α', yet no step of that task occurs after that point in α'. Then the correspondence implies that the same user task is enabled from some point on in α, but no step of that task occurs; this is a contradiction to the fairness of α with respect to that user task.

Second, there might be some i and r such that the $user\text{-}receive_i$ task for round r is enabled from some point on in α', yet no step of that task occurs. This implies that, from the given point on in α', $user\text{-}sent(j, r) = true$ for all $j \in nbrs_i \cup \{i\}$, and $user\text{-}rcvd(i, r) = false$. The correspondence then implies that from the corresponding point in α, $user\text{-}sent(r)_j = true$ for all $j \in nbrs_i \cup \{i\}$, and $user\text{-}rcvd(r)_i = false$.

We use the following assertion.

> **Assertion 16.2.2** *In any reachable state of the SimpleSynch system, the following holds. If $pkt\text{-}sent(i, r)_j = true$, then either channel $C_{j,i}$ contains a message or $pkt\text{-}rcvd(j, r)_i = true$.*

Then for each $j \in nbrs_i$, fairness for the $send$ task at round r implies that eventually in α, $pkt\text{-}sent(j, r)_i$ becomes $true$. Then Assertion 16.2.2 and channel fairness imply that eventually $pkt\text{-}rcvd(j, r)_i$ becomes $true$. Then fairness for the $user\text{-}receive_i$ task at round r in S implies that a step of this task eventually occurs in α, a contradiction. $\square$

Note that the proof of Lemma 16.3 actually shows that $fairtraces(S) \subseteq fairtraces(L)$, in addition to showing indistinguishability to the individual users. Lemmas 16.1 and 16.3 imply

Theorem 16.4 *If α is any fair execution of the SimpleSynch system, then there is a fair execution α' of the GlobSynch system that is indistinguishable from α to each U_i.*

Complexity analysis. Each round requires $2|E|$ messages, one in each direction on each edge of the graph. Suppose that c is an upper bound on the time for any $user\text{-}send_i$ event to occur, once all $user\text{-}receive_i$ events for any smaller rounds have occurred; that ℓ is an upper bound on the time for any task of any process;

and that d is an upper bound on the time for delivering the oldest message in any channel. Then the total amount of time required to simulate r rounds is at most $r(c + d + O(\ell))$.

16.3 The Safe Synchronizer

It is impossible to reduce the time complexity of the *SimpleSynch* algorithm significantly, but it is possible to reduce the communication complexity. Namely, if there is no message from U_i to neighbor U_j at round r in the underlying synchronous algorithm, then we may be able to avoid a round r message from process i to process j in the asynchronous algorithm. But we cannot simply omit these messages. Each process needs to determine that it has already received all the messages that its neighbors will ever send it for round r, before it can perform a *user-receive* output for round r. The messages of the *SimpleSynch* algorithm are used to help determine this, as well as to deliver the user's messages. The basic strategy for reducing communication is to separate these two functions.

Thus, we decompose the implementation of *LocSynch* into several pieces: a "front end," *FrontEnd* for each node, communicating with the *FrontEnds* of neighboring nodes over special channels $D_{i,j}$, and a "safe synchronizer," *Safe-Synch*. See Figure 16.3 for this new architecture. The job of each *FrontEnd$_i$* is to deliver the messages received from the local user U_i in *user-send$_i$* events. At each particular round r, after receiving a *user-send$_i$*, *FrontEnd$_i$* sorts all the outgoing messages for round r into "outboxes." Then it sends the contents of each nonempty *outbox* to the appropriate neighbor j using channel $D_{i,j}$ and waits to receive an acknowledgment on $D_{j,i}$. When *FrontEnd$_i$* has received acknowledgments for all of its messages, it is said to be *safe*; this implies that all of i's messages have been received by the appropriate neighboring *FrontEnds*. Meanwhile, *FrontEnd$_i$* collects and acknowledges messages sent to it by its neighboring *FrontEnds*.

When is it permissible for *FrontEnd$_i$* to perform a *user-receive$_i$* for round r, that is, to deliver to U_i all the round r messages it has collected from its neighbors? It can only do this when it knows that it already has received all the messages it will ever receive for round r. It is therefore sufficient for *FrontEnd$_i$* to determine that *all its neighboring FrontEnds are safe* for round r, that is, that those neighbors know that all *their* messages for round r have been received by the appropriate *FrontEnd* automata.

Thus, the job of the safe synchronizer automaton *SafeSynch* is to tell each *FrontEnd* automaton when all its neighbors are safe. To do this, *SafeSynch* has *ok* input actions, outputs of the *FrontEnd* automata, by which the *FrontEnd* automata tell *SafeSynch* that they are safe. *SafeSynch* sends *go$_i$* to *FrontEnd$_i$* when it has received an *ok* from each of i's neighbors, as well as from i itself.

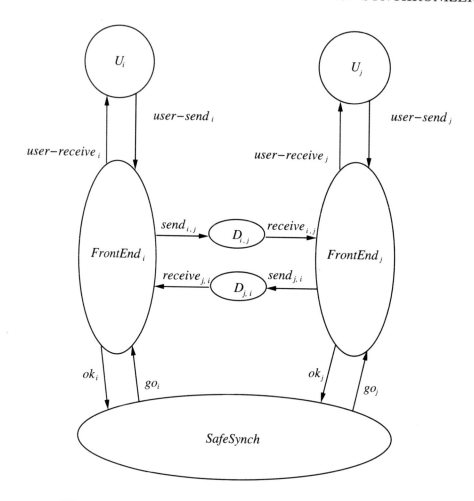

Figure 16.3: Decomposition of *LocSynch* using *SafeSynch*.

After *FrontEnd$_i$* receives *go$_i$*, it can perform a *user-receive$_i$*. In the rest of this section, we describe this decomposition in more detail.

16.3.1 Front-End Automata

***FrontEnd$_i$* automaton:**

Signature:

Input:

    user-send$(T, r)_i$, T a set of tagged messages, $r \in \mathbb{N}^+$

    receive("*msgs*", $N, r)_{j,i}$, N a set of messages, $r \in \mathbb{N}^+$, $j \in nbrs$

    receive("*ack*", $r)_{j,i}$, $r \in \mathbb{N}^+$, $j \in nbrs$

    go$(r)_i$, $r \in \mathbb{N}^+$

Output:
> $user\text{-}receive(T,r)_i$, T a set of tagged messages, $r \in \mathbb{N}^+$
> $send(\text{``}msgs\text{''}, N, r)_{i,j}$, N a set of messages, $r \in \mathbb{N}^+$, $j \in nbrs$
> $send(\text{``}ack\text{''},r)_{i,j}$, $r \in \mathbb{N}^+$, $j \in nbrs$
> $ok(r)_i$, $r \in \mathbb{N}^+$

States:
user-sent, *user-rcvd*, each a vector indexed by $\mathbb{N}^+$ of Booleans, initially all *false*
pkt-for, *pkt-sent*, *pkt-rcvd*, *ack-rcvd*, each an array indexed by $nbrs \times \mathbb{N}^+$ of Booleans,
>   initially all *false*

ack-sent, an array indexed by $nbrs \times \mathbb{N}^+$ of Booleans, initially all *false*
outbox, an array indexed by $nbrs \times \mathbb{N}^+$ of sets of messages, initially all $\emptyset$
inbox, a vector indexed by $\mathbb{N}^+$ of sets of tagged messages, initially all $\emptyset$
ok-given, *go-seen*, each a vector indexed by $\mathbb{N}^+$ of Booleans, initially all *false*

Transitions:

$user\text{-}send(T,r)_i$
>   Effect:
>> $user\text{-}sent(r) := true$
>>   for all $j \in nbrs$ such that $\exists m, (m,j) \in T$ do
>>> $outbox(j,r) := \{m | (m,j) \in T\}$
>>> $pkt\text{-}for(j,r) := true$

$send(\text{``}msgs\text{''}, N, r)_{i,j}$
>   Precondition:
>> $pkt\text{-}sent(j,r) = false$
>> $pkt\text{-}for(j,r) = true$
>> $N = outbox(j,r)$
>   Effect:
>> $pkt\text{-}sent(j,r) := true$

$receive(\text{``}ack\text{''}, r)_{j,i}$
>   Effect:
>> $ack\text{-}rcvd(j,r) := true$

$receive(\text{``}msgs\text{''}, N, r)_{j,i}$
>   Effect:
>> $inbox(r) := inbox(r) \cup \{(m,j) | m \in N\}$
>> $pkt\text{-}rcvd(j,r) := true$

$send(\text{``}ack\text{''},r)_{i,j}$
>   Precondition:
>> $pkt\text{-}rcvd(j,r) = true$
>> $ack\text{-}sent(j,r) = false$
>   Effect:
>> $ack\text{-}sent(j,r) := true$

$ok(r)_i$
>   Precondition:
>> $user\text{-}sent(r) = true$
>>   for all $j \in nbrs$
>>>   if $pkt\text{-}for(j,r) = true$ then
>>> $ack\text{-}rcvd(j,r) = true$
>> $ok\text{-}given(r) = false$
>   Effect:
>> $ok\text{-}given(r) := true$

$go(r)_i$
>   Effect:
>> $go\text{-}seen(r) := true$

$user\text{-}receive(T,r)_i$
>   Precondition:
>> $go\text{-}seen(r) = true$
>> $T = inbox(r)$
>> $user\text{-}rcvd(r) = false$
>   Effect:
>> $user\text{-}rcvd(r) := true$

Tasks:
for every r:
$\quad$ {*user-receive*$(T, r)_i : T$ a set of tagged messages}
$\quad$ {*ok*$(r)_i$}
for every j and every r:
$\quad$ {*send*("*msgs*", $N, r)_{i,j} : N$ a set of messages}
$\quad$ {*send*("*ack*", $r)_{i,j}$}

16.3.2　Channel Automata

Each pair of front end automata, *FrontEnd*$_i$ and *FrontEnd*$_j$, communicate by means of two channel automata, $D_{i,j}$ and $D_{j,i}$. These are reliable send/receive channels from i to j and from j to i respectively, as defined in Section 14.1.2.

16.3.3　The Safe Synchronizer

The entire job of the safe synchronizer, *SafeSynch*, is to wait until it has received *ok*s from all of the neighbors of *FrontEnd*$_i$ and from *FrontEnd*$_i$ itself before performing *go*$_i$.

SafeSynch automaton:

Signature:

Input:
$\quad$ *ok*$(r)_i$, $r \in \mathbb{N}^+$, $1 \leq i \leq n$

Output:
$\quad$ *go*$(r)_i$, $r \in \mathbb{N}^+$, $1 \leq i \leq n$

States:
ok-seen, go-given, each an array indexed by $\{1, \dots, n\} \times \mathbb{N}^+$ of Booleans, initially all *false*

Transitions:

ok$(r)_i$
$\quad$ Effect:
$\quad\quad$ *ok-seen*$(i, r) := true$

go$(r)_i$
$\quad$ Precondition:
$\quad\quad$ for all $j \in nbrs_i \cup \{i\}$
$\quad\quad\quad$ *ok-seen*$(j, r) = true$
$\quad\quad$ *go-given*$(i, r) = false$
$\quad$ Effect:
$\quad\quad$ *go-given*$(i, r) := true$

Tasks:
for every i, r:
$\quad$ {*go*$(r)_i$}

16.3.4 Correctness

Lemma 16.5 *If α is any fair execution of the SafeSynch system (i.e., Front-End, channel, SafeSynch, and user automata, as depicted in Figure 16.3), then there is a fair execution α' of the LocSynch system that is indistinguishable from α to each U_i.*

Proof Sketch. This is proved using a simulation relation from the *SafeSynch* system to the *LocSynch* system. The strategy is the same as the one used in the proof of Lemma 16.3 for the *SimpleSynch* algorithm, using exactly the same simulation relation f, but the details are a little more complicated here because the algorithm is more complicated. Again, the only interesting case in the simulation proof is the *user-receive* action, which here requires this invariant assertion.

> **Assertion 16.3.1** *In all reachable states of the SafeSynch system, the following holds. If $go\text{-}seen(r)_i = true$, then for all $j \in nbrs_i$,*
>
> *1. $user\text{-}sent(r)_j = true$*
> *2. $\{m : (m, j) \in inbox(r)_i\} = outbox(i, r)_j$*

This assertion in turn needs some auxiliary invariants for its proof, for example,

> **Assertion 16.3.2** *In all reachable states of the SafeSynch system, the following holds. If $ok\text{-}seen(j, r) = true$, then[3]*
>
> *1. $user\text{-}sent(r)_j = true$*
> *2. $\{m : (m, j) \in inbox(r)_i\} = outbox(i, r)_j$ for all $i \in nbrs_j$*

Further details are left to the reader. $\qquad\square$

Now Lemmas 16.1 and 16.5 imply

Lemma 16.6 *If α is any fair execution of the SafeSynch system, then there is a fair execution α' of the GlobSynch system that is indistinguishable from α to each U_i.*

It still remains to implement the *SafeSynch* automaton with a distributed algorithm. We describe several ways of doing this in the following section. It is also necessary to implement the $D_{i,j}$ channels using the actual send/receive channels $C_{i,j}$. This is done by "multiplexing" the $C_{i,j}$ so that they implement not only the channels of the distributed implementation of *SafeSynch* but the $D_{i,j}$'s as well. The multiplexing strategy is described in Exercise 14.6.

---

[3]Recall that *ok-seen* is part of the state of the *SafeSynch* component.

16.4   Safe Synchronizer Implementations

In this section, we describe several implementations of *SafeSynch* by distributed algorithms. There are two main implementations, *Alpha* and *Beta*, plus a way of combining them to obtain a hybrid implementation *Gamma*.

Recall that the job of *SafeSynch* is, for each round and each i, to wait until it has received *ok*s from all of the neighbors of *FrontEnd$_i$* and from *FrontEnd$_i$* itself, and then to perform *go$_i$*.

16.4.1   Synchronizer Alpha

The most straightforward implementation of *SafeSynch* is the *Alpha* synchronizer, which works as follows.

> **Alpha synchronizer:**
>
> When any process *Alpha$_i$* receives an *ok$_i$* for any round r, it sends this information to all of its neighbors. When *Alpha$_i$* has heard that all its neighbors have received *ok*s for round r and *Alpha$_i$* itself has also received an *ok* for round r, then *Alpha$_i$* outputs *go$_i$*.

We leave to the reader the task of writing the precondition-effect code for each *Alpha$_i$*; the structure of the code is somewhat similar to that of *SimpleSynch$_i$*. Correctness—both safety and liveness—is easy to show, using simulation techniques to relate the *Alpha* system (*Alpha$_i$*, *FrontEnd*, $D_{i,j}$, and user automata) to the *SafeSynch* system.[4] We obtain

Theorem 16.7 *If α is any fair execution of the Alpha system, then there is a fair execution α' of the GlobSynch system that is indistinguishable from α to each U_i.*

Complexity analysis.   We analyze the complexity of the entire *Alpha* system. The communication complexity depends on the number of messages sent by the underlying synchronous algorithm: if the synchronous algorithm sends a total of m non-*null* messages in r rounds, then the *Alpha* system sends a total of at most $2m + 2r|E|$ messages to simulate r rounds. The $2m$ is for the *msgs* and *ack* messages sent by the *FrontEnd*s, while the $2r|E|$ term is for the messages sent

---

[4]This strategy may not seem very modular, since the same user, *FrontEnd* and $D_{i,j}$ automata appear in both systems. However, they can be handled in a trivial way, letting the simulation relation leave them unchanged. An alternative approach would involve formulating a more abstract (and more general) environment for the *SafeSynch* automaton.

within *Alpha* itself. This term accounts for a message in each direction on each edge at each round.

If c, ℓ, and d are defined as for the *SimpleSynch* algorithm, then the total amount of time required to simulate r rounds is at most $r(c + 3d + O(\ell))$. (This does take pileups in the underlying channels into account.) Thus, both the communication complexity and the time complexity of *Alpha* are worse than the corresponding costs for *SimpleSynch*.

Like *SimpleSynch*, *Alpha* has a reasonable time complexity but high communication complexity. In the following subsection, we give an alternative implementation of *SafeSynch* that has better communication complexity but at the cost of additional time complexity.

16.4.2 Synchronizer Beta

Synchronizer *Beta* assumes the existence of a rooted spanning tree of the entire graph G, preferably one of small height.

> **Beta synchronizer:**
>
> At round r, all processes convergecast all their *ok* information to the root, along the edges of the spanning tree. After the root has collected this information from all the processes, it broadcasts permission to perform *go* outputs, also along the edges of the spanning tree.

Again, we leave to the reader the task of writing the precondition-effect code for each process *Beta$_i$* of *Beta*. The ideas are similar to those used for broadcast and convergecast in Section 15.3. Again, correctness is easy to show, using simulation techniques to relate the *Beta* system to the *SafeSynch* system.

Theorem 16.8 *If α is any fair execution of the Beta system (Beta$_i$, FrontEnd, $D_{i,j}$, and user automata), then there is a fair execution α' of the GlobSynch system that is indistinguishable from α to each U_i.*

Complexity analysis. If the underlying synchronous algorithm sends a total of m non-*null* messages in r rounds, then the *Beta* system sends a total of at most $2m + 2rn$ messages to simulate r rounds. The $2m$ is as for *Alpha*, while the $2rn$ is for the broadcast and convergecast messages. If h is an upper bound on the height of the spanning tree, then the total amount of time to simulate r rounds is at most $r(c + 2d + O(\ell) + 2h(d + O(\ell)))$, or $r(c + O(hd) + O(h\ell))$.

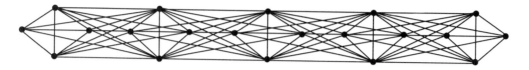

Figure 16.4: Network graph G.

16.4.3   Synchronizer Gamma

By combining the ideas of synchronizers *Alpha* and *Beta*, we can get a hybrid algorithm, *Gamma*, that (depending on the structure of the graph G) can simultaneously do as well as *Alpha* in terms of time and as well as *Beta* in terms of communication.

Algorithm *Gamma* assumes a spanning forest of G, where each tree in the forest is rooted. We call each tree a *cluster*; for each cluster C, we write $nodes(C)$ for its set of nodes. (Constructing a suitable spanning forest is itself an interesting problem, but we do not describe how to do this here.) *Gamma* uses a version of *Beta* to synchronize the nodes within each cluster and a version of *Alpha* to synchronize among clusters.

In the extreme case where each cluster consists of a single node, *Gamma* is the same as *Alpha*, whereas in the case where there is only a single cluster containing all the nodes, *Gamma* is the same as *Beta*. For intermediate cases, both the communication and time complexity measures of *Gamma* are intermediate between those of *Alpha* and *Beta*.

Example 16.4.1   Cluster decomposition

Consider a network graph G consisting of p complete graphs, each with k nodes. The complete graphs are arranged in a line, with all the nodes of adjacent pairs of complete graphs connected to each other. See Figure 16.4 for the case where $p = 5$ and $k = 4$. (In the diagram, some edges are not visible because they are "under" other edges.) Now consider the cluster decomposition for G depicted in Figure 16.5.

Figure 16.5: Cluster decomposition for G.

Each cluster C of this decomposition is a tree for one of the k-node complete graphs in G. The root for each cluster tree is the node at the top. Algorithm *Gamma* uses a version of *Beta* to synchronize within each of the k-node trees, and a version of *Alpha* to synchronize among the p trees.

Since *Gamma* is a combination of two algorithms, we begin with a high-level decomposition of *SafeSynch* into two kinds of automata, which we call *ClusterSynch* and *ForestSynch* automata. There is a *ClusterSynch*$_k$ automaton for each cluster C_k, and a single *ForestSynch* automaton. See Figure 16.6 for the architecture.

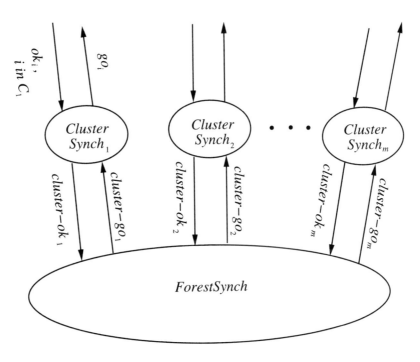

Figure 16.6: Decomposition of *SafeSynch* into *ClusterSynch* and *ForestSynch* automata.

For each cluster C_k and any round r, the automaton *ClusterSynch*$_k$ has two jobs. First, after it receives ok_i inputs for all nodes i in C_k, it outputs a single *cluster-ok*$_k$ to *ForestSynch*. And second (in a completely independent task), after a *cluster-go*$_k$ input arrives from *ForestSynch*, *ClusterSynch*$_k$ produces a go_i for each node i in C_k. This combination of jobs is a lot like the activities of *Beta*. Written as an abstract automaton:

ClusterSynch$_k$ automaton:

Signature:

Input:
$ok(r)_i,\ r \in \mathbb{N}^+,\ i \in nodes(C_k)$
$cluster\text{-}go(r)_k,\ r \in \mathbb{N}^+$

Output:
$go(r)_i,\ r \in \mathbb{N}^+,\ i \in nodes(C_k)$
$cluster\text{-}ok(r)_k,\ r \in \mathbb{N}^+$

States:
ok-seen, *go-given*, each an array indexed by $nodes(C_k) \times \mathbb{N}^+$ of Booleans, initially all *false*
cluster-ok-given, *cluster-go-seen*, each a vector indexed by $\mathbb{N}^+$ of Booleans, initially all *false*

Transitions:

$ok(r)_i$
  Effect:
    $ok\text{-}seen(i,r) := true$

$cluster\text{-}go(r)_k$
  Effect:
    $cluster\text{-}go\text{-}seen(r) := true$

$cluster\text{-}ok(r)_k$
  Precondition:
    for all $i \in nodes(C_k)$
      $ok\text{-}seen(i,r) = true$
    $cluster\text{-}ok\text{-}given(r) = false$
  Effect:
    $cluster\text{-}ok\text{-}given(r) := true$

$go(r)_i$
  Precondition:
    $cluster\text{-}go\text{-}seen(r) = true$
    $go\text{-}given(i,r) = false$
  Effect:
    $go\text{-}given(i,r) := true$

Tasks:
for every r:
  $\{cluster\text{-}ok(r)_k\}$
for every i, r:
  $\{go(r)_i\}$

   The *ForestSynch* automaton is (up to renaming of external actions) a safe synchronizer for the *cluster graph* G' of G, where the nodes of G' correspond to the clusters of G, and there is an edge in G' from C_k to C_ℓ exactly if there is an edge in G from *some node* in C_k to *some node* in C_ℓ. Define the *ClusterForest* system to consist of the *ClusterSynch*, *ForestSynch*, *FrontEnd*, $D_{i,j}$, and user automata.

Lemma 16.9 *If α is any fair execution of the ClusterForest system, then there is a fair execution α' of the SafeSynch system that is indistinguishable from α to each U_i.*

Proof Sketch. A simulation proof can be used, but, for variety, we sketch an operational argument, based on executions. The main thing that needs to be shown is that if $go(r)_i$ occurs, then previously $ok(r)_j$ must have occurred, for each $j \in nbrs_i \cup \{i\}$. There are two cases.

1. i and j are in the same cluster C_k (possibly with $i = j$).
   Then the code for $ClusterSynch_k$ implies that prior to the $go(r)_i$, there must be a $cluster\text{-}go(r)_k$. Then the definition of $ForestSynch$ implies that prior to the $cluster\text{-}go(r)_k$, there must be a $cluster\text{-}ok(r)_k$. But this in turn implies that there is a previous $ok(r)_j$, which suffices.

2. i is in cluster C_k, and j is in cluster C_ℓ, $k \neq \ell$.
   Since $j \in nbrs_i$, it must be that the two clusters C_k and C_ℓ are neighbors in the cluster graph G' (by definition of neighboring clusters in the cluster graph). As before, prior to the $go(r)_i$, there must be a $cluster\text{-}go(r)_k$. Then the definition of $ForestSynch$ implies that, prior to this, there must be a $cluster\text{-}ok_\ell$. This implies as before that there is a previous $ok(r)_j$.

$\square$

To finish the description of synchronizer *Gamma*, we describe how to implement the *ForestSynch* and *ClusterSynch* automata with distributed algorithms. $ClusterSynch_k$ can be implemented using a variant of synchronizer *Beta* on the rooted tree C_k. That is, a convergecast is first carried out, collecting the *ok*s at the root, which then performs a *cluster-ok* output. The root also receives *cluster-go*, then broadcasts to all the nodes in $nodes(C_k)$ to tell them to perform *go*. (These two activities could actually be formalized using two separate automata.)

Any implementation of *SafeSynch* may, with suitable renaming, be used to implement *ForestSynch*; we choose synchronizer *Alpha*. A technical complication is that we cannot run *Alpha* directly on the given distributed network, because *Alpha* is supposed to run on processes that correspond to the entities being synchronized (which in this case are whole clusters), using channels that correspond to edges between neighboring entities (here, clusters). The given model only allows processes and channels corresponding to the nodes and edges of G. However, it is not hard to implement the needed processes and channels: we run the process for any cluster at the cluster's root node and simulate direct communication between processes for neighboring clusters using a designated path between the root nodes in the two clusters. Such a path must exist, because the clusters are connected and there exist nodes in the two clusters that are neighbors in G. Again, some preprocessing is needed to determine these paths, but

we ignore this issue here. The *cluster-ok* and *cluster-go* actions are implemented
as internal actions of the processes at the root nodes of the clusters.

Example 16.4.2   Implementing *Alpha*

> Consider the network graph G and cluster decomposition of Exam-
> ple 16.4.1. For that graph and decomposition, we run the *Alpha*
> process for each cluster at the root (the top node, in Figure 16.5) of
> that cluster's tree. Communication between the *Alpha* processes for
> neighboring clusters could be simulated using the direct edge in the
> underlying graph G (in Figure 16.4) between the roots of the clusters.

In the complete implementation *Gamma*, the process associated with each
node i of G is, formally, a composition of three processes: $FrontEnd_i$, process
i in the *ClusterSynch* implementation, and process i in the *ForestSynch* implementation. Each channel $C_{i,j}$ is used to implement three channels: $D_{i,j}$ and
the channels from i to j in the *ClusterSynch* and *ForestSynch* implementations.
Defining the *Gamma* system to be the entire implementation, we can use simulation techniques to prove the following.

Theorem 16.10 *If α is any fair execution of the Gamma system, then there is
a fair execution α' of the GlobSynch system that is indistinguishable from α to
each U_i.*

Orthogonal decompositions.   You may find it interesting to observe that
the complete *Gamma* system has two natural decompositions. One is logical, in
terms of the functions (data communication, cluster synchronization, and forest
synchronization) being performed. The other is spatial, in terms of processes and
channels in the complete implementation. These two decompositions correspond
to different orders of composing the primitive I/O automata that constitute the
algorithm. Since the composition operation is associative, we end up with the
same algorithm either way we look at it.

Complexity analysis.   Let h be the maximum height of any cluster tree and
let e' be the total number of edges on all the paths used for communication
among the roots. If the underlying synchronous algorithm sends a total of m
non-*null* messages in r rounds, then the *Gamma* system sends a total of at most
$2m + O(r(n + e'))$ messages. The $O(rn)$ is for the messages sent within all the
cluster trees in the *ClusterSynch* implementation. The $O(re')$ is for the messages
sent between roots in the *ForestSynch* implementation. The time required to
simulate r rounds is $O(r(c + O(hd) + O(h\ell)))$. If $n + e' \ll |E|$, then *Gamma*

uses fewer messages than *Alpha*, and if the maximum height of a cluster spanning tree is much less than the maximum height of a spanning tree of the entire network, then *Gamma* takes less time than *Beta*.

Example 16.4.3   Comparative complexity of *Alpha*, *Beta*, and *Gamma*

Again consider the network graph G and cluster decomposition of Example 16.4.1. For that graph and decomposition, we compare the costs of the three safe synchronizer implementations we have given. Costs are per round, and we neglect the costs incurred by the users, *FrontEnds*, and $D_{i,j}$'s, which are the same for all three algorithms; we also neglect local processing time. For *Beta*, we assume that the tree used has the minimum possible height, approximately p.

	Messages	Time
Alpha:	$O\left(pk^2\right)$	$O\left(d\right)$
Beta:	$O\left(pk\right)$	$O\left(pd\right)$
Gamma:	$O\left(pk\right)$	$O\left(d\right)$

If p and k are approximately equal, then *Gamma* represents an order-of-magnitude improvement over each of *Alpha* and *Beta*.

16.5   Applications

The synchronizer algorithms given in the previous sections allow a fault-free asynchronous network to implement any non-fault-tolerant synchronous network algorithm. (The synchronizers do not work for fault-tolerant algorithms such as those in Chapter 6.) In this section, we give a few examples of asynchronous algorithms constructed using synchronizers.

Recall that we are considering only undirected networks in this chapter. In all the analyses in this section, we neglect local process step times.

16.5.1   Leader Election

Using synchronizers, synchronous ring leader-election algorithms such as *LCR* and *HS* can be run in an asynchronous ring. But this is not interesting, because these algorithms already work in an asynchronous network, without the overhead introduced by synchronizers.

In an asynchronous network based on an arbitrary undirected graph with a known diameter, *diam*, a synchronizer can be used to run the *FloodMax* synchronous leader-election algorithm. Using synchronizer *Alpha*, the resulting algorithm sends $O\left(|E| \cdot diam\right)$ messages and takes $O\left(diam \cdot d\right)$ time to simulate the necessary *diam* synchronous rounds.

A synchronizer can also be used to run the *OptFloodMax* synchronous leader-election algorithm, which is like *FloodMax* except that nodes only send messages when they have new information to send. If synchronizer *Alpha* is used, the advantage of the optimization is lost, since the synchronizer itself sends messages on all channels at all rounds. However, if synchronizer *Beta* is used, then communication complexity is kept reasonably low (at the cost of additional time).

16.5.2   Breadth-First Search

Recall that the *SynchBFS* algorithm in Section 4.2 requires $O\left(|E|\right)$ messages and $O\left(diam\right)$ rounds in a network with diameter *diam*; the processes are not required to know *diam*. Using synchronizers, the *SynchBFS* algorithm can be run in an asynchronous network. With synchronizer *Alpha*, the resulting algorithm sends $O\left(|E| \cdot diam\right)$ messages and requires $O\left(diam \cdot d\right)$ time to simulate the *diam* rounds needed for all processes to output their parent information. With *Beta* (using a tree of height at most *diam*), the algorithm sends only $O\left(|E| + n \cdot diam\right)$ messages and takes $O\left(diam^2 \cdot d\right)$ time, which is the same as the *LayeredBFS* algorithm given in Section 15.4. Some improvement in the time complexity is possible using *Gamma*, at the expense of extra communication complexity.

There is a technicality: it is not obvious how the BFS algorithms obtained using the synchronizers are supposed to terminate. As described, the implementation continues to simulate rounds forever, thus generating an infinite number of messages. (If the processes knew *diam*, then they could simply stop after simulating *diam* rounds, but we have assumed here that the processes do not know *diam*.) An ad hoc solution to this problem is to have each user automaton that determines its parent perform only one additional round to notify its neighbors and then halt.

16.5.3   Shortest Paths

For the problem of finding shortest paths from a designated source, the use of a synchronizer is a big win. Recall that the *AsynchBellmanFord* algorithm has both message and time complexities that are exponential in the number of nodes. However, the synchronous *BellmanFord* algorithm has communication complexity "only" $O(n|E|)$ and round complexity only $O(n)$, for a network with known size n. We can run the synchronous *BellmanFord* algorithm using, say, synchronizer *Alpha*, obtaining an algorithm that sends $O(n|E|)$ messages and uses $O(nd)$ time to simulate the required n rounds. Synchronizer *SimpleSynch* would work just as well.

16.5.4 Broadcast and Acknowledgment

It is possible to design a synchronous algorithm that allows a process to broadcast a message to all other processes and receive an acknowledgment in return and that uses $O(|E|)$ messages and $O(diam)$ rounds (see Exercise 4.8). We can run this algorithm using synchronizer *Alpha*, thus obtaining an asynchronous algorithm for broadcast and acknowledgment that uses $O(|E| \cdot diam)$ messages and $O(diam \cdot d)$ time. Compare this with the complexity of *AsynchBcastAck* in Section 15.3.

16.5.5 Maximal Independent Set

Synchronizers can also be used with randomized synchronous algorithms such as *LubyMIS*. We leave the details for you to work out.

16.6 Lower Bound on Time

An informal paraphrase of the results about synchronizers is as follows:

> Any (non-fault-tolerant) synchronous algorithm can be transformed into a corresponding asynchronous algorithm without too great an increase in costs.

In particular, by using synchronizer *Alpha* or *SimpleSynch*, it is possible not to increase the time cost at all. In this section, we show a limitation on the synchronizer approach, by giving a lower bound on the time required for an asynchronous network algorithm to solve a particular problem. Since there is a very fast synchronous algorithm to solve the same problem, this means (informally speaking) that

> Not every synchronous algorithm can be transformed to a corresponding asynchronous algorithm with a similar time complexity.

These two informal paraphrases appear to be contradictory. It turns out that the reason for the difference is the *locality* of the correctness condition guaranteed by the synchronizers. We return to this point after the lower bound proof.

The result of this section is the only lower bound in this book for the time complexity of a problem in an asynchronous distributed system.

The problem we consider is called the "session problem." Let $G = (V, E)$ be a graph, with *diam* its diameter as usual. The system's interface with its environment includes $flash_i$ output actions, one for each node i of G; $flash_i$ is an output of the process automaton at node i. We treat the *flash* actions as abstract actions, but you might want to think of them as signals that the corresponding processes have completed some computation task.

Define a *session* to be any sequence of *flash* events containing at least one $flash_i$ for every i. For any nonnegative integer k, the *k-session problem* requires simply that the algorithm should perform at least k disjoint sessions, in any fair execution.

Example 16.6.1   Motivation for the *k*-session problem

The k-session problem was originally inspired by a matrix computation problem for the asynchronous shared memory model. Consider a collection of asynchronous parallel processes performing a coordinated calculation of the transitive closure of an $m \times m$ Boolean matrix. The matrix starts out in shared memory, and all the partial results and final outputs are written to shared memory.

There is a process $P_{i,j,k}$ for every $i, j, k, 1 \le i, j, k \le m$. Each process $P_{i,j,k}$ is responsible simply for writing 1 in location (i, j) of the output matrix in case it ever sees 1s in both locations (i, k) and (k, j). Thus, each goes through a simple loop, reading locations (i, k) and (k, j), then (possibly) writing (i, j). Each individual read or write operation on shared memory is represented abstractly as a *flash* output.

Basic properties of matrices then imply that the calculation is performed correctly if there is "enough" interleaving among the process steps. Specifically, $O(\log n)$ sessions suffice. It does not matter if the processes do excess reading and writing—as long as enough interleaving occurs, the correct output will be produced.

A simpler version of the problem for which a similar lower bound could be proved is one in which each process is required to perform *exactly one flash* in each session. The version of the problem that we use is less constrained, so it leads to a stronger lower bound result.

It is trivial to solve the k-session problem in the synchronous network setting. All we need is for each process i to perform a single $flash_i$ output at each of k rounds. No communication between processes is required. The number of rounds needed is exactly k.

In the asynchronous network setting, we model the processes as I/O automata as usual, connected by reliable FIFO send/receive channels. Without loss of generality, we assume that the channels are universal. We associate times with events as usual, with ℓ as an upper bound for the time of each process task and d as an upper bound for the delivery time of the oldest message in each channel. We assume that $\ell \ll d$ and in fact will ignore ℓ in our result and proof. Recall from Section 8.6 that a fair execution with times associated with all events, subject to the given restrictions, is called a *timed execution*.

Next, we define the *time measure* $T(A)$ for algorithm A. For each timed execution α of A, define $T(\alpha)$ to be the supremum of the times at which a *flash* event occurs in α. (We use a supremum instead of a maximum here because there could be infinitely many such events.) Then define

$$T(A) = \sup\{T(\alpha) : \alpha \text{ is a timed execution of } A\}.$$

That is, $T(A)$ is the supremum of the times at which a *flash* occurs in any timed execution of A.

We can now state and prove the lower bound.

Theorem 16.11 *Suppose A is an asynchronous network algorithm that solves the k-session problem on graph G. Then $T(A) \geq (k-1)\,diam \cdot d$.*

In order to compare this result with the simple upper bound of k rounds for the synchronous setting, it is probably reasonable to charge time d, the maximum message-delivery time, for each round. Then the discrepancy between the inherent lower bound of Theorem 16.11 and the small upper bound of kd is approximately a factor of $diam$. This proves that the inherent overhead due to asynchrony, for the session problem, is a factor of $diam$.

Proof. We assume without loss of generality that all actions of A are external. We proceed by contradiction.

Suppose that there exists an algorithm A with $T(A) < (k-1) \cdot diam \cdot d$. Define a timed execution of A to be *slow* if all the message deliveries take the maximum time d. Let α be any slow timed execution of A; note that α with its time information suppressed must be a fair execution of A. Since A is correct, α must contain k sessions. By assumption, no *flash* event occurs in α at or after time $(k-1) \cdot diam \cdot d$. So we can write α as a concatenation $\alpha' \cdot \alpha''$, where the time of the last event in α' is strictly less than $(k-1) \cdot diam \cdot d$ and where there are no *flash* events in α''. Moreover, we can decompose α' into $k-1$ smaller pieces, as a concatenation $\alpha_1 \cdot \alpha_2 \cdot \ldots \cdot \alpha_{k-1}$, where in each of the fragments α_r, $1 \leq r \leq k-1$, the difference between the times associated with the first and last events is strictly less than $diam \cdot d$.

We now construct a fair trace β of A; β will be an ordinary *untimed* fair trace—without times associated with its events. It is constructed as a concatenation of the form $\beta = \beta_1 \cdot \beta_2 \cdot \ldots \cdot \beta_{k-1} \beta''$, where each β_r is obtained by reordering the actions in α_r (and removing the times) and β'' is just the sequence of actions in α'' (with the times removed). We will show that β contains fewer than k sessions, which will contradict the correctness of A.

All the reordering that we do in constructing β will preserve the important dependencies among actions in α, in particular, the dependency of a *receive* event on the corresponding *send* event and the (possible) dependency of any event of any process i on any prior event of the same process. We use the notation $\rightarrow_{trace(\alpha)}$, as defined in Section 14.1.4, for the irreflexive partial order that describes these dependencies. Theorem 14.1 will be used to show that β is in fact a fair trace of A.

The following claim describes the properties we require of our reordered sequences β_r. Fix j_0 and j_1 to be any two nodes of G whose distance is equal to *diam*, and define

$$i_r = \begin{cases} j_0, & \text{if } r \text{ is even} \\ j_1, & \text{if } r \text{ is odd} \end{cases}$$

Claim 16.12 *For every* r, $1 \leq r \leq k - 1$, *there exists a sequence* β_r *of actions of A such that the following properties hold:*

1. *β_r is obtained from the sequence of actions in α_r by reordering, preserving the $\rightarrow_{trace(\alpha)}$ order.*

2. *β_r can be written as a concatenation $\gamma_r \delta_r$, where γ_r contains no event of process i_{r-1} and δ_r contains no event of process i_r.*

We first show how to complete the proof of the theorem using Claim 16.12. Since the only reordering of events is for individual β_r sequences and since that reordering respects the $\rightarrow_{trace(\alpha)}$ dependencies, Theorem 14.1 implies that β is a fair trace of A. But we can show that β contains at most $k - 1$ sessions: No session can be entirely contained within γ_1, since γ_1 contains no event of i_0. Likewise, no session can be entirely contained within any segment of the form $\delta_{r-1}\gamma_r$, since this sequence contains no event of process i_{r-1}. This implies that each session must contain events on *both sides* of some γ_r–δ_r boundary. But there are only $k - 1$ such boundaries, hence at most $k - 1$ sessions. Thus, β violates the correctness guarantees of A, which yields a contradiction.

It remains to construct the sequences β_r required for Claim 16.12. So fix any arbitrary r, $1 \leq r \leq k - 1$. We consider the following cases:

1. α_r contains no event of i_{r-1}.

Then let β_r be the sequence of actions in α_r, without any reordering. Taking $\gamma_r = \beta_r$ and $\delta_r = \lambda$ (the empty sequence) gives the needed properties.

2. α_r contains no event of i_r.

Then let β_r be the sequence of actions in α_r, without any reordering. Taking $\gamma_r = \lambda$ and $\delta_r = \beta_r$ suffices.

3. α_r contains at least one event of i_{r-1} and at least one event of i_r.

Then let π be the first event of i_{r-1} in α_r and let ϕ be the last event of i_r in α_r. We claim that we cannot have $\pi \rightarrow_{trace(\alpha)} \phi$, that is, ϕ cannot depend on π. This is so because α is a slow execution, so the time for a message to propagate from process i_{r-1} to process i_r in α is at least $diam \cdot d$; however, the time between the first and last events in α_r is strictly less than $diam \cdot d$.

Then we claim (and leave as an exercise to show) that it is possible to reorder the events of α_r so that ϕ precedes π, while still preserving the $\rightarrow_{trace(\alpha)}$ partial order. Let β_r be the resulting sequence of events, γ_r the prefix of β_r ending with ϕ, and δ_r the rest of β_r. These sequences have all the needed properties.

$\square$

We emphasize again that the trace β that we construct in the proof of Theorem 16.11 does not have times associated with its events. The contradiction arises because β does not contain enough sessions, not because of any timing properties of β. Timing information is used in the proof to deduce that certain events cannot depend on others, in the slow timed execution α.

Local notion of correctness. Theorem 16.11 looks almost like a contradiction to some of the synchronizer results—those that give transformations from synchronous to asynchronous algorithms with only constant time overhead. The difference is that the synchronizers only guarantee a "local" notion of correctness. Rather than preserving the behavior of the collection of users (i.e., synchronous processes) as a whole, they only preserve the behavior of each user separately, permitting reordering of the events at different users.

For many distributed applications, the order of events at different users does not matter; for instance, typical data processing and financial applications can generally withstand out-of-order processing of the transactions of different users. However, for applications in which there is significant communication among the users outside of the distributed system, the order of events at different users may be important.

16.7   Bibliographic Notes

Awerbuch [29] introduced the general notion of a synchronizer, as well as the decomposition of the synchronizer problem into a data communication part and a safe synchronizer. Awerbuch's paper also defines the *Alpha*, *Beta* and *Gamma* synchronizers and contains algorithms for obtaining good cluster decompositions for *Gamma*. Applications of synchronizers to obtain efficient asynchronous algorithms for breadth-first search and maximum flow are presented in [29, 30]. Further work on efficient cluster decompositions appears in [35, 36, 32]. The formal presentation of synchronizers using I/O automata is due to Devarajan [89], following an earlier development by Fekete, Lynch, and Shrira [109].

The lower bound proof is due to Arjomandi, Fischer, and Lynch [14], who presented the result for a shared memory model. The presentation in this chapter uses some simplifications by Attiya and Mavronicolas [17]. Attiya and Mavronicolas [17] also extended the lower bound result to the setting of partially synchronous systems. Raynal has written a book entirely about synchronizers [250].

16.8   Exercises

16.1. State and prove a close correspondence between the synchronous model of Chapter 2 and the asynchronous model consisting of user automata U_i and *GlobSynch* that is given in Section 16.1.

16.2. Fill in the details of the proof of Lemma 16.1. Specifically, Claim 16.2 needs a proof, as does the claim that it is possible to reorder the events of β to obtain γ without violating the $\rightarrow_\beta$ ordering.

16.3. Let L and G denote the *LocSynch* and *GlobSynch* systems, respectively, modified slightly so that the external actions are exactly all the actions of the user automata. (That is, the internal actions of the users are reclassified as outputs.) Prove, by exhibiting a counterexample execution, that it is not the case that $fairtraces(L) \subseteq fairtraces(G)$.

16.4. Fill in all the details of the proof and complexity analysis for the *SimpleSynch* system. In particular,

(a) State and prove all needed invariants.

(b) Prove that f is a simulation relation.

(c) Carry out the fairness argument carefully in terms of Theorem 8.13.

(d) Give a careful proof of the time complexity claim. (Don't forget that the assumed bound of d only refers to the delivery of the *oldest* message currently in any channel.)

16.5. Let S and G denote the *SimpleSynch* and *GlobSynch* systems, respectively, modified so that the external actions are exactly all the actions of the user automata. (That is, the internal actions of the users are reclassified as outputs, and the *send* and *receive* actions are "hidden"—that is, reclassified as internal.)

(a) Prove, by exhibiting a counterexample execution, that it is not the case that $fairtraces(S) \subseteq fairtraces(G)$.

(b) Modify S to obtain a new system S', also composed of user automata plus a distributed algorithm, such that $fairtraces(S') \subseteq fairtraces(G)$. Analyze its complexity.

16.6. Fill in the details in the proof of Lemma 16.5.

16.7. Write precondition-effect code for the $Alpha_i$ automaton and prove its correctness theorem, Theorem 16.7. Use a simulation relation from the *Alpha* system to the *SafeSynch* system.

16.8. Write precondition-effect code for the $Beta_i$ automaton and prove its correctness theorem, Theorem 16.8. Use a simulation relation from the *Beta* system to the *SafeSynch* system.

16.9. True or false?

Let B and G denote the *Beta* and *GlobSynch* systems, respectively, again modified so that the actions that are classified as external are exactly all the actions of the user automata. Then $fairtraces(B) \subseteq fairtraces(G)$.

Prove your answer.

16.10. Give precondition-effect code for the node processes in the implementations of the *ClusterSynch* and *ForestSynch* automata, in the *Gamma* synchronizer. Prove Theorem 16.10.

16.11. Give a distributed algorithm that operates in an arbitrary network graph G and produces a minimum-height rooted spanning tree for the use of the *Beta* synchronizer. You may assume the nodes have UIDs, but there is no distinguished node. How efficient an algorithm can you design?

16.12. Give a distributed algorithm that operates in an arbitrary network graph G and obtains a "good" spanning forest for the use of the *Gamma* synchronizer. Also, produce the distinguished paths for communication between the roots of neighboring clusters. You may assume the nodes have UIDs, but there is no distinguished node. Your algorithm should yield trees of small height, as well as short communication paths.

16.13. Consider a square grid graph G, consisting of $\sqrt{n} \times \sqrt{n}$ nodes. Consider a partition P_k into k^2 equal-sized clusters, obtained by dividing each side into k equal intervals. In terms of n and k, what are the communication and time complexity bounds for synchronizer *Gamma* based on partition P_k? (You may assume the best possible spanning trees and communication paths for the given decomposition.)

16.14. A programmer at the Flaky Computer Corporation who has substantial experience with fault-tolerant algorithms has just had a brilliant idea for a synchronizer to be used in fault-tolerant asynchronous network programming. He admits that his idea only works for a completely connected network G but still thinks it is a big win.

His synchronizer is like *GlobSynch*, except that at each round r, it waits to obtain *user-sends* for round r from at least $n-f$ of the processes (including i), rather than from all n processes, before performing a *user-receive$_i$* event for round r.

Show his superiors that his algorithm is incorrect before they install it in a fault-tolerant aircraft-control system. (*Hint:* You can consider a correct synchronous consensus algorithm such as *FloodSet* in conjunction with the proposed synchronizer. Produce an incorrect execution of the combined algorithm.)

16.15. Prove that the termination strategy described for *SynchBFS* with a synchronizer works correctly.

16.16. State and prove a result giving the important properties guaranteed by the asynchronous algorithm obtained by running *LubyMIS* with your favorite synchronizer.

16.17. Prove that $O\left(\log n\right)$ sessions suffice to solve the Boolean matrix, transitive closure problem described in Example 16.6.1. What is the best constant you can prove?

16.18. Prove the missing claim in the proof of Theorem 16.11, that is, that it is possible to reorder the events of α_r so that ϕ precedes π while still preserving $\rightarrow_{trace(\alpha)}$.

16.19. Obtain the best *upper bound* you can for the time complexity of an asynchronous solution to the k-session problem. Generalize your algorithm to the asynchronous implementation of arbitrary synchronous algorithms. What correctness conditions are guaranteed?

16.20. Redo Exercise 15.40, this time using some of the algorithm decomposition ideas presented in this chapter. Try to use all the modularity you can. For example, you should give abstract automata to represent the behavior required of the MST algorithm and of the algorithm that uses the MST to elect a leader.

Chapter 17

Shared Memory versus Networks

In the previous chapter, we described synchronizers, which comprise one method for simplifying the programming of asynchronous networks. This method enables (non-fault-tolerant) synchronous network algorithms such as those described in Chapter 4 to be used in asynchronous networks. In this chapter, we describe a second strategy for simplifying the programming of asynchronous networks: using them to simulate *asynchronous shared memory systems*. This enables asynchronous shared memory algorithms such as those described in Chapters 10, 11, and 13 to be used in asynchronous networks. Many other asynchronous shared memory algorithms can also be adapted to run in asynchronous networks, including practical algorithms for scientific programming and financial databases. The premise underlying this strategy is that the asynchronous shared memory model is easier to program than the asynchronous network model.

More generally, this chapter deals with relationships between the asynchronous shared memory model and the asynchronous network model. It turns out that there are strong transformation results in both directions, some of which preserve even some fault-tolerance properties. This leads to the conclusion that (except for differences in efficiency) the two models are pretty much the same.

There are other consequences of these transformation results besides just the provision of a simpler programming model for asynchronous networks. For example, a fault-tolerant transformation from the network model to the shared memory model implies that certain impossibility results for the asynchronous shared memory model yield corresponding impossibility results for the asynchronous network model.

A different kind of transformation from the asynchronous shared memory model to the asynchronous network model appears in Section 18.3.3. That transformation rests on the establishment of a notion of *logical time* in an asynchronous network.

17.1 Transformations from the Shared Memory Model to the Network Model

In this section, we describe several ways of transforming asynchronous shared memory systems into asynchronous send/receive network systems. Subsection 17.1.1 gives the correctness conditions to be satisfied by the transformations. Subsection 17.1.2 contains non-fault-tolerant strategies, while Subsection 17.1.3 contains fault-tolerant strategies. The only types of failures we consider here are process stopping failures.

17.1.1 The Problem

We start with a shared memory system A in the model of Chapter 9. As usual, we assume that A interacts with its environment using a set of n ports, numbered $1, \ldots, n$; on port i, A interacts with user automaton U_i. As for the user automata in Chapters 10–13, we assume that the external actions of each U_i are exactly those actions by which it interacts with A. In this chapter, we permit each process i of A to have any number of tasks. Because some of our transformations preserve fault-tolerance properties, we also include $stop_i$ input actions, as discussed in Section 9.6, and assume that each $stop_i$ event permanently disables all the tasks of process i.

It turns out that we need a technical restriction on A in order for our transformations to work correctly. This technical restriction is the same one we used in Section 13.1.4. That is, consider A in combination with any collection of user automata. We assume that for each port i, there is a function $turn_i$ that, for any finite execution α of the combined system, yields either the value *system* or *user*. This is supposed to indicate whose turn it is to take the next step, after α. We require that if $turn_i(\alpha) = system$, then U_i has no output step enabled in its state after α, while if $turn_i(\alpha) = user$, then process i of A has no output or internal step—that is, no locally controlled step—enabled in its state after α. Thus, we assume the same shared memory model as we did in Section 13.1.4.

The general problem (including a fault-tolerance requirement for an arbitrary set I of ports) is to design an asynchronous send/receive network system B with processes P_i, $1 \leq i \leq n$, that is an *I-simulation* of A, defined as follows. For any execution α of B with any collection of users U_i, there should be an execution α' of A with the same users such that the following conditions hold:

1. α and α' are indistinguishable[1] to U (the composition of the users U_i).

2. For each i, a *stop$_i$* occurs in α exactly if a *stop$_i$* occurs in α'.

Moreover, if α is a fair execution and if every i for which *stop$_i$* appears in α is in I, then α' is also a fair execution. If B is an I-simulation of A for every I with $|I| \leq f$, then we say that B is an *f-simulation* of A.

You might recognize these conditions as being similar to the ones that are asserted in Theorem 13.7. This connection will be exploited in this chapter, in proving that certain network systems simulate shared memory systems.

As described in Section 14.1.1, in system B, each *stop$_i$* event permanently disables all the tasks of process P_i. However, a *stop* event has no effect on the channels.

17.1.2   Strategies Assuming No Failures

In the absence of failures, there are simple strategies that work. Most of these can be classified as *single-copy* or *multi-copy* schemes, based on the number of copies of each shared variable that are maintained in the network.

Single-copy schemes.   The simplest simulation strategy involves just distributing the shared variables of A arbitrarily among the processes of B, with each shared variable located at a single process. This strategy works for shared variables of arbitrary types.

> *SimpleShVarSim* algorithm:
>
> Each shared variable x of A is assumed to be "owned" by a single process P_i of B. The job of process P_i is twofold: to simulate the corresponding process i of A and to manage the shared variables that it owns.
>
> For each i, process P_i has the same actions at the user interface as does process i of A. P_i's steps simulate those of process i directly, with the following exceptions: When process i of A performs an access to a shared variable x, P_i instead sends a message containing the invocation to the process P_j that owns variable x. (If P_i itself is the owner, it just passes the invocation request to a "subroutine.") Then P_i suspends all locally controlled steps of its simulation of process i, pending a response to the invocation. When a response arrives, P_i resumes simulating process i of A as usual.
>
> When the owner of a shared variable x receives a message (or a local invocation request) containing an invocation of x, it simply applies it to x,

---

[1] This uses the formal notion of "indistinguishable" from Section 8.7.

in one indivisible step. The response is sent in a response message to the sender of the invocation (or passed back to the main simulation task, if the request is local).

The *SimpleShVarSim* algorithm has some interesting modularity. We can express each process P_i as the composition of an I/O automaton Q_i, which is responsible for simulating process i of A, and an I/O automaton $R_{x,i}$ for each shared variable x.[2]

For Q_i, we simply use automaton P_i of the *Trans(A)* algorithm of Section 13.1.4. More precisely, we assume that the outputs of automaton Q_i include actions of the form $a_{x,i}$, where a is an invocation that process i of A uses on shared variable x, and that the inputs include actions of the form $b_{x,i}$, where b is a response to process i from shared variable x.

Each $R_{x,i}$ has inputs $a_{x,i}$ and outputs $b_{x,i}$. For convenience, we assume that for any particular shared variable x, all the automata $R_{x,i}$ have reliable FIFO send/receive channels by which they communicate with each other. As in Exercise 14.6, the channels for the individual x can all be simulated by the given FIFO reliable channels. It will turn out that, for each x, the composition of all the automata $R_{x,i}$, together with the channels between them, constitute an atomic object of x's variable type.

Figure 17.1 shows the architecture for *SimpleShVarSim*, for the special case of two processes and two shared variables. We have not explicitly represented the *stop* actions—we assume that each $stop_i$ is an input to Q_i and to all the $R_{x,i}$.

The code for $R_{x,i}$ is as follows. It is presented in two parts, based on whether or not P_i is the owner of x. Because the $stop_i$ action is included in the signature of $R_{x,i}$, we include an explicit description of the handling of the $stop_i$ action: it simply sets a *stopped* flag, which disables all locally controlled actions and prevents any changes associated with input actions. (This handling is not particularly interesting here, because we do not make any claims about the behavior of this algorithm in the presence of faults.) For the purpose of disambiguation, we subscript channel actions by the name of the variable as well as the nodes at both ends.

$R_{x,i}$, P_i the owner of x:

Signature:

Input:

    $a_{x,i}$, a an invocation of x by process i
    receive("*invoke*", $a)_{x,j,i}$, a an invocation of x by j, $j \neq i$
    $stop_i$

---

[2]We also hide the communication actions between them.

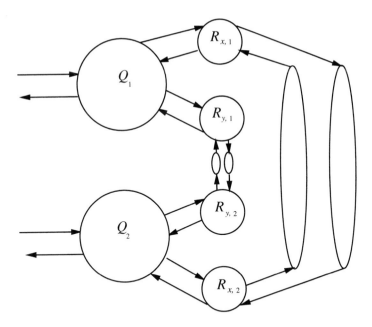

Figure 17.1: Architecture for *SimpleShVarSim*—two processes and two shared variables.

Output:
    $b_{x,i}$, b a response of x to process i
    $send(\text{``respond''}, b)_{x,i,j}$, b a response of x to j, $j \neq i$
Internal:
    $perform(a, j)_{x,i}$, a an invocation of x, $1 \leq j \leq n$

States:
val, a value in the domain of x, initially the initial value of x
inv-buffer, a set of pairs (a, j), a an invocation, $1 \leq j \leq n$, initially empty
resp-buffer, a set of responses b, initially empty
stopped, a Boolean, initially *false*
for every $j \neq i$:
    send-buffer(j), a FIFO queue of responses, initially empty

Transitions:

$a_{x,i}$
    Effect:
        if *stopped* = *false* then
            inv-buffer := *inv-buffer* $\cup \{(a, i)\}$

$receive(\text{``invoke''}, a)_{x,j,i}$
    Effect:
        if *stopped* = *false* then
            inv-buffer := *inv-buffer* $\cup \{(a, j)\}$

$perform(a, j)_{x,i}$
    Precondition:
        $stopped = false$
        $(a, j) \in inv\text{-}buffer$
    Effect:
        $inv\text{-}buffer := inv\text{-}buffer - \{(a, j)\}$
        $(b, val) := f(a, val)$
        if $j = i$ then
          $resp\text{-}buffer := resp\text{-}buffer \cup \{b\}$
        else
          add b to $send\text{-}buffer(j)$

$send(\text{``respond''}, b)_{x,i,j}$
    Precondition:
        $stopped = false$
        b is first on $send\text{-}buffer(j)$
    Effect:
        remove first element of $send\text{-}buffer(j)$

$stop_i$
    Effect:
        $stopped := true$

$b_{x,i}$
    Precondition:
        $stopped = false$
        $b \in resp\text{-}buffer$
    Effect:
        $resp\text{-}buffer := resp\text{-}buffer - \{b\}$

Tasks:
$\{b_{x,i} : b$ is a response$\}$
for every j:
    $\{send(\text{``respond''}, b)_{x,i,j} : b$ is a response$\}$
    $\{perform(a, j)_{x,i} : a$ is an invocation$\}$

$R_{x,i}$, P_i not the owner of x:

Signature:

Input:
    $a_{x,i}$, a an invocation of x by process i
    $receive(\text{``respond''}, b)_{x,j,i}$, a an invocation of x by i, j the owner of x
    $stop_i$
Output:
    $b_{x,i}$, b a response of x to process i
    $send(\text{``invoke''}, a)_{x,i,j}$, a an invocation of x by i, j the owner of x

States:

$resp\text{-}buffer$, a set of responses b, initially empty
$send\text{-}buffer$, a FIFO queue of responses, initially empty
$stopped$, a Boolean, initially *false*

Transitions:

$a_{x,i}$
    Effect:
        if *stopped* = *false* then
            add *a* to *send-buffer*

send("*invoke*", $a)_{x,i,j}$
    Precondition:
        stopped = *false*
        a is first on *send-buffer*
    Effect:
        remove first element of *send-buffer*

receive("*respond*", $b)_{x,j,i}$
    Effect:
        if *stopped* = *false* then
            resp-buffer := *resp-buffer* $\cup$ {*b*}

$b_{x,i}$
    Precondition:
        stopped = *false*
        b $\in$ *resp-buffer*
    Effect:
        resp-buffer := *resp-buffer* $-$ {*b*}

$stop_i$
    Effect:
        stopped := *true*

Tasks:
{$b_{x,i}$: *b* is a response}
{*send*("*invoke*", $a)_{x,i,j}$: *a* is an invocation}

Theorem 17.1 *The SimpleShVarSim algorithm based on A is a 0-simulation of A. (We do not claim any fault-tolerance properties.)*

Proof Sketch. We first claim that for each x, the composition of all the automata $R_{x,i}$, $1 \leq i \leq n$, plus the channels between them (with hiding of *send* and *receive* actions), constitute an atomic object B_x of x's variable type and of the interface specified for the definition of *Trans* in Section 13.1.4. (We do not claim any fault-tolerance properties for B_x, however.) With these atomic objects B_x, system B is exactly the system *Trans*(A). This allows us to apply Theorem 13.7, with $I = \emptyset$: if α is any execution of B with users U_i, then Theorem 13.7 yields an execution α' of A with the same users, satisfying all the conditions in the definition of a 0-simulation. $\square$

Location of shared variables. The *SimpleShVarSim* algorithm permits the variables to be owned by arbitrary processes. As a general guideline, however, the best performance is obtained by locating variables at the processes that access them most frequently.

For example, if a single-writer/multi-reader read/write shared variable x is written more frequently than it is read, then it is natural to locate it at the process corresponding to the writer. If we do this, then *write* accesses are fast, since they are performed locally. Of course, in this case all *read* accesses by processes other than the writer are slow, since they involve message exchanges over the network. If *write* accesses are frequent relative to *read* accesses, this arrangement works well, but it may not be the best if *writes* are relatively rare.

Fault-tolerance. The *SimpleShVarSim* algorithm does not have any interesting fault-tolerance properties. For example, if a $stop_i$ occurs, then all processes are thereafter prevented from accessing any of the variables owned by process P_i.

Busy-waiting. Some shared memory algorithms, such as the *Bakery* mutual exclusion algorithm of Section 10.7 and the *RightLeftDP* Dining Philosophers algorithm of Section 11.3, include *busy-waiting loops* in which a process repeatedly checks a shared variable, waiting for a particular condition to become satisfied. The *SimpleShVarSim* algorithm could be modified to remove such loops, by instead having the owner of the variable notify the busy-waiting process when the value of the variable changes (or when the awaited condition becomes true). This serves to reduce the communication complexity.

Multi-copy schemes. It is sometimes useful to allow several processes to maintain copies of the same shared variable x. Consider, for example, the case where x is a read/write shared variable for which *read* operations are frequent but *write* operations are rare. (This is the situation in many databases.) Then, if many processes maintain "cached" copies of x, many *reads* can be performed locally and therefore at low cost. The problem, however, is that *write* operations become more expensive than before, since they must be performed on all copies of x. This means that messages have to be sent from a writer process to all the processes that maintain copies of x.

The problem is even worse than this, though. Suppose, for example, that x is a multi-writer register. Then two processes, say P_1 and P_2, could simultaneously attempt to *write* to x, and two processes maintaining copies of x, say P_3 and P_4, could receive the messages from P_1 and P_2 in opposite orders. This could lead them to apply the *writes* to their copies in different orders, yielding inconsistent results for subsequent *reads*.

Even in the case where x is a single-writer register, anomalies can occur. If the writer sends out messages for a *write*, its message might arrive much earlier at one process, say P_1, than at another, say P_2. A local *read* could occur at P_1 after it receives the message, obtaining the new value, then another local *read* could later occur at P_2 before it receives the message, obtaining the old value. If the first *read* finishes before the second *read* begins, this behavior is not allowable for a read/write atomic object.

Thus, a more clever protocol is required to manage the *writes*. For instance, a writer could work in two phases: "locking" and modifying all the copies of x in the first phase, then releasing the locks in the second. A *read* operation would be delayed while the local copy is locked. In this case, some care must be taken that all invoked operations eventually get performed.

This type of algorithm is an example of a *concurrency control algorithm*. Specifically, the algorithm we just sketched is a *read/write locking algorithm* implementing an *atomic transaction* that writes to all the copies of x. This means that it appears to the processes performing operations on x that writes to all copies are performed instantaneously, at some "serialization point" within the interval of the containing *write* operation. There are many other kinds of concurrency control protocols, including locking algorithms for other types of shared variables besides read/write variables, *timestamp-based algorithms*, *hybrid algorithms* that combine the use of locking and timestamps, and *optimistic algorithms*. We do not present these here, but instead refer you to the book *Atomic Transactions*, by Lynch, Merritt, Weihl, and Fekete for a complete presentation (in the same style as this book).

A popular multi-copy algorithm for read/write shared variables is the *MajorityVoting algorithm*. The heart of this algorithm is the implementation, for each read/write shared variable x, of a read/write atomic object for x. This implementation is in turn based on an underlying implementation of atomic transactions.

MajorityVotingObject algorithm (informal):

Each of the n processes maintains a copy of x, initially the initial value of x, together with a nonnegative integer *tag*, initially 0.

A process that wants either to *read* or to *write* x performs an atomic transaction involving some of the copies of x. The atomic transaction consists of a series of operations that appear to be performed instantaneously at some "serialization point" during the execution of the transaction. (An incomplete operation might or might not have a serialization point.) The transactions can be implemented using two-phase locking, or timestamp-based, hybrid, or optimistic concurrency control methods, augmented by some priority mechanism to ensure that (if no process fails) each transaction eventually completes.

In order for process P_i to perform a *read* of x, it reads at least a majority of the copies of x. Among these, it chooses one with the largest *tag* and returns the associated value of x. All these steps are part of the same atomic transaction and so are executed "as if" instantaneously.

In order for process P_i to perform a *write(v)* to x, it first performs an *embedded-read*, which is exactly like a *read* as described just above. From the result of this *embedded-read*, P_i determines the largest *tag*, t. Then it writes $(v, t + 1)$ to at least a majority of the copies of x. All these steps—those of the *embedded-read* and those that write the copies—are part of the same atomic transaction and so are executed "as if" instantaneously.

Lemma 17.2 *The MajorityVotingObject algorithm is a read/write atomic object.*

Proof Sketch.   We verify the conditions in the definition of an atomic object, as given in Section 13.1.1. Well-formedness and failure-free termination should be easy to see. For the atomicity condition, fix any execution α of the *Majority-VotingObject* algorithm (with any set of user automata). We choose the subset Φ of incomplete operations to be exactly those that are assigned serialization points in the underlying transaction implementation and adopt the responses for the operations in Φ and the serialization points from the transaction implementation. To see that the shrinking property holds, we need to know that each *read* obtains the value written by the *write* serialized just before it, if there is one; if not, it obtains the initial value v_0.

The keys to seeing this are the following facts:

1. The *write* operations obtain *tags* $1, 2, \ldots$, in the order of their serialization points.

2. Each *read* or *embedded-read* obtains the largest *tag* that has been written by a *write* operation serialized before it (or 0 if there are none), together with the accompanying value.

These facts are true because each *read* or *embedded-read* reads a majority of the copies, the largest *tag* has been written to a majority of the copies, and all majorities intersect.   □

Now, if the shared memory system A uses read/write shared variables, we define the *MajorityVoting* algorithm based on A to consist of the same Q_i components that are used in *SimpleShVarSim*, together with *MajorityVotingObject*s for all the read/write shared variables. Then Lemma 17.2 implies

Theorem 17.3 *Suppose that A uses read/write shared variables. Then the MajorityVoting algorithm based on A is a 0-simulation of A.*

Fault-tolerance. Although the *Majority Voting Object* algorithm allows flexibility in the choice of which majority is read or written, it does not, in general, provide a fault-tolerant implementation of an atomic object for x. This is because the standard transaction implementations are not fault-tolerant. For example, in a read/write locking algorithm, a process performing a *read* transaction might send out messages to read a majority of the copies, causing a majority of the copies to become locked. Then the process might fail without releasing its locks. This would prevent any later *write* transaction from ever obtaining the locks it requires. In practice, this problem can be handled by using timeouts to detect process failures (which we cannot do in the asynchronous network model) and/or weakening the resiliency requirements.

17.1.3 An Algorithm Tolerating Process Failures

As we noted, the strategies described in Section 17.1.2 do not have any interesting fault-tolerance properties. In this section, we present the *ABD algorithm* of Attiya, Bar-Noy, and Dolev, which works in the presence of a limited number f of process stopping failures; the network is assumed to be reliable. We assume that n, the total number of processes, is strictly greater than $2f$, that is, that a *majority* of the processes do not fail. We only consider the case of single-writer/multi-reader read/write shared memory.

The heart of the *ABD* algorithm is the implementation, for each read/write shared variable x, of a read/write atomic object guaranteeing f-failure termination. For simplicity, we describe this implementation assuming that only *write* operations occur on port 1 and only *read* operations on ports $2, \ldots, n$; we will later have to modify this implementation slightly in order to use it in the general simulation. The algorithm uses ideas from the *Majority Voting* algorithm and from the *VitanyiAwerbuch* algorithm of Section 13.4.3. The main idea is that the result of each *write* is stored at a majority of the nodes in the network, before the *write* completes.

ABDObject algorithm (informal):

Each of the n processes maintains a copy of x, initially the initial value of x, together with a nonnegative integer *tag*, initially 0.

When the unique writer process wants to perform a *write(v)* on x, it first lets t be the smallest *tag* that it has not yet assigned to any *write*. Then it sets its local copy of x and local *tag* to v and t, respectively, and sends (*"write"*, v, t) messages to all the other processes. A process receiving such a message updates its copy of x and its *tag* in the same way, provided that t is greater than its current *tag*; in any case, it sends an acknowledgment to the writer. When the writer knows (via the acknowledgments and its knowledge of its own local behavior) that a majority of the processes have their *tag* values equal to t, it returns *ack*.

When any process P_i wants to perform a *read* of x, it sends *read* messages to all the other processes and also reads its own value of x and its own *tag*. A process receiving such a message responds with its latest value of x and *tag*. When P_i has learned the x and *tag* values of a majority of the processes, it prepares to return the value v of x associated with the largest *tag* t it has seen. But before doing this, P_i propagates (v, t) to a majority of the processes: it updates its own value of x and *tag* and also sends a second round of messages to all the other processes (except for the writer). A process receiving such a message updates its copy of x and its *tag* accordingly, provided that t is greater than its current *tag*; in any case, it sends an acknowledgment to P_i. When P_i knows (via the acknowledgments and its knowledge of its own local behavior) that a majority of the processes have their *tag* values at least equal to t, it returns v.

The code is as follows. ABD_1 is the writer process and $ABD_2, \ldots, ABD_n$ are reader processes. For simplicity, we do not include explicit mention of *stop* actions, which we assume are handled as for *SimpleShVarSim*. Also, we omit the explicit subscript x on the various actions. (The code is already long enough without these details.) We assume that V is the domain of values and v_0 the initial value for x.

$ABDObject_1$ automaton (formal):

Signature:

Input:
    $write(v)_1$, $v \in V$
    $receive(\text{``write-ack''}, t)_{j,1}$, $t \in \mathbb{N}^+$, $j \neq 1$
    $receive(\text{``read''}, u)_{j,1}$, $u \in \mathbb{N}^+$, $j \neq 1$
Output:
    ack_1
    $send(\text{``write''}, v, t)_{1,j}$, $v \in V$, $t \in \mathbb{N}^+$, $j \neq 1$
    $send(\text{``read-ack''}, v, t, u)_{1,j}$, $v \in V$, $t \in \mathbb{N}$, $u \in \mathbb{N}^+$, $j \neq 1$

States:
$val \in V$, initially v_0
$tag \in \mathbb{N}$, initially 0
$status \in \{idle, active\}$, initially *idle*
$count \in \mathbb{N}$, initially 0
for every $j \neq 1$:
    send-buffer(j), a FIFO queue of messages, initially empty

Transitions:

$write(v)_1$
    Effect:
        $val := v$
        $tag := tag + 1$
        $status := active$
        $count := 1$
        for all $j \neq 1$ do
            add (*"write"*, v, tag) to *send-buffer*(j)

$send(m)_{1,j}$
    Precondition:
        m is first on *send-buffer*(j)
    Effect:
        remove first element of *send-buffer*(j)

$receive($ *"write-ack"*$, t)_{j,1}$
    Effect:
        if $status = active$ and $t = tag$ then
            $count := count + 1$

ack_1
    Precondition:
        $status = active$
        $count > \frac{n}{2}$
    Effect:
        $count := 0$
        $status := idle$

$receive($ *"read"*$, u)_{j,1}$
    Effect:
        add (*"read-ack"*, val, tag, u)
            to *send-buffer*(j)

Tasks:
$\{ack_1\}$
for every j:
    $\{send(m)_{1,j} : m$ a message$\}$

Note that, in contrast to the *Majority Voting* and *Vitanyi Awerbuch* algorithms, the choice of a new *tag* is simple in the *ABDObject* algorithm, because there is only one writer. The following is the code for the reader processes.

ABDObject$_i$ automaton, $2 \leq i \leq n$ (formal):

Signature:

Input:
    $read_i$
    $receive($ *"write"*$, v, t)_{1,i}$, $v \in V$, $t \in \mathbb{N}^+$
    $receive($ *"read-ack"*$, v, t, u)_{j,i}$, $v \in V$, $t \in \mathbb{N}$, $u \in \mathbb{N}^+$, $j \neq i$
    $receive($ *"prop-ack"*$, u)_{j,i}$, $u \in \mathbb{N}^+$, $j \notin \{1, i\}$
    $receive($ *"read"*$, u)_{j,i}$, $u \in \mathbb{N}^+$, $j \notin \{1, i\}$
    $receive($ *"propagate"*$, v, t, u)_{j,i}$, $v \in V$, $t \in \mathbb{N}$, $u \in \mathbb{N}^+$, $j \notin \{1, i\}$
Output:
    v_i, $v \in V$
    $send($ *"write-ack"*$, t)_{i,1}$, $t \in \mathbb{N}^+$
    $send($ *"read"*$, u)_{i,j}$, $u \in \mathbb{N}^+$, $j \neq i$
    $send($ *"propagate"*$, v, t, u)_{i,j}$, $v \in V$, $t \in \mathbb{N}$, $u \in \mathbb{N}^+$, $j \notin \{1, i\}$
    $send($ *"read-ack"*$, v, t, u)_{i,j}$, $v \in V$, $t \in \mathbb{N}$, $u \in \mathbb{N}^+$, $j \notin \{1, i\}$
    $send($ *"prop-ack"*$, u)_{i,j}$, $u \in \mathbb{N}^+$, $j \notin \{1, i\}$

States:
$val \in V$, initially v_0
$tag \in \mathbb{N}$, initially 0
$response\text{-}val \in V$, initially v_0
$read\text{-}tag \in \mathbb{N}$, initially 0
$status \in \{idle, active1, active2\}$, initially $idle$
$count \in \mathbb{N}$, initially 0
for every $j \neq i$:
    $send\text{-}buffer(j)$, a FIFO queue of messages, initially empty

Transitions:

$read_i$
    Effect:
        $read\text{-}tag := read\text{-}tag + 1$
        $status := active1$
        $count := 1$
        for all $j \neq i$ do
            add (*"read"*, $read\text{-}tag$)
                to $send\text{-}buffer(j)$

$send(m)_{i,j}$
    Precondition:
        m is first on $send\text{-}buffer(j)$
    Effect:
        remove first element of $send\text{-}buffer(j)$

$receive(\text{"read-ack"}, v, t, u)_{j,i}$
    Effect:
        if $status = active1$ and $u = read\text{-}tag$ then
           $count := count + 1$
           if $t > tag$ then
               $val := v$
               $tag := t$
           if $count > \frac{n}{2}$ then
               $response\text{-}val := val$
               $status := active2$
               $count := 1$
               for all $j \notin \{1, i\}$ do
                   add (*"propagate"*, val, tag, $read\text{-}tag$)
                       to $send\text{-}buffer(j)$

$receive(\text{"prop-ack"}, u)_{j,i}$
    Effect:
        if $status = active2$ and $u = read\text{-}tag$
           then $count := count + 1$

v_i
    Precondition:
        $status = active2$
        $count > \frac{n}{2}$
        $v = response\text{-}val$
    Effect:
        $count := 0$
        $status := idle$

$receive(\text{"write"}, v, t)_{1,i}$
    Effect:
        if $t > tag$ then
           $val := v$
           $tag := t$
           add (*"write-ack"*, t) to $send\text{-}buffer(1)$

$receive(\text{"read"}, u)_{j,i}$
    Effect:
        add (*"read-ack"*, val, tag, u)
           to $send\text{-}buffer(j)$

$receive(\text{"propagate"}, v, t, u)_{j,i}$
    Effect:
        if $t > tag$ then
           $val := v$
           $tag := t$
         add (*"prop-ack"*, u) to $send\text{-}buffer(j)$

Tasks:

$\{v_i\}$

for every j:

$\quad \{send(m)_{i,j} : m$ a message$\}$

In this code, the *read-tag* is used to keep track of which acknowledgments belong to the current operation. The *response-val* is used to remember the value to be returned while it is being propagated. Note that it is not necessary to propagate the response value to the writer, since the writer must already have the latest information.

Theorem 17.4 *The ABDObject algorithm, for $n > 2f$, is a read/write atomic object guaranteeing f-failure termination.*

Proof Sketch. This is similar to the proofs of the *VitanyiAwerbuch* and *Integer-Bloom* algorithms in Chapter 13. Well-formedness is easy to see. It is also easy to prove f-failure termination, because each operation requires the participation of only a majority of the processes and $n > 2f$. So, as usual, atomicity is the key property to show. We use Lemma 13.16.

Let α be any execution of the *ABDObject* algorithm. Using a restatement of Lemma 13.10 for the asynchronous network setting, we may assume without loss of generality that α contains no incomplete operations.

Define Π to be the set of operations occurring in α. We define a partial ordering on Π as follows. First, order the *write* operations in the order in which they are performed, that is, in the order of their *tags*. Then order each *read* right after the *write* whose *tag* it obtains, if any, otherwise prior to all the *write* operations.

The key properties that need to be shown are

1. If a *write* π with *tag* $= t$ completes before a *read* ϕ is invoked, then ϕ obtains a *tag* that is at least as large as t.

   This is because π's *tag* is received by a majority of the copies, ϕ reads a majority of the copies, and all majorities intersect.

2. If *read* π completes before *read* ϕ is invoked, then the *tag* obtained by ϕ is at least as great as that obtained by π.

   This is by a similar argument, because π propagates its information to a majority of the copies.

Using these two properties, it is not hard to show that the four conditions required for Lemma 13.16 hold, which implies the atomicity condition.   □

Obviously, we can modify the *ABDObject* algorithm so that any other port i is the *write* port, rather than port 1. It is also easy to modify the algorithm so that *read* operations are also permitted on the single *write* port. The results of such modifications still guarantee f-failure termination. The complete *ABD* algorithm based on A is then constructed by using the processes of *Trans(A)*, as we did for *SimpleShVarSim* and *MajorityVoting*, plus an atomic object for each shared variable x. Each atomic object is the appropriately modified version of the *ABDObject*.

Theorem 17.5 *Suppose that A uses single-writer/multi-reader shared memory and that $n > 2f$. Then the ABD algorithm based on A is an f-simulation of A.*

Proof.   By Theorems 17.4 and 13.7.   □

Bounded *tags*.   The *ABD* algorithm uses unbounded *tag* values. It is possible to modify the algorithm so that it uses bounded *tag*s instead. We leave this for an exercise.

Applications.   The *ABD* algorithm can be used to obtain distributed implementations for many interesting fault-tolerant shared memory algorithms based on single-writer/multi-reader registers. For example, the atomic snapshot and atomic multi-writer register algorithms in Chapter 13 can be transformed using *ABD* into algorithms implementing the same objects in the asynchronous send/receive network model. But note that although the original algorithms in these cases guarantee wait-free termination, the transformed versions only tolerate f failures, where $n > 2f$.

17.1.4 An Impossibility Result for $\frac{n}{2}$ Failures

It is not hard to see that the *ABD* algorithm does not tolerate f failures if $n \le 2f$. This is because the failure of this many processes makes the other processes permanently unable to secure the majorities that they need to complete their work. It turns out that this limitation is inherent. The key result is the following, giving a limitation on the fault-tolerance of read/write atomic object implementations in asynchronous networks. To get a stronger statement, we state the result in terms of broadcast systems rather than send/receive systems.

Theorem 17.6 *Let* $n = m + p$, *where* $m, p \geq 1$, *and suppose that* $n \leq 2f$. *Then there is no algorithm in the asynchronous broadcast model (with a reliable broadcast channel) that implements a read/write atomic object with m writers and p readers, guaranteeing f-failure termination.*

Proof. Suppose for the sake of contradiction that there is such an algorithm, say A. As usual for such impossibility proofs, we assume that the users are the most nondeterministic possible.

Let G_1 be the set $1, \ldots, n - f$ and G_2 the set $n - f + 1, \ldots, n$. By assumption, $|G_1| \leq f$ and $|G_2| \leq f$.

Consider a fair execution α_1 of the system (A plus users) that contains an invocation $write(v)_1$ on port 1, where $v \neq v_0$, and no other invocations. Furthermore, suppose that *stop* inputs occur on exactly the ports in G_2 and that these events occur right at the start of the execution; this implies that processes with indices in G_2 never perform any locally controlled actions. By f-failure termination, the *write* must eventually terminate with a matching ack_1. Let α_1' be the prefix of α_1 ending with the ack_1.

Now consider a second fair execution α_2 containing an invocation $read_n$ on port n and no other invocations. Furthermore, suppose that *stop* events occur on exactly the ports in G_1, at the start of the execution. Again by f-failure termination, the *read* must eventually terminate, and the response value must be v_0. Let α_2' be the prefix of α_2 ending with this response.

Now we construct a finite execution α that does not satisfy the atomicity property, thus yielding a contradiction. Execution α satisfies the following conditions:

1. α is indistinguishable from α_1' to the processes with indices in G_1.

2. α is indistinguishable from α_2' to the processes with indices in G_2.

3. In α, the ack_1 response event precedes the $read_n$ invocation event.

This violates the atomicity condition, which says that the *read* is supposed to return v, the value written by the *write*, rather than the initial value v_0.

Execution α is constructed as follows. It contains no *stop* events. It begins with all the activity of α_1' except for the *stop* events and the *receive* events at processes with indices in G_2. Since the processes in G_2 fail right at the start in α_1', anyhow, the result of eliminating all of these events is still an execution and is indistinguishable from α_1' to the processes in G_1. Execution α then finishes with all the activity of α_2', except for the *stop* events and the *receive* events at processes with indices in G_1.

Thus, in α, the processes in each group, G_1 or G_2, behave independently of the processes in the other group. None of the messages broadcast by processes in G_1 are delivered to processes in G_2, and vice versa. It is easy to see that α satisfies all the required properties. $\square$

Theorem 17.6 implies that, for any fixed n and f, where $n \geq 2$ and $f \geq \frac{n}{2}$, there can be no general method for producing f-simulations of n-process shared memory algorithms, even if the underlying shared variables are restricted to be single-writer/single-reader registers. To see this, note that for any such n, there is a trivial wait-free shared memory algorithm A that implements a 1-writer/$n-1$-reader read/write atomic object using a single 1-writer/$n-1$-reader read/write register. An f-simulation of A, if it existed, would yield a send/receive network algorithm that implemented a 1-writer/$n-1$-reader read/write atomic object with f-failure termination. (The argument for this is similar to the proof of Corollary 13.9.) But this contradicts Theorem 17.6.

17.2   Transformations from the Network Model to the Shared Memory Model

Now we describe transformations in the opposite direction, from the asynchronous network model to the shared memory model. These transformations tolerate process stopping failures: a shared memory system with at most f process failures can simulate a network with at most f process failures (and reliable communication). Now there is no special requirement on the number of failures—unlike the transformations in the opposite direction, these constructions work even if $n \leq 2f$. Moreover, the constructions are much simpler than the transformations in the opposite direction.

The reason why these constructions are simpler and yield stronger results is that the asynchronous shared memory model is, in a sense, *more powerful* than the asynchronous network model. The extra power comes from the availability of reliable shared memory.

It is possible to use these transformations to run asynchronous network algorithms in asynchronous shared memory systems. But this is probably not a very interesting thing to do, because the shared memory model is easier to program. A more important use is to allow impossibility results for the asynchronous shared memory model to be carried over to the asynchronous network model. For example, the impossibility of consensus in the presence of failures, proved in Theorem 12.8 for the shared memory model, can be extended to the network model using these transformations.

We present two transformations: one for send/receive systems and one for broadcast systems.

17.2.1 Send/Receive Systems

Suppose that we are given an asynchronous send/receive system A in the model of Chapter 14, based on a directed graph G, with processes P_i, $1 \leq i \leq n$, and reliable FIFO channels $C_{i,j}$. As before, each $stop_i$ event immediately disables all tasks of P_i but has no effect on the channels.

The general problem (including fault-tolerance requirements) is to produce a shared memory system B with n processes, using single-writer/single-reader shared registers, that "simulates" A. The sense in which it should simulate A is exactly the same as for the transformation in the reverse direction. For any execution α of B with any set of users U_i, there should be an execution α' of A with the same users such that the following conditions hold:

1. α and α' are indistinguishable to U.

2. For each i, a $stop_i$ occurs in α exactly if a $stop_i$ occurs in α'.

Moreover, if α is a fair execution and if every i for which $stop_i$ appears in α is in I, then α' is also a fair execution. If B simulates A in this way, for a particular I, then we say that B is an *I-simulation* of A. If B is an I-simulation of A for every I with $|I| \leq f$, then we say that B is an *f-simulation* of A.

We give an algorithm, *SimpleSRSim*, that works for arbitrary failures, that is, an n-simulation.

> ### *SimpleSRSim* algorithm (informal):
>
> For each directed edge (i, j) in the underlying directed graph G, B includes a single-writer/single-reader read/write shared variable $x(i, j)$, writable by process i and readable by process j. It contains a queue of messages, initially empty. Process i only adds messages to the queue; no messages are ever removed.
>
> Process i of B simulates process P_i of A. Simulations of user interface steps and internal steps of P_i are direct. In order to simulate a $send(m)_{i,j}$ action of P_i, process i of A adds the message m to the end of the queue in the variable $x(i, j)$. (It can do this using only a *write* operation by keeping a duplicate local copy of the queue.) Also, from time to time, process i checks all its "incoming" variables $x(j, i)$ in order to determine if there are any new messages that have been placed there since the last time it checked. If so, process i handles those messages in the same way that P_i handles them.

The code is as follows. Note that each process has several tasks. In the code for $check(j)_i$, we use the notation $receive(M)_{j,i}$ as shorthand for the sequence of actions $receive(m_1)_{j,i}$, $receive(m_2)_{j,i}$, ... , where M is the sequence of messages $m_1, m_2, \ldots$. In that code fragment, the sequence M contains the new messages that have been placed in $x(j, i)$ since the last time process i checked.

***SimpleSRSim* algorithm (formal):**

Shared variables:
for every edge (i, j) of G:
    $x(i, j)$, a FIFO queue of messages, initially empty

Actions of i:
As for P_i, except:

Input:	Internal:
Omit all *receive* actions.	$send(m, j)_i$ for every $send(m)_{i,j} \in out(P_i)$
Output:	$check(j)_i$ for every $j \in$ *in-nbrs*
Omit all *send* actions.	

States of i:
$pstate \in states(P_i)$, initially a start state
for every $j \in$ *out-nbrs*:
    out-msgs(j), a FIFO queue of messages, initially empty
for every $j \in$ *in-nbrs*:
    in-msgs(j), a FIFO queue of messages, initially empty
    processed-msgs(j), a FIFO queue of messages, initially empty

Transitions of i:

π, an input of $P_i \neq receive$
    Effect:
        $pstate :=$ any s such that
            $(pstate, \pi, s) \in trans(P_i)$

π, a locally controlled action of $P_i \neq send$
    Precondition:
        π is enabled in $pstate$
    Effect:
        $pstate :=$ any s such that
            $(pstate, \pi, s) \in trans(P_i)$

$send(m, j)_i$
    Precondition:
        $send(m)_{i,j}$ is enabled in $pstate$
    Effect:
        add m to *out-msgs*(j)
        $x(i, j) :=$ *out-msgs*(j)
        $pstate :=$ any s such that
            $(pstate, send(m)_{i,j}, s) \in trans(P_i)$

$check(j)_i$
    Precondition:
        true
    Effect:
        processed-msgs$(j) :=$ *in-msgs*(j)
        in-msgs$(j) := x(j, i)$
        $pstate :=$ last state of any execution
            fragment starting with $pstate$ and
            with action sequence $receive(M)_{j,i}$,
            where *processed-msgs*$(j) \cdot M =$ *in-msgs*(j)

Tasks of i:
As for P_i, except:
  replace each $send(m)_{i,j}$ by $send(m, j)_i$
  add, for every j:
    $\{ check(j)_i \}$

Then it should not be hard to see that the simulation is correct.

Theorem 17.7 *If A is an asynchronous send/receive system with reliable FIFO send/receive channels, then the SimpleSRSim algorithm is an n-simulation of A.*

Proof.   We leave the proof for an exercise.   □

17.2.2   Broadcast Systems

A similar construction to *SimpleSRSim* can be used to simulate an asynchronous broadcast system having a reliable broadcast channel. The correctness conditions for the simulation are the same as for send/receive systems. The main difference is that the new simulation uses single-writer/*multi-reader* registers instead of single-writer/single-reader registers.

> **$SimpleBcastSim$ algorithm:**
>
> For each i, $1 \leq i \leq n$, B includes a single-writer/multi-reader shared variable $x(i)$, writable by i and readable by all processes (including i). It contains a queue of messages, initially empty.
>
> As before, process i of B simulates process P_i of A, with direct simulations of user interface steps and internal steps of P_i. In order to simulate a $bcast(m)_i$ action of P_i, process i of A adds the message m to the end of the queue in the variable $x(i)$. Also, from time to time, process i checks all variables $x(j)$ (including $x(i)$) in order to determine if there are any new messages. If so, process i handles those messages in the same way that P_i handles them.

Theorem 17.8 *If A is an asynchronous broadcast system with a reliable broadcast channel, then the SimpleBcastSim algorithm is an n-simulation of A.*

17.2.3   Impossibility of Agreement in Asynchronous Networks

Theorem 17.8 can be used to prove the impossibility of solving the fundamental agreement problem of Chapter 12 in an asynchronous network, *even if the network guarantees reliable broadcast, there is guaranteed to be no more than one process failure, and the only type of failure is stopping!* This impossibility result represents a fundamental limitation on the computing capabilities of asynchronous networks.

This result should be contrasted with the results in Chapter 6 for the stopping agreement problem in the synchronous network model. In that setting, the problem is solvable, although it has a nontrivial inherent time cost that depends on the number of tolerated failures. The proof of Theorem 6.33, the lower bound on the time, rests on the possibility that a process might stop *in the middle of a broadcast.* In contrast, in the asynchronous model, the impossibility result still holds even without the possibility of partial broadcasts.

We use the problem statement given in Section 12.1 for the agreement problem with 1-failure termination. (Note that that statement can be formulated in terms of trace properties and so makes sense for asynchronous network systems as well as for shared memory systems.)

Theorem 17.9 *There is no algorithm in the asynchronous broadcast model with a reliable broadcast channel that solves the agreement problem and guarantees 1-failure termination.*

Proof.   Suppose for the purpose of obtaining a contradiction that there is such an algorithm A. Then Theorem 17.8 yields an algorithm B in the single-writer/ multi-reader shared memory model that is an n-simulation of A. The definition of an n-simulation implies that B is a solution to the agreement problem and that it guarantees 1-failure termination. But this contradicts Theorem 12.8, the impossibility of solving the agreement problem in the read/write shared memory model.   □

17.3   Bibliographic Notes

Good references for concurrency control algorithms for implementing atomic transactions are the books by Lynch, Merritt, Weihl, and Fekete [207] and by Bernstein, Hadzilacos, and Goodman [50].

The *MajorityVoting* algorithm is due to Gifford [137]. It has been generalized by Herlihy [154, 149] and by Goldman and Lynch [140]; this latter extension also appears in [207].

The *ABD* algorithm is due to Attiya, Bar-Noy, and Dolev [18]. Their paper also includes an algorithm that uses bounded *tags*, based on the ideas of Israeli and Li [162], plus additional applications for the *ABD* simulation. The impossibility result for $n \leq 2f$ is adapted from similar proofs by Bracha and Toueg [56] and by Attiya, Bar-Noy, Dolev, Peleg, and Reischuk [20].

Theorem 17.9, the impossibility of agreement in fault-prone asynchronous networks, is due to Fischer, Lynch, and Paterson [123]. They proved the result directly, in terms of the network model, rather than via a transformation as we have presented.

17.4 Exercises

17.1. Prove the claim within the proof sketch for Theorem 17.1—that for each x, the composition of all the automata $R_{x,i}$ plus the channels between them (with hiding of *send* and *receive* actions) constitute an atomic object B_x of the appropriate type and interface.

17.2. State and prove a result relating the time complexity of the system B obtained by applying the *SimpleShVarSim* algorithm to a shared memory system A, to the time complexity of the original system A. Be sure to state carefully any assumptions you make.

17.3. Let B be an asynchronous network algorithm obtained by applying *SimpleShVarSim* to the *PetersonNP* algorithm of Section 10.5.2. Obtain the best upper bound you can on the time complexity of B, more specifically, on the time from any *try*$_i$ event to the corresponding *crit*$_i$ event. How does this compare to the general upper bound obtained for Exercise 17.2?

17.4. *Research Question:* State and prove a result describing what is guaranteed when the *SimpleShVarSim* transformation is applied to a *randomized* shared memory system such as the *LehmannRabin* algorithm in Section 11.4.

17.5. Give precondition-effect code for the read/write locking algorithm outlined in Section 17.1.2, for simulating single-writer/multi-reader shared memory algorithms in an asynchronous network. (This outline appears a couple of paragraphs before the description of the *MajorityVotingObject* algorithm.) Each reader of a shared variable x should keep a local copy of x and read it (if it is available). The writer should perform its writes to individual copies using a two-phase locking protocol. All operations should be guaranteed to terminate. State and prove a correctness result.

17.6. Generalize your answer to Exercise 17.5 to multi-writer/multi-reader shared memory algorithms.

17.7. Consider the *Bakery* mutual exclusion algorithm of Section 10.7, transformed to run in asynchronous networks in two different ways:

(a) Using *SimpleShVarSim*.

(b) Using the two-phase locking strategy developed in Exercise 17.5.

Compare the time and communication complexity of the two resulting algorithms.

17.8. Generalize the *MajorityVotingObject* algorithm to allow each *read* operation to access a *read quorum* of copies instead of a majority of copies, and each *write* operation to access a *write quorum* of copies. Read and write quorums do not have to be strict majorities; what conditions do they need to satisfy? Describe the algorithm using precondition-effect notation and prove its correctness.

17.9. Is the "propagation phase" of the reader code in the *ABDObject* implementation necessary? Either argue that the algorithm works without it or exhibit a counterexample.

17.10. Extend the *ABDObject* algorithm so that it implements a multi-writer/multi-reader read/write atomic object, guaranteeing f-failure termination, if $n > 2f$. Show how to incorporate this extension into a fault-tolerant asynchronous network simulation of the shared memory model with multi-writer/multi-reader shared registers.

17.11. Modify the *ABDObject* algorithm so that it uses bounded instead of unbounded *tags*. (*Hint:* It is not enough just to use the integers mod k for some fixed k; a finite data type D with more interesting structure is needed. See [162] for one data type that works. The writer needs to choose successively "larger" *tags*, according to data type D, knowing that any old *tags* that are held by slow processes can be detected by those processes to be "smaller" than the newer *tags*. So when the writer chooses a new *tag*, it needs to take account of all the *tags* that could possibly be held by any process. In order for the writer to keep track of this set, whenever any process modifies its local *tag*, it first ensures that a majority of the processes know that it is adopting the new *tag*. Then the writer can always determine the possible *tags* at all processes, simply by querying a majority of the processes for this information. See [18] for more hints.)

17.12. State and prove a result similar to Theorem 17.6 for the problem of implementing a snapshot atomic object in an asynchronous network with $n \leq 2f$.

17.13. Prove Theorem 17.7.

17.14. Give precondition-effect code for the *SimpleBcastSim* algorithm, in the same style as we gave for the *SimpleSRSim* algorithm. Prove its correctness (Theorem 17.8).

Chapter 18

Logical Time

In this chapter we present the third of our major methods for simplifying the job of programming an asynchronous network: the introduction of a notion of *logical time*. In our asynchronous network model, there is no built-in notion of *real time*. It is, however, possible to impose a notion of logical time by means of special protocols. Logical time can sometimes be used in place of real time, in cases where the users of the system do not care about the relative order of events that occur at different network locations.

18.1 Logical Time for Asynchronous Networks

The basic idea is for every event of an execution of an asynchronous network system A to be assigned a "logical time," which is an element of some fixed totally ordered set T.[1] Typically, this set T is either the nonnegative integers or the nonnegative reals (perhaps with other types of values such as process indices as tiebreakers). These logical times need not have any particular relationship to real time. However, the logical times of different events are required to respect all the possible dependencies among the events within system A, as described in Section 14.1.4. Under these assumptions, we will be able to prove that the logical-time assignment "looks like" a real-time assignment to the processes.

We consider logical time for send/receive systems and broadcast systems separately. We assume throughout the chapter that the channels are the particular *universal* channels defined in Chapter 14. We do not consider faults.

---

[1]T must satisfy one technical assumption: there must be a sequence $t_1, t_2, \ldots$ of increasing elements of T such that every $t \in T$ is bounded above by some t_i.

18.1.1   Send/Receive Systems

We consider an asynchronous send/receive network system with universal reliable
FIFO send/receive channels. We assume that the underlying network graph G
is an arbitrary strongly connected directed graph. Recall that the events of
such a system are of the following types: user interface events by which process
automata communicate with the system's users, *send* and *receive* events by which
process automata interact with channel automata, and internal events of process
automata. (We do not need to consider internal events for channels, because the
particular universal channels we are using do not have any internal events.)

Let α be an execution of an asynchronous send/receive network system A.
Then a *logical-time assignment* for α is defined to be an assignment of a value in
T to every event in α, in a way that is "consistent" with all possible dependencies
among events in α. Specifically, we require the following four properties:

1. No two events get assigned the same logical time.

2. The logical times of events at each process are strictly increasing, according
   to their order of occurrence in α.

3. The logical time of any *send* event is strictly smaller than that of the
   corresponding *receive* event.

4. For any particular value $t \in T$, there are only finitely many events that get
   assigned logical times smaller than t.

Properties 2 and 3 imply that the order of logical times must be consistent with
the ordering $\rightarrow_{trace(\alpha)}$, as defined in Section 14.1.4. However, we allow some
events at different processes to have their logical times ordered in the opposite
order from their order in α.

We claim that any logical-time assignment "looks like" a real-time assignment
to every process in the network. Specifically, any fair execution α with a logical-
time assignment *ltime* looks to every process like another fair execution α' in
which the *ltimes* behave like real times—that is, in which events occur in the
order of their *ltimes*.

Theorem 18.1 *Let α be a fair execution of a send/receive network system A
with universal reliable FIFO channels and let ltime be a logical-time assignment
for α. Then there is another fair execution α' of A such that*

1. α' contains the same events as α.

2. The events in α' occur in the order of their ltimes in α.

3. α' *is indistinguishable from* α *to every process automaton.*[2]

Theorem 18.1 specifies that the order of the events of each particular process must be the same in α and α'. However, it permits events at different processes to be reordered.

Proof. Let γ be the sequence obtained by reordering the events of α in the order of their *ltimes*. Properties 1 and 4 of the definition of logical time imply that a unique such sequence exists. Then we can use Corollary 14.2 to infer the existence of the needed fair execution α'. In applying Corollary 14.2, we regard (i.e., reclassify) all process actions as external. Properties 2 and 3 of the logical-time definition then imply that the reordering preserves $\rightarrow_{trace(\alpha)}$. This is as needed for Corollary 14.2. □

Example 18.1.1 Send/receive diagram

Consider a send/receive system A based on a three-node complete undirected graph. Consider an execution α of A in which messages are sent and received according to the pattern in Figure 18.1.

In this *send/receive diagram*, each process's execution is represented by a vertical line, with time proceeding downward. The dots indicate *send* and *receive* events, and each slanted line joins the *send* event to the *receive* event for a single message. Here we do not depict other events, that is, internal events of processes and events by which the processes communicate with the users. These could be represented by other dots on the vertical lines.

Figure 18.2 shows a logical-time assignment *ltime* for α (assuming that α contains only *send* and *receive* events). Since time proceeds downward, the *ltime* order does not coincide with the order of events in α. However, it is consistent with all possible dependencies among events in α.

Figure 18.3 depicts the reordering of the events of α in the order of their *ltimes*, yielding α' as described in Theorem 18.1. Note that the order of events at each process is the same in α and α'.

Notice the close parallel between the ideas of this section and those used in Section 16.2 to relate local and global synchronizers. In each case, a dependency order is defined on events in an execution, capturing all possible dependencies among events. Then, in each case, the events of the execution are reordered, preserving all dependencies but realigning them according to a global notion of time

---

[2]We use the formal definition of "indistinguishable" from Section 8.7.

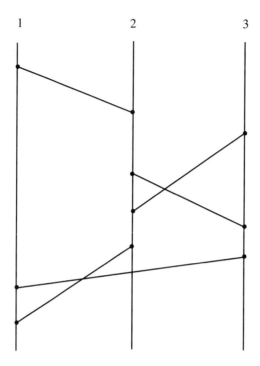

Figure 18.1: Send/receive diagram for execution α.

(synchronous rounds or logical time). (The definitions of a local synchronizer and of logical time are used to show that this can be done.) In each case, the conclusion is that the reordered execution is locally indistinguishable from the original execution. Thus, it looks to all the participants in the original execution as if they are operating in global synchrony.

18.1.2   Broadcast Systems

We can also define logical time for reliable asynchronous broadcast systems with universal reliable broadcast channels. In this case, the events are user-interface events, *bcast* and *receive* events, and internal events of processes.

Let α be an execution of an asynchronous broadcast system. A logical-time assignment for α is defined to be an assignment of a value in T to every event in α, in such a way as to satisfy the same properties as for send/receive systems, except that Property 3 now says:

3′. The logical time of any *bcast* event is strictly smaller than that of each corresponding *receive* event.

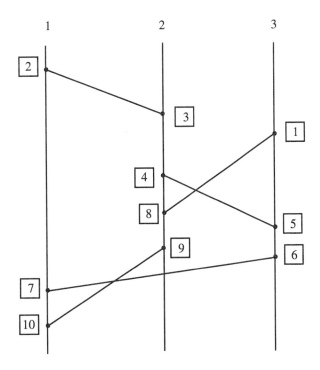

Figure 18.2: A logical-time assignment for α.

As for send/receive systems, we have

Theorem 18.2 *Let α be a fair execution of a broadcast system A with a universal reliable broadcast channel, and let ltime be a logical-time assignment for α. Then there is another fair execution α' of A such that*

1. α' contains the same events as α.

2. The events in α' occur in the order of their ltimes in α.

3. α' is indistinguishable from α to every process automaton.

Proof Sketch. Similar to the proof of Theorem 18.1, but this time based on Corollary 14.4. It is left as an exercise. $\qquad\square$

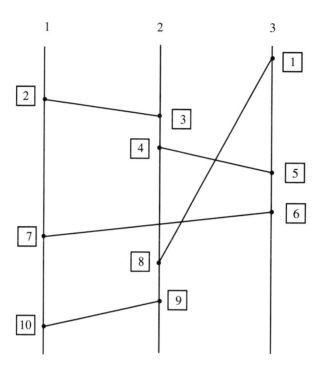

Figure 18.3: Send/receive diagram for reordered execution α'.

18.2   Adding Logical Time to Asynchronous Algorithms

In the previous section, we defined the notion of logical time for asynchronous send/receive and broadcast systems. Now we give two algorithms for generating logical times for the events of a given asynchronous send/receive network algorithm A. Each of these algorithms is really an algorithm transformation that "transforms" the given algorithm A into a new asynchronous send/receive algorithm $L(A)$ with the same underlying network digraph. The transformation works process by process, defining $L(A)_i$ (process i of the $L(A)$ system) in terms of A_i (process i of the A system). The processes in $L(A)$ cooperate to somehow "simulate" a fair execution of A, where each $L(A)_i$ simulates the corresponding A_i. Whenever a process of $L(A)$ simulates a step of A, it also "generates" a logical-time value. The fact that we have included quotes around some terms (i.e., "transform," "simulate," "generate") indicates that we do not have a single clear meaning for these terms but will interpret them slightly differently in different situations.

Both the transformations we describe can be modified for use in broadcast systems.

18.2.1 Advancing the Clock

The following is a simple algorithm transformation for producing logical times for an execution of a given asynchronous send/receive network algorithm A. We call it the *LamportTime transformation* after Lamport, its discoverer. It is based on maintaining local clocks, advancing them when messages are received in order to keep them adequately synchronized. The logical-time domain T is the set of pairs (c, i), where c is a nonnegative integer and i is a process index; the ordering of pairs is lexicographic.

> ### *LamportTime* transformation:
>
> Process *LamportTime*$(A)_i$ maintains the state of process A_i, plus a local variable *clock* that takes on nonnegative integer values, initially 0. The *clock* variable gets increased by at least 1 at every event (including user interface events, *send* and *receive* events, and internal events) that occurs at process i. The logical time of any event is defined to be the value of the *clock* variable *immediately after* the event, paired with the process index i as a tiebreaker.
>
> Whenever process i performs a *send* event, it first increments its *clock* variable to get the *clock* value v for the *send* event, then it attaches value v to the message being sent, as a *timestamp*. When process i performs a *receive* event, it increases its *clock* variable to be not only strictly larger than its previous value, but also strictly larger than the timestamp of the message. The new *clock* value gets assigned to the *receive* event.

More precisely, the code for process i in the *LamportTime*(A) algorithm is as follows.

LamportTime$(A)_i$:

Signature:
As for A_i, except that *send*$(m)_i$ and *receive*$(m)_i$ actions are replaced,
    respectively, with *send*$(m, c)_i$ and *receive*$(m, c)_i$ actions, where $c \in \mathbb{N}$.

States:
As for A_i, plus:
clock $\in \mathbb{N}$, initially 0

Transitions:
As for A_i, with the following modifications:

Input action $\neq$ *receive*
    Effect:
        As for A_i, plus:
        $clock := clock + 1$

Locally controlled action $\neq$ *send*
    Precondition:
        As for A_i.
    Effect:
        As for A_i, plus:
        $clock := clock + 1$

$send(m, c)_i$
    Precondition:
        As for $send(m)_i$ in A_i, plus:
        $c = clock + 1$
    Effect:
        As for $send(m)_i$ in A_i, plus:
        $clock := c$

$receive(m, c)_i$
    Effect:
        As for $receive(m)_i$ in A_i, plus:
        $clock := \max(clock, c) + 1$

Tasks:
As for A_i (modulo the replacements).

Because each process increments its *clock* at every step and because of the tiebreaker, it is easy to see that $LamportTime(A)$ satisfies Properties 1 and 2 of the definition of logical time. Property 3 follows from the handling of the *receive* events. Property 4 follows from the fact that each event causes its associated *clock* variable to be increased by at least 1.

In terms of the informal conditions mentioned at the beginning of this section, the "transformation" of each A_i that produces $LamportTime(A)_i$ simply adds the new *clock* component, plus statements to maintain it. It does not, for example, add entirely new types of actions or delay events. The "simulation" is step by step, directly producing a fair execution of A. When process $LamportTime(A)_i$ simulates a step of A_i, the logical-time value that is "generated" is just the pair (c, i), where c is the value of *clock* after the step.

Broadcast. It is easy to modify the $LamportTime$ transformation to work in asynchronous broadcast systems.

18.2.2 Delaying Future Events

Now we give an alternative algorithm transformation for producing logical times in an execution of a send/receive network algorithm A. We call this one *Welch-Time*, after Welch, its discoverer. Like $LamportTime$, $WelchTime$ is based on maintaining local clocks, only this time the clocks are not advanced in response to message receipts; rather, messages that arrive "too soon" are delayed. In a sense, this transformation is more "intrusive" than the *LamportTime* transformation, because it introduces delays in the events of the underlying execution. The logical time domain T is the set of triples (c, i, k), where c is a nonnegative real, i is a process index, and $k \in \mathbb{N}^+$.

WelchTime transformation:

Each process *WelchTime*$(A)_i$ maintains a local variable *clock*, with nonnegative real values. We assume that the *clock* values of process i are maintained by a separate task, which ensures that the values of the *clock* are monotonically nondecreasing and unbounded.

The logical time of any event is defined to be the value of *clock* when the event occurs, with the process index as a first-order tiebreaker and (for events at the same process when the *clock* has the same value) a sequence number giving the order of execution as a second-order tiebreaker. Note that the *clock* value does not change during the performance of any event of the underlying algorithm A. The *clock* value of a *send* event is attached as a *timestamp* to the message being sent.

Each process i maintains a FIFO queue *receive-buffer*, in order to hold messages whose timestamps are greater than or equal to the local *clock* value. When a message arrives at process i, its timestamp is examined. If the timestamp is less than the current *clock* value, the message is processed immediately; otherwise, it is placed in the *receive-buffer*. At each locally controlled step, process i first removes from the *receive-buffer* and processes all messages whose timestamps are less than its current *clock* value; these messages are processed in the order in which they appear in the *receive-buffer*.

This algorithm is said to simulate a *receive*$(m)_i$ event of A when the corresponding message is processed (rather than when it first arrives at process i). The *clock* value that gets associated with the *receive* event is the *clock* value at the time the message is processed.

Property 4 of *WelchTime*(A) follows from the unboundedness of the local *clock* variables. The unboundedness of the local *clock* variables also implies that every message in a *receive-buffer* is eventually processed, so every *receive* event is eventually simulated and assigned a logical time. Thus, every event does indeed obtain a logical time. Then Properties 1 and 2 follow from the tiebreakers and the monotonicity of the local clocks. Property 3 is guaranteed by the *receive-buffer* discipline.

In terms of the informal conditions mentioned earlier, the "transformation" of each A_i that produces *WelchTime*$(A)_i$ adds and manages the *clock*, *receive-buffer*, and sequence-number tiebreaker components. In this transformation, *receive* actions of A_i can be delayed. The "simulation" now produces a fair execution of A that reorders some *receive* events of A with respect to other events. Each time process i simulates a step of A, the logical-time value that is "generated" is just the triple $(clock, i, k)$, where k is a sequence number used as a second-order tiebreaker.

Note that the amount of delay introduced by the *WelchTime* transformation is especially great when the local clocks are far out of synchronization. This algorithm works best when the clocks happen to stay closely synchronized.

Broadcast. It is easy to modify the *WelchTime* algorithm transformation to work in asynchronous broadcast systems.

18.3   Applications

In this section, we present some simple applications of the addition of logical time to asynchronous network algorithms.

18.3.1   Banking System

We consider the problem, given in Exercise 15.43, of counting the total amount of money in a banking system in which there are no external deposits or withdrawals but in which money is transferred between processes via messages.

The banking system is modelled as an asynchronous send/receive network algorithm A with no actions at its user interface. Each process has a local variable *money* that contains the amount of money currently residing at that location. The *send* and *receive* actions have arguments that represent amounts of money. The processes in A decide when and where to send money and how much to send. We make one technical assumption: that each process sends infinitely many messages to each of its neighbors. This is not a serious restriction—it is always possible to add dummy messages containing $0.

We would like an asynchronous send/receive network algorithm in which each process decides on a local balance, in such a way that the total of all the balances is the correct amount of money in the system. The execution of this algorithm should be triggered by signals arriving from the outside, at one or more of the system locations. (These signals could happen at any time and could happen at different times at different locations.)

So, we suppose that algorithm A is transformed somehow (e.g., using *Lamport-Time* or *WelchTime*) to a new system $L(A)$, which simulates A and generates logical times for its events. Then the required algorithm, *CountMoney*, is obtained as a further transformation of $L(A)$, where each process *CountMoney*$_i$

of *CountMoney* is responsible for "monitoring" the work of the corresponding process $L(A)_i$ of $L(A)$.[3]

CountMoney algorithm:

The heart of the algorithm is a "subroutine" that uses a predetermined logical time $t \in T$, assumed to be known to all processes. Assuming that t is known, the general strategy is

1. For each process of A, determine the value of the *money* variable after all events with logical times less than or equal to t and before all events with logical times greater than t.

2. For each channel, determine the amount of money in all the messages sent at logical times less than or equal to t but received at logical times strictly greater than t.

Specifically, each process $CountMoney_i$ is responsible for determining the value of the *money* variable of process A_i, as well as the amounts of money in all the channels incoming to A_i.

To determine these amounts, process $CountMoney_i$ attaches the logical time of each *send* event to the message being sent, as a timestamp. In order to determine the value of the *money* variable of process A_i, process $CountMoney_i$ keeps track of the *money* values before and after the event of A_i most recently simulated. When it simulates the first event of A_i having a logical time strictly greater than t, $CountMoney_i$ returns the recorded value of the *money* variable before this event. (There must be such an event, because A_i performs infinitely many events and there are only finitely many events with logical time less than or equal to t.)

In order to determine the amount of money in the channel from j to i, process $CountMoney_i$ needs to determine the messages whose $send_j$ events have logical time less than or equal to t and whose $receive_i$ events have logical time strictly greater than t. Thus, starting with the first event of A_i with logical time exceeding t (i.e., the one at which $CountMoney_i$ determines the value of *money* at A_i), process $CountMoney_i$ records messages coming in on the channel. It continues recording them as long as the attached timestamp is less than or equal to t. When a message arrives on the channel with timestamp strictly greater than t, $CountMoney_i$ returns the

---

[3]This construction makes some technical assumptions about the transformed algorithm $L(A)$: that the simulation is step by step, and that it produces steps of A and logical times in a form that is identifiable by the *CountMoney* processes.

sum of the amounts of money in the recorded messages. (Such a message must arrive, because A_j sends infinitely many messages to A_i.)

The balance computed by each process $CountMoney_i$ (in the subroutine) is the sum of the values it determines for process A_i and for all the incoming channels.

Recall that all of this assumed a predetermined logical time t. Since there is really no such predetermined t, the processes need some mechanism to determine one. (Just choosing an arbitrary t does not work, because that logical time might have already passed at some process before it begins executing the subroutine.) For example, the processes might use a predetermined sequence $t_1, t_2, \ldots$ of increasing logical times such that every $t \in T$ is $\leq t_i$ for some i, and attempt to complete the subroutines for all of them (in parallel). By broadcasting their results, the processes can determine the first t_i whose subroutine succeeds everywhere and use the results of that subroutine.

We argue correctness for the subroutine, for any particular t. First, to see that the general strategy yields the correct total amount of money, consider any fixed fair execution of $CountMoney$. This execution simulates a fair execution α of A, together with a logical-time assignment $ltime$ for α. Then Theorem 18.1 implies that there is another fair execution α' of A that contains the same events, that is indistinguishable from α to all processes A_i, and in which all events occur in the order of their $ltimes$. What the general strategy does is to "cut" execution α' immediately after any events that have $ltime = t$ and to record the money that is at all the processes and in all the channels, at this instant. Thus, the general strategy gives an *instantaneous global snapshot* of the system during execution α', which must certainly yield the correct total amount of money in the banking system.

It should be straightforward to see that the distributed algorithm in fact correctly implements the general strategy.

Example 18.3.1   Execution of the *CountMoney* algorithm

Figure 18.4 shows a send/receive diagram for a fair execution α of banking algorithm A, with associated logical times as assigned by $L(A)$, with the initial amounts of money at each process at the tops of the respective time lines, and with the amounts of transferred money labelling the message edges.

Now consider a fair execution of the *CountMoney* algorithm that simulates execution α. Suppose the value of $t = 7.5$ is used in this

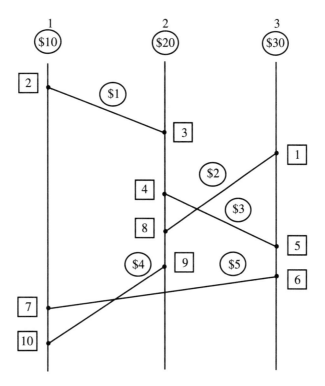

Figure 18.4: Execution α of banking algorithm A.

execution. Figure 18.5 adds a dotted line to the previous diagram, indicating (and connecting) the places where logical time 7.5 intersects the process time lines.

In the execution of *CountMoney*, process 1 determines the value of *money* for process A_1 to be $\$10 - \$1 + \$5 = \$14$; process 2 determines the value for A_2 to be $\$20 + \$1 - \$3 = \$18$; and process 3 determines the value for A_3 to be $\$30 - \$2 + \$3 - \$5 = \$26$. All the channels are determined to be empty except for the channel from process 3 to process 2, which process 2 determines to contain $\$2$. The total amount determined is thus $\$14 + \$18 + \$26 + \$2 = \$60$, which is the correct total.

Figure 18.6 contains the send/receive diagram for the reordered execution α', in which the events appear in logical-time order. Here, the dotted line corresponding to $t = 7.5$ is horizontal and cuts exactly one edge, the unique edge from process 3 to process 2. It is easy to

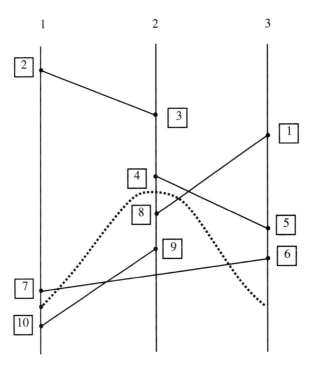

Figure 18.5: Dotted line for $t = 7.5$.

see that the calculated amounts describe exactly the situation at the processes and in the channels at time 7.5 in α'.

We remark that the *CountMoney* algorithm does not introduce any new delays in the operation of A, in addition to those already imposed by $L(A)$.

18.3.2   Global Snapshots

The idea of the *CountMoney* algorithm can be generalized beyond just a banking system, to an arbitrary asynchronous send/receive system A. (As before, we assume that each process A_i sends infinitely many messages to each of its neighbors.) Suppose we want an instantaneous global snapshot of the system state at some point during an execution of A. This might be useful, for instance, for debugging, for establishing a backup version of the system state in case of failure, or for detecting certain global properties such as whether the algorithm has terminated everywhere. It is possible to obtain an instantaneous global snapshot by delaying all the processes and messages for as long as it takes to record all the

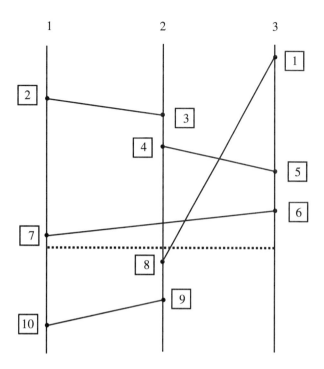

Figure 18.6: Reordered execution α' with horizontal line for $t = 7.5$.

needed information; however, this strategy is not practical in most distributed systems of any realistic size.

But for some applications, a true instantaneous global snapshot may not be needed; a system state that "looks like" an instantaneous global snapshot to all processes may be good enough. We listed some examples of such applications in the previous paragraph; others will be given later, in Chapter 19. In such a case, the strategy used for determining the total amount of money in a banking system can be adapted to provide an acceptable global snapshot of asynchronous send/ receive network system A. As before, A is first augmented with logical times.

LogicalTimeSnapshot algorithm:

As for *CountMoney*, the heart of the algorithm is a subroutine that uses a predetermined logical time $t \in T$, assumed to be known to all processes. Assuming that t is known, the strategy is

1. Determine the state of each process of A after all events with logical times less than or equal to t and before all events with logical times greater than t.

2. For each channel, determine the sequence of messages sent at logical times less than or equal to t but received at logical times strictly greater than t.

This information is determined using the same distributed algorithm that is used in *CountMoney*.

Any fair execution of *LogicalTimeSnapshot* simulates a fair execution α of A, together with a logical-time assignment *ltime* for α. Then Theorem 18.1 implies that the global state returned is an instantaneous global snapshot of another fair execution α' of A that contains the same events in *ltime* order and that is indistinguishable from α to all processes. This should be sufficient, for example, for establishing an acceptable backup version of the system state.

18.3.3 Simulating a Single State Machine

Logical time can also be used to allow a distributed system to simulate a centralized state machine, or, in other words, a single shared variable. Recall the formal notion of a *variable type* from Section 9.4; it consists of a set V of values, an initial value v_0, sets of *invocations* and *responses*, and a function $f : invocations \times V \to responses \times V$. We show how to "implement" a shared variable x of a given variable type in the asynchronous broadcast network model.

We consider a setting in which there are n user processes submitting invocations to x and receiving responses from x, one user process U_i at each node i of the network. We assume that each user process issues invocations sequentially, that is, it waits until it has received a response for any previous invocation before issuing a new invocation. We would like the users to obtain a view that is consistent with there being a single copy of x to which all the operations are applied. More precisely, the network as a whole (with *send* and *receive* actions hidden) should be an *atomic object* of the given type, as defined in Section 13.1. We impose no resiliency requirements here; we only require well-formedness, atomicity and failure-free termination.

There are many possible solutions to this problem, some of which are discussed in Section 17.1. For instance, one process could maintain a single copy of x, performing all the operations on this one copy—see the *SimpleShVarSim* algorithm. Here we consider a solution in which *every* process keeps a private copy of x; all invocations are broadcast to all processes, who perform them on their copies. The process originating an operation can determine the needed response when it performs the operation on its local copy. In order for this strategy to work correctly—that is, to guarantee that all processes perform the operations on their copies in the same order and that the points at which the operations appear to occur are within their respective invocation-response intervals—some synchronization is needed. We use the notion of logical time to obtain the needed synchronization.

ReplicatedStateMachine algorithm:

The algorithm starts with a trivial asynchronous algorithm A. Each process A_i simply receives invocations from user U_i and broadcasts them. (It does not matter what processes do with these messages when they are received.) In addition, A_i broadcasts dummy messages, if necessary, to ensure that it broadcasts infinitely often. Then logical time is added to A by a transformation, yielding $L(A)$, as before.

The main algorithm uses $L(A)$. Besides a local copy of x, each process i has a local variable *invocation-buffer* in which it stores all the invocations it has ever heard about, together with the logical times of their *bcast* events. Process i places a local invocation in its *invocation-buffer* when it performs the *bcast* for that invocation, and places a remote invocation (that is, one occurring at another process) in its *invocation-buffer* when it performs the *receive* for that invocation.

Process i also maintains a vector *known-time*, which keeps track of the largest logical time it has heard about for each process, initially 0. Thus, *known-time* $(i)_i$ is just the logical time of the most recent event at process i, and *known-time* $(j)_i$ for any $j \neq i$ is the logical time of the *bcast* event for the last message received by i from j.

Process i is permitted to apply an invocation π in its *invocation-buffer* to its copy of x when the following conditions are both true.

1. Invocation π has the smallest logical time of any invocation in *invocation-buffer$_i$* that has not yet been applied by process i to x.

2. For every j, *known-time* $(j)_i$ is at least as great as the logical time of π.

When process i applies an operation that was invoked locally to its copy of x, it conveys the response from x to the user.

Lemma 18.3 *The ReplicatedStateMachine algorithm implements an atomic object.*

Proof. Well-formedness is easy to see. We argue termination. Consider any fair execution α. Property 1 of logical time implies that each invocation in α is assigned a unique logical time. Property 4 implies that there are only finitely many invocations in α with logical times smaller than any particular t. Thus, there is a uniquely defined sequence Π of invocations in α, arranged in the order of the logical times of their *bcast* events.

The reliable broadcast ensures that each process eventually places each invocation in its *invocation-buffer*. Since infinitely many events occur at each process of A, Property 4 implies that the logical time at each process grows without bound. The fact that each process broadcasts infinitely many times implies that each component in each process's *known-time* vector also grows without bound. Then we can argue, by induction on the positions of invocations in sequence Π, that every invocation eventually is applied to every copy of x. This implies that a response is produced for every invocation, showing termination.

Now we argue atomicity. Consider any (finite or infinite) execution α. As before (see, e.g., the proof of Theorem 17.4), we may assume that there are no incomplete operations in α.

We first claim that each process applies operations to its local copy of x in the order of their logical times, with no gaps. This is because when process i applies an operation π with logical time t to x, it checks explicitly that it does not know of any pending invocations with logical times smaller than t and that its *known-times* for all processes are at least equal to t. Then the FIFO property of the broadcast channel between each pair of processes implies that process i will never hear of any other invocations with logical times smaller than t.

Now we define a serialization point for each operation of α. Namely, for each operation π originating at process i whose *bcast* event has logical time t, choose the serialization point to be the earliest point at which all processes in the system have reached logical time $\geq t$. (Break ties by arranging the serialization points in the order of logical times.) We know that such a point must be reached in α, because we have already argued that process i must apply operation π to its local copy of x; however, it cannot do this until all its *known-times* are at least t, which implies that all processes have reached logical time at least t.

Note that the serialization point of any operation π cannot be before π's invocation, because of Property 2 of logical time and the fact that t is the logical time of π's *bcast*. On the other hand, the serialization point of π cannot be after π's response, because π's originating process does not respond to the user until after all its *known-times* are at least t. Thus, the serialization points occur within the operation intervals.

Since the serialization points occur in logical time order, which is the same order as that in which the operations are performed on the local copies, the "shrinking" property required for the atomicity condition holds. $\square$

It is not obvious that the *ReplicatedStateMachine* algorithm has any advantages over the simple centralized *SimpleShVarSim* algorithm; after all, *Replicated-StateMachine* essentially requires every process to perform the work done by one process in the centralized algorithm. One advantage can be seen in the case where the logical times at the different processes happen to remain closely synchronized. In this case, the time to perform an operation in the *SimpleShVarSim* algorithm is approximately a two-way message delay. In *ReplicatedStateMachine*, on the other hand, an operation π can be performed by the originating process i as soon as it learns that all the other processes have reached the logical time assigned to the *bcast* event of π. If the clocks are closely synchronized, this requires only approximately a one-way message delay.

ReplicatedStateMachine can be used to implement all the shared variables in a distributed implementation of a shared memory system. This approach is an alternative to the implementation techniques suggested in Section 17.1.

Special handling of read operations. Suppose that some of the operations on the shared variable x being implemented are *read* operations (or, more generally, any operations that do not modify the value of the variable but only return a response). Then *ReplicatedStateMachine* could be modified to perform these operations locally, without using the *invocation-buffer* mechanism at all. This modification yields weaker correctness guarantees than those of an atomic object, but it may still be reasonable for many applications.

Banking distributed database. The *ReplicatedStateMachine* algorithm can be used in a setting where the shared variable x represents an entire banking database. Typical operations for this case would be *deposit, withdraw, add-interest,* and so on. The database might be replicated, say, at each branch of the bank. For many operations in such a database, the order of the updates is important. For example, different results can be obtained if a *withdraw* operation is invoked before a *deposit* rather than after, if the balance is low. Thus, consistent order of application of operations, as ensured by the *ReplicatedStateMachine* algorithm, is important.

It is often useful for the individual branches to be able to read information from the local copy of the database, even when the information is not completely up-to-date. In this case, the special handling of *read* operations described above can be useful.

Mutual exclusion. The mutual exclusion problem is defined in Chapter 10 for the asynchronous shared memory model and in Chapter 20 for the asynchronous network model. Briefly, users request exclusive use of a resource via *try* actions, and the system grants it via *crit* actions. Users return the resource via *exit* actions, and the system responds with *rem*. The system is supposed to guarantee that at most one user has the resource at a time and that the resource continues to be granted if there are requests. Here, we will also require *lockout-freedom*, that is, that every request is eventually granted.

The *ReplicatedStateMachine* algorithm can be used to help solve the mutual exclusion problem in a broadcast network. In this case, the shared variable x is a FIFO queue of process indices, supporting operations $add(i)$, $first(i)$, and $remove(i)$. The $add(i)$ operation adds the indicated index to the end of the queue. The $first(i)$ operation is a query that returns *true* if i is the first element on the queue, but otherwise returns *false*. The $remove(i)$ operation removes all occurrences of index i from the queue. Let B_x be an atomic object for x, where port i supports all the operations with argument i.

When user i requests access to the critical region via a try_i event, process i invokes an $add(i)$ operation on atomic object B_x, which has the effect of adding i to the end of the queue. Then process i repeatedly invokes the $first(i)$ operation, waiting for the answer *true*, which indicates that i has reached the first position on the queue. When i receives the answer *true*, it allows user i to go to the critical region with a $crit_i$ event. When user i exits the critical region with an $exit_i$ event, process i invokes a $remove(i)$ operation on atomic object B_x. When this operation returns, process i allows user i to go to the remainder region with a rem_i operation. (This is essentially the *QueueME* algorithm from Section 10.9.2.) This solves the mutual exclusion problem (with lockout-freedom), using any implementation of atomic object B_x, in particular, using *ReplicatedStateMachine*.

However, if *ReplicatedStateMachine* is used, a simple optimization is possible. Namely, modify the $add(i)$ operation so that it has a return value: either the index of i's predecessor j on the queue, if there is one, or else *null*. If the return value is *null*, then there is no predecessor and process i can immediately perform $crit_i$. Otherwise, process i simply waits until it performs $remove(j)$ for i's predecessor j on its local copy of the queue (at which point it knows that user j has returned the resource). Then it performs $crit_i$. The $exit_i$ is handled as before.

18.4 Transforming Real-Time Algorithms to Logical-Time Algorithms*

Each of the algorithms we have described so far has been built upon an asynchronous algorithm A, augmented with logical time. Another design strategy is to start with an algorithm that uses a notion of "real time," and then to transform it into one that uses logical time instead of real time.

Suppose that we begin with an asynchronous send/receive network system

A in which each process A_i has a local variable *real-time* with values in $R^{\geq 0}$, initially 0. Suppose that all the processes' *real-time* variables are maintained by a global *RealTime* I/O automaton, via $tick(t)$ outputs that simultaneously set all the processes' *real-time* variables to t. (The I/O automaton model permits a single output action to synchronize with more than one input action.) The only requirement on the *RealTime* automaton is that the times occurring as arguments in its output events should be nondecreasing and unbounded in any fair execution.[4] The processes A_i are not permitted to modify the *real-time* variables.

Then it is possible to transform each process A_i into a process B_i that works without *RealTime*, using logical time instead. B_i does not have a *real-time* variable but instead has a *clock* variable that it uses in the same way as A_i uses *real-time*. The *clock* variables are maintained by the B_i using an implementation of logical time for which the logical-time domain is $R^{\geq 0}$ (or a subset of $R^{\geq 0}$).

In order to describe what this transformation guarantees, we consider both system A and its transformed version B, each composed with user automata U_i, one per node i. Then we obtain

Theorem 18.4 *For every fair execution α of the B system (i.e., B plus user automata), there is a fair execution α' of the A system (A plus RealTime automaton plus users) that is indistinguishable from α to each U_i.*

That is, each fair execution of B looks like an execution of A to each individual user.

Example 18.4.1   Banking system

It is possible to design an algorithm similar to *CountMoney* but using real time, to count the total amount of money in a bank. Namely, each process i records the value of its *money* variable just before the step where it finds that its *real-time* variable exceeds t. Then it records all incoming messages sent when the sender's *real-time* variable is less than or equal to t, but received when process i's *real-time* variable is greater than t.

The resulting algorithm can be transformed as above into an algorithm that uses logical time.

---

[4]Since *RealTime* is just an ordinary I/O automaton, we cannot assume anything about the "rate" at which its outputs occur. In Chapters 23–25, we consider a model in which such rate assumptions can be expressed.

18.5   Bibliographic Notes

The notion of logical time is due to Lamport, in his famous paper "Time, Clocks and the Ordering of Events in a Distributed System" [176]. That paper also contains the *LamportTime* algorithm transformation, as well as a short description of the key ideas of the *ReplicatedStateMachine* algorithm. Lamport later extended the replicated state machine approach to tolerate a limited number of failures [179]. Schneider [255] has written a survey of the uses of replicated state machines to implement fault-tolerant services.

The *WelchTime* algorithm transformation is due to Welch [286]; the same transformation is also studied by Neiger and Toueg [232] and is extended to a partially synchronous model by Chaudhuri, Gawlick, and Lynch [74].

The *CountMoney* and *LogicalTimeSnapshot* algorithms are closely related to the consistent global snapshot algorithm of Chandy and Lamport [68].

Banking database examples such as those in this chapter are discussed extensively by Lynch, Merritt, Fekete, and Weihl in [207]; the focus there is on atomic transactions for banking and other databases.

The "vector clocks" algorithm outlined in Exercise 18.17 is due to Mattern [222], Liskov and Ladin [197], and Fidge [115]. It is used in the Isis system [52]. A survey of applications of vector clocks appears in [256].

18.6   Exercises

18.1. Prove Theorem 18.2.

18.2. Write "code" for the *WelchTime* algorithm transformation in the same general style as the *LamportTime* code.

18.3. Describe an implementation of logical time for a send/receive network system in which the logical time domain is $R^{\geq 0}$.

18.4. During a Friday late-night work session, over pizza, several of the programmers at the Flaky Computer Corporation have invented four notions of "illogical time" for asynchronous send/receive network systems. Each of the four notions of illogical time results from dropping exactly one of the four properties required for logical time. They think that these notions might be useful for some applications. For each of their four notions,

   (a) Describe an algorithm transformation that imposes that kind of illogical time on executions of a given asynchronous network algorithm A.

(b) Discuss possible applications.

18.5. The *CountMoney* algorithm is formulated as a double algorithm transformation applied to the underlying banking system A, which may make it difficult to see what is going on. For this exercise, you will combine the various pieces into a single algorithm.

(a) Write precondition-effect code for any specific banking system A of the type allowed in Section 18.3.1. That is, you need to specify the initial amounts of money at all the processes, plus some rules determining when and to whom money is transferred, and how much is sent.

(b) Write precondition-effect code for a modified version of your algorithm A from part (a) that includes logical times. You may choose your favorite algorithm for generating logical times.

(c) Write precondition-effect code for a modification of your algorithm from part (b) that uses the strategy of *CountMoney* to produce the required balances. Be sure to include a mechanism for determining an appropriate logical time t.

18.6. Reconsider the banking system example in Section 18.3.1. Now suppose that the underlying banking system A allows deposits and withdrawals (modelled as input actions at the user interface of the system) in addition to transfers. If we apply the same *CountMoney* transformation as before, what can be claimed about the output of the resulting system?

18.7. Adapt the *LogicalTimeSnapshot* algorithm to broadcast systems rather than send/receive systems. State carefully what your algorithm guarantees.

18.8. In the *CountMoney* and *LogicalTimeSnapshot* algorithms, the logical time is piggybacked on each message. Develop an alternative algorithm that does not piggyback logical time but instead sends a single extra *marker* message on each channel to indicate the dividing point between the messages sent at logical times less than or equal to t and those sent at logical times greater than t. Prove its correctness.

18.9. Give an alternative proof of Lemma 18.3 based on Exercise 13.21.

18.10. Suppose that "illogical time," in particular, the kind of logical time that satisfies Properties 1, 2, and 4 but not Property 3', is used in the *ReplicatedStateMachine* algorithm. What properties are guaranteed?

18.11. Develop the modified implementation of a shared variable described in Section 18.3.3, which handles *read* operations locally. Show that it does *not*, in general, implement an atomic object. State carefully what correctness conditions it does satisfy.

18.12. The optimized mutual exclusion algorithm at the end of Section 18.3.3 is described in several pieces: a simple asynchronous algorithm A with logical time imposed upon it, the *ReplicatedStateMachine* algorithm, and a main algorithm that uses the replicated queue. Combine all these pieces into a single algorithm. Write precondition-effect code for your algorithm and sketch a correctness proof.

18.13. The *ReplicatedStateMachine* algorithm uses logical time to implement an atomic object in the broadcast network model. How can it be modified to work in the send/receive network model?

18.14. Give a careful proof of Theorem 18.4; this will require describing the transformation precisely.

18.15. Design an algorithm based on *logical time* for simulating single-writer/ multi-reader shared memory algorithms in an asynchronous send/receive network. This method should be an alternative to the *two-phase locking* strategy described in Section 17.1.2. Each reader of a shared variable x should should keep a local copy of x. Each *read* and *write* operation on x should be assigned a logical time, and the operations should be performed on each local copy in the order of their logical times. All operations must be guaranteed to terminate.

Give precondition-effect code, state and prove a correctness result, and analyze the complexity.

18.16. Generalize your answer to Exercise 18.15 to multi-writer/multi-reader shared memory algorithms.

18.17. Consider weakening the definition of logical time to *weak logical time*, by allowing T to be a partially ordered set rather than a totally ordered set. However, Properties 1–4 in the definition of logical time must still hold. Thus, not all events are required to be related in the logical time order, but events that depend on each other (events at the same node, or *sends* and corresponding *receives*) must still be related.

(a) Give a version of Theorem 18.1 that holds for a weak logical-time assignment. It should be stated in terms of an arbitrary total order consistent with the given partial order. Prove your result.

(b) Develop an algorithm transformation for producing a *weak logical-time assignment* for an execution of a given asynchronous network algorithm A. The times associated with events should only be related in the underlying partial order T if there is a dependency between the events. (*Hint:* An algorithm can be based on the set T of length n vectors of nonnegative integers. We say that $C <_T C'$ provided that $C(i) \leq C'(i)$ for all i and $C(i) < C'(i)$ for some i; that is, the vector C' is at least as large as C in all components and strictly larger in some component.

Each process i maintains a local *clock* that is a vector in T, initialized at all 0s. When any event occurs at process i, $clock_i(i)$ is increased by at least 1. When process i sends a message, it first increments $clock_i(i)$, then attaches the resulting vector to the message as a timestamp. When process i receives a message, it first increments $clock_i(i)$, then sets its *clock* vector to be the component-wise maximum of the newly incremented *clock* vector and the vector timestamp of the message.)

Show that your transformation in fact produces a weak logical-time assignment and that the times of events are only related by T if there is a dependency between the events.

Chapter 19

Consistent Global Snapshots and Stable Property Detection

In this chapter, we present the last of our four methods for simplifying the programming of asynchronous networks, namely, monitoring an asynchronous network algorithm A while it runs. For instance, a monitoring algorithm might

- assist in debugging A, say by checking for violation of desired invariants

- produce backup versions of A's global state

- detect when A has terminated execution

- detect whether some of the processes of A are involved in a "deadlock," that is, a situation in which several processes are all waiting for each other to do something

- compute some global quantity (e.g., the total amount of money) being managed by A

We focus on two notions in this chapter: *consistent global snapshots* and *stable property detection*. A global snapshot returns a global state of A, that is, a collection of states for all processes and channels of A. The snapshot is said to be "consistent" if it looks to the processes as if it were taken *at the same instant everywhere in the system*. Such a snapshot is useful for all the tasks listed above. A stable property of A is any property of the global state of A that, if it ever becomes true, will remain true forever. Examples of stable properties are system termination and deadlock.

Each monitoring algorithm is described as a transformed version $B(A)$ of the original algorithm A; more specifically, $B(A)$ is based on the same underlying graph as A, and each process $B(A)_i$ is defined only in terms of the corresponding process A_i. $B(A)_i$ is *not* expressed as a simple composition of some new I/O automaton with A_i, because the new process $B(A)_i$ needs access to the state of A_i. Rather, $B(A)_i$ is described as adding some new state components and actions and making some modifications to old actions. We constrain these changes so that they do not interfere much with the operation of A.

19.1 Termination-Detection for Diffusing Algorithms

We begin by considering just the termination-detection problem, for an asynchronous send/receive algorithm A of a particularly simple type known as a *diffusing algorithm*.

19.1.1 The Problem

We assume that the underlying graph G is an arbitrary connected undirected graph. We assume that in algorithm A, all processes' initial states are *quiescent* (as defined in Section 8.1). That is, only input actions are enabled. We consider A in an environment that only supplies a single input event to a single (arbitrary) process. According to the I/O automaton definitions, the arrival of such an input at a process can enable the process to perform locally controlled actions, including sending messages to other processes. These messages may then awaken the recipient processes, who may then send additional messages, and so on. The algorithm A is said to be *diffusing* because all activity begins at the location where the input occurs and "diffuses" through some portion of the network via messages.

A global state of A is said to be *quiescent* provided that no process is enabled to perform any locally controlled action and there are no messages in the channels. (This again coincides with the definition of *quiescent* in Section 8.1, this time applied to the single I/O automaton representing the entire algorithm A.) The *termination-detection problem*[1] for A is as follows: if, sometime after an input occurs at some process A_i, algorithm A ever reaches a quiescent global state, then eventually a special *done_i* output should be performed at node i.

The actual termination detection, including the *done* output, is to be performed by a *monitoring algorithm* $B(A)$. $B(A)$ should also be a send/receive network algorithm, based on the same graph G as A. Each process automaton

---

[1]In this chapter, we use "termination" to mean quiescence; in most other places in the book, we use it to mean that the system produces an answer.

$B(A)_i$ of the monitoring algorithm $B(A)$ should be defined in terms of the corresponding process automaton A_i. The changes we permit to A_i in order to get $B(A)_i$ are as follows.

- $B(A)_i$ may contain new state components in addition to all the state components of A_i.

- The projection of the start states of $B(A)_i$ on the state components of A_i must be exactly the start states of A_i.

- $B(A)_i$ may contain new input, output, and internal actions, in addition to the actions of A_i.

- The actions of A_i may have new information piggybacked on them in $B(A)_i$, for example, a $send(m)_i$ action may be transformed into a $send(m, c)_i$ action. The actions of A_i retain their preconditions and remain in the same classes of the task partition in $B(A)_i$. They have the same effects as before on the state components of A_i, but they may also affect the new state components.

- The new input actions of $B(A)_i$ can change the values of the new state components of $B(A)_i$ only.

- The preconditions of the new locally controlled actions of $B(A)_i$ may involve the entire state of $B(A)_i$, including both old and new state components. However, the new locally controlled actions may affect only the new state components of $B(A)_i$. They are grouped into new classes in the task partition of $B(A)_i$.

19.1.2   The *DijkstraScholten* Algorithm

We present the *DijkstraScholten algorithm* for termination detection for diffusing algorithms. The idea of the algorithm is to augment the underlying algorithm A with the construction and maintenance of a spanning tree of the graph nodes currently involved in A. This tree is rooted at the *source node*, that is, the node at which the input occurs. The construction of the spanning tree is similar to the *AsynchSpanningTree* algorithm in Section 15.3, but it is more complicated because it allows the tree to shrink and grow repeatedly, incorporating the same node many times. (The same sorts of complications appeared in the termination protocol for *AsynchBFS* in Section 15.4.)

DijkstraScholten algorithm (informal):

The messages used by the algorithm are the messages of A plus an *ack* message. The messages of A are treated like the *search* messages in the *AsynchSpanningTree* algorithm. Each process other than the source designates the neighbor from which its first receives an A message as its parent in the spanning tree. Any subsequent A message is immediately acknowledged; only the first remains unacknowledged (for now). Also, the source process immediately acknowledges any A message it receives. Thus, as A messages get sent around the network, a spanning tree of the nodes involved in the protocol is constructed.

Now, we allow the spanning tree to "shrink," using a convergecast procedure, in order to report termination back to the source process. Specifically, each process $DijkstraScholten(A)_i$ looks for a situation when both of the following local conditions hold simultaneously:

1. The state of A_i is quiescent.

2. All its outgoing A messages have been acknowledged.

When it finds this, it "cleans up": a non-source process sends an acknowledgment to its parent and deletes all information about this protocol, while a source process reports that it is done.

A similar cleanup procedure to the one used here was described for the *AsynchBcastAck* algorithm in Section 15.4. But in the present case, after a process cleans up, it may receive another A message, causing it to participate once again in the spanning tree construction. In fact, this may happen any number of times, depending on the message transmission pattern of the underlying algorithm A. That is, the spanning tree in the $DijkstraScholten(A)$ algorithm can grow and shrink repeatedly and can grow in different ways at different times.

Example 19.1.1 Growing and shrinking spanning tree

Suppose the underlying graph G consists of nodes 1, 2, 3, and 4, connected as in Figure 19.1, and consider the following scenario, depicted in that figure. Here we use the notation $DS(A)_i$ as shorthand for the process $DijkstraScholten(A)_i$.

(a) Process A_1 receives an input, awakens, and sends messages to its neighbors, A_2 and A_3.

(b) Processes $DS(A)_2$ and $DS(A)_3$ receive the messages from A_1 and set their *parent* pointers to point to node 1. Then A_2 and A_3 awaken and send messages to each other. Since each of $DS(A)_2$ and

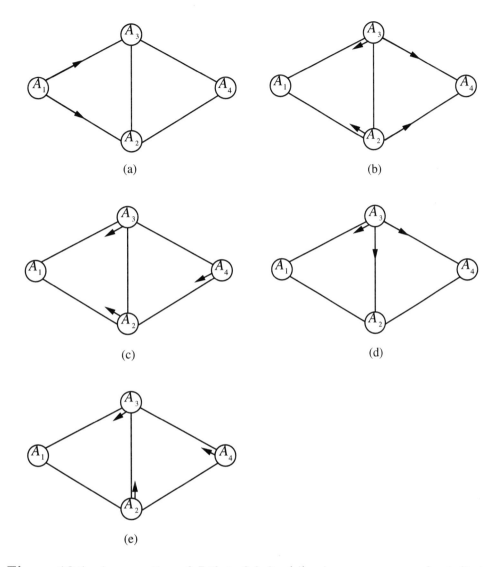

Figure 19.1: An execution of *DijkstraScholten(A)*. An arrow on an edge indicates a message in transit; an arrow parallel to an edge indicates a parent pointer.

$DS(A)_3$ already has a parent, it responds with an acknowledgment. Next, each of A_2 and A_3 sends a message to A_4.

(c) A_2's message reaches process $DS(A)_4$ first, so $DS(A)_4$ sets its *parent* pointer to 2 and immediately acknowledges the message from A_3. Now processes A_1, A_2, A_3, and A_4 continue their work for a while, sending messages to each other as needed; each message is immediately acknowledged. Next, A_2 reaches a quiescent state. $DS(A)_2$ cannot yet clean up, because it still has not received an acknowledgment for its initial message to A_4.

(d) Now A_4 reaches a quiescent state. Since $DS(A)_4$ has no unacknowledged A messages, it sends an acknowledgment to its parent, $DS(A)_2$, and then cleans up, forgetting everything about its participation in the protocol. When $DS(A)_2$ receives this acknowledgment, A_2 is still in a quiescent state and $DS(A)_2$ has now received acknowledgments for all its outgoing A messages; therefore, $DS(A)_2$ sends an acknowledgment to its parent, $DS(A)_1$, and then cleans up. Next, A_3 sends messages to A_2 and A_4.

(e) When A_2 and A_4 receive these messages, they awaken just as they did earlier, reset their *parent* pointers to point to 3, and continue carrying out the work of algorithm A.

This execution can continue in this fashion indefinitely, with portions of the spanning tree growing and shrinking as corresponding portions of algorithm A quiesce. But if all of algorithm A ever becomes quiescent, then the tree eventually shrinks down to the source node 1. If A_1 reaches a quiescent state and $DS(A)_1$ has acknowledgments for all its outgoing messages, then $DS(A)_1$ can announce termination.

The code for process i in the *DijkstraScholten*(A) algorithm is as follows. The *deficit* variable is used to keep track of the number of outstanding acknowledgments.

DijkstraScholten(A)$_i$ automaton (formal):

Signature:

As for A_i, plus:

Input: Internal:
    receive("*ack*")$_{j,i}$, $j \in nbrs$ *cleanup*$_i$

Output:
    send("*ack*")$_{i,j}$, $j \in nbrs$
    done$_i$

States:

As for A_i, plus:
status $\in \{idle, source, non\text{-}source\}$, initially *idle*
parent $\in nbrs \cup \{null\}$, initially *null*
for every $j \in nbrs$:
    send-buffer(j), a FIFO queue of *ack* messages, initially empty
    deficit(j) $\in \mathbb{N}$, initially 0

Transitions:

Input of $A_i \neq receive$
    Effect:
        As for A_i, plus:
        status := *source*

$receive(m)_{j,i}$, m an A message
    Effect:
        As for A_i, plus:
        if *status* = *idle* then
            status := *non-source*
            parent := j
        else add "*ack*" to *send-buffer(j)*

Locally controlled action of $A_i \neq send$
    Precondition:
        As for A_i.
    Effect:
        As for A_i.

$send(m)_{i,j}$, m an A message
    Precondition:
        As for A_i.
    Effect:
        As for A_i, plus:
        $deficit(j) := deficit(j) + 1$

$send(\text{"}ack\text{"})_{i,j}$
    Precondition:
        "*ack*" is first on *send-buffer(j)*
    Effect:
        remove first element of *send-buffer(j)*

$receive(\text{"}ack\text{"})_{j,i}$
    Effect:
        $deficit(j) := deficit(j) - 1$

$cleanup_i$
    Precondition:
        status = *non-source*
        state of A_i is quiescent
        for all $k \in nbrs$
            $deficit(k) = 0$
    Effect:
        add "*ack*" to *send-buffer(parent)*
        status := *idle*
        parent := *null*

$done_i$
    Precondition:
        status = *source*
        state of A_i is quiescent
        for all $k \in nbrs$
            $deficit(k) = 0$
    Effect:
        status := *idle*

Tasks:
As for A_i, plus:
$\{done_i\}$
$\{cleanup_i\}$
for every $j \in nbrs$:
   $\{send(\text{"}ack\text{"})_{i,j}\}$

It should be clear that any global state of *DijkstraScholten(A)* projects to give a global state of A, and that any fair execution of *DijkstraScholten(A)* projects to give a fair execution of A. To see that *DijkstraScholten(A)* correctly detects termination of A, we first prove a multipart invariant assertion lemma. The key invariants are the last two: the next to last says that the *parent* pointers form a spanning tree for the non-*idle* processes, while the last implies that a *done* report means that A has become quiescent.

Lemma 19.1 *In any state of DijkstraScholten(A) after an execution containing an input at node i, the following are true:*

1. *$status_i \in \{source, idle\}$ and $parent_i = null$.*

2. *For every $j \neq i$, $status_j \in \{idle, non\text{-}source\}$, and if $status_j = non\text{-}source$, then $parent_j \neq null$.*

3. *For every j, if $status_j = idle$, then the projected state of A_j is quiescent, $parent_j = null$, and $deficit(k)_j = 0$ for every k.*

4. *For every j and k, $deficit(k)_j$ is the sum of the following four quantities: the number of A messages in the channel from j to k, the number of acks in send-buffer$(j)_k$, the number of acks in the channel from k to j, plus 1 if $parent_k = j$.*

5. *If $status_i = source$, then the parent pointers form a directed tree rooted at i and spanning exactly the set of nodes with $status \neq idle$.*

6. *If $status_i = idle$, then $status_j = idle$ for all j and all channels are empty.*

Proof.   The proof is left as an exercise.   □

Theorem 19.2 *The DijkstraScholten(A) algorithm detects termination for a diffusing algorithm A.*

Proof.   Parts 6 and 3 of Lemma 19.1 imply that if *DijkstraScholten(A)* announces termination then in fact *A* has become quiescent. We must also show the required liveness property: if *A* becomes quiescent, then eventually *Dijkstra-Scholten(A)* announces termination.

So consider, for the sake of contradiction, a fair execution α of *Dijkstra-Scholten(A)* in which algorithm *A* becomes quiescent and in which no *done* event occurs. Then, after the point of quiescence, no further *A* messages are sent or received; it follows that the tree formed by the *parent* pointers (as described in Part 5 of Lemma 19.1) cannot grow any further. Eventually, this tree must stop shrinking, stabilizing to a fixed tree *T*. (This tree *T* must contain at least the source node, because we are assuming that no *done* event is ever performed.) Since there are no further *A* messages or changes to the tree, eventually there are no further *ack* messages anywhere in the global state. Thereafter, the first three terms in the sum for any $deficit(k)_j$ as described in Part 4 of Lemma 19.1 must be 0, and the only way any $deficit(k)_j$ might be non-zero is if $parent_k = j$. But then any leaf node *i* of *T* is enabled to perform a *cleanup*, so it eventually does so. But this means that *T* shrinks further, a contradiction. It follows that eventually in α, a *done* event must occur.   □

Complexity analysis. Consider an execution of the *DijkstraScholten*(*A*) algorithm containing a *done* event. The total number of messages sent in α is $2m$, where m is the number of messages sent in the contained execution of A. An upper bound on the time from when A quiesces until the *done* event is $O\left(m(\ell + d)\right)$, where ℓ and d are defined as usual. Note that the communication and time complexity do not depend directly on the size of the network, but rather on the number of A messages sent. If A only operates for a short time in a small portion of the network, then it will normally send only a small number of messages, so *DijkstraScholten*(*A*) only incurs correspondingly small costs. On the other hand, if A sends a large number of messages then *DijkstraScholten*(*A*) can be quite expensive.

Example 19.1.2 Breadth-first search

> Recall the *AsynchBFS* algorithm from Section 15.4, in which processes correct erroneous *parent* information until this information stabilizes. As presented, the algorithm does not terminate, since the processes have no way of knowing when the algorithm has become quiescent.
>
> To express *AsynchBFS* as a diffusing algorithm, we make a tiny change, letting process i_0 be initially quiescent and awakening it with a *wakeup* input action. Then we apply the *DijkstraScholten* algorithm to obtain a terminating BFS algorithm. This is a systematic version of the ad hoc termination strategy presented for *AsynchBFS*.

19.2 Consistent Global Snapshots

Now we turn to the problem of taking a *consistent global snapshot* of a running asynchronous send/receive network algorithm A. Informally speaking, we say that a snapshot is "consistent" if it looks to the processes as if it were taken at the same instant everywhere in the system.

19.2.1 The Problem

Once again, we assume that the underlying graph G is an arbitrary connected undirected graph. Now the underlying algorithm A is an arbitrary send/receive network algorithm. The snapshot is to be taken by a monitoring algorithm $B(A)$, also a send/receive network algorithm based on graph G. Again, each process automaton $B(A)_i$ of the monitoring algorithm $B(A)$ should be defined in terms of the corresponding A_i.

The types of changes we allow this time are a little more general than those we allowed in Section 19.1.1, but they still are enough to ensure that any fair execution of $B(A)$ "contains" a fair execution of A. The difference is that now we also allow $B(A)_i$ to "delay" a $send(m)_{i,j}$ action of A_i until after $B(A)_i$ places another message ahead of m in the channel from i to j.

We assume that each $B(A)_i$ has an input action $snap_i$ that signals it to begin taking a snapshot of A. We require that in any fair execution of $B(A)$ containing at least one $snap$ input event, eventually every $B(A)_i$ will perform a $report_i$ output containing a state of A_i and states for all the channels of A incoming to A_i.

The various states reported by all the $B(A)_i$ constitute a global state of A. We require that this state satisfy a consistency property. Namely, let α be the fair execution of A that is contained in the given fair execution of $B(A)$. There should be another fair execution α' of A such that all of the following conditions hold:

1. α' is indistinguishable from α to each process A_i.

2. α' begins with the prefix α_1 of α occurring before the first $snap$ event in the given execution of $B(A)$.

3. α' ends with the suffix α_2 of α occurring after the last $report$ event in the given execution of $B(A)$.

4. The returned state is exactly the global state after a prefix of α' that includes all of α_1 and none of α_2.

Thus, as far as the processes can tell, the returned global state is extracted instantaneously at some point in the execution of A. Moreover, this point is somewhere between the beginning and the end of the execution of the snapshot algorithm.

Example 19.2.1   Banking system

Let A be the banking system of Example 18.3.1. Figure 18.4 depicts an execution of A containing five transfers of money among the three processes in the system. (Ignore the logical time labels in the diagrams.) Suppose that some process of the monitoring algorithm $B(A)$ receives a $snap$ input at the beginning of the execution. Then one example of a global state that might be returned by a consistent global snapshot algorithm is the one given in Figure 18.5. That is, $B(A)_1$, $B(A)_2$, and $B(A)_3$ return $14, $18, and $26 as the respective states of A_1, A_2, and A_3. All channels are determined to be empty except for the channel from A_3 to A_2, which $B(A)_2$ reports as containing a single message with value \$2. The needed alternative execution α' is depicted in Figure 18.6.

19.2.2 The Chandy-Lamport Algorithm

We have already described one solution to the consistent global snapshot problem—the *LogicalTimeSnapshot* algorithm of Section 18.3.2. Now we present an alternative algorithm, the *ChandyLamport global snapshot algorithm*, which is very much like *LogicalTimeSnapshot* but does not use an explicit logical time t. Instead (as suggested in Exercise 18.8) it uses new *marker* messages to indicate the dividing points between the messages sent at times $\leq t$ and those sent at times $> t$.

> ***ChandyLamport* algorithm (informal):**
>
> When a process $ChandyLamport(A)_i$ that has not previously been involved in the snapshot algorithm receives a $snap_i$ input, it records the current state of A_i. Then it immediately sends a *marker* message on each of its outgoing channels; this *marker* indicates the boundary between the messages that are sent out before the local state was recorded and the messages sent out afterward.[2]
>
> Then $ChandyLamport(A)_i$ begins recording the messages arriving on each incoming channel in order to obtain a state for that channel; it records messages on the channel just until it encounters a *marker*. At this point, $ChandyLamport(A)_i$ has recorded all the messages sent on that channel before the neighbor at the other end recorded its local state.[3]
>
> There is one remaining situation to consider: suppose that process $Chandy$-$Lamport(A)_i$ receives a *marker* message before it has recorded the state of A_i. In this case, immediately upon receiving the first *marker* message, $ChandyLamport(A)_i$ records the current state of A_i, sends out *marker* messages, and begins recording incoming messages. The channel upon which it has just received the *marker* is recorded as empty.

The code appears below.

---

[2] For example, if A is a banking system as described in Example 19.2.1, then money sent before the marker is *not* included in the recorded local state of the sender, but money sent after the marker *is* included.

[3] In the banking example, this means that $ChandyLamport(A)_i$ has counted all the money that was sent out by the neighbor before recording its local state and hence was not counted by the neighbor.

ChandyLamport(A)$_i$ automaton (formal):

Signature:

As for A_i, plus:

Input:
> $snap_i$
> $receive(\text{``marker''})_{j,i}$, $j \in nbrs$

Output:
> $report(s, C)_i$, $s \in states(A_i)$, C a mapping from $nbrs$ to finite sequences of A messages
> $send(\text{``marker''})_{i,j}$, $j \in nbrs$

Internal:
> $internal\text{-}send(m)_{i,j}$, $j \in nbrs$, m a message of A

States:

As for A_i, plus:
$status \in \{start, snapping, reported\}$, initially $start$
$snap\text{-}state$, a state of A_i or $null$, initially $null$
for every $j \in nbrs$:
> $channel\text{-}snapped(j)$, a Boolean, initially $false$
> $send\text{-}buffer(j)$, a FIFO queue of A messages and $markers$, initially empty
> $snap\text{-}channel(j)$, a FIFO queue of A messages, initially empty

Transitions:

$snap_i$
>   Effect:
>>   if $status = start$ then
>> $snap\text{-}state :=$ state of A_i
>> $status := snapping$
>>   for all $j \in nbrs$ do
>>   add ``marker'' to $send\text{-}buffer(j)$

Input of $A_i \neq receive$
>   Effect:
>>   As for A_i.

$receive(m)_{j,i}$, m an A message
>   Effect:
>>   As for A_i, plus:
>>   if $status = snapping$
>>   and $channel\text{-}snapped(j) = false$ then
>>   add m to $snap\text{-}channel(j)$

$receive(\text{``marker''})_{j,i}$
>   Effect:
>>   if $status = start$ then
>> $snap\text{-}state :=$ state of A_i
>> $status := snapping$
>>   for all $j \in nbrs$ do
>>   add ``marker'' to $send\text{-}buffer(j)$
>> $channel\text{-}snapped(j) := true$

Locally controlled action of $A_i \neq send$
>   Precondition:
>>   As for A_i.
>   Effect:
>>   As for A_i.

$internal\text{-}send(m)_{i,j}$
>   Precondition:
>>   As for $send(m)_{i,j}$ in A_i.
>   Effect:
>>   add m to $send\text{-}buffer(j)$

$send(m)_{i,j}$
    Precondition:
        m is first on $send\text{-}buffer(j)$
    Effect:
        remove first element of $send\text{-}buffer(j)$

$report(s, C)_i$
    Precondition:
        $status = snapping$
        for all $j \in nbrs$
            $channel\text{-}snapped(j) = true$
        $s = snap\text{-}state$
        for all $j \in nbrs$
            $C(j) = snap\text{-}channel(j)$
    Effect:
        $status := reported$

Tasks:
As for A_i, except:
internal-sends are in tasks corresponding to *sends* in A_i,
plus there are new tasks:
    $\{report(s, C)_i : s \in states(A_i), C$ a mapping$\}$
    for every $j \in nbrs$:
        $\{send(m)_{i,j} : m$ a message$\}$

Theorem 19.3 *The ChandyLamport(A) algorithm determines a consistent global snapshot for A.*

Proof. Fix any fair execution of *ChandyLamport(A)* in which some process receives a *snap* input. We first argue that every process eventually performs a *report* output. As soon as any *snap* input occurs at some process *ChandyLamport(A)$_i$*, that process records the state of A_i and sends out *markers* on all its channels. As soon as any other process *ChandyLamport(A)$_j$* receives a *marker* on any channel, it records the state of A_j and sends out *markers* on all its channels, if it has not previously done so. Because of the connectivity of the graph, *markers* thus eventually propagate to all processes, and all processes record their local states. Also, every process *ChandyLamport(A)$_i$* eventually finishes collecting the messages on all its incoming channels (when it has received a *marker* on each channel). Then each *ChandyLamport(A)$_i$* eventually performs a *report*, as claimed.

Now we argue that the returned global state is consistent. That is, we let α denote the contained fair execution of A (where the *send* events in α correspond to the *internal-send* events in the execution of *ChandyLamport(A)*), and we produce the required alternative execution α' and its required prefix. Namely, let α_1 be the portion of α before the first *snap* and α_2 the portion of α after the last *report*. Execution α' begins with α_1 and ends with α_2; the only reordering involves the events of α between the first *snap* and the last *report*.

Each event of α between the first *snap* and the last *report* occurs at some process $ChandyLamport(A)_i$. These events can be divided into two sets: S_1— those that precede the event ($snap_i$ or $receive(marker)_{j,i}$) of $ChandyLamport(A)_i$ at which the state of A_i is recorded, and S_2—those that follow this event. The reordering places all S_1 events before all S_2 events while preserving the order of events of each A_i and the order of each *send* (derived from an *internal-send*) with respect to the corresponding *receive*. The fact that such a reordering is possible depends on the fact that there is no *internal-send*$(m)_{i,j}$ event that follows the recording of the state at A_i and whose corresponding *receive*$(m)_{i,j}$ event precedes the recording of the state of A_j. (If an *internal-send*$(m)_{i,j}$ follows the recording of the state of A_i, then m is placed in *send-buffer*$(j)_i$ after the *marker*. But this implies that the *marker* arrives at $ChandyLamport(A)_j$ before m does, which means that the state of A_j is already recorded by the time m arrives.) Reordering the events of α in this way and filling in states of each A_i as in α yields the sequence α'.

Now consider the prefix α_3 of α' ending just after all the events in S_1. We claim that α' and its prefix α_3 satisfy all the needed properties; the key fact is that the results returned by all the processes constitute exactly the global state of A after α_3. It should be obvious that the returned state of each A_i is exactly the state of A_i after α_3, because α_3 is defined to include exactly the events of A_i preceding the recording of the state of A_i. We must also check that the channel recordings give exactly the messages that are in transit in the channels of A after α_3. But the messages in transit from i to j after α_3 are exactly the messages whose *internal-send*$(m)_{i,j}$ events occur before the recording of the state of A_i and whose *receive*$(m)_{i,j}$ events occur after the recording of the state of A_j. These are exactly the messages that arrive at $ChandyLamport(A)_j$ from $ChandyLamport(A)_i$ ahead of the *marker* and after $ChandyLamport(A)_j$ records the state of A_j, which are exactly the messages recorded by $ChandyLamport(A)_j$ for this channel.   □

Directed graphs. It is easy to see that the *ChandyLamport* algorithm works in strongly connected directed graphs as well as in connected undirected graphs.

Example 19.2.2   Two-dollar bank

Let A be a simple special case of the banking system of Example 18.3.1 in which the underlying graph G has only two nodes, 1 and 2, and in which the total amount of money in the system is \$2. Suppose that each process begins with \$1. We use the notation $CL(A)_i$ as shorthand for the process $ChandyLamport(A)_i$.

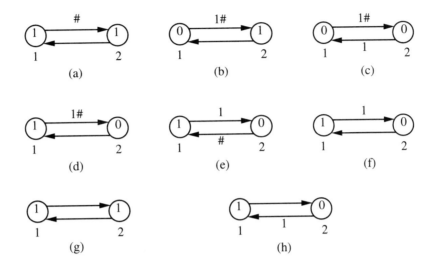

Figure 19.2: Execution of *ChandyLamport(A)*, for the two-dollar bank.

Consider the fair execution of *ChandyLamport(A)* depicted in Figure 19.2. In this diagram, the # symbols denote *markers*.

(a) $snap_1$ occurs, causing $CL(A)_1$ to record the state of A_1 as $1. Then $CL(A)_1$ sends a *marker* to $CL(A)_2$ and starts recording incoming messages.

(b) A_1 sends $1 to A_2; the dollar enters the channel from $CL(A)_1$ to $CL(A)_2$, behind the *marker*.

(c) A_2 sends $1 to A_1.

(d) A_1 receives the dollar and $CL(A)_1$ records it in *snap-channel*$(2)_1$.

(e) $CL(A)_2$ receives the *marker* from $CL(A)_1$, records the state of A_2 as $0, sends a *marker* to $CL(A)_1$, records the state of the incoming channel as empty, and reports its results.

(f) $CL(A)_1$ receives the *marker* from $CL(A)_2$, records the state of the incoming channel as the sequence consisting of one message (the $1 it received before the *marker*), and reports its results.

(g) A_2 receives the dollar.

The global state returned by the algorithm is shown in (h). It consists of $1 at A_1, $1 in the channel from A_2 to A_1, and no money at A_2 or in the channel from A_1 to A_2. This yields the correct total, $2.

Note that the global state returned by the snapshot algorithm does not actually appear in the contained fair execution α of A. It does, however, appear in an alternative fair execution α' of A in which

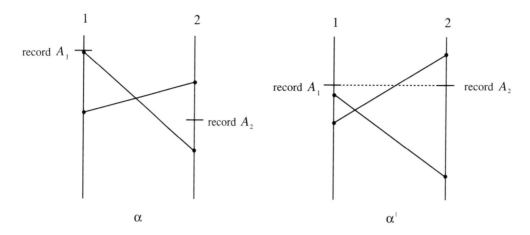

Figure 19.3: Send/receive diagrams for α and α'.

events occur in the following order: (a) A_2 sends \$1 to A_1. (b) A_1 sends \$1 to A_2. (c) A_1 receives \$1. (d) A_2 receives \$1. Figure 19.3 shows send/receive diagrams for α and α'. The diagram for α includes indications of where the states of A_1 and A_2 are recorded in the execution of *ChandyLamport*(A). The diagram for α' shows how these two recording points are aligned in the construction of α'. The state returned by the snapshot algorithm is the state represented by the horizontal line in the second diagram.

Complexity analysis. The *ChandyLamport*(A) algorithm uses $O\left(|E|\right)$ messages, in addition to the messages of A. The time from the first *snap* event until the last *report* event depends on the number of A messages that pile up in the channels and *send-buffers*. If we ignore these pileups, we obtain a time bound of only $O\left(diam(\ell + d)\right)$, but it is probably not reasonable to ignore them. More realistic time bounds can be obtained in terms of the number of A messages that appear anywhere in the global state during the time of the snapshot.

19.2.3   Applications

In this subsection, we give some applications for consistent global snapshots.

Banking system. The *ChandyLamport* algorithm—or any other algorithm that produces a consistent global snapshot—can be used to count the total amount of money in the banking system described in this chapter. This strategy can be generalized to allow the computation of other quantities being managed by the underlying algorithm A.

Distributed debugging. A consistent global snapshot algorithm can be used to help debug distributed algorithms. The designer of a distributed algorithm A can (and should) describe key properties of A by invariant assertions about the global state of A. A debugger can allow A to run, obtaining consistent global snapshots from time to time and checking that the invariants are true for each snapshot. Since each global state returned by the snapshot algorithm is a reachable global state of A, the invariants ought to be true for those states. The designer can carry out such checking before attempting detailed inductive proofs for the invariants. For example, the *AsynchSpanningTree* algorithm of Section 15.3 has two invariants, Assertions 15.3.1 and 15.3.2, which could be checked in this way.

Some work is required to verify that the invariants are true of the returned global state. For example, the global state information can be transmitted to a single process, which can check the invariants locally. Or, a distributed algorithm can be used, using the information returned by the snapshot algorithm as input data. For example, Assertion 15.3.1 can be checked using a distributed algorithm to verify that a set of given *parent* pointers comprise a directed spanning tree rooted at a given node i_0; we leave the development of such an algorithm for an exercise. Assertion 15.3.2 can also be checked by a distributed algorithm. In this case, the distributed algorithm is particularly simple because the invariant is representable as the conjunction of a set of properties, each of which can be verified locally. (The results of local verification can be convergecast to i_0.)

An alternative debugging strategy is to use a centralized simulation of A on a single processor. In this case, the invariants can be verified after every simulated step of A (or from time to time), using the simulated state of A. No global snapshot algorithm is needed in this case; the disadvantage is that the simulation takes longer, since it is all carried out on a single processor.

Stable property detection. A *stable property* P of an asynchronous send/receive algorithm condition: if P is true of any reachable state s of A, then P is true of all states reachable from s. Informally speaking, this says that if P ever becomes true in an execution of A, then P remains true from that point onward.

A simple strategy to determine whether or not a stable property P is true of the global state of an algorithm A is to obtain a consistent global state using a global snapshot algorithm and then to determine whether P is true or false of the returned global state. Again, this determination can be made either by collecting the information at a single process, which can determine P locally, or by a distributed algorithm using the information returned by the snapshot algorithm as input data. The correctness conditions for a consistent global snapshot algorithm imply the following:

1. If P is true of the snapshot state, then P is also true of the global state of A just after the last *report* of the snapshot algorithm.

2. If P is false for the snapshot state, then P is also false for the global state of A just before the first *snap* of the snapshot algorithm.

The first of these facts is true because the state of A after the last *report* is reachable from the snapshot state, while the second is true because the snapshot state is reachable from the state of A before the first *snap*. The algorithm provides no information about whether P is true of the global states of A that arise while the snapshot algorithm is in progress.

Termination detection.   Now we return to the termination-detection problem. This time, consider a send/receive algorithm A with no external inputs but in which the start states are not necessarily quiescent. If A ever reaches a quiescent global state (in which no process is enabled to perform any locally controlled action and there are no messages in the channels), a termination-detection algorithm should eventually output *done*.

Since A has no external inputs, quiescence is a stable property. So termination can be detected using the general strategy for detecting stable properties: take a global snapshot, then determine if the returned global state is quiescent. In this case, once the snapshot has been performed, each process i can determine whether its recorded state of A_i is quiescent and whether its recorded incoming channel states are empty. The results (a bit for each process saying whether or not its information indicates quiescence) can then be convergecast to some distinguished process along a spanning tree. In fact, each process only needs to convergecast a single bit, saying whether or not all the processes in its subtree have reported quiescence.

If this strategy concludes that A has terminated, then this is guaranteed to be the case. Moreover, if the snapshot is executed repeatedly, this strategy is guaranteed eventually to detect termination.

Example 19.2.3   Breadth-first search and shortest paths

The strategy just described can be used to detect termination for the *AsynchBFS* and *AsynchBellmanFord* algorithms. The snapshot can be initiated by the source node i_0. If the answer is positive, that is, that the underlying algorithm has terminated, then process i_0 can broadcast a message to all the processes, telling them to output their results. On the other hand, if the answer is negative, that is, that the underlying algorithm still has not terminated, then process i_0 must continue to perform snapshots until one returns a positive answer.

Example 19.2.4   Leader election

The asynchronous *OptFloodMax* leader-election algorithm of Section 15.2 can be augmented with termination detection based on the *ChandyLamport* snapshot algorithm to produce a terminating algorithm for leader election in an arbitrary connected undirected graph. A snapshot can be initiated, for example, by any process whose maximum known UID changes. Several snapshots may have to be performed before termination is detected. Messages of the various snapshots can be tagged with identifying numbers for the snapshots in order to keep the snapshots separate.

It is interesting to compare the costs of this termination-detection strategy with those of the *DijkstraScholten* algorithm, even though they work for somewhat different types of algorithms. Recall that the communication and time complexity for *DijkstraScholten(A)* depend on the total number of A messages sent, not on the size of the network. Thus, if A only operates for a short time in a small portion of the network, then *DijkstraScholten(A)* incurs correspondingly small costs. On the other hand, the snapshot strategy always involves all the processes in the network, so its costs must depend on the network size. But in the case where the snapshot only needs to be executed once (and there is no pileup of A messages), the costs of the snapshot strategy do not depend on the total number of A messages sent. Thus, if A operates for a long time, sending many messages, the snapshot strategy should perform better than *DijkstraScholten(A)*.

Deadlock detection. We give only one version of the *deadlock-detection problem*; there are many variants. Consider a send/receive network algorithm A in which each process A_i has local states that indicate that it is "waiting for" some subset of its neighboring processes (say, to release resources). We assume that when A_i is waiting for a nonempty set of neighbors, it is in a quiescent state; in fact, it cannot perform any locally controlled steps until it has received a message from each of the neighbors for which it is waiting (say, informing it that a resource has been released). After A_i receives a message from any of the processes for which it is waiting, it continues to wait for the remaining processes. We assume further that A has no external inputs.

A *deadlock* in a global state of A consists of a cycle of two or more processes, each waiting for the next in the cycle, with no messages en route from any process to its predecessor in the cycle. Deadlock is a stable property, because once such a cyclic pattern is established, none of the processes in the cycle can ever perform any more locally controlled steps. Thus, we can detect deadlock using the general strategy for detecting stable properties: take a global snapshot, then determine if there is a deadlock in the returned global state. This determination can be made by collecting the information at a single process and carrying out a sequential cycle-detection algorithm (say, using depth-first search). Alternatively, this determination can be made by a distributed cycle-detection algorithm operating on the snapshot results.

This strategy is guaranteed to only detect true deadlocks. Moreover, if the snapshot is executed repeatedly, it is guaranteed eventually to detect any deadlock that occurs.

19.3 Bibliographic Notes

The *DijkstraScholten* algorithm was invented by Dijkstra and Scholten [92]. The presentation in their paper is quite different from ours; it provides a "derivation" of the algorithm along with a proof. A generalization of *DijkstraScholten* in which activity is allowed to begin at multiple locations was studied by Francez and Shavit. Other work on termination detection appears in a paper by Francez [126]. The *ChandyLamport* consistent global snapshot algorithm and its use for detecting stable properties are due to Chandy and Lamport [68]. The algorithm is derived from Lamport's earlier work on logical time [176]. Fischer, Griffeth, and Lynch [118] designed another algorithm for consistent global snapshots, this one tailored for transaction-based systems (as discussed in Exercise 19.8).

The restrictions we listed on the modifications to the underlying algorithm A are derived from the definition of the *superposition* operation in the Unity programming language, as designed by Chandy and Misra [69]. Some representative papers on distributed deadlock detection are those by Isloor and Marsland [161], Menasce and Muntz [224], Gligor and Shattuck [138], Obermarck [234], Ho and Ramamoorthy [157], Chandy, Misra, and Haas [70], and Bracha and Toueg [57]. The approach of this chapter to deadlock detection is closest to that of Bracha and Toueg [57]. Tay and Loke have designed a model that can be used to understand some deadlock-detection algorithms [274].

19.4 Exercises

19.1. In the *DijkstraScholten* algorithm, the spanning tree of processes involved in the algorithm can grow and shrink repeatedly, incorporating the same process many times. This behavior does not arise in the version of *Asynch-BcastAck* with garbage collection—there, once a process has cleaned up its state, it will never again need to participate in the algorithm. What causes this difference in behavior?

19.2. Prove Lemma 19.1.

19.3. Give the best upper bounds you can for the communication and time complexity of the terminating breadth-first search algorithm described in Section 19.1, obtained by applying *DijkstraScholten* to *AsynchBFS*.

19.4. Describe how to obtain a terminating shortest paths algorithm by using *DijkstraScholten* together with the *AsynchBellmanFord* algorithm of Section 15.4. Give the best upper bounds you can for its communication and time complexity.

19.5. Consider an algorithm A that begins in a quiescent global state (as does a diffusing algorithm) but that is used with an environment that can submit inputs at any number of locations (one per location). Design an algorithm to detect when A reaches a quiescent global state. Now we say that termination is detected when *done* outputs are performed by all processes that have received inputs from the environment.

19.6. Give more details for the proof of Theorem 19.3.

19.7. Example 19.2.1 describes an execution α of a banking system A, together with a global state that is a correct result for a consistent global snapshot algorithm.

   (a) Describe a specific execution of *ChandyLamport*(A) that returns this global snapshot. You may allow *snap* inputs to occur at any subset of the processes, at any time.

   (b) Generalize your result for part (a).

19.8. We consider a generalization of the banking system discussed in this chapter. Suppose we are given a send/receive system A in which the processes maintain a distributed database, with each process managing some of the data items. The only activity performed by A involves *transactions*. Here, we define a transaction to be simply a sequential program consisting of a series of operations on data items; atomicity for the entire transaction is not required.

The problem is to design a new system $B(A)$, as a transformation of A, to determine a "reasonable" *transaction-consistent snapshot* of A. A transaction-consistent snapshot consists of a state for each A_i that can result after some set of transactions has run to completion. A snapshot is considered reasonable if it includes all transactions that finish before the snapshot algorithm begins, along with an arbitrary subset of the other transactions that start before the snapshot ends.

The transformation B should not interfere unnecessarily with the operation of A; for example, it is not allowed to stop all transactions while it is obtaining the snapshot.

19.9. Prove an upper bound on the time complexity for *ChandyLamport*(A), in terms of the number of A messages that appear in the global state during the time of the snapshot.

19.10. Consider a connected undirected graph G with a distinguished node i_0. Design an asynchronous send/receive algorithm A with underlying graph G to verify that a given, fixed set of *parent* pointers constitute a directed spanning tree of a subgraph of G rooted at i_0. More precisely, assume that each process of A has a *parent* pointer whose value is either the index of a neighboring process or else *null*. The output should be produced by process i_0. Give precondition-effect code for your algorithm, prove that it is correct, and analyze its complexity.

19.11. Consider the *AsynchBFS* algorithm augmented with the *ChandyLamport* snapshot algorithm to detect termination, as described in Example 19.2.3.

(a) Describe an explicit execution (for a graph G of your choice) in which process i_0 first initiates *AsynchBFS* and then initiates a snapshot, and in which the state returned by the snapshot is not quiescent.

(b) Suppose that i_0 initiates another snapshot each time the previous one returns a negative answer. Is there an upper bound on the number of snapshots that can be invoked before one must succeed in returning a positive answer?

19.12. Comparison of the *DijkstraScholten* and snapshot approaches to termination is only meaningful for algorithms A to which both types of termination strategy are applicable. Describe the largest class of algorithms you can find to which both strategies can be applied.

19.13. Consider a collection of processes, each of which might be waiting for some of its neighbors. That is, each process has a fixed local value *waiting-for*, indicating the set of neighbors for which that process is waiting.

   (a) Design (i.e., give precondition-effect code for) a distributed cycle-detection algorithm for this collection of processes. Your algorithm should determine whether or not there is a cycle of two or more processes, each waiting for the next in the cycle, with no messages en route from any process to its predecessor in the cycle.

   (b) Prove that your algorithm is correct and analyze its complexity.

   (c) Show how your algorithm can be used to detect deadlocks in an underlying asynchronous algorithm A, according to the problem description in Section 19.2.3.

19.14. In another version of the deadlock problem, processes wait for sets of neighbors as in Section 19.2.3, but now each waiting process only needs to hear from *any one* of these neighbors rather than all of them. Define an appropriate notion of deadlock for this version of the problem and design an algorithm based on consistent global snapshots for detecting this new type of deadlock.

19.15. Describe some other applications of consistent global snapshots for monitoring send/receive network algorithms.

Chapter 20

Network Resource Allocation

Having now finished Chapters 16–19, on general methods for programming asynchronous networks, we now resume our study of specific problems in asynchronous networks. In this chapter, we revisit the problem of mutual exclusion and the more general problem of resource allocation, which we studied in Chapters 10 and 11 in the asynchronous shared memory setting. Next, in Chapter 21, we consider consensus and other problems in asynchronous networks in which some of the processes might fail. The final chapter on asynchronous computing is Chapter 22, in which we study the problem of reliable communication over unreliable channels.

20.1 Mutual Exclusion

We begin with the mutual exclusion problem.

20.1.1 The Problem

The problem statement is much the same as in Section 10.2. We assume that we have n *users*, $U_1, \ldots, U_n$, defined to be I/O automata preserving well-formedness, just as in Section 10.2. Now we assume that the system A being used to solve the problem is an asynchronous network system, with one process P_i corresponding to each user U_i. We assume that the actions try_i, $crit_i$, $exit_i$, and rem_i are used for communication between I/O automata U_i and P_i. In the case of a send/ receive network, the processes P_i communicate via reliable FIFO channels $C_{i,j}$, as depicted in Figure 20.1. We will also consider broadcast systems, as well as systems containing a combination of send/receive and broadcast channels. (Such a combination can be regarded as a special case of a multicast channel—see Section 14.3.2.)

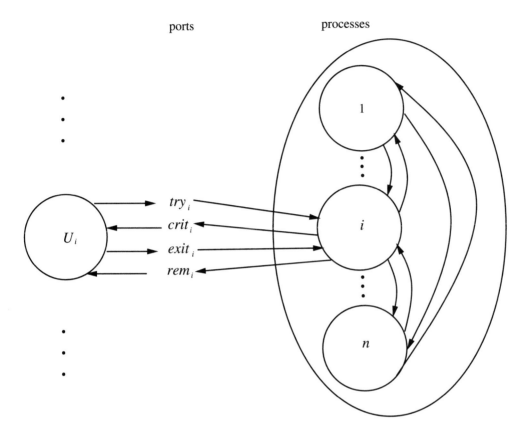

ports   processes

Figure 20.1: Interactions between components for the mutual exclusion problem. The
arrows inside the system oval represent send/receive channels.

The basic correctness conditions to be guaranteed by the system are the same
as the ones we defined in Section 10.2. Namely, we require that the combination
of system A and the users must satisfy the following properties:

Well-formedness: In any execution, and for any i, the subsequence describing
the interaction between U_i and A is well-formed for U_i.

Mutual exclusion: There is no reachable system state (i.e., a combination of
a global state for A and states for all the U_i) in which more than one user
is in the critical region C.

Progress: At any point in a *fair execution*,

1. (Progress for the trying region) If at least one user is in T and no
   user is in C, then at some later point some user enters C.

2. (Progress for the exit region) If at least one user is in E, then at some later point some user enters R.

We say that an asynchronous network system A *solves the mutual exclusion problem* provided that it solves it for every collection of users.

In this chapter, we drop the restriction, made in Section 10.2, that a process can perform locally controlled actions only when its user is in the trying region or exit region. That restriction is workable in the shared memory setting, because there the shared variables maintain information so that it is always available to all the processes. However, in the network setting, there are no shared variables, so the processes need to do the work of maintaining this information and communicating it to other processes whenever it is required.

We also use the same lockout-freedom condition as in Section 10.4, namely,

Lockout-freedom: In any fair execution, the following hold:

1. (Lockout-freedom for the trying region) If all users always return the resource, then any user that reaches T eventually enters C.

2. (Lockout-freedom for the exit region) Any user that reaches E eventually enters R.

In this chapter, we will sometimes analyze the communication and time complexity for requests that operate "in isolation." We say that a request by a user is *isolated* provided that, during the time from its *try* to its *crit*, all other users remain in their remainder regions.

In the rest of this section, we present several mutual exclusion algorithms for asynchronous networks.

20.1.2 Simulating Shared Memory

Chapter 10 contains many shared memory algorithms for mutual exclusion. Using the techniques of Chapter 17, we can transform these into algorithms for the asynchronous network model. For instance, the *Bakery* algorithm of Section 10.7 can be implemented reasonably efficiently in an asynchronous send/receive network.

20.1.3 Circulating Token Algorithm

The simplest mutual exclusion algorithm for the asynchronous send/receive network setting works when the network is a unidirectional ring.

Circulating Token algorithm (informal):

A *token* representing control of the resource circulates continuously around the ring. When process P_i receives the token, it checks whether or not there is an outstanding request from user U_i. If there is no such request, P_i passes the token to P_{i+1}. On the other hand, if there is an outstanding request, P_i grants the resource to U_i and holds the token until U_i returns the resource. When U_i returns the resource, P_i passes the token to P_{i+1}.

The formal code appears below.

Circulating Token$_i$ automaton (formal):

Signature:

Input: Output:
   try_i $crit_i$
   $exit_i$ rem_i
   $receive(\text{``token''})_{i-1,i}$      $send(\text{``token''})_{i,i+1}$

States:
$token\text{-}status \in \{not\text{-}here, available, in\text{-}use, used\}$, initially $available$ if $i = 1$, $not\text{-}here$ otherwise
$region \in \{R, T, C, E\}$, initially R

Transitions:

try_i
   Effect:
      $region := T$

$crit_i$
   Precondition:
      $region = T$
      $token\text{-}status = available$
   Effect:
      $region := C$
      $token\text{-}status := in\text{-}use$

$exit_i$
   Effect:
      $region := E$

rem_i
   Precondition:
      $region = E$
   Effect:
      $region := R$
      $token\text{-}status := used$

$receive(\text{``token''})_{i-1,i}$
   Effect:
      $token\text{-}status := available$

$send(\text{``token''})_{i,i+1}$
   Precondition:
      $token\text{-}status = used$ or
         ($token\text{-}status = available$ and $region = R$)
   Effect:
      $token\text{-}status := not\text{-}here$

Tasks:
Each locally controlled action comprises a task by itself.

Theorem 20.1 *The CirculatingToken algorithm solves the mutual exclusion problem and guarantees lockout-freedom.*

Proof Sketch. Straightforward. Mutual exclusion is guaranteed, because there is only one token, and only the user where the token is located can be in C. Progress is guaranteed, because the token keeps circulating until it finds a request. Lockout-freedom is guaranteed, because no process satisfies two consecutive requests without allowing the token to circulate around the ring in the interim, thus giving every other process a chance. □

Complexity analysis. First we consider the communication complexity of the *CirculatingToken* algorithm. It is not clear what we should measure, because the messages are not naturally apportioned to particular requests. For example, messages are sent even when there are no active requests. One thing we can say is that the total number of messages sent between a try_i and its corresponding $crit_i$ is at most n. We can also give an amortized analysis for the "heavy load" case, where there is always an active request at each node. (Formally, each rem_i is immediately followed by a try_i). In this case, there are only a constant number of messages per request.

For the time complexity, we assume as usual that ℓ is an upper bound on time for each process task and d is an upper bound on the delay for the oldest message in any channel. We also assume that c is an upper bound on the time any user spends in the critical region. Then the time from a try_i event until the corresponding $crit_i$ event is at most $c(n-1) + dn + O(\ell n)$. Note that this time bound has a dn term, which can appear even in the case of a very light load, for instance, an isolated request.

Virtual rings. The *CirculatingToken* algorithm can be used in an arbitrary send/receive network based on a strongly connected directed graph G, if the processes are configured into a virtual ring. The consecutive processes on the ring need not be neighbors in G—communication between any pair of processes can be simulated by a series of communications along a directed path in the underlying network, because of the strong connectivity of G. The performance of the resulting algorithm depends strongly on the graph G and the order in which the processes are arranged in the ring—it is important to minimize the total length of the paths used in the simulation.

Fault-tolerance. In practice, the *CirculatingToken* algorithm can be made resilient to some types of failures. For example, if a process fails cleanly, in a way that is detectable to the other processes, then the other processes can reconfigure themselves into a new ring. For another example, if the token is lost, again in a way that is detectable, a new token can be generated using a leader-election protocol on the ring, for instance, one of those in Section 15.1.

In the asynchronous model, ordinary process stopping failures and message losses cannot be detected, because there is no way processes can distinguish such failures from situations in which the processes or messages are simply delayed. Thus, in order to achieve fault-tolerance, it is necessary to assume a stronger model that includes events that announce such failures. In practice, these events are usually implemented by timeouts.

20.1.4 An Algorithm Based on Logical Time

In Section 18.3.3, we described another solution to the mutual exclusion problem for an asynchronous network system, in particular, for a broadcast network system. That solution used the *ReplicatedStateMachine* algorithm to implement an atomic object representing a queue of requesting process indices. The *Replicated-StateMachine* algorithm in turn used logical time. Thus, the algorithm was described in several pieces.

In this section we present a similar algorithm, but to compare it more easily with the other algorithms in this chapter, we put the pieces together. For simplicity, we do not handle local operations in a special way as described in Section 18.3.3. We call the resulting algorithm the *LogicalTimeME algorithm*.

> ### *LogicalTimeME* algorithm (informal):
>
> This algorithm generates logical times for events using the *LamportTime* strategy, based on local nonnegative integer *clock* values. A logical time is a pair (c, i), where $c \in \mathbb{N}$ and i is a process index; logical time pairs are ordered lexicographically.
>
> The algorithm uses both broadcast and send/receive communication, where send/receive communication is allowed for all pairs of distinct processes. In place of the separate *invocation-buffer* and queue, each process P_i maintains a single *history* data structure. For each j, $history(j)_i$ records all the messages P_i has ever received from P_j, each with a nonnegative integer c, which is the *clock* value associated with that message's *bcast* or *send* event. The *try* and *exit* requests are broadcast, much as before. Instead of broadcasting dummy messages, each process acknowledges each *try* message with an *ack* message.
>
> P_i can perform a *crit$_i$* when its latest *try* request has reached its *history(i)*, provided that every other request that P_i has heard of with a smaller logical time has already been granted and provided that P_i has received a mes-

sage with greater logical time from every other process. (These latter two properties together ensure that there is no current request with a smaller logical time.) P_i can perform a rem_i as soon as its latest $exit$ request has reached its $history(i)$.

We let $\leq$ denote lexicographic order on logical time pairs.

LogicalTimeME$_i$ automaton (formal):

Signature:

Input:

    try_i

    $exit_i$

    $receive(m)_{j,i}$, $m \in \{$ *"try"*, *"exit"*, *"ack"*$\}$
        $\times \mathbb{N}$, $1 \leq j \leq n$,

Output:

    $crit_i$

    rem_i

    $send(m)_{i,j}$, $m \in \{$ *"ack"*$\} \times \mathbb{N}$, $j \neq i$

    $bcast(m)_i$, $m \in \{$ *"try"*, *"exit"*$\} \times \mathbb{N}$

States:

$region \in \{R, T, C, E\}$, initially R

$clock \in \mathbb{N}$, initially 0

$bcast\text{-}buffer$, a FIFO queue of $\{$ *"try"*, *"exit"*$\}$, initially empty

for every $j, 1 \leq j \leq n$:

    $history(j)$, a subset of $\{$ *"try"*, *"exit"*, *"ack"*$\} \times \mathbb{N}$, initially $\emptyset$

for every $j \neq i$:

    $send\text{-}buffer(j)$, a FIFO queue of $\{$ *"ack"*$\} \times \mathbb{N}$, initially empty

Transitions:

try_i

    Effect:

        $clock := clock + 1$

        $region := T$

        add *"try"* to $bcast\text{-}buffer$

$bcast(m, c)_i$

    Precondition:

        m is first on $bcast\text{-}buffer$

        $c = clock + 1$

    Effect:

        $clock := c$

        remove first element of $bcast\text{-}buffer$

$receive(m, c)_{j,i}$

    Effect:

        $clock := \max(clock, c) + 1$

        $history(j) := history(j) \cup \{(m, c)\}$

        if $m =$ *"try"* and $j \neq i$ then

            add *"ack"* to $send\text{-}buffer(j)$

$send(m, c)_{i,j}$

    Precondition:

        m is first on $send\text{-}buffer(j)$

        $c = clock + 1$

    Effect:

        $clock := c$

        remove first element of $send\text{-}buffer(j)$

$crit_i$

    Precondition:

        $region = T$

        (*"try"*, c) $\in history(i)$

        $\nexists($ *"exit"*, $c') \in history(i)$ with $c' > c$

        for all $j \neq i$

            if (*"try"*, $c') \in history(j)$, $(c', j) < (c, i)$

            then

                $\exists($ *"exit"*, $c'') \in history(j)$ with $c'' > c'$

                $\exists(m, c') \in history(j)$ with $(c, i) < (c', j)$

    Effect:

        $clock := clock + 1$

        $region := C$

$exit_i$
>   Effect:
>   > $clock := clock + 1$
>   > $region := E$
>   >   add "exit" to *bcast-buffer*

rem_i
>   Precondition:
>   > $region = E$
>   > $(\text{"exit"}, c) \in history(i)$
>   > $\nexists (\text{"try"}, c') \in history(i)$ with $c' > c$
>   Effect:
>   > $clock := clock + 1$
>   > $region := R$

Tasks:
$\{crit_i\}$
$\{rem_i\}$
$\{bcast(m)_i : m \in \{\text{"try"}, \text{"exit"}\} \times \mathbb{N}\}$
for every $j \neq i$:
> $\{send(m)_{i,j} : m \in \{\text{"ack"}\} \times \mathbb{N}\}$

Theorem 20.2 *The LogicalTimeME algorithm solves the mutual exclusion problem and guarantees lockout-freedom.*

Proof.   We give an operational argument. To see that the algorithm guarantees mutual exclusion, we proceed by contradiction. Suppose that, in some reachable system state, two processes, P_i and P_j, are in C at the same time. Assume (without loss of generality) that the logical time t_i of P_i's latest *try* message is smaller than the logical time t_j of P_j's latest *try* message. Then, in order to perform $crit_j$ and enter C, P_j had to see, in its $history(i)$, a message from P_i with logical time greater than t_j and hence greater than t_i. Then the FIFO property of the communication channel from P_i to P_j implies that P_j must have seen P_i's current *try* message when it performed $crit_j$. But then the precondition of $crit_j$ implies that P_j must have seen a subsequent *exit* message from P_i. This implies that P_i must have already left C at the time P_j performed $crit_j$, a contradiction.

Next, we argue lockout-freedom, which implies progress. Lockout-freedom for the trying region follows from the fact that requests are serviced in the order of the logical times of their *try* messages. We argue that a *try* message with the smallest logical time among those for current requests eventually receives a *crit* response. Since there are only finitely many *try* messages that get assigned logical times smaller than that of any particular *try* message, an inductive argument can then be used to show that all requests are granted.

So suppose that P_i is in T and has the *try* message with the smallest logical time, t_i, among those for current requests. We argue that eventually the preconditions for $crit_i$ must become satisfied and must remain satisfied until $crit_i$

occurs. The fairness properties for the broadcast channel implies that eventually P_i receives its own *try* message and places it in $history(i)_i$. Also, since *try* messages receive corresponding *ack*s and the *clock* variables are managed using the *LamportTime* discipline, eventually P_i obtains a message from each of the other processes with a logical time greater than t_i. Finally, since P_i's request is the current request with the smallest logical time, any request with a smaller logical time must have already had a corresponding *exit* event. Then the fairness properties of the broadcast channel imply that eventually P_i receives these *exit* messages. In this way, all the preconditions for $crit_i$ must eventually become satisfied.

Lockout-freedom for the exit region is straightforward. □

Complexity analysis. For the communication complexity, we note that in *LogicalTimeME*, unlike in *CirculatingToken*, all messages are naturally apportioned to particular requests. So we count the number of messages per request. For every request, there is one *try* broadcast and one *exit* broadcast, for a total of $2n$ individual messages, plus $n - 1$ *ack* messages sent in response to the *try* messages. The total is therefore exactly $3n - 1$ messages per request.

For the time complexity, we consider first the case of an isolated request by a user U_i. In fact, we consider a "strongly isolated" request, for which we also require that no residual messages arising from prior requests remain in the system state when the try_i event occurs. In this case, the time from try_i to $crit_i$ is only at most $2d + O(\ell)$, where d is an upper bound on the delivery of the oldest (broadcast or point-to-point) message from any process i to any other process j. In contrast, recall that the time complexity of the *CirculatingToken* algorithm has a dn term, even in the case of an isolated request.

We leave the general worst-case upper bound on the time from a try_i event to the corresponding $crit_i$ event for an exercise.

20.1.5 Improvements to the LogicalTimeME Algorithm

Now we describe a simple variation on the *LogicalTimeME* algorithm that is designed to reduce the communication complexity. The algorithm, called the *RicartAgrawalaME algorithm* after its designers, uses only $2n - 1$ messages per request. It improves on *LogicalTimeME* by acknowledging requests in a careful manner that eliminates the need for *exit* messages. The algorithm uses both broadcast and send/receive communication, where send/receive communication is allowed for all pairs of distinct processes.

RicartAgrawalaME algorithm:

Logical times for events are generated as in *LogicalTimeME*. The only message that is broadcast is *try*, and the only message that is sent on a send/receive channel is *ok*. Each message carries the *clock* value of its *bcast* or *send* event.

After a try_i input, P_i broadcasts *try* just as in *LogicalTimeME* and can go to C after it receives subsequent *ok* messages from all the other processes. The interesting part of the algorithm is a rule for when a process P_i can send an *ok* message to another process P_j. The idea is to use a priority scheme. In response to a *try* message from P_j, P_i does the following:

1. If P_i is in E or R, or in T prior to broadcasting the *try* message for its current request, then P_i replies with *ok*.

2. If P_i is in C, then P_i defers replying until it reaches E, and then immediately sends any deferred *ok*s.

3. If P_i is in T and its current request has already been broadcast, then P_i compares the logical time t_i of (the *bcast* event of) its own request to the logical time t_j associated with the incoming *try* message of P_j. If $t_i > t_j$, then P_i's own request is given lower priority and P_i replies with an *ok* message. Otherwise, P_i's own request has higher priority, so it defers replying until such time as it finishes its next critical region. At that time, it immediately sends any deferred *ok*s.

   P_i can perform a rem_i at any time after it receives an $exit_i$.

In other words, when there is a conflict, the *RicartAgrawalaME* algorithm resolves it in favor of the "earlier" request, as determined by the logical times.

Theorem 20.3 *The RicartAgrawalaME algorithm solves the mutual exclusion problem and guarantees lockout-freedom.*

Proof. We give an operational proof. First, we prove mutual exclusion by contradiction. Suppose that, in some reachable system state, two processes, P_i and P_j, are in C at the same time. Assume (without loss of generality) that the logical time t_i of P_i's latest *try* message is smaller than the logical time t_j of P_j's latest *try* message. Then there must have been *try* messages and *ok* messages sent from each of P_i and P_j to the other, prior to their entry into C. Moreover, at each process, the receipt of the *try* from the other precedes its sending of the corresponding *ok*. This still leaves several possible orderings of the various events. See Figure 20.2 for some possibilities.

Now we claim that the *receive* event for P_j's latest *try* message occurs after P_i broadcasts its own latest *try* message. If not, then properties of logical time

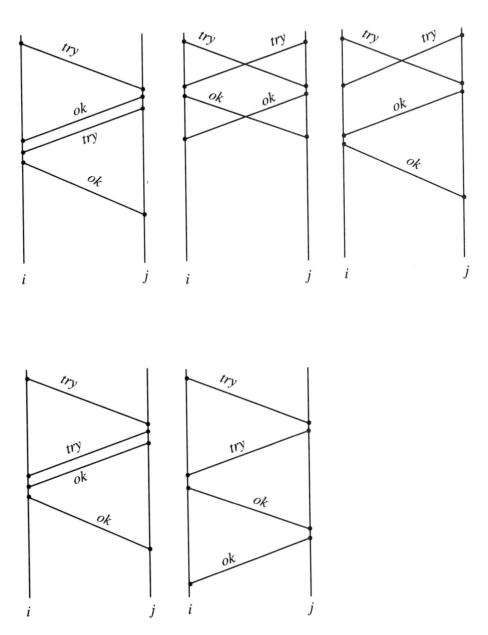

Figure 20.2: Some possible orders of events in the *RicartAgrawalaME* algorithm.

imply that the logical time of this *receive* event is greater than t_j and that the logical time t_i of the *bcast* event by P_i is greater than the logical time of this *receive* event. Thus, $t_i > t_j$, a contradiction.

Therefore, at the time P_i receives P_j's *try* message, P_i is either in T or in C. But in either of these cases, P_i's rules say that it should defer sending an *ok* message until it finishes its own critical region. Thus, P_j could not enter C before P_i leaves, a contradiction.

Now we prove progress, also by contradiction. Progress for the exit region is immediate. Suppose that in fair execution α a point is reached at which some user is in T and no user is in C and after which no user ever enters C. Then (arguing as in the proof of Lemma 10.4), in some suffix α_1 of α, all the users are either in R or T and no further region changes occur. Then there is some suffix α_2 of α_1 in which all processes in T have assigned logical times to their latest requests and in which no messages are ever in transit. Among all the processes in T in α_2, let P_i be the process whose latest request has the smallest logical time, say t_i.

Since P_i is stuck forever in T, it must be that some other process P_j never replies with an *ok* message to P_i's last *try* message. There are only two reasons why P_j might not send the *ok* immediately upon receiving the *try* from P_i:

1. P_j is in C when it receives the *try*. In this case, since there are no processes in C during α_2, P_j must finish its critical region before the start of α_2 and must thereafter send the deferred *ok* message to P_i.

2. P_j is in T when it receives the *try*, with a logical time $t_j < t_i$ assigned to its request. In this case, since P_i's request has the smallest logical time among the processes stuck in T in α_2, it must be that P_j reaches and completes its critical region after it receives the *try* from P_i and before the beginning of α_2. But once again, this means that P_j must send the deferred *ok* message to P_i.

In either case, P_i receives all the needed *ok* messages and proceeds to C, a contradiction.

We leave the lockout-freedom property for an exercise.   □

Complexity analysis. It is easy to see that exactly $2n - 1$ messages are sent per request. The time complexity is left as an exercise.

Another optimization. It is possible to improve further on the *Ricart-AgrawalaME* algorithm by giving a different interpretation to the *ok* messages. Now when some process P_i sends an *ok* to some other process P_j, not only does it approve P_j's current request, but it also gives P_j process P_i's permission to reenter C any number of times—until P_j sends an *ok* to P_i in response to a *try* message from P_i. The rules for responding to a *try* message are the same as for *RicartAgrawalaME*.

This version of the algorithm performs particularly well in the situation where a single user requests the resource repeatedly, without any intervening requests by other users. In this case, the requesting user can go to its critical region repeatedly, without any messages being sent after those for the first request.

20.2 General Resource Allocation

We now consider more general resource-allocation problems in asynchronous networks.

20.2.1 The Problem

The problem definition is much the same as in Section 11.1, using the notions of *explicit resource specification* and *exclusion specification* defined there. We assume the same kinds of user automata as in Section 20.1.

The basic correctness conditions to be guaranteed by the system are the same as those in Section 11.1. Namely, for a given exclusion specification $\mathcal{E}$, we require that the combination of the system and the users satisfy the following properties:

Well-formedness: In any execution, and for any i, the subsequence describing the interaction between U_i and A is well-formed for U_i.

Exclusion: There is no reachable system state in which the set of users in their critical regions is a set in $\mathcal{E}$.

Progress: At any point in a *fair execution*,

    1. (Progress for the trying region) If at least one user is in T and no user is in C, then at some later point some user enters C.

    2. (Progress for the exit region) If at least one user is in E, then at some later point some user enters R.

We say that an asynchronous network system *solves the general resource-allocation problem* provided that it solves it for every collection of users. For explicit resource specifications, we also consider

Independent progress: At any point in a *fair execution*,

1. (Independent progress for the trying region) If U_i is in T and all conflicting users are in R, then at some later point either U_i enters C or some conflicting user enters T.

2. (Independent progress for the exit region) If U_i is in E and all conflicting users are in R, then at some later point either U_i enters R or some conflicting user enters T.

We also consider the same lockout-freedom condition as for mutual exclusion. As we did for mutual exclusion, we drop the restriction that a process can perform locally controlled actions only when its user is in the trying or exit region.

For a given resource specification $\mathcal{R}$, we say that a request by a user is *isolated* provided that, during the time from *try* to *crit*, all other users with conflicting requests are in their remainder regions.

Drinking Philosophers. A variant of the general resource-allocation problem that we will consider in Section 20.2.5 allows for the same user U_i to request different resources at different times. This version of the problem is based on a given resource specification $\mathcal{R}$, and we assume that, for every i, the try_i action is parameterized by an arbitrary *subset* of R_i, the set of resources specified for user U_i. The *exclusion* condition is reinterpreted to refer to the *actual* resources that have most recently been requested rather than the potential resource requirements described by $\mathcal{R}$. That is, we require that there be no reachable system state in which two users whose most recent request sets intersect are simultaneously in their critical regions. The *progress* condition and *lockout-freedom* condition are the same as before. The *independent progress* condition and the definition of an *isolated* request are reinterpreted to refer to the *actual* requests.

This version of the resource-allocation problem is sometimes known as the *Drinking Philosophers problem*, and its resources are sometimes called *bottles*.

20.2.2 Coloring Algorithm

The *Coloring* algorithm of Section 11.3.3 can be modifed to solve the generalized resource-allocation problem in an asynchronous send/receive network based on a connected undirected graph G, for a given resource specification $\mathcal{R}$. One way to do this is by using one of the simulations of shared memory algorithms described in Chapter 17. However, a special-purpose simulation works more efficiently.

Coloring **algorithm:**

We include a process to manage each resource, in addition to processes that simulate the processes of the shared memory *Coloring* algorithm. Each process P_i of the network algorithm simulates exactly one process of the shared memory algorithm plus some subset of the resource processes. When user U_i performs try_i, process P_i collects the needed resources one at a time, in increasing order according to color as before, this time by sending messages to the appropriate resource processes. After sending each message, P_i waits to receive a response. Each resource process maintains a FIFO queue of requesting users, adding each newly received request to the end of the queue. When the index i reaches the front of a resource process's queue, the resource process sends a message back to P_i, which then goes on to request its next resource. When P_i has obtained all its needed resources, it performs $crit_i$. When $exit_i$ occurs, P_i sends messages to all the involved resource processes to tell the resource processes to remove index i from their queues. After sending out all these messages, and without waiting for responses, P_i can perform rem_i.

This algorithm requires that each process P_i be able to communicate with all processes P_j that manage resources assigned to i by the given resource specification $\mathcal{R}$. As usual, this communication can be performed directly if the relevant nodes are all connected directly in the underlying graph G, or else can be simulated by a path of edges in G.

The analysis of this version of the *Coloring* algorithm for networks is similar to the analysis in Section 11.3.3 for shared memory. In this case, the time bound depends on upper bounds on process step time, message-delivery time, and critical region time, plus the number of colors used to color the resource graph, and the maximum number of users for a single resource. However, as before, the time bound is not directly dependent on the size of the underlying graph G.

20.2.3 Algorithms Based on Logical Time

The *RicartAgrawalaME* algorithm can be generalized to solve the resource-allocation problem for an arbitrary resource specification $\mathcal{R}$. Now we assume that we have a combination of multicast and send/receive communication. (Technically, this can be regarded as a special case of multicast communication—see Section 14.3.2.) Multicast must be permitted from any process to the set of all the others that share resources with it, and send/receive communication must be permitted between any two processes that share resources.

RicartAgrawalaRA algorithm:

Processes compute logical times using the *LamportTime* algorithm.

After a try_i input, process i multicasts a try message with an associated *clock* value to all the processes with which it shares resources. Process

i can go to C after it receives subsequent ok messages from all these processes. Processes use the same rule for sending ok messages as in *RicartAgrawalaME*, using the logical times to determine priority.

Process i can perform a rem_i at any time after it receives an $exit_i$.

Theorem 20.4 *The RicartAgrawalaRA algorithm solves the general resource-allocation problem for a given resource specification and guarantees lockout-freedom and independent progress.*

As for the *RicartAgrawalaME* algorithm, we can modify the *RicartAgrawalaRA* algorithm so that the ok messages extend permission until it is explicitly revoked.

20.2.4 Acyclic Digraph Algorithm

In the *RicartAgrawalaRA* algorithm, logical times are used to assign priorities to conflicting requests, thereby breaking ties. Alternative strategies can be used to break ties, for example, maintaining an acyclic digraph involving all the processes.

For simplicity, we consider an explicit resource specification $\mathcal{R}$ satisfying the following two restrictions:

1. Each resource is in the resource sets of exactly two users.

2. Each pair of users share at most one resource.

We leave the extensions to remove these restrictions for an exercise.

We assume a send/receive network based on a connected undirected graph G. We assume that any two processes that share a resource are connected directly by an edge in G. Also, just to make things simple, we assume that the *all* edges in G are between processes that share resources.

AcyclicDigraphRA algorithm:

The algorithm is based on maintaining orientations of all the edges of G in such a way that, at any time, the digraph H consisting of all the oriented edges is acyclic. The orientation of each edge is recorded in local *orientation* variables at the two endpoint processes and is changed by means of a *change* message sent from the process at the head of the directed edge to the process at the tail of the edge. We must assume that the digraph determined by the initial edge orientations is acyclic.

If process i is in the trying region and has all its incident edges oriented inward, then it can perform a $crit_i$ output. If process i is in the exit region, then it can perform rem_i, set all its *orientation* variables to point outward, and send a *change* message on each incident edge, all in one step. (The *change* messages are placed simultaneously in local *send-buffers* directed to all the neighbors.) Also, if process i is in the remainder region with all its edges oriented inward, then process i can set all its *orientation* variables to point outward and send a *change* message on each incident edge, again in one step.

Theorem 20.5 *The AcyclicDigraphRA algorithm solves the resource-allocation problem (with Restrictions 1 and 2 above) and guarantees lockout-freedom.*

Proof Sketch. We begin by giving a somewhat more careful definition of the orientation of each edge in an arbitrary reachable state. Namely, we say that an edge (i, j) is oriented from i to j provided that P_i's *orientation* variable for the edge indicates "outward" and either P_j's *orientation* variable indicates "inward," or else there is a *change* message on the way from P_i to P_j (in the *send-buffer(j)$_i$* or in the channel from i to j). An invariant can be used to show that this rule determines a unique orientation for each edge, in each reachable state.

Then we prove the invariant that when a process P_i is in the critical region, then all its incident edges are oriented inward and no *change* messages are in transit in either direction on any of those edges. This implies the exclusion property.

Next we prove the key invariant that the digraph H is acyclic. We have assumed that this is true initially. The only steps that can falsify this assertion are those in which some edge orientations change. But every step that changes edge orientation simultaneously changes the orientation for *all* the edges incident on some particular node i in such a way that all the edges are directed outward after the step. Because no edge is directed inward toward i after this step, there can be no cycle after the step involving the newly directed edges. It follows that no cycle can be created by the step.

Next we prove lockout-freedom, which implies progress. We consider only lockout-freedom for the trying region; as usual, the condition for the exit region is trivial. Since the graph is always acyclic, at any point in an execution, we may define the *height* of a graph node i to be the maximum length of a directed path starting at i in the digraph H. We first note that the height of a node never increases until the node reaches height 0 (and gives the process at that node a chance to enter the critical region). We then show that any node at height 0 eventually directs all its incoming edges away from itself. Using these facts, we show that any node with height $h > 0$ eventually attains a smaller height, h', which implies that any node with height $h > 0$ eventually attains height 0. This gives the process at that node a chance to enter the critical region. □

Identical processes. An interesting feature of the *AcyclicDigraphRA* algorithm is that the processes are "almost" identical: they do not use UIDs or any other distinguishing information other than the initial orientations of all the edges. In order to solve this problem in arbitrary graphs, arguments such as the one for Theorem 11.2 imply that some method of breaking symmetry is needed. Here, symmetry is broken by the condition that the digraph H is initially acyclic.

20.2.5   Drinking Philosophers*

Now we describe a particular solution to the Drinking Philosophers problem for a given resource specification $\mathcal{R}$, in a send/receive network with reliable FIFO channels based on a connected undirected graph G. This solution is modular—it uses an arbitrary lockout-free algorithm that solves the general resource-allocation problem for $\mathcal{R}$. The architecture for this solution, which we call *ModularDP*, is depicted in Figure 20.3. The communication between each U_i and the corresponding D_i uses $try(B)_i$, $crit_i$, $exit_i$, and rem_i actions. Here, $B \subseteq B_i$, where B_i is the set of bottles (resources) specified by $\mathcal{R}$ for i.

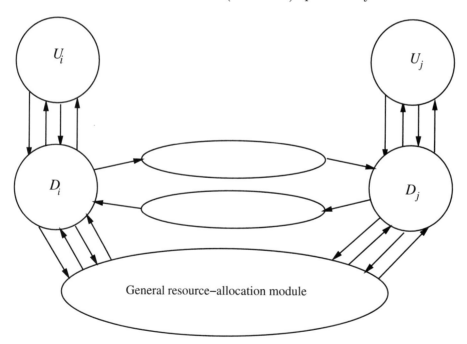

Figure 20.3: Architecture for *ModularDP*.

The communication between each D_i and the general resource-allocation algorithm uses *internal-try$_i$*, *internal-crit$_i$*, *internal-exit$_i$*, and *internal-rem$_i$* actions; we rename these actions to avoid ambiguity.

A complete solution to the Drinking Philosophers problem in the given model must include an implementation of the general resource-allocation module in Figure 20.3 by a send/receive network algorithm A, based on the same underlying graph G. Each process P_i in the complete solution is the composition of D_i and a corresponding process of A. Each channel $C_{i,j}$ in the complete solution must implement both the channel from D_i to D_j in Figure 20.3 and also the corresponding channel of A.

For simplicity, we again make one of the assumptions about $\mathcal{R}$ that we made for *AcyclicDigraphRA*: each bottle is in the resource sets of exactly two users. We also assume that any two processes that share a bottle are connected by an edge in G.

ModularDP algorithm:

When D_i receives $try(B)_i$, it sends *request* messages for those bottles that it needs but currently lacks. The recipient D_j of a *request* satisfies it if U_j is in E or R. If U_j is in T or C, then D_j defers the *request* so that it can satisfy it when U_j finishes its critical region.

In order to prevent two processes from deferring each other's requests and thus blocking progress, a *general resource-allocation module* is used to establish a priority between the processes. Thus, as soon as a process D_i in its trying region is able to do so, it invokes *internal-try$_i$* to try to gain priority. When D_i receives an *internal-crit$_i$* input while it is still in its trying region—that is, when it enters its *internal critical region*—it sends *demand* messages for needed bottles that are still missing. The recipient D_j of a *demand* always satisfies it if it has the bottle, unless U_j is actually in the critical region using the bottle; in this case, D_j defers the *demand* and satisfies it when U_j finishes its critical region.

Once D_i is in its internal critical region, we can show that it eventually receives all its needed bottles. When D_i is in the trying region and has all its bottles, it can enter its critical region. Once D_i enters its critical region, it can output *internal-exit$_i$*, since it no longer needs the priority associated with the internal critical region.

D_i automaton:

Signature:

Input:
> $try(B)_i$, $B \subseteq B_i$
> $exit_i$
> $internal$-$crit_i$
> $internal$-rem_i
> $receive(m)_{j,i}$, $m \in \{$ *"request"*, *"bottle"*, *"demand"*$\} \times (B_i \cap B_j)$, $j \in nbrs$

Output:
> $crit_i$
> rem_i
> $internal$-try_i
> $internal$-$exit_i$
> $send(m)_{i,j}$, $m \in \{$ *"request"*, *"bottle"*, *"demand"*$\} \times (B_i \cap B_j)$, $j \in nbrs$

States:

$region \in \{R, T, C, E\}$, initially R
$internal$-$region \in \{R, T, C, E\}$, initially R
$need \subseteq B_i$, initially $\emptyset$
$bottles \subseteq B_i$; initially arbitrary, subject to the global restriction that the *bottle* sets for
> all processes partition the set of all bottles of $\mathcal{R}$.

$deferred \subseteq B_i$, initially $\emptyset$
$current$, a Boolean, initially *false*
for every $j \in nbrs$:
> $send$-$buffer(j)$, a FIFO queue of messages in $\{$ *"request"*, *"bottle"*, *"demand"*$\} \times (B_i \cap B_j)$,
> initially empty

Transitions:

$try(B)_i$
> Effect:
>> $region := T$
>> $need := B$
>> for all $j \in nbrs$,
>>> all $b \in (need \cap B_j) - bottles$, do
>>> add (*"request"*, b) to $send$-$buffer(j)$

$send(m)_{i,j}$
> Precondition:
>> m is first on $send$-$buffer(j)$
> Effect:
>> remove first element of $send$-$buffer(j)$

$internal$-try_i
> Precondition:
>> $region = T$
>> $internal$-$region = R$
> Effect:
>> $internal$-$region := T$

$receive($ *"request"*, $b)_{j,i}$
> Effect:
>> if $region \in \{T, C\}$ and $b \in need$ then
>>> $deferred := deferred \cup \{b\}$
>> else
>>> add (*"bottle"*, b) to $send$-$buffer(j)$
>>> $bottles := bottles - \{b\}$

$internal$-$crit_i$
> Effect:
>> $internal$-$region := C$
>> if $region = T$ then
>>> $current := true$
>>> for all $j \in nbrs$,
>>>> all $b \in (need \cap B_j) - bottles$, do
>>>> add (*"demand"*, b) to $send$-$buffer(j)$

receive("demand", b)$_{j,i}$
    Effect:
        if $b \in bottles$ and $(region \neq C$ or $b \notin need)$
        then
            add *("bottle", b)* to *send-buffer(j)*
            bottles := *bottles* − {b}
            deferred := *deferred* − {b}

receive("bottle", b)$_{j,i}$
    Effect:
        bottles := *bottles* ∪ {b}

crit$_i$
    Precondition:
        region = T
        need ⊆ *bottles*

    Effect:
        region := C
        current := *false*

internal-exit$_i$
    Precondition:
        internal-region = C
        current = *false*
    Effect:
        internal-region = E

internal-rem$_i$
    Effect:
        internal-region := R

exit$_i$
    Effect:
        region := E
        for all $j \in nbrs$,
            all $b \in deferred \cap B_j$ do
                add *("bottle", b)* to *send-buffer(j)*
        bottles := *bottles* − *deferred*
        deferred := ∅

rem$_i$
    Precondition:
        region = E
    Effect:
        region := R

Tasks:
{*crit$_i$*}
{*exit$_i$*}
{*internal-try$_i$*}
{*internal-exit$_i$*}
for every $j \in nbrs$:
    {*send(m)$_{i,j}$* : $m \in$ { *"request"*, *"bottle"*, *"demand"*} × $(B_i \cap B_j)$}

Two points about the code need explanation. First, we can show that when D_i receives a *("request", b)* message, it actually has the bottle b. Thus, it is not necessary for D_i to check that $b \in bottles$ before satisfying or deferring the *request*. On the other hand, it is possible for D_i to receive a *("demand", b)* message when it does not have the bottle b. So before satisfying a *demand*, D_i checks that $b \in bottles$.

Second, the flag *current$_i$* keeps track of whether there is a current internal critical region that is still being used to grant priority to the current request by U_i. The *current$_i$* flag is set to *true* when an *internal-crit$_i$* occurs while *region$_i$* =

T. It is set to *false* when $crit_i$ occurs. When $current_i = false$, D_i can perform *internal-exit$_i$*, thus terminating the internal critical region.

Theorem 20.6 *The ModularDP algorithm, using any lockout-free solution to the general resource-allocation problem, solves the Drinking Philosophers problem and guarantees lockout-freedom.*

Proof Sketch. Well-formedness is easy to see. The exclusion condition follows from the fact that the *bottles* sets and *bottle* messages explicitly represent the bottles, plus the fact that a process must have all needed *bottles* in order to perform a *crit* output. We argue lockout-freedom, which implies progress. For this, we use the properties of the general resource-allocation module.

First, it is easy to see from the code that the environment of the resource-allocation module preserves well-formedness for that module. Then the properties of the module imply that every execution of the system satisfies the well-formedness and exclusion conditions for the module. Also, every fair execution satisfies the lockout-freedom condition for the module.

Claim 20.7 *In any fair execution of the ModularDP system, if every crit is followed by a corresponding exit, then every internal-crit is followed by a corresponding internal-exit.*

Proof Sketch. Suppose that an *internal-crit$_i$* occurs at some point in a fair execution α and that *internal-exit$_i$* never occurs thereafter; let α_1 be the suffix of α starting immediately after the *internal-crit$_i$*. Then it must be that $current_i$ remains *true* throughout α_1, since if it ever became *false*, the precondition of *internal-exit$_i$* would be true and *internal-exit$_i$* would eventually occur. Also, by the exclusion condition for the module, no neighbor of D_i can be in its internal critical region during α_1.

When the *internal-crit$_i$* event occurs, it must be that $region_i = T$, because $current_i$ is set to *true*. Therefore, as part of the *internal-crit$_i$* event, D_i sends *demand* messages for all its needed bottles. Consider any recipient D_j of such a (*"demand"*, b) message. If D_j has bottle b and is not actually using it (i.e., is not in its critical region, with $b \in need_j$), then it sends (*"bottle"*, b) to D_i. On the other hand, if D_j is using b, then, since every $crit_j$ is followed by an $exit_j$, D_j eventually finishes the critical region and satisfies the deferred *demand*. Thus, eventually, D_i gets all the needed bottles. We claim that it must keep those bottles until it performs $crit_i$. This is because it does not receive a *demand* for any of them during α_1; this can be proved using the fact that no neighbor of D_i is in its internal critical region during α_1. (Some invariants are needed here.)

Since D_i gets all the needed bottles, D_i eventually performs $crit_i$. But this event causes *current* to be set to *false*, a contradiction. □

Claim 20.7 allows us to prove the key claim.

Claim 20.8 *In any fair execution of the ModularDP system, if every crit is followed by a corresponding exit, then every try is followed by a corresponding crit (i.e., every request is granted).*

Proof Sketch. Suppose that try_i occurs at some point in a fair execution α and that $crit_i$ never occurs thereafter; let α_1 be the suffix of α starting immediately after try_i.

If an *internal-crit* occurs in α_1, then Claim 20.7 implies that there is a subsequent *internal-exit*. But because of the handling of the *current* flag, the only way this could happen is if, in the interim, a $crit_i$ occurs. This is a contradiction. So we may assume that no *internal-crit* occurs in α_1.

If *internal-region* is ever equal to T during α_1, the lockout-freedom property for the module implies that eventually an *internal-crit* must occur, a contradiction. So we can assume that *internal-region* $\neq T$ throughout α_1. If *internal-region* is ever equal to R during α_1, then eventually an *internal-try$_i$* occurs, leading to *internal-region* $= T$, again a contradiction. So we can assume that *internal-region* $\neq R$ throughout α_1. Using lockout-freedom for the module, we can show that *internal-region* $\neq E$ throughout α_1.

The only remaining possibility is that *internal-region* $= C$ throughout α_1. But since α_1 immediately follows a try_i event, it must be that *current* $=$ *false* throughout α_1. But then eventually an *internal-exit$_i$* occurs, leading to *internal-region* $= E$, a contradiction. □

Claim 20.8 yields lockout-freedom for the trying region for the *ModularDP* system; lockout-freedom for the exit region is easy.

Complexity analysis. The complexity bounds for *ModularDP* depend on the costs of the implementation of the general resource-allocation module. The D_i components of the algorithm send at most $3k$ messages per request, if k is the maximum degree of any node in the underlying graph G.

For the time complexity, let ℓ and d be as usual and let c be an upper bound on the length of any critical region, for any U_i. Suppose that T_1 and T_2 are upper bounds on the respective times a single process spends in its internal trying and internal exit regions. (T_1 will typically be a function of an upper bound on the length of an internal critical region. An upper bound on the length of an internal critical region is $c + 3d + O(\ell)$.) Then the time from a *try* to the corresponding *exit* can be bounded by $T_1 + T_2 + c + 3d + O(\ell)$.

For a "strongly isolated" request, that is, an isolated request in which any residual messages from prior requests have already been delivered, the time complexity is at most $2d + O(\ell)$.

20.3 Bibliographic Notes

The *CirculatingToken* algorithm is due to Le Lann [191]. His paper includes a discussion of various forms of fault-tolerance for mutual exclusion algorithms, including regeneration of a lost token using a leader-election algorithm. The *LogicalTimeME* algorithm is due to Lamport [176], and the *RicartAgrawalaME* algorithm to Ricart and Agrawala [252]. The optimization at the end of Section 20.1 is due to Carvalho and Roucairol [64]. Raynal's book [250] contains a large collection of mutual exclusion algorithms, for both the asynchronous network and asynchronous shared memory models.

The Drinking Philosophers problem was defined by Chandy and Misra [67]. Their paper also contains a general resource-allocation algorithm very similar to the *AcyclicDigraphRA* algorithm, as well as a Drinking Philosophers solution constructed by modifying their general resource-allocation algorithm. Welch and Lynch [285] developed the *ModularDP* algorithm in the form presented here, based on the ideas of Chandy and Misra. In particular, they made explicit the modularity that was implicit in the Chandy-Misra algorithm.

Other recent work on resource-allocation problems in networks includes that of Styer and Peterson [272], Choy and Singh [80], and Awerbuch and Saks [37]. These papers focus on obtaining improved running time and/or fault-tolerance.

20.4 Exercises

20.1. Give precondition-effect code for an implementation of the *Bakery* mutual exclusion algorithm in the asynchronous send/receive network setting. Analyze the complexity of your algorithm. (*Note:* Your implementation need not be, but may be, obtained using a general transformation applied to the original *Bakery* algorithm.)

20.2. Give precondition-effect code for an implementation of the *PetersonNP* mutual exclusion algorithm in the asynchronous send/receive network setting. Analyze the complexity of your algorithm.

20.3. Fill in the details of the proof of Theorem 20.1.

20.4. Suppose that G is a connected undirected graph. Design an efficient send/ receive network algorithm based on G that causes all the processes in the network to configure themselves into a virtual ring. More specifically, assume that the processes have UIDs. Each process must output the UID of its ring successor, plus the UIDs of all the nodes along a path to that successor. Try to minimize the total length of all the paths.

20.5. Repeat Exercise 20.4, but for the case where G is a strongly connected directed graph.

20.6. Give an invariant assertion proof for the mutual exclusion property of the *LogicalTimeME* algorithm. (*Hint:* The key invariant says that if a process i is in C, then the logical time associated with its *try* message is less than that of any other *try* message that does not have a subsequent *exit* message.)

20.7. Prove a general worst-case upper bound on the time between a try_i event and the corresponding $crit_i$ event, in the *LogicalTimeME* algorithm. Remember not to neglect possible channel pileups.

20.8. "Optimize" the *LogicalTimeME* algorithm so that the *history* variables do not keep all the messages that have ever been received. That is, condense the information that is retained, while permitting each process to exhibit the same behavior as before. Prove the correctness of your optimized algorithm using a simulation relation relating it to *LogicalTimeME*.

20.9. Suppose that we modify the *LogicalTimeME* algorithm so that each process increments its local clock when it receives a message but does not increase it additionally to guarantee that the new clock value is larger then the value in the received message. (This yields one of the notions of "illogical time" described in Exercise 18.4.) Which correctness properties does the modified algorithm retain? Prove your claims (both positive and negative).

20.10. Write precondition-effect code for the *RicartAgrawalaME* algorithm and use it as the basis for a formal correctness proof. Use invariant assertions in your proof of mutual exclusion.

20.11. Prove that the *RicartAgrawalaME* algorithm is lockout-free and prove an upper bound on the time from any try_i event until the corresponding $crit_i$ event.

20.12. Write precondition-effect code for the improved version of the *RicartAgrawalaME* algorithm in which *ok* messages convey permission to access the critical region repeatedly. Prove its correctness.

20.13. Analyze the communication and time complexity of the modified *Coloring* algorithm described in Section 20.2.2.

20.14. Do the following for the *RicartAgrawalaRA* algorithm:

   (a) Write precondition-effect code.

   (b) Prove its correctness.

   (c) Analyze its complexity.

   (d) Construct an execution in which the time from a try_i event until the corresponding $crit_i$ event is as large as you can make it.

20.15. Write precondition-effect code for the improved version of the *RicartAgrawalaRA* algorithm in which *ok* messages convey permission to access the critical region repeatedly. Prove its correctness.

20.16. Do the following for the *AcyclicDigraphRA* algorithm:

   (a) Write precondition-effect code.

   (b) Give a careful proof of correctness.

   (c) Determine whether it guarantees independent progress.

   (d) Analyze its complexity.

   (e) Construct an execution in which the time from a *try* event until the corresponding *crit* event is as large as you can make it.

   (f) Prove an upper bound on the time for an isolated request.

20.17. Explain how the *CirculatingToken* algorithm can be regarded as a special case of the *AcyclicDigraphRA* algorithm.

20.18. Generalize the *AcyclicDigraphRA* algorithm to remove the two given restrictions on the resource specification.

20.19. Give an efficient algorithm for a send/receive network based on a connected undirected graph G, to orient all the edges to form an acyclic digraph H. You may assume that the processes have UIDs.

20.20. State and prove an analogue of Theorem 11.2 for the asynchronous network setting.

20.21. Define a notion of *waiting chain* similar to the one described in Section 11.3.1, but that makes sense for algorithms such as *RicartAgrawalaRA* and *AcyclicDigraphRA*, in which processes do not explicitly acquire individual resources. Use your definition to analyze the lengths of the waiting chains for the resource-allocation algorithms in this chapter.

20.22. The programmers at the Flaky Computer Corporation have decided to try to improve the *AcyclicDigraphRA* algorithm. Namely, a process that is in the remainder region with all edges oriented inward does not change the orientation of the edges to point outward *unless* it receives an explicit *try* message from a neighbor. A process P_i sends *try* messages to all its neighbors when it receives a try_i input from user U_i.

What is wrong with this strategy?

20.23. *Research Question:* Design a send/receive network algorithm for the general resource-allocation problem, based on a given resource specification $\mathcal{R}$. Assume that any two processes that share a resource are connected by an edge in the underlying graph G. Design your algorithm to achieve low time complexity for a request that has a small number k of "overlapping" conflicting requests. Try for a bound that is linear in k.

20.24. *Research Question:* Design a send/receive network algorithm for the general resource-allocation problem, based on a given resource specification $\mathcal{R}$. Assume that any two processes that share a resource are connected by an edge in the underlying graph G. Design your algorithm so that it guarantees lockout-freedom for any particular process i, even in the face of stopping failures of processes whose distances from i in G are greater than or equal to k. Try to minimize k.

20.25. Fill in all the details in the proof of Theorem 20.6. In particular, you will need to prove some invariant assertions, including

> **Assertion 20.4.1** *If $b \in bottles_i$ and a ("demand", b) message is in transit from D_j to D_i, then $region_j = T$, internal-region$_j = C$, and current$_j = true$.*

20.26. Prove the $T_1 + T_2 + c + 3d + O(\ell)$ upper bound on the time complexity for *ModularDP*.

20.27. Consider the *ModularDP* Drinking Philosophers algorithm using the *Coloring* algorithm (adapted for networks) to implement the general resource-allocation module. State and prove an upper bound on the time a user must wait for a request to be satisfied.

20.28. Generalize the *ModularDP* algorithm to remove the restriction on the resource specification.

Chapter 21

Asynchronous Network Computing with Process Failures

In this chapter, we consider what can and what cannot be computed in asynchronous networks in the presence of process stopping failures. Here, we only consider process failures and assume that communication is reliable.

We begin by showing that, for the purpose of obtaining computability results, it does not matter whether we consider send/receive or broadcast systems.

Then we (re-)state the fundamental impossibility result for the problem of distributed agreement in the asynchronous network model. This result says that the agreement problem cannot be solved in asynchronous networks, even if there is guaranteed to be no more than one process failure. In Chapter 12, we discussed this problem and gave an analogous impossibility result for the asynchronous shared memory setting. As we noted at the beginning of Chapter 12, such impossibility results have practical implications for distributed applications in which agreement is required. These include database systems requiring agreement on whether transactions commit or abort, communication systems requiring agreement on message delivery, and process control systems requiring agreement on fault diagnoses. The impossibility results imply that no purely asynchronous algorithm can work correctly.

In the rest of this chapter, we describe some ways around this fundamental difficulty: using randomization, strengthening the model with mechanisms for failure detection, agreeing on a set of values rather than just one, and agreeing approximately rather than exactly.

This chapter rests heavily on previous chapters, especially Chapters 7, 12, and 17. In particular, many results about computability in asynchronous networks follow directly from analogous results about computability in asynchronous read/write shared memory systems, by means of general transformations.

21.1   The Network Model

The model we assume throughout this chapter is an asynchronous broadcast system with reliable broadcast channels and process stopping failures (modelled with *stop* events). We could equally well have considered send/receive systems with reliable FIFO send/receive channels between all pairs of distinct processes: it turns out that the two models are the same from the point of view of computability. It is not hard to see that the broadcast model is at least as powerful as the send/receive model. The following theorem shows that it is not more powerful.

Theorem 21.1 *If A is any asynchronous broadcast system with a reliable broadcast channel, then there is an asynchronous send/receive system B with reliable FIFO send/receive channels that has the same user interface as A and that "simulates" A, as follows. For every execution α of B, there is an execution α' of A such that the following conditions hold:*

1. α and α' are indistinguishable to U (the composition of the users U_i).

2. For each i, a $stop_i$ occurs in α exactly if it does in α'.

Moreover, if α is fair, then α' is also fair.

Proof Sketch.   System B has one process Q_i for each process P_i of A. Each Q_i is responsible for simulating P_i, plus participating in the simulation of the broadcast channel.

Q_i simulates a $bcast(m)_i$ output of P_i by performing $send(m,t)_{i,j}$ outputs for all $j \neq i$, where t is a local integer-valued *tag*, and then performing an internal step simulating $receive(m)_{i,i}$. The *tag* values used by Q_i start with 1 and are incremented with each successive *bcast*. If Q_i receives a message (m,t) sent by Q_j, it helps in the simulation of P_j's broadcast by relaying the message— specifically, it sends (m,t,j) to all processes other than i and j. If Q_i receives (m,t,j) from k, it continues helping by sending (m,t,j) to all processes other than i, j, and k to which Q_i has not already sent (m,t,j).

Meanwhile, Q_i collects tagged messages (m,t) originally broadcast by each P_j, $j \neq i$; these are either received directly from Q_j or via relays. At certain times, Q_i is allowed to perform an internal step simulating a $receive(m)_{j,i}$ event of the A system. Specifically, Q_i can do this when Q_i has a message (m, t) originally broadcast by P_j, Q_i has already relayed (m, t, j) to all processes other than i and j, and Q_i has already simulated $receive_{j,i}$ events for messages from P_j with all *tag* values strictly less than t.

Some key facts for the proof are as follows. First, note that no process Q_i simulates a $receive(m)_{j,i}$ event for any j until after it has succeeded in sending the corresponding (m, t) to all the other processes, and thus after it has been guaranteed that all processes will eventually receive (m, t) from j. Second, note that although a process Q_i can receive messages originally broadcast by P_j out of the order in which they were broadcast by P_j, the *tags* allow Q_i to sort these messages into the proper order. Third, note that if a message with tag t is sent by any process Q_i, then it must be that messages originating at P_i with all smaller *tag* values have previously been sent to all processes. $\qquad\square$

Theorem 21.1 implies that it does not matter, from the point of view of computability, whether we consider broadcast systems or send/receive systems. Of course, the complexity is different—the total number of *receive* events might be multiplied by approximately n in the simulation described above—but we will not worry much about complexity in this chapter. We choose to consider broadcast systems because they make the impossibility results appear slightly stronger and because they make the algorithms easier to write.

21.2 Impossibility of Agreement in the Presence of Faults

We use the definition of the agreement problem in Section 12.1. Although it was formulated there for shared memory systems, it also makes sense for asynchronous (broadcast or send/receive) network systems. We review it here.

The user interface of the system A consists of $init(v)_i$ input actions and $decide(v)_i$ output actions, where $v \in V$ and $1 \le i \le n$; A also has $stop_i$ input actions. All the actions with subscript i are said to occur on *port* i. Each user U_i has outputs $init(v)_i$ and inputs $decide(v)_i$, $v \in V$. U_i is assumed to perform at most one $init_i$ action in any execution.

A sequence of $init_i$ and $decide_i$ actions is *well-formed* for i provided that it is some prefix of a sequence of the form $init_i(v), decide_i(w)$. We consider the following conditions on the combined system consisting of A and the users U_i:

Well-formedness: In any execution, and for any i, the interactions between U_i and A are well-formed for i.

Agreement: In any execution, all decision values are identical.

Validity: In any execution, if all *init* actions that occur contain the same value v, then v is the only possible decision value.

Failure-free termination: In any fair failure-free execution in which *init* events occur on all ports, a *decide* event occurs on each port.

We say that an asynchronous network system *solves the agreement problem* if it guarantees well-formedness, agreement, validity, and failure-free termination (for all collections of users). We also consider

f-failure termination, $0 \leq f \leq n$: In any fair execution in which *init* events occur on all ports, if there are *stop* events on at most f ports, then a *decide* event occurs on every non-failing port.

Wait-free termination is defined to be the special case of f-failure termination where $f = n$.

Of course, it is easy to solve the agreement problem in the asynchronous broadcast model if there are no fault-tolerance requirements. For example, each process could simply broadcast its initial value and apply some appropriate agreed-upon function to the vector of initial values it receives. Since all processes are guaranteed to receive the same vector of values, all will obtain the same result.

The main impossibility result for broadcast systems (repeated from Section 17.2.3) is

Theorem 21.2 *There is no algorithm in the asynchronous broadcast model with a reliable broadcast channel that solves the agreement problem and guarantees 1-failure termination.*

The proof given in Section 17.2.3 is based on a transformation from asynchronous broadcast systems to asynchronous shared memory systems (Theorem 17.8) and an impossibility result for the agreement problem in the asynchronous shared memory model (Theorem 12.8). It is also possible to prove the impossibility result directly, using a proof similar to that of Theorem 12.8. We leave this alternative proof for an exercise.

21.3   A Randomized Algorithm

Theorem 21.2 says that the agreement problem cannot be solved in an asynchronous network system, even for only a single stopping failure. However, the problem is so fundamental to distributed computing that it is important to find ways around this inherent limitation. In order to obtain an algorithm, we must be willing either to weaken the correctness requirements, strengthen the model, or both.

In this section, we do both. We show that the agreement problem can be solved in a *randomized* asynchronous network. This model is stronger than the ordinary asynchronous network model, because it allows the processes to make random choices during the computation. On the other hand, the correctness conditions are slightly weaker than before: although well-formedness, agreement, and validity are still guaranteed, the termination condition is now probabilistic. Namely, all the nonfaulty processes will decide by time t after the arrival of all inputs, with probability at least $p(t)$, where p is a particular monotone nondecreasing, unbounded function. This implies eventual termination with probability 1.

In the subsequent sections, we consider other ways around the inherent limitation expressed by Theorem 21.2, including the use of failure detectors, allowing more than one decision value, and allowing approximate instead of exact agreement.

The algorithm, by Ben-Or, works for $n > 3f$ and $V = \{0, 1\}$. Formally, it is an instance of the probabilistic model described in Section 8.8.

BenOr algorithm:

Each process P_i has local variables x and y, initially *null*. An $init(v)_i$ input causes process P_i to set $x := v$. P_i executes a series of *stages* numbered $1, 2, \ldots$, each stage consisting of two *rounds*. P_i begins stage 1 after it receives its initial value in an $init_i$ input. It continues performing the algorithm forever, even after it decides.

At each stage $s \geq 1$, P_i does the following:

Round 1: P_i broadcasts (*"first"*, s, v), where v is its current value of x, then waits to obtain $n - f$ messages of the form (*"first"*, $s, *$). If all of these have the same value v, then P_i sets $y := v$; otherwise it sets $y := null$.

Round 2: P_i broadcasts (*"second"*, s, v), where v is its current value of y, then waits to obtain $n - f$ messages of the form (*"second"*, $s, *$). There are three cases: First, if all of these have the same value $v \neq null$, then P_i sets $x := v$ and performs a $decide(v)_i$ if it has not already done so. Second, if at least $n - 2f$ of these messages, but not all of the messages, have the same value $v \neq null$, then P_i sets $x := v$ (but does not decide). (The assumption that $n > 3f$ implies that there cannot be two different such values v.) Otherwise, P_i sets x to either 0 or 1, choosing randomly with equal probability.

Notice the similarity between the organization of the *BenOr* algorithm and that of the *TurpinCoan* algorithm in Section 6.3.3.

Lemma 21.3 *The BenOr algorithm guarantees well-formedness, agreement, and validity.*

Proof.   Well-formedness is straightforward. For validity, suppose that all *init* events that occur in an execution contain the same value v. Then it is easy to see that any process that completes stage 1 must decide on v in that stage. This is because the only value sent or received by any process in a (*"first"*, $1, *$) message is v, so the only value sent in a (*"second"*, $1, *$) message is v.

For agreement, suppose that process P_i decides v at stage s and no process decides at any smaller-numbered stage. Then it must be that P_i receives $n - f$ (*"second"*, s, v) messages. This implies that any other process P_j that completes stage s receives at least $n - 2f$ (*"second"*, s, v) messages, since it hears from all but at most f of the processes that P_i hears from. This means that P_j cannot decide on a value different from v at stage s; moreover, P_j sets $x := v$ at stage s. Since this is true for all P_j that complete stage s, it follows (as in the argument for validity) that any process that completes stage $s + 1$ must decide v at stage $s + 1$.   □

Now we consider termination. First, it is not hard to see that the algorithm continues to progress through successive stages; this fact does not depend on the probabilities.

Lemma 21.4 *In every fair execution of the BenOr algorithm in which init events occur on all ports, each nonfaulty process completes infinitely many stages. Moreover, if ℓ is an upper bound on the time for each process task, and d is an upper bound on the delivery time for the oldest message in transit from each P_i to each P_j, then each nonfaulty process completes each stage s by $O(s(d + \ell))$ time after the last init event.*

However, Lemma 21.4 does not imply that each nonfaulty process eventually decides. It turns out that this property is not guaranteed by the *BenOr* algorithm, but only holds *probabilistically*.

Example 21.3.1   An execution with no decisions

We describe a fair execution of the *BenOr* algorithm for $n = 3f + 1$ in which no process ever decides. Every stage s proceeds in the same way, as follows.

Some number m of the processes, $f + 1 \le m \le 2f$, start with $x = 0$, and the rest start with $x = 1$. After round 1, all processes have $y = null$, and at round 2, all processes choose their new values of x randomly. Then some number m' of the random choices, $f + 1 \leq m' \leq 2f$, turn out to be 0 and the rest 1, leading to a situation where m' of the processes begin stage $s + 1$ with $x = 0$ and the rest with $x = 1$.

As in Section 11.4, we imagine that all the nondeterministic choices in the algorithm—here, which action occurs next and when, and what is the resulting state—are under the control of an *adversary*. We constrain the adversary to enforce the fairness conditions of all the process I/O automata and the broadcast channel automaton. We also constrain it to observe the usual time restrictions: an upper bound of ℓ on time for tasks within processes and an upper bound of d on the delivery time for the oldest message in transit from each P_i to each P_j. Finally, we require that the adversary allow *init* events on all ports. We assume that the adversary has complete knowledge of the past execution. Any such adversary determines a probability distribution on the executions of the algorithm.

Lemma 21.5 *For any adversary and any $s \geq 0$, with probability at least $1 - (1 - \frac{1}{2^n})^s$, all nonfaulty processes decide within $s + 1$ stages.*

Proof Sketch. The case $s = 0$ is trivial. Consider any stage $s \geq 1$. We argue that with probability at least $\frac{1}{2^n}$, all nonfaulty processes choose the same value of x at the end of stage s (no matter how the random choices are resolved for other stages). In this case, by the argument for agreement, all nonfaulty processes decide by the end of stage $s + 1$.

For this stage s, consider any shortest finite execution α in which some nonfaulty process, say P_i, has received $n - f$ (*"first"*, $s, *$) messages. (Thus, α ends with the delivery of one of these messages.) If at least $f + 1$ of these messages contain a particular value v, then define v to be a *good* value after α; there can be either one or two good values. We claim that if there is only one good value v after α, then every (*"second"*, $s, *$) message that is sent in any extension of α must contain either value v or value *null*. This is because if P_i receives $f + 1$ copies of v, then every other process receives at least one copy of v and so cannot send a (*"second"*, $s, \bar{v}$) message. (Here we use the notation $\bar{v}$ to denote the value $1 - v$.) Similarly, if there are two good values after α, then every (*"second"*, $s, *$) message that is sent in any extension of α must contain *null*.

It follows that if there is only one good value v, then v is the only value that can be "forced" to be any process's value of x at the end of stage s by a *nonrandom* assignment, in any extension of α. Similarly, if there are two good values, then no value can be forced in this way. Since no process makes a random choice for stage s in α, the determination of values that can be forced at stage s is made before any random choices for stage s.

Thus, if there is exactly one good value, then with probability at least $\frac{1}{2^n}$, all processes that choose their values of x randomly will choose the good value, thus agreeing with those that choose nonrandomly. Similarly, if there are two good values, then with probability at least $\frac{1}{2^n}$, all processes will (randomly) choose the same value of x. In either case, with probability at least $\frac{1}{2^n}$, all nonfaulty processes end up with the same value of x at the end of stage s.

Now, the argument for each stage s only depends on the random choices at stage s, and these are independent of the choices at other stages. So we can combine the probabilities for different stages, to see that with probability at least $1 - (1 - \frac{1}{2^n})^s$, all nonfaulty processes obtain the same value of x at the end of some stage s', $1 \leq s' \leq s$. Therefore, with probability at least $1 - (1 - \frac{1}{2^n})^s$, all nonfaulty processes decide within $s + 1$ stages. $\square$

Now define a function T from $\mathbb{N}^+$ to $R^{\geq 0}$ such that each nonfaulty process completes each stage s by $T(s)$ time after the last *init* event. By Lemma 21.4, we can choose $T(s)$ to be $O(s(d + \ell))$. Also, define $p(t)$ to be 0 if $t < T(1)$ and $1 - (1 - \frac{1}{2^n})^{s-1}$ if $s \geq 1$ and $T(s) \leq t < T(s + 1)$. Lemmas 21.5 and 21.4 then imply

Lemma 21.6 *For any adversary and any $t \geq 0$, with probability $p(t)$, all nonfaulty processes decide within time t after the last init event.*

The main correctness result is

Theorem 21.7 *The BenOr algorithm guarantees well-formedness, agreement, and validity. It also guarantees that, with probability 1, all nonfaulty processes eventually decide.*

Proof.   By Lemmas 21.3, 21.6, and 21.4. (Lemma 21.4 is needed to show that $p(t)$ is unbounded.) $\square$

Randomized versus nonrandomized protocols.   One reason the *BenOr* algorithm is significant is that it demonstrates an inherent difference between the randomized and nonrandomized asynchronous network models. Namely, the agreement problem cannot be solved at all in the presence of process failures in the nonrandomized model, but can be solved easily (with probability 1) in the randomized model. A similar contrast is shown by the *LehmannRabin* algorithm in Section 11.4.

Reducing the complexity. The *BenOr* algorithm is not practical, because its probabilistic time bound is high. It is possible to improve the time complexity by increasing the probability that different processes' random values at the same stage are the same. However, this requires the use of cryptographic techniques, which are outside the model given here.

21.4 Failure Detectors

Another way to solve the agreement problem in fault-prone asynchronous networks is to strengthen the model by adding a new type of system component known as a *failure detector*. A failure detector is a module that provides information to the processes in an asynchronous network about previous process failures. There are different sorts of failure detectors, based on whether the information about stopping is always correct and on whether it is complete. The simplest one is a *perfect failure detector*, which is guaranteed to report only failures that have actually happened and to eventually report all such failures to all other non-failed processes.

Formally, we consider a system A that has the same structure as an asynchronous network system, except that it has additional input actions *inform-stopped*$(j)_i$ for each pair i and j of ports, $i \neq j$. A *perfect failure detector* for system A is a single I/O automaton that has the actions $stop_i$, $1 \leq i \leq n$, as inputs, and the actions *inform-stopped*$(j)_i$, $1 \leq i, j \leq n$, $i \neq j$, as outputs. The idea is that the failure detector learns about stopping failures that occur anywhere in the network and informs the other processes about them. An *inform-stopped*$(j)_i$ action is intended as an announcement at port i that process j has stopped. Figure 21.1 shows the architecture for a simple three-process system. The following algorithm solves the agreement problem when used with a perfect failure detector:

PerfectFDAgreement algorithm (informal):

Each process P_i attempts to stabilize two pieces of data:

1. A vector *val*, indexed by $\{1, \ldots, n\}$, with values in $V \cup \{null\}$. If *val*$(j) = v \in V$, it means that P_i has learned that P_j's initial value is v.

2. A set *stopped* of process indices. If $j \in$ *stopped*, it means that P_i has learned that P_j has stopped.

Process P_i continually broadcasts its current *val* and *stopped* data and updates it upon receipt of new data from processes not in *stopped*. It

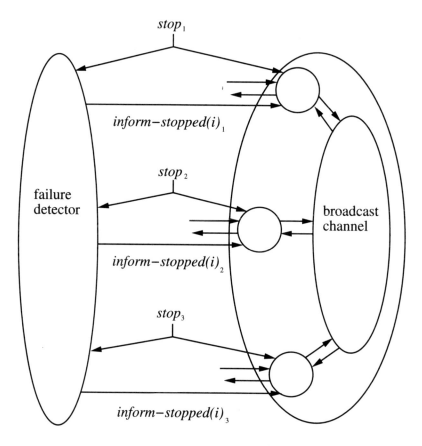

Figure 21.1: Architecture for asynchronous broadcast system with a perfect failure detector.

ignores messages from processes it has already placed in *stopped*. P_i also keeps track of processes that "ratify" its data, that is, from which it receives the same (*val, stopped*) data that it already has. When P_i reaches a point where its data has "stabilized," that is, when it has received ratifications for its current data from all non-stopped processes, then P_i decides on the non-*null* value corresponding to the smallest index in its *val* vector.

The code follows. Let W denote the set of vectors indexed by $\{1, \ldots, n\}$, of elements of $V \cup \{null\}$. We define a partial ordering on pairs (w, I), where $w \in W$ and $I \subseteq \{1, \ldots, n\}$. Namely, we write $(w, I) \leq_d (w', I')$ and say that (w', I') *dominates* (w, I), provided that both of the following hold:

1. For all k, if $w(k) \in V$, then $w(k) = w'(k)$.

2. $I \subseteq I'$.

This captures the idea that (w', I') contains at least all the information that (w, I) does.

To avoid confusion, we do not explicitly describe the behavior of P_i after a $stop_i$ event occurs. It is just as usual—the process stops.

$PerfectFDAgreement_i$ automaton (formal):

Signature:

Input:
  $init(v)_i$, $v \in V$
  $receive(w, I)_{j,i}$, $w \in W$, $I \subseteq \{1, \ldots, n\}$,
    $1 \leq j \leq n$
  $inform\text{-}stopped(j)_i$, $j \neq i$

Output:
  $bcast(w, I)_i$, $w \in W$, $I \subseteq \{1, \ldots, n\}$
  $decide(v)_i$, $v \in V$

States:
$val \in W$, initially identically *null*
$stopped \subseteq \{1, \ldots, n\}$, initially $\emptyset$
$ratified \subseteq \{1, \ldots, n\}$, initially $\emptyset$
decided, a Boolean, initially *false*

Transitions:

$init(v)_i$
  Effect:
    $val(i) := v$
    $ratified := \{i\}$

$inform\text{-}stopped(j)_i$
  Effect:
    $stopped := stopped \cup \{j\}$
    $ratified := \{i\}$

$bcast(w, I)_i$
  Precondition:
    $w = val$
    $I = stopped$
  Effect:
    none

$receive(w, I)_{j,i}$
  Effect:
    if $j \notin stopped$ then
      if $(w, I) = (val, stopped)$ then
        $ratified := ratified \cup \{j\}$
      else if $(w, I) \not\leq_d (val, stopped)$ then
        $stopped := stopped \cup I$
        for all k, $1 \leq k \leq n$, do
          if $val(k) = null$ then $val(k) := w(k)$
        $ratified := \{i\}$

$decide(v)_i$
  Precondition:
    $ratified \cup stopped = \{1, \ldots, n\}$
    $v = val(j)$, where j is the smallest index
      with $v(j) \neq null$
    $decided = false$
  Effect:
    $decided := true$

Tasks:
$\{bcast(w, I)_i : w \in W, I \subseteq \{1, \ldots, n\}\}$
$\{decide(v)_i : v \in V\}$

Theorem 21.8 *PerfectFDAgreement, when used with any perfect failure detector, solves the agreement problem and guarantees wait-free termination.*

Proof.   Well-formedness and validity are easy to see. For wait-free termination, consider a fair execution α in which *init* events occur on all ports and let i be any non-failing port; we show that P_i eventually decides in α. Note that every time P_i's data $(val_i, stopped_i)$ changes in α, it must be that the new pair dominates the old pair. Since there are only finitely many possible pairs, eventually this data reaches final values (w_{final}, I_{final}). If P_i decides before this point, then we are done, so suppose that it does not. Then we claim that eventually thereafter, $ratified_i \cup stopped_i = \{1, \dots, n\}$, which is enough to imply that a $decide_i$ event occurs. To prove this claim, it is enough to show that every process $j \neq i$ that never fails eventually ratifies this pair (w_{final}, I_{final}).

So consider any $j \neq i$ that never fails. Eventually, a message containing (w_{final}, I_{final}) is broadcast by P_i and received by P_j, after which P_j's pair always dominates (w_{final}, I_{final}). But P_j's pair can never *strictly* dominate (w_{final}, I_{final}), since if it did, P_j would eventually succeed in communicating this new information to P_i. So, eventually, P_j's pair becomes and remains equal to (w_{final}, I_{final}). Then, eventually, a message containing (w_{final}, I_{final}) is broadcast by P_j and received by P_i. This places j in $ratified_i$, as needed.

Finally we argue agreement. Suppose that P_i is the first process that decides and let w and I be the values of val_i and $stopped_i$, respectively, when the $decide_i$ event, π, occurs. Then all processes in I fail in α prior to π and so can never decide. Let $J = \{1, \dots, n\} - I$; we argue that all processes in J that decide must decide on the same value as P_i.

Each process j in J must be in $ratified_i$ when π occurs, so must have (w, I) as its local data at some point t_j before π. We claim that each process j in J must keep $val = w$ forever after point t_j in α, which implies that if it decides, it agrees with P_i.

So suppose that this is not the case and let j be the first process in J to acquire a *val* vector containing information that is not in w (i.e., some element of the vector is in V, whereas the corresponding element of w is *null*). Then this acquisition must occur as a result of a $receive_{k,j}$ event occurring after point t_j, where the broadcasting process P_k has, at the time of the broadcast, a *val* vector containing information not in w. Since P_j ignores all processes in I after point t_j, it must be that the broadcasting process P_k is in J. But this contradicts the choice of j as the first process in J to acquire information not in w.   □

Complexity.   The communication complexity and time complexity of the *PerfectFDAgreement* algorithm are unbounded. This is not so terrible, because we are only addressing computability issues in this chapter. However, it is possible to devise similar protocols with bounded complexity. We leave this for an exercise.

21.5 *k*-Agreement

Now we consider weakening the problem statement. The *k-agreement problem*, as described in Sections 7.1 and 12.5 for the synchronous network setting and asynchronous shared memory setting, respectively, is a variation on the agreement problem that can be solved in asynchronous networks with a limited number $(f < k)$ of faults. We use the same problem definition as in Section 12.5: that is, this problem has the same well-formedness and termination conditions as the ordinary agreement problem, and the agreement and validity conditions are replaced by the following, where k is any integer, $k \geq 1$.

Agreement: In any execution, there is a subset W of V, $|W| = k$, such that all decision values are in W.

Validity: In any execution, any decision value for any process is the initial value of some process.

The agreement condition is weaker than that for ordinary agreement in that it permits k decision values rather than just 1. The validity condition is a slight strengthening of the validity condition for ordinary agreement. There is a trivial algorithm to solve the k-set agreement problem in an asynchronous broadcast network, where $f < k$:

> *TrivialKAgreement* **algorithm:**
>
> Processes $P_1, P_2, \ldots P_k$ (only) broadcast their initial values. Every process P_i decides on the first value it receives.

Theorem 21.9 *TrivialKAgreement solves the k-agreement problem and guarantees f-failure termination, if $f < k$.*

It is also not hard to devise a k-agreement algorithm that is similar to *Perfect-FDAgreement*, based on stable vectors. We leave this for an exercise. Alternatively, we can obtain k-agreement algorithms for the asynchronous network model from algorithms for the asynchronous shared memory model, using Theorem 17.5 to translate from the shared memory model to the network model; however, this approach has the disadvantage that it only works if $n > 2f$, whereas *TrivialKAgreement* and the algorithm based on stable vectors also work if $n \leq 2f$.

It turns out that the k-agreement problem cannot be solved if the number of failures is $\geq k$.

Theorem 21.10 *The k-agreement problem is not solvable with k-failure termination in the asynchronous broadcast model.*

Proof.   By Theorems 12.13 and 17.8.   □

21.6   Approximate Agreement

Again we weaken the problem statement. Another variation on the agreement problem is the *approximate agreement problem,* as described in Sections 7.2 and 12.5 for the synchronous network setting and the asynchronous shared memory setting, respectively. We use the same problem definition as in Section 12.5. That is, the set V of values is the set of real numbers, and processes are permitted to send real-valued data in messages. Instead of having to agree exactly, as in the agreement problem, the requirement is that they agree to within a small positive tolerance ϵ. The problem has the same well-formedness and termination conditions as the ordinary agreement problem, and the agreement and validity conditions are replaced by the following.

Agreement: In any execution, any two decision values are within ϵ of each other.

Validity: In any execution, any decision value is within the range of the initial values.

An algorithm similar to the *ConvergeApproxAgreement* algorithm of Section 7.2 works for the asynchronous setting with stopping failures, provided that $n > 3f$. Each process P_i executes a series of stages, at each of which it waits to hear from any $n - f$ processes rather than from all n processes. (It cannot wait to hear from all processes, because up to f processes might stop.) Because we are now considering stopping failures only, it is not necessary for P_i to "reduce" its multiset of values by discarding the extreme values. The *mean* and *select* functions used in the following description, as well as some notions like the *width* of a multiset of reals, are defined in Section 7.2.

> ***AsynchApproxAgreement* algorithm:**
>
> We assume that $n > 3f$. Each P_i maintains a variable *val* containing its latest estimate. This gets initialized to the value v that arrives in an $init(v)_i$ input. At each stage, P_i does the following: First, it broadcasts its *val* value, tagged with the stage number s. Then it collects the first $n - f$ values it receives for stage s into a multiset W. Finally, it sets *val* to $mean(select(W))$.

It should be obvious that the *val* chosen by any process at any stage s is in the range of the *vals* chosen by all the processes at stage $s - 1$ (or the initial *val* values, if $s = 1$). We claim that, at each stage, the width of the multiset of *vals* is reduced by a factor of at least $\left\lfloor \frac{n-f-1}{f} \right\rfloor + 1$. Since $n > 3f$, this yields convergence.

Lemma 21.11 *Let v and v' be the values of val_i and $val_{i'}$ chosen by two processes P_i and $P_{i'}$ at stage s of an execution of AsynchApproxAgreement. Then*

$$|v - v'| \leq \frac{d}{\left\lfloor \frac{n-f-1}{f} \right\rfloor + 1},$$

where d is the width of the range of the val values chosen at stage $s - 1$, if $s \geq 2$, and d is the width of the initial values, if $s = 1$.

Proof. Analogous to that of Lemma 7.17. □

Termination. So far everything we have said about *AsynchApproxAgreement* works if we just assume that $n > 2f$ (rather than $n > 3f$). But we do not yet have a complete algorithm, because we have not said when processes actually decide. We use the extra processes to help in achieving termination.

We cannot use the simple termination strategy that we used for *Converge-ApproxAgreement*, because a process cannot wait to hear from all processes at stage 1 and thus cannot always determine an upper bound on the range of the multiset of initial values. However, we can modify this strategy slightly by adding a special *initialization stage*, stage 0, to the beginning of the algorithm. In stage 0, each process P_i broadcasts its *val*, collects a multiset of $n - f$ *vals*, and chooses the *median* of the multiset as its new *val* for use in stage 1. Since $n > 3f$, it is easy to check that any *val* chosen by any process P_i at stage 0 is in the range of the multiset collected by any process P_j at stage 0. Thus, each P_i can use the range of the multiset it collects at stage 0 to compute a stage number by which it is sure that the *val* values of any two processes at stage s are at most ϵ apart. The rest of this strategy is as for *ConvergeApproxAgreement*.

The *AsynchApproxAgreement* algorithm is not optimal, in the sense that the problem can actually be solved for any $n > 2f$. However, a more complicated algorithm is needed. For example, an algorithm that works for $n > 2f$ can be obtained from a shared memory approximate agreement algorithm A, based on single-writer/multi-reader shared registers, that guarantees wait-free termination. Theorem 12.14 asserts that such an algorithm A exists (and you can find one in [24]). Then Theorem 17.5 can be used to infer the existence of an asynchronous network algorithm that solves the approximate agreement problem and guarantees f-failure termination, for $n > 2f$.[1] On the other hand, it is not hard to see that the approximate agreement problem cannot be solved if $n \leq 2f$.

Theorem 21.12 *The approximate agreement problem is not solvable with f-failure termination in the asynchronous broadcast model if $n \leq 2f$.*

Proof Sketch.   The proof is similar to that of Theorem 17.6. Briefly, we suppose that such an algorithm exists and let G_1 be the set $1, \ldots, n - f$ and G_2 be the set $n - f + 1, \ldots, n$. We consider a fair execution α_1 in which all processes begin with value v_1 and all processes with indices in G_2 fail right at the start. By f-failure termination, all processes in G_1 must eventually decide, and the validity condition implies that they must decide v_1. Symmetrically, we consider a second fair execution α_2 in which all processes begin with v_2, where $|v_1 - v_2| > \epsilon$, and all processes with indices in G_1 fail at the start. In α_2, all processes in G_2 must eventually decide v_2.

We then construct a finite execution α as in the proof of Theorem 17.6, by combining α_1 and α_2. In α, the processes in G_1 decide v_1 and those in G_2 decide v_2, which contradicts the agreement condition. $\square$

21.7   Computability in Asynchronous Networks*

The same construction that is used in the proofs of Theorems 17.6 and 21.12 can be used to show that many other problems of global coordination cannot be solved in asynchronous networks if half of the processes might fail.

As we did in Section 12.5, we can consider the solvability of arbitrary *decision problems* in asynchronous networks. Ordinary agreement, k-agreement, and approximate agreement problems are all examples of decision problems, and we have already given the main results about the computability of these problems in asynchronous networks. As for the read/write shared memory model, we state a theorem that gives some conditions that imply that a problem cannot be solved with 1-failure termination in the asynchronous network model.

Theorem 21.13 *Let D be a decision mapping whose decision problem is solvable with 1-failure termination in the asynchronous broadcast model. Then there must be a decision mapping D' with $D'(w) \subseteq D(w)$ for all w, such that both of the following hold:*

---

[1]In order to apply Theorem 17.5, we need for A to satisfy the "turn" restriction given in Section 17.1.1. The shared memory approximate agreement algorithm can be constructed so as to satisfy this condition.

1. *If input vectors w and w' differ in exactly one position, then there exist $y \in D'(w)$ and $y' \in D'(w')$ such that y and y' differ in at most one position.*

2. *For each w, the graph defined by $D'(w)$ is connected.*

Proof. By Theorems 12.15 and 17.8. □

In general, impossibility results for computabiliy in the read/write shared memory setting carry over to the network setting using Theorem 17.8. Algorithms carry over also, using Theorem 17.5, but only under the restrictions needed for Theorem 17.5, including the requirement that $n > 2f$.

21.8 Bibliographic Notes

Theorem 21.2, the impossibility of agreement in the presence of stopping failures, was first proved by Fischer, Lynch, and Paterson [123]. Their original proof was given directly in terms of the asynchronous broadcast model rather than via a transformation. Loui and Abu-Amara [199] observed that Theorem 21.2 could be extended to the read/write shared memory model, using essentially the same proof. Our proof of Theorem 12.8 follows the presentation of Loui and Abu-Amara. The original proof by Fischer, Lynch, and Paterson, reorganized somewhat according to suggestions by Bridgland and Watro [58] is outlined in Exercises 21.2, 21.3, and 21.4.

The *BenOr* algorithm was invented by Ben-Or [46]. Later work by Rabin [248] and by Feldman [114] produced other randomized algorithms with much better (in fact, constant) time complexity. These use "secret sharing" techniques to increase the probability that the random values chosen by different processes at the same stage are the same.

The notion of a failure detector was defined and developed by Chandra and Toueg [66] and by Chandra, Hadzilacos, and Toueg [65]. Those papers describe not only the perfect failure detector discussed here but also many less perfect variations, including failure detectors that falsely identify processes as faulty and failure detectors that fail to notify all processes about failures. Such weaker failure detectors can also be used to solve the agreement problem, and some can be implemented in practical distributed systems using timeouts. Failure detectors are also discussed by Hadzilacos and Toueg [143].

We have already discussed the origins of the k-agreement problem and the approximate agreement problem in the Bibliographic Notes for Chapters 7 and 12. Attiya, Bar-Noy, Dolev, Koller, Peleg, and Reischuk [19, 20, 40] describe some other interesting problems that are solvable in asynchronous networks with failures, including a problem of process *renaming* and a problem of *slotted exclusion*. Bridgland and Watro [58] describe a resource-allocation problem that is solvable in asynchronous networks with failures. The idea of a stable vector algorithm is due to Attiya et al. [20].

The proof of Theorem 21.12 is adapted from proofs by Bracha and Toueg [56] and Attiya, Bar-Noy, Dolev, Peleg, and Reischuk [20]. Biran, Moran, and Zaks [51] characterized the decision problems that can be solved in an asynchronous network with 1-failure termination, based on an earlier impossibility result by Moran and Wolfstahl [230]. Theorem 21.13 is adapted from these two papers.

21.9 Exercises

21.1. Prove Theorem 21.1.

21.2. Suppose $V = \{0, 1\}$. If A is an asynchronous broadcast system that solves the agreement problem, then define 0-*valence*, 1-*valence*, *univalence* and *bivalence* for finite executions of A, and also define *initializations* of A, in the same way as in Section 12.2.2.

(a) Give an example of such a system A in which there is a bivalent initialization.

(b) Given an example of such a system A in which all initializations are univalent.

(c) Prove that if A guarantees 1-failure termination, then there is a bivalent initialization.

21.3. Let V, A be as in Exercise 21.2. Define a *decider* execution α to be a finite failure-free input-first execution satisfying the following conditions, for some i:

(a) α is bivalent.

(b) There exists a 0-valent failure-free extension α_0 of α such that the portion of α_0 after α consists of steps of process i only.

(c) There exists a 1-valent failure-free extension α_1 of α such that the portion of α_1 after α consists of steps of process i only.

That is, a single process i can operate on its own in two different ways (e.g., interleaving locally controlled and message-receiving steps in two different ways, or else receiving two different sequences of messages), in such a way as to resolve the final decision in two different ways.

Prove that if A has a bivalent initialization, then A has a decider. Note that we have assumed only that A solves the agreement problem; we have made no fault-tolerance assumptions. (*Hint:* Consider the proof of Lemma 12.7.)

21.4. Use the results of Exercises 21.2 and 21.3 to prove Theorem 21.2.

21.5. Reconsider the agreement problem of this chapter, using the broadcast model. This time consider a more constrained fault model than general stopping failures, in which processes can only fail at the beginning of computation. (That is, all *stop* events precede all other events.) Can the agreement problem be solved in this model, guaranteeing

   (a) 1-failure termination?

   (b) f-failure termination, where $n > 2f$?

   (c) wait-free termination?

   In each case, give either an algorithm or an impossibility proof.

21.6. Design a variant of the *BenOr* algorithm in which all nonfaulty processes eventually halt.

21.7. Design variants of the *BenOr* randomized agreement algorithm that work for the following cases:

   (a) The synchronous network model with stopping failures.

   (b) The synchronous network model with Byzantine failures.

   (c) The asynchronous network model with Byzantine failures. (As mentioned in Section 14.1.1, a Byzantine failure of a process P_i is modelled by allowing P_i to be replaced by an arbitrary I/O automaton with the same external interface.)

   In each case, try to design the algorithm to work for as few processes as possible, relative to the number f of tolerated failures.

21.8. Design a randomized asynchronous algorithm for agreement with stopping failures, using an arbitrary value set V rather than just $\{0, 1\}$. Try to minimize the number of processes. (*Hint:* Combine the ideas of the *TurpinCoan* algorithm with those of the *BenOr* algorithm.)

21.9. Repeat Exercise 21.8 for the case of Byzantine failures.

21.10. Devise an alternative protocol to *PerfectFDAgreement* that also uses a perfect failure detector to achieve wait-free agreement but that has "small" communication and time complexity. Try to obtain the smallest communication and time complexity that you can.

21.11. Define an *imperfect failure detector* as follows. It has the same external interface as a perfect failure detector, with the addition of an *inform-not-stopped(j)$_i$* action for each j and i, $j \neq i$. This is used to correct a previous *inform-stopped(j)$_i$* action, that is, to notify process P_i that P_j has in fact not stopped, in spite of a previous erroneous notification. An imperfect failure detector can alternate *inform-stopped(j)$_i$* and *inform-not-stopped(j)$_i$* events any number of times. However, in any fair execution α of the failure detector, there can be only finitely many such events for any i and j, and the final such event must contain the correct information—saying whether or not *stop$_j$* occurs in α.

Suppose that $n > 2f$. Devise an algorithm that solves the agreement problem guaranteeing f-failure termination, using any imperfect failure detector.

21.12. Prove that there is no algorithm to solve the agreement problem guaranteeing f-failure termination, using an arbitrary imperfect failure detector as defined in Exercise 21.11, in case $n \leq 2f$.

21.13. Give precondition-effect code for a "stable vector" algorithm similar to *PerfectFDAgreement*, to solve the k-agreement problem. Prove that it works correctly, if $f < k$. (*Hint:* The state only contains the components *val*, *ratified*, and *decided* but not the *stopped* component. A decision can be made when $|ratified| \geq n - f$.)

21.14. Define a finite execution α of a k-agreement algorithm to be *m-valent* if there are exactly m distinct decision values that appear in extensions of α, and define an *initialization* as in Section 12.2.2. Prove (without using Theorem 21.10) that any k-agreement algorithm in the asynchronous broadcast model that guarantees k-failure termination must have a $k + 1$–valent initial execution. (*Hint:* Use ideas from Section 7.1, including Sperner's Lemma.)

21.15. Give complete precondition-effect code for the *AsynchApproxAgreement* algorithm, including the termination protocol. Prove correctness.

21.16. Modify the *AsynchApproxAgreement* algorithm and its proof to work for the case of Byzantine failures. How many processes are needed? (*Hint:* Use ideas from the *ConvergeApproxAgreement* algorithm for the synchronous Byzantine setting.)

21.17. Prove the most general impossibility result you can, using the construction in the proof of Theorem 21.12.

21.18. Give a general characterization of the *decision problems* (as defined in Section 12.5) that can be solved in asynchronous networks with 1-failure termination. (*Warning:* This is very hard.)

Chapter 22

Data Link Protocols

In this chapter, we consider the problem of implementing reliable FIFO communication using less reliable channels. This is one of the most fundamental problems solved by communication networks. The "less reliable channels" we consider include channels that exhibit failures such as the loss and duplication of messages, as well as channels that reorder messages. We also consider process crashes that lose process state information. We only consider the problem in the very special case of a two-node network.

We begin by presenting two simple, well-known algorithms: Stenning's protocol and the Alternating Bit protocol. In Stenning's protocol, the process at the sending end attaches (unbounded) integer tags to messages submitted by the user; this protocol tolerates loss, duplication, and reordering of messages on the channels. The Alternating Bit protocol, on the other hand, uses only bounded tags and tolerates loss and duplication, but not reordering. We then consider whether it is possible to tolerate reordering using bounded tags. Finally, we consider the case of crashes that lose process state information (the contents of volatile memory).

Throughout this chapter, we discuss messages at two levels: the level of the users of the communication system and the level of the underlying channels. In order to distinguish between these two types of messages, we call them *high-level* and *low-level* messages, respectively. We generally let M and M' denote the high-level and low-level message alphabets, respectively. Also, we usually capitalize the actions at the user interface, for example, *SEND* and *RECEIVE*, while we continue to use lowercase for the actions at the channel interface, for example, *send* and *receive*.

The techniques that we use for modelling the algorithms in this chapter (using I/O automata, composition, and simulation relations) are suitable for modelling layered communication architectures such as the ISO hierarchy.

22.1   The Problem

We consider the problem in an asynchronous send/receive network with an underlying graph G consisting of two nodes, 1 and 2, connected by a single undirected edge. The problem is to implement reliable FIFO communication between users U_1 and U_2 located at the two nodes. High-level messages submitted by U_1 to the process P_1 located at node 1 are supposed to be delivered subsequently to U_2. Each message should be delivered exactly once, and the deliveries should occur in the order in which the messages are submitted.

Formally, we let F denote the universal reliable FIFO send/receive channel from 1 to 2 with alphabet M, as defined in Section 14.1.2 and Example 8.1.1; here, we rename the external actions as $SEND(m)_{1,2}$ and $RECEIVE(m)_{1,2}$, $m \in M$. Then the correctness requirement for a protocol is that it should "implement" F, in the sense that each of its fair executions α, when projected on the external actions of F, should yield a fair trace of F. More precisely, in terms of the formal notation for I/O automata introduced in Chapter 8, the requirement is that $\alpha|ext(F) \in fairtraces(F)$.

Note that the universal reliable FIFO channel F is essentially an unbounded queue, so any implementation of F will also need unbounded storage. An alternative way of modelling the problem would be to use an explicit handshake between U_1 and the channel, by which the channel tells U_1 when it may submit the next high-level message. This would avoid the need for unbounded storage. However, it would introduce the additional complication of modelling the handshake protocol.

The two processes executing the code to implement F are modelled as I/O automata. The channels connecting them in both directions are also I/O automata, but they are generally not reliable FIFO channels. In particular, they may lose, duplicate, or reorder low-level messages.

We do not consider certain other types of unreliability, however, such as the manufacture of spurious messages. Also, we impose some limitations on message loss—we usually assume some liveness property that says, roughly speaking:

> If infinitely many messages are sent, then infinitely many of them are delivered.

There are basically two ways to formalize this property—using the *strong loss limitation (SLL)* and *weak loss limitation (WLL)* conditions defined in Section 14.1.2. The difference is that the SLL condition specifies that the channel is fair to each particular type of message. In this chapter, we use both conditions, as needed. We also usually impose a finite limit on message duplication.

Formal descriptions of the allowed behavior for most of the channels we need in this chapter appear in Section 14.1.2. Some of these descriptions are themselves I/O automata (and use I/O automaton fairness to express the needed liveness conditions). Others are axiomatic, in terms of a *cause* function from *receive* events to *send* events. Still others consist of a combination of an automaton and some extra liveness constraints. In this chapter, we use all three types of descriptions, as convenient.

The architecture we consider throughout this chapter is depicted in Figure 22.1. It consists of two process automata, P_1 and P_2, and two channel automata, $C_{1,2}$ and $C_{2,1}$, one in each direction. The processes interact with the users by means of *SEND* and *RECEIVE* actions and with the channels by means of *send* and *receive* actions. In Section 22.5, we also introduce additional actions to model process crashes.

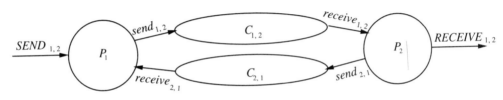

Figure 22.1: Architecture for data link protocols.

22.2 Stenning's Protocol

The simplest protocol for ensuring reliable FIFO message delivery in terms of less reliable channels is due to Stenning. It tolerates all three types of channel unreliability: (limited) loss, (finite) duplication, and reordering.

Stenning protocol (informal):

Process P_1 places high-level messages submitted by user U_1 in a buffer, $buffer_1$, tagging them with successive integers starting with 1. P_1 repeatedly sends the first message in $buffer_1$ to P_2 with its tag attached. Process P_2 accepts the first message tagged with 1 that it receives. Then P_2 accepts each subsequent message exactly if its tag is one greater than the tag of the message previously accepted. P_2 places the accepted messages in $buffer_2$ and delivers the messages in $buffer_2$, in order, to U_2.

P_2 acknowledges a high-level message by sending its tag back to P_1. When P_1 receives an acknowledgment for its current tag, it moves on to begin processing the next high-level message.

The following is the code for process P_1 of the *Stenning* protocol.

Stenning$_1$ automaton (formal):

Signature:

Input:
    $SEND(m)_{1,2}, m \in M$
    $receive(k)_{2,1}, k \in \mathbb{N}$

Output:
    $send(m,k)_{1,2}, m \in M, k \in \mathbb{N}$

States:
buffer, a FIFO queue of elements of M, initially empty
$tag \in \mathbb{N}$, initially 1

Transitions:

$SEND(m)_{1,2}$
    Effect:
        add m to *buffer*

$send(m,k)_{1,2}$
    Precondition:
        m is first on *buffer*
        $k = tag$
    Effect:
        none

$receive(k)_{2,1}$
    Effect:
        if $k = tag$ then
            remove first element (if any) of *buffer*
            $tag := tag + 1$

Tasks:
$\{send(m,k)_{1,2} : m \in M, k \in \mathbb{N}\}$

The following is the code for process P_2.

Stenning$_2$ automaton (formal):

Signature:

Input:
    $receive(m,k)_{1,2}, m \in M, k \in \mathbb{N}$

Output:
    $RECEIVE(m)_{1,2}, m \in M$
    $send(k)_{2,1}, k \in \mathbb{N}$

States:
buffer, a FIFO queue of elements of M, initially empty
$tag \in \mathbb{N}$, initially 0

Transitions:

$RECEIVE(m)_{1,2}$
    Precondition:
        m is first on *buffer*
    Effect:
        remove first element of *buffer*

$send(k)_{2,1}$
    Precondition:
        $k = tag$
    Effect:
        none

$receive(m, k)_{1,2}$
    Effect:
        if $k = tag + 1$ then
           add m to *buffer*
           $tag := tag + 1$

Tasks:
$\{RECEIVE(m)_{1,2} : m \in M\}$
$\{send(k)_{2,1} : k \in \mathbb{N}\}$

The channels $C_{1,2}$ and $C_{2,1}$ in the *Stenning* protocol are any I/O automata that satisfy the specification of a *lossy reordering channel* given in Example 14.1.2 (with suitable renaming of actions). That is, they allow limited loss, finite duplication, and reordering. The allowed channel behavior is specified in Example 14.1.2 using a combination of a basic automaton and some additional liveness properties. We want this form of specification here because it yields an explicit state that we can use in invariant assertions and simulation relations. The complete *Stenning* protocol is obtained by composing P_1, P_2, $C_{1,2}$, and $C_{2,1}$.

In order to prove the correctness of the *Stenning* protocol, we begin with some invariants. But note the following technicality: since we need invariants that mention the channel states, we must give them in terms of particular automata for the channels. Thus, we state the invariants in terms of the basic I/O automata $A_{1,2}$ and $A_{2,1}$ defined in Example 14.1.2. The *in-transit* variables are state components of the $A_{1,2}$ and $A_{2,1}$ automata.

Lemma 22.1 *In every reachable state of the Stenning protocol using channels $A_{1,2}$ and $A_{2,1}$, the following are true.*

1. *$tag_2 \leq tag_1 \leq tag_2 + 1$.*

2. *If (m, k) is in in-transit$_{1,2}$, then $k \leq tag_1$.*

3. *If (m, tag_1) is in in-transit$_{1,2}$, then m is the first element of buffer$_1$.*

4. *If k is in in-transit$_{2,1}$, then $k \leq tag_2$.*

5. *If $tag_2 = tag_1$, or if any message in in-transit$_{1,2}$ or in-transit$_{2,1}$ has its tag value equal to tag_1, then buffer$_1$ is nonempty.*

Proof.   By a straightforward induction. Left as an exercise.   □

Our goal is to show that the *Stenning* protocol, using any allowable channels, guarantees reliable FIFO message delivery. We first give a technical lemma that asserts correctness in terms of the *channel specifications* rather than in terms of *arbitrary allowable channels*. This lemma implies the result for arbitrary allowable channels.

The statement of Lemma 22.2 is slightly heavy on notation, but it is not really that complicated. The assumptions just say that α projects to give fair executions of the node processes P_1 and P_2, as well as executions allowed by the lossy reordering channel specifications. The conclusion says that α yields a fair trace of F, that is, it exhibits reliable FIFO message delivery.

Lemma 22.2 *Let α be any execution of the Stenning protocol with $A_{1,2}$ and $A_{2,1}$. Suppose that*

1. *$\alpha|P_1$ and $\alpha|P_2$ are fair.*

2. *$\alpha|A_{1,2}$ and $\alpha|A_{2,1}$ satisfy the liveness properties in Example 14.1.2.*

Then $\alpha|ext(F) \in fairtraces(F)$.

Proof Sketch.   Let $\beta = trace(\alpha)$. It is not hard to see that $\beta \in traces(F)$, which is another way of saying that the sequence of high-level messages in *RECEIVE* events in β is a prefix of the sequence of high-level messages in *SEND* events in β. This can be proved using a (single-valued) simulation relation from the *Stenning* protocol with $A_{1,2}$ and $A_{2,1}$ to F, and then invoking Theorem 8.13. The proof of the simulation relation uses Lemma 22.1. Assumptions 1 and 2 in the statement of the theorem are not even needed in this part of the proof, because they deal only with liveness. We leave this proof as an exercise.

It remains to show the fairness condition of F, that is, that any high-level message that is submitted to P_1 eventually gets delivered by P_2. (The correspondence between sending and delivery events is uniquely determined by the definition of F.) So suppose not; consider the first high-level message m that is submitted but not delivered and let k denote its associated *tag*. This message can never be accepted by P_2 for addition to its *buffer*, since, if it were, the fairness properties of P_2 would imply that the message would be delivered to U_2. So it follows that tag_2 remains $\leq k - 1$ forever.

We claim that this message m eventually reaches the front of $buffer_1$. This is obvious if it is the first message ever sent, that is, if $k = 1$. If $k \geq 1$, then the previous message must eventually get accepted by P_2, since it is delivered to U_2. Thus, tag_2 eventually reaches, and stays equal to, $k - 1$. But then the fairness properties of P_2 imply that P_2 keeps sending $k - 1$ messages forever, and the weak loss limitation (WLL) condition for $A_{2,1}$ implies that eventually a copy of $k - 1$ is received by P_1. This means that the message with $tag = k - 1$ gets removed from $buffer_1$, so m reaches the front.

Once this message m reaches the front of $buffer_1$, it must stay there forever (since it is never accepted by P_2). Then the fairness of P_1 implies that P_1 keeps sending (m, k) messages forever, and the WLL condition for $A_{1,2}$ implies that eventually a copy of (m, k) is received, and hence accepted, by P_2. This is a contradiction. □

It is also possible to prove the fairness condition by means of an execution correspondence, using Theorem 8.13 and a simulation from *Stenning* to F. We leave this for an exercise.

Lemma 22.2 implies the main correctness result for the *Stenning* protocol, given in the following theorem. It says that the *Stenning* protocol with lossy reordering channels guarantees reliable FIFO message delivery.

Theorem 22.3 *The Stenning protocol, using any lossy reordering channels (according to the specification in Example 14.1.2), implements F, in the following sense: For every fair execution α (of the protocol plus the channels), $\alpha|ext(F) \in fairtraces(F)$.*

Proof Sketch. This follows from Lemma 22.2 and basic properties of I/O automaton composition, in particular, Theorems 8.4 and 8.2. The proof is left as an exercise. □

22.3 Alternating Bit Protocol

An interesting variation on the *Stenning* protocol is the *Alternating Bit protocol*, which we abbreviate as *ABP*. The behavior of the *ABP* is very similar to that of the *Stenning* protocol, but the *ABP* only uses $\{0, 1\}$–valued tags instead of integer-valued tags. In fact, the *ABP* can be viewed as an *optimized* version of *Stenning*, in which the integer-valued tags are simply replaced by their low-order bits. Of course, this means that the *ABP* makes stronger requirements on its underlying channels in order to work correctly.

In addition to being interesting on its own, the *ABP* has for many years served as a standard example for demonstrating the use of various protocol verification techniques.

ABP (informal):

Process P_1 places high-level messages submitted by U_1 in *buffer*$_1$, tagging each with a binary value, 0 or 1, in an alternating fashion. P_1 repeatedly sends the first message in its *buffer* to P_2, with its tag attached. P_2 accepts the first message tagged with 1 that it receives. Then P_2 accepts each subsequent message exactly if its tag is different from the tag of the message previously accepted. P_2 places accepted messages in *buffer*$_2$ and delivers the messages in *buffer*$_2$, in order, to U_2.

P_2 acknowledges a high-level message by sending its tag back to P_1. When P_1 receives an acknowledgment for its current tag, it moves on to begin processing the next high-level message.

The code for process P_1 follows.

ABP$_1$ automaton (formal):

Signature:

Input: Output:
  $SEND(m)_{1,2}$, $m \in M$ $send(m, b)_{1,2}$, $m \in M$, $b \in \{0, 1\}$
  $receive(b)_{2,1}$, $b \in \{0, 1\}$

States:
buffer, a FIFO queue of elements of M, initially empty
tag $\in \{0, 1\}$, initially 1.

Transitions:

$SEND(m)_{1,2}$ $receive(b)_{2,1}$
  Effect: Effect:
    add m to *buffer*   if $b = tag$ then
                                                  remove first element (if any) of *buffer*
$send(m, b)_{1,2}$ *tag* := *tag* + 1 mod 2
  Precondition:
    m is first on *buffer*
    $b = tag$
  Effect:
    none

Tasks:
$\{send(m,b)_{1,2} : m \in M, b \in \{0,1\}\}$

And now we give the code for process P_2.

ABP_2 automaton (formal):

Signature:

Input:
    $receive(m,b)_{1,2}, m \in M, b \in \{0,1\}$

Output:
    $RECEIVE(m)_{1,2}, m \in M$
    $send(b)_{2,1}, b \in \{0,1\}$

States:
buffer, a FIFO queue of elements of M, initially empty
$tag \in \{0,1\}$, initially 0.

Transitions:

$RECEIVE(m)_{1,2}$
    Precondition:
        m is first on *buffer*
    Effect:
        remove first element of *buffer*

$send(b)_{2,1}$
    Precondition:
        $b = tag$
    Effect:
        none

$receive(m,b)_{1,2}$
    Effect:
        if $b \neq tag$ then
            add m to *buffer*
            $tag := tag + 1 \bmod 2$

Tasks:
$\{RECEIVE(m)_{1,2} : m \in M\}$
$\{send(b)_{2,1} : b \in \{0,1\}\}$

The *ABP* requires channels with stronger reliability conditions than those we assumed for the *Stenning* protocol: now we must assume that the channels do not reorder low-level messages, though they can still lose and duplicate them. Thus, the channels $C_{1,2}$ and $C_{2,1}$ are any I/O automata that satisfy the specification of a *lossy FIFO channel* given in Example 14.1.1 (with suitable renaming of actions). That is, they allow limited loss, finite duplication, and no reordering. As before, the allowed channel behavior is specified using a combination of a basic automaton and some additional liveness properties. The complete ABP is obtained by composing P_1, P_2, $C_{1,2}$, and $C_{2,1}$.

Our strategy for proving the correctness of ABP is to relate it to the *Stenning* protocol using a simulation relation. In this simulation, we consider the *Stenning* processes in combination with lossy FIFO channels rather than the more general lossy reordering channels we considered in Section 22.2.

In the rest of this section, we let $A_{1,2}$ and $A_{2,1}$ denote the basic automata from Example 14.1.1 with external interfaces appropriate to the ABP. We let $A'_{1,2}$ and $A'_{2,1}$ denote the same automata but with external interfaces appropriate to the *Stenning* protocol. Finally, we let P'_1 and P'_2 denote the processes *Stenning*$_1$ and *Stenning*$_2$, in order to distinguish them from the processes P_1 and P_2 of the ABP.

A key to the simulation proof is a new invariant about the *Stenning* protocol with channels $A'_{1,2}$ and $A'_{2,1}$.

Lemma 22.4 *In every reachable state of the Stenning protocol using channels $A'_{1,2}$ and $A'_{2,1}$, the following is true.*

Let T be the sequence of integers consisting of the tags in queue$_{2,1}$ (in order from first to last on the queue), followed by tag$_2$, followed by the tag components of the elements of queue$_{1,2}$, followed by tag$_1$. Then the integers in T are nondecreasing, and the difference between the first and last integer in T is at most 1.

Proof. The proof is left as an exercise.   □

Now we can relate the ABP and the *Stenning* protocol. Lemma 22.5 says that for any execution α of the ABP with lossy FIFO channels, there is an execution α' of the *Stenning* protocol with lossy FIFO channels, such that α and α' look the same at the external interface.

Lemma 22.5 *Let α be any execution of ABP with $A_{1,2}$ and $A_{2,1}$. Suppose that*

  1. $\alpha|P_1$ and $\alpha|P_2$ are fair.

  2. $\alpha|A_{1,2}$ and $\alpha|A_{2,1}$ satisfy the liveness properties in Example 14.1.1.

Then there exists α', an execution of the Stenning protocol with $A'_{1,2}$ and $A'_{2,1}$, such that

  1. $\alpha|P'_1$ and $\alpha|P'_2$ are fair.

  2. $\alpha|A'_{1,2}$ and $\alpha|A'_{2,1}$ satisfy the liveness properties in Example 14.1.1.

3. $\alpha|ext(F) = \alpha'|ext(F)$.

Proof Sketch. We first produce a simulation relation f from ABP with channels $A_{1,2}$ and $A_{2,1}$ to the *Stenning* protocol with the corresponding channels $A'_{1,2}$ and $A'_{2,1}$ This relation expresses the fact that the binary *tags* in ABP are simply the low-order bits of the integer *tags* in the *Stenning* protocol. Specifically, if s and u are states of ABP and *Stenning*, respectively, then we define $(s, u) \in f$ exactly if

1. $s.buffer_1 = u.buffer_1$ and $s.buffer_2 = u.buffer_2$

2. $s.tag_1 = u.tag_1 \bmod 2$ and $s.tag_2 = u.tag_2 \bmod 2$

3. $s.queue_{1,2}$ and $u.queue_{1,2}$ contain the same number of elements. Moreover, for any j, if (m, k) is the jth element of $u.queue_{1,2}$, then $(m, k \bmod 2)$ is the jth element of $s.queue_{1,2}$.

4. $s.queue_{2,1}$ and $u.queue_{2,1}$ contain the same number of elements. Moreover, for any j, if k is the jth element of $u.queue_{2,1}$, then $k \bmod 2$ is the jth element of $s.queue_{2,1}$.

It is straightforward to show that f is a simulation relation. Most of what we must show follows immediately from the definition of f and the transitions of ABP and *Stenning*. Lemma 22.4 is used in the proof of Condition 2 (the step condition) of the definition of a simulation relation, for *receive* actions. In particular, for each *receive* step of ABP in which the message is accepted, we must argue that the corresponding *receive* step of the *Stenning* protocol also causes the message to be accepted. For example, consider an $(s, receive(m, b)_{1,2}, s')$ step of ABP in which m is accepted by P_2. The condition that causes m to be accepted is that $b \neq s.tag_2$. In the corresponding state u of the *Stenning* protocol, the simulation relation implies that the incoming low-level message has a tag k that is different from $u.tag_2$, modulo 2. But in order to show that m is accepted in state u, we must show that $k = tag_2 + 1$. Lemma 22.4 can be used to show that this must be the case.

Just producing a simulation relation is not enough to show the liveness properties, however. But, actually, it turns out that f is stronger than an ordinary simulation relation: it maps each step of ABP to a step of the *Stenning* protocol with the same type of action. In fact, the actions are identical, except where the *Stenning* action contains an integer k and the corresponding ABP action contains the low-order bit b.

Now fix α as in the hypothesis of the theorem. Then simulation f yields a "corresponding" execution α' of the *Stenning* system. This correspondence guarantees that both of the following hold:

1. α and α' have the same sequences of actions, with the one exception mentioned just above.

2. States in the same positions in α and α' are related by f.

These conditions are sufficiently strong that they allow us to infer the needed conditions for α' from the conditions for α.   □

See Section 8.5.5 for another version of this execution correspondence idea, and Section 10.9.4 and Chapter 16 for similar arguments involving execution correspondence.

Lemma 22.5 implies the following technical lemma for the *ABP*. It says that any fair execution of the *ABP* protocol whose channel behavior is allowed by the specification of a lossy FIFO channel exhibits reliable FIFO message delivery.

Lemma 22.6 *Let* α *be any execution of the ABP protocol with* $A_{1,2}$ *and* $A_{2,1}$. *Suppose that*

 1. $\alpha|P_1$ *and* $\alpha|P_2$ *are fair.*

 2. $\alpha|A_{1,2}$ *and* $\alpha|A_{2,1}$ *satisfy the liveness properties in Example 14.1.1.*

Then $\alpha|ext(F) \in fairtraces(F)$.

Proof Sketch.   By Lemmas 22.5 and 22.2.   □

Lemma 22.6 in turn implies the main correctness result for the *ABP*, given in the following theorem. It says that the *ABP* with lossy FIFO channels guarantees reliable FIFO message delivery.

Theorem 22.7 *The ABP, using any lossy FIFO channels (according to the specification in Example 14.1.1), implements F, in the following sense: For every fair execution* α *(of the protocol plus the channels),* $\alpha|ext(F) \in fairtraces(F)$.

Proof Sketch.   By Lemma 22.6 and basic properties of composition, in particular, Theorems 8.4 and 8.2. The proof is left as an exercise.   □

Infinite duplication.   Note that the *ABP* still works with slightly more general channels that allow infinite duplication. These channels still do not reorder messages, and losses are limited by the WLL condition. The only real difference between such channels and the lossy FIFO channels described above is that the new channels can make infinitely many duplicates of the *last* message sent, in the case where only finitely many messages are sent. The reason we did not present Lemmas 22.5 and 22.6 and Theorem 22.7 in terms of these slightly more general channels is that we wanted to use invariant assertions and simulations in the proof, and these more general channels are easier to describe in terms of axioms than in terms of automata.

22.4 Bounded Tag Protocols Tolerating Reordering

So far, we have seen that it is possible to achieve reliable FIFO communication in the presence of limited loss, finite duplication, and arbitrary reordering of low-level messages, using the *Stenning* protocol with unbounded tags. With bounded tags, using the *ABP*, it is possible to tolerate limited loss and finite duplication, but not reordering. In this section, we consider the question of whether it is possible to design bounded tag protocols that tolerate reordering of low-level messages.

Consider first what goes wrong when the *ABP* is used with channels that can reorder low-level messages: process P_2 can get fooled into accepting an old high-level message m that happens to arrive tagged with the same bit as the one currently expected. This behavior can cause duplicate delivery to U_2 of the same high-level message, violating the requirements for reliable communication.

For example, the send/receive diagram in Figure 22.2 depicts an execution in which process P_2 accepts a duplicate copy of m after it has already accepted a later message m'.

Thus, we see that the *ABP* does not work with channels that can reorder low-level messages, but of course this does not imply that there cannot be *other* bounded tag protocols that do tolerate reordering.

We give three results. First, in Section 22.4.1, we show the nonexistence of bounded tag protocols that tolerate both reordering and duplication. Next, in Section 22.4.2, we present a bounded tag protocol that tolerates loss and reordering, but not duplication. Unfortunately, this protocol has very high complexity. Finally, in Section 22.4.3, we prove the nonexistence of "efficient" protocols that tolerate loss and reordering. This implies that the high complexity of the protocol in Section 22.4.2 is unavoidable.

Throughout this section, we formalize the notion of a "bounded tag" protocol by simply assuming that the high-level message alphabet M and the low-level message alphabet M' are both finite.

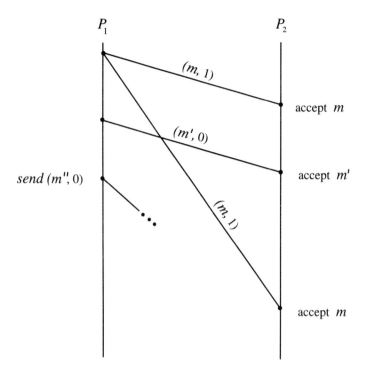

Figure 22.2: P_2 is fooled into accepting m.

22.4.1   Impossibility Result for Reordering and Duplication

We show that there is no protocol that solves the reliable FIFO communication
problem using channels that can both reorder and duplicate low-level messages.
For convenience, we now base our formal statement on axiomatic specifications
of the allowed channel behavior.

   We need some general terminology to describe the interaction between process
automata and channel trace properties. Namely, if P_1 and P_2 comprise a protocol,
and $Q_{1,2}$ and $Q_{2,1}$ are trace properties for the two channels between P_1 and P_2,
then we say that an execution α of $P_1 \times P_2$ is *consistent with* $Q_{1,2}$ provided that
$\alpha|ext(Q_{1,2}) \in traces(Q_{1,2})$. We define consistency with $Q_{2,1}$ analogously. Also,
we say that a finite execution α of $P_1 \times P_2$ is *finitely consistent with* $Q_{1,2}$ provided
that $\alpha|ext(Q_{1,2})$ is a finite prefix of a sequence in $traces(Q_{1,2})$, and analogously
for $Q_{2,1}$.

Example 22.4.1   Consistency and I/O automata

   Consider the special case where $A_{1,2}$ and $A_{2,1}$ are any I/O automata
   with the appropriate channel external interfaces, and $traces(Q_{1,2})$ and

$traces(Q_{2,1})$ are defined to be exactly the fair traces of $A_{1,2}$ and $A_{2,1}$, respectively.

Then the traces of the fair executions of $P_1 \times P_2$ that are consistent with $Q_{1,2}$ and with $Q_{2,1}$ are exactly the fair traces of the composition $P_1 \times P_2 \times A_{1,2} \times A_{2,1}$. Similarly, the traces of the finite executions of $P_1 \times P_2$ that are finitely consistent with $Q_{1,2}$ and with $Q_{2,1}$ are exactly the finite traces of the composition $P_1 \times P_2 \times A_{1,2} \times A_{2,1}$.

These facts can be shown using the compositionality results in Chapter 8, in particular, Theorems 8.1, 8.3, 8.4, and 8.6.

For the result of this subsection, we fix $Q_{1,2}$ to be the trace property with inputs $send(m)_{1,2}$, $m \in M'$, and outputs $receive(m)_{1,2}$, $m \in M'$, and whose traces are exactly those containing no losses and only finite duplication. Arbitrary reordering is allowed. (Formally, there is a *cause* function as in Section 14.1.2 that is onto, and finitely many to one.) Let $Q_{2,1}$ be the analogous trace property, for the opposite channel direction. Then we just say that executions are *consistent* and *finitely consistent*, as a short way of saying that they are consistent or finitely consistent with both $Q_{1,2}$ and $Q_{2,1}$.

The following theorem says that there is no bounded tag protocol that guarantees reliable FIFO message delivery using channels that can reorder and duplicate messages.

Theorem 22.8 *There is no bounded tag protocol (P_1, P_2) that implements F using the reordering, duplicating channels $Q_{1,2}$ and $Q_{2,1}$ (in the sense that if α is a consistent fair execution of $P_1 \times P_2$, then $\alpha|ext(F) \in fairtraces(F)$).*

Proof.   Suppose for the sake of contradiction that there is such an implementation, (P_1, P_2). We construct an execution with incorrect behavior.

First, we run the system as far as we can, until it is no longer possible for process P_1 to send any additional low-level messages with new values. Formally, we construct a finitely consistent execution α_1 of $P_1 \times P_2$, such that if an event $send(m)_{1,2}$ occurs in any finitely consistent extension of α_1, then an event $send(m)_{1,2}$ also occurs in α_1. This construction can be carried out by successive extension, where we attempt to send a new low-level message in each extension until we can no longer do this; the finiteness of the low-level message alphabet M' implies that this construction must eventually terminate. Suppose there are n (user-interface) *SEND* events in α_1.

Now let α_2 be a fair, consistent extension of α_1 that contains exactly one additional *SEND* event, for a total of $n+1$ *SEND* events in all. By the correctness condition, all messages submitted by U_1 in α_2 must eventually get delivered to

U_2, so that there are exactly $n + 1$ *RECEIVE* events in α_2. Let α_3 be the finite prefix of α_2 up to and including the last *RECEIVE* event.

Now we construct a finitely consistent execution α_4 with the following properties:

1. α_4 is an extension of α_1.

2. α_4 is indistinguishable from α_1 to P_1.

3. α_4 is indistinguishable from α_3 to P_2.

We construct α_4 by preventing all events involving P_1 immediately after α_1 while allowing all events of P_2 to proceed exactly as in α_3. The additional events of P_2 might include *receive* events, *send* events, and internal events, as well as the required *RECEIVE* events. In showing that α_4 is a finitely consistent execution, the only difficulty is the *receive* events: we must show that P_2 can be permitted to receive the same low-level messages after α_1 as it does in α_3, even though P_1 does not send any additional low-level messages after α_1. But this is possible because all low-level messages sent by P_1 in α_3 after α_1 contain values that P_1 has already sent in α_1. Thus, any low-level message that is received by P_2 after α_1 could just as well be considered to be a duplication of some low-level message sent in α_1.

In α_4, there are exactly n *SEND* events and $n + 1$ *RECEIVE* events. To complete the contradiction, we extend α_4 to a fair, consistent execution without introducing any new *SEND* events. The resulting execution has more *RECEIVE* events than *SEND* events, contradicting the correctness conditions. □

Thus, if the channels permit finite duplication and arbitrary reordering of low-level messages, then even though no low-level messages can be lost, reliable FIFO delivery of high-level messages is impossible.

22.4.2 A Bounded Tag Protocol Tolerating Loss and Reordering

Although it is far from obvious, it turns out that it is possible to tolerate loss and reordering of messages (though, of course, not duplication), using bounded tags. We present an algorithm, the *Probe algorithm*, that accomplishes this. The *Probe* algorithm is *not* a practical communication protocol; it is a *counterexample algorithm* whose main purpose is to show that there can be no impossibility proof for the task in question.

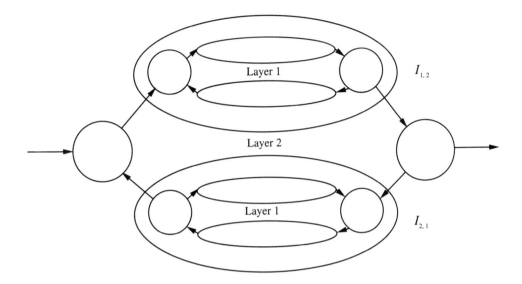

Figure 22.3: Layered structure of the *Probe* protocol.

Probe algorithm (informal):

This algorithm is most easily presented in two layers, combined using I/O automaton composition. Layer 1 uses the given channels to implement intermediate channels, $I_{1,2}$ and $I_{2,1}$, that do not reorder messages, but can lose or duplicate them. More precisely, each intermediate channel satisfies an axiomatic specification in terms of a *cause* function as in Section 14.1.2. In this case, the *cause* function is required not to reorder messages, but to satisfy the WLL loss limitation condition. Infinite duplication is allowed. Layer 2 uses the resulting FIFO channels to implement reliable FIFO communication.

Layers 1 and 2 are combined as in Figure 22.3, with one instance of the Layer 1 protocol used to implement each channel needed for the Layer 2 protocol. Process P_1 of the complete algorithm is obtained by composing process P_1 of the Layer 2 protocol with the sending process in the Layer 1 implementation of $I_{1,2}$ and the receiving process in the Layer 1 implementation of $I_{2,1}$. Symmetrically, P_2 of the complete algorithm is obtained by composing process P_2 of the Layer 2 protocol with the receiving process in the Layer 1 implementation of $I_{1,2}$ and the sending process in the Layer 1 implementation of $I_{2,1}$. Also, each channel in the complete algorithm must be "multiplexed" to implement one channel of each Layer 1 implementation.

Layer 2 is straightforward—for example, *ABP* can be used. (Note that the channels $I_{1,2}$ and $I_{2,1}$ are slightly more general than the lossy FIFO channels that we considered in Section 22.3 in that they allow infinite duplication; however, a remark at the end of that section indicates that the *ABP* still works with these more general channels.) Layer 1, which involves implementing the intermediate channels in terms of the given channels (which can lose and reorder messages but not duplicate them) is more difficult.

Each Layer 1 implementation works as follows. Process P_1 sends a low-level message to P_2 only in response to an explicit *probe* message from P_2. The low-level message that P_1 sends always contains the value of the most recent high-level message that it has received from U_1, which it keeps track of in *latest*. Thus, in this protocol, P_1 does not remember all the messages that are submitted by U_1, but only the most recent one. (The justification for this is that the intermediate channel being implemented is permitted to lose some high-level messages, anyway.) To ensure that P_1 only sends messages in response to *probes*, P_1 keeps a variable *unanswered*, which it increments whenever it receives a *probe* and decrements whenever it sends a low-level message.

Process P_2 continually sends *probes* to P_1, keeping track, in *pending*, of the number of *probes* that it has ever sent. Meanwhile, P_2 counts, in *count(m)*, the number of copies of each high-level message m received since the last time it delivered a high-level message to U_2 (or since the beginning of the execution if no message has yet been delivered to U_2). Initially, and whenever it delivers a message to U_2, P_2 sets *old* to *pending*. When *count(m)* exceeds *old*, P_2 can output m.

The code for the Layer 1 protocol to implement $I_{1,2}$ follows. Of course, the code for $I_{2,1}$ is symmetric. In this description, we use M for the high-level message alphabet of the Layer 1 protocol.

Probe Layer 1, process P_1:

Signature:

Input:
  $SEND(m)_{1,2}$, $m \in M$
  $receive(\text{"probe"})_{2,1}$

Output:
  $send(m)_{1,2}$, $m \in M$

States:
$latest \in M \cup \{null\}$, initially *null*
$unanswered \in \mathbb{N}$, initially 0

Transitions:

$SEND(m)_{1,2}$
    Effect:
        $latest := m$

$receive($ "probe" $)_{2,1}$
    Effect:
        $unanswered := unanswered + 1$

$send(m)_{1,2}$
    Precondition:
        $unanswered > 0$
        $m = latest$
    Effect:
        $unanswered := unanswered - 1$

Tasks:
$\{send(m)_{1,2} : m \in M\}$

Probe Layer 1, process P_2:

Signature:

Input:
    $receive(m)_{1,2}, m \in M$

Output:
    $RECEIVE(m)_{1,2}, m \in M$
    $send($ "probe" $)_{2,1}$

States:
$pending \in \mathbb{N}$, initially 0
$old \in \mathbb{N}$, initially 0
for every $m \in M$:
    $count(m) \in \mathbb{N}$, initially 0

Transitions:

$RECEIVE(m)_{1,2}$
    Precondition:
        $count(m) > old$
    Effect:
        for all $m' \in M$ do
            $count(m') := 0$
        $old := pending$

$send($ "probe" $)_{2,1}$
    Precondition:
        $true$
    Effect:
        $pending := pending + 1$

$receive(m)_{1,2}$
    Effect:
        $count(m) := count(m) + 1$

Tasks:
$\{RECEIVE(m)_{1,2} : m \in M\}$
$\{send($ "probe" $)_{2,1}\}$

The channels $C_{1,2}$ and $C_{2,1}$ used by the Layer 1 protocol do not duplicate messages, but can reorder and lose messages. Formally, their specifications are given in terms of a *cause* function, as in Section 14.1.2. In this case, the *cause* function is required to be one-to-one but need not be onto or monotonic. However, message loss is limited by the WLL condition. Channels $C_{1,2}$ and $C_{2,1}$ are any I/O automata (with the appropriate external interfaces) whose fair traces satisfy this specification. The full Layer 1 protocol is obtained by composing P_1, P_2, and the two channels.

The following lemma says that Layer 1 of the *Probe* protocol, with the given nonduplicating channels, implements the intermediate channel $I_{1,2}$.

Lemma 22.9 *Layer 1 of the Probe protocol, using any nonduplicating channels (as defined by $C_{1,2}$ and $C_{2,1}$ above), implements the intermediate channel $I_{1,2}$, in the following sense: For every fair execution α, $\alpha|ext(I_{1,2}) \in traces(I_{1,2})$.*

Proof Sketch. We first show that $I_{1,2}$ does not reorder messages. To see that this is the case, note that when P_2 performs any *RECEIVE* after the first one, it checks that $count(m) > old$, where m is the high-level message being delivered. The management of the *old* variable, plus the facts that P_1 only sends messages in response to *probes* and that the channels do not duplicate messages, imply that there were at most *old* low-level messages in transit from P_1 to P_2 at the point of the preceding *RECEIVE* event. Therefore, at least one of the messages containing m must have been sent by P_1 since the preceding *RECEIVE* event. This implies that m must have been the value of $latest_1$ at some point after the preceding *RECEIVE* event. This implies that no reordering occurs.

It remains to show that $I_{1,2}$ guarantees the WLL condition—that if there are infinitely many *SEND* events, then infinitely many of them must have corresponding *RECEIVE* events. So suppose that there are infinitely many *SEND* events. Then the fact that P_2 keeps sending *probes*, the fact that P_1 keeps responding to received *probe* messages, the liveness assumptions for the channels, and the finiteness of the high-level message alphabet M all combine to imply that P_2 performs infinitely many *RECEIVE* events. But as we argued in the previous paragraph, any message that is delivered to U_2 after the first one must in fact have been the value of $latest_1$ at some point after the previous *RECEIVE* event. This is enough to imply that the *RECEIVE* events must correspond to infinitely many different *SEND* events. $\qquad\square$

Now we consider the complete *Probe* protocol. As described earlier, each process is the composition of a Layer 2 process and two Layer 1 processes, as depicted in Figure 22.3. Each channel is "multiplexed" to implement one channel of each of the two Layer 1 protocols.

The channels needed for the complete *Probe* protocol are similar to the channels $C_{1,2}$ and $C_{2,1}$ used for the Layer 1 implementations in that they cannot duplicate messages but can reorder and lose messages. Formally, the channel specifications are given in terms of a *cause* function, as in Section 14.1.2. As for $C_{1,2}$ and $C_{2,1}$, the *cause* function is required to be one-to-one but need not be onto or monotonic.

However, it turns out that we need a slightly stronger loss limitation condition than the WLL condition used in channels $C_{1,2}$ and $C_{2,1}$. Namely, each channel of the complete *Probe* protocol must satisfy the WLL condition for *each* of the two channels it implements. We do something simpler and more conservative— we require the SLL condition. (This actually guarantees SLL for each of the two implemented channels.) See Exercise 14.7 for a description of the channel multiplexing strategy.

Now the channels are any I/O automata (with the appropriate external interfaces) whose fair traces satisfy these new channel specifications. The full *Probe* protocol is obtained by composing P_1, P_2, and the two channels.

The following theorem says that the full *Probe* protocol, with the given nonduplicating SLL channels, guarantees reliable FIFO delivery.

Theorem 22.10 *The Probe protocol, using any nonduplicating SLL channels (as described above), implements the reliable FIFO channel F, in the following sense:*
For every fair execution α, $\alpha|ext(F) \in fairtraces(F)$.

Proof. This follows from the correctness of the implementations of Layer 1 (as proved in Lemma 22.9) and Layer 2. Note that the SLL condition for each of the given channels implies the weaker WLL conditions for each of the two Layer 1 channels it implements. □

Complexity analysis. We do not attempt a formal complexity analysis of the *Probe* protocol (nor for the other protocols in this chapter). However, notice that the *Probe* protocol has a serious complexity problem: it can require more and more low-level messages to deliver later and later high-level messages. More specifically, in the Layer 1 protocol, once k low-level messages have been lost, it requires at least $k + 1$ low-level messages to deliver each subsequent high-level message, even if no further losses occur. In the following subsection, we consider whether it is possible to avoid this cost.

22.4.3   Nonexistence of Efficient Protocols Tolerating Loss and Reordering

We have just described the *Probe* protocol, which implements reliable FIFO communication using channels that can lose and reorder, but not duplicate, messages. In this section, we show that any protocol that accomplishes this *must* incur the sort of cost that the *Probe* protocol exhibits, requiring more and more low-level messages to deliver later and later high-level messages.

As for our previous impossibility result, Theorem 22.8, we base our formal statement on an axiomatic characterization of the trace properties defining the allowed channel behavior. We use the general terminology introduced in Section 22.4.1 to describe the interaction between process automata and channel trace properties, in particular, the definition of an execution of $P_1 \times P_2$ being *consistent with* a trace property for either channel interface and the definition of a finite execution α of $P_1 \times P_2$ being *finitely consistent with* a trace property.

For this subsection, we fix $Q_{1,2}$ to be the trace property with inputs $send(m)_{1,2}$, $m \in M'$, and outputs $receive(m)_{1,2}$, $m \in M'$, and whose traces are exactly those containing no duplication and whose losses are limited by the SLL condition. Arbitrary reordering is allowed. Let $Q_{2,1}$ be the analogous trace property, for the opposite channel direction. Then we just say that executions are *consistent* and *finitely consistent*, without explicitly mentioning the channel trace properties.

The *Probe* protocol works (i.e., implements reliable FIFO communication) using any channels satisfying these specifications. We show that any protocol that does this must be costly, in terms of the number of low-level messages needed to deliver later high-level messages. To do this, we need a precise definition of cost.

First, we say that a finitely consistent execution α of $P_1 \times P_2$ is *complete* if the number of *SEND* events is equal to the number of *RECEIVE* events in α. This means that the protocol has succeeded in delivering to U_2 all the high-level messages that have been submitted by U_1.

The following definition expresses the idea that, in order to successfully deliver any high-level message, the protocol only needs *in the best case* to send a *bounded* number of low-level messages. If α is a complete execution, $k \in \mathbb{N}^+$, and $m \in M$, then we say that an extension α' is a *k-extension* of α for m provided that the following conditions hold:

1. In the portion of α' after α, the user-interface events are exactly the two events $SEND(m)_{1,2}$ and $RECEIVE(m)_{1,2}$. (This means that exactly one high-level message, m, is sent by user U_1 and delivered successfully to U_2, in the portion of α' after α. This condition implies that α' is also a complete execution.)

2. All low-level messages received by P_2 in α' after α are sent after α. (That is, no old low-level messages are received.)

3. The number of $receive_{1,2}$ events in α' after α is less than or equal to k.

A protocol is *k-message-bounded* if for every complete execution α and every $m \in M$, there is a k-extension of α for m. A protocol is *message-bounded* if it is k-message-bounded for some $k \in \mathbb{N}^+$.

Thus, a message-bounded protocol satisfies only a very minimal requirement on its cost: that in the best case, presumably where no further low-level messages are lost, the number of low-level messages needed to deliver a high-level message should not grow without bound. But even though this requirement is so weak, we can still show that there is no message-bounded protocol that implements reliable FIFO communication using channels that can lose and reorder messages.

Theorem 22.11 *There is no message-bounded, bounded tag protocol (P_1, P_2) that implements F using the lossy, reordering channels $Q_{1,2}$ and $Q_{2,1}$ (in the sense that if α is a consistent fair execution of $P_1 \times P_2$, then $\alpha|ext(F) \in fairtraces(F)$).*

Proof. Assume for the sake of contradiction that there is such a protocol, (P_1, P_2), and fix k such that (P_1, P_2) is k-message-bounded.

Suppose that we could produce a multiset T of elements of M', a complete execution α of $P_1 \times P_2$, and a k-extension α' of α (for any m) satisfying both of the following conditions:

1. All the messages in T are "in transit" (i.e., they have been sent but not received) from P_1 to P_2 after the execution α.[1]

2. The multiset of low-level messages received by P_2 in the portion of α' after α is a submultiset of T.

In this case, we could derive a contradiction as follows. Using a construction similar to the one in the proof of Theorem 22.8, we produce an alternative finitely consistent execution α_1 such that all of the following hold:

1. α_1 is an extension of α.

2. α_1 is indistinguishable from α to P_1.

3. α_1 is indistinguishable from α' to P_2.

---

[1]The multiset of messages that are sent but not received is uniquely determined by the execution α.

We do this by preventing all events involving P_1 immediately after α while allowing all events of P_2 to proceed exactly as in α'. We can do this, because the additional *receive* events of P_2 can be generated by the low-level messages that are already in transit from P_1 to P_2 after α. Then a contradiction is reached as in the proof of Theorem 22.8, by generating a fair, consistent execution with more *RECEIVE* events than *SEND* events.

Thus, it would be enough to manufacture this bad situation. The following key claim says that if a multiset T of low-level messages is in transit from P_1 to P_2, then either the bad situation already exists, or else we can increase T to a larger multiset T'.

Claim 22.12 *Suppose α is a complete execution and T is a multiset of low-level messages in transit from P_1 to P_2 after α, where T contains at most k copies of any element. Then at least one of the following conditions holds:*

1. *There is a k-extension α' of α (for some m) such that the multiset of low-level messages received by P_2 in α' after α is a submultiset of T.*

2. *There is a complete extension α' of α and a new multiset T' of low-level messages in transit from P_1 to P_2 after α', where T' contains at most k copies of any element and $T \subset T'.$[2]*

First suppose that Claim 22.12 is true. We show that, in this case, it is possible to manufacture the bad situation described earlier, which we already said was enough to prove the theorem. For this, we define two sequences, a sequence $\alpha_0, \alpha_1, \ldots$ of complete executions, and a sequence $T_0, T_1, \ldots$ of multisets of low-level messages, each with at most k copies of any element. Each α_i is an extension of the previous one, and for each i, we have $T_i \subset T_{i+1}$. Moreover, for each i, the multiset T_i is in transit from P_1 to P_2 after α_i.

We begin with α_0 consisting simply of initial states for P_1 and P_2, and T_0 equal to the empty multiset. If Case 1 in Claim 22.12 holds, then we have produced the bad situation and we are done. Otherwise, Case 2 of Claim 22.12 must hold. In this case, let $\alpha_1 = \alpha'$ and let $T_1 = T'$. In general, if Case 1 holds for α_i and T_i, then we are done; otherwise we can use Case 2 to define α_{i+1} and T_{i+1}.

Now we claim that Case 1 must eventually hold. For, if not, Case 2 holds for every i, and we produce two infinite sequences. In particular, we obtain an infinite chain $T_0 \subset T_1 \subset T_2 \subset \cdots$. But since each T_i is defined to have at most k copies of each element of M', this chain cannot have more than $k|M'|+1$

---

[2]This says that T is a proper submultiset of T', that is, that there is at least one more copy of at least one element of M' in T' than there is in T.

terms. This is finite, because we have assumed that $|M'|$ is finite. So Case 1 must eventually hold, as claimed.

So it remains only to prove Claim 22.12.

Proof (of Claim 22.12). Fix an arbitrary $m \in M$ and obtain a k-extension α' of α for message m; this is possible because the protocol is assumed to be k-message-bounded. If the multiset of low-level messages received by P_2 in α' after α is a submultiset of T, then Case 1 is satisfied and we are done. So assume that this is not the case. Then there is some $p \in M'$ for which the number of new $receive(p)_{1,2}$ events in α' after α is strictly greater than the number of copies of p in T. Let $T' = T \cup \{p\}$ (using union of multisets). Since α' is a k-extension, the number of these new $receive(p)_{1,2}$ events is at most k, which implies that the number of copies of each element in T' is still at most k. We obtain a complete extension of α that leaves T' in transit.

We know that there is at least one $send(p)_{1,2}$ event in α' after α, since all low-level messages received by P_2 after α' are assumed to be sent after α'. Let α_1 be the prefix of α' ending with the first such $send(p)_{1,2}$ event; then α_1 is a finitely consistent extension of α. Then the multiset T' of low-level messages is in transit after α_1. If α_1 contains either both or neither of the new $SEND(m)_{1,2}$ event and the $RECEIVE(m)_{1,2}$ event, then α_1 is complete and thus satisfies Case 2.

The remaining case is where α_1 contains only the $SEND(m)_{1,2}$ event but not the $RECEIVE(m)_{1,2}$ event. In this case, we extend α_1 to a finitely consistent α_2 containing one additional $RECEIVE(m)_{1,2}$ event, but in which no low-level message from T' is received by P_2. We can achieve this because of the following basic fact: Any finitely consistent execution of $P_1 \times P_2$ can be extended to a fair, consistent execution in such a way that no new $SEND_{1,2}$ events occur and all new $receive_{1,2}$ events are caused by new $send_{1,2}$ events. Applying this fact to α_1, we obtain a fair, consistent extension α_3 of α_1, which, because of the correctness conditions, must contain a $RECEIVE(m)_{1,2}$ event corresponding to the last $SEND(m)_{1,2}$. The needed complete execution α_2 is the prefix of α_3 ending with this $RECEIVE$ event. $\square$

The proof of Theorem 22.11 is now complete. $\square$

22.5 Tolerating Crashes

The results presented so far in this chapter settle pretty much every question regarding the implementability of reliable FIFO communication using unreliable channels, at least if the processes are assumed to be reliable. With only two nodes, there is not much point in considering stopping failures or Byzantine failures of processes. It is useful, however, to consider what happens when processes can *crash* and later *recover*. If a process crash amounts simply to stopping and a subsequent recovery involves simply resuming where the process left off, then a process that crashes and recovers is formally no different from a correct process that pauses for a while. However, if a process crash involves loss of some or all of the information in the state, then new considerations arise.

In this section, we consider the reliable FIFO communication problem in the presence of processes that can *crash*, losing information, and later *recover*. The processes in this setting model physical processors that have volatile memory, or a combination of stable and volatile memory. In a crash of such a processor, all contents of volatile memory are lost. Recovery involves resuming from the previous state of stable memory, together with some default state of volatile memory. The first thing that is normally done when a processor recovers is that a *recovery protocol* is run, using the information in stable memory to restore the volatile memory to some sensible state. In the formal model, we treat the whole recovery protocol as a single *recover* step.

In Section 22.5.1, we show the impossibility of implementing, in the presence of crashes, the same type of reliable FIFO communication that we considered for reliable processes. This motivates weakening the problem requirements for the new setting. In Section 22.5.2, we give a second impossibility result, this time for a much weaker problem statement. Finally, in Section 22.5.3, we present a practical algorithm that tolerates crashes as well as unreliable channels.

Throughout this section, we assume that each process P_i has an additional input action $CRASH_i$ and an additional output action $RECOVER_i$, this latter considered to comprise a new task. The occurrence of a $CRASH_i$ is assumed to enable a corresponding $RECOVER_i$ and to disable all other locally controlled actions until a $RECOVER_i$ occurs. It follows that such a $RECOVER_i$ must eventually occur, in any fair execution of P_i. We assume that, in the interval between a $CRASH_i$ and the next $RECOVER_i$, any inputs that occur (including additional $CRASH_i$ events) have no effect on the state.

The new interfaces are depicted in Figure 22.4.

22.5.1   A Simple Impossibility Result

We consider the case where the $RECOVER_i$ action sets the entire state of process P_i back to an arbitrary start state. Thus, in this case, a $CRASH_i$ and subsequent $RECOVER_i$ cause all state information to be lost. In such a model, it is not hard to see that it is impossible to solve the reliable FIFO communication problem, even if the underlying channels themselves are reliable FIFO channels!

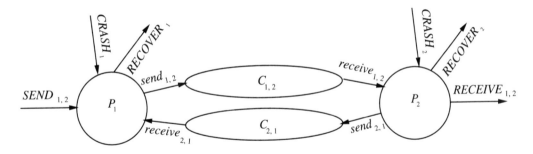

Figure 22.4: External interfaces of processes that crash.

Theorem 22.13 *There is no protocol in the given crash failure model that implements F using reliable FIFO channels (in the sense that for every fair execution α, $\alpha|ext(F) \in fairtraces(F)$).*

Proof. Assume for the purpose of obtaining a contradiction that there is such a protocol. The basic idea of the proof is that after a crash of P_2, the protocol is unable to tell whether or not a high-level message has just been delivered to U_2.

Let α_1 be any fair execution of the protocol in which a single *SEND* event occurs but no *CRASH* event occurs. Then correctness implies that the *SEND* event is followed by a later corresponding *RECEIVE* event. Let α_2 be the prefix of α_1 ending just *before* this *RECEIVE* event and let α_2' be the prefix ending just *after* the *RECEIVE* event.

Now let α_3 be an extension of α_2 with a single $CRASH_2$ event followed immediately by a corresponding $RECOVER_2$ event. Then α_3 can be extended to a fair execution α_4 containing no further *SEND* events or crashes. Since α_4 must also satisfy the correctness conditions, α_4 must contain a *RECEIVE* event corresponding to the *SEND* event in α_4, and this *RECEIVE* must occur sometime after the *CRASH* and *RECOVER* events.

Now we construct an alternative fair execution α_5. Execution α_5 starts with α_2', then continues with $CRASH_2$ and $RECOVER_2$, and then finishes with the portion of α_4 that comes after the *RECOVER*. Then α_5 is also a fair execution. But α_5 contains two *RECEIVE* events and only one *SEND* event, which contradicts the correctness conditions. ☐

Notice that the proof of Theorem 22.13 still works in a stronger model in which the *CRASH* and *RECOVER* events always occur consecutively and in which only finitely many crashes ever occur.

22.5.2   A Harder Impossibility Result

Theorem 22.13 suggests that the problem statement that we have been using
is too strong for the setting with crashes. The logical thing to do is to try to
weaken the problem statement in order to obtain a version that *can* be solved in
this setting. Unfortunately, it turns out that even when the problem statement
is weakened quite a lot, the problem still cannot be solved. In this section, we
present an impossibility result for a much weaker version of the problem. (Of
course, now the proof is harder.)

The crash model we use is the same as in Section 22.5.1—in particular, all
state information is lost when a process crashes.

We weaken the problem statement by requiring less at the external interface.
Namely, the channel to be implemented permits no duplication but does allow
reordering. For losses, we now only require that a message be delivered if its
SEND event has no following *RECOVER* event. That is, we allow loss of any
message whose *SEND* event precedes any *RECOVER* event. So if there are
infinitely many *CRASH* and *RECOVER* events, no messages are required to be
delivered at all. But if there are only finitely many such events, any message
sent after the last *RECOVER* must be delivered. We use B to denote this
specification (formally, a trace property).

We also weaken the problem statement by assuming more about the channels
to be used in the implementation. Namely, we do not permit duplication or
reordering. All the channels can do is lose messages, with losses limited by the
SLL condition. We use $Q_{1,2}$ and $Q_{2,1}$ to denote the specifications for the two
channels. Now we say that an execution of a protocol is *consistent* or *finitely
consistent* to mean that it has these properties for both of the specific channels
$Q_{1,2}$ and $Q_{2,1}$.

For either of these channel specifications, $Q_{1,2}$ or $Q_{2,1}$, it makes sense to talk
about a *sequence* T of messages being "in transit" at some point in a finitely
consistent execution. This means that T is any *subsequence* of the sequence
of messages that have been sent since the sending of the last message that has
already been delivered (for some *cause* function). A consequence of this definition
is that any sequence T of messages in transit is a possible sequence of messages
that might next be delivered by the channel, even if there are no further *send*
events.

The impossibility result is as follows. It says that there is no protocol using
lossy low-level channels that guarantees communication with no duplication and
with no losses after all crashes and recoveries have ceased.

Theorem 22.14 *There is no protocol* (P_1, P_2) *in the given crash failure model* *that implements B using the lossy channels $Q_{1,2}$ and $Q_{2,1}$ (in the sense that if α is a fair, consistent execution of $P_1 \times P_2$, then $\alpha|ext(B) \in traces(B)$).*

In the proof, we use the notation $\bar{i}$ to denote the opposite process to i, that is, $\bar{1} = 2$ and $\bar{2} = 1$. Also, if α is any finitely consistent execution of $P_1 \times P_2$ and $i \in \{1, 2\}$, then we define

- $in(\alpha, i)$ to be the sequence of low-level messages received by P_i during α

- $out(\alpha, i)$ to be the sequence of low-level messages sent by P_i during α

- $state(\alpha, i)$ to be the state of P_i after α

Proof. Assume for the purpose of obtaining a contradiction that there is such a protocol. The key to the proof is the following claim. It says that for any crash-free finitely consistent execution α, it is possible, using crashes, to create a situation in which both processes have the same states that they have at the end of α, but in which one of the channels has in transit the *entire* sequence of low-level messages sent along that channel in α.

Claim 22.15 *Let α be any crash-free finitely consistent execution. Let $i \in \{1, 2\}$. Suppose that either α contains no steps or the last step in α is a step of P_i. Then there is a finitely consistent execution α' of $P_1 \times P_2$ at the end of which all of the following hold:*

1. *The state of P_i is $state(\alpha, i)$.*

2. *The state of $P_{\bar{i}}$ is $state(\alpha, \bar{i})$.*

3. *The sequence $out(\alpha, i)$ is in transit from P_i to $P_{\bar{i}}$.*

Execution α' may contain CRASH and RECOVER events, but there are no unmatched CRASH events—that is, each CRASH has a following corresponding RECOVER.

Proof (of Claim 22.15). The proof is by induction on the number of steps in α.

Basis: 0 steps. Then $\alpha' = \alpha$ suffices.

Inductive step: k steps, $k > 0$.

If α contains no steps of $P_{\bar{i}}$ then $\alpha' = \alpha$ suffices, so assume that α contains at least one step of $P_{\bar{i}}$. Then let α_1 be the longest prefix of α that ends with a step of $P_{\bar{i}}$. Note that α_1 is a proper prefix of α, because we have assumed that the last step of α is a step of P_i. Note that $state(\alpha, \bar{i}) = state(\alpha_1, \bar{i})$. Also, $in(\alpha, i)$ is a subsequence of $out(\alpha_1, \bar{i})$.

Then by inductive hypothesis, there is a finitely consistent execution α_1' at the end of which the following hold:

1. The state of P_i is $state(\alpha_1, i)$.

2. The state of $P_{\bar{i}}$ is $state(\alpha_1, \bar{i})$.

3. The sequence $out(\alpha_1, \bar{i})$ is in transit from $P_{\bar{i}}$ to P_i.

Moreover, α_1' does not contain any unmatched $CRASH$ events. Since $in(\alpha, i)$ is a subsequence of $out(\alpha_1, \bar{i})$, it is also the case that the sequence $in(\alpha, i)$ is in transit from $P_{\bar{i}}$ to P_i after α_1'.

Now we construct the needed execution α'. Execution α' begins with α_1'. The rest of α' involves P_i only (which is fine because $P_{\bar{i}}$ is already in the needed final state). First, a $CRASH_i$ and a $RECOVER_i$ occur, returning P_i to its initial state in α. Then P_i runs on its own exactly as it does in α, extracting low-level messages from the incoming channel as needed. This is possible because the sequence $in(\alpha, i)$ is in transit from $P_{\bar{i}}$ to P_i after α_1'. This brings the state of P_i to $state(\alpha, i)$ and puts the needed low-level messages, those in $out(\alpha, i)$, in the outgoing channel. Also, α_1' contains no unmatched $CRASH$ events.

Figure 22.5 illustrates the change in system state that occurs when P_i is run after α_1'.   □

Now we use Claim 22.15 to complete the proof of Theorem 22.14. Let α be any crash-free finitely consistent execution containing exactly one $SEND$ event and its corresponding $RECEIVE$ event and assume without loss of generality that α ends with the $RECEIVE$ event.

We construct an execution α_1 whose final process states are the same as those in α but that has a $SEND$ as its last external interface event. (That is, there are no following $SEND$, $RECEIVE$, $CRASH$, or $RECOVER$ events.) First, Claim 22.15 yields a finitely consistent execution α' that ends with the process states equal to $state(\alpha, 1)$ and $state(\alpha, 2)$, respectively, and with $out(\alpha, 2)$ in transit from P_2 to P_1, and that has no unmatched $CRASH$ events. Then we construct α_1 by extending α' as in the inductive step of Claim 22.15, by crashing and recovering P_1, then running it on its own just as in α. (Again, the needed input sequence $in(\alpha, 1)$ is in transit in the incoming channel.) This allows P_1 to reach $state(\alpha, 1)$ again. Note that there is a $SEND$ step, but no other user interface step, in the portion of α_1 after α'. This yields the claimed properties for α_1.

Now we can get a contradiction. Let α_2 be an extension of α_1 to a fair, consistent execution that contains no further $SEND$, $CRASH$, or $RECOVER$ events, and in which every low-level message received after α_1 is sent after α_1.

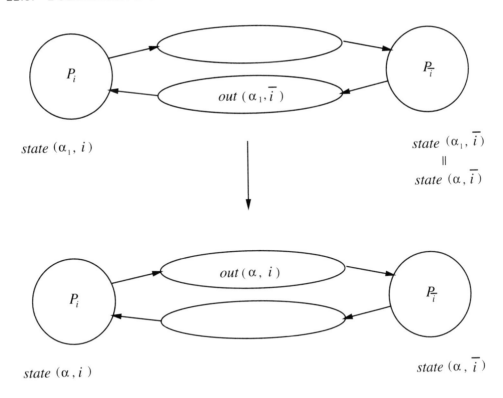

Figure 22.5: Change in system state from α'_1 to α'.

(That is, all old low-level messages are lost.) By the correctness requirements, there is at least one *RECEIVE* event in the suffix, to correspond to the last *SEND* event in α_1. But note that the portion of α_2 after α_1 could also be attached after α, again yielding a fair consistent execution; this is because the two processes are in the same states after α and α_1 and because all old low-level messages are lost. But this violates correctness, since α already has an equal number of *SEND* and *RECEIVE* events (one of each) and the suffix contains at least one more *RECEIVE* but no more *SEND*s. $\qquad\square$

Theorem 22.14 says that it is impossible to solve even a very weak version of the reliable FIFO message-delivery problem, if we have to contend with crashes that lose all state information.

22.5.3 A Practical Protocol

In spite of the impossibility results given in the last two subsections, it is important in practice to have message-delivery protocols that guarantee some sort of reliable FIFO message delivery in spite of process crashes. In this section, we describe one important protocol, the *FivePacketHandshake protocol*. This protocol is the standard method for setting up network connections, used in TCP, ISO TP-4, and many other transport protocols. We use the word "packet" in this subsection synonymously with "low-level message."

The *FivePacketHandshake* protocol satisfies the correctness specification B of Section 22.5.2, which allows no duplication and requires that messages submitted after the last *RECOVER* not be lost. In fact, it guarantees more, in that it does not reorder messages. It tolerates not only process crashes, but also a wide range of channel failures. The reason that this does not contradict the impossibility result of Theorem 22.14 is that *FivePacketHandshake* depends on the ability of the system to provide unique identifiers (UIDs) for messages, which can be thought of (and modelled formally) as a kind of stable memory.

Why is it reasonable to model UIDs in terms of stable memory? The key property of UIDs is that no UID is ever generated twice, even if there is an intervening crash. In the formal model, we can express this abstractly by allowing the protocol to remember, even after a crash, which UIDs have previously been generated, and to check that it never generates any of them a second time. More specifically, we can keep a component *used* in the protocol state, containing all the UIDs that have ever been generated. When the protocol chooses a new UID, it picks one that is not already in the *used* set. The *used* set is assumed to survive crashes, that is, to reside in stable memory.

In reality, there are many different ways to generate UIDs—for example, using a random number generator or a real-time clock. However, it turns out to be simple and informative to model all these techniques formally by keeping the used UIDs in stable memory.

We permit the underlying channels to lose, duplicate, and reorder messages. However, we permit only finite duplication, and the losses are limited by the SLL condition.

FivePacketHandshake protocol (informal):

P_1 maintains a buffer of high-level messages submitted by U_1, as in *Stenning* and *ABP*, and works on getting the messages to P_2 one at a time.

This time, for each high-level message that P_1 tries to send, there is an initial two-way exchange of packets (low-level messages) between P_1 and P_2 to establish a commonly accepted message identifier. In this exchange, P_1 first sends a new UID v to P_2 in a (*"needuid"*, v) packet. P_2 pairs this UID v with another new UID u and sends the pair (u, v) back to P_1 in an (*"accept"*, u, v) packet. P_1 can recognize that this packet is recent

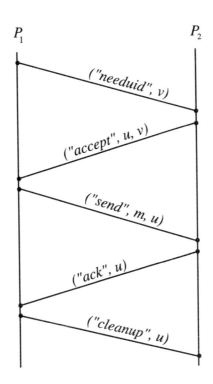

Figure 22.6: The five packets of the *FivePacketHandshake* protocol.

because it contains P_1's latest UID v. P_1 then chooses u as the UID for the high-level message it is trying to send.

Now P_1 sends the latest high-level message m to P_2, paired with the new UID u, in a (*"send"*, m, u) packet. P_2 can recognize that the packet is recent because it contains P_2's latest UID u. After accepting a message, P_2 sends an acknowledgment packet of the form (*"ack"*, u).

The fifth packet, of the form (*"cleanup"*, u), is used by P_1 to tell P_2 when it should discard a current UID.

The five packets of the *FivePacketHandshake* protocol are illustrated in Figure 22.6.

The code follows. For convenience, we include a component *used* in *each* process state containing all the UIDs that have ever been generated by that process. The *used* components are the only components to survive crashes.

FivePacketHandshake, process P_1:

Signature:

Input:

    $SEND(m)_{1,2}$, $m \in M$

    $receive(p)_{2,1}$, $p \in \{(\text{``accept''}, u, v) : u, v \text{ UIDs}\} \cup \{(\text{``ack''}, u) : u \text{ a UID}\}$

    $CRASH_1$

Output:

    $send(p)_{1,2}$, $p \in \{(\text{``needuid''}, v) : v \text{ a UID}\} \cup \{(\text{``send''}, m, u) : m \in M, u \text{ a UID}\}$

        $\cup \{(\text{``cleanup''}, u) : u \text{ a UID}\}$

    $RECOVER_1$

Internal:

    $choose(v)_i$, v a UID

States:

$status \in \{idle, needuid, send, crashed\}$, initially $idle$

$buffer$, a FIFO queue of M, initially empty

$uid\text{-}v$, a UID or $null$, initially $null$

$uid\text{-}u$, a UID or $null$, initially $null$

$used$, a set of UIDs, initially empty

$send\text{-}buffer$, a FIFO queue of packets, initially empty

Transitions:

$SEND(m)_{1,2}$
    Effect:
        if $status \neq crashed$ then
            add m to $buffer$

$choose(v)_1$
    Precondition:
        $status = idle$
        $buffer$ is nonempty
        $v \notin used$
    Effect:
        $uid\text{-}v := v$
        $used := used \cup \{v\}$
        $status := needuid$

$send(\text{``needuid''}, v)_{1,2}$
    Precondition:
        $status = needuid$
        $v = uid\text{-}v$
    Effect:
        none

$receive(\text{``accept''}, u, v)_{2,1}$
    Effect:
        if $status \neq crashed$ then
            if $status = needuid$
                and $uid\text{-}v = v$ then
            $uid\text{-}u := u$
            $status := send$
            else if $uid\text{-}u \neq u$ then
                add $(\text{``cleanup''}, u)$ to $send\text{-}buffer$

$send(\text{``send''}, m, u)_{1,2}$
    Precondition:
        $status = send$
        m is first on $buffer$
        $u = uid\text{-}u$
    Effect:
        none

receive("ack", u)$_{2,1}$
    Effect:
        if *status* $\neq$ *crashed* then
           if *status* = *send*
             and *u* = *uid-u* then
               remove first element of *buffer*
               uid-v := *null*
               uid-u := *null*
               status := *idle*
               add ("cleanup", u) to *send-buffer*

send("cleanup", u)$_{1,2}$
    Precondition:
        status $\neq$ *crashed*
        ("cleanup", u) is first on *send-buffer*
    Effect:
        remove first element of *send-buffer*

$CRASH_1$
    Effect:
        status := *crashed*

$RECOVER_1$
    Precondition:
        status = *crashed*
    Effect:
        buffer := empty sequence
        uid-v := *null*
        uid-u := *null*
        send-buffer := empty sequence
        status := *idle*

Tasks:
$\{send(\text{ "neeuid"}, v)_{1,2} : v \text{ a UID}\}$
$\{send(\text{ "send"}, m, u)_{1,2} : m \in M, u \text{ a UID}\}$
$\{send(\text{ "cleanup"}, u)_{1,2} : u \text{ a UID}\}$
$\{RECOVER_1\}$
$\{choose(v)_1 : v \text{ a UID}\}$

FivePacketHandshake, process P_2:

Signature:

Input:
    $receive(p)_{1,2}, p \in \{(\text{ "neeuid"}, v) : v \text{ a UID}\} \cup \{(\text{ "send"}, m, u) : m \in M, u \text{ a UID}\}$
        $\cup \{(\text{ "cleanup"}, u) : u \text{ a UID}\}$
    $CRASH_2$
Output:
    $RECEIVE(m)_{1,2}, m \in M$
    $send(p)_{2,1}, p \in \{(\text{ "accept"}, u, v) : u, v \text{ UIDs}\} \cup \{(\text{ "ack"}, u) : u \text{ a UID}\}$
    $RECOVER_1$

States:
status $\in \{idle, accept, rcvd, ack, crashed\}$, initially *idle*
buffer, a FIFO queue of M, initially empty
uid-v, a UID or *null*, initially *null*
uid-u, a UID or *null*, initially *null*
last, a UID or *null*, initially *null*
used, a set of UIDs, initially empty
send-buffer, a FIFO queue of packets, initially empty

Transitions:

$receive(\text{"needuid"}, v)_{1,2}$
    Effect:
        if $status = idle$ then
            $u := $ any UID $\notin used$
            $used := used \cup \{u\}$
            $uid\text{-}v := v$
            $uid\text{-}u := u$
            $status := accept$

$send(\text{"accept"}, u, v)_{2,1}$
    Precondition:
        $status = accept$
        $u = uid\text{-}u$
        $v = uid\text{-}v$
    Effect:
        none

$receive(\text{"send"}, m, u)_{1,2}$
    Effect:
        if $status \neq crashed$ then
           if $status = accept$
              and $u = uid\text{-}u$ then
              add m to $buffer$
              $last := u$
              $status := rcvd$
           else if $u \neq last$ then
              add $(\text{"ack"}, u)$ to $send\text{-}buffer$

$RECEIVE(m)_{1,2}$
    Precondition:
        $status = rcvd$
        m is first on $buffer$
    Effect:
        remove first element of $buffer$
        $status := ack$

$send(\text{"ack"}, u)_{2,1}$
    Precondition:
        $status \neq crashed$
        $(status = ack$ and $last = u)$
           or $(\text{"ack"}, u)$ is first on $send\text{-}buffer$
    Effect:
        if $(\text{"ack"}, u)$ is first on $send\text{-}buffer$ then
           remove first element of $send\text{-}buffer$

$receive(\text{"cleanup"}, u)_{1,2}$
    Effect:
        if $status = accept$ and $u = uid\text{-}u$
           or if $status = ack$ and $u = last$ then
           $uid\text{-}v := null$
           $uid\text{-}u := null$
           $last := null$
           $status := idle$

$CRASH_2$
    Effect:
        $status := crashed$

$RECOVER_2$
    Precondition:
        $status = crashed$
    Effect:
        $buffer := $ empty sequence
        $uid\text{-}v := null$
        $uid\text{-}u := null$
        $last := null$
        $send\text{-}buffer := $ empty sequence
        $status := idle$

Tasks:
$\{RECEIVE(m)_{1,2} : m \in M\}$
$\{send(\text{"accept"}, u, v)_{2,1} : u, v \text{ UIDs}\}$
$\{send(\text{"ack"}, u)_{2,1} : u \text{ a UID}\}$
$\{RECOVER_2\}$

This code is somewhat tricky. For example, there are two situations in which P_1 adds a *cleanup* packet to its *send-buffer*. One is the "normal" situation described above, in which P_1 has just received an *ack* packet from P_2. The other is when P_1 has just received an (*"accept"*, u, v) packet for a UID u that is not P_1's current *uid-u*; it is possible in this case that P_2 still has u as its current *uid-u* and that a *cleanup* packet may be needed to dislodge it.

Likewise, there are two situations in which P_2 generates an *ack* packet. One is the "normal" situation in which P_2 is in *ack* mode, while the other is when P_2 has just received a (*"send"*, m, u) packet for some "old" u. In this latter situation, it is possible that P_1 still has *status* = *send* and *uid-u* = u and that an *ack* packet may be needed to dislodge u.

The following theorem says that the *FivePacketHandshake* protocol guarantees the specification B, using very weak channel assumptions. Namely, the channels are allowed to lose, reorder, and duplicate messages, subject only to the SLL condition and the finiteness restriction on duplication.

Theorem 22.16 *The FivePacketHandshake protocol, using any finitely duplicating SLL channels, implements the specification B, in the following sense: For every fair execution α, $\alpha|ext(B) \in traces(B)$.*

Proof Sketch. The safety properties—that the protocol does not reorder or duplicate messages—are fairly easy to see. The tricky part of the proof is the liveness argument. It is not at all obvious that this algorithm continues to make progress, delivering successive messages to U_2.

A key piece of the liveness argument deals with the situation where P_1 has *status* = *needuid*, while P_2 has *status* = *accept* but *uid-v* equal to a value v that is different from P_1's current value of *uid-v*. This situation implies that any current *needuid* packet from P_1 is ignored by P_2. We must show that the value v is eventually dislodged from P_2, thereby allowing the current *needuid* packets an opportunity to reach P_2. So suppose that v is never dislodged. Then fairness for P_2 implies that P_2 sends infinitely many (*"accept"*, u, v) packets. Then the channel liveness condition implies that infinitely many of these arrive at P_1, and the code of P_1 implies that each of these causes a (*"cleanup"*, u) packet to be sent. Again by channel liveness, eventually one of these (*"cleanup"*, u) packets must arrive at P_2. This causes v to become dislodged.

But things can get more complicated than this. Note that after v is dislodged, it is possible for P_2 to acquire another value of *uid-v* that is also not the current value at P_1. This can happen if P_1 receives an old *needuid* packet. But then the same argument as above shows that this value of *uid-v* is also dislodged. This can happen any number of times, but since we have assumed that the channels permit only finite duplication, it can happen only finitely many times before a current *needuid* packet finally arrives at P_2. $\square$

Eventual quiescence. An important property of the *FivePacketHandshake* protocol in practice is that in case there are only finitely many *SEND*, *CRASH*, and *RECOVER* events, eventually both processes reach and remain in states that are the same as their initial states, except for the *used* sets. Informally speaking, the protocol eventually "forgets" everything that has happened so far. This means that no memory needs to be reserved for the use of this protocol when it is not actively processing messages from U_1 to U_2. In practice, this allows the same pair of processes in a network to simulate the *FivePacketHandshake* protocol in parallel for a very large number of distinct pairs (U_1, U_2) of users. (The instances of the protocol are combined using I/O automaton composition at each process.) If at any time only a small number of pairs (U_1, U_2) are actively engaged in communication, then the total amount of required memory for all the parallel executions of *FivePacketHandshake* is reasonably small.

Finite UID sets. In practice, the number of available UIDs is very large, but it is not infinite as we have been assuming. For example, UIDs can be chosen to be successively increasing integers modulo n, for some very large number n. This "finite version" of the protocol works correctly (and in fact, its correctness can be proved via a simulation relation relating it to the ordinary *FivePacketHandshake* protocol), provided that by the time the UIDs "wrap around" to reuse a value u, any old packets carrying the same UID u have already been eliminated from the system. It may be possible to assert this in a practical setting, because of known limits on the message-delivery time, local processing time, and rate of submission of high-level messages, or because of an explicit policy of discarding old packets.

22.6 Bibliographic Notes

The ISO layered communication architecture is described in [54, 290, 273]. The *Stenning* protocol is due to Stenning [270]. The *ABP* was first presented by Bartlett, Scantlebury, and Wilkenson [42]. Besides being an interesting and useful protocol on its own, the *ABP* has served as a test case for protocol verification techniques. Correctness proofs for the *ABP* appear, for example, in [177, 59, 229, 38, 146, 260, 280].

The simple impossibility result for reordering and duplication is derived from the work of Wang and Zuck [284]. The *Probe* protocol was developed by Afek, Attiya, Fekete, Fischer, Lynch, Mansour, Wang, and Zuck [4], using ideas from an earlier Probe protocol by Afek and Gafni [5]. An earlier protocol to solve the same problem, but without the modularity presented here, was developed by

Attiya, Fischer, Wang, and Zuck [23]. Afek et al. [4] also proved the impossibility result of Theorem 22.11. Mansour and Schieber [220], Wang and Zuck [284], and Tempero and Ladner [278, 277] proved related impossibility results.

The nontrivial impossibility result for the setting with crashes, Theorem 22.14, is due to Lynch, Mansour, and Fekete [206] and, independently, to Spinelli [268]. The two results are combined into a single paper [112]. Spinelli [268] also proved a number of other results about the implementability of reliable communication. Baratz and Segall [41] showed how to tolerate crashes using a very small amount of stable data and also conjectured the impossibility result for the case without stable data. Attiya, Dolev, and Welch [21] proved related impossibility results.

The *FivePacketHandshake* protocol is one of a series designed by Belsnes [44]; the protocols in the series guarantee stronger correctness conditions and tolerate successively stronger types of faulty behavior on the part of the channels as additional packets are added to the exchange. The *FivePacketHandshake* protocol is the standard protocol for setting up network connections, used in TCP, ISO TP-4, and many other transport protocols. A complete correctness proof for a generalized version of this protocol, plus a proof of another protocol that uses timing, has been carried out by Lampson, Lynch, and Søgaard-Andersen [188, 190, 264].

22.7 Exercises

22.1. Prove Lemma 22.1.

22.2. Show the existence of a simulation relation from the *Stenning* protocol using channels $A_{1,2}$ and $A_{2,1}$ from Example 14.1.2 to F, the corresponding universal reliable FIFO channel. Specifically, if s and u are states of the *Stenning* protocol and F, respectively, then we define $(s, u) \in f$ exactly if the following are true:

(a) If $s.tag_1 = s.tag_2$ then $u.queue$ is obtained by first removing the first element[3] of $s.buffer_1$, then appending the "reduced" $buffer_1$ at the end of $s.buffer_2$.

(b) Otherwise, $u.queue$ is obtained by appending $s.buffer_1$ at the end of $s.buffer_2$.

Prove that f is a simulation relation.

22.3. Use the results of Exercise 22.2 to prove Lemma 22.2. In particular, use the simulation and an execution correspondence to prove the fairness property.

---

[3]Lemma 22.1 implies that $s.buffer_1$ is nonempty in this case.

22.4. Prove Theorem 22.3.

22.5. Consider the *Stenning* protocol with the channels that are like the ones considered in Section 22.2 but that allow infinite duplication. That is, the code for automaton A in Example 14.1.2 is modified by removing the finiteness restriction on the effect of the *send* action.

(a) Show that the protocol no longer works correctly, in particular, that it violates the fairness of the reliable FIFO channel it is supposed to be implementing.

(b) Show how to strengthen the liveness conditions on the channels slightly to restore the correctness of the *Stenning* protocol.

22.6. Prove Lemma 22.4.

22.7. Prove that f in the proof of Lemma 22.5 is a simulation relation.

22.8. Prove Theorem 22.7.

22.9. Design a generalized version of the ABP that uses tags that are integers mod k, $k \geq 2$, instead of integers mod 2. Your new protocol should still use the same (FIFO) channels as ABP and should still implement F. However, in your new protocol, P_1 should be able to send the first p messages at the front of its *buffer* while waiting for an acknowledgment for the first message. In terms of k, what is the largest value of p that you can achieve?

22.10. Show that the ABP still works if the channels are permitted unlimited duplication of messages. The channels still cannot reorder messages, and the losses are limited by the WLL condition.

22.11. Is Theorem 22.8 still true if the channels are constrained to make at most k duplicates of any low-level message, for some known bound k? We still assume that the channels do not lose messages, but are allowed to reorder them arbitrarily. Give either an impossibility proof or an algorithm.

22.12. Fill in the details of the proof of Lemma 22.9. In particular, give a careful definition of the *cause* function and show that it satisfies the required properties for the $I_{1,2}$ specification.

22.13. Suppose that Layer 1 of the *Probe* protocol is modified by adding the line "*pending* := *pending* − 1" to the effect of the *receive*$(m)_{1,2}$ action. Is the resulting protocol still correct? Prove that it is or give a counterexample.

22.14. Prove the fact used in the proof of Claim 22.12, namely that any finitely consistent execution of $P_1 \times P_2$ can be extended to a fair, consistent execution in such a way that no new $SEND_{1,2}$ events occur and all new $receive_{1,2}$ events are caused by new $send_{1,2}$ events.

22.15. Strengthen the result of Theorem 22.11 to include a lower bound on the rate of growth of the best-case number of low-level messages needed to deliver successive high-level messages.

22.16. Suppose that specification B of Section 22.5.2 is weakened so that some messages sent after the last $RECOVER$ are allowed to be lost. However, if there are only finitely many $CRASH$ and $RECOVER$ events, then all messages *after the first k* that are sent after the $RECOVER$ must be delivered. As before, no duplication is permitted, but reordering is allowed.

Using the same channel specifications $Q_{1,2}$ and $Q_{2,1}$ that are used in Section 22.5.2, either extend the impossibility result in Theorem 22.14 to this weaker specification or devise an algorithm that solves the problem.

22.17. *Research Question:* Answer the same question as in Exercise 22.16, but this time weaken the specification B some more, as follows. This time, if there are only finitely many $CRASH$ and $RECOVER$ events, then, *eventually*, all messages that are sent must be delivered.

22.18. Prove that the *FivePacketHandshake* protocol does not reorder or duplicate messages.

22.19. Construct an execution of the *FivePacketHandshake* protocol in which the second type of *ack* packet, produced when P_2 receives an old *send* message, is needed to dislodge a UID from P_1.

22.20. Give a careful proof of the required liveness property of the *FivePacketHandshake* protocol. That is, prove that any message sent after the last $RECOVER$ event must eventually be delivered to U_2.

22.21. Consider the *FivePacketHandshake* protocol in case there are only finitely many $SEND$, $CRASH$, and $RECOVER$ events. Prove that, in this case, eventually both processes reach and remain in states that are the same as their initial states, except for the *used* sets.

22.22. Design an efficient algorithm to implement reliable FIFO communication between two users, in terms of a network based on an arbitrary undirected graph. Assume that there is a process at each node of the graph, as usual, and a reliable FIFO send/receive channel on each edge.

Part III

Partially Synchronous Algorithms

The final part of this book consists of Chapters 23–25. These chapters contain algorithms and lower bound results for the *partially synchronous model*, in which system components have some information about timing, although not complete information as they do in the synchronous model. Such partial information can provide a realistic model of the timing knowledge that is available in real distributed systems.

As usual, the first chapter, Chapter 23, contains our formal model. Then there are only two algorithm chapters: Chapter 24 on *mutual exclusion* in partially synchronous shared memory systems and Chapter 25 on *consensus* in partially synchronous network systems. These chapters represent the beginnings of what is likely to become an interesting new part of the theory of distributed algorithms.

Chapter 23

Modelling V: Partially Synchronous System Models

The final three chapters of this book comprise a short introduction to the study of *partially synchronous*, or *timing-based*, distributed algorithms. Recall that Part I (Chapters 2–7) examined *synchronous* distributed algorithms, while Part II (Chapters 8–22) dealt with *asynchronous* distributed algorithms. It turns out that there is an interesting class of models and algorithms between these two extremes, which we call *partially synchronous*. In a partially synchronous system, the components have some information about time, although the information might not be exact. For example, processes in a partially synchronous network might have access to almost-synchronized clocks, or might know approximate bounds on process step time or message-delivery time.

Partially synchronous models are probably more realistic than either completely synchronous or completely asynchronous models, since real systems typically do use some timing information. However, the theory of partially synchronous systems is not nearly so well developed as the theories of synchronous and asynchronous systems. The ideas that we present here are only the beginning of what we think will be a large amount of interesting research on the foundations of timing-based computing.

In this chapter, we give an introduction to models and proof methods for timing-based distributed algorithms. We begin in Section 23.1 by presenting a *timed automaton* model that we call the *MMT model* after its discoverers, Merritt, Modugno, and Tuttle. The MMT model is a simple variant of the I/O automaton model that is adequate for modelling most timing-based algorithms. In order to use certain basic proof methods—in particular, the invariant and simulation methods—with this model, we find it useful to be able to transform each MMT automaton into another type of automaton that we call a *general timed automaton (GTA)*. We present the GTA model in Section 23.2, along with the transformation from MMT automata to GTAs. In Section 23.3, we discuss verification techniques that can be used with these models.

In Chapters 24 and 25, we give preliminary results about mutual exclusion and consensus in the partially synchronous setting.

23.1 MMT Timed Automata

An MMT timed automaton model is obtained by simply replacing the fairness conditions of the I/O automaton model with lower and upper bounds on time. Notice that replacing the fairness conditions with just upper bounds would not add any interesting power to the model, because upper bounds alone do not restrict the set of executions that are produced by an I/O automaton. (In fact, throughout the "asynchronous" chapters of the book, we have already been associating upper bounds with tasks of an algorithm, in order to analyze time complexity. The usefulness of this analysis depends on the fact that these bounds do not restrict the algorithm's behavior.) However, introducing both lower and upper bounds does give extra power, because this allows us to restrict the set of executions. Indeed, for many timing-based algorithms, correctness depends crucially on the restrictions on executions that are imposed by the time bounds.

23.1.1 Basic Definitions

We start with an I/O automaton A having only finitely many tasks. A *boundmap* b for A is a pair of mappings, *lower* and *upper*, that give lower and upper bounds for all the tasks. For each task C, we require that $lower(C)$ and $upper(C)$ must satisfy the conditions $0 \leq lower < \infty$, $0 < upper(C) \leq \infty$, and $lower(C) \leq upper(C)$. That is, the lower bounds are not allowed to be ∞, the upper bounds are not allowed to be 0, and the lower bounds cannot be greater than the upper bounds. An *MMT automaton* is an I/O automaton A together with a boundmap for A.

Now we define how an MMT automaton executes. A *timed execution* of an MMT automaton $B = (A, b)$ is defined to be a finite sequence $\alpha = s_0, (\pi_1, t_1)$, $s_1, (\pi_2, t_2), \ldots, (\pi_r, t_r), s_r$ or an infinite sequence $\alpha = s_0, (\pi_1, t_1), s_1, (\pi_2, t_2)$, $\ldots, (\pi_r, t_r), s_r, \ldots$, where the s's are states of the I/O automaton A, the π's are actions of A, and the t's are times in $R^{\geq 0}$. We require that the sequence $s_0, \pi_1, s_1, \ldots$—that is, the sequence α with the times ignored—be an ordinary execution of I/O automaton A. We also require that the successive times t_r in α

be nondecreasing and that they satisfy the lower and upper bound requirements expressed by the boundmap b.

What does it mean to satisfy the lower and upper bound requirements? To say this formally, we define r to be an *initial index* for a task C provided that C is enabled in s_r and one of the following is true:

1. $r = 0$.

2. C is not enabled in s_{r-1}.

3. $\pi_r \in C$.

The initial indices represent the points at which we begin to measure the time bounds. Then, for every initial index r for a task C, we require that the following conditions hold. (We let $t_0 = 0$.)

Upper bound: If there exists $k > r$ with $t_k > t_r + upper(C)$, then there exists $k' > r$ with $t_{k'} \leq t_r + upper(C)$ such that either $\pi_{k'} \in C$ or C is not enabled in $s_{k'}$.

Lower bound: There does not exist $k > r$ with $t_k < t_r + lower(C)$ and $\pi_k \in C$.

The upper bound condition says that, from any initial index for a task C, if time ever passes beyond the specified upper bound for C, then in the interim, either an action in C must occur, or else C must become disabled. The lower bound condition says that, from any initial index for C, no action in C can occur before the specified lower bound.

We denote the set of timed executions of B by $texecs(B)$. A state is said to be *reachable* in B if it is the final state of some finite timed execution of B.

The upper and lower bound properties are safety properties. We are also interested in one basic liveness property: we say that a timed execution is *admissible* provided that the following condition is satisfied:

Admissibility: If timed execution α is an infinite sequence, then the times of the actions approach ∞. If α is a finite sequence, then in the final state of α, if task C is enabled, then $upper(C) = \infty$.

The admissibility condition says that time advances normally and that processing does not stop if the automaton is scheduled to perform some more work. We denote the set of admissible timed executions of B by $atexecs(B)$. In this book, we will focus mainly on the admissible timed executions.

Note that in an admissible timed execution, an *upper* bound of ∞ for a task C does not impose any requirement that actions in task C ever occur.

This is somewhat different from what we did in the asynchronous chapters: In Section 8.6, we defined another notion of timed execution which specified that all tasks satisfied the fairness condition and, *in addition*, that some of them satisfied upper time bounds. We used this combined notion in analyzing time complexity. Now we are dropping the fairness conditions entirely and just considering time bounds. It is possible to define a version of the MMT model in which some tasks have time bounds and some have fairness conditions, but we will not do this formally in this book. Instead, we will discuss the issue of combining time bounds and fairness conditions informally, when it arises in particular algorithms.

Some sort of admissibility condition is needed in any useful model for timing-based computing, in order to rule out some rather strange behavior, such as an automaton performing infinitely many outputs in a finite amount of time.[1] Although such executions make some formal sense, they are meaningless in reality and hard to think about. A good model for timed systems should make it possible to avoid thinking about this issue.

In order to describe the external behavior of MMT automata, we define *timed traces*. The *timed trace* of a timed execution α of B, denoted by $ttrace(\alpha)$, is the subsequence of α consisting of all the external actions, each paired with its associated time. The *admissible timed traces* of B, which we denote by $attraces(B)$, are the timed traces of admissible timed executions of B.

MMT automata can be used for describing many types of components in timing-based systems. They are especially good for modelling computer systems at a low level, since the task structure and associated time bounds provide natural ways of modelling physical system components and their speeds. However, they are somewhat less well suited for describing systems at a high level or for providing correctness specifications. This is because their rather stylized conventions about tasks and bounds do not always provide the best "language" for expressing the desired behavior.

Example 23.1.1   Channel MMT automaton

We define an MMT automaton $D_{i,j} = (C_{i,j}, b)$ based on the universal reliable FIFO send/receive channel automaton $C_{i,j}$ of Example 8.1.1. The boundmap b of $D_{i,j}$ imposes an upper bound of d, where d is some fixed positive real, on the delivery time for the oldest message in the channel. It does not impose any lower bound. $D_{i,j}$ is a formal description of a channel we have used frequently in the chapters

---

[1] This behavior is sometimes called *Zeno behavior*, in reference to Zeno's paradox. In Zeno's paradox, the runner Achilles takes infinitely many steps, each successively shorter, approaching closer and closer to his goal (a tortoise) but never quite reaching it.

on asynchronous algorithms in order to carry out time performance analysis.

Thus, if *rec* denotes the single task of $C_{i,j}$, then we define b to be the pair $(lower, upper)$, where $lower(rec) = 0$ and $upper(rec) = d$, for some fixed $d \in R^+$. All of the following are admissible timed traces of $D_{i,j}$:

$$(send(1)_{i,j}, 0), (send(2)_{i,j}, 0), (receive(1)_{i,j}, d), (receive(2)_{i,j}, 2d)$$

$$(send(1)_{i,j}, 0), (send(2)_{i,j}, 0), (receive(1)_{i,j}, 0), (receive(2)_{i,j}, 0)$$

$$(send(1)_{i,j}, 0), (receive(1)_{i,j}, d), (send(2)_{i,j}, d), (receive(2)_{i,j}, 2d),$$
$$(send(3)_{i,j}, 2d), (receive(3)_{i,j}, 3d), \ldots$$

On the other hand, the following are not admissible timed traces of $D_{i,j}$:

$$(send(1)_{i,j}, 0), (send(2)_{i,j}, 0), (receive(1)_{i,j}, d)$$

$$(send(1)_{i,j}, 0), (receive(1)_{i,j}, 2d)$$

$$(send(1)_{i,j}, 0), (receive(1)_{i,j}, d), (send(2)_{i,j}, d), (receive(2)_{i,j}, d),$$
$$(send(3)_{i,j}, d), (receive(3)_{i,j}, d), \ldots$$

The first of these three sequences fails to be an admissible timed trace because it is finite, yet the *rec* task is enabled at the end. In general, any admissible timed execution that contains at least k *send* inputs must also contain at least k corresponding *receive* outputs, because the upper bound condition and the admissibility condition together imply the usual fairness condition for the *rec* task. The second sequence fails to be an admissible timed trace because it violates the upper bound condition. The third sequence fails because it violates the admissibility condition—it does not allow time to increase beyond d, even though an infinite amount of activity occurs.

Example 23.1.2   Timeout MMT automaton

We define an MMT automaton P_2 that awaits the receipt of a message from another process P_1 and, if no such message arrives within a certain amount of time, performs a *timeout* action. P_2 measures the elapsed time by counting a fixed number $k \geq 1$ of its own steps, which are assumed to observe known lower and upper bounds ℓ_1 and ℓ_2, $0 < \ell_1 \leq \ell_2 < \infty$. Its *timeout* is performed at most time ℓ after *count* reaches 0. Notice that we write the lower and upper bounds for each task in the form of a closed interval—we will use this convention frequently.

P_2 automaton:

Signature:

Input: Internal:
    $receive(m)_{1,2}, m \in M$ $decrement$
Output:
    $timeout$

States:

$count \in \mathbb{N}$, initially k
$status \in \{active, done, disabled\}$, initially $active$

Transitions:

$decrement$ $timeout$
    Precondition: Precondition:
        $status = active$ $status = active$
        $count > 0$ $count = 0$
    Effect: Effect:
        $count := count - 1$ $status := done$

$receive(m)_{1,2}$
    Effect:
        if $status = active$ then
          $status := disabled$

Tasks and bounds:

$\{decrement\}$, bounds $[\ell_1, \ell_2]$
$\{timeout\}$, bounds $[0, \ell]$

In an admissible timed execution, P_2 simply decreases its *count*
until $count = 0$ or until a $receive(m)$ occurs to disable the timeout.
After *count* reaches 0, P_2 performs a *timeout* (provided that no *receive* occurs previously). It is not hard to see that, in any timed
execution of P_2, if a *timeout* occurs, then it occurs at some time in
the interval $[k\ell_1, k\ell_2 + \ell]$. Moreover, if a *timeout* occurs, then there
is no previous *receive*. Finally, in an admissible timed execution of
P_2, if no *receive* occurs, then a *timeout* does in fact occur.

Example 23.1.3   Two-task race

We define a simple MMT automaton *Race* with two tasks, *main* and
int (interrupt). The *main* task increments a counter *count* as long as
a Boolean *flag* is *false*. The *int* task simply sets *flag* := *true*. When
flag = *true*, the *main* task decrements *count* until it reaches 0, then

reports completion. The *main* task has associated bounds of ℓ_1 and ℓ_2, $0 < \ell_1 \le \ell_2 < \infty$, while the *int* task just has an upper bound of ℓ.

Race automaton:

Signature:

Input:	Internal:
none	*increment*
Output:	*decrement*
report	*set*

States:

$count \in \mathbb{N}$, initially 0
flag, a Boolean, initially *false*
reported, a Boolean, initially *false*

Transitions:

increment
    Precondition:
        flag = *false*
    Effect:
        $count := count + 1$

decrement
    Precondition:
        flag = *true*
        $count > 0$
    Effect:
        $count := count - 1$

set
    Precondition:
        flag = *false*
    Effect:
        flag := *true*

report
    Precondition:
        flag = *true*
        $count = 0$
        reported = *false*
    Effect:
        reported := *true*

Tasks and bounds:
$main = \{increment, decrement, report\}$, bounds $[\ell_1, \ell_2]$
$int = \{set\}$, bounds $[0, \ell]$

In every admissible timed execution of *Race*, a *report* eventually occurs. In Section 23.3.3, we will sketch a proof that this *report* must occur by time $\ell + \ell_2 + L\ell$, where $L = \ell_2/\ell_1$. (L can be regarded as a measure of the *timing uncertainty* in the system.)

23.1.2 Operations

We define composition and hiding operations for MMT automata, analogous to those for I/O automata.

Composition. MMT automata can be composed in much the same way as ordinary I/O automata, by identifying actions having the same name in different automata. However, unlike what we did for I/O automata, we only define composition for a *finite* collection of MMT automata. This is because an MMT automaton is only allowed to have a finite number of tasks.

We define a finite collection of MMT automata to be *compatible* if their underlying I/O automata are compatible, according to the definition of compatibility in Section 8.2.1. Then the *composition* $(A, b) = \prod_{i \in I}(A_i, b_i)$ of a finite compatible collection of MMT automata $\{(A_i, b_i)\}_{i \in I}$ is the MMT automaton defined as follows:

- $A = \prod_{i \in I} A_i$, that is, A is the composition of the underlying I/O automata A_i for all the components.

- For each task C of A, b's *lower* and *upper* bounds for C are the same as those of b_i, where A_i is the unique component I/O automaton having task C.

As for I/O automata, we sometimes use the infix operation symbol $\times$ to denote composition. For instance, if $I = \{1, \ldots, n\}$, then we sometimes write $\prod_{i \in I} A_i$ as $A_1 \times \cdots \times A_n$.

Example 23.1.4   Composition of MMT automata

We consider the composition of three MMT automata. The first is a process P_1 that might be alive or dead (which one is determined nondeterministically by the initial state). If it is alive, it sends messages from a fixed message alphabet M periodically, with intervening times at most $\ell > 0$, on an outgoing channel.

P_1 automaton:

Signature:

Input: Output:
    none $send(m)_{1,2}$, $m \in M$

States:
$status \in \{alive, dead\}$, initially arbitrary

Transitions:

$send(m)_{1,2}$
       Precondition:
             $status = alive$
       Effect:
             none

Tasks and bounds:
$\{send(m)_{1,2} : m \in M\}$, bounds $[0, \ell]$

The other two automata are channel $D_{1,2}$, as defined in Example 23.1.1, and timeout process P_2, as defined in Example 23.1.2. If $k\ell_1 > \ell + d$, then in any admissible timed execution, the composition performs a *timeout* exactly if P_1 is *dead*. Moreover, this *timeout* is performed no later than time $k\ell_2 + \ell$.

We close this subsection with three basic results analogous to Theorems 8.1–8.3. These relate the admissible timed executions and admissible timed traces of a composition to those of the component MMT automata. The first says that an admissible timed execution or admissible timed trace of a composition projects to yield admissible timed executions or admissible timed traces of the component automata.

Let $\{(A_i, b_i)\}_{i \in I}$ be a compatible collection of MMT automata and let $(A, b) = \prod_{i \in I}(A_i, b_i)$. Let B_i denote the MMT automaton (A_i, b_i) for each i and let B denote (A, b). For any timed execution $\alpha = s_0, (\pi_1, t_1), s_1, \ldots$ of B, let $\alpha | B_i$ be the sequence obtained by deleting each pair $(\pi_r, t_r), s_r$ for which π_r is not an action of A_i, and replacing each remaining s_r by $(s_r)_i$, that is, automaton A_i's piece of the state s_r. Also, for any timed trace β of B (or, more generally, any sequence of actions paired with times), let $\beta | B_i$ be the subsequence of β consisting of all the pairs containing actions of A_i.

Theorem 23.1 *Let $\{B_i\}_{i \in I}$ be a compatible collection of MMT automata and let $B = \prod_{i \in I} B_i$.*

1. *If $\alpha \in atexecs(B)$, then $\alpha | B_i \in atexecs(B_i)$ for every $i \in I$.*

2. *If $\beta \in attraces(B)$, then $\beta | B_i \in attraces(B_i)$ for every $i \in I$.*

Proof. The proof is left as an exercise. $\qquad\square$

The other two are converses of Theorem 23.1. The next theorem says that, under certain conditions, admissible timed executions of component MMT automata can be pasted together to form an admissible timed execution of the composition.

Theorem 23.2 *Let $\{B_i\}_{i \in I}$ be a compatible collection of MMT automata and let $B = \prod_{i \in I} B_i$. Suppose α_i is an admissible timed execution of B_i for every $i \in I$ and suppose β is a sequence of (action,time) pairs, where all the actions* *in β are in $ext(A)$, such that $\beta|B_i = ttrace(\alpha_i)$ for every $i \in I$. Then there is an admissible timed execution α of B such that $\beta = ttrace(\alpha)$ and $\alpha_i = \alpha|B_i$ for every $i \in I$.*

Proof.   The proof is left as an exercise. $\square$

The final theorem says that admissible timed traces of component MMT automata can also be pasted together to form an admissible timed trace of the composition.

Theorem 23.3 *Let $\{B_i\}_{i \in I}$ be a compatible collection of MMT automata and let $B = \prod_{i \in I} B_i$. Suppose β is a sequence of (action,time) pairs, where all the actions in β are in $ext(A)$. If $\beta|B_i \in attraces(B_i)$ for every $i \in I$, then $\beta \in attraces(B)$.*

Proof.   The proof is left as an exercise. $\square$

Hiding.   The hiding operation for MMT automata is defined in terms of the hiding operation for ordinary I/O automata, as given in Section 8.2.2. Namely, if $B = (A, b)$ is an MMT automaton and $\Phi \subseteq out(A)$, then $hide_\Phi(B)$ is the MMT automaton $(hide_\Phi(A), b)$. As for I/O automata, this operation simply reclassifies output actions as internal.

23.2   General Timed Automata

The timing restrictions in MMT automata are specified by means of upper and lower bound conditions imposed on executions. An alternative approach is to encode timing restrictions *directly into the states and transitions of the automaton*. This approach has the advantage that it allows some important state-based proof methods, such as the methods of invariant assertions and of simulation relations, to be used to reason about correctness and timing properties of timed systems.

In this section, we describe a second timed automaton model, which we call the *general timed automaton* (*GTA*) model. General timed automata have no "external" timing restrictions—all their time constraints are explicitly encoded into their states and transitions. As we will show, MMT automata can be viewed as a special case of general timed automata, by encoding the timing restrictions. There are GTAs that are not MMT automata, however; in fact, there are some GTAs that exhibit behavior that cannot be exhibited by any MMT automaton.

23.2.1 Basic Definitions

We assume a universal set of *actions*, including special *time-passage actions* $\nu(t)$, $t \in R^+$. The time-passage action $\nu(t)$ denotes the passage of time by the amount t. A *timed signature* S is a quadruple consisting of four disjoint sets of actions: the *input actions* $in(S)$, the *output actions* $out(S)$, the *internal actions* $int(S)$, and the time-passage actions. We define

- the *visible actions*, $vis(S)$, to be the input and output actions, $in(S) \cup out(S)$

- the *external actions*, $ext(S)$, to be the visible and time-passage actions, $vis(S) \cup \{\nu(t) : t \in R^+\}$

- the *discrete actions*, $disc(S)$, to be the visible and internal actions, $vis(S) \cup int(S)$

- the *locally controlled actions*, $local(S)$, to be the output and internal actions, $out(S) \cup int(S)$

- $acts(S)$ to be all the actions of S

A GTA A consists of the following four components:

- $sig(A)$, a timed signature

- $states(A)$, a set of *states*

- $start(A)$, a nonempty subset of $states(A)$ known as the *start states* or *initial states*

- $trans(A)$, a *state transition relation*, where $trans(A) \subseteq states(A) \times acts(sig(A)) \times states(A)$

Unlike I/O automata and MMT automata, GTAs do not have $tasks(A)$ components. As before, we use $acts(A)$ as shorthand for $acts(sig(A))$, and similarly $in(A)$, and so on. There are two simple axioms that A is required to satisfy:

A1: If $(s, \nu(t), s')$ and $(s', \nu(t'), s'')$ are in $trans(A)$, then $(s, \nu(t + t'), s'')$ is in $trans(A)$.

A2: If $(s, \nu(t), s') \in trans(A)$ and $0 < t' < t$, then there is a state s'' such that $(s, \nu(t'), s'')$ and $(s'', \nu(t - t'), s')$ are in $trans(A)$.

Axiom A1 allows repeated time-passage steps to be combined into one step, while Axiom A2 is a kind of converse to A1 that allows a time-passage step to be split in two.

A *timed execution fragment* of a GTA, A, is defined to be either a finite sequence $\alpha = s_0, \pi_1, s_1, \pi_2, \ldots, \pi_r, s_r$ or an infinite sequence $\alpha = s_0, \pi_1, s_1, \pi_2, \ldots, \pi_r, s_r, \ldots$, where the s's are states of A, the π's are actions (either input, output, internal, or time-passage) of A, and $(s_k, \pi_{k+1}, s_{k+1})$ is a transition of A for every k. Note that if the sequence is finite, it must end with a state. A timed execution fragment beginning with a start state is called a *timed execution*.

If α is any timed execution fragment and π_r is any discrete action in α, then we say that the *time of occurrence* of π_r is the sum of all the reals in the time-passage actions preceding π_r in α. We define a timed execution fragment α to be *admissible* provided that the sum of all the reals in the time-passage actions in α is ∞. We denote the set of admissible timed executions of A by $atexecs(A)$. We will mainly consider the admissible timed executions, though we will also sometimes consider the *finite* timed executions, that is, those that are finite sequences. A state is said to be *reachable* in A if it is the final state of a finite timed execution of A.

The *timed trace* of a timed execution fragment α is the sequence of visible events in α, each paired with its time of occurrence. The *admissible timed traces* of A, which we denote by $attraces(A)$, are the timed traces of admissible timed executions of A. Note that an admissible timed trace of A can be finite, even though it is derived from an (infinite) admissible timed execution.

Because of Axioms A1 and A2, there is not much difference between timed execution fragments that differ only by splitting and combining time-passage steps. So we define an equivalence relation on timed execution fragments that says that they are the same except for time-passage. Namely, we say that one timed execution fragment α is a *time-passage refinement* of another timed execution fragment α' provided that α and α' are identical except for the fact that, in α, some of the time-passage steps of α' are replaced with finite sequences of time-passage steps, with the same initial and final states and the same total amount of time-passage. We say that timed execution fragments α and α' are *time-passage equivalent* if they have a common time-passage refinement.

Example 23.2.1   A general timed automaton

We describe a general timed automaton $D'_{i,j}$ that corresponds closely to the MMT automaton $D_{i,j}$ of Example 23.1.1. In particular, it has the same set of admissible timed traces. $D'_{i,j}$ simply encodes the timing restriction of $D_{i,j}$—the upper bound of d on the time to deliver the oldest message in the channel—into its states and transitions. It does this by keeping explicit track of the current time, in a variable *now*, and by keeping track of the latest time at which the next message delivery can occur, in a variable *last*. Note that the values of *last* represent absolute times, not incremental times.

We describe $D'_{i,j}$ using the same sort of precondition-effect notation that we have been using for other automata, only now we include code for the time-passage actions as well as for the discrete actions.

When a *send* event occurs, the *queue* is modified as before, but now, in addition, if there was no previously scheduled message delivery, the *last* variable is set to $now + d$ to reflect the requirement that the next message delivery must occur within time d. When a *receive* occurs, the *last* bound is reset to $now + d$ if the *queue* is still nonempty after the event, to reflect the time requirement for the next message delivery; on the other hand, if the *queue* is emptied, then *last* is set to ∞ to reflect the fact that there is no scheduled message delivery.

The code for the time-passage actions $\nu(t)$ is written in much the same way as that for other actions. The effect of $\nu(t)$ is simply to increase the current time *now* by t. Note that $\nu(t)$ also includes a nontrivial precondition: $now + t \leq last$. This says that time is not allowed to pass beyond the scheduled deadline for the next message delivery. This may at first seem somewhat strange—after all, how can a program or machine block the passage of time? But this style of specification for time-passage actions is just a formal way of saying that the automaton is guaranteed to perform some action before a designated amount of time has elapsed.

$D'_{i,j}$ automaton:

Timed Signature:

Input:
    $send(m)_{i,j}$, $m \in M$
Output:
    $receive(m)_{i,j}$, $m \in M$

Internal:
    none
Time-passage:
    $\nu(t)$, $t \in R^+$

States:
queue, a FIFO queue of elements of M, initially empty
$now \in R^{\geq 0}$, initially 0
$last \in R^+ \cup \{\infty\}$, initially ∞

Transitions:

$send(m)_{i,j}$
    Effect:
        add m to *queue*
        if $|queue| = 1$ then
          $last := now + d$

$\nu(t)$
    Precondition:
        $now + t \leq last$
    Effect:
        $now := now + t$

$receive(m)_{i,j}$
    Precondition:
        m is first on *queue*
    Effect:
        remove first element of *queue*
        if *queue* is nonempty then
          $last := now + d$
        else $last := \infty$

It should not be hard to see that $D'_{i,j}$ has the same set of admissible timed traces as $D_{i,j}$. We leave it as an exercise to show this.

Example 23.2.1 should give you an idea of how MMT automata can be regarded as a special case of general timed automata: the time requirements specified by the boundmap b of an MMT automaton (A, b) can be encoded into the states and transitions of a corresponding GTA. This can be done using *last* state components to keep track of the upper bound requirements, plus additional *first* state components to keep track of the lower bound requirements. We give the detailed construction in Section 23.2.2.

The GTA model is more general than the MMT automaton model, however. The next example contains another channel expressed as a GTA; it turns out that this one cannot be expressed as an MMT automaton.

Example 23.2.2   A non-MMT general timed automaton

We describe another GTA, $D''_{i,j}$, that represents a reliable FIFO channel, but this time the time bound of d is required for *every* message in the channel, not only the oldest. This time, the message-delivery deadlines are stored along with the messages on the *queue* instead of in separate *last* components. The handling of the deadlines is similar, however.

$D''_{i,j}$ automaton:

Timed Signature:

Input:
    $send(m)_{i,j}$, $m \in M$
Output:
    $receive(m)_{i,j}$, $m \in M$

Internal:
    none
Time-passage:
    $\nu(t)$, $t \in R^+$

States:
queue, a FIFO queue of elements of $M \times R^+$, initially empty
$now \in R^{\geq 0}$, initially 0

Transitions:

$send(m)_{i,j}$
    Effect:
        add $(m, now + d)$ to *queue*

$receive(m)_{i,j}$
    Precondition:
        (m, t) is first on *queue*, for some t
    Effect:
        remove first element of *queue*

$\nu(t)$
    Precondition:
        if *queue* is nonempty then
            $now + t \leq t'$, where t' is the time
            in the first pair of *queue*
    Effect:
        $now := now + t$

We claim (and leave it as an exercise to show) that there is no MMT automaton with the same set of admissible timed traces as $D''_{i,j}$. This could be interpreted to mean that $D''_{i,j}$ is not physically implementable. However, as we have seen in earlier chapters, $D''_{i,j}$ can be a convenient abstraction for use in analyzing the time complexity of algorithms when we do not want to bother considering the pileups of messages in the channels.

The next example shows an anomaly: a GTA that has *no* admissible timed executions. Although this is a strange situation, there is nothing in the general model that prevents this. For the special case of MMT automata (and consequently for the GTAs that correspond to MMT automata as described in Section 23.2.2), this anomaly does not occur. (See Exercise 23.1.) Additional restrictions can be added to the GTA model to rule out this situation, but since we will mainly focus in this book on algorithms that can be expressed by MMT automata, we do not describe these restrictions here.

Example 23.2.3   A general timed automaton with no admissible timed executions

Consider a "process automaton" A that sends the same message m infinitely many times. However, successive sending times are closer and closer together, approaching a time limit of 1.

A automaton:

Timed Signature:

Input: Internal:
    none   none
Output: Time-passage:
    $send(m)$ $\nu(t),\, t \in R^+$

States:
$now \in R^{\geq 0}$, initially 0
$last \in R^{\geq 0} \cup \{\infty\}$, initially 0

Transitions:

$send(m)$ $\nu(t)$
    Precondition: Precondition:
        $now = last$ $now + t \leq last$
    Effect: Effect:
        $last := now + \frac{1-now}{2}$ $now := now + t$

In fact, things can be even worse—the definition of a GTA even allows timed automata that have no time-passage steps at all!

The GTA model is not the most general model possible for timing-based computing. For example, it has no features for expressing liveness properties (except for admissibility). Liveness considerations are somewhat less important in the timed setting than they are in the untimed setting, since many liveness conditions (e.g., a condition saying that something eventually happens) can be replaced by corresponding upper time bound conditions (e.g., a condition saying that the event happens within time t). However, sometimes it is useful to be able to express both time bounds and liveness conditions for the same system.

The GTA model is also not general enough to provide detailed descriptions of *hybrid systems*—systems composed of analog physical components as well as discrete computer components. However, the model is sufficient for our purposes in this book.

23.2.2 Transforming MMT Automata into General Timed Automata

We have spoken of the general timed automaton model as a generalization of the MMT timed automaton model. However, this is not formally true, because of the different ways in which they specify timing restrictions: the MMT automaton model uses boundmaps, while the GTA model encodes the restrictions into the states and transitions. In order to view the MMT model as a special case of the GTA model, we need to do some work. In this section, we show how to transform any MMT automaton (A, b) into a naturally corresponding general timed automaton $A' = gen(A, b)$.

The construction is similar to the one used in Example 23.2.1 to obtain $D'_{i,j}$ from $D_{i,j}$. That is, it involves building time deadlines into the state and not allowing time to pass beyond those deadlines while they are still in force. We also add new constraints on non-time-passage actions to express the lower bound conditions.

Specifically, the state of the underlying I/O automaton A is augmented with a *now* component, plus $first(C)$ and $last(C)$ components for each task C. The $first(C)$ and $last(C)$ components represent, respectively, the earliest and latest times at which the next action in task C is allowed to occur. The *now*, *first*, and *last* components all take on values that represent *absolute* times, not incremental times. The time-passage actions $\nu(t)$ are also added.

The *first* and *last* components get updated in the natural way by the various steps, according to the *lower* and *upper* bounds specified by the boundmap b. The time-passage actions $\nu(t)$ have an explicit precondition saying that time cannot pass beyond any of the $last(C)$ values; this is because these represent deadlines for the various tasks. Restrictions are also added on actions in any task C, saying that the current time *now* must be at least as great as the lower bound $first(C)$.

In more detail, the timed signature of $A' = gen(A, b)$ is the same as the signature of A, with the addition of the time-passage actions $\nu(t)$, $t \in R^+$. Each state of A' consists of the following components:

> $basic \in states(A)$, initially a start state of A
> $now \in R^{\geq 0}$, initially 0
> for each task C of A:
>> $first(C) \in R^{\geq 0}$, initially $lower(C)$ if C is enabled in state $basic$, otherwise 0
>> $last(C) \in R^+ \cup \{\infty\}$, initially $upper(C)$ if C is enabled in $basic$, otherwise ∞

The transitions are defined as follows.

If $\pi \in acts(A)$, then $(s, \pi, s') \in trans(A')$ exactly if all the following conditions hold:

1. $(s.basic, \pi, s'.basic) \in trans(A)$.

2. $s'.now = s.now$.

3. For each $C \in tasks(A)$,

   (a) If $\pi \in C$, then $s.first(C) \leq s.now$.

   (b) If C is enabled in both $s.basic$ and $s'.basic$ and $\pi \notin C$, then $s.first(C) = s'.first(C)$ and $s.last(C) = s'.last(C)$.

   (c) If C is enabled in $s'.basic$ and either C is not enabled in $s.basic$ or $\pi \in C$, then $s'.first(C) = s.now + lower(C)$ and $s'.last(C) = s.now + upper(C)$.

   (d) If C is not enabled in $s'.basic$, then $s'.first(C) = 0$ and $s'.last(C) = \infty$.

If $\pi = \nu(t)$, then $(s, \pi, s') \in trans(A')$ exactly if all the following conditions hold:

1. $s'.basic = s.basic$.

2. $s'.now = s.now + t$.

3. For each $C \in tasks(A)$,

   (a) $s'.now \leq s.last(C)$.

   (b) $s'.first(C) = s.first(C)$ and $s'.last(C) = s.last(C)$.

Theorem 23.4 *If (A, b) is any MMT timed automaton, then $gen(A, b)$ is a general timed automaton. Moreover, $attraces(A, b) = attraces(gen(A, b))$.*

Lemma 23.5 *The following hold in any reachable state of $gen(A, b)$ and for any task C of A.*

1. $now \leq last(C)$.

2. If C is enabled, then $last(C) \leq now + upper(C)$.

3. $first(C) \leq now + lower(C)$.

4. $first(C) \leq last(C)$.

Omitting trivial components. If some of the timing requirements specified by b are trivial—that is, if some lower bounds are 0 or some upper bounds are ∞—then it is possible to simplify the automaton $gen(A, b)$ just by omitting mention of these components. We will do this in our examples.

Example 23.2.4   Transformed MMT automaton

Let (A, b) be the composition MMT automaton described in Example 23.1.4, composed of P_1, P_2, and the channel $D_{1,2}$. We give explicit code for the transformed MMT automaton $A' = gen(A, b)$. As just discussed, we omit trivial bounds. Thus, the only bounds we need to incorporate are the upper bounds for all tasks, plus the lower bound for the decrementing task of P_2. We use the following names for the tasks: *send* for the unique task of P_1, *rec* for the unique task of the channel $D_{1,2}$, and *dec* and *timeout* for the two tasks of P_2.

A' automaton:

Timed Signature:

Input:
    none

Output:
    $send(m)_{1,2}$, $m \in M$
    $receive(m)_{1,2}$, $m \in M$
    timeout

Internal:
    decrement

Time-passage:
    $\nu(t)$, $t \in R^+$

States:

$status_1 \in \{alive, dead\}$, initially arbitrary
queue, a FIFO queue of elements of M, initially empty
$count_2 \in \mathbb{N}$, initially k
$status_2 \in \{active, done, disabled\}$, initially *active*

$now \in R^{\geq 0}$, initially 0
$last(send) \in R^+ \cup \{\infty\}$, initially ℓ if $status = alive$, otherwise ∞
$last(rec) \in R^+ \cup \{\infty\}$, initially ∞
$first(dec) \in R^{\geq 0}$, initially ℓ_1
$last(dec) \in R^+ \cup \{\infty\}$, initially ℓ_2
$last(timeout) \in R^+ \cup \{\infty\}$, initially ∞

Transitions:

$send(m)_{1,2}$
    Precondition:
        $status_1 = alive$
    Effect:
        add m to *queue*
        $last(send) := now + \ell$
        if $|queue| = 1$ then
            $last(rec) := now + d$

$receive(m)_{1,2}$
    Precondition:
        m is first on *queue*
    Effect:
        remove first element of *queue*
        if $status_2 = active$ then
            $status_2 := disabled$
        if *queue* is nonempty then
            $last(rec) := now + d$
        else $last(rec) := \infty$
        $first(dec) := 0$
        $last(dec) := \infty$
        $last(timeout) := \infty$

decrement
    Precondition:
        $status_2 = active$
        $count_2 > 0$
        $now \geq first(dec)$
    Effect:
        $count_2 := count_2 - 1$
        if $count_2 > 0$ then
            $first(dec) := now + \ell_1$
            $last(dec) := now + \ell_2$
        else
            $first(dec) := 0$
            $last(dec) := \infty$
            $last(timeout) := \ell$

timeout
    Precondition:
        $status_2 = active$
        $count_2 = 0$
    Effect:
        $status_2 := done$
        $last(timeout) := \infty$

$\nu(t)$
    Precondition:
        $now + t \leq last(send)$
        $now + t \leq last(rec)$
        $now + t \leq last(dec)$
        $now + t \leq last(timeout)$
    Effect:
        $now := now + t$

23.2.3 Operations

Composition. We define a composition operation for general timed automata, generalizing the composition operation we have already defined for MMT automata. First, we define a finite collection $\{S_i\}_{i \in I}$ of timed signatures to be *compatible* if for all $i, j \in I$, $i \neq j$, we have

1. $int(S_i) \cap acts(S_j) = \emptyset$

2. $out(S_i) \cap out(S_j) = \emptyset$

We say that a collection of GTAs is *compatible* if their timed signatures are compatible.

The *composition* $S = \prod_{i \in I} S_i$ of a finite compatible collection of timed signatures $\{S_i\}_{i \in I}$ is defined to be the timed signature with

- $out(S) = \cup_{i \in I} out(S_i)$

- $int(S) = \cup_{i \in I} int(S_i)$

- $in(S) = \cup_{i \in I} in(S_i) - \cup_{i \in I} out(S_i)$

The *composition* $A = \prod_{i \in I} A_i$ of a finite compatible collection of GTAs $\{A_i\}_{i \in I}$ is defined as follows:[2]

---

[2]The $\prod$ notation in the definition of $start(A)$ and $states(A)$ refers to the ordinary Cartesian product, while the $\prod$ notation in the definition of $sig(A)$ refers to the composition of timed signatures just defined. Also, we are here using the notation s_i to denote the ith component of the state vector s.

- $sig(A) = \prod_{i \in I} sig(A_i)$

- $states(A) = \prod_{i \in I} states(A_i)$

- $start(A) = \prod_{i \in I} start(A_i)$

- $trans(A)$ is the set of triples (s, π, s') such that, for all $i \in I$, if $\pi \in acts(A_i)$, then $(s_i, \pi, s_i') \in trans(A_i)$; otherwise $s_i = s_i'$

The transitions of the composition are obtained by allowing all the components that have a particular action π in their signature to participate, simultaneously, in steps involving π, while all the other components do nothing. Note that this implies that all the components participate in time-passage steps, with the same amount of time passing for all of them. Again, we sometimes use the infix operation symbol $\times$ to denote composition.

Theorem 23.6 *The composition of a compatible collection of general timed automata is a general timed automaton.*

Composition versus gen. For a given compatible collection of MMT automata, it turns out that it does not matter whether we compose first and then apply the *gen* transformation to the composition, or first apply the *gen* transformation to the components and then compose. The resulting GTAs are the same, up to isomorphism (of the reachable portions of the machines).

Once again, we obtain projection and pasting theorems analogous to Theorems 8.1–8.3. Let $\{B_i\}_{i \in I}$ be a compatible collection of GTAs and let $B = \prod_{i \in I} B_i$. For any timed execution $\alpha = s_0, \pi_1, s_1, \ldots$ of B, let $\alpha | B_i$ be the sequence obtained by deleting each pair π_r, s_r for which π_r is not an action of B_i, and replacing each remaining s_r by $(s_r)_i$, that is, automaton A_i's piece of the state s_r. Also, for any timed trace β of B (or, more generally, any sequence of actions paired with times), let $\beta | B_i$ be the subsequence of β consisting of all the pairs containing actions of B_i.

Theorem 23.7 *Let $\{B_i\}_{i \in I}$ be a compatible collection of general timed automata and let $B = \prod_{i \in I} B_i$.*

1. *If $\alpha \in atexecs(B)$, then $\alpha | B_i \in atexecs(B_i)$ for every $i \in I$.*

2. *If $\beta \in attraces(B)$, then $\beta | B_i \in attraces(B_i)$ for every $i \in I$.*

Proof. The proof is left as an exercise. $\Box$

The first pasting theorem, Theorem 23.8, has a small technicality that is a consequence of the fact that the GTA model allows consecutive time-passage steps to appear in an execution. Namely, the admissible timed execution α that is produced by "pasting together" individual admissible timed executions α_i might not project to give exactly the original α_i's, but rather admissible timed executions that are time-passage equivalent to the original α_i's.

Theorem 23.8 *Let $\{B_i\}_{i \in I}$ be a compatible collection of general timed automata and let $B = \prod_{i \in I} B_i$. Suppose α_i is an admissible timed execution of B_i for every $i \in I$, and suppose β is a sequence of (action,time) pairs, with all the actions in $vis(B)$, such that $\beta | B_i = ttrace(\alpha_i)$ for every $i \in I$. Then there is an admissible timed execution α of B such that $\beta = ttrace(\alpha)$ and α_i is time-passage equivalent to $\alpha | B_i$ for every $i \in I$.*

Proof.   The proof is left as an exercise.   □

Theorem 23.9 *Let $\{B_i\}_{i \in I}$ be a compatible collection of general timed automata and let $B = \prod_{i \in I} B_i$. Suppose β is a sequence of (action,time) pairs, where all the actions in β are in $vis(A)$. If $\beta | B_i \in attraces(B_i)$ for every $i \in I$, then $\beta \in attraces(B)$.*

Proof.   The proof is left as an exercise.   □

Hiding.   If A is a GTA and $\Phi \subseteq out(A)$, then $hide_\Phi(A)$ is the GTA that is identical to A, except that the actions in Φ are reclassified as internal.

23.3   Properties and Proof Methods

The correctness of timing-based algorithms and systems, as well as their performance, often depends critically on timing assumptions. Unlike in the asynchronous setting, drastic changes of behavior of timing-based algorithms can result from small changes in timing assumptions. However, reasoning about this timing-dependence can be extraordinarily difficult, even for extremely simple "algorithms" such as those in the examples in this chapter. Systematic proof methods can be a great help in this setting.

In this section, we describe two important proof techniques for timing-based algorithms: the method of *invariant assertions* and the method of *simulation relations*. Since these methods have been used so successfully in the synchronous and asynchronous settings, it is natural to try to adapt them for use in the timing-based setting. We also define a notion of *timed trace property*, analogous to the notion of *trace property* introduced in Section 8.5.2.

23.3.1 Invariant Assertions

We define an *invariant assertion* for a general timed automaton A to be any property that is true of all reachable states of A.

This definition is formally the same as the one we used in the asynchronous setting. But there is a difference: In an asynchronous system, the state typically consists of ordinary data such as the values of local and shared variables and sequences of messages in transit in channels. But in a timing-based system, the state typically also contains *timing information* such as the current time and scheduled deadlines for future events. For example, if a message is in transit in a channel, the state may contain information giving the range of future times at which it might be delivered. This means that in the timed setting, invariant assertions may involve timing information in addition to ordinary data.

Although the type of information included in the state is richer in the timed setting, the proof method for invariants is the same as before—induction. This time, the induction is on the number of steps in a timed execution leading to the state in question.

Note that we present the method of invariant assertions in the context of general timed automata. If we want to use this method for an MMT automaton, we must first transform it into a GTA.

Example 23.3.1   Invariant for the timeout system

Consider the timeout system A' of Example 23.2.4, with the assumption that $k\ell_1 > \ell + d$. It would be nice to prove that the system only performs a *timeout* in case the contained process P_1 is actually *dead*. The following invariant assertion can be used to prove this.

Assertion 23.3.1 *In any reachable state of A', if $status_1 = alive$, then $count_2 > 0$.*

Unfortunately, as usual, Assertion 23.3.1 cannot be proved alone by induction—auxiliary assertions are needed. In this case, we first prove the following (by a trivial induction).

Assertion 23.3.2 *In any reachable state of A', if $status_2 = done$, then $count_2 = 0$.*

Then we prove the following strengthened version of Assertion 23.3.1, by a not-so-trivial induction. Notice that this assertion involves statements about the *first* and *last* time components of the state.

Assertion 23.3.3 *In any reachable state of A', if $status_1 = alive$, then the following are true:*

1. $count_2 > 0$

2. *Either last(send) + d < first(dec) + (count$_2$ − 1)ℓ_1, queue is nonempty, or status$_2$ = disabled.*

3. *If queue is nonempty, then either last(rec) < first(dec)+ (count$_2$ − 1)ℓ_1 or status$_2$ = disabled.*

Condition 1 is just a restatement of Assertion 23.3.1. Each of Conditions 2 and 3 uses the expression $first(dec) + (count_2 - 1)\ell_1$ in an inequality. This expression describes the earliest time at which $count_2$ might reach 0, assuming that it is currently positive. That is, $first(dec)$ is the earliest time for the next *decrement,* and there are $count_2 - 1$ additional decrements required to get $count_2$ down to 0, with ℓ_1 as the minimum time for each. Condition 2 says that either a message is scheduled to be sent, in sufficient time to arrive before $count_2$ reaches 0, or else a message is already in transit, or else one has already arrived (thus disabling the timeout). Condition 3 says that if a message is in transit, then either some message will arrive before the $count_2$ reaches 0 or else one has already arrived. Thus, some claims about the timing of events are concisely formulated as invariants, using the *first* and *last* deadline components of the states.

Assertion 23.3.3 can be proved by induction on the number of actions in a timed execution. The argument is straightforward (in fact, boring), but we include it here because it provides a good model for other such proofs.

Basis: Initially, $count_2 = k > 0$, *queue* is empty, and $first(dec) = \ell_1$. These imply Conditions 1 and 3. Moreover, if $status_1 = alive$, then $last(send) = \ell$. So

$$last(send) + d = \ell + d < k\ell_1 = count_2\ell_1 = first(dec) + (count_2 - 1)\ell_1$$

This shows Condition 2.

Inductive step: As usual, we carry out a case analysis based on the different types of actions, only this time, the time-passage actions $\nu(t)$ must also be included in the analysis. Suppose that $(s, \pi, s') \in trans(A')$ and that s satisfies the invariant. Assume that $s'.status_1 = alive$; then also $s.status_1 = alive$.

1. $\pi = send(m)_{1,2}$

   Then $s.first(dec) = s'.first(dec)$, $s.count_2 = s'.count_2$, and $s.status_2 = s'.status_2$. This step does not affect Condition 1 and it makes Condition 2 true. We consider Condition 3. If $s.queue$ is nonempty, then $s.last(rec) = s'.last(rec)$, so Condition 3 for s implies Condition 3 for s'.

So suppose that $s.queue$ is empty. Then by inductive hypothesis (Condition 2), either $s.last(send)+d < s.first(dec)+(s.count_2-1)\ell_1$ or $s.status_2 = disabled$. In the latter case we are done, so assume the former. Then $s'.last(rec) = s.now+d \leq s.last(send)+d$ by Lemma 23.5, $< s.first(dec)+(s.count_2-1)\ell_1 = s'.first(dec)+(s'.count_2 - 1)\ell_1$, which suffices.

2. $\pi = receive(m)_{1,2}$

   By inductive hypothesis, $s.count_2 > 0$. This statement is unaffected by the step, so Condition 1 holds. Also, Assertion 23.3.2 implies that $s.status_2 \neq done$. Therefore, $s'.status_2 = disabled$, which implies Conditions 2 and 3.

3. $\pi = timeout$

   By inductive hypothesis, $s.count_2 > 0$. So $timeout$ is not enabled in s, which says that this case cannot arise.

4. $\pi = decrement$

   For Condition 1, we argue by contradiction. If $s'.count_2 = 0$, then $s.count_2 = 1$, so by inductive hypothesis (Conditions 2 and 3), either $s.last(send) + d < s.first(dec)$, $s.last(rec) < s.first(dec)$, or $s.status_2 = disabled$. By the precondition of $decrement$, the last of these is impossible. So we have that

   $$\min (s.last(send), s.last(rec)) < s.first(dec) \leq s.now.$$

   But $s.now \leq s.last(send)$ and $s.now \leq s.last(rec)$, by Lemma 23.5; thus, $s.now \leq \min (s.last(send), s.last(rec))$. This is a contradiction.

   For Conditions 2 and 3, it is enough to show that the value of $first(dec) + (count_2 - 1)\ell_1$ is not decreased by this step. This follows because the second term is decreased by exactly ℓ_1, while the first term is increased by at least ℓ_1. (This is because $s.first(dec) \leq s.now$ and $s'.first(dec) = s.now + \ell_1$.)

5. $\pi = \nu(t)$

   This step does not affect any of the three conditions, because only now is changed, and now is not mentioned anywhere.

23.3.2 Timed Trace Properties

Recall that many of the properties to be proved for asynchronous systems can be naturally formulated as properties of their traces or fair traces. It turns out that, analogously, many interesting properties of timed systems can be formulated as properties of their admissible timed traces. Properties that can be specified in this way include performance properties as well as ordinary correctness properties.

A *timed trace property* P is defined to consist of the following:

- $sig(P)$, a timed signature containing no internal actions

- $ttraces(P)$, a set of sequences of (action,time) pairs; the time components in each sequence must be monotone nondecreasing, and, if the sequence is infinite, they must be unbounded

We will usually interpret the statement that a GTA A satisfies a trace property P to mean that $in(A) = in(P)$, $out(A) = out(P)$ and $attraces(A) \subseteq ttraces(P)$.

Example 23.3.2   Timed trace property

Let P be the timed trace property defined as follows. The signature $sig(P)$ is

Input:	Internal:
$receive(m)_{1,2}, m \in M$	none
Output:	Time-passage:
$timeout$	$\nu(t), t \in R^+$

The set $ttraces(P)$ of timed traces is exactly the set of sequences β of (action,time) pairs that satisfy the monotonicity and boundedness conditions and are such that,

1. If there is a $(timeout, t)$ pair in β, then $k\ell_1 \leq t \leq k\ell_2 + \ell$.

2. If there is a $timeout$ pair in β, then there is no preceding $receive$ pair.

3. If there is no $receive$ pair in β, then there is a $timeout$ pair in β.

Then $gen(P_2)$, where P_2 is the MMT automaton of Example 23.1.2, satisfies the timed trace property P, in the sense that $attraces(gen(P_2)) \subseteq ttraces(P)$.

23.3.3   Simulations

The simulation method can be used for reasoning about timing-based systems as well as synchronous and asynchronous systems. To do this, we define the notion of a "timed simulation relation" between states of two general timed automata. The definition is very similar to the definition of a simulation relation for I/O automata in Section 8.5.5.

Let A and B be two general timed automata with the same input and output actions. Suppose that f is a binary relation over $states(A)$ and $states(B)$; we use the notation $u \in f(s)$ as an alternative way of writing $(s, u) \in f$. Then f is a *timed simulation relation* from A to B provided that both of the following are true:

1. If $s \in start(A)$, then $f(s) \cap start(B) \neq \emptyset$.

2. If s is a reachable state of A, $u \in f(s)$ is a reachable state of B, and $(s, \pi, s') \in trans(A)$, then there is a timed execution fragment α starting with u and ending with some $u' \in f(s')$, such that

   (a) $ttrace(\alpha) = ttrace(s, \pi, s')$.
   (b) The total amount of time-passage in α is the same as the total amount of time-passage in (s, π, s').

Thus, the start condition is the same as for a simulation relation for I/O automata. The step condition is a little different—now we require that the correspondence preserve the timed trace, that is, the sequence of visible actions, each paired with its time of occurrence, plus the total amount of time-passage. Note that in the step condition, π can be a time-passage action as well as a discrete action. If π is a visible action, then α must consist of a π step, possibly with some preceding and/or following internal steps. If π is an internal action, then α must consist of internal steps only. If $\pi = \nu(t)$, then α must consist of time-passage steps interspersed with internal steps, with the total amount of time-passage equal to t.

As before, since the states s and u in the step condition are assumed to be reachable, invariant assertions about the states of A and B can be used in a proof that f is a timed simulation relation.

The following theorem gives the key property of timed simulation relations.

Theorem 23.10 *If there is a timed simulation relation from A to B, then* $attraces(A) \subseteq attraces(B)$.

Proof. The proof is left as an exercise. $\square$

In the rest of this section, we give examples to show how timed simulations can be used to prove properties of timed systems. One interesting use of such simulations is to prove time bounds for systems with timing assumptions. This can be done by formalizing the timing specification as a GTA, B, with *last* and *first* deadline components expressing the required timing behavior (upper and lower bounds, respectively). The implementation is also formalized as a GTA,

A, with *last* and *first* components representing the timing assumptions. The existence of a timed simulation from A to B then implies that A satisfies the timing requirements.

Since simulations can be used in the timed setting to prove timing properties, the simulation method is more powerful in the timed setting than it is in the asynchronous setting. In the asynchronous setting, we are often interested in *liveness properties*, whereas in the timed setting, we are more often interested in *time bounds*. Formal proofs of liveness conditions often use extra machinery such as temporal logic in addition to simulations, but time bounds can be proved just using simulations.

Example 23.3.3 Simulation proof of time bounds for a timeout process

We show that P_2, the timeout MMT automaton of Example 23.1.2, must perform a *timeout* within the interval $[k\ell_1, k\ell_2 + \ell]$, if no messages are received. To simplify matters, we define a variant A of P_2 that does not even have a *receive* action in its signature. The code for A is as follows.

A automaton:

Signature:

Input: Internal:
   none   *decrement*
Output:
   timeout

States:

$count \in \mathbb{N}$, initially k
$status \in \{active, done\}$, initially *active*

Transitions:

decrement   *timeout*
   Precondition: Precondition:
      $status = active$ $status = active$
      $count > 0$ $count = 0$
   Effect: Effect:
      $count := count - 1$ $status := done$

Tasks and bounds:

$dec = \{decrement\}$, bounds $[\ell_1, \ell_2]$
$timeout = \{timeout\}$, bounds $[0, \ell]$

Then the code for $gen(A)$ is as follows.

$gen(A)$ automaton:

Timed Signature:

Input: Internal:
    none   *decrement*
Output: Time-passage:
    timeout $\nu(t),\, t \in R^+$

States:
$count \in \mathbb{N}$, initially k
$status \in \{active, done\}$, initially $active$

$now \in R^{\geq 0}$, initially 0
$first(dec) \in R^{\geq 0}$, initially ℓ_1
$last(dec) \in R^+ \cup \{\infty\}$, initially ℓ_2
$last(timeout) \in R^+ \cup \{\infty\}$, initially ∞

Transitions:

decrement
    Precondition:
       $status = active$
       $count > 0$
       $now \geq first(dec)$
    Effect:
       $count := count - 1$
       if $count > 0$ then
          $first(dec) := now + \ell_1$
          $last(dec) := now + \ell_2$
       else
          $first(dec) := 0$
          $last(dec) := \infty$
          $last(timeout) := \ell$

timeout
    Precondition:
       $status = active$
       $count = 0$
    Effect:
       $status := done$
       $last(timeout) := \infty$

$\nu(t)$
    Precondition:
       $now + t \leq last(dec)$
       $now + t \leq last(timeout)$
    Effect:
       $now := now + t$

Automaton A simply counts down from k to 0 and then performs a *timeout*. Informally, it is easy to see that a single *timeout* occurs within the claimed time interval $[k\ell_1, k\ell_2 + \ell]$. To prove this formally, we express these timing requirements using a trivial high-level GTA. This GTA is of the form $gen(B)$, where B is the following trivial MMT automaton.

B automaton:

Signature:

Input: Output:
    none   *timeout*

States:
$status \in \{active, done\}$, initially *active*

Transitions:

timeout
    Precondition:
        $status = active$
    Effect:
        $status := done$

Tasks and bounds:
$timeout = \{timeout\}$, bounds $[k\ell_1, k\ell_2 + \ell]$

Now we produce a timed simulation relation f from $gen(A)$ to $gen(B)$, thereby showing that A satisfies the timing requirements. If s and u are states of $gen(A)$ and $gen(B)$, respectively, then we define $(s, u) \in f$ provided that the following conditions hold:

1. $s.now = u.now$.

2. $s.status = u.status$.

3. $u.last(timeout) \geq$
$$\begin{cases} s.last(dec) + (s.count - 1) \cdot \ell_2 + \ell & \text{if } s.count > 0, \\ s.last(timeout) & \text{otherwise.} \end{cases}$$

4. $u.first(timeout) \leq$
$$\begin{cases} s.first(dec) + (s.count - 1) \cdot \ell_1 & \text{if } s.count > 0, \\ s.first(timeout) & \text{otherwise.} \end{cases}$$

The relationships involving the *now* and *status* values are straightforward. The interesting relationships involve the *last* and *first* deadlines. The $u.last(timeout)$ value (in $gen(B)$) is constrained to be at least as large as a certain quantity that is calculated in terms of the state (including deadline components) of $gen(A)$. This quantity is a calculated upper bound on the last time when a *timeout* action might be performed by $gen(A)$. There are two cases: If $count > 0$, then this time is bounded by the last time at which the first *decrement* can occur, plus the additional time required to do $count - 1$ additional *decrement* steps followed by a *timeout* step; since each of these $count$ steps can take at most time ℓ_2 and the *timeout* can take at most time ℓ, this additional time is at most $(count - 1) \cdot \ell_2 + \ell$. On the other hand, if $count = 0$, then this time is bounded by the last time at which the *timeout* can occur. The inequality expresses the fact that this calculated bound on the actual time until *timeout* is at most equal to the upper bound to be proved.

The interpretation of the *first(timeout)* inequality is symmetric—the values of *first(timeout)* should be no larger than a calculated lower bound on the earliest time until a *timeout* action is performed by $gen(A)$.

In order to prove that f is a timed simulation, we first prove an easy invariant.

Assertion 23.3.4 *In any reachable state of $gen(A)$, if count > 0, then status = active.*

Then the proof proceeds in the usual way for simulations, verifying the start condition and the step condition. The inequalities are treated in just the same manner as any other type of relation between the states. As in Example 23.3.1, we include some details as a model for other such proofs; the rest of the details are left for an exercise.

For the start condition, let s and u be the unique start states of $gen(A)$ and $gen(B)$, respectively. We must show that $u \in f(s)$. Conditions 1 and 2 of the definition of f are immediate. Consider Condition 3. The definition of $gen(B)$ implies that $u.last(timeout) = k\ell_2 + \ell$, and the definition of $gen(A)$ implies that $s.count > 0$ and $s.last(dec) + (s.count - 1) \cdot \ell_2 + \ell = \ell_2 + (k - 1)\ell_2 + \ell = k\ell_2 + \ell$. Therefore, $u.last(timeout) = s.last(dec) + (s.count - 1) \cdot \ell_2 + \ell$, which shows Condition 3. Condition 4 is analogous to Condition 3.

For the step condition, we suppose that $(s, \pi, s') \in trans(gen(A))$, s is reachable, and u is a reachable state in $f(s)$. We consider cases based on types of actions, including time-passage actions.

For example, consider the case where $\pi = decrement$. By the precondition of *decrement*, $s.count > 0$. The fact that $u \in f(s)$ means that $s.now = u.now$; $s.status = u.status$; $u.last(timeout) \geq s.last(dec) + (s.count - 1) \cdot \ell_2 + \ell$; and $u.first(timeout) \leq s.first(dec) + (s.count - 1) \cdot \ell_1$. It suffices to show that $u \in f(s')$.

Conditions 1 and 2 carry over immediately. Suppose that $s'.count > 0$. For Condition 3, note that the left side of the inequality, *last*(*timeout*), is not changed by this step, while the right side is not increased. This latter property is true because *last*(*dec*) is increased by at most ℓ_2, while the second term decreases by exactly ℓ_2 and the third term is unchanged. (The reason why *last*(*dec*) is increased by at most ℓ_2 is that $s.now \leq s.last(dec)$ and $s'.last(dec) = s.now + \ell_2$.) This means that the inequality still holds after the step. Similar arguments can be made for Condition 4 and for the case where $s'.count = 0$.

Other arguments in the same style can be made for the other types of actions. For the case where $\pi = timeout$, the interesting thing to show is that the precondition $first(timeout) \leq now$ is satisfied in state u. This inequality holds because the precondition of π in $gen(A)$ implies that $s.first(timeout) \leq s.now = u.now$, and Condition 4 implies that $u.first(timeout) \leq s.first(timeout)$.

For the case where π is a time-passage action, the interesting thing to show is the precondition $u'.now \leq u.last(timeout)$. This inequality holds because the precondition of π in $gen(A)$ implies that $u'.now = s'.now \leq \min(s.last(dec), s.last(timeout))$, and Condition 3 implies that $\min(s.last(dec), s.last(timeout)) \leq u.last(timeout)$. Time-passage steps do not change anything mentioned in the definition of f except for *now*, so it is easy to see that they preserve all the relationships in f.

Since f is a timed simulation, Theorem 23.10 implies that $attraces(gen(A)) \subseteq attraces(gen(B))$, and then Theorem 23.4 implies that $attraces(A) \subseteq attraces(B)$. This says that A satisfies the timing requirements.

Of course, there are other ways to prove time bounds for timing-based systems besides using timed simulations. For example, operational arguments based on the invariants in Exercise 23.13 can be used to prove the upper bound of $k\ell_2 + \ell$ on the time until a *timeout* occurs.

Example 23.3.4   Two-task race

We outline a simulation proof that $\ell + \ell_2 + L\ell$ is an upper bound on the time until the *Race* automaton of Example 23.1.3 performs a *report* output. Now the specification is $gen(B')$, where B' is an MMT automaton similar to the specification automaton B of Example 23.3.3.

B' automaton:

Signature:

Input: Output:

   none   *report*

States:

reported, a Boolean, initially *false*

Transitions:

report
    Precondition:
       reported = false
    Effect:
       reported := true

Tasks and bounds:
report = {*report*}, bounds $[0, \ell + \ell_2 + L\ell]$

Intuitively, the reason that $\ell + \ell_2 + L\ell$ is a correct upper bound is as follows. Within time ℓ, the *int* task sets the *flag* to *true*. During this time, the largest value that *count* could reach is $\frac{\ell}{\ell_1}$. Then it takes time at most $\frac{\ell}{\ell_1}\ell_2 = L\ell$ for the *main* task to decrement *count* to 0, and then an additional time at most ℓ_2 to perform a *report*.

Now we define a timed simulation relation g from $gen(Race)$ to $gen(B')$. If s and u are states of $gen(Race)$ and $gen(B')$, respectively, then we define $(s, u) \in g$ provided that the following conditions hold:

1. $s.now = u.now$.

2. $s.reported = u.reported$.

3. $u.last(report) \geq$
$$\begin{cases} s.last(int) + (s.count + 2)\ell_2 + L(s.last(int) - s.first(main)) \\ \quad \text{if } s.flag = false \text{ and } s.first(main) \leq s.last(int). \\ s.last(main) + (s.count)\ell_2 \\ \quad \text{otherwise.} \end{cases}$$

The idea of the third condition is as follows. If *flag* = *true*, then the time remaining until *report* is just the time for the *main* task to do the remaining *decrement* steps, followed by the final *report*. The same reasoning holds if *flag* is still *false*, but must become *true* before there is time for another *increment* to occur, that is, if $s.first(main) >$

s.last(*int*). Otherwise, *s.flag* = *false* and *s.first*(*main*) ≤ *s.last*(*int*), which means that there is time for at least one more *increment* to occur. Then the first case of the inequality for *last*(*report*) applies.

In this case, after the *set*, it might take as long as time (*count* + 1)ℓ_2 for the *main* task to count down from the current *count* and then to *report*. But the current *count* could be increased before the *set* by some additional *increment* events. The largest number of these that might occur is 1 + [*last*(*int*) − *first*(*main*)]/ℓ_1. Multiplying this by ℓ_2 gives the extra time required to decrement this additional count.

The proof that *g* is a timed simulation relation follows the same general outline as the proof in Example 23.3.3. We leave this as an exercise.

23.4   Modelling Shared Memory and Network Systems

We close this chapter by indicating how partially synchronous shared memory systems and partially synchronous network systems can be modelled using MMT automata and GTAs. These models will be used in Chapters 24 and 25.

23.4.1   Shared Memory Systems

We model a partially synchrononous shared memory system as an MMT automaton (*A*, *b*). Here, we assume that I/O automaton *A* is an asynchronous shared memory system, according to the definitions in Chapter 9; the only new constraint is that *A* has only finitely many tasks. The boundmap *b* adds time bounds for each task.

Most of the time, we will assume that each process has only one task and that the boundmap assigns a lower bound of ℓ_1 and an upper bound of ℓ_2 to each task, where $0 < \ell_1 \leq \ell_2 < \infty$. In this case, we will write $L = \ell_2/\ell_1$; as before, *L* is a measure of the *timing uncertainty* in the system.

23.4.2   Networks

In the partially synchronous setting, we will only consider send/receive networks, not broadcast or multicast networks. We assume an underlying directed graph $G = (V, E)$. We model a partially synchronous send/receive network system as a collection of process automata, one for each vertex, plus a collection of channel automata, one for each edge.

The process automaton associated with each vertex i is an MMT automaton P_i. P_i has input and output actions by which it communicates with the external users, plus outputs of the form $send(m)_{i,j}$, where m is a message and j is an outgoing neighbor, and inputs of the form $receive(m)_{j,i}$, where j is an incoming neighbor. To model process stopping failures, we include a $stop_i$ input action. The effect of this action is to permanently disable all tasks of P_i. We will usually assume that each process P_i has time bounds of ℓ_1 and ℓ_2 for each of its (finitely many) tasks, where $0 < \ell_1 \leq \ell_2 < \infty$.

The channel automaton associated with each directed edge (i, j) is a GTA $C_{i,j}$. Its "visible interface" consists of inputs of the form $send(m)_{i,j}$ and outputs of the form $receive(m)_{i,j}$. Restrictions on the external behavior of a channel are expressed by a timed trace property P; the channels defined by P are those GTAs whose visible actions are the same as those of P and whose admissible timed traces are in $ttraces(P)$. There are two common cases:

1. Each $C_{i,j}$ is the GTA $D'_{i,j}$ with the appropriate timed signature described in Example 23.2.1, that is, a reliable FIFO channel with an upper bound of d on the delivery of the oldest message.

2. Each $C_{i,j}$ is the GTA $D''_{i,j}$ with the appropriate timed signature described in Example 23.2.2, that is, a reliable FIFO channel with an upper bound of d on the delivery of every message.

Again, we will write $L = \ell_2/\ell_1$ and use L as a measure of the timing uncertainty in the system.

23.5 Bibliographic Notes

The MMT timed automaton model was designed by Merritt, Modugno, and Tuttle [227]. Their model is somewhat more general than the one we use in this book, in that they allow eventual upper bounds as well as real-valued upper bounds. The variant of the model we use here is close to the one defined by Lynch and Attiya [215]. The two-task race example was suggested by Pnueli [243] as a test case for proof methods for timing-based systems.

The general timed automaton model is based on the timed automaton model of Lynch and Vaandrager [210, 212, 211]; it is similar to the timed automaton model of Alur and Dill [9]. Issues involving the existence of admissible timed executions are studied by Gawlick, Segala, Søgaard-Andersen, and Lynch [136]. The transformation from MMT automata to general timed automata was developed by Lynch and Attiya [215]. The operations for GTAs are derived from [212]; that paper describes many other operations on GTAs besides composition and hiding, including sequential composition and various forms of choice, interrupt, and timeout.

Invariants that include time deadlines have been used by Tel [275], Lewis [194], Shankar [259], Abadi and Lamport [1], Lynch [204], and others. The simulation method of proving timing properties was first used by Lynch and Attiya [215]. The simulation proofs of time bounds in Examples 23.3.3 and 23.3.4 are derived from [215], as well as from the survey papers [204, 205]. Other types of simulations for GTAs are defined by Lynch and Vaandrager [210, 211].

Other timed simulation proofs have been carried out by Søgaard-Andersen, Lampson, and Lynch [264, 190], Heitmeyer and Lynch [148], and Luchangco [201]. Some preliminary work has been carried out by Luchangco, Söylemez, Garland, and Lynch, in using the assistance of an automatic theorem-prover in checking and carrying out timed simulation proofs [202]. This work uses the Larch Prover [134].

23.6 Exercises

23.1. Let (A, b) be any MMT automaton and let α be any finite timed execution of (A, b). Prove the following:

  (a) There is an (admissible) timed execution of (A, b) that starts with α.

  (b) Let β be any finite sequence of input actions paired with times, in which the times are nondecreasing and at least as great as the largest time occurring in α. Then there is an (admissible) timed execution α' of (A, b) such that α' starts with α and such that β is the subsequence of inputs and associated times occurring in α' after α.

  (c) Let β be any infinite sequence of input actions paired with times, in which the times are nondecreasing and unbounded and at least as great as the largest time occurring in α. Then there is an (admissible) timed execution α' of (A, b) such that α' starts with α and such that β is the subsequence of inputs and associated times occurring in α' after α.

23.2. Suppose that the definition of an MMT automaton were weakened to allow *countably* many tasks instead of only finitely many. Show that there exists an automaton (A, b) satisfying this new definition that has *no* (admissible) timed executions.

23.3. Describe carefully the behavior of the composed MMT automaton in Example 23.1.4, in the case where $k\ell_1 \leq \ell + d$.

23.4. Prove Theorems 23.1, 23.2, and 23.3.

23.5. Consider a time-bounded variant of the *AsynchBellmanFord* algorithm of Section 15.4, in which

- Each process automaton is the MMT automaton consisting of the given I/O automaton and bounds $[\ell_1, \ell_2]$ for each task, where $0 < \ell_1 \le \ell_2 < \infty$.
- Each channel is the appropriate MMT automaton $D_{i,j}$, from Example 23.1.1.

Analyze the communication and time complexity of the resulting algorithm.

23.6. Prove that the GTA $D'_{i,j}$ in Example 23.2.1 and the MMT automaton $D_{i,j}$ in Example 23.1.1 have the same sets of admissible timed traces.

23.7. Prove that there is no MMT automaton with the same set of admissible timed traces as the GTA $D''_{i,j}$ in Example 23.2.2.

23.8. Give precondition-effect code for a GTA A with the following behavior. In any admissible timed execution, A performs exactly two outputs, a and b, in that order, both by time 1. Moreover, A should, in various admissible timed executions, allow for a and b to occur at *any time*, subject to the given limitations. Prove that there is no MMT automaton with the same set of admissible timed traces as A.

23.9. Give explicit precondition-effect code for the transformed automaton *gen(Race)*, where *Race* is the MMT automaton defined in Example 23.1.3. The style of your code should be similar to the code in Example 23.2.4.

23.10. Prove Theorems 23.7, 23.8, and 23.9.

23.11. Show that the simpler restatement of Theorem 23.8, asserting that $\alpha_i = \alpha | B_i$ rather than just that they are time-passage equivalent, is false.

23.12. Prove Theorem 23.10.

23.13. Prove the following multipart invariant of the system A' of Example 23.2.4. If $status_1 = dead$, then

(a) *queue* is empty.

(b) $status_2 \ne disabled$.

(c) If $count_2 > 0$, then $last(dec) + (count_2 - 1)\ell_2 \le k\ell_2$.

(d) If $count_2 = 0$, then $last(timeout) \leq k\ell_2 + \ell$.

23.14. Prove Lemma 11.3, the time bound for the *RightLeftDP* algorithm, using the simulation method of Section 23.3.3.

23.15. Fill in the details of the proof that f is a timed simulation relation, from Example 23.3.3.

23.16. Prove that the relation g defined in Example 23.3.4 is a timed simulation relation.

Chapter 24

Mutual Exclusion with Partial Synchrony

In this chapter, we visit the mutual exclusion problem for the third time, this time in the partially synchronous shared memory setting. We present only very basic results: simple timing-based algorithms and their analysis, and simple impossibility results.

24.1 The Problem

The setting is very much the same as in Chapter 10—a shared memory system with n ports, interacting with users $U_1, \dots, U_n$. The external interface, consisting of try_i, $crit_i$, $exit_i$, and rem_i actions, is exactly the same as before. This time, however, the users and the shared memory system are modelled as MMT automata, as defined in Section 23.1, rather than as I/O automata. Figure 10.4 can still be used to represent the architecture we consider in this chapter.

As before, each user U_i is required to preserve well-formedness. We allow arbitrary timing constraints for the users. Formally, each MMT automaton U_i is of the form (A_i, b_i), where A_i is any I/O automaton that was allowed in Section 10.2 and that has only finitely many tasks, and b_i is an arbitrary boundmap. Included among the allowable boundmaps is the trivial boundmap giving trivial lower bounds of 0 and trivial upper bounds of ∞.

The rest of the system consists of a single MMT automaton $B = (A, b)$ representing the shared memory system. The underlying I/O automaton A is of the form we considered in Chapter 10 for solving the mutual exclusion problem in the asynchronous shared memory model. In particular, it consists of n processes, one per port. We assume throughout this chapter that each process has just one task. The boundmap b assigns a lower bound of ℓ_1 and an upper bound of ℓ_2 to each task, where $0 < \ell_1 \leq \ell_2 < \infty$. As before, we write $L = \ell_2/\ell_1$; L is a measure of the *timing uncertainty* in the system.

We make three other restrictions in this chapter. First, we restrict process activity in the same way that we did in Chapter 10: the single task of each process i in the shared memory system can only be enabled when U_i is in the trying or exit region. Second, we assume that the single task of process i is in fact always enabled when U_i is in the trying or exit region. (However, we allow the possibility that the only action enabled might be a dummy action that causes no state changes.) Third, we only consider shared memory systems with read/write shared variables.

The correctness conditions we require are much the same as in Chapter 10. Restating them for timed automata, we have

Well-formedness: In any timed execution of the combined system, and for any i, the subsequence describing the interaction between U_i and $B = (A, b)$ is well-formed for i.

Mutual exclusion: There is no reachable system state in which more than one user is in the critical region C.

Progress: At any point in an *admissible timed execution*,[1]

1. (Progress for the trying region) If at least one user is in T and no user is in C, then at some later point some user enters C.

2. (Progress for the exit region) If at least one user is in E, then at some later point some user enters R.

We say that B *solves the mutual exclusion problem* provided that it solves it (i.e., guarantees well-formedness, mutual exclusion, and progress) for every collection of users. These correctness conditions could alternatively be formulated in terms of a timed trace property P, as defined in Section 23.3.2.

24.2   A Single-Register Algorithm

In this section, we present a partially synchronous mutual exclusion algorithm, the *FischerME algorithm*, that uses only a single read/write register. This simple algorithm already demonstrates that the partially synchronous model is very different from the asynchronous model, because, as we showed in Theorem 10.33,

---

[1]As in Section 23.1, this is defined to mean that time passes normally and that processing does not stop if there is more work to be done.

any asynchronous read/write shared memory mutual exclusion algorithm requires at least n shared registers.

The starting point for the algorithm is the following incorrect *asynchronous* algorithm.

IncorrectFischerME algorithm (informal):

The algorithm uses a single read/write shared variable *turn*, writable and readable by all processes. Each process i that wants to obtain the resource repeatedly tests *turn* until it finds the value equal to 0. After it finds $turn = 0$, process i sets *turn* equal to its own index i. Then it checks that *turn* is still equal to i. If so, process i proceeds to the critical region; otherwise, it goes back to the beginning, testing for $turn = 0$. When a process i exits, it resets *turn* to 0.

In the style used for shared memory programs in Chapter 10, this is written as

---

IncorrectFischerME algorithm (formal):

Shared variables:
$turn \in \{0, 1, \ldots, n\}$, initially 0, writable and readable by all processes

Process i:

    ** Remainder region **

    try_i
L: if $turn \neq 0$ then goto L
    $turn := i$
    if $turn \neq i$ then goto L
    $crit_i$

    ** Critical region **

    $exit_i$
    $turn := 0$
    rem_i

The *IncorrectFischerME* algorithm is incorrect in that it fails to guarantee mutual exclusion. (We know that it must be incorrect, because otherwise it would violate Theorem 10.33.)

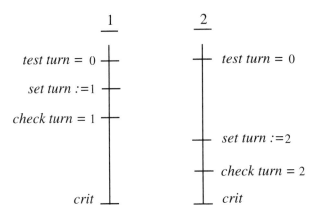

Figure 24.1: Bad execution of the *IncorrectFischerME* algorithm.

Example 24.2.1   Bad execution of *IncorrectFischerME*

Consider an execution in which two processes, say 1 and 2, both test *turn* and find *turn* = 0. Next, process 1 sets *turn* := 1 and immediately checks and finds *turn* = 1. Then process 2 sets *turn* := 2 and immediately checks and finds *turn* = 2. Then both processes 1 and 2 proceed to the critical region. This execution is illustrated in Figure 24.1.

In order to avoid this bad interleaving of events, we can add a simple timing restriction. Namely, any process i that sets *turn* := i can delay its check of *turn* for longer than time ℓ_2, the assumed upper bound on process step time. All other steps proceed at the normal rate, with some time in the interval $[\ell_1, \ell_2]$ between successive steps of the same process. This restriction prevents the bad interleaving in Figure 24.1 as follows: Any process i that sets *turn* := i is made to wait long enough before checking to ensure that any other process j that tested *turn* before i set *turn* (and therefore might subsequently set *turn* to its own index) has already set *turn* to its index. That is, there will be no processes left at the point of setting *turn*, when i finally checks.

Here is the precondition-effect code. In this code, we assume that a_1 and a_2 are two positive reals with $\ell_2 < a_1 \leq a_2$. Note that this code has two tasks for each process i, the *main$_i$* task with bounds $[\ell_1, \ell_2]$ and the *check$_i$* task with bounds $[a_1, a_2]$. This is technically not permitted by the model, which only allows one task per process, with bounds $[\ell_1, \ell_2]$. However, we could easily modify this algorithm by inserting a number $k - 1$ of explicit *delay* steps before any *check*, where $k\ell_1 > \ell_2$, and putting all the actions of each process in one task with bounds $[\ell_1, \ell_2]$. The resulting version of the algorithm "behaves like" the *FischerME* algorithm with $a_1 = k\ell_1$ and $a_2 = k\ell_2$. We omit the formal details.

FischerME algorithm:

Shared variables:
$turn \in \{0, 1, \ldots, n\}$, initially 0

Actions of i:

Input: Internal:
    try_i $test_i$
    $exit_i$ set_i
Output: $check_i$
    $crit_i$ $reset_i$
    rem_i

States of i:
$pc \in \{rem, test, set, check, leave\text{-}try, crit, reset, leave\text{-}exit\}$, initially rem

Transitions of i:

try_i
    Effect:
        $pc := test$

$test_i$
    Precondition:
        $pc = test$
    Effect:
        if $turn = 0$ then $pc := set$

set_i
    Precondition:
        $pc = set$
    Effect:
        $turn := i$
        $pc := check$

$check_i$
    Precondition:
        $pc = check$
    Effect:
        if $turn = i$ then $pc := leave\text{-}try$
        else $pc := test$

$crit_i$
    Precondition:
        $pc = leave\text{-}try$
    Effect:
        $pc := crit$

$exit_i$
    Effect:
        $pc := reset$

$reset_i$
    Precondition:
        $pc = reset$
    Effect:
        $turn := 0$
        $pc := leave\text{-}exit$

rem_i
    Precondition:
        $pc = leave\text{-}exit$
    Effect:
        $pc := rem$

Tasks and bounds:
$main_i = \{test_i, set_i, crit_i, reset_i, rem_i\}$, bounds $[\ell_1, \ell_2]$
$check_i = \{check_i\}$, bounds $[a_1, a_2]$

Theorem 24.1 *The FischerME algorithm with $\ell_2 < a_1$ solves the mutual exclusion problem.*

Proof.   We consider the *FischerME* algorithm together with any collection of users. Well-formedness is easy to see. For the mutual exclusion property, we wish to prove the following invariant of the combined system (algorithm plus users).

> **Assertion 24.2.1** *In any reachable state, there do not exist i and j, $i \neq j$, such that $pc_i = pc_j = crit$.*

As usual, proving this assertion by induction requires auxiliary invariants. Now, however, we need auxiliary invariants that involve time information as well as ordinary program variables.

Therefore, we transform the system into a general timed automaton (GTA), as described in Section 23.2.2. This transformation encodes all timing constraints into the states and transitions of the system rather then expressing them as "external" restrictions on timed executions. In particular, the state includes components $first(check_i)$ and $last(main_i)$, representing the first time that the next $check_i$ action might occur and the last time that the next action in $main_i$ might occur, respectively. We consider Assertion 24.2.1 and the other assertions below as properties of the state of the GTA obtained by this transformation.

The key claim, which can be proved by induction, is the following. It says that the earliest future time a successful $check_i$ can happen is after the set_j of any other process j that has already passed the test $test_j$. This lemma is used to rule out the bad interleaving in Example 24.2.1.

> **Assertion 24.2.2** *In any reachable state, if $pc_i = check$, $turn = i$, and $pc_j = set$, then $first(check_i) > last(main_j)$.*

Assertion 24.2.2 can be proved by a simple induction on the number of steps in a timed execution leading to the state in question. Here, the steps include time-passage steps as well as ordinary input, output, and internal steps. See Example 23.3.1 for a model of how such proofs proceed. For Assertion 24.2.2, the interesting arguments are those involving steps of the form (s, π, s') where π is either a set_i or a successful $test_j$, $j \neq i$. (Here, the indices i and j are the ones that appear in the assertion.)

1. $\pi = set_i$.

   In this case, $s'.first(check_i) = s.now + a_1$. Also, if $s'.pc_j = set$, then $s'.last(main_j) \leq s.now + \ell_2$, by Lemma 23.5. Since $\ell_2 < a_1$, the inequality follows.

2. $\pi = test_j$ and $s.turn = 0$ (i.e., the test is successful).

   In this case, $s'.turn = 0$, making the statement true vacuously.

Assertion 24.2.2 can be used to prove the following assertion. This one says that if a process i is in the critical region (or just before it or just after it), then $turn = i$ and no other process can be about to set $turn$. Note that, unlike Assertion 24.2.2, Assertion 24.2.3 does not mention any timing information. However, timing information is used in its inductive proof.

Assertion 24.2.3 *In any reachable state, if $pc_i \in \{leave\text{-}try, crit, reset\}$, then $turn = i$ and, for all j, $pc_j \neq set$.*

The proof is again by induction. Now the interesting arguments are those involving steps (s, π, s'), where π is either a successful $check_i$, a set_j or $reset_j$, $j \neq i$, or a successful $test_j$, $j \neq i$.

1. $\pi = check_i$ and $s.turn = i$ (i.e., the check is successful).

   Then $s'.turn = i$. Suppose that there is some j such that $s'.pc_j = set$. Then also $s.pc_j = set$. Then Assertion 24.2.2 implies that $s.first(check_i) > s.last(main_j)$. But Lemma 23.5 says that $s.now \leq s.last(main_j)$, so $s.first(check_i) > s.now$. This contradicts the timing constraints of the GTA. It follows that there is no j such that $s'.pc_j = set$.

2. $\pi = set_j$, $j \neq i$.

   Suppose that $s'.pc_i \in \{leave\text{-}try, crit, reset\}$. Then $s.pc_i \in \{leave\text{-}try, crit, reset\}$. Then the inductive hypothesis implies that there is no j such that $s.pc_j = set$. But then π cannot be enabled in s, a contradiction.

3. $\pi = reset_j$, $j \neq i$.

   Suppose that $s'.pc_i \in \{leave\text{-}try, crit, reset\}$. Then $s.pc_i \in \{leave\text{-}try, crit, reset\}$, and the inductive hypothesis implies that $s.turn = i$. But also, the fact that π is enabled in s implies that $s.pc_j = reset$, so the inductive hypothesis implies that $s.turn = j$. This is a contradiction.

4. $\pi = test_j$, $j \neq i$, and $s.turn = 0$ (i.e., the test is successful).

   Then the inductive hypothesis implies that $s.pc_i \notin \{leave\text{-}try, crit, reset\}$, so $s'.pc_i \notin \{leave\text{-}try, crit, reset\}$, which implies that the condition is true vacuously.

The mutual exclusion property, Assertion 24.2.1, then follows immediately from Assertion 24.2.3.

Finally, we consider the progress condition. For this, it is useful to have one more invariant, this one proved by an easy induction.

Assertion 24.2.4 *In any reachable state, if turn $= i$, then $pc_i \in$ {check, leave-try, crit, reset}.*

Using Assertion 24.2.4, we can argue progress operationally along the lines of the proof of Lemma 10.4, the progress lemma for the *DijkstraME* algorithm. That is, consider an admissible timed execution α that reaches a point where there is at least one user in T and no user in C and suppose for the sake of contradiction that, after this point, no user ever enters C. Then we can show that eventually in α, no further region changes occur, every process is in T or R, and some process is in T. Then we can argue (using Assertion 24.2.4) that eventually *turn* acquires the index of a contender (i.e., a process in T). Then, subsequently, *turn* must always be equal to some contender's index, although it may change to the index of different contenders. However, eventually *turn* stabilizes to a final (contender's) index, say i. Again using Assertion 24.2.4, we argue that, subsequently, process i enters C.

This completes the proof of Theorem 24.1. $\square$

Now we consider the time complexity of *FischerME*.

Theorem 24.2 *In any timed execution of the FischerME algorithm,*

1. *The time from any point when some process i is in the trying region until some process is in the critical region is at most $2a_2 + 5\ell_2$.*

2. *The time from any point when any process i is in the exit region until process i is in the remainder region is at most $2\ell_2$.*

Proof. The bound for the exit region is straightforward. For the trying region bound, we could use an operational argument, but for variety, we give a proof using a timed simulation, as described in Section 23.3.3. Notice that the proof of progress for *FischerME* (in the proof of Theorem 24.1) is based on the execution reaching certain "milestones"—for example, the "seizing" of the *turn* variable by some contender and the "stabilizing" of the *turn* variable to some particular contender's index. We incorporate these milestones, together with their time bounds, into an "abstract mutual exclusion algorithm" B. We then show the time bounds for *FischerME* using a simulation from *FischerME* to B. The strategy is the same as in Section 23.3.3.

The abstract algorithm B is the following MMT automaton.

B automaton:

Signature:

Input: Internal:
    try_i, $1 \leq i \leq n$ *seize*
    $exit_i$, $1 \leq i \leq n$ *stabilize*
Output:
    $crit_i$, $1 \leq i \leq n$
    rem_i, $1 \leq i \leq n$

States:
status, an element of $\{start, seized, stab\}$, initially *start*
for every i, $1 \leq i \leq n$:
    $region_i$, an element of $\{R, T, C, E\}$, initially R

Transitions:

try_i
    Effect:
        $region_i := T$

seize
    Precondition:
        $\exists i, region_i = T$
        $\forall i, region_i \neq C$
        $status = start$
    Effect:
        $status := seized$

stabilize
    Precondition:
        $status = seized$
    Effect:
        $status := stab$

$crit_i$
    Precondition:
        $region_i = T$
        $status = stab$
    Effect:
        $region_i := C$
        $status := start$

$exit_i$
    Effect:
        $region_i := E$

rem_i
    Precondition:
        $region_i = E$
    Effect:
        $region_i := R$

Tasks and bounds:
$seize = \{seize\}$, bounds $[0, a_2 + 3\ell_2]$
$stab = \{stabilize\}$, bounds $[0, \ell_2]$
$crit = \{crit_i : 1 \leq i \leq n\}$, bounds $[0, a_2 + \ell_2]$
for every i, $1 \leq i \leq n$:
    $rem_i = \{rem_i\}$, $1 \leq i \leq n$, bounds $[0, 2\ell_2]$

Algorithm B is very abstract—it just expresses the well-formedness and mutual exclusion conditions, plus the global milestones in the trying region (with time bounds), plus the time bounds for individual processes in the exit region. Since the bounds for the milestones add up to the time bound of $[2a_2 + 5\ell_2]$ that we want to prove for the trying region, it is not hard to see that B solves the mutual exclusion problem and has the required time bounds. We now present a timed simulation f from the *FischerME* system (algorithm plus users) to the B system (with the same users). Since f is a timed simulation, this implies (in view of Theorem 23.10) that the *FischerME* algorithm also observes the required bounds.

Define $(s, u) \in f$ if the following hold. (We assume that all unbound uses of process indices are implicitly universally quantified.)

1. $s.now = u.now$.

2. All user states are identical in s and u.

3. $u.region_i = \begin{cases} R & \text{if } s.pc_i = rem, \\ T & \text{if } s.pc_i \in \{test, set, check, leave\text{-}try\}, \\ C & \text{if } s.pc_i = crit, \\ E & \text{if } s.pc_i \in \{reset, leave\text{-}exit\}. \end{cases}$

4. $u.status = \begin{cases} start & \text{if } s.turn = 0 \text{ or } \exists i : s.pc_i \in \{crit, reset\}, \\ seized & \text{if } s.turn \neq 0, \not\exists i : s.pc_i \in \{crit, reset\}, \text{ and } \exists i : s.pc_i = set, \\ stab & \text{if } s.turn \neq 0 \text{ and } \not\exists i : s.pc_i \in \{crit, reset, set\}. \end{cases}$

5. $u.last(seize) \geq s.last(main_i) + a_2 + 2\ell_2$ if $s.pc_i = reset$.

6. $u.last(seize) \geq \min_i \{g(i)\}$ if $s.turn = 0$, where

$$g(i) = \begin{cases} s.last(check_i) + 2\ell_2 & \text{if } s.pc_i = check, \\ s.last(main_i) + \ell_2 & \text{if } s.pc_i = test, \\ s.last(main_i) & \text{if } s.pc_i = set, \\ \infty & \text{otherwise.} \end{cases}$$

7. $u.last(stab) \geq s.last(main_i)$ if $s.pc_i = set$.

8. $u.last(crit) \geq \begin{cases} s.last(check_i) + \ell_2 & \text{if } s.pc_i = check \wedge s.turn = i, \\ s.last(main_i) & \text{if } s.pc_i = leave\text{-}try. \end{cases}$

9. $u.last(rem_i) \geq \begin{cases} s.last(main_i) + \ell_2 & \text{if } s.pc_i = reset, \\ s.last(main_i) & \text{if } s.pc_i = leave\text{-}exit. \end{cases}$

The *now*, user, and region correspondences are all straightforward. The *status* correspondence gives the natural definition of the *status* of the competition in the *FischerME* algorithm: If $turn = 0$ or some process is in (or just after) the critical region, then the competition has status *start*. If *turn* is equal to the index of a competing process (i.e., is non-zero and is not equal to the index of a process that is in or just after the critical region) and if some process is still able to modify *turn*, then the competition has status *seized*. If *turn* is equal to the index of a competitor and no process is still able to set *turn*, then the competition has status *stab*.

The first inequality for *last*(*seize*) says that if some process is about to *reset*, then the time until the *turn* variable is seized is at most an additional $a_2 + 2\ell_2$ after the *reset* occurs. The second inequality for *seize* says that if *turn* = 0 (which implies that no process is at *crit* or *reset*), then the time until the *turn* variable is seized is determined by the minimum of a set of possible times, each corresponding to some candidate process that might set *turn*. For instance, if $pc_i = set$—that is, if process i is about to set *turn*—then the corresponding time is just the latest time at which it can take its next step; however, if $pc_i = test$— that is, if process i is about to *test* the variable—then the corresponding time is an additional ℓ_2 after the *test* occurs. The interpretations for the remaining inequalities are similar.

Then it is not hard to show that f is a timed simulation relation; the argument follows the style of those in Examples 23.3.3 and 23.3.4. Assertions 24.2.3 and 24.2.4 are used in this proof; Assertion 24.2.3 is used in the *set*, *crit*, and *reset* cases, while Assertion 24.2.4 is used in the time-passage case. In this simulation, each external step of the *FischerME* system simulates a corresponding external step of the B system. A *set* step that changes *turn* from 0 to a process index simulates *seize*, and a *set* step that leaves no other processes at *set* simulates *stabilize*. A *set* step that satisfies both of these conditions simulates both *seize* and *stabilize* (in that order). Each other step simulates a trivial timed execution fragment with no actions. We leave the details for an exercise.

It follows from Theorem 23.10 that the admissible timed traces of the *FischerME* system are included among those of the B system. This implies the needed time bounds.   □

When the *FischerME* algorithm is modified to fit our model, including $k - 1$ explicit *delay* steps as we discussed just before the code, where $k\ell_1 > \ell_2$, the time bound for the trying region is $2k\ell_2 + 5\ell_2$. Choosing k to be as small as possible, that is, $k = \lfloor L \rfloor + 1$, where $L = \ell_2/\ell_1$, yields a time bound of $2L\ell_2 + O(\ell_2)$.

Stretching.   The time bound of $2L\ell_2 + O(\ell_2)$ illustrates how timing uncertainty can "stretch" the time complexity of an algorithm. If $L = 1$, that is, if $\ell_1 = \ell_2$, then there is no timing uncertainty in the system. In this case, the time bound is just $O(\ell_2)$—it depends only on the upper bound ℓ_2 on the real time between each process's steps. But if L is not equal to 1, the time bound increases accordingly. In fact, the real time ℓ_2 in the time bound is *multiplied* by the timing uncertainty L.

The term of $L\ell_2$ arises in the *FischerME* algorithm as follows. In order to be sure that a certain amount of real time, say t, has elapsed, a process counts its own steps. It must count enough steps so that even if the steps take the smallest amount of time possible, ℓ_1, real time t must have elapsed; thus, the number of steps must be at least t/ℓ_1. But these steps could in fact take the largest amount of time possible, ℓ_2, for a total real time of at least $(t/\ell_1)\ell_2 = Lt$.

Roughly speaking, it requires real time Lt for processes in a system with timing uncertainty t to be sure that real time t has elapsed. In this sense, the time complexity is "stretched" by a factor equal to the timing uncertainty. This stretching phenomenon has already appeared in the timeout example in Example 23.1.4. There, the inequality $k\ell_1 > \ell + d$ was required for the timeout to work correctly—the timeout process essentially checks that real time greater than $\ell + d$ has elapsed. But then a *timeout* might occur as late as time $k\ell_2 + \ell > L(\ell + d) + \ell$.

Mixing time bounds and fairness. We can consider a variant of the *FischerME* algorithm in which the only time constraints are a lower bound on the time from when a *check* action is enabled until it occurs, and an upper bound on the time for a *set* action. Any enabled, locally controlled action other than a *check* action is just required to occur *eventually*. It is not hard to see that this variant still solves the mutual exclusion problem. This variant cannot be represented using the MMT model as we have presented it in this book; rather, it requires a version of the model allowing time bounds for some tasks and fairness conditions for others. Of course, no time bounds can be proved for this version of the algorithm.

24.3   Resilience to Timing Failures

The correctness of the *FischerME* algorithm depends critically on timing restrictions. Even its most basic correctness condition, mutual exclusion, can fail to hold in a timed execution in which the important timing constraints—the lower bound of a_1 for *check* steps and the upper bound of ℓ_2 for *set* steps—are violated. It would be nice to improve this algorithm so that at least the mutual exclusion condition is always satisfied, no matter what happens to the timing. As a general design principle, it is desirable for timing-based algorithms to guarantee their most crucial safety properties, regardless of timing variations.

One idea for improving the *FischerME* algorithm in this way is to replace its critical region by the trying, critical, and exit regions of a second algorithm S. Algorithm S should always guarantee the mutual exclusion condition for its critical region, regardless of the timing of its steps. However, S should also not impede the progress of the *FischerME* algorithm when the timing constraints are satisfied. We could let S be any asynchronous algorithm that solves the mutual exclusion problem (satisfying the well-formedness, mutual exclusion, and progress conditions), but, unfortunately, Theorem 10.33 implies that such an algorithm would require at least n shared registers. Fortunately, we do not need such a strong progress condition for S; instead, we can use the following weaker progress condition.

1-concurrent progress: In any *admissible timed execution* in which there is never more than one user outside of R at once,

1. (1-concurrent progress for the trying region) If U_i is in T, then at some later point it enters C.
2. (1-concurrent progress for the exit region) If U_i is in E, then at some later point it enters R.

Here, of course, the users and regions are those of the second algorithm S.

An example of an asynchronous algorithm S with the needed conditions follows. Note that this algorithm uses only two shared registers.

S:

Shared variables:
x, a process index, initially arbitrary, writable and readable by all processes
$y \in \{0, 1\}$, initially 0, writable and readable by all processes

Process i:

** Remainder region **

try_i
M: $x := i$
     if $y \neq 0$ then goto M
     $y := 1$
     if $x \neq i$ then goto M
     $crit_i$

** Critical region **

$exit_i$
$y := 0$
rem_i

Theorem 24.3 *Asynchronous shared memory algorithm S guarantees the well-formedness, mutual exclusion, and 1-concurrent-progress conditions.*

Proof.   Left for an exercise. It is similar to many of the other proofs of mutual exclusion algorithms in this book. □

The combination of the *FischerME* algorithm and S can be described by the following code.

FischerS algorithm:

Shared variables:
$turn \in \{0, 1, \ldots, n\}$, initially 0, writable and readable by all processes
x, a process index, initially arbitrary, writable and readable by all processes
$y \in \{0, 1\}$, initially 0, writable and readable by all processes

Process i:

** Remainder region **

```
        try_i
L:   if turn ≠ 0 then goto L
        turn := i
        if turn ≠ i then goto L

M:   x := i
        if y ≠ 0 then goto M
        y := 1
        if x ≠ i then goto M
        crit_i
```

** Critical region **

```
        exit_i
        y := 0

        turn := 0
        rem_i
```

The *FischerS* code can be regarded as denoting either an asynchronous algorithm or a partially synchronous algorithm. When it denotes an asynchronous algorithm, we assume fairness conditions for all processes. We obtain

Theorem 24.4 *The FischerS algorithm, regarded as an asynchronous algorithm, guarantees the well-formedness and mutual exclusion conditions.*

Proof. Well-formedness is easy, and mutual exclusion follows from the fact, claimed in Theorem 24.3, that S guarantees mutual exclusion. □

We leave the determination of progress properties of *FischerS* for the exercises.

On the other hand, when the *FischerS* code denotes a partially synchronous algorithm, we assume as for *FischerME* that there are two tasks for each process i, one with bounds $[a_1, a_2]$ and the other with bounds $[\ell_1, \ell_2]$, where $\ell_2 < a_1$. The first task includes only the step where process i checks the value of *turn*, and the second task includes everything else.

Theorem 24.5 *The FischerS algorithm, regarded as a partially synchronous algorithm, solves the mutual exclusion problem, that is, it guarantees well-formedness, mutual exclusion, and progress.*

Proof. The well-formedness and mutual exclusion conditions follow from Theorem 24.4. The progress condition for the exit region is easy. We argue the progress condition for the trying region. In this argument, R, T, C, and E denote the regions of the *FischerS* algorithm. We also define the *FischerME trying region* to be the portion of T prior to label M, and define the S *trying region* to be the rest of T. Likewise, we define the S *exit region* to be the portion of E before the assignment $y := 0$ and the *FischerME exit region* to be the rest of E. We also define the *FischerME critical region* to be the combination of the S trying region, C, and the S exit region.

Suppose that at some point in an admissible timed execution, at least one user is in T and no user is in C. If at any subsequent point, some process is in the S trying region, then (using the fact that *FischerME* guarantees mutual exclusion) the 1-concurrent-progress condition for S implies that eventually some process enters C, as needed.

On the other hand, assume that no process ever subsequently reaches the S trying region. Then the 1-concurrent-progress condition for S implies that eventually the S exit region becomes empty. This means that the *FischerME* critical region is empty, so the progress condition for the *FischerME* algorithm implies that eventually some process enters the *FischerME* critical region. But this means it enters the S trying region, which is a contradiction. □

24.4 Impossibility Results

We finish this chapter with two impossibility results. The first is a lower bound on the time required to solve the mutual exclusion problem in the partially synchronous model. The second is an impossibility result for the case where time bounds are required to hold *eventually*.

24.4.1 A Lower Bound on the Time

The *FischerME* algorithm solves the mutual exclusion problem in the partially synchronous shared memory model and achieves a worst-case time bound of $2L\ell_2 + O\left(\ell_2\right)$ for progress in the trying region. It is possible to improve this to obtain a time bound of $L\ell_2 + O\left(\ell_2\right)$. (We leave this improvement for an exercise.) But is it possible to do better? That is, does there exist a faster algorithm that solves the mutual exclusion problem in this model, still using only a constant number of variables? We give a simple result for the special case of one variable; the statement is closely related to that of Theorem 10.34.

Theorem 24.6 *There is no algorithm in the partially synchronous read/write shared memory model that solves the mutual exclusion problem for two processes using only one read/write shared variable, and that has an upper bound of $L\ell_2$ on the time for progress in the trying region.*

The proof of Theorem 24.6 uses an interesting argument involving "stretching" and "shrinking" timed executions, while still observing the timing constraints. It is based closely on the proof of Theorem 10.34.

Proof.   Suppose for the sake of contradiction that there is such an algorithm, A, using a single shared register x. We construct a timed execution of A that violates mutual exclusion.

Consider an admissible timed execution α_1 of A in which process 1 runs alone, taking steps at the slowest possible rate—that is, with time ℓ_2 between its successive steps. By the time bound assumption, process 1 must reach C by time $L\ell_2$ in α_1. As in the arguments in Section 10.8, process 1 must write to the shared variable before entering C. Let α_2 be the prefix of α_1 ending just before process 1 writes to x for the first time.

Similarly, consider a slow admissible timed execution α_3 involving process 2 alone, starting from the same start state as α_1, in which process 2 reaches C by time $L\ell_2$. Let α_4 be the prefix of α_3 ending when process 2 enters C. Let α_5 be an alternative finite timed execution of A that is just like α_4 except that everything is sped up ("shrunk") by a factor of $L = \ell_2/\ell_1$. Then in α_5, process 2 enters C by time ℓ_2.

The counterexample timed execution α begins with α_2, thus bringing process 1 to the point of writing x. At this point, we allow process 1 to pause. Now we allow process 2 to take steps, executing as in the fast timed execution α_5. (Since process 1 does not write to x in α_2, process 2 cannot tell that process 1 is active and so can execute as if it were alone.) Thus, within time ℓ_2 after process 2 begins operating, it reaches C. We allow process 1 to pause for time exactly ℓ_2, which is enough time to allow process 2 to reach C. Next, we resume process 1, allowing it to continue as in α_1. The first thing it does is write x, thereby overwriting anything process 2 might have written there on its way to C. This eliminates all evidence of process 2's execution, thus allowing process 1 to run just as it does in α_1, eventually reaching C. But this puts both processes in C simultaneously, which contradicts the mutual exclusion requirement. $\square$

It is possible to extend the lower bound in Theorem 24.6 to cases where there are more shared variables, but the results that are currently known for these cases are not very tight. The methods of Section 10.8 yield some partial results.

24.4.2 Impossibility Result for Eventual Time Bounds*

The *FischerS* algorithm solves the mutual exclusion problem (including the progress condition) if it runs partially synchronously, and it guarantees at least the mutual exclusion property if it runs asynchronously. Is it possible to guarantee progress under weaker conditions, for example, if the algorithm runs asynchronously for a while, but *eventually* starts to satisfy its timing constraints? It is not hard to see that the *FischerS* algorithm does not make this guarantee; we leave this for an exercise. We show that in fact no algorithm does so.

Theorem 24.7 *There is no asynchronous algorithm A for $n \geq 2$ processes that does all of the following:*

1. *Guarantees well-formedness and mutual exclusion when run asynchronously*

2. *Guarantees progress when run in such a way that each process's step bounds are eventually in the range $[\ell_1, \ell_2]^2$*

3. *Uses fewer than n shared read/write registers*

Proof Sketch.   The proof follows that of Theorem 10.33 very closely. In particular, the main lemma is analogous to Lemma 10.37—it asserts the existence

---

[2]Formally, we would define an *eventually timed execution* of an MMT automaton and state this condition in terms of eventually timed executions. We omit the formal treatment.

of a k-reachable system state in which k distinct variables are "covered" by k processes. No timing restrictions appear in the statement of this lemma.

The main lemma is proved by induction using the same construction as in the proof of Lemma 10.37. The only difference is that wherever the earlier proof used the general progress condition, we must now make do with the weaker "eventually time-bounded" progress condition. Now, whenever we want to force processes to make progress, we simply begin running them in such a way that their timing constraints are satisfied from that point on.

There is one slightly tricky aspect of the construction: When we splice the computation of process $k + 1$ into the main computation involving processes $1, \ldots, k$, we must "shrink" the computation of $k + 1$ to fit it in before the other processes take their next steps, and then must allow process $k + 1$ to pause sufficiently long to allow the other processes to finish their computation. These timing adjustments may cause timing constraints to be violated. But that is not a problem—the lemma does not require that the execution constructed satisfy any particular timing constraints.   ☐

24.5   Bibliographic Notes

The *FischerME* algorithm was designed by Fischer [116]. This algorithm has been used recently as a test case for demonstrating the power of formal methods for reasoning about timing-based systems. The proof that *FischerME* satisfies the mutual exclusion property is derived from proofs by Abadi and Lamport [1] and Luchangco [201]. The proof of the time bound for *FischerME* is due to Luchangco and Lynch [201, 204, 205]. Proof of an improved time bound also appears in [201]. All the proofs for the *FischerME* algorithm have been checked by computer using the Larch theorem prover [202]. A sketch of a time bound proof for the *DijkstraME* algorithm appears in [204].

The *FischerS* algorithm is due to Lynch and Shavit [209], as are the impossibility results in Section 24.4. Alur and Taubenfeld [10] have obtained partially synchronous mutual exclusion algorithms with good time complexity in the face of a limited number of concurrent requests; their model and measure are somewhat different from the one used here. Attiya and Lynch [25] have some upper and lower bound results for the time complexity of mutual exclusion in partially synchronous networks. Their problem is different from the one considered here in that the system is not given explicit notification of when critical regions are completed.

24.6 Exercises

24.1. Prove Assertion 24.2.4.

24.2. Fill in the details of the operational proof of progress for Theorem 24.1.

24.3. Show that the *FischerME* algorithm permits a process to be locked out.

24.4. Does the *IncorrectFischerME* algorithm satisfy the progress condition? Give a proof or a counterexample.

24.5. Fill in the details of the simulation argument in the proof of Theorem 24.2.

24.6. Prove an improved time bound of $2a_2 + 5\ell_2 - a_1$ for the *FischerME* algorithm.

24.7. Describe a timed execution of the *FischerME* algorithm that takes as long a time as possible from when some process is in T until some process is in C. How does the coeffecient of 2 before the a_2 arise?

24.8. Devise an alternative mutual exclusion algorithm for the partially synchronous shared memory model, using one read/write shared variable. This one should have a time bound that is of the form $L\ell_2 + O(\ell_2)$, without the coefficient of 2 before the $L\ell_2$ term.

24.9. Let P be an MMT automaton with no input actions and only the single output action a. Suppose that P has only a single task, with associated bounds $[\ell_1, \ell_2]$, where $0 < \ell_1 \le \ell_2 < \infty$, and that this task is always enabled. Suppose that, in every admissible timed execution, P performs exactly one output of a, at a real time that is greater than or equal to d. Prove that there is some admissible timed execution of P in which a is output at a real time greater than or equal to Ld, where $L = \ell_2/\ell_1$.

24.10. Reconsider the *DijkstraME* algorithm of Section 10.3. Prove a time bound of $(3n + 11)\ell$ for the time from when some process is in the trying region until some process is in the critical region, assuming that ℓ is an upper bound on process step time. Do this by regarding this algorithm as an MMT automaton and using a timed simulation similar to the one in the proof of Theorem 24.2.

24.11. Prove Theorem 24.3. (*Hint:* Let I_1 be the set of processes i such that $x = i$ and i is about to set y. Let I_2 be the set of processes i such that $x = i$ and i is about to test x. Let I_3 be the set of processes that are either in, just before, or just after C. The following invariants may be useful:

(a) $|I_1 \cup I_2 \cup I_3| \le 1$.

(b) If $|I_2 \cup I_3| > 0$, then $y = 1$.

(c) If all processes are in R, then $y = 0$.)

24.12. Show that algorithm S does not guarantee progress (in the presence of concurrent requests). Do this by giving an explicit execution in which the progress condition is violated.

24.13. Does the *FischerS* algorithm, regarded as an asynchronous algorithm, satisfy the 1-concurrent-progress condition? Prove or give a counterexample.

24.14. Give an explicit execution of the *FischerS* algorithm regarded as an asynchronous algorithm, in which the progress condition is violated.

24.15. Give another algorithm that has all the correctness properties we claimed for the *FischerS* algorithm (i.e., it guarantees well-formedness and mutual exclusion when run asynchronously and progress when run partially synchronously), but that only uses two read/write shared variables instead of three.

24.16. Prove that there is no algorithm that has all the correctness properties we claimed for the *FischerS* algorithm but that only uses one read/write shared variable instead of three.

24.17. *Research Question:* Consider the k-concurrent-progress condition, defined in Exercise 10.32. Design an algorithm that satisfies the well-formedness, mutual exclusion, and k-concurrent-progress conditions when run asynchronously and also satisfies the progress condition when run partially synchronously. Try to minimize the number of shared registers.

24.18. *Research Question:* Design a timing-based algorithm that solves the mutual exclusion problem (guaranteeing well-formedness, mutual exclusion, and progress). Moreover, it should satisfy all of the following time bound requirements:

(a) The worst-case time from when some user is in T until some user is in C is $O(L\ell_2)$.

(b) The worst-case time from when some user i is in T and all other users are in R until either user i enters C or some other user enters T is $O(\ell_2)$.

(c) The worst-case time from when any user is in E until that user reaches R is $O(\ell_2)$.

Also try to generalize your result by designing another algorithm for the same problem, but this time generalizing the second requirement to one that asserts a good upper bound for progress in the trying region, in the case where there are at most k users concurrently outside of R. (Here, k is fixed, $1 \le k \le n$.)

24.19. Obtain a lower bound on the time for progress in the trying region in the partially synchronous model, for the case of two shared read/write variables. (*Hint:* Consider the proofs in Section 10.8. The lower bound will be of the form $cL\ell_2$, where c is a small constant.)

24.20. *Research Question:* For every k, $1 \le k \le n$, obtain tight upper and lower bounds on the worst-case time for progress, for mutual exclusion algorithms in the partially synchronous read/write shared memory model with k shared variables.

24.21. Give a particular execution that demonstrates that the *FischerS* algorithm does not satisfy the requirements listed in the statement of Theorem 24.7.

24.22. Give a more detailed proof of Theorem 24.7.

24.23. Consider the solvability of the mutual exclusion problem in the *unknown time bound* model. In this model, we assume lower and upper time bounds ℓ_1 and ℓ_2 on process step times, but these bounds are "unknown" to the processes. (That is, they can be different in different executions, though each execution observes fixed bounds throughout.)

Prove an analogue to Theorem 24.7 for the unknown time bound model.

24.24. *Research Question:* Develop a theory of partially synchronous algorithms for more general resource-allocation problems.

Chapter 25

Consensus with Partial Synchrony

In this, the final chapter, we visit consensus problems for the fourth time, this time in the partially synchronous network setting. We consider only stopping failures. It turns out that the results for consensus in the partially synchronous setting are quite different from those in either the synchronous or asynchronous setting. We first present a basic algorithm and a basic lower bound, both derived from corresponding results for the synchronous setting; there is a gap in time complexity between these two results, based on the timing uncertainty. Then we give a more difficult algorithm and a more difficult lower bound result that mostly close this gap. We finish with some results for weaker timing models and a look ahead to some possible future work.

25.1 The Problem

We define the *agreement problem* in much the same way as we did in Sections 12.1 and 21.2. Namely, the external interface of the system A consists of $init(v)_i$ input actions and $decide(v)_i$ output actions, where $1 \leq i \leq n$ and $v \in V$, plus $stop_i$ input actions. Each user U_i has $init(v)_i$ outputs and $decide(v)_i$ inputs, $v \in V$. Now U_i is an MMT automaton that performs at most one $init_i$ action in any timed execution.

A sequence of $init_i$ and $decide_i$ actions is *well-formed* for i provided that it is some prefix of a sequence of the form $init(v)_i, decide(w)_i$. We consider the following conditions on the combined system consisting of A and the users U_i:

Well-formedness: In any timed execution of the combined system, and for any port i, the interactions between U_i and A are well-formed for i.

Agreement: In any timed execution, all decision values are identical.

Validity: In any timed execution, if all *init* actions that occur contain the same
value v, then v is the only possible decision value.

Failure-free termination: In any admissible failure-free timed execution in
which *init* events occur on all ports, a *decide* event occurs on each port.

f-failure termination, $0 \leq f \leq n$: In any admissible timed execution in
which *init* events occur on all ports, if there are *stop* events on at most f
ports, then a *decide* event occurs on every non-failing port.

Wait-free termination is defined to be the special case of f-failure termination
where $f = n$.

We assume that A is a partially synchronous send/receive network system,
as described in Section 23.4.2. Each process P_i is an MMT automaton with time
bounds of ℓ_1 and ℓ_2 for each of its (finitely many) tasks, where $0 < \ell_1 \leq \ell_2 < \infty$;
let $L = \ell_2/\ell_1$. The processes are subject to stopping failures. Channels are
assumed to be of the second type defined in Section 23.4.2, that is, reliable FIFO
channels with an upper bound of d on the delivery time for *every message*.

We say that A *solves the agreement problem* if it guarantees well-formedness,
agreement, validity, and failure-free termination for every collection of users. We
consider algorithms that guarantee f-failure termination for various values of
f. The question we consider is how much time it takes after the arrival of all
inputs for all nonfaulty processes to decide. We focus here on the role of L, the
uncertainty parameter, in this time complexity.

Throughout this chapter, we consider a special case of the problem. Namely,
we assume that $V = \{0, 1\}$ and that the network graph is completely connected.
We assume that ℓ_1 and ℓ_2 are much smaller than d, in fact, we assume that even
$n\ell_2$ and $L\ell_2$ are small relative to d.

We need one more technical assumption: each process task of a non-failed
process is always enabled (though the only action of the task that is enabled
might be a dummy action that causes no state changes). This assumption allows
us to consider simple patterns of step times in our lower bound proofs.

25.2   A Failure Detector

A useful building block for the algorithms in this chapter is a "perfect failure
detector" F. We defined failure detectors for the asynchronous setting in Section 21.4. Recall that a failure detector has *stop*$_i$ actions as inputs and *inform-
stopped$(j)_i$* actions as outputs, $j \neq i$. An *inform-stopped$(j)_i$* action is intended

as an announcement, at location i, that process j has stopped. A perfect failure detector is guaranteed to report only failures that have actually happened and to eventually report all such failures to all other non-failed processes. The only difference here from Section 21.4 is that we no longer assume that a failure detector is an I/O automaton but, rather, that it is a general timed automaton (GTA).

We give a partially synchronous network system (in the model assumed in this chapter) that implements a perfect failure detector. The idea is similar to that used in the timeout MMT automaton of Example 23.1.2.

> ### *PSynchFD* algorithm:
>
> Each process P_i continually sends messages to all the other processes P_j, using one task per process. If a process P_i performs a sufficiently large number m of steps without receiving a message from P_j, it records that P_j has stopped and outputs *inform-stopped*$(j)_i$.
>
> The number m of steps is taken to be the smallest integer that is strictly greater than $(d + \ell_2)/\ell_1 + 1$.

Theorem 25.1 *PSynchFD is a perfect failure detector.*

Proof.   It should be obvious that all failures are eventually detected by all other non-failed processes. We must argue that only actual failures are detected. So suppose that P_i outputs *inform-stopped*$(j)_i$. Then prior to this, P_i performs more than $(d + \ell_2)/\ell_1 + 1$ steps without receiving a message from P_j. This implies that time strictly greater than $d + \ell_2$ passes without P_i receiving any messages from P_j. But since the time between P_i's successive *send*s to P_j is at most ℓ_2, and each message takes at most time d to arrive, the time between successive receive events must be at most $d + \ell_2$. Thus, it must be that P_j has stopped. $\square$

We will also need two timing properties of *PSynchFD*. The first says that a failure notification can only occur after more than time d has elapsed since a failure. The second provides an upper bound on the time until failure notification occurs.

Theorem 25.2

1. *In any timed execution of PSynchFD containing both a stop$_j$ event and an inform-stopped$(j)_i$ event, the time from the stop$_j$ event until the inform-stopped$(j)_i$ event is strictly greater than d.*

2. *In any admissible timed execution of PSynchFD in which a stop$_j$ event occurs, within time $Ld + d + O(L\ell_2)$ after the stop$_j$ event, either an inform-stopped$(j)_i$ event or a stop$_i$ event occurs.*

Proof.

1. As in the proof of Theorem 25.1, at the point when the *inform-stopped(j)*$_i$ occurs, no message has been received by P_i from P_j for some amount of time $a > d + \ell_2$. Suppose that the *inform-stopped(j)*$_i$ event occurs at time t. Then no message from P_j arrives at P_i in the time interval $(t - a, t)$. Then it must be that no message is sent by P_j to P_i during the time interval $(t - a, t - a + \ell_2]$, for otherwise it would arrive at P_i in the time interval $(t - a, t - a + \ell_2 + d]$, which is included in the interval $(t - a, t)$. But this means that P_j must stop by time $t - a + \ell_2 < t - d$, as needed.

2. Consider an admissible timed execution of *PSynchFD* in which a *stop*$_j$ occurs, say at time t. Then no message is sent from P_j to P_i after time t, so no message is received by P_i from P_j after time $t + d$. After receiving the last message, the time for P_i to count m steps is at most $m\ell_2$. Since m is just greater than $(d + \ell_2)/\ell_1 + 1$, $m\ell_2 = Ld + O\left(L\ell_2\right)$. So if P_i does not fail in the meantime, the total time from *stop*$_j$ to *inform-stopped(j)*$_i$ is $Ld + d + O\left(L\ell_2\right)$, as needed.

$\square$

Part 1 of Theorem 25.2 has an important consequence. It implies that when any process P_i times out another process P_j, it knows that all messages that were sent by P_j prior to its failure have already arrived at their destinations.

Since we are assuming that $L\ell_2$ is small relative to d, we can think of the time bound for failure notification as approximately $Ld + d$.

25.3 Basic Results

We begin by considering what we know about the agreement problem from results in earlier chapters and attempting to extend the results to the partially synchronous setting. The main relevant results turn out to be the matching upper and lower bounds of $f + 1$ rounds, for agreement with f failures, in the synchronous model. These appear in Sections 6.2 and 6.7, respectively.

25.3.1 Upper Bound

Section 6.2 contains several algorithms that solve the agreement problem in the synchronous network model with stopping failures. Most of the algorithms that tolerate f stopping failures require exactly $f + 1$ rounds. It is possible to transform any of these algorithms to run in the partially synchronous setting. The transformation works as follows.

Let A be any synchronous network algorithm for a complete graph network. Recall that the conventions of the synchronous model imply that inputs appear in the initial states and outputs are written to write-once local variables. In terms of A, we describe an algorithm A' for the partially synchronous network model.

A' algorithm:

Each process P_i is the composition of two MMT automata: Q_i, which is node i's portion of the *PSynchFD* algorithm, plus a main automaton R_i. R_i has the *inform-stopped$_i$* actions as inputs. R_i maintains a variable *stopped*, in which it records the set of processes j for which it has received *inform-stopped$(j)_i$* inputs, that is, those that it has learned have failed. R_i also maintains a variable containing the simulated state of process i of A.

In order to simulate each round r, process R_i first determines and sends out all its round r messages from algorithm A (using one task per destination process). This determination is made using the *msgs$_i$* function of A. Next R_i waits, for each $j \neq i$, until it has either received a round r message from R_j or sees that $j \in stopped$. Then R_i determines the new simulated state of A from the old state, using the received messages (and using a *null* message for any process from which R_i has not received a round r message).

Now fix f and suppose that A is any f-fault-tolerant, $f+1$–round algorithm that solves the agreement problem in the synchronous network model. We construct a partially synchronous version A' of A as above. This is *almost*, but not quite, what we need—the difference is just that A' uses different input/output conventions from the ones that we use in this chapter. So we modify A' to obtain an algorithm B as follows: First, in B, R_i does not begin the simulation of A until it receives an *init$(v)_i$* input. At that time, it places the value v in its simulated input variable and begins the simulation of round 1. (However, Q_i begins its timeout activity right at the start of the timed execution.) Second, in B, when R_i simulates the write of value v to its output variable, it immediately thereafter performs a *decide$(v)_i$* output action.

Theorem 25.3 *B solves the agreement problem in the partially synchronous network model, and guarantees f-failure termination. Moreover, in any admissible timed execution in which inputs arrive on all ports and at most f failures occur, the time from the last init event until all nonfaulty processes have decided is at most $f(Ld + d) + d + O(fL\ell_2)$.*

Proof. It should be easy to see that B simulates A correctly, which implies that B solves the agreement problem. For the time bound, we give an operational argument. Fix an admissible timed execution α of B. Let S be an upper bound for the *PSynchFD* algorithm, where $S = Ld + d + O(L\ell_2)$. Such an S exists, by Theorem 25.2. We define a series of time milestones, $T(0), T(1), T(2), \ldots$. The milestone $T(r)$ will be shown to be an upper bound on the time for all not-yet-failed processes to complete the simulation of round r.

First, define $T(0)$ to be the time at which the last *init* occurs in α. Second, define

$$T(1) = \begin{cases} T(0) + \ell_2 + S, & \text{if some process fails by time } T(0) + \ell_2, \\ T(0) + \ell_2 + d, & \text{otherwise.} \end{cases}$$

Finally, for $r \geq 2$, define

$$T(r) = \begin{cases} T(r-1) + \ell_2 + S, & \text{if some process fails in the time interval} \\ & \quad (T(r-2) + \ell_2, T(r-1) + \ell_2], \\ T(r-1) + \ell_2 + d, & \text{otherwise.} \end{cases}$$

Because S is an upper bound for the time to detect failures, it is easy to see that

Claim 25.4 *Let $r \geq 0$ and let j be any process index. If process j fails by time $T(r) + \ell_2$, then j is detected as failed by all not-yet-failed processes by time $T(r+1)$.*

Now we can show the key claim.

Claim 25.5 *For all $r \geq 0$, $T(r)$ is an upper bound on the time for all not-yet-failed processes to complete their simulation of r rounds of A.*

Proof (of Claim 25.5).   By induction on r.

Basis: $r = 0$. This is trivial.

Inductive step: $r \geq 1$. If a process j fails by time $T(r-1) + \ell_2$, then Claim 25.4 implies that it is timed out by all not-yet-failed processes by time $T(r)$. On the other hand, if process j does not fail by time $T(r-1) + \ell_2$, then it succeeds in sending out all its round r messages by time $T(r-1) + \ell_2$. These all arrive at their destinations by time $T(r-1) + \ell_2 + d \leq T(r)$. Thus, all processes complete round r by time $T(r)$.   □

Now we show the required time bound, thereby completing the proof of Theorem 25.3. By Claim 25.5, $T(f+1)$ is an upper bound on the time for all nonfaulty processes to complete their simulation of $f + 1$ rounds, so $T(f+1) + O(\ell_2)$ is an upper bound on the time for all nonfaulty processes to perform their *decide* output actions. But the definition of the milestones and the fact that there are at most f failures imply that

$$T(f+1) \leq T(0) + f(\ell_2 + S) + (\ell_2 + d).$$

Plugging in the bound for S yields

$$T(f+1) \leq T(0) + f(Ld + d) + d + O\left(fL\ell_2\right).$$

This implies the needed bound.

25.3.2 Lower Bound

In Theorem 6.33, we showed a lower bound of $f + 1$ on the number of rounds required to solve the agreement problem in the synchronous network model with f faulty processes. With a little work, we can extend this bound to the partially synchronous model, giving a lower bound of $(f+1)d$ time. Note that there is no mention in this bound of the timing uncertainty L.

Theorem 25.6 *Suppose that $n \geq f + 2$. Then there is no n-process agreement algorithm for the partially synchronous network model that guarantees f-failure termination, in which all nonfaulty processes always decide strictly before time $(f+1)d$.*

Proof Sketch. Suppose for the sake of contradiction that there is such an algorithm A. We transform A into an f-round synchronous algorithm A', thus contradicting Theorem 6.33.

Algorithm A must, of course, work correctly when we restrict attention to a special case of the partially synchronous model, in which we only consider timed executions satisfying certain interleaving and timing constraints:

1. All inputs arrive right at the beginning, at time 0.

2. All tasks proceed as slowly as possible, subject to the ℓ_2 upper bound; therefore, all locally controlled steps of the processes occur at times that are integer multiples of ℓ_2.[1] Moreover, for each process, the task steps occur in a prespecified order.

3. For every $r \in \mathbb{N}$, all messages sent at times in the interval $[rd, (r+1)d)$ are delivered at exactly time $(r+1)d$. Moreover, messages delivered to a single process i at the same time are delivered in order of sender indices.

---

[1]Recall that we have assumed that each task always has a step enabled.

4. At a time that is a multiple of both ℓ_2 and d, all the message deliveries occur prior to all the locally controlled process steps.

Call the partially synchronous model with these restrictions the *strongly timed model*. We regard A as an algorithm for the strongly timed model. Without loss of generality, we may assume that A is "deterministic," in the sense that each process task has at most one locally controlled action enabled in any state, and that for each state and each action, there is at most one possible new state. Also, since all messages are delivered at times that are multiples of d and processes decide strictly before time $(f + 1)d$, we may assume without loss of generality that the processes decide at their first step after the time fd message deliveries.

It turns out that the behavior of algorithm A in the strongly timed model is very close to the behavior of an f-round synchronous network algorithm. In particular, for every $r \geq 1$, since no messages arrive between times $(r - 1)d$ and rd, the messages sent in the interval $[(r - 1)d, rd)$ are all determined by the process states just after the time $(r - 1)d$ message deliveries. So we might try to regard all these messages as the round r messages of a synchronous algorithm.

However, there is one significant technical difference. In the synchronous model, if a process i fails at round r, then for each $j \neq i$, process i either succeeds in sending *all* or *none* of its round r information to process j. If it succeeds in sending all its round r information to j and none to j', then this corresponds to sending *all* its messages in the interval $[(r - 1), rd)$ to j, but *none* of messages in the interval $[(r - 1), rd)$ to j', in algorithm A. But this is not a possible behavior in the strongly timed model, if i sends several messages to each of j and j' in that interval.

In order to transform A into a synchronous algorithm, it is helpful to generalize the synchronous model slightly. Namely, instead of allowing each process i, at each round r, to send only one message to each other process, we allow it to send a *finite sequence of messages*, each to an arbitrary, specified destination. We allow a failure of i to interrupt this sequence after any prefix. It is not hard to see that the proof of Theorem 6.33 extends to this slightly generalized model. It is only necessary to include extra steps in the chain constructed in the proof of Theorem 6.33 for adding and removing the messages in the sequences one at a time.

Now it is possible to transform the given agreement algorithm A into an agreement algorithm A' in this stronger synchronous model, in such a way that every execution of A' corresponds to a timed execution of A. The sequence of messages process i sends at round r of A' consists of all the messages it sends in the interval $[(r - 1)d, rd)$ of A, in the order of its steps in A. Now the behavior caused by a failure in A' does correspond to possible behavior of A.

The resulting algorithm A' is an f-round agreement algorithm for the stronger synchronous model, for $n \geq f + 2$. This is a contradiction to Theorem 6.33. $\square$

An alternative way of proving Theorem 25.6 is to carry out a new chain argument similar to the one in the proof of Theorem 6.33, but directly in terms of the strongly timed model. Again, extra steps must be included in the chain for adding and removing messages sent "in the middle" of rounds.

25.4 An Efficient Algorithm

The two results described in Section 25.3 leave an interesting gap in time complexity. The upper bound is approximately $fLd + (f+1)d$, while the lower bound is $(f+1)d$. The most notable difference is the fact that the timing uncertainty L appears in the upper bound but not in the lower bound. We would like to understand how the inherent complexity of this problem depends on the timing uncertainty.

The practical importance of understanding the impact of L on the time complexity depends on the size of L. If each process P_i of an algorithm A is run on a dedicated processor, so that the speed of P_i's steps is governed by a highly accurate processor clock, then L will typically be very small and the dependency of A's complexity on L will not matter much. On the other hand, if process speeds are determined by other factors such as process swapping, then L could be quite large and this dependency could be important. In any case, the question is interesting theoretically.

Initially, you might guess that it is possible to improve the lower bound result of Theorem 25.6 to incorporate a multiplicative factor of L. But this cannot be done: it turns out that there is a clever algorithm that runs in time approximately $Ld + (2f + 2)d$. This means, roughly speaking, that only one message delivery is "stretched" by the timing uncertainty L. There is also a more difficult lower bound proof that yields a lower bound of $Ld + (f-1)d$. We present the algorithm in this section and the lower bound in Section 25.5.

25.4.1 The Algorithm

We describe a partially synchronous algorithm, *PSynchAgreement*, which guarantees wait-free termination and which has a time bound of $Ld + (2f + 2)d + O(f\ell_2 + L\ell_2)$ when there are at most f failures. *PSynchAgreement* has a very simple description, but its behavior is rather tricky to understand. We suggest that before reading about this algorithm, you try to design a solution of your own.

In the *PSynchAgreement* algorithm, we specify that a process should send certain messages to "all processes"; this includes sending to the sender itself. The model does not actually permit this, but as usual, this can be simulated using internal steps.

PSynchAgreement algorithm:

The algorithm uses the *PSynchFD* failure detector just as algorithm B in Section 25.3.1 does. That is, each process P_i of *PSynchAgreement* is the composition of two MMT automata: Q_i, which is node i's portion of the *PSynchFD* algorithm, plus a main automaton R_i. R_i has the *inform-stopped$_i$* actions as inputs. R_i maintains a variable *stopped*, in which it records the set of processes j for which it has received *inform-stopped$(j)_i$* inputs—that is, those that it has learned have failed.

The algorithm proceeds in "rounds," numbered $0, 1, \ldots$. At each round, each R_i tries to reach a decision; however, it is only allowed to decide 0 at an even-numbered round and 1 at an odd-numbered round. R_i only begins its round 0 after it receives its input. R_i maintains a variable *decided*, to keep track of processes from which it has received a *decided* message.

Round 0: If R_i's input is 1, then R_i does the following, in order:
    send *goto*(1) to all processes
    go to round 1
If R_i's input is 0, then R_i does the following, in order:
    send *goto*(2) to all processes
    output *decide*(0)$_i$
    send *decided* to all processes

Round $r > 0$: R_i waits until a point where either it has received a *goto*$(r + 1)$ message or else it has received a *goto*(r) message from every process that is not in *stopped* $\cup$ *decided*. At that point, if R_i has received a *goto*$(r + 1)$ message, then it does the following, in order:
    send *goto*$(r + 1)$ to all processes
    go to round $r + 1$
Otherwise—that is, if R_i has not received any *goto*$(r + 1)$ message but has received a *goto*(r) message from every process that is not in *stopped* $\cup$ *decided*—R_i does the following, in order:
    send *goto*$(r + 2)$ to all processes
    output *decide*$(r \bmod 2)_i$
    send *decided* to all processes

Thus, R_i starts off by examining its initial value. If the initial value is 1, R_i advances to round 1, after telling the other processes to do the same. On the other hand, if its initial value is 0, then R_i actually decides on 0, once it has told the other processes to advance to round 2. This is to prevent the others from deciding (in a conflicting way) at round 1. (Note that the algorithm favors a decision of 0 at the beginning.)

At any later round r, if R_i is told to advance to round $r+1$, then it does so, after telling the other processes to do the same. On the other hand, if R_i has not been told to advance to round $r+1$ and it hears that every process that has not failed or decided has reached round r, then it can decide on $r \bmod 2$.

25.4.2 Safety Properties

We first show the safety properties: well-formedness, agreement, and validity. These are based on two lemmas. We say that a process i *tries to decide* at a round $r \geq 0$ provided that it sends at least one $goto(r+2)$ message in preparation for a *decide* event at round r.

Lemma 25.7 *In any timed execution of PSynchAgreement and for any $r \geq 0$, the following are true:*

1. *If any process sends a $goto(r + 2)$ message, then some process tries to decide at round r.*

2. *If any process reaches round $r + 2$, then some process tries to decide at round r.*

Proof. The first $goto(r+2)$ message must be generated in this way. A process advances to round $r + 2$ only after receiving a $goto(r + 2)$ message. □

Lemma 25.8 *In any timed execution of PSynchAgreement and for any $r \geq 0$, if a process i decides at round r, then the following are true:*

1. *R_i sends no $goto(r + 1)$ messages.*

2. *R_i sends a $goto(r + 2)$ message to every process.*

3. *No process tries to decide at round $r + 1$.*

Proof. The first two parts should be clear from the algorithm description. For the third part, suppose for the sake of contradiction that R_j tries to decide at round $r + 1$. This means that at some point in round $r + 1$, process R_j has not received a $goto(r + 2)$ message but has received a $goto(r + 1)$ message from every process that is not in $stopped_j \cup decided_j$. Since R_i sends no $goto(r + 1)$ messages, it must be that at the designated point, $i \in stopped_j \cup decided_j$.

If $i \in stopped_j$ at this point, then Theorem 25.2 implies that R_j must have already received all messages sent by R_i before R_i failed. But by Part 2, this includes a $goto(r + 2)$ message, which is a contradiction.

On the other hand, if $i \in decided_j$ at this point, then R_j must have received a *decided* message from R_i. But R_i sends such a message only after it has sent its $goto(r + 2)$ message to R_j. Then the FIFO property of the channels implies that R_j must have already received the $goto(r + 2)$ message at the designated point, which is again a contradiction.   □

Now we can show the safety properties.

Theorem 25.9 *The PSynchAgreement algorithm guarantees well-formedness, agreement, and validity.*

Proof.   Well-formedness is straightforward. For validity, if all processes start with 0, then no process can ever leave round 0. Since 1 can only be decided at odd-numbered rounds, no process can decide 1. On the other hand, if all processes start with 1, then no process tries to decide 0 at round 0. Then Lemma 25.7 implies that no process reaches round 2. It follows that no process decides 0.

For agreement, suppose that R_i decides at round r and no process decides at any earlier round. Then by Lemma 25.8, no process tries to decide at round $r + 1$. Then by Lemma 25.7, no process can reach round $r + 3$. So the only possible rounds at which processes may decide are r and $r + 2$. Since these have the same parity, all the decisions must be the same.   □

25.4.3   Liveness and Complexity

Now we prove wait-free termination, as well as the time bound. We begin with a liveness claim for admissible timed executions.

Lemma 25.10 *In any admissible timed execution of PSynchAgreement, each process continues to advance from round to round until it either fails or decides.*

Proof.   If not, then let r be the first round at which some process gets stuck; note that r must be at least 1. Let i be the index of any process that gets stuck at round r. For any other process R_j that ever fails, R_i must eventually detect the failure and place j in $stopped_i$. Also, for any other process R_j that ever decides but never fails, R_i must eventually discover that j has decided and place j in $decided_i$. Let I be the set of remaining processes—that is, all processes except those that ever fail or decide.

Then all processes in I must eventually reach round r, because r is the first round at which any process gets stuck. Since $r \geq 1$, this implies that each process $R_j, j \in I$, must send a $goto(r)$ message to R_i, which R_i eventually receives. But then R_i's condition for deciding is satisfied, so R_i must either decide or advance to round $r + 1$. This contradicts the assumption that R_i gets stuck at round r. $\square$

Now we define a notion that is useful for the liveness and complexity proofs and prove some of its properties. In a given admissible timed execution of *PSynchAgreement*, we define a round r to be *quiet* if there is *some* process that never receives a $goto(r + 1)$ message from any other process. Combining this new definition with some of the earlier lemmas, we get

Lemma 25.11 *In any admissible timed execution of PSynchAgreement and for any $r \geq 0$, the following are true:*

1. *If no process tries to decide at round r, then round $r + 1$ is quiet.*

2. *If some process decides at round r, then round $r + 2$ is quiet.*

Proof. Part 1 follows immediately from Lemma 25.7. For Part 2, if some process decides at round r, then Lemma 25.8 implies that no process tries to decide at round $r + 1$, and then Part 1 implies that $r + 2$ is quiet. $\square$

The reason that the notion of a quiet round is important is that no process can ever advance past a quiet round:

Lemma 25.12 *In any admissible timed execution of PSynchAgreement, if round r is quiet, then no process ever advances to round $r + 1$.*

Proof. If a process R_i advances to round $r + 1$, it first sends a $goto(r + 1)$ message to all processes. These are eventually received, which means that round r is not quiet. $\square$

Now we show that a quiet round must occur.

Lemma 25.13 *In any admissible timed execution of PSynchAgreement in which there are at most f failures, there is a quiet round numbered at most $f + 2$.*

Proof.   If any process decides by round f, this follows from Lemma 25.11. So suppose that no process decides by round f. Since there are at most f failures, there must be some round r, $0 \le r \le f$, in which no process fails.

We claim that no process tries to decide at round r. Suppose for the sake of contradiction that some process i does try. Then, since process i does not fail at round r, admissibility implies that process i must actually decide at round r. But this contradicts the assumption that no process decides by round f.

Since no process tries to decide at round r, Lemma 25.11 implies that round $r + 1$ is quiet. $\square$

We can now prove wait-free termination.

Theorem 25.14 *The PSynchAgreement algorithm guarantees wait-free termination.*

Proof.   Consider an admissible timed execution in which *init* events occur on all ports. Let i be any non-failing port. We argue that R_i eventually decides.

By Lemma 25.10, R_i continues to advance from round to round until it decides. But Lemma 25.13 implies that there is some quiet round r, and then Lemma 25.12 implies that R_i cannot advance to round $r + 1$. This implies that R_i must decide. $\square$

Finally, we prove the complexity bound. At this point, we fix f to be any number of failures, $0 \le f \le n$.

Theorem 25.15 *In any admissible timed execution of PSynchAgreement in which inputs arrive on all ports and there are at most f failures, the time from the last init event until all nonfaulty processes have decided is at most $Ld + (2f + 2)d + O\left(f\ell_2 + L\ell_2\right)$.*

Proof Sketch.   The proofs of Theorem 25.14 and its supporting lemmas show that the execution must consist of a series of non-quiet rounds, numbered up to at most $f + 1$, followed by a single quiet round, say round r. All processes that do not fail must decide without advancing past round r.

Let S be an upper bound for the *PSynchFD* algorithm, where $S = Ld + d + O\left(L\ell_2\right)$. Define a series of time milestones, $T', T(0), T(1), \ldots, T(r)$. T' is the time at which the last *init* occurs. For each k, $0 \le k \le r$, $T(k)$ is the earliest time at which every process has either failed, decided, or advanced to the next round, $k + 1$. Thus, all nonfaulty processes decide by time $T(r)$. It is not hard to see that $T(0) - T'$, the time for round 0, is $O\left(\ell_2\right)$. Also, for $k \ge 1$, $T(k) - T(k-1)$, the time for round k is at most $S + O\left(\ell_2\right)$, that is, slightly more than the time required to detect a failure. Thus, $T(k) - T(k-1) \le Ld + d + O\left(L\ell_2\right)$.

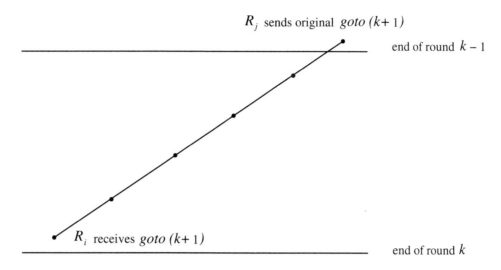

Figure 25.1: $goto(k+1)$ messages relayed from R_j to R_i.

A more interesting fact is that the time $T(k) - T(k-1)$ for any *non-quiet* round k, $1 \leq k \leq r-1$, does not depend on the timing uncertainty L. To see this, we consider any particular process R_i. Since round k is not quiet, R_i receives a $goto(k+1)$ message; we bound the time by which this happens.

This message must have originated, possibly via a series of relays, from some original $goto(k+1)$ message sent by a process R_j trying to decide at round $k-1$. See Figure 25.1.

Claim 25.16 *Let f_k denote the number of processes that fail in the middle of sending $goto(k+1)$ messages. Then the total time that elapses from the sending of the original $goto(k+1)$ message by R_j until the receipt of the $goto(k+1)$ message by R_i is at most $(f_k + 1)d + O(f_k \ell_2)$.*

Proof. R_j sends its $goto(k+1)$ message as part of an attempt to send such messages to all processes, including R_i. If R_j does not fail in the middle of this attempt, then R_j succeeds in sending this message to R_i, and R_i receives it within time d of when R_j sends it. Even if R_j does fail in the middle of this attempt, all the messages it succeeds in sending arrive within time d of when they are sent.

Likewise, each process $R_{j'}$ involved in relaying the message from R_j to R_i sends its $goto(k+1)$ message as part of an attempt to send such messages to all processes, including R_i. Again, if $R_{j'}$ does not fail in the middle of this attempt, then $R_{j'}$ succeeds in sending the message to R_i, and R_i receives it within time d

of when $R_{j'}$ sends it. Even if $R_{j'}$ does fail in the middle of this attempt, all the messages it succeeds in sending arrive within time d of when they are sent.

It follows that the total time from when the original $goto(k+1)$ message is sent by R_j until i receives some $goto(k+1)$ message is at most $(f_k+1)d+O(f_k\ell_2)$. (The ℓ_2 accounts for the time from when a relay process receives a $goto(k+1)$ message until it sends its own $goto(k+1)$ messages.)

Since the original $goto(k+1)$ message is sent by R_j while it is in round $k-1$, it follows that it is sent by time $T(k-1)$. Since all processes receive $goto(k+1)$ messages within time $(f_k+1)d+O(f_k\ell_2)$, it follows that each will either advance to round $k+1$, fail, or decide by time $T(k-1)+(f_k+1)d+O(f_k\ell_2)+O(\ell_2) = T(k-1)+(f_k+1)(d+O(\ell_2))$. This implies that $T(k)-T(k-1) \leq (f_k+1)(d+O(\ell_2))$. As we said earlier, this does not depend on the timing uncertainty L.

Since $T(0)-T'$ is $O(\ell_2)$, $T(k)-T(k-1) \leq (f_k+1)(d+O(\ell_2))$ for all k, $1 \leq k \leq r-1$, and $T(r)-T(r-1) \leq Ld+d+O(L\ell_2)$, it follows that

$$T(r)-T' \leq \Sigma_{k=1}^{r-1}(f_k+1)(d+O(\ell_2)) + Ld+d+O(L\ell_2).$$

Since $\Sigma_{k=1}^{r-1}f_k \leq f$ and $r \leq f+2$, we obtain

$$T(r)-T' \leq Ld+(2f+2)d+O(f\ell_2+L\ell_2).$$

This is the needed complexity bound.   □

25.5 A Lower Bound Involving the Timing Uncertainty*

In Section 25.4, we presented a partially synchronous agreement algorithm, *PSynchAgreement*, which works in time approximately $Ld+(2f+2)d$. The *PSynchAgreement* algorithm goes a long way toward closing the complexity gap between the simple upper bound of approximately $fLd+(f+1)d$ and the simple lower bound of $(f+1)d$ proved in Section 25.3. In particular, the *PSynch-Agreement* algorithm demonstrates that there is no hope of proving a lower bound containing a term of fLd. In this section, we prove a lower bound that does depend on L, specifically, $Ld+(f-1)d$. This still leaves a gap between the upper and lower bounds, though at least the form of the dependency of the time complexity on the timing uncertainty L is clear.

Theorem 25.17 *Suppose that $n \geq f+1$. Then there is no n-process agreement algorithm for the partially synchronous model that guarantees f-failure termination, in which all nonfaulty processes always decide strictly before time $Ld+(f-1)d$.*

The proof of Theorem 25.17 is quite interesting, because it uses a combination of several techniques from earlier chapters, including chain arguments as in Chapter 6, arguments based on reachability of various decision values as in Chapter 12, and arguments about stretching and shrinking timed executions as in Chapter 24.

Throughout the rest of this section we suppose for the sake of contradiction that A is an n-process agreement algorithm for the partially synchronous network model that guarantees f-failure termination, and in which all nonfaulty processes always decide strictly before time $Ld + (f-1)d$. Without loss of generality, we assume that A is "deterministic," as we did in the proof of Theorem 25.6. We prove a series of lemmas leading to the conclusion that A cannot exist.

First, in Lemma 25.18, we show that a certain "bad combination" of timed executions cannot occur if algorithm A is correct. This bad combination involves a "0-valent" timed execution α_0 and a "1-valent" timed execution α_1, both reaching time at least $(f-1)d$, together having few failures, and distinguishable to at most one non-failed process. Lemma 25.18 is proved using a stretching and shrinking argument. Second, in Lemma 25.19, we show that a related combination does in fact exist—one with the same conditions, except that we only require that 0 be reachable from α_0 and that 1 be reachable from α_1, rather than requiring 0-valence and 1-valence. Lemma 25.19 is proved using a chain argument. Third, in Lemma 25.20, we produce a single "bivalent" timed execution α reaching time at least $(f-1)d$ and having few failures. Lemma 25.20 follows immediately from Lemmas 25.18 and 25.19. Fourth, in Lemma 25.21, we strengthen Lemma 25.20 to include a "maximality" property, which yields two immediate extensions of α, a 0-valent extension α_0 and a 1-valent extension α_1. But this α_0 and α_1 comprise a "bad combination," yielding a contradiction.

Now we give the details. We begin by distinguishing among all the timed executions of A a subset that we call the "synchronous" timed executions. A *synchronous* infinite timed execution is one for which there is an infinite sequence of times $t_0 = 0, t_1, t_2, \ldots$ where $\ell_1 \leq t_{k+1} - t_k \leq \ell_2$ for $k \geq 0$, satisfying the following constraints:

1. All inputs arrive right at the beginning, at time t_0.

2. All the tasks of non-failed processes take steps exactly at times $t_1, t_2, \ldots$; we call these the *active times*.[2] Moreover, for each process, the task steps occur in a prespecified order.

3. Messages delivered to a single process i at the same time are delivered in order of sender indices.

---

[2]Recall once again that we have assumed that each task always has a step enabled.

4. At each active time, any message deliveries occur prior to all the locally controlled process steps.

These conditions are somewhat similar to those used in the proof sketch for Theorem 25.6. A synchronous infinite timed execution can be divided up into infinitely many "blocks" $B_0, B_1, B_2, \ldots$, where each B_k includes all the input and message delivery steps at time t_k but no locally controlled process steps at time t_k. Thus, block B_0 includes only the input events, whereas each block B_k, $k \geq 1$, starts with the locally controlled steps at time t_{k-1} and finishes with the message delivery steps at time t_k. A *synchronous* finite timed execution is a prefix of a synchronous infinite timed execution consisting of some finite number of complete blocks.

If α and α' are synchronous timed executions, where α is a finite prefix of α', we say that α is a *k-block prefix* of α', $k \geq 0$, if it consists of exactly the complete blocks $B_0, B_1, \ldots, B_k$ of α'. (In particular, a 0-block prefix contains one block, B_0.) If α is a k-block prefix of α' for some $k \geq 0$, we say that α is a *block prefix* of α', and that α' is a *block extension* of α.

We will be especially interested in certain particular kinds of block extensions. Namely, if α is a synchronous finite execution, α' is a synchronous (finite or infinite) execution, and α is a k-block prefix of α', $k \geq 0$, then we say that α' is

1. A *fast extension* of α if all steps in α' after α take the minimum time ℓ_1, that is, $t_{i+1} - t_i = \ell_1$ for all $i \geq k$.

2. A *slow extension* of α if all steps in α' after α take the maximum time ℓ_2, that is, $t_{i+1} - t_i = \ell_2$ for all $i \geq k$.

3. A *failure-free extension* of α if there are no *stop* events in α' after α.

4. An *fff-extension* of α if it is a fast, failure-free extension of α.

We emphasize that all of these types of extensions are block extensions, by complete blocks only. Note that the designation "fast" or "slow" refers only to process step time, not message-delivery time, which can still be any number in $[0, d]$.

Now we define some notions that are similar to notions used in the impossibility results for agreement in the asynchronous model in Chapter 12. We say that a value $v \in \{0, 1\}$ is *fff-reachable* from a synchronous finite timed execution α if there is some fff-extension α' of α in which some process decides v. (This decision might occur either in α or in the portion of α' after α.) We define a synchronous finite timed execution α to be 0-valent if only the value 0 is fff-reachable from α, 1-valent if only 1 is fff-reachable, and bivalent if both are fff-reachable. Timed execution α is *univalent* if it is either 0-valent or 1-valent.

We need one more notion—a notion of "indistinguishability" of two synchronous finite timed executions to a particular process i. Similar notions have been used in the synchronous and asynchronous chapters of this book. Here, the notion we need is a bit more complicated than before, because it takes into account messages that are in transit to i at the end of the executions. Namely, if α and α' are two synchronous finite timed executions with the same active times, then we say that α and α' are *indistinguishable* to i if the following conditions hold.

1. The projections of α and α' on i, that is, $\alpha|P_i$ and $\alpha'|P_i$, are time-passage equivalent.[3]

2. The same messages are sent to P_i in α and α', by the same processes, in the same order, and at the same times.

The following lemma describes a certain bad combination of timed executions that cannot occur if the algorithm A is correct.

Lemma 25.18 *There do not exist two k-block synchronous timed executions, α_0 and α_1, such that all of the following hold:*

1. *α_0 and α_1 have the same active times, $t_1, \ldots, t_k$, where $t_k \geq (f-1)d$.*

2. *α_0 is 0-valent.*

3. *α_1 is 1-valent.*

4. *$|F| \leq f - 1$, where F is the set of processes that fail in either α_0 or α_1.*

5. *α_0 and α_1 are distinguishable to at most one process not in F.*

Figure 25.2 depicts this bad combination.

Proof. Suppose for the sake of contradiction that such α_0 and α_1 exist. We will construct slow extensions β_0 and β_1, of α_0 and α_1, respectively, both leading to the same decision, say 0. Then we will speed up β_1 and remove some of the failures to obtain an fff-extension β_1', also with decision 0. This will contradict the 1-valence of α_1.

In more detail, let G be F together with the process, if any, to which the two timed executions α_0 and α_1 are distinguishable; thus, $|G| \leq f$. We produce the slow extensions β_0 and β_1, of α_0 and α_1, respectively, as follows.

---

[3]The projection operation | is defined in Section 23.2.3 and the notion of time-passage equivalence is defined in Section 23.2.1.

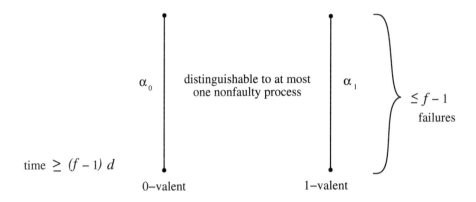

time $\geq (f-1)\, d$

Figure 25.2: Bad combination of timed executions for Lemma 25.18.

First, at time t_k, we provide *stop* events for all processes in G that have not yet failed. Then we extend α_0 and α_1 in the same way, with slow extensions having no additional failures. It is possible to extend them in the same way, because α_0 and α_1 are indistinguishable to all processes except those in G. By the assumed upper bound for A, all nonfaulty processes must decide in β_0 and β_1 strictly before time $Ld + (f-1)d \leq t_k + Ld$. Thus, strictly less than Ld time passes in the new parts of the two timed executions before decisions occur. Moreover, since α_0 and α_1 are extended in the same way, the same decision is reached in β_0 and β_1. Suppose without loss of generality that this common decision is 0. See Figure 25.3.

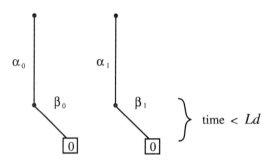

Figure 25.3: Extensions β_0 and β_1 in the proof of Lemma 25.18.

Now consider extending α_1 to an alternative synchronous timed execution β_1'; unlike β_1, β_1' will be an fff-extension of α_1. Timed execution β_1' is the same as β_1, except that the portion after α_1 is "sped up" by a factor of L to become *fast*. Moreover, no processes fail in β_1' after α_1; however, any messages sent by processes in G in β_1' after α_1 take the maximum amount d of time to arrive.

Thus, β_1' behaves, prior to time $t_k + d$, exactly like a sped-up version of β_1. (Note that once the messages sent by the processes in G arrive, things can look quite different in β_1 and β_1', but this does not matter.) Then, since all processes not in G decide 0 in β_1 strictly before time $t_k + Ld$, they will decide 0 in β_1' strictly before time $t_k + d$. See Figure 25.4.

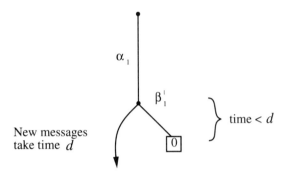

Figure 25.4: Extension β_1' in the proof of Lemma 25.18.

But since β_1' is an fff-extension of α_1, this contradicts the 1-valence of α_1. □

We will get a contradiction by showing that a bad combination of timed executions of the sort described in Lemma 25.18 must in fact occur. First we get a related combination.

Lemma 25.19 *For some k, there exist two k-block synchronous timed executions, α_0 and α_1, such that all of the following hold:*

1. *α_0 and α_1 have the same active times, $t_1, \ldots, t_k$, where $t_k \geq (f-1)d$.*

2. *0 is fff-reachable from α_0.*

3. *1 is fff-reachable from α_1.*

4. *$|F| \leq f - 1$, where F is the set of processes that fail in either α_0 or α_1.*

5. *α_0 and α_1 are distinguishable to at most one process not in F.*

Notice that the only difference between these conditions and those in the bad combination is that Conditions 2 and 3 only require that 0 and 1 be fff-reachable rather than requiring that α_0 be 0-valent and α_1 be 1-valent. See Figure 25.5.

Proof Sketch. This can be proved using a chain argument similar to the one in the proof of Theorem 6.33. The proof is left as an exercise. □

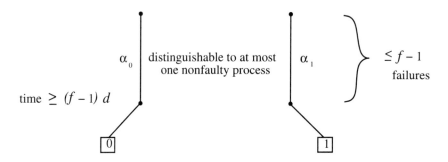

Figure 25.5: Timed executions α_0 and α_1 for Lemma 25.19.

Combining Lemmas 25.18 and 25.19 immediately yields

Lemma 25.20 *There exists a synchronous finite timed execution α such that all of the following hold:*

1. *The final active time t_k of α is at least $(f-1)d$.*

2. *α is bivalent.*

3. *At most $f - 1$ processes fail in α.*

See Figure 25.6.

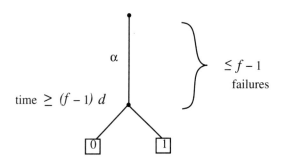

Figure 25.6: Timed execution α for Lemma 25.20.

Proof.   Let α_0 and α_1 be the two synchronous timed executions whose existence is asserted by Lemma 25.19. By Lemma 25.18, it cannot be the case that α_0 is 0-valent and also α_1 is 1-valent. Therefore, at least one of α_0 and α_1 must be bivalent, which means that it satisfies all the required conditions.   □

Now we strengthen Lemma 25.20 to include a "maximality" property.

Lemma 25.21 *There exists a synchronous finite timed execution α such that all of the following hold:*

1. *The final active time t_k of α is at least $(f-1)d$.*

2. *α is bivalent.*

3. *At most $f-1$ processes fail in α.*

4. *There are two fff-extensions of α, β_0 and β_1, each by a single block, such that*

   (a) *β_0 is 0-valent.*
   (b) *β_1 is 1-valent.*
   (c) *β_0 and β_1 are distinguishable to at most one process.*

See Figure 25.7. (Note the similarity between the configuration whose existence is asserted here and the notion of a *decider* in the proof of Theorem 12.6.)

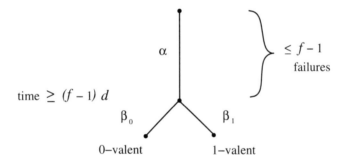

Figure 25.7: α, β_0, and β_1 for Lemma 25.21.

Proof Sketch. Let α be the synchronous finite timed execution whose existence is asserted by Lemma 25.20. Then we extend α by executing the following "program":

> while there exists a proper bivalent fff-extension of α do
> $\alpha :=$ any such extension

We know that this program eventually terminates, because decisions are required in all failure-free extensions of α before time $Ld + (f-1)d$. Consider the final α that results from this program.

We claim that this α has all the properties we need. It satisfies the needed time bound, bivalence, and failure conditions. Moreover, because it is bivalent but cannot be extended to a longer bivalent timed execution, there must be two fff-extensions of α, γ_0 and γ_1, each by a single block, such that

1. γ_0 is 0-valent.

2. γ_1 is 1-valent.

This is not quite what we need, however, because it might be that γ_0 and γ_1 are distinguishable to more than one process.

So we carry out one more chain construction between γ_0 and γ_1 to produce the needed β_0 and β_1. Starting from γ_0, at each step in the chain we simply modify all the message deliveries to one of the processes P_i so that they are the same as in γ_1. Each two consecutive timed executions in the chain are distinguishable to only one process. Since all of these timed executions must be univalent, there are two consecutive executions in the chain, β_0 and β_1, such that β_0 is 0-valent and β_1 is 1-valent. These give all the required properties.   □

Now we can obtain the contradiction.

Lemma 25.22 *A does not exist.*

Proof.   The two synchronous timed executions β_0 and β_1 whose existence is asserted by Lemma 25.21 satisfy all the requirements for a bad combination listed in the statement of Lemma 25.18. This is a contradiction.   □

This proves Theorem 25.17.

25.6   Other Results*

In this section, we consider what happens to the results about the agreement problem if we weaken the timing model in several ways. Our treatment here is informal.

25.6.1   Synchronous Processes, Asynchronous Channels*

Suppose that we weaken the model to use reliable FIFO channels, as defined in Chapter 14, with no upper bound on message-delivery time but only a guarantee of eventual delivery. However, the processes still observe the $[\ell_1, \ell_2]$ bounds. In this case, it is not hard to see that the agreement problem cannot be solved for even one stopping failure. This is so even if $\ell_1 = \ell_2$, that is, if the process step times are completely predictable.

Theorem 25.23 *There is no algorithm in the model with synchronous processes and asynchronous channels that solves the agreement problem and guarantees 1-failure termination.*

Proof Sketch. Suppose for the sake of contradiction that A is such an algorithm. Then A can be "simulated" in the asynchronous model, using an implementation of logical time as defined in Chapter 18. In this way, an algorithm for agreement in the asynchronous network model, guaranteeing 1-failure termination, can be produced, contradicting Theorem 21.2. We leave the details for an exercise.   □

25.6.2 Asynchronous Processes, Synchronous Channels*

Now suppose we weaken the partially synchronous model, this time keeping the upper bound of d on delivery of all messages, but imposing only fairness, and no time bounds, on the processes. Again, it is not hard to see that the agreement problem cannot be solved for even one stopping failure.

Theorem 25.24 *There is no algorithm in the model with asynchronous processes and d-bounded channels that solves the agreement problem and guarantees 1-failure termination.*

Proof. Suppose for the sake of contradiction that A is such an algorithm. Run the same algorithm A in the asynchronous model. Then any fair execution α of A in the asynchronous model can be "timed" in such a way that all the messages observe the upper bound of d. This means that the execution satisfies all of the conditions required for the agreement problem with 1-failure termination. Since none of these conditions depends on the times, the same conditions hold for the given fair execution α. Since this works for any fair execution α of A, it follows that A solves the agreement problem with 1-failure termination in the asynchronous model. Once again, this contradicts Theorem 21.2.   □

25.6.3 Eventual Time Bounds*

For the final result of the book, we consider the case of eventual time bounds, as we did in Section 24.4.2. That is, we consider the model where the algorithm runs asynchronously for a while, but *eventually* starts to satisfy its timing constraints. It turns out that the agreement problem is solvable in this model. However, unlike in the partially synchronous model, where the time bounds always hold, a solution requires $n > 2f$. Using an argument similar to that in the proof of Theorem 17.6, it is not hard to show that the problem is not solvable in this model if $n \leq 2f$. We leave this for an exercise.

Theorem 25.25 *The agreement problem is solvable, with f-failure termination, in the model where process task time bounds of $[\ell_1, \ell_2]$ and bounds of d for all messages hold eventually, provided that $n > 2f$.*

Designing a solution to this problem in this model is not easy. Strategies like the one used in the *PSynchAgreement* protocol, based on timing out failed processes, do not work, because before the time bounds hold, processes can conclude incorrectly that other processes have failed. We sketch an algorithm based on a different strategy.

The heart of the algorithm is an algorithm A for a variant of the *synchronous* model of Chapter 2 in which, in addition to up to f process failures, there may be some loss of messages. We assume that any messages may be lost, but that messages can only be lost for a finite number of rounds. After some point, all messages are guaranteed to be delivered. The processes do not know when this point is, however.

Algorithm A works as follows. We assume again that processes send messages to themselves as well as to the other processes.

A algorithm:

The rounds are organized into "stages" $1, 2, \ldots$ where each stage s consists of the four consecutive rounds $4s - 3$, $4s - 2$, $4s - 1$, and $4s$. Stage s is "owned" by a process, $owner(s)$; this is the process whose index is equivalent to s, modulo n.

At various times, a process may *lock* a value $v \in \{0, 1\}$, together with an associated stage number s. If process i locks (v, s), it means that process i thinks that $owner(s)$ might decide v at stage s. Process i continues to hold *some lock* for v as long as it continues to think that $owner(s)$ might decide v at stage s. A value v is *acceptable* to i if i does not have a lock on $\bar{v}$. Initially, no value is locked.

The processing during any particular stage s with owner i is as follows.

Round $4s - 3$: All processes send all their acceptable values to process i. Process i then attempts to choose a value to *propose*. In order for process i to propose v, it must hear that at least $n - f$ processes (possibly including itself) find value v acceptable at stage s. There might be more than one value that is suitable for i to propose; in this case, i chooses its own initial value.

Round $4s - 2$: If process i has determined a value v to propose, then it sends a (*"lock"*, v) message to all processes. Any process that receives such a message locks (v, s) and releases any earlier lock on the same value v.

Round 4s – 1: Any process that received a (*"lock"*, v) message at round $4s - 2$ sends an *ack* message to process i. If process i receives *ack*s from at least $f + 1$ processes, then process i decides on its proposed value v.

Round 4s: Every process sends messages containing all its current locks to every other process. Any process i that has a lock on some (v, s') and receives a message $(\bar{v}, s'')$, $s'' > s'$, that is, a newer lock for the opposite value, releases the earlier lock.

Lemma 25.26 *Algorithm A, for $n > 2f$, solves the agreement problem and guarantees f-failure termination.*

Proof. First note that

Claim 25.27 *For each stage s, there is at most one value v that is proposed at stage s, and so at most one v for which any process ever holds a lock on (v, s).*

Then an easy induction on the number of rounds (using the fact that a process favors its own initial value) implies

Claim 25.28 *If all processes begin with initial value v, then $\bar{v}$ is never proposed or locked.*

Since a process only decides on a value it has proposed, validity follows. Then we show

Claim 25.29 *If process i decides on value v at stage s, then at the end of every stage $\geq s$, at least $f + 1$ processes have locks on v with associated stage numbers $\geq s$.*

Proof. The algorithm ensures that at least $f + 1$ processes lock (v, s) at round $4s - 2$. We claim that none of these processes ever releases a lock on v without immediately acquiring another lock on the same value v.

Suppose for the sake of contradiction that one of these processes, say process i, does release a lock on v without immediately acquiring another lock on v. Then process i must release the lock because it learns about a lock on $(\bar{v}, s')$ for some $s' > s$, which means that $owner(s')$ proposes $\bar{v}$ at stage s'. Fix s' to be the first stage $> s$ at which $\bar{v}$ is proposed.

But then just prior to stage s', there must still be at least $f + 1$ locks on v, which would prevent $owner(s')$ from obtaining approval for $\bar{v}$ at round $4s' - 3$ from the required $n - f$ processes. This is a contradiction. $\qquad\square$

Now we resume the proof of Lemma 25.26. We show agreement. Suppose that process i decides v at stage s. Then no process can decide $\bar{v}$ at the same stage. Moreover, by Claim 25.29, there are always at least $f + 1$ locks on v from stage s onward. This prevents any process from obtaining approval for $\bar{v}$ from the $n - f$ processes that would be required for it to propose $\bar{v}$. So $\bar{v}$ never gets proposed, and no process ever decides $\bar{v}$.

To see termination, consider what happens after we reach the assumed point after which all messages are delivered reliably. After any subsequent stage s, it is not hard to see that there can be at most one locked value among all the non-failed processes in the system. This is because of Claim 25.27 and the lock-release rule at round $4s$. Once this is so, the owner of any stage will succeed in obtaining all the necessary approval and acknowledgments to allow it to decide (if it does not fail). □

Proof Sketch (of Theorem 25.25). We give only the general idea for the construction of an algorithm B for the model with eventual time bounds. Each process P_i of B maintains a nonnegative integer-valued local variable *clock*, initially 0. Each *clock* variable is monotonically nondecreasing. Let $C = \max\{clock_i : 1 \le i \le n\}$. Then C can be regarded as a sort of "global clock" maintained by the system. By a protocol involving repeated sending and updating of *clock* values (which we omit here), the processes can ensure that, starting soon after the point p when the time bounds begin to be satisfied:

1. The rate of growth of C with respect to real time is bounded from below and from above, by known constant bounds.

2. Each *clock* is within a known (additive) constant of C.

Thus, the processes eventually achieve rather synchronized *clock*s.

In addition to maintaining its *clock*, each process P_i of B also simulates its counterpart in algorithm A, using its local *clock* to determine what round to simulate. A fairly large (but predictable) number of clock values are devoted to the simulation of each round r—enough to ensure that after point p in the execution, any message sent by a process P_i at the beginning of P_i's simulated round r is in fact delivered to every process P_j before the end of P_j's simulated round r.

Note that prior to point p, some P_i might not finish its simulation of some round r before its *clock* advances too far. In this case, there is no harm if P_i simply omits sending the extra messages—after all, in A, they might be lost, anyhow. However, P_i must simulate the state transition for round r. It can do this at the first step after its simulation of round r is interrupted.

In this way, B simulates algorithm A and achieves the same correctness conditions. □

25.7 Postscript

In this chapter and the previous one, we have presented a few basic results for two fundamental problems of distributed computing—mutual exclusion and consensus—in partially synchronous models. These few results already demonstrate that the theory for partially synchronous distributed computing is quite different from that for either synchronous or asynchronous distributed computing.

However, much work remains to be done in this area. There are many other problems of interest in distributed computing that can be considered in the partially synchronous setting. These include many problems described in this book, for example, problems of network searching, construction of spanning trees, resource allocation, snapshots, and stable property detection. They also include many other problems that arise in real communication systems, distributed operating systems, and real-time process control systems.

It would also be useful to have general characterization results describing exactly what can be computed in partially synchronous systems, and with what time complexity. Transformation results relating the power of partially synchronous models to that of the synchronous and asynchronous models would also be good to have.

25.8 Bibliographic Notes

Most of the constructions and results in the chapter, including the *PSynchFD* failure detector, the simple upper and lower bound results in Theorems 25.3 and 25.6, and the more difficult upper and lower bound results in Theorems 25.15 and 25.17, were proved by Attiya, Dwork, Lynch, and Stockmeyer [22]. Ponzio [247, 245] extended the algorithm of Section 25.4.1 to the stronger "sending-omission" failure model and gave a less efficient algorithm for the case of Byzantine failures. Berman and Bharali [48] improved the complexity of Ponzio's sending-omission algorithm. Ponzio also obtained good upper and lower bounds on the time complexity for failure detection, in a two-node system [246]. The impossibility result for synchronous processes and asynchronous channels, Theorem 25.23, was proved first by Dolev, Dwork, and Stockmeyer [95]. The proof sketched here, based on *WelchTime*, is due to Welch [287].

Theorem 25.25, for the model with eventual time bounds, was proved by Dwork, Lynch, and Stockmeyer [104]. That paper also contains a similar result for the unknown time bound model, as well as results for other failure models. Lamport's Paxos algorithm [183] is very similar to the algorithms in [104].

Other results in the partially synchronous model include upper and lower bounds by Attiya and Mavronicolas [17] on the time to solve the session problem of Section 16.6; bounds by Wang and Zuck [284] on the size of the low-level message alphabet needed for reliable high-level message transmission; and trade-off upper and lower bounds by Kleinberg, Attiya, and Lynch [167] on the time for message delivery and the time for system quiescence, in connection management protocols.

25.9 Exercises

25.1. Give precondition-effect code for process P_i in the *PSynchFD* algorithm.

25.2. Suppose that instead of using channels that guarantee delivery of all messages in time d, we instead use channels that only guarantee delivery of the oldest message within time d.

(a) Modify the *PSynchFD* algorithm for use with such a model, trying to minimize the resulting time complexity.

(b) Prove a lower bound on the time complexity of failure detectors for this setting.

25.3. *Research Question:* Design the most efficient algorithm you can for simulating synchronous network algorithms with stopping failures in the partially synchronous model. Can you achieve an upper bound of $Ld + rd$ (plus low-order terms) on the time required to simulate r rounds?

25.4. The following alternative strategy can be used to solve the agreement problem in a partially synchronous network, in the special case where all inputs are assumed to arrive at time 0.

The processes simulate the *EIGStop* algorithm of Section 6.2.3 by relaying the information they receive as soon as they receive it, recording the values in their *EIG* trees just as before. Each process must determine when it has finished recording values in its tree. It does this by ensuring that time at least $(f + 1)(d + \ell)$ has elapsed.

Give detailed code for such an algorithm, prove that it works correctly, and analyze its time complexity.

25.5. Prove the analogue of Theorem 6.33 for the generalized synchronous model defined and used in the proof of Theorem 25.6. (*Hint:* The proof is very similar to that of Theorem 6.33.)

25.6. Fill in the details in the proof of Theorem 25.15. In particular, prove that $T(0) - T'$, the time for round 0, is $O(\ell_2)$ and for $k \geq 1$, $T(k) - T(k-1)$, the time for round k, is at most $S + O(\ell_2)$.

25.7. For an arbitrary f, $0 \leq f \leq n$, describe a particular admissible timed execution of *PSynchAgreement* in which inputs arrive on all ports and there are at most f failures, and in which the time until every process fails or decides is as long as you can manage.

25.8. Suppose that instead of using channels that guarantee delivery of all messages in time d, we instead use channels that only guarantee delivery of the oldest message within time d. Modify the *PSynchAgreement* algorithm for use with such a model, trying to minimize the resulting time complexity.

25.9. *Research Question:* Design a more efficient agreement algorithm than *PSynchAgreement* for the partially synchronous model. Can you achieve an upper bound of $Ld + fd$ (plus lower-order terms) on the time?

25.10. Prove Lemma 25.19. (*Hint:* Use a chain argument similar to the one in the proof of Theorem 6.33. Base it on a subset of the synchronous timed executions that satisfy the timing constraint that for every $r \in \mathbb{N}$, all messages sent at times in the interval $[rd, (r+1)d)$ are delivered at exactly time $(r+1)d$. The timed executions in this subset are similar to executions in the synchronous model, and the same sort of chain argument can be used.)

25.11. *Research Question:* Prove a better lower bound than the one in Theorem 25.17 for the time to reach agreement in the partially synchronous model. Can you achieve a lower bound of $Ld + fd$? Can you do better?

25.12. *Research Question:* Obtain the best upper and lower bounds you can for the problem of Byzantine agreement in the partially synchronous model.

25.13. *Research Question:* Consider the problem of k-agreement, as defined in Section 21.5, in the partially synchronous network model with f stopping failures. Obtain good upper and lower bounds on the time for all nonfaulty processes to decide. Can you achieve bounds of approximately $Ld + \frac{f}{k}d$? (This bound is suggested by the *FloodMin* algorithm and Theorem 7.14 for the synchronous network setting.)

25.14. Prove Theorem 25.23, the impossibility result for the agreement problem
in a send/receive network with synchronous processes and asynchronous
channels. (*Hint:* Show how to simulate an algorithm for this model using
the asynchronous model, using the *WelchTime* implementation of logical
time. The *clock* values used by the *WelchTime* algorithm can be maintained by counting steps.)

25.15. Prove that the agreement problem cannot be solved in the model in which
time bounds eventually hold, if $n \leq 2f$.

25.16. Complete the proof of Theorem 25.25. That is,

(a) Define the *clock* management strategy precisely.

(b) State carefully the needed claims about the degree of synchronization
and the rate of growth.

(c) Complete the description of algorithm B by describing precisely the
simulation based on the clock.

(d) Prove that B guarantees the correctness conditions for the agreement
problem, with f-failure termination.

25.17. Analyze the time complexity of the algorithm B you constructed for Exercise 25.16.

25.18. Consider the solvability of the agreement problem in the *unknown time
bound* model. In this model, we assume lower and upper time bounds ℓ_1
and ℓ_2 on process step times, $0 < \ell_1 \leq \ell_2 < \infty$, and an upper bound of d
on delivery time for each message, but these bounds are "unknown" to the
processes. (That is, they can be different in different executions, though
each execution observes fixed bounds throughout.)

Prove an analogue to Theorem 25.25 for the unknown time bound model.

25.19. *Research Question:* Redo the proofs of the time bound results for *PSynchFD*
and *PSynchAgreement* using the simulation methods of Section 23.3.3.

25.20. Obtain good upper and lower bounds for the time complexity of the *session
problem* of Section 16.6, in the partially synchronous network model.

25.21. Obtain good upper and lower bounds for the time complexity of the problem
of implementing a snapshot atomic object, as defined in Section 13.3, in the
partially synchronous shared memory model. (Be sure to describe carefully
what you are measuring.)

25.22. *Research Question*: Obtain upper and lower bounds for the time complexity of other problems of interest in distributed computing, in the partially synchronous setting. Look beyond the problems mentioned in this book to others that arise in actual communication systems, distributed operating systems, and real-time process control systems. You may also want to look beyond the specific formulation of the partially synchronous setting used in this book.

25.23. *Research Question*: Obtain general characterization results describing exactly what can be computed in partially synchronous systems, and with what time complexity, and transformation results relating the power of partially synchronous models to that of the synchronous and asynchronous models.

Bibliography

[1] Martin Abadi and Leslie Lamport. An old-fashioned recipe for real time. In J. W. de Bakker et al., editors, *Real-Time: Theory in Practice* (REX Workshop, Mook, The Netherlands, June 1991), volume 600 of *Lecture Notes in Computer Science*, pages 1–27. Springer-Verlag, New York, 1992.

[2] Karl Abrahamson. On achieving consensus using a shared memory. In *Proceedings of the Seventh Annual ACM Symposium on Principles of Distributed Computing*, pages 291–302, Toronto, Ontario, Canada, August 1988.

[3] Yehuda Afek, Hagit Attiya, Danny Dolev, Eli Gafni, Michael Merritt, and Nir Shavit. Atomic snapshots of shared memory. *Journal of the ACM*, 40(4):873–890, September 1993.

[4] Yehuda Afek, Hagit Attiya, Alan Fekete, Michael Fischer, Nancy Lynch, Yishay Mansour, Da-Wei Wang, and Lenore Zuck. Reliable communication over unreliable channels. *Journal of the ACM*, 41(6):1267–1297, November 1994.

[5] Yehuda Afek and Eli Gafni. End-to-end communication in unreliable networks. In *Proceedings of the Seventh Annual ACM Symposium on Principles of Distributed Computing*, pages 131–148, Toronto, Ontario, Canada, August 1988. ACM, New York.

[6] Yehuda Afek and Eli Gafni. Time and message bounds for election in synchronous and asynchronous complete networks. *SIAM Journal on Computing*, 20(2):376–394, April 1991.

[7] Gul A. Agha. *Actors: A Model of Concurrent Computation in Distributed Systems*. MIT Press, Cambridge, 1986.

[8] Bowen Alpern and Fred B. Schneider. Defining liveness. *Information Processing Letters*, 21(4):181–185, October 1985.

[9] Rajeev Alur and David L. Dill. A theory of timed automata. *Theoretical Computer Science*, 126(2):183–235, April 1994.

[10] Rajeev Alur and Gadi Taubenfeld. Results about fast mutual exclusion. In *Proceedings of the Real-Time Systems Symposium*, pages 12–21, Phoenix, December 1992. IEEE, Los Alamitos, Calif.

[11] James H. Anderson. Composite registers. *Distributed Computing*, 6(3):141–154, April 1993.

[12] James H. Anderson. Multi-writer composite registers. *Distributed Computing*, 7(4):175–195, May 1994.

[13] Dana Angluin. Local and global properties in networks of processors. In *Proceedings of the 12th Annual ACM Symposium on Theory of Computing*, pages 82–93, Los Angeles, April 1980.

[14] Eshrat Arjomandi, Michael J. Fischer, and Nancy A. Lynch. Efficiency of synchronous versus asynchronous distributed systems. *Journal of the ACM*, 30(3):449–456, July 1983.

[15] E. A. Ashcroft. Proving assertions about parallel programs. *Journal of Computer and System Sciences*, 10(1):110–135, February 1975.

[16] James Aspnes and Maurice Herlihy. Fast randomized consensus using shared memory. *Journal of Algorithms*, 11(3):441–461, September 1990.

[17] H. Attiya and M. Mavronicolas. Efficiency of semisynchronous versus asynchronous networks. *Mathematical Systems Theory*, 27(6):547–571, November/December 1994.

[18] Hagit Attiya, Amotz Bar-Noy, and Danny Dolev. Sharing memory robustly in message-passing systems. *Journal of the ACM*, 42(1):124–142, January 1995.

[19] Hagit Attiya, Amotz Bar-Noy, Danny Dolev, Daphne Koller, David Peleg, and Rüdiger Reischuk. Achievable cases in an asynchronous environment. In *28th Annual Symposium on Foundations of Computer Science*, pages 337–346. IEEE, Los Alamitos, Calif., October 1987.

[20] Hagit Attiya, Amotz Bar-Noy, Danny Dolev, David Peleg, and Rüdiger Reischuk. Renaming in an asynchronous environment. *Journal of the ACM*, 37(3):524–548, July 1990.

[21] Hagit Attiya, Shlomi Dolev, and Jennifer L. Welch. Connection management without retaining information. In *Proceedings of the 28th Annual Hawaii International Conference on System Sciences*, volume II (Software Technology), pages 622–631, Wailea, Hawaii, January 1995. IEEE, Los Alamitos, Calif.

[22] Hagit Attiya, Cynthia Dwork, Nancy Lynch, and Larry Stockmeyer. Bounds on the time to reach agreement in the presence of timing uncertainty. *Journal of the ACM*, 41(1):122–152, January 1994.

[23] Hagit Attiya, Michael Fischer, Da-Wei Wang, and Lenore Zuck. Reliable communication using unreliable channels. Manuscript, 1989.

[24] Hagit Attiya, Nancy Lynch, and Nir Shavit. Are wait-free algorithms fast? *Journal of the ACM*, 41(4):725–763, July 1994.

[25] Hagit Attiya and Nancy A. Lynch. Time bounds for real-time process control in the presence of timing uncertainty. *Information and Computation*, 110(1):183–232, April 1994.

[26] Hagit Attiya and Ophir Rachman. Atomic snapshots in $O(n \log n)$ operations. In *Proceedings of the 12th Annual ACM Symposium on Principles of Distributed Computing*, pages 29–40, Ithaca, N.Y., August 1993.

[27] Hagit Attiya, Marc Snir, and Manfred K. Warmuth. Computing in an anonymous ring. *Journal of the ACM*, 35(4):845–875, October 1988.

[28] Hagit Attiya and Jennifer L. Welch. Sequential consistency versus linearizability. *ACM Transactions on Computer Systems*, 12(2):91–122, May 1994.

[29] Baruch Awerbuch. Complexity of network synchronization. *Journal of the ACM*, 32(4):804–823, October 1985.

[30] Baruch Awerbuch. Reducing complexities of the distributed max-flow and breadth-first search algorithms by means of network synchronization. *Networks*, 15(4):425–437, winter 1985.

[31] Baruch Awerbuch. Optimal distributed algorithms for minimum weight spanning tree, counting, leader election and related problems. In *Proceedings of the 19th Annual ACM Symposium on Theory of Computing*, pages 230–240, New York, May 1987.

[32] Baruch Awerbuch, Bonnie Berger, Lenore Cowen, and David Peleg. Near-linear cost sequential and distributed constructions of sparse neighborhood covers. In *34th Annual Symposium on Foundations of Computer Science*, pages 638–647, Palo Alto, Calif., November 1993. IEEE, Los Alamitos, Calif.

[33] Baruch Awerbuch and Robert G. Gallager. Distributed BFS algorithms. In *26th Annual Symposium on Foundations of Computer Science*, pages 250–256, Portland, Ore., October 1985. IEEE, Los Alamitos, Calif.

[34] Baruch Awerbuch, Oded Goldreich, David Peleg, and Ronen Vainish. A tradeoff between information and communication in broadcast protocols. *Journal of the ACM*, 37(2):238–256, April 1990.

[35] Baruch Awerbuch and David Peleg. Sparse partitions. In *31st Annual Symposium on Foundations of Computer Science*, volume II, pages 503–513, St. Louis, October 1990. IEEE, Los Alamitos, Calif.

[36] Baruch Awerbuch and David Peleg. Routing with polynomial communication-space trade-off. *SIAM Journal of Discrete Mathematics*, 5(2):151–162, 1992.

[37] Baruch Awerbuch and Michael Saks. A Dining Philosophers algorithm with polynomial response time. In *31st Annual Symposium on Foundations of Computer Science*, volume I, pages 65–74, St. Louis, October 1990. IEEE, Los Alamitos, Calif.

[38] J. C. M. Baeten and W. P. Weijland. *Process Algebra*. Cambridge Tracts in Theoretical Computer Science 18. Cambridge University Press, Cambridge, U.K., 1990.

[39] Amotz Bar-Noy, Danny Dolev, Cynthia Dwork, and H. Raymond Strong. Shifting gears: Changing algorithms on the fly to expedite Byzantine agreement. In *Proceedings of the Sixth Annual ACM Symposium on Principles of Distributed Computing*, pages 42–51, Vancouver, British Columbia, Canada, August 1987.

[40] Amotz Bar-Noy, Danny Dolev, Daphne Koller, and David Peleg. Fault-tolerant critical section management in asynchronous environments. *Information and Computation*, 95(1):1–20, November 1991.

[41] Alan E. Baratz and Adrian Segall. Reliable link initialization procedures. *IEEE Transactions on Communications*, 36(2):144–152, February 1988.

[42] K. A. Bartlett, R. A. Scantlebury, and P. T. Wilkinson. A note on reliable full-duplex transmission over half-duplex links. *Communications of the ACM*, 12(5):260–261, May 1969.

[43] Richard Bellman. On a routing problem. *Quarterly of Applied Mathematics*, 16(1):87–90, 1958.

[44] Dag Belsnes. Single-message communication. *IEEE Transactions on Communications*, COM-24(2):190–194, February 1976.

[45] M. Ben-Ari. *Principles of concurrent programming.* Prentice Hall, Englewood Cliffs, N.J., 1982.

[46] Michael Ben-Or. Another advantage of free choice: Completely asynchronous agreement protocols. In *Proceedings of the Second Annual ACM Symposium on Principles of Distributed Computing*, pages 27–30, Montreal, Quebec, Canada, August 1983.

[47] Claude Berge. *Graphs and Hypergraph.* North-Holland, Amsterdam, 1973.

[48] Piotr Berman and Anupam A. Bharali. Distributed consensus in semi-synchronous systems. In *Proceedings of the Sixth International Parallel Processing Symposium*, pages 632–635, Beverly Hills, March 1992. IEEE, Los Alamitos, Calif.

[49] Piotr Berman and Juan A. Garay. Cloture voting: $n/4$-resilient distributed consensus in $t + 1$ rounds. *Mathematical Systems Theory—An International Journal on Mathematical Computing Theory*, 26(1):3–20, 1993. Special issue on Fault-Tolerant Distributed Algorithms.

[50] P. A. Bernstein, V. Hadzilacos, and N. Goodman. *Concurrency Control and Recovery in Database Systems.* Addison-Wesley, Reading, Mass., 1987.

[51] Ofer Biran, Shlomo Moran, and Shmuel Zaks. A combinatorial characterization of the distributed 1-solvable tasks. *Journal of Algorithms*, 11(3):420–440, September 1990.

[52] Kenneth P. Birman and Thomas A. Joseph. Reliable communication in the presence of failures. *ACM Transactions on Computer Systems*, 5(1):47–76, February 1987.

[53] Bard Bloom. Constructing two-writer atomic registers. *IEEE Transactions on Communications*, 37(12):1506–1514, December 1988.

[54] Gregor Bochmann and Jan Gecsei. A unified method for the specification and verification of protocols. In B. Gilchrist, editor, *Information Processing 77* (Toronto, August 1977), volume 7 of *Proceedings of IFIP Congress*, pages 229–234. North-Holland, Amsterdam, 1977.

[55] Elizabeth Borowsky and Eli Gafni. Generalized FLP impossibility result for *t*-resilient asynchronous computations. In *Proceedings of the 25th Annual ACM Symposium on Theory of Computing*, pages 91–100, San Diego, May 1993.

[56] Gabriel Bracha and Sam Toueg. Asynchronous consensus and broadcast protocols. *Journal of the ACM*, 32(4):824–840, October 1985.

[57] Gabriel Bracha and Sam Toueg. Distributed deadlock detection. *Distributed Computing*, 2(3):127–138, December 1987.

[58] Michael F. Bridgland and Ronald J. Watro. Fault-tolerant decision making in totally asynchronous distributed systems. In *Proceedings of the Sixth Annual ACM Symposium on Principles of Distributed Computing*, pages 52–63, Vancouver, British Columbia, Canada, August 1987.

[59] Manfred Broy. Functional specification of time sensitive communicating systems. In W. P. de Roever, J. W. de Bakker, and G. Rozenberg, editors, *Stepwise Refinement of Distributed Systems: Models, Formalisms, Correctness* (REX Workshop, Mook, The Netherlands, May/June 1989), volume 430 of *Lecture Notes in Computer Science*, pages 153–179. Springer-Verlag, New York, 1990.

[60] James E. Burns. Mutual exclusion with linear waiting using binary shared variables. *ACM SIGACT News*, 10(2):42–47, summer 1978.

[61] James E. Burns. A formal model for message passing systems. Technical Report TR-91, Computer Science Department, Indiana University, Bloomington, September 1980.

[62] James E. Burns, Paul Jackson, Nancy A. Lynch, Michael J. Fischer, and Gary L. Peterson. Data requirements for implementation of N-process mutual exclusion using a single shared variable. *Journal of the ACM*, 29(1):183–205, January 1982.

[63] James E. Burns and Nancy A. Lynch. Bounds on shared memory for mutual exclusion. *Information and Computation*, 107(2):171–184, December 1993.

[64] O. S. F. Carvalho and G. Roucairol. On mutual exclusion in computer networks. *Communications of the ACM*, 26(2):146–148, February 1983.

[65] Tushar Deepak Chandra, Vassos Hadzilacos, and Sam Toueg. The weakest failure detector for solving consensus. In *Proceedings of the 11th Annual ACM Symposium on Principles of Distributed Computing*, pages 147–158, Vancouver, British Columbia, Canada, August 1992. To appear in *Journal of ACM*.

[66] Tushar Deepak Chandra and Sam Toueg. Unreliable failure detectors for asynchronous systems. In *Proceedings of the 10th Annual ACM Symposium on Principles of Distributed Computing*, pages 325–340, Montreal, Quebec, Canada, August 1991. To appear in the *Journal of the ACM*.

[67] K. M. Chandy and J. Misra. The Drinking Philosophers problem. *ACM Transactions on Programming Languages and Systems*, 6(4):632–646, October 1984.

[68] K. Mani Chandy and Leslie Lamport. Distributed snapshots: Determining global states of distributed systems. *ACM Transactions on Computer Systems*, 3(1):63–75, February 1985.

[69] K. Mani Chandy and Jayadev Misra. *Parallel Program Design: A Foundation*. Addison-Wesley, Reading, Mass., 1988.

[70] K. Mani Chandy, Jayadev Misra, and Laura M. Haas. Distributed deadlock detection. *ACM Transactions on Computer Systems*, 1(2):144–156, May 1983.

[71] Ernest Chang and Rosemary Roberts. An improved algorithm for decentralized extrema-finding in circular configurations of processes. *Communications of the ACM*, 22(5):281–283, May 1979.

[72] Ernest J. H. Chang. Echo algorithms: Depth parallel operations on general graphs. *IEEE Transactions on Software Engineering*, SE-8(4):391–401, July 1982.

[73] Soma Chaudhuri. More *choices* allow more *faults*: Set consensus problems in totally asynchronous systems. *Information and Computation*, 105(1):132–158, July 1993.

[74] Soma Chaudhuri, Rainer Gawlick, and Nancy Lynch. Designing algorithms for distributed systems with partially synchronized clocks. In *Proceedings*

of the 12th Annual ACM Symposium on Principles of Distributed Computing, pages 121–132, Ithaca, N.Y., August 1993.

[75] Soma Chaudhuri, Maurice Herlihy, Nancy A. Lynch, and Mark R. Tuttle. Tight bounds for k-set agreement. Technical Report 95/4, Digital Equipment Corporation, Cambridge Research Lab, Cambridge, Mass. To appear.

[76] Soma Chaudhuri, Maurice Herlihy, Nancy A. Lynch, and Mark R. Tuttle. A tight lower bound for k-set agreement. In *34th Annual Symposium on Foundations of Computer Science*, pages 206–215, Palo Alto, Calif., November 1993. IEEE, Los Alamitos, Calif.

[77] Soma Chaudhuri, Maurice Herlihy, Nancy A. Lynch, and Mark R. Tuttle. A tight lower bound for processor coordination. In Donald S. Fussell and Miroslaw Malek, editors, *Responsive Computer Systems: Steps Toward Fault-Tolerant Real-Time Systems*, chapter 1, pages 1–18. Kluwer Academic, Boston, 1995. (Selected papers from *Second International Workshop on Responsive Computer Systems*, Lincoln, N.H., September 1993.)

[78] Benny Chor, Amos Israeli, and Ming Li. On processor coordination using asynchronous hardware. In *Proceedings of the Sixth Annual ACM Symposium on Principles of Distributed Computing*, pages 86–97, Vancouver, British Columbia, Canada, 1987.

[79] Ching-Tsun Chou and Eli Gafni. Understanding and verifying distributed algorithms using stratified decomposition. In *Proceedings of the Seventh Annual ACM Symposium on Principles of Distributed Computing*, pages 44–65, Toronto, Ontario, Canada, August 1988.

[80] Manhoi Choy and Ambuj K. Singh. Efficient fault tolerant algorithms for resource allocation in distributed systems. In *Proceedings of the 24th Annual ACM Symposium on Theory of Computing*, pages 593–602, Victoria, British Columbia, Canada, May 1992.

[81] William Douglas Clinger. *Foundations of Actor Semantics*. Ph.D. thesis, Department of Mathematics, Massachusetts Institute of Technology, Cambridge, June 1981. University Microfilms, Ann Arbor, Mich.

[82] Brian A. Coan. *Achieving Consensus in Fault-Tolerant Distributed Computer Systems: Protocols, Lower Bounds, and Simulations*. Ph.D. thesis, Department of Electrical Engineering and Computer Science, Massachusetts Institute of Technology, Cambridge, June 1987.

[83] Thomas H. Cormen, Charles E. Leiserson, and Ronald L. Rivest. *Introduction to Algorithms*. MIT Press/McGraw-Hill, Cambridge, Mass./New York, 1990.

[84] Armin B. Cremers and Thomas N. Hibbard. Mutual exclusion of N processors using an $O(N)$-valued message variable. In G. Ausiello and C. Böhm, editors, *Automata, Languages and Programming: Fifth Colloquium* (5th ICALP, Udine, Italy, July 1978), volume 62 of *Lecture Notes in Computer Science*, pages 165–176. Springer-Verlag, New York, 1978.

[85] Armin B. Cremers and Thomas N. Hibbard. Arbitration and queueing under limited shared storage requirements. Technical Report 83, Department of Informatics, University of Dortmund, March 1979.

[86] N. G. de Bruijn. Additional comments on a problem in concurrent programming control. *Communications of the ACM*, 10(3):137–138, March 1967.

[87] W. P. de Roever and F. A. Stomp. A correctness proof of a distributed minimum-weight spanning tree algorithm. In *Proceedings of the Seventh International Conference on Distributed Computing Systems*, pages 440–447, Berlin, September 1987. IEEE, Los Alamitos, Calif.

[88] Richard A. DeMillo, Nancy A. Lynch, and Michael J. Merritt. Cryptographic protocols. In *Proceedings of the 14th Annual ACM Symposium on Theory of Computing*, pages 383–400, San Francisco, May 1982.

[89] Harish Devarajan. A correctness proof for a network synchronizer. Master's thesis, Department of Electrical Engineering and Computer Science, Massachusetts Institute of Technology, Cambridge, May 1993. Technical Report MIT/LCS/TR-588.

[90] E. W. Dijkstra. Solution of a problem in concurrent programming control. *Communications of the ACM*, 8(9):569, September 1965.

[91] E. W. Dijkstra. Hierarchical ordering of sequential processes. *Acta Informatica*, 1(2):115–138, 1971.

[92] Edsger W. Dijkstra and C. S. Scholten. Termination detection for diffusing computations. *Information Processing Letters*, 11(1):1–4, August 1980.

[93] D. Dolev and H. R. Strong. Authenticated algorithms for Byzantine agreement. *SIAM Journal of Computing*, 12(4):656–666, November 1983.

[94] Danny Dolev. The Byzantine generals strike again. *Journal of Algorithms*, 3(1):14–30, March 1982.

[95] Danny Dolev, Cynthia Dwork, and Larry Stockmeyer. On the minimal synchronism needed for distributed consensus. *Journal of the ACM*, 34(1):77–97, January 1987.

[96] Danny Dolev, Michael J. Fischer, Rob Fowler, Nancy A. Lynch, and H. Raymond Strong. An efficient algorithm for Byzantine agreement without authentication. *Information and Control*, 52(3):257–274, March 1982.

[97] Danny Dolev, Maria Klawe, and Michael Rodeh. An $O(n \log n)$ unidirectional distributed algorithm for extrema finding in a circle. *Journal of Algorithms*, 3(3):245–260, September 1982.

[98] Danny Dolev, Nancy A. Lynch, Shlomit S. Pinter, Eugene W. Stark, and William E. Weihl. Reaching approximate agreement in the presence of faults. *Journal of the ACM*, 33(3):499–516, July 1986.

[99] Danny Dolev, Rudiger Reischuk, and H. Raymond Strong. Early stopping in Byzantine agreement. *Journal of the ACM*, 37(4):720–741, October 1990.

[100] Danny Dolev and Nir Shavit. Bounded concurrent time-stamp systems are constructible. In *Proceedings of the 21st Annual ACM Symposium on Theory of Computing*, pages 454–466, Seattle, May 1989. To appear in *SIAM Journal of Computing*.

[101] Danny Dolev and H. Raymond Strong. Polynomial algorithms for multiple processor agreement. In *Proceedings of the 14th Annual ACM Symposium on Theory of Computing*, pages 401–407, San Francisco, May 1982.

[102] Cynthia Dwork, Maurice Herlihy, Serge A. Plotkin, and Orli Waarts. Time-lapse snapshots. In D. Dolev, Z. Galil, and M. Rodeh, editors, *Theory of Computing and Systems* (ISTCS '92, Israel Symposium, Haifa, May 1992), volume 601 of *Lecture Notes in Computer Science*, pages 154–170. Springer-Verlag, New York, 1992.

[103] Cynthia Dwork, Maurice P. Herlihy, and Orli Waarts. Contention in shared memory algorithms. In *Proceedings of the 25th Annual ACM Symposium on Theory of Computing*, pages 174–183, San Diego, May 1993. Expanded version in Technical Report CRL 93/12, Digital Equipment Corporation, Cambridge Research Lab, Cambridge, Mass.

[104] Cynthia Dwork, Nancy Lynch, and Larry Stockmeyer. Consensus in the presence of partial synchrony. *Journal of the ACM*, 35(2):288–323, April 1988.

[105] Cynthia Dwork and Yoram Moses. Knowledge and common knowledge in a Byzantine environment: Crash failures. *Information and Computation*, 88(2):156–186, October 1990.

[106] Cynthia Dwork and Dale Skeen. The inherent cost of nonblocking commitment. In *Proceedings of the Second Annual ACM Symposium on Principles of Distributed Computing*, pages 1–11, Montreal, Quebec, Canada, August 1983.

[107] Cynthia Dwork and Orli Waarts. Simple and efficient bounded concurrent timestamping and the traceable use abstraction. In *Proceedings of the 24th Annual ACM Symposium on Theory of Computing*, pages 655–666, Victoria, British Columbia, Canada, May 1992. Preliminary. Final version to appear in *Journal of the ACM*.

[108] Murray A. Eisenberg and Michael R. McGuire. Further comments on Dijkstra's concurrent programming control problem. *Communications of the ACM*, 15(11):999, November 1972.

[109] A. Fekete, N. Lynch, and L. Shrira. A modular proof of correctness for a network synchronizer. In J. van Leeuwen, editor, *Distributed Algorithms* (2nd International Workshop, Amsterdam, July 1987), volume 312 of *Lecture Notes in Computer Science*, pages 219–256. Springer-Verlag, New York, 1988.

[110] A. D. Fekete. Asymptotically optimal algorithms for approximate agreement. *Distributed Computing*, 4(1):9–29, March 1990.

[111] A. D. Fekete. Asynchronous approximate agreement. *Information and Computation*, 115(1):95–124, November 15, 1994.

[112] Alan Fekete, Nancy Lynch, Yishay Mansour, and John Spinelli. The impossibility of implementing reliable communication in the face of crashes. *Journal of the ACM*, 40(5):1087–1107, November 1993.

[113] Paul Feldman and Silvio Micali. An optimal probabilistic protocol for synchronous Byzantine agreement. To appear in *SIAM Journal on Computing*. Preliminary version appeared as Technical Report MIT/LCS/TM-425.b, Laboratory for Computer Science, Massachusetts Institute of Technology, Cambridge, December 1992.

[114] Paul Neil Feldman. *Optimal Algorithms for Byzantine Agreement*. Ph.D. thesis, Department of Mathematics, Massachusetts Institute of Technology, Cambridge, June 1988.

[115] Colin J. Fidge. Timestamps in message-passing systems that preserve the partial ordering. In *Proceedings of the 11th Australian Computer Science Conference*, pages 56–66, Brisbane, Australia, February 1988.

[116] Michael Fischer. Re: Where are you? E-mail message to Leslie Lamport. Arpanet message number 8506252257.AA07636@YALE-BULLDOG .YALE.ARPA (47 lines), June 25, 1985.

[117] Michael J. Fischer. The consensus problem in unreliable distributed systems (a brief survey). Research Report YALEU/DCS/RR-273, Yale University, Department of Computer Science, New Haven, Conn., June 1983.

[118] Michael J. Fischer, Nancy D. Griffeth, and Nancy A. Lynch. Global states of a distributed system. *IEEE Transactions on Software Engineering*, SE-8(3):198–202, May 1982.

[119] Michael J. Fischer and Nancy A. Lynch. A lower bound for the time to assure interactive consistency. *Information Processing Letters*, 14(4):183–186, June 1982.

[120] Michael J. Fischer, Nancy A. Lynch, James E. Burns, and Allan Borodin. Resource allocation with immunity to limited process failure. In *20th Annual Symposium on Foundations of Computer Science*, pages 234–254, San Juan, Puerto Rico, October 1979. IEEE, Los Alamitos, Calif.

[121] Michael J. Fischer, Nancy A. Lynch, James E. Burns, and Allan Borodin. Distributed FIFO allocation of identical resources using small shared space. *ACM Transactions on Programming Languages and Systems*, 11(1):90–114, January 1989.

[122] Michael J. Fischer, Nancy A. Lynch, and Michael Merritt. Easy impossibility proofs for distributed consensus problems. *Distributed Computing*, 1(1):26–39, January 1986.

[123] Michael J. Fischer, Nancy A. Lynch, and Michael S. Paterson. Impossibility of distributed consensus with one faulty process. *Journal of the ACM*, 32(2):374–382, April 1985.

[124] Robert W. Floyd. Assigning meanings to programs. In *Mathematical Aspects of Computer Science* (New York, April 1966), volume 19 of *Proceedings of the Symposia in Applied Mathematics*, pages 19–32. American Mathematical Society, Providence, 1967.

[125] L. R. Ford, Jr. and D. R. Fulkerson. *Flows in Networks*. Princeton University Press, Princeton, N.J., 1962.

[126] Nissim Francez. Distributed termination. *ACM Transactions on Programming Languages and Systems*, 2(1):42–55, January 1980.

[127] Greg N. Frederickson and Nancy A. Lynch. Electing a leader in a synchronous ring. *Journal of the ACM*, 34(1):98–115, January 1987.

[128] Harold N. Gabow. Scaling algorithms for network problems. *Journal of Computer and System Sciences*, 31(2):148–168, October 1985.

[129] Eli Gafni. Personal communication, April 1994.

[130] R. G. Gallager, P. A. Humblet, and P. M. Spira. A distributed algorithm for minimum-weight spanning trees. *ACM Transactions on Programming Languages and Systems*, 5(1):66–77, January 1983.

[131] Robert G. Gallager. Distributed minimum hop algorithms. Technical Report LIDS-P-1175, Laboratory for Information and Decision Systems, Massachusetts Institute of Technology, Cambridge, January 1982.

[132] Juan A. Garay, Shay Kutten, and David Peleg. A sub-linear time distributed algorithm for minimum-weight spanning trees. In *34th Annual Symposium on Foundations of Computer Science*, pages 659–668, Palo Alto, Calif., November 1993. IEEE, Los Alamitos, Calif.

[133] Juan A. Garay and Yoram Moses. Fully polynomial Byzantine agreement in $t + 1$ rounds. In *Proceedings of the 25th Annual ACM Symposium on Theory of Computing*, pages 31–41, San Diego, May 1993.

[134] Stephen J. Garland and John V. Guttag. A guide to LP, the Larch Prover. Research Report 82, Digital Systems Research Center, Palo Alto, Calif., December 1991.

[135] Rainer Gawlick, Nancy Lynch, and Nir Shavit. Concurrent time-stamping made simple. In D. Dolev, Z. Galil, and M. Rodeh, editors, *Theory of Computing and Systems* (ISTCS '92, Israel Symposium, Haifa, May 1992), volume 601 of *Lecture Notes in Computer Science*, pages 171–185. Springer-Verlag, New York, 1992.

[136] Rainer Gawlick, Roberto Segala, Jørgen Søgaard-Andersen, and Nancy Lynch. Liveness in timed and untimed systems. In Serge Abiteboul and Eli Shamir, editors, *Automata, Languages and Programming* (21st International Colloquium, ICALP '94, Jerusalem, July 1994), volume 820 of *Lecture Notes in Computer Science*, pages 166–177. Springer-Verlag, New York, 1994.

[137] David K. Gifford. Weighted voting for replicated data. In *Proceedings of the Seventh Symposium on Operating Systems Principles*, pages 150–162, Pacific Grove, Calif., December 1979. ACM, New York.

[138] Virgil D. Gligor and Susan H. Shattuck. On deadlock detention in distributed systems. *IEEE Transactions on Software Engineering*, SE-6(5):435–440, September 1980.

[139] Kenneth Goldman and Kathy Yelick. A unified model for shared-memory and message-passing systems. Technical Report WUCS–93–35, Washington University, St. Louis, June 1993.

[140] Kenneth J. Goldman and Nancy Lynch. Quorum consensus in nested transaction systems. *ACM Transactions on Database Systems*, 19(4):537–585, December 1994.

[141] Kenneth J. Goldman and Nancy A. Lynch. Modelling shared state in a shared action model. In *Proceedings of the Fifth Annual IEEE Symposium on Logic in Computer Science*, pages 450–463, Philadelphia, June 1990.

[142] J. N. Gray. Notes on data base operating systems. In R. Bayer, R. M. Graham, and G. Seegmüller, editors, *Operating Systems: An Advanced Course*, volume 60 of *Lecture Notes in Computer Science*, chapter 3.F, page 465. Springer-Verlag, New York, 1978.

[143] Vassos Hadzilacos and Sam Toueg. Fault-tolerant broadcasts and related problems. In Sape Mullender, editor, *Distributed Systems*, second edition, chapter 5, pages 97–145. ACM Press/Addison-Wesley, New York/Reading, Mass., 1993.

[144] S. Haldar and K. Vidyasankar. Constructing 1-writer multireader multivalued atomic variables from regular variables. *Journal of the ACM*, 42(1):186–203, January 1995.

[145] Joseph Y. Halpern, Yoram Moses, and Orli Waarts. A characterization of eventual byzantine agreement. In *Proceedings of the Ninth Annual ACM*

Symposium on Principles of Distributed Computing, pages 333–346, Quebec City, Quebec, Canada, August 1990.

[146] Joseph Y. Halpern and Lenore D. Zuck. A little knowledge goes a long way: Knowledge-based proofs for a family of protocols. *Journal of the ACM*, 39(3):449–478, July 1992.

[147] Frank Harary. *Graph Theory*. Addison-Wesley, Reading, Mass., 1972.

[148] Constance Heitmeyer and Nancy Lynch. The generalized railroad crossing: A case study in formal verification of real-time systems. Technical Memo MIT/LCS/TM-511, Laboratory for Computer Science, Massachusetts Institute of Technology, Cambridge, November 1994. Abbreviated version in *Proceedings of the Real-Time Systems Symposium*, pages 120–131, San Juan, Puerto Rico, December 1994. IEEE, Los Alamitos, Calif. Later version to appear in C. Heitmeyer and D. Mandrioli, editors *Formal Methods for Real-time Computing*, chapter 4, *Trends in Software* series, John Wiley & Sons, New York.

[149] Maurice Herlihy. A quorum-consensus replication method for abstract data types. *ACM Transactions on Computer Systems*, 4(1):32–53, February 1986.

[150] Maurice Herlihy. Wait-free synchronization. *ACM Transactions on Programming Languages and Systems*, 13(1):124–149, January 1991.

[151] Maurice Herlihy and Nir Shavit. A simple constructive computatability theorem for wait-free computation. In *Proceedings of the 26th Annual ACM Symposium on Theory of Computing*, pages 243–262, Montreal, Quebec, Canada, May 1994.

[152] Maurice P. Herlihy and Nir Shavit. The asynchronous computability theorem for *t*-resilient tasks. In *Proceedings of the 25th Annual ACM Symposium on Theory of Computing*, pages 111–120, San Diego, May 1993.

[153] Maurice P. Herlihy and Jeannette M. Wing. Linearizability: A correctness condition for concurrent objects. *ACM Transactions on Programming Languages and Systems*, 12(3):463–492, July 1990.

[154] Maurice Peter Herlihy. *Replication Methods for Abstract Data Types*. Ph.D. thesis, Department of Electrical Engineering and Computer Science, Massachusetts Institute of Technology, Cambridge, May 1984. Technical Report MIT/LCS/TR-319.

[155] Lisa Higham and Teresa Przytycka. A simple, efficient algorithm for maximum finding on rings. In André Schiper, editor, *Distributed Algorithms* (7th International Workshop, WDAG '93, Lausanne, Switzerland, September 1993), volume 725 of *Lecture Notes in Computer Science*, pages 249–263. Springer-Verlag, New York, 1993.

[156] D. S. Hirschberg and J. B. Sinclair. Decentralized extrema-finding in circular configurations of processes. *Communications of the ACM*, 23(11):627–628, November 1980.

[157] Gary S. Ho and C. V. Ramamoorthy. Protocols for deadlock detection in distributed database systems. *IEEE Transactions on Software Engineering*, SE-8(6):554–557, November 1982.

[158] C. A. R. Hoare. Proof of correctness of data representations. *Acta Informatica*, 1(4):271–281, 1972.

[159] C. A. R. Hoare. *Communicating Sequential Processes*. Prentice-Hall International, United Kingdom, 1985.

[160] Pierre A. Humblet. A distributed algorithm for minimum weight directed spanning trees. *IEEE Transactions on Communications*, COM-31(6):756–762, June 1983.

[161] Sreekaanth S. Isloor and T. Anthony Marsland. An effective "on-line" deadlock detection technique for distributed database management systems. In *Proceedings of COMPSAC 78: IEEE Computer Society's Second International Computer Software and Applications Conference*, pages 283–288, Chicago, November 1978.

[162] Amos Israeli and Ming Li. Bounded time-stamps. *Distributed Computing*, 6(4):205–209, July 1993.

[163] Amos Israeli and Meir Pinhasov. A concurrent time-stamp scheme which is linear in time and space. In A. Segall and S. Zaks, editors, *Distributed Algorithms: Sixth International Workshop* (WDAG '92, Haifa, Israel, November 1992), volume 647 of *Lecture Notes in Computer Science*, pages 95–109. Springer-Verlag, New York, 1992.

[164] Wil Janssen and Job Zwiers. From sequential layers to distributed processes: Deriving a distributed minimum weight spanning tree algorithm. In *Proceedings of the 11th Annual ACM Symposium on Principles of Distributed Computing*, pages 215–227, Vancouver, British Columbia, Canada, August 1992.

[165] Bengt Jonsson. Compositional specification and verification of distributed systems. *ACM Transactions on Programming Languages and Systems*, 16(2):259–303, March 1994.

[166] Richard M. Karp and Vijaya Ramachandran. Parallel algorithms for shared-memory machines. In Jan Van Leeuwen, editor, *Algorithms and Complexity*, volume A of *Handbook of Theoretical Computer Science*, chapter 17, pages 869–942. Elsevier/MIT Press, New York/Cambridge, 1990.

[167] Jon Kleinberg, Hagit Attiya, and Nancy Lynch. Trade-offs between message delivery and quiesce times in connection management protocols. In *Proceedings of ISTCS 1995: The Third Israel Symposium on Theory of Computing and Systems*, pages 258–267, Tel Aviv, January 1995. IEEE, Los Alamitos, Calif.

[168] Donald E. Knuth. Additional comments on a problem in concurrent programming control. *Communications of the ACM*, 9(5):321–322, May 1966.

[169] Donald E. Knuth. *Fundamental Algorithms*, volume 1 of *The Art of Computer Programming*, second edition. Addison-Wesley, Reading, Mass., 1973.

[170] Dénes König. Sur les correspondances multivoques des ensembles. *Fundamenta Mathematicae*, 8:114–134, 1926.

[171] Clyde P. Kruskal, Larry Rudolph, and Marc Snir. Efficient synchronization on multiprocessors with shared memory. In *Proceedings of the Fifth Annual ACM Symposium on Principles of Distributed Computing*, pages 218–228, Calgary, Alberta, Canada, August 1986.

[172] Jaynarayan H. Lala. A Byzantine resilient fault-tolerant computer for nuclear power plant applications. In *FTCS: 16th Annual International Symposium on Fault-Tolerant Computing Systems*, pages 338–343, Vienna, July 1986. IEEE, Los Alamitos, Calif.

[173] Jaynarayan H. Lala, Richard. E. Harper, and Linda S. Alger. A design approach for ultrareliable real-time systems. *Computer*, 24(5):12–22, May 1991. Issue on Real-time Systems.

[174] Leslie Lamport. A new solution of Dijkstra's concurrent programming problem. *Communications of the ACM*, 17(8):453–455, August 1974.

[175] Leslie Lamport. Proving the correctness of multiprocess programs. *IEEE Transactions on Software Engineering*, SE-3(2):125–143, March 1977.

[176] Leslie Lamport. Time, clocks, and the ordering of events in a distributed system. *Communications of the ACM*, 21(7):558–565, July 1978.

[177] Leslie Lamport. Specifying concurrent program modules. *ACM Transactions on Programming Languages and Systems*, 5(2):190–222, April 1983.

[178] Leslie Lamport. The weak Byzantine generals problem. *Journal of the ACM*, 30(3):669–676, July 1983.

[179] Leslie Lamport. Using time instead of timeout for fault-tolerant distributed systems. *ACM Transactions on Programming Languages and Systems*, 6(2):254–280, April 1984.

[180] Leslie Lamport. The mutual exclusion problem. Part II: Statement and solutions. *Journal of the ACM*, 33(2):327–348, April 1986.

[181] Leslie Lamport. On interprocess communication, Part I: Basic formalism. *Distributed Computing*, 1(2):77–85, April 1986.

[182] Leslie Lamport. On interprocess communication, Part II: Algorithms. *Distributed Computing*, 1(2):86–101, April 1986.

[183] Leslie Lamport. The part-time parliament. Research Report 49, Digital Systems Research Center, Palo Alto, Calif., September 1989.

[184] Leslie Lamport. The temporal logic of actions. *ACM Transactions on Programming Languages and Systems*, 16(3):872–923, May 1994.

[185] Leslie Lamport and Nancy Lynch. Distributed computing: Models and methods. In Jan Van Leeuwen, editor, *Formal Models and Semantics*, volume B of *Handbook of Theoretical Computer Science*, chapter 18, pages 1157–1199. Elsevier/MIT Press, New York/Cambridge, 1990.

[186] Leslie Lamport and Fred B. Schneider. Pretending atomicity. Research Report 44, Digital Equipment Corporation, Systems Research Center, Palo Alto, Calif., May 1989.

[187] Leslie Lamport, Robert Shostak, and Marshall Pease. The Byzantine generals problem. *ACM Transactions on Programming Languages and Systems*, 4(3):382–401, July 1982.

[188] Butler Lampson, Nancy Lynch, and Jørgen Søgaard-Andersen. At-most-once message delivery: A case study in algorithm verification. In W. R. Cleaveland, editor, *CONCUR'92* (Third International Conference on Concurrency Theory, Stony Brook, N.Y., August 1992), volume 630 of *Lecture*

Notes in Computer Science, pages 317–324. Springer-Verlag, New York, 1992.

[189] Butler Lampson, William Weihl, and Umesh Maheshwari. Principles of Computer Systems: Lecture Notes for 6.826, Fall 1992. Research Seminar Series MIT/LCS/RSS 22, Laboratory for Computer Science, Massachusetts Institute of Technology, Cambridge, July 1993.

[190] Butler W. Lampson, Nancy A. Lynch, and Jørgen F. Søgaard-Andersen. Correctness of at-most-once message delivery protocols. In Richard L. Tenney, Paul D. Amer, and M. Ümit Uyan, editors, *Formal Description Techniques VI* (Proceedings of the IFIP TC6/WG6.1 Sixth International Conference on Formal Description Techniques, FORTE '93, Boston, October, 1993) *IFIP Transactions C*, pages 385–400. North-Holland, Amsterdam, 1994.

[191] Gérard Le Lann. Distributed systems—towards a formal approach. In Bruce Gilchrist, editor, *Information Processing 77* (Toronto, August 1977), volume 7 of *Proceedings of IFIP Congress*, pages 155–160. North-Holland, Amsterdam, 1977.

[192] Daniel Lehmann and Michael O. Rabin. On the advantages of free choice: A symmetric and fully distributed solution to the Dining Philosophers problem. In *Proceedings of Eighth Annual ACM Symposium on Principles of Programming Languages*, pages 133–138, Williamsburg, Va., January 1981.

[193] F. Thomson Leighton. *Introduction to Parallel Algorithms and Architectures: Arrays, Trees, Hypercubes*. Morgan Kaufmann, San Mateo, Calif., 1992.

[194] Harry R. Lewis. Finite-state analysis of asynchronous circuits with bounded temporal uncertainty. Technical Report TR-15-89, Center for Research in Computing Technology, Aiken Computation Laboratory, Harvard University, Cambridge, Mass., 1989.

[195] Harry R. Lewis and Christos H. Papadimitriou. *Elements of the Theory of Computation*. Prentice Hall, Englewood Cliffs, N.J., 1981.

[196] Ming Li and Paul M. B. Vitányi. How to share concurrent asynchronous wait-free variables. In G. Ausiello et al., editors, *Automata, Languages and Programming* (16th International Colloquium, ICALP '89, Stresa, Italy,

July 1989), volume 372 of *Lecture Notes in Computer Science*, pages 488–505. Springer-Verlag, New York, 1989. Final version (with John Tromp) submitted for publication.

[197] Barbara Liskov and Rivka Ladin. Highly-available distributed services and fault-tolerant distributed garbage collection. In *Proceedings of the Fifth Annual ACM Symposium on Principles of Distributed Computing*, pages 29–39, Calgary, Alberta, Canada, August 1986.

[198] Barbara Liskov, Alan Snyder, Russell Atkinson, and Craig Schaffert. Abstraction mechanisms in CLU. *Communications of the ACM*, 20(8):564–576, August 1977.

[199] Michael C. Loui and Hosame H. Abu-Amara. Memory requirements for agreement among unreliable asynchronous processes. In Franco P. Preparata, editor, *Parallel and Distributed Computing*, volume 4 of *Advances in Computing Research*, pages 163–183. JAI Press, Greenwich, Conn., 1987.

[200] Michael Luby. A simple parallel algorithm for the maximal independent set problem. *SIAM Journal of Computing*, 15(4):1036–1053, November 1986.

[201] Victor Luchangco. Using simulation techniques to prove timing properties. Master's thesis, Department of Electrical Engineering and Computer Science, Massachusetts Institute of Technology, Cambridge, June 1995.

[202] Victor Luchangco, Ekrem Söylemez, Stephen Garland, and Nancy Lynch. Verifying timing properties of concurrent algorithms. In Dieter Hogrefe and Stefan Leue, editors, *Formal Description Techniques VII: Proceedings of the 7th IFIP WG6.1 International Conference on Formal Description Techniques* (FORTE '94, Berne, Switzerland, October 1994), pages 259–273. Chapman and Hall, New York, 1995.

[203] N. Lynch. Concurrency control for resilient nested transactions. In *Proceedings of the Second ACM SIGACT-SIGMOD Symposium on Principles of Database Systems*, pages 166–181, Atlanta, March 1983.

[204] Nancy Lynch. Simulation techniques for proving properties of real-time systems. In W. P. de Roever, J. W. de Bakker, and G. Rozenberg, editors, *A Decade of Concurrency: Reflections and Perspectives* (REX School/Symposium, Noordwijkerhout, The Netherlands, June 1993), volume 803 of *Lecture Notes in Computer Science*, pages 375–424. Springer-Verlag, New York, 1994.

[205] Nancy Lynch. Simulation techniques for proving properties of real-time systems. In Sang H. Son, editor, *Advances in Real-Time Systems*, chapter 13, pages 299–332. Prentice Hall, Englewood Cliffs, N.J., 1995.

[206] Nancy Lynch, Yishay Mansour, and Alan Fekete. The data link layer: Two impossibility results. In *Proceedings of the Seventh Annual ACM Symposium on Principles of Distributed Computing*, pages 149–170, Toronto, Ontario, Canada, August 1988.

[207] Nancy Lynch, Michael Merritt, William Weihl, and Alan Fekete. *Atomic Transactions*. Morgan Kaufmann, San Mateo, Calif., 1994.

[208] Nancy Lynch, Isaac Saias, and Roberto Segala. Proving time bounds for randomized distributed algorithms. In *Proceedings of the 13th Annual ACM Symposium on Principles of Distributed Computing*, pages 314–323, Los Angeles, August 1994.

[209] Nancy Lynch and Nir Shavit. Timing-based mutual exclusion. In *Proceedings of the Real-Time Systems Symposium*, pages 2–11, Phoenix, December 1992. IEEE, Los Alamitos, Calif.

[210] Nancy Lynch and Frits Vaandrager. Forward and backward simulations for timing-based systems. In J. W. de Bakker et al., editors, *Real-Time: Theory in Practice* (REX Workshop, Mook, The Netherlands, June 1991), volume 600 of *Lecture Notes in Computer Science*, pages 397–446. Springer-Verlag, New York, 1992.

[211] Nancy Lynch and Frits Vaandrager. Forward and backward simulations—Part II: Timing-based systems. Technical Memo MIT/LCS/TM-487.b, Laboratory for Computer Science, Massachusetts Institute of Technology, Cambridge, April 1993. To appear in *Information and Computation*.

[212] Nancy Lynch and Frits Vaandrager. Action transducers and timed automata. Technical Memo MIT/LCS/TM-480.b, Laboratory for Computer Science, Massachusetts Institute of Technology, Cambridge, October 1994.

[213] Nancy A. Lynch. Upper bounds for static resource allocation in a distributed system. *Journal of Computer and System Sciences*, 23(2):254–278, October 1981.

[214] Nancy A. Lynch. Multivalued possibilities mappings. In W. P. de Roever, J. W. de Bakker, and G. Rozenberg, editors, *Stepwise Refinement of Distributed Systems: Models, Formalisms, Correctness* (REX Workshop,

Mook, The Netherlands, May/June 1989), volume 430 of *Lecture Notes in Computer Science*, pages 519–543. Springer-Verlag, New York, 1990.

[215] Nancy A. Lynch and Hagit Attiya. Using mappings to prove timing properties. *Distributed Computing*, 6(2):121–139, September 1992.

[216] Nancy A. Lynch and Michael J. Fischer. On describing the behavior and implementation of distributed systems. *Theoretical Computer Science*, 13(1):17–43, 1981. Special issue on Semantics of Concurrent Computation.

[217] Nancy A. Lynch and Mark R. Tuttle. Hierarchical correctness proofs for distributed algorithms. Master's thesis, Department of Electrical Engineering and Computer Science, Massachusetts Institute of Technology, Cambridge, April 1987. Technical Report MIT/LCS/TR-387. Abbreviated version in *Proceedings of the Sixth Annual ACM Symposium on Principles of Distributed Computing*, pages 137–151, Vancouver, British Columbia, Canada, August, 1987.

[218] Nancy A. Lynch and Mark R. Tuttle. An introduction to input/output automata. *CWI-Quarterly*, 2(3):219–246, September 1989. Centrum voor Wiskunde en Informatica, Amsterdam. Technical Memo MIT/LCS/TM-373, Laboratory for Computer Science, Massachusetts Institute of Technology, Cambridge, November 1988.

[219] Zohar Manna and Amir Pnueli. *The Temporal Logic of Reactive and Concurrent Systems: Specification*. Springer-Verlag, New York, 1992.

[220] Yishay Mansour and Baruch Schieber. The intractability of bounded protocols for on-line sequence transmission over non-FIFO channels. *Journal of the ACM*, 39(4):783–799, October 1992.

[221] John C. Martin. *Introduction to Languages and the Theory of Computation*. McGraw-Hill, New York, 1991.

[222] Friedemann Mattern. Virtual time and global states of distributed systems. In Michel Cosnard et al., editors, *Parallel and Distributed Algorithms: Proceedings of the International Workshop on Parallel and Distributed Algorithms* (Chateau de Bonas, Gers, France, October, 1988), pages 215–226. North-Holland, Amsterdam, 1989.

[223] John M. McQuillan, Gilbert Falk, and Ira Richer. A review of the development and performance of the ARPANET routing algorithm. *IEEE Transactions on Communications*, COM-26(12):1802–1811, December 1978.

[224] Daniel A. Menasce and Richard R. Muntz. Locking and deadlock detection in distributed data bases. *IEEE Transactions on Software Engineering*, SE-5(3):195–202, May 1979.

[225] Karl Menger. Zur allgemeinen Kurventheorie. *Fundamenta Mathematicae*, 10:96–115, 1927.

[226] Michael Merritt, 1985. Unpublished Notes.

[227] Michael Merritt, Francemary Modugno, and Mark R. Tuttle. Time constrained automata. In J. C. M. Baeten and J. F. Goote, editors, *CONCUR '91: 2nd International Conference on Concurrency Theory* (Amsterdam, August 1991), volume 527 of *Lecture Notes in Computer Science*, pages 408–423. Springer-Verlag, New York, 1991.

[228] Robin Milner. An algebraic definition of simulation between programs. In *2nd International Joint Conference on Artificial Intelligence*, pages 481–489, Imperial College, London, September 1971. British Computer Society, London.

[229] Robin Milner. *Communication and Concurrency*. Prentice-Hall International, United Kingdom, 1989.

[230] Shlomo Moran and Yaron Wolfstahl. Extended impossibility results for asynchronous complete networks. *Information Processing Letters*, 26(3):145–151, November 1987.

[231] Yoram Moses and Orli Waarts. Coordinated traversal: $(t+1)$-round Byzantine agreement in polynomial time. *Journal of Algorithms*, 17(1):110–156, July 1994.

[232] Gil Neiger and Sam Toueg. Simulating synchronized clocks and common knowledge in distributed systems. *Journal of the ACM*, 40(2):334–367, April 1993.

[233] Tobias Nipkow. Formal verification of data type refinement: Theory and practice. In W. P. de Roever, J. W. de Bakker, and G. Rozenberg, editors, *Stepwise Refinement of Distributed Systems: Models, Formalisms, Correctness* (REX Workshop, Mook, The Netherlands, May/June 1989), volume 430 of *Lecture Notes in Computer Science*, pages 561–591. Springer-Verlag, New York, 1990.

[234] Ron Obermarck. Distributed deadlock detection algorithm. *ACM Transactions on Database Systems*, 7(2):187–208, June 1982.

[235] Susan Owicki and David Gries. An axiomatic proof technique for parallel programs, I. *Acta Informatica*, 6(4):319–340, 1976.

[236] David Park. Concurrency and automata on infinite sequences. In Peter Deussen, editor, *Theoretical Computer Science* (5th GI Conference, Karlsruhe, Germany, March 1981), volume 104 of *Lecture Notes in Computer Science*, pages 167–183. Springer-Verlag, New York, 1981.

[237] M. Pease, R. Shostak, and L. Lamport. Reaching agreement in the presence of faults. *Journal of the ACM*, 27(2):228–234, April 1980.

[238] G. L. Peterson. Myths about the mutual exclusion problem. *Information Processing Letters*, 12(3):115–116, June 1981.

[239] Gary L. Peterson. An $O(n \log n)$ unidirectional distributed algorithm for the circular extrema problem. *ACM Transactions on Programming Languages and Systems*, 4(4):758–762, October 1982.

[240] Gary L. Peterson. Concurrent reading while writing. *ACM Transactions on Programming Languages and Systems*, 5(1):46–55, 1983.

[241] Gary L. Peterson and James E. Burns. Concurrent reading while writing II: The multi-writer case. In *28th Annual Symposium on Foundations of Computer Science*, pages 383–392, Los Angeles, October 1987. IEEE, Los Alamitos, Calif.

[242] Gary L. Peterson and Michael J. Fischer. Economical solutions for the critical section problem in a distributed system. In *Proceedings of the Ninth Annual ACM Symposium on Theory of Computing*, pages 91–97, Boulder, Colo., May 1977.

[243] Amir Pnueli. Personal communication, 1988.

[244] Amir Pnueli and Lenore Zuck. Verification of multiprocess probabilistic protocols. *Distributed Computing*, 1(1):53–72, January 1986.

[245] Stephen Ponzio. Consensus in the presence of timing uncertainty: Omission and Byzantine failures. In *Proceedings of the 10th Annual ACM Symposium on Principles of Distributed Computing*, pages 125–138, Montreal, Quebec, Canada, August 1991.

[246] Stephen Ponzio. Bounds on the time to detect failures using bounded-capacity message links. In *Proceedings of the Real-time Systems Symposium*, pages 236–245, Phoenix, December 1992. IEEE, Los Alamitos, Calif.

[247] Stephen J. Ponzio. The real-time cost of timing uncertainty: Consensus and failure detection. Master's thesis, Department of Electrical Engineering and Computer Science, Massachusetts Institute of Technology, Cambridge, June 1991. Technical Report MIT/LCS/TR-518.

[248] Michael O. Rabin. Randomized Byzantine generals. In *24th Annual Symposium on Foundations of Computer Science*, pages 403–409, Tucson, November 1983. IEEE, Los Alamitos, Calif.

[249] M. Raynal. *Algorithms for Mutual Exclusion*. MIT Press, Cambridge, 1986.

[250] Michel Raynal. *Networks and Distributed Computation: Concepts, Tools, and Algorithms*. MIT Press, Cambridge, 1988.

[251] Michel Raynal and Jean-Michel Helary. *Synchronization and Control of Distributed Systems and Programs*. John Wiley & Sons, Ltd., Chichester, U.K., 1990.

[252] Glenn Ricart and Ashok K. Agrawala. An optimal algorithm for mutual exclusion in computer networks. *Communications of the ACM*, 24(1):9–17, January 1981. Corrigendum in *Communications of the ACM*, 24(9):578, September 1981.

[253] Michael Saks and Fotios Zaharoglou. Wait-free k-set agreement is impossible: The topology of public knowledge. In *Proceedings of the 25th Annual ACM Symposium on the Theory of Computing*, pages 101–110, San Diego, May 1993.

[254] Russell Schaffer. On the correctness of atomic multi-writer registers. Technical Memo MIT/LCS/TM-364, Laboratory for Computer Science, Massachusetts Institute of Technology, Cambridge, June 1988.

[255] Fred B. Schneider. Implementing fault-tolerant services using the state machine approach. *ACM Computing Surveys*, 22(4):299–319, December 1990.

[256] Reinhard Schwarz and Friedemann Mattern. Detecting causal relationships in distributed computations: In search of the holy grail. *Distributed Computing*, 7(3):149–174, March 1994.

[257] Roberto Segala and Nancy Lynch. Probabilistic simulations for probabilistic processes. *Nordic Journal of Computing*, 2(2):250–273, August 1995. Special issue on selected papers from CONCUR'94.

[258] Adrian Segall. Distributed network protocols. *IEEE Transactions on Information Theory*, IT-29(1):23–35, January 1983.

[259] A. Udaya Shankar. A simple assertional proof system for real-time systems. In *Proceedings of the Real-Time Systems Symposium*, pages 167–176, Phoenix, December 1992. IEEE, Los Alamitos, Calif.

[260] A. Udaya Shankar and Simon S. Lam. A stepwise refinement heuristic for protocol construction. *ACM Transactions on Programming Languages and Systems*, 14(3):417–461, July 1992.

[261] Nir Shavit. *Concurrent Time Stamping*. Ph.D. thesis, Department of Computer Science, Hebrew University, Jerusalem, Israel, January 1990.

[262] Abraham Silberschatz, James L. Peterson, and Peter B. Galvin. *Operating System Concepts*, third edition. Addison-Wesley, Reading, Mass., 1992.

[263] Ambuj K. Singh, James H. Anderson, and Mohamed G. Gouda. The elusive atomic register. *Journal of the ACM*, 41(2):311–339, March 1994.

[264] Jørgen Søgaard-Andersen. *Correctness of Protocols in Distributed Systems*. Ph.D. thesis, Department of Computer Science, Technical University of Denmark, Lyngby, December 1993. ID-TR: 1993-131.

[265] Jørgen F. Søgaard-Andersen, Stephen J. Garland, John V. Guttag, Nancy A. Lynch, and Anna Pogosyants. Computer-assisted simulation proofs. In Costas Courcoubetis, editor, *Computer-Aided Verification* (5th International Conference, CAV '93, Elounda, Greece, June/July 1993), volume 697 of *Lecture Notes in Computer Science*, pages 305–319. Springer-Verlag, New York, 1993.

[266] Edwin H. Spanier. *Algebraic Topology*. McGraw-Hill, New York, 1966.

[267] E. Sperner. Neuer beweis für die invarianz der dimensionszahl und des gebietes. *Abhandlungen Aus Dem Mathematischen Seminar Der Hamburgischen Universität*, 6:265–272, 1928.

[268] John M. Spinelli. Reliable communication on data links. Technical Report LIDS-P-1844, Laboratory for Information and Decision Systems, Massachusetts Institute of Technology, Cambridge, December 1988.

[269] T. K. Srikanth and Sam Toueg. Simulating authenticated broadcasts to derive simple fault-tolerant algorithms. *Distributed Computing*, 2(2):80–94, August 1987.

[270] N. V. Stenning. A data transfer protocol. *Computer Networks*, 1(2):99–110, September 1976.

[271] Tom Stoppard. *Rosencrantz & Guildenstern Are Dead*. Grove Press, New York, 1968.

[272] Eugene Styer and Gary L. Peterson. Improved algorithms for distributed resource allocation. In *Proceedings of the Seventh Annual ACM Symposium on Principles of Distributed Computing*, pages 105–116, Toronto, Ontario, Canada, August 1988.

[273] Andrew S. Tanenbaum. *Computer Networks*, second edition. Prentice Hall, Englewood Cliffs, N.J., 1988.

[274] Y. C. Tay and W. Tim Loke. On deadlocks of exclusive AND-requests for resources. *Distributed Computing*, 9(2):77–94, October 1995.

[275] Gerard Tel. Assertional verification of a timer based protocol. In Timo Lepistö and Arto Salomaa, editors, *Automata, Languages and Programming* (15th International Colloquium, ICALP '88, Tempere, Finland, July 1988), volume 317 of *Lecture Notes in Computer Science*, pages 600–614. Springer-Verlag, New York, 1988.

[276] Gerard Tel. *Introduction to Distributed Algorithms*. Cambridge University Press, Cambridge, U.K., 1994.

[277] Ewan Tempero and Richard Ladner. Recoverable sequence transmission protocols. *Journal of the ACM*, 42(5):1059–1090, September 1995.

[278] Ewan Tempero and Richard E. Ladner. Tight bounds for weakly-bounded protocols. In *Proceedings of the Ninth Annual ACM Symposium on Principles of Distributed Computing*, pages 205–218, Quebec City, Quebec, Canada, August 1990.

[279] Russell Turpin and Brian A. Coan. Extending binary Byzantine agreement to multivalued Byzantine agreement. *Information Processing Letters*, 18(2):73–76, February 1984.

[280] Jan L. A. van de Snepscheut. The sliding-window protocol revisited. *Formal Aspects of Computing*, 7(1):3–17, 1995.

[281] George Varghese and Nancy A. Lynch. A tradeoff between safety and liveness for randomized coordinated attack protocols. In *Proceedings of the 11th Annual ACM Symposium on Principles of Distributed Computing*, pages 241–250, Vancouver, British Columbia, Canada, August 1992.

[282] Paul M. B. Vitányi. Distributed elections in an Archimedean ring of pro-
      cessors. In *Proceedings of the 16th Annual ACM Symposium on Theory of
      Computing*, pages 542–547, Washington, D.C., April/May 1984.

[283] Paul M. B. Vitányi and Baruch Awerbuch. Atomic shared register access
      by asynchronous hardware. In *27th Annual Symposium on Foundations
      of Computer Science*, pages 233–243, Toronto, Ontario, Canada, October
      1986. IEEE, Los Alamitos, Calif. Corrigendum in *28th Annual Symposium
      on Foundations of Computer Science*, page 487, Los Angeles, October
      1987.

[284] Da-Wei Wang and Lenore D. Zuck. Tight bounds for the sequence trans-
      mission problem. In *Proceedings of the Eighth Annual ACM Symposium
      on Principles of Distributed Computing*, pages 73–83, Edmonton, Alberta,
      Canada, August 1989.

[285] Jennifer Welch and Nancy Lynch. A modular Drinking Philosophers algo-
      rithm. *Distributed Computing*, 6(4):233–244, July 1993.

[286] Jennifer Lundelius Welch. Simulating synchronous processors. *Information
      and Computation*, 74(2):159–171, August 1987.

[287] Jennifer Lundelius Welch. *Topics in Distributed Computing: The Impact
      of Partial Synchrony, and Modular Decomposition of Algorithms*. Ph.D.
      thesis, Department of Electrical Engineering and Computer Science, Mas-
      sachusetts Institute of Technology, Cambridge, March 1988.

[288] Jennifer Lundelius Welch, Leslie Lamport, and Nancy Lynch. A lattice-
      structured proof technique applied to a minimum spanning tree algorithm.
      In *Proceedings of the Seventh Annual ACM Symposium on Principles of
      Distributed Computing*, pages 28–43, Toronto, Ontario, Canada, August
      1988.

[289] John H. Wensley et al. SIFT: Design and analysis of a fault-tolerant
      computer for aircraft control. *Proceedings of the IEEE*, 66(10):1240–1255,
      October 1978.

[290] Hubert Zimmerman. OSI reference model—the ISO model of architecture
      for open systems interconnection. *IEEE Transactions on Communications*,
      COM-28(4):425–432, April 1980.

Index

Italicized page numbers indicate places where terms are defined or introduced.

Related Titles from Morgan Kaufmann

Atomic Transactions
Nancy Lynch, Michael Merritt, William Weihl, and Alan Fekete
This book develops a theory for transactions that provides practical solutions for systems developers, focusing on the interface between the user and the database. The authors present a formal approach to system design that is as relevant to practitioners as it is elegant.
1993; 500 pages; cloth; ISBN 1-55860-104-X

Transaction Processing: Concepts and Techniques
Jim Gray and Andreas Reuter
Using transactions as a unifying conceptual framework, the authors show how to build high-performance distributed systems and high-availability applications with finite budgets and risk.
1993; 1070 pages; cloth; ISBN 1-55860-190-2

Distributed Object Management
Edited by M. Tamer Ozsu, Umeshwar Dayal, and Patrick Valduriez
A groundbreaking collection of articles focusing on the use of object-oriented technologies in distributed computer systems. Product developers, researchers, and database technology watchers will find this an indispensable guide to a rapidly growing field.
1993; 441 pages; cloth; ISBN 1-55860-256-9

Active Database Systems: Triggers and Rules for Advanced Database Processing
Edited by Jennifer Widom and Stefano Ceri
This significant collection focuses on the most prominent research projects in active database systems. A comprehensive introduction to the core topics of the fields includes the motivation and history as well as a broader survey of research topics and information on forthcoming standards.
1995; 332 pages; cloth; ISBN 1-55860-304-2